Conceiving the Inconceivable

Other Books by Ashish Dalela:

The Science of God
Time and Consciousness
The Balanced Organization
The Yellow Pill
Cosmic Theogony
Emotion
Mystic Universe
Moral Materialism
Signs of Life
Uncommon Wisdom
Gödel's Mistake
Quantum Meaning
Sāñkhya and Science
Is the Apple Really Red?
Six Causes

Conceiving the Inconceivable

PART 1

A Scientific Commentary on
Vedānta Sūtras

Original Text Composed by
Sage Vyāsa

Ashish Dalela

SHABDA
PRESS

Conceiving the Inconceivable Part 1—A Scientific Commentary on
Vedānta Sūtras
by Ashish Dalela
www.shabda.co

Copyright © 2020, 2021 by Ashish Dalela
All Rights Reserved
Interior Design: Ciprian Begu

All rights reserved. No part of this book may be reproduced in any form
without the express permission of the author. This includes reprints, excerpts,
photocopying, recording, or any future means of reproducing. If you would
like to do any of the above, please seek permission first by contacting the
author on www.shabda.co.

Published by Shabda Press
press.shabda.co
ISBN 978-93-85384-31-8
v1.2(06/2021)

SHABDA
PRESS

"We have to explain what is meant by Vedānta. Veda means knowledge and anta means end; we have already explained. So, everyone is searching after knowledge, inquisitiveness. The science is also the same process. Science is trying to find out the ultimate cause, starting point. Is it not? That is scientific research. So, we have our departments of knowledge. He can study even a flower. Go on studying, you can come to the seed, the potential. This is scientific research. To find out the ultimate cause. So, there are so many departments of knowledge. Department of science, department of art. Vedānta means the Ultimate knowledge, the Original. That is called brahma-jijñāsā. … [it] means this human form of life is specially meant for enquiring Absolute Truth. If the human being does not enquire about it then he's animal. You have to prove it logically, scientifically. This is first sūtra. So, you write on upon one sūtra, then I give you next sūtra. Every one of you can write according to understanding, athātho-brahma-jijñāsā. Now, this is the life for enquiring about the Ultimate goal, Absolute Truth."

—His Divine Grace A.C. Bhaktivedānta Swami Prabhupāda
From a recording by H.H. Bhaktisvarūpa Dāmodara Swami

We should always be enthusiastic to try for capturing the rhinoceros. That way, if we fail, everyone will say, "Never mind, nobody can catch a rhinoceros anyway," and if we succeed, then everyone will say, "Just see what a wonderful thing they have done!"

—His Divine Grace A.C. Bhaktivedānta Swami Prabhupāda
Quoted in "Chasing Rhinos with the Swami" by Syāmasundar Das

CONTENTS

Series Preface

At present, the Vedic philosophical system suffers from many misconceptions—(a) the Vedic texts comprise many disparate or conflicting doctrines that don't form a coherent system, (b) these texts advocate the worship of different deities so the Vedic system must be polytheistic, (c) due to the differences between the various Vedic texts, they must have been authored by different people so they cannot be of divine origin, and (d) the texts produced by various human minds must have originated at different ages and times in history.

Those who want to correct these misconceptions are also making many mistakes. First, they defend the history as being a few thousand years older than modern estimates (when the Vedic tradition is sanātana or eternal). Second, they accept impersonalism as a solution to the supposed polytheism of the Vedas (even though it is solemnly rejected by the Vedic texts). Third, they apologize for the diversity of texts as the intellectual virtue of plural viewpoints (when plurality is different perspectives on a single understanding of reality). Fourth, they visualize Vedic knowledge through the mundane lens of geographical contiguity and genetic resemblances confusing the correction of mistakes with pedestrian ideals of nationalism, political unity, cultural pride, etc., and the true spiritual foundations under which all material identities of body, gender, society, and nation are rejected as a waste of time, are ignored.

This series of books differs from the above-mentioned goals and aspirations. This may potentially reduce the reader list to a smaller number of people who are truly interested in the truth, not a race, nationality, language, etc. But that risk must be taken in the interest of truth, and broader objectives of Vedic knowledge. The sacrifice of immediate interests is hence a necessary evil.

The primary goal of this series of books is to establish that the Vedas constitute a coherent description of reality, which has to be understood from multiple perspectives to grasp its true nature. This understanding can be broadly classified into the following categories—(a) the study of matter as concepts and qualities, (b) the understanding of the soul and its relation to God, (c) the practices by which this nature of the soul and God are practically realized and experienced, and (d) the system of reasoning and logic that is used to explain it to anyone who might be interested. The study of the nature of the soul and God is theology. The practice by which this nature is realized is religion. The description of matter as categories and qualities is philosophy. And the system of reasoning and logic used to explain it to those who are interested is science.

Each perspective can be, in principle, described and understood without the others. For example, we can practice religious mysticism without perfectly knowing theology. We can know the philosophy of reality without religion or theology. And we can understand the science without practicing mysticism.

Nevertheless, the Vedic texts do not put these into separate boxes. Every text discusses all the subjects—science, philosophy, religion, and theology—but with different relative emphases. Some texts are more focused on science, others more on theology and religion, while others more on philosophy. This unifying tendency in the Vedic system is the antithesis of the modern tendency to compartmentalize, separate one issue from another, focus on narrow problems, and create the illusion of progress by going round and round in circles.

The Vedic system looks at all inquiries holistically and their answers to one question cannot contradict the answers to any other potential question. If you progress in philosophy, then you also progress in religion, theology, and science. Scientific progress is not contrary to ethics and morality; spiritual development is not contrary to the necessities of life. The Vedic system is not divided into physics, chemistry, mathematics, sociology, economics, psychology, cosmology, theology, and so on, as its purpose is to create wise people—who know everything—rather than professional academics whose solutions are conceived within the narrow ambits of their primary expertise, rather than broadly concerned with several aspects of the problem needed for a wise person.

The understanding of the knowledge and its application to various areas of human knowledge should be the primary goal because by achieving that goal, the other goals can be achieved automatically. If the knowledge is useful and true, then each path meant to attain it can be useful for people with different abilities and interests. If the Vedic texts describe reality correctly, then the timelessness of the knowledge would be more important than the age of the text. If the philosophy is consistent and complete, then even plural authorship of the texts would indicate a multitude of mutually coherent viewpoints. If the personalistic and aspected nature of reality is understood correctly, then the myriad personalities would not be contradictory to a single person of God. And the universal applicability and the non-sectarian nature of knowledge would make any national, social, cultural, and political pride completely redundant.

Even as the Vedas are divine knowledge, and many times described as the word of God and transmitted through the creator of the universe—Brahma—nobody has to accept their divinity a priori. Vedas recommend faith in the teachers because no student approaches a teacher without some faith. But blind faith—as the antithesis of reason and experience—is rejected. The philosophy of the Vedas is meant to be studied, debated, and discussed by all qualified people (the restriction of the Vedas to a certain class is the restriction of qualification). And the knowledge of the Vedas is beyond race, nation, and society. In all these ways, the Vedas constitute a "secular science"—not atheistic, but secular—as they are amenable to reason and experience, open to sincere inquiry and discussion, and not to be conflated with narrow political objectives.

The primary aim of this series of books is to help the readers understand the knowledge. If the truth of the Vedic texts is known, then we can talk about their history. If the unity of Vedic philosophy is known, then we can talk about whether they had different authors. If by learning this philosophy, we can master every subject, then we can talk about its divine and eternal nature. And if all these are achieved, then we can speak of the intellectual, cultural, and social superiority of the people who have preserved, advanced, and propagated this knowledge selflessly. In fact, by establishing the truth, all other questions about history, authorship, and divinity will become moot—we will accept them without an argument, based on their superiority. Without proving the consistency, completeness, pervasive usefulness, and the empirical truth of this knowledge, there is no point in talking about history, authorship, divinity, geographical heritage, and socio-cultural identities. Without understanding the nature of reality, pride in ancient history makes no difference to the present. And without putting that knowledge into practice, all claims remain the subject of endless subjective opinions and pointless debates. If instead, we focus on the truth in the Vedas, then even the temporaneous goals can also be achieved naturally.

The Vedas in fact describe the history of their appearance, but because people don't believe in the Vedic truth, therefore, they don't accept the history. Because the academics have become accustomed to numerous mythological texts in the West, which were repeatedly modified and curated by religious institutions to suit their political objectives, they think that the Vedas too must be myths. But where is the evidence for the doctoring of the Vedas? We can find that evidence in the case of the Bible and the Koran for instance, where books have been revised many times, and the ideas of the doctors were inserted into the books. But the Vedic tradition gives us no such evidence. Instead, there is clear evidence of the separation of the texts from the commentaries on the texts. The texts are always separate from the commentaries by various authors. Therefore, if we rely on the Vedic texts, we can also understand their own history.

To understand the Six Systems of Philosophy, we need to take note of their historical appearance. The Vedas state that their knowledge has existed since time immemorial, and originated in the four Vedas compiled by Brahma—the creator of the universe—after being inspired in the heart by Lord Viṣṇu. Brahma imparted this knowledge to his sons—the seven sages, Manu, the four Kumaras, and others. These disciples and their successors then produced a broader oral tradition, which was called the "Vedic system"—because it was based on the original four Vedas that were narrated by Brahma to others. This oral tradition was significantly larger than what we know as the Vedic texts today.

Vedic cosmology divides time into cycles of yugas, which are further divided into four sub-ages called Satya-yuga, Treta-yuga, Dvapara-yuga, and Kali-yuga. The Kali-yuga is the smallest age and is 432,000 years. Dvapara is twice that of Kali-yuga, Treta is three times of Kali-yuga, and Satya is four times Kali-yuga. The present age is Kali-yuga. In the bygone ages—Satya, Treta, and Dvapara—which amounts to 3,888,000 solar years, the Vedas existed as an oral tradition, because the people following the system had a great memory.

At the beginning of Kali-yuga, these texts were scribed by Vyāsa, who is also sometimes called Bādarāyana. This is when the oral tradition became a written one. Vyāsa performed a selection from the oral tradition, and the texts he produced by scribing the oral tradition were a subset of the oral tradition.

Vyāsa also divided the oral tradition into many parts, which are today known as Samhita, Upaniśad, Tantra, Purāna, Itihāsa, etc. Each of these classes is further divided into many sub-classes and texts. For instance, there are 108 Upaniśad and 18 Purāna. He then also *composed* the Vedānta Sūtra after *compiling* the other Vedic texts. There is a subtle difference between compiling and composing. A compilation is the selective scribing of the oral tradition. But the composition is solely attributable to Bādarāyana (although he often quotes other sages even in this text). Quite simply, Vedānta Sūtra is Bādarāyana's summary of the oral tradition, after the selective scribing of the oral tradition.

While dividing, scribing, and compiling the Vedic texts, Vyāsa referred to the philosophies of some of the Six Systems such as Sāñkhya and Yoga and included them into the Vedic texts. He left out some of the philosophies such as Nyāya, Vaiśeṣika, and Mīmāṃsā as they were, and still are, considered supplementary. We might wonder why. And the answer is that Nyāya is a system of logic, Mīmāṃsā is the use of reason for semantic analysis, and Vaiśeṣika is the application of semantic analysis to the study of material nature. These are, strictly speaking, the applications of Vedic philosophy, which are of great interest to the experts, but not of primary interest to the general population. This exclusion of some philosophies from the primary Vedic texts means that logic, semantic analysis, and its applications to the study of nature, were considered to be not of interest to the people primarily interested in the conclusions.

The selective inclusions and exclusions of some philosophies do not mean that they weren't part of the Vedic tradition. For example, practically everyone undergoing scientific education at present uses logic and mathematics, but the foundations of logic and mathematics are studied only by experts. Similarly, practically everyone masters some language, but the foundations of linguistics are outside the scope for everyone except the experts. The doctors who treat patients learn medicine, but they don't study biochemistry because that is too much unnecessary detail that is not of primary interest to their needs.

Therefore, the inclusion of philosophies of Sāñkhya and Yoga should be viewed as based on the fact that these were considered general information for everyone's use, while the exclusion of philosophies like Nyāya, Vaiśeṣika, and Mīmāṃsā should be viewed as something that was needed only for experts.

Quite separately, complete systems of philosophy existed as the Sūtra texts that this series is about. They were authored by other sages (Sāñkhya by Kapila, Yoga by Patanjali, Nyāya by Gautama, Vaiśeṣika by Kanāda, and Mīmāṃsā by Jaimini). These other systems of philosophy are also based on the oral Vedic tradition, which preceded Bādarāyana's selected scribing of the tradition, although Nyāya, Vaiśeṣika, and Mīmāṃsā were not included in the scribing. They too existed as an oral tradition and were scribed by their tradition followers, but their names are not known at present because (a) the texts are relatively small compared to the texts that Vyāsa scribed, and (b) there was no selection performed in the scribing of these texts; they were presented as they were. In that light, we can view Vyāsa as an editor of the Vedic tradition, while the other systems of philosophy had scribes that did not try to edit the Sūtra texts.

The result of this difference between Bādarāyana's selected scribing, and the texts of the other five systems, is that we can sometimes find it hard to cite the claims in the philosophies of Sāñkhya, Yoga, Nyāya, Vaiśeṣika, and Mīmāṃsā from the Saṃhita, Upaniśad, Tantra, Purāna, and Itihāsa. This inability to find direct references for one system in another one should not be taken to mean that they are at variance, or that they are not Vedic, or that they were created after the scribing of Vedic texts by other philosophers who did not agree with Bādarāyana's view. We must rather understand that all the Six Systems are based on the oral tradition. Specifically, Sāñkhya, Yoga, Vaiśeṣika, Nyāya, and Mīmāṃsā had their oral tradition before Bādarāyana scribing a select portion of the oral tradition, followed by composing the Vedānta Sūtra. As far as the historical dates of composing are concerned, Vedānta Sūtra is later. It is for this reason that it is sometimes called Uttara Mīmāṃsā (later analysis).

When we study the Six Systems of philosophy, in one sense, we are studying the much older oral tradition—as it was understood by six different sages. And when we study the Saṃhita, Upaniśad, Tantra, Purāna, and Itihāsa, we are studying the Vedic system as it was selectively scribed by Bādarāyana. The differences in these systems do not indicate a contradiction, but the fact that the oral tradition was bigger than the combinations of all the texts at present.

The point is this: The Six Systems are Vedic because they are all based on the oral tradition. They are also Vedic because Bādarāyana's texts directly reference Sāñkhya and Yoga, which are also referenced by Nyāya, Vaiśeṣika, and Mīmāṃsā. Then, several doctrines about the nature of the soul and God are common across the Six Systems and can be found in Bādarāyana's texts. Therefore, the Six Systems are not divergent philosophies, but different streams within the oral tradition that emphasized different aspects, and were thereby encoded as the Sūtra texts, that came to be studied by different students, and that inherited method of teacher-disciple succession created many schools.

And yet, there is widespread perception at present that the Six Systems of Philosophy are divergent, or even contradictory. This perception of divergence is not entirely fictional; it is indeed based on fact. But its appearance is relatively recent. Such deviations appear in the age of Kali-yuga, where people tend to replace understanding with argument, and incommensurate ideas that deviate from the Vedic philosophy appear. To support their contentions, they also reject many essential aspects of the cohesive system of philosophy.

To understand this divergence, we need to consider the last few thousand years of history, in which three philosophies—materialism, voidism, and impersonalism—have dominated. Each of the Six Systems of Philosophy rejects these doctrines. The world, in Vedic philosophy, reflects the properties of God like a mirror reflects a person's image. The mirror is real, and hence, matter is real. The form in the mirror is objective—the image in the mirror is real. Similarly, the reflection in the mirror is not a creation of the mirror, or an illusion, because there is a person outside the mirror. Since there is a transcendent person, therefore, the mirror and the reflection in it are not the only reality;

there is also a transcendent reality. By acknowledging a transcendent reality, materialism is rejected. By acknowledging that this transcendent reality is a person, impersonalism is rejected. And by recognizing that the person exists even if not reflected in the mirror—i.e., if the world doesn't exist—voidism is rejected.

The Six Systems texts delve into the details of why materialism, voidism, and impersonalism are false. They describe why God desires to see His reflection—namely, that it is a process of self-awareness and self-cognition. They describe how God is reflected in the mirror—the mirror is also a person, not an impersonal thing; the reflection in the mirror is the mirror "knowing" God; the mirror is then identified as God's energy or Śakti, and two realities—one masculine and the other feminine—are seen as the basis of the world. The immense variety in the reflection is attributed to the myriad aspects of God, which are integrated in God but separated in the Śakti. Thus, the created world is called *duality* whereas God is described as *non-duality*. The separation of the integrated reality is then understood as a mechanism by which God knows Himself—quite like a person looking into a mirror to see his varied features.

Each of the Six Systems of Vedic philosophy goes over these themes in different orders, emphasizing different aspects of this ideology, dwelling more on some things and less on others. Each philosophy refutes impersonalism, voidism, and materialism as these doctrines are contrary to the Vedic system.

In the modern context, the criticism of materialism can be equated to the rejection of modern science, and the ideas that underpin it. The Six Systems texts provide alternative descriptions of matter too, unparalleled by any other system in the past or present in its breadth and cohesiveness. The methods of realizing the truth of this description—i.e., the methods for practical and empirical confirmations—are also presented. The alternative to materialism is hence also rational and empirical, and without changing the definition of science—i.e., empirical, and rational truth—the reality is presented differently. It is rather the change of the doctrine of matter, with far wider empiricism, that covers the experiences of the senses, mind, intellect, ego, and the moral sense. The criticism of materialism therefore also constitutes an alternative science.

Similarly, in the modern context, the criticism of voidism can be equated to the rejection of Buddhism and allied traditions, which reject the reality of the soul and God. This rejection, similar to the rejection of materialism, is relatively easier, and the Six Systems of Philosophy don't dwell upon it as much.

The greatest focus in these systems—apart from the description of their position on the nature of reality—is to distinguish it from impersonalism because impersonalism uses more Vedic terminology than voidism. All over the Six Systems texts, we can find the rejection of all the contentions of impersonalism, namely—(a) that nature is a deluding agency, (b) that nature is inert, (c) that Oneness is the ultimate reality instead of diversity, (d) that this Oneness is formless, (e) that the desire and individuality of the soul are temporary.

All the followers of the Vedic tradition easily accept the rejections of materialism and voidism, but the rejection of impersonalism has become contentious because impersonalism used to be a non-Vedic system until Shankaracharya authored a commentary on the Vedānta Sūtra, to establish that impersonalism was Vedic. This commentary replaced the void of the Buddhists with two realities—called Brahman and māyā—with Brahman being an undivided consciousness, and māyā being inert matter (sort of like the Cartesian mind-body dualism). Since Brahman is undivided, therefore, the analogy of a person reflected in a mirror is modified to say that the mirror—i.e., māyā—creates an illusory picture of the formless. Since māyā is originally formless, and Brahman is always formless, this doctrine runs into difficulties in explaining the origin of forms. Calling something an illusion doesn't make it go away. The doctrine might also sometimes say that even māyā is a conscious entity, which deliberately tries to mislead Brahman into an illusion. This is also problematic, because if māyā is a deluding agency, then everything in the world—including the Vedic scriptures—must be illusory, as they are byproducts of māyā. The evil nature of māyā would entail that Brahman can never be liberated out of māyā because even the supposed sources of enlightenment are merely delusions.

The fact is that Vedānta does not support such an interpretation, because there are explicit statements about devotion to the Lord, the difference between the soul and God, and the divine relationship between God and His Sakti. Hence, Shankaracharya's commentary was an ill-conceived misrepresentation. His position was, in fact, subsequently criticized by other Vedānta views, and owing to these successive interpretations, the Vedānta system is popular today.

The Vedic practitioners of that time could have protested Shankaracharya's commentary, but they welcomed it on pragmatic grounds— they saw Indian society afflicted by Buddhism and considered that to be a bigger and more urgent problem. In voidism, every book is a delusion, because the whole world is unreal. Therefore, even the Vedas must be a delusion. Shankaracharya argued against that idea, and his key contribution was to explain why the Vedic texts are not delusions. But he married an un-Vedic doctrine of impersonalism to the acceptance of the Vedic texts as divine knowledge and divine authority.

To support his impersonal doctrine, Shankaracharya also created a schism between the Six Systems, rejecting the other five systems in his Vedānta commentary. Shankaracharya could not comment on Vedānta alone, if the integrity of the other five systems of philosophy—namely, Sāñkhya, Mīmāṃsā, Nyāya, Vaiśeṣika, and Yoga—wasn't challenged. Historically, these six systems had always supported each other and used each other's doctrines. The schism between the Six Systems of philosophy owes to the criticism of the other five systems by Shankaracharya. Since that time, people began to consider the Six Systems as divergent and inconsistent philosophies, and their teachers began to grow apart, instead of being considered a part of a single coherent system.

Even as later Ācharyas tried to correct this problem by commenting again on Vedānta Sūtra, the results were less than desirable. Three specific problems arose quickly out of these successive commentaries. First, the commentaries of Rāmanujāchārya, Mādhavāchārya, and others, emphasized the worship of Lord Viṣṇu, instead of Lord Shiva, thus creating a schism between Vaishnavism and Shaivism. Second, they restricted themselves to the discussion of the soul and God, neglecting His Śakti. Third, the study of material nature and Śakti was embraced by the Tantra system, and the Vedic system split again into the third sect of Shaktism, which seemed different from Shaivism and Vaishnavism.

The specific outcome of Shankaracharya's commentary was the schism between the Six Systems, and the specific outcome of the later commentaries was the schism between Vaishnavism, Shaivism, and Shaktism. Once these two types of schisms were created, the unity in the Vedic system was effectively lost. The Vaishnavas and Shaivas focused on Vedānta, and the Shaktas took a greater interest in the other five systems of philosophy. Over time, each of these three systems was further split into many subsects, each based on different Vedic texts, but each of them neglecting the principles presented in the other texts. To the outsider, this reinforced the belief that the Vedic system is not just diverse but also disparate; that it is a collection of many contradictory ideologies.

These schisms continue to play havoc on the understanding of the Vedic system even today. For instance, Sāñkhya is included in all Puranas, but practically everyone who reads these Puranas glosses over Sāñkhya and proceeds into the stories because the teachers of the Puranas are mostly Vaishnavas and they deemphasize everything other than select aspects of Vedānta. Similarly, the discussion of Yoga forms a core aspect of all the Upanishads, but the teachers of these Upanishads, who are mostly Shaivas, gloss over Yoga philosophy because they are focused on Vedānta. When outsiders look at these discrepancies, they find it justifiable to create even more discrepancies. For instance, the Yoga Sūtra doesn't speak about the Kundalini, although Tantra does. There is no discussion about Chakras in the Yoga Sūtra, although it is present in the Tantras. The Yoga Sūtra speaks of only one Asana or meditative posture, while Tantras speak of 8,400,000 such postures. While Tantra practitioners indulge in sexual practices, the Yoga Sūtra speaks of celibacy. While Yoga Sūtra rejects the pursuit of mystical powers, the Tantra system advocates it. The modern practitioners of Yoga have therefore effectively transformed it into Tantra. This means that even more people who are interested in the transcendental nature of the Six Systems of Philosophy, are repelled from it, as it is now Tantric.

The schisms between the various systems are also exacerbated because the Vedānta school emphasizes the urgency of liberation from the material world, while other systems discuss the nature of the material world. If you think of the material world as a raging firestorm, then Vedānta says that you must quickly get out of it. Sāñkhya explains how the fire started. Yoga explains how to get out of the firestorm. Nyāya explains how that fire is a logical outcome of the incompatibility between soul and matter. Vaiśeṣika explains how the fire burns. And Mīmāṃsā discusses the protections while trying to get out of the firestorm. Now, it is up to the reader to decide—Do you want to treat the methods of protecting yourself against the fire as a recommendation for permanently living in the fire, or a method to defend yourself while you are trying to escape? Do you want to consider the description of fire and how it burns just an intellectual curiosity or urgent information that matches the urge to escape the fire?

The divergences in the Six Systems are exacerbated when their position in the larger scheme of things is not understood. Then, a method for protection against the burning fire is treated as a recommendation to stay in the fire. Or, information about the fire's burning is used just for intellectual curiosity. This recommendation then is seen as a contrast against the exhortation to escape the fire, and, lo and behold, a contradiction between the texts is produced.

To avoid such misinterpretations, one must study all the Six Systems, because that gives one the conviction that there is a fire (in case you don't believe it), there is a reason why it was started (in case you are looking for a rational justification), there is a method to escape it, and there are methods to avoid its harmful effects while you are trying to run out of the firestorm. Wearing a mask is not contradictory to running out; understanding that the fire will not die on its own is not contradictory to deciding that one must run out of the fire. In this way, the Six Systems of philosophy are consistent and coherent, despite their diverging emphases. By studying them, we obtain a view into the larger oral tradition, how this tradition was adapted for different purposes, and why all the systems of philosophy are important for different aspects of the problem. These books are the manuals for life—useful for different kinds of issues.

Finally, a few words must be said about the prevalent commentaries, and how the present commentaries differ. The prevalent commentaries today fall into two broad categories. First, experts in one system, trained by their tradition, comment on only one system of philosophy. Second, academics not trained in any system by the tradition, but having some expertise in the Sanskrit language, comment on multiple systems; they produce false interpretations of things that they don't understand because the context in which the text is written completely escapes them. Both these classes seem interesting to historians, but they mean little to most people because their ideas are not compared to modern thinking. The experts are restricted to one system; the non-experts are misleading; and neither experts nor non-experts demonstrate the relevance of an ancient system in a modern world—when so much around has changed.

These commentaries aim to carry out an unthinkable marriage between (a) the text, (b) the broader Vedic context, (c) demonstrate how this knowledge is relevant today, and (d) make it assimilable to people who know little about Vedic philosophy (or even about Western philosophy and modern science).

This series of books is subtitled "Scientific Commentaries", by which I mean reason and experience—something that can be rationally explained, put into practice, and confirmed by experience. I also mean a contrast or similarity to modern science, Western philosophy, and other prevalent systems of thinking. The former is meant to demonstrate that this is not based on "faith"—although enough faith is needed to read the books, put some of it in practice, and realize the truth. The latter is meant to assist the understanding of the modern mind which is accustomed to almost everything other than Vedic doctrines.

We progress from what we know to what we don't. If what we know is true, then it must be confirmed. If what we know is false, then it must be rejected by reason and evidence. The books are meant to provide adequate background to help people understand. This is a different approach to commentaries than those that have been done in the past: The past commentators relied exclusively on referencing other Vedic texts, and that was acceptable in a society where the Vedic texts were popular and their tenets were accepted. It is not useful for a global audience, or those who are educated in modern science but know very little about Vedic texts. They need an alternative, and these books can help.

From an academic viewpoint, the purpose of writing scientific commentaries is also to transform the discussion of Vedic texts from one of history, linguistics, and religious studies to one about science, philosophy, and empirical merit. Unless Vedic texts are seen as technical information, rather than poetry and literature, their content cannot be truly evaluated and appreciated.

Any ambitious project is hard, and anything hard is likely to have flaws. But it is said that thoroughly honest people enjoy and appreciate reading about the truth even if imperfectly composed. I sincerely hope that you will too.

Book Preface

Science, by the common definition, is the study of reality through reason and experience, as opposed to faith. In Vedic epistemology, observation, reason, and faith are called pratyakśa, anumāna, and śabda, and the last method (which rests on the authority of the Vedas) is given greater importance over the first two. By this distinction, however, faith is emphasized, whereas reason and experience are not. Hence, in what way can the knowledge of God be "scientific", if the legitimacy of observation and reason is rejected? The answer to this question is that we need to redefine the nature of reason and experience.

The Vedic doctrine of experience is that it comprises three aspects. In the material world, these are called sattva, rajas, and tamas. In the description of a conscious person (e.g., soul and God), they are called sat, chit, and ānanda. These are also described as sambanda, abhidheya, and prayojana. In my earlier books, I have termed these relation, cognition, and emotion. In Greek philosophy, these were called ethos, logos, and pathos. We can understand them as the three criteria employed while judging and choosing: right, truth, and good. And there are other names by which these are described in different places.

All of these components are necessary for experience, but each of them is sufficient to cause experience (the other two). This leads to the doctrine that each of these three modes is sometimes dominant and sometimes subordinate. When the mode is dominant, then it is the cause, and at that time, it is sufficient to cause experience. But the effect (experience) requires all the three modes.

Thus, the variety of experience is constructed by the innumerable combinations of the modes, and it is described as an inverted tree whose root is the 'balanced' state of the three modes in which they are inseparable, but which then 'expands' into three 'branches', each of which then divides successively by the three modes creating infinite variety which is called the manifest world.

This description of reality however creates three problems. First, context determines which mode is dominant and in different contexts, different things are superior. Second, the superior is understood as the whole which is then divided into its parts; however, due to the modes, the whole in one situation becomes the part in another. Third, the cause in one context becomes the effect in another. The result is that this inverted tree-like structure involves infinite contradictions. The same thing is a cause and an effect; the same thing is the whole and the part; the same thing is considered dominant and subordinate.

Commentaries on Vedānta Sutra have tried to address these contradictions. To resolve one contradiction, we can remove one branch, twig, or leaf in the tree, and the tree is now incomplete. But if the branch, twig, or leaf is restored, then the contradiction returns. This is the basis of the problem—now well known in modern mathematics—that knowledge is either inconsistent or incomplete. The problem also exists in Vedānta Sutra commentaries: (1) if everything is described, then there are many contradictions, and (2) as contradictions reduce, more aspects of reality are rejected, as they are incompatible with other aspects. A consistent description is also the description of nothingness.

The Acintyabhedābheda doctrine says that the complete description is 'inconceivable' as the same thing is a cause and effect, whole and part, dominant and subordinate. That leads to the collapse of rationality. But this is not a problem unique to Vedānta. Any scientific theory that tries to be complete, will be ridden with contradictions; fewer contradictions mean more incompleteness; that is, a consistent theory will describe fewer aspects of our experience.

The doctrine of the three modes, with their dominant-subordinate, whole-part, and cause-effect relations, addresses this central problem of knowledge through experience. However, to formulate a scientific understanding, we must now update our understanding of the meaning of rationality or logic.

The problem with logic is that it describes universal truth—logical truth is true in all possible worlds. For example, $2 + 2 = 4$ is universally true. Logic is hence incapable of dealing with contextual truth. To solve this problem of universal truth, we must define what we mean by contextual truth: it is the answer to a question; if the question is changed, then the answer is changed.

Logic, therefore, must now be redefined not as the pair of premises and conclusions, but as the triad of the premise, question, and answer. Each premise gives rise to some questions, which then gives rise to an answer. The answer is not universal, because the question is contextual. And yet, it is true—in relation to the question, when the question is posed. The original premise, which leads to all questions and answers, is called the Absolute Truth. But all subsequent emanations from this truth are Relative Truths. The relative truth is not falsity. But it is true only in a context. It is one of the many branches of the tree.

The Absolute Truth is the primordial premise which creates everything else, by giving rise to questions and problems—which are termed as the 'desire' in the Absolute Truth. Due to this desire, the Absolute Truth is a person, and the premise doesn't exist merely as an idea. Once these questions and problems are created, then the answer to these are also created. The answer is a part of the premise, and it is connected to the premise through a question. However, since the premise becomes a question, and then becomes an answer, therefore, the same thing is alternately known as a premise, a problem, and an answer.

'Truth' must thus be defined as the relation between a question and an answer. If an answer solves a problem, then, it is true. But many answers can address a problem. Therefore, aside from the 'truth', we must also judge the 'good' and 'right'. If surgery is successful but the patient dies, then the surgery is not 'good'. A surgery performed by an unqualified person is not 'right'. Thus, the connection between solutions and problems is judged in three ways: (a) it solves a problem, (b) the solution increases happiness, and (c) we are permitted to it. By this definition, the 'Absolute Truth' is the answer to all questions, increases happiness in all situations, and everyone is permitted to use the solution.

With the redefinition of experience (as the combination of the three modes), causality (as one of the three modes), reality (as the tree of all mode combinations), and reason (as the choice of one of the tree branches), we meet the rational criterion for knowledge—it must be consistent and complete. The tests of truth, right, and good constitute the empirical criteria for knowledge. When rational and empirical criteria are met, then the knowledge is 'scientific'. Since these criteria are met, therefore, the knowledge of the Absolute Truth is 'scientific', i.e., rational and empirical. It need not necessarily be accepted on faith, although if it were accepted on faith, it will still be true, right, and good.

This interpretation shows how the above understanding is presented in the Vedānta Sutra. Vedānta has progressed over centuries through Advaita, Śuddhādvaita, Viśiṣṭādvaita, Dvaita, Bhedābheda, and Acintyabhedābheda. As the doctrines have become more complete, they have also become more inconsistent. The Advaita doctrine describes the soul, without matter and God. As successive doctrines add more aspects of reality, more contradictions are created. The Bhedābheda doctrine says that God, matter, and the soul are at once different and identical. And the Acintyabhedābheda doctrine acknowledges the failure of physical ideas of identity and difference. The next step in the progression of Vedānta is to make the complete understanding of reality also rational. And this rationality requires us to revisit the nature of whole and parts.

If wholes and parts are physical, then we are led to reductionism. For example, if the whole is an ocean, and the part is a drop, then removing a drop reduces the ocean. Indeed, there is no ocean apart from the drops. All physical analogies of whole and part have failed to correctly describe the Vedānta doctrine. Hence, this interpretation redefines the wholes and parts as ideas.

For example, a 'mammal' is the whole, and a 'cow' is the part. We can say: a cow is a mammal, but we cannot say that a mammal is a cow. The mammal exists independent of the cow, but the cow doesn't exist independent of the mammal. If cows ceased to exist, the definition of mammal would not change. But if the mammal ceased to exist, then cows will cease to exist as well.

The use of concepts as wholes and parts breaks the principles of modern logic. Since cows are mammals, but mammals are not cows, therefore, the principle of identity is broken (A is B, but B is not A). Similarly, the principle of mutual exclusion is broken (something is either A or not-A) because a mammal is neither a cow nor a tiger. Likewise, the principle of non-contradiction is broken (something cannot be A and not-A) because both cows and tigers are mammals. The failure of modern logic is pervasive, but it is not understood because we view the world physically. If the notion of whole and part is changed, then the principles of modern logic are rejected, and a new logic is needed.

This new logic is based on the hierarchy of concepts, and because the conventional separation and identity is rejected while understanding this hierarchy, therefore, we can say that the reality is Bhedābheda—i.e., neither different nor identical. Since conventional logic cannot be used with the hierarchy of concepts, therefore, we can say that reality is Achintya or inconceivable. But because everything can be understood through an alternative conception of reality as concepts, and its associated logic, therefore, the reality is conceivable.

As a result, every past doctrine about Vedānta is considered true, although from a certain perspective, i.e., that doctrine becomes a form of contextual truth. The Acintyabhedābheda doctrine describes the Absolute Truth, but within current logic. And the present interpretation transcends the current logic.

The summary of Vedānta is that the Absolute Truth has a masculine and a feminine aspect. In different contexts, they are called superior to each other, equal to each other, different from each other, inseparable from each other, the cause of each other, and the effect of each other. The soul is sometimes called a part of the masculine, sometimes of the feminine, sometimes their child, sometimes similar to the whole, and sometimes dissimilar from the whole. The material world is sometimes called a part of God, sometimes separate from God, sometimes an expression of God, and sometimes God is said to be immanent in the world, and yet, the world is not considered identical to God. Every position is considered, debated, rejected in one sense, and accepted in another.

Vedānta is therefore not for the faint-hearted. Those who want to think of reality in terms of absolutely true and false claims are likely to be perplexed by these descriptions. Similarly, those who come to religion hoping to find an absolute set of unchanging ideas, are likely to be baffled. Vedānta is for the advanced student of Vedic philosophy, and it explains how seemingly contradictory positions are true, although they are not true universally. There is a sense in which one position is true, and another sense in which the opposite position is true. To employ these meanings, we must acknowledge that reality is itself meaning. Otherwise, these meanings and their truth would be attributed only to our minds, not to reality, and philosophy would be mere speculation.

The novelty of this interpretation is two-fold. First, it advocates a novel understanding of reality, which is semantic rather than physical.

Second, it describes how every other Vedānta position becomes simultaneously true if such a view is adopted. The different Vedānta doctrines are therefore not false or contradictory. They are all true, and the study of Vedānta is the study of from different perspectives. The unity of Vedic philosophy exists even within Vedānta, even though the doctrines have ostensibly seemed contradictory.

Introduction

Background Information

The Problem of Knowledge

Commentaries on Vedānta Sūtra have been written once every few centuries, and only when there was something new to be said. This is one such commentary. It is not that the passing of time has made it inevitable. It is that there are some unsolved problems in Vedānta, and this commentary presents the solution. The central problem is that of the consistency and completeness of knowledge. Completeness means that everything can be known, and consistency means that it is known without contradictions. Regrettably, this goal of knowledge has seemed to be impossible. We now know—through many attempts in Western logic and mathematics, as well through previous attempts to solve this problem in Vedic philosophy—that no rational description is both consistent and complete. We are therefore compelled to sacrifice either consistency or completeness. The sacrifice of completeness is unsatisfactory, as it entails that everything cannot be known. The alternative seems appealing: everything can be known, but the knowledge will have contradictions. However, any contradiction also makes the truth of the entire system seem suspect.

There are many ways to understand such contradictions. Philosophies like Buddhism believe that reality is itself inconsistent and therefore consistent knowledge of reality cannot exist. Others like Advaita take the view that reality is consistent, but our language and experience produce inconsistencies in knowledge; therefore, we must reject experience and language. Then, there are Vaishnava doctrines that indicate that our experience can be consistent, however, our language is never consistent; therefore, the complete truth can be experienced although not described. And some philosophies aren't even aware of the problem, or even if they are aware, they do not try to find a solution.

There are two main sources of the problem, and both arise when we consider meanings as a part of reality. The first issue is that meanings are always defined through opposites such as hot vs. cold, bitter vs. sweet, big vs. small. In this world, these opposites exist in different things—i.e., something is either hot or cold—but the origin of everything must have both. Due to the coexistence of opposites, the source of everything becomes self-contradictory. However, if one side of the opposition is discarded, then the source becomes incomplete.

The second issue with meanings is that they exist in three modes—universal, individual, and contextual. For example, there is a universal idea of a circle, there are individual circles, and something not perfectly circular may be called a 'circle' sometimes. If we use the word 'circle', are we referring to the universal idea, the individual things, or the contextual use? It turns out that we need each of the three modes to obtain completeness, however, their coexistence creates contradictions if we are not careful to distinguish between the three modes. For example, if we call an imperfect round a 'circle' and treat that designation as the universal idea of a circle, then perfect circles would no longer be circles. Likewise, if an individual thing is circular and black, and we do not distinguish between the individual and the universal, then blackness becomes a part of the definition of a circle, and circles that are not black can no longer be circles.

The source of the consistency vs. completeness debate in Indian philosophy rests on the contradictories such as hot vs. cold, while the source of the same debate in Western philosophy lies in the existence of modalities. Naturally, if we combine them—and we must—then, the problem is bigger. However, there is also a bright side to this dilemma: By combining the contradictories with the modalities, we can open the doors to a solution. On the other hand, there is no solution to the problem of contradictories without modalities or vice versa. The solution with modalities must say that even the opposites are modalities; therefore, they are not simultaneously experienced, although they exist at once.

The Problem of Modalities

But even before we set out to solve any of these problems, we need a very profound change: We must give up the idea that the world is physical because in a physical world knowledge is impossible. For example, when you see a cow, there is a symbol of the cow in your mind. The external cow is also a symbol of the idea of a cow. The difference between the two is that the external symbol elucidates the idea in greater detail—and is hence 'bigger'—than the internal symbol. This means that even the external cow is not a physical object. It is as much a symbol of an idea as an internal symbol. Similarly, our minds are the symbols of the universal concept of mind. When the idea of cow exists in our minds, both of which are symbols, then the symbol of cow exists within a symbol of mind. Consequently, the symbol of the cow is a symbol within a symbol. Thus, the external cow, our minds, and the knowledge in our minds are all symbols. There is factually nothing physical in this world; everything must be treated as a symbol of some idea. Hence, when we speak of the modalities of reality, they pertain to the symbols. Each symbol has a universal, individual, and contextual modality. The universal modality is the idea in the symbol; the individual modality is that the symbol is an instance of the idea, and the contextual modality is that this symbol is related to other kinds of symbols.

These relations between the symbols also come in three modalities—each idea in a symbol is a part of a more abstract idea, the idea is distinct from other ideas that are also part of the more abstract idea and yet not this particular idea, and that there are potentially other symbolic instances of the same idea. Let us consider these three types of relations between the symbols one by one.

First, when you say that something is a cow, you also accept that it is a mammal. Now, most people today don't accept this claim. They say that ideas like mammal and animal are simply in our minds and that there is nothing objectively mammalian about the cow. That should also imply that we stop using the terms mammals and animals in relation to the cow. But we cannot do that either. Removing words such as mammal and animal from our vocabulary would create new problems—e.g., we would not be able to put horses and cows in the same category. Therefore, some philosophers like to live in the doublethink in which the cow is not objectively a mammal (as the mammal is in the mind), but use the word mammal in relation to the cow (otherwise, we will lose the capacity to group other animals together). In this doublethink, we don't accept that there is a symbolic representation of mammals in a cow. Owing to physical thinking, if a mammal were inside the cow, then it could not exist in other species such as tigers, horses, cats, and dogs. This is because something can only be inside the cow, and not outside, or vice versa. The physicalist in fact insists that a mammal is neither inside nor outside. It is only in our minds.

Second, when you say that something is a cow, you also mean that it is not a horse, cat, dog, tiger, etc. If you don't adopt this way of thinking, then saying that something is a cow would not be contradictory to stating that the same thing is a tiger. But how does the assertion that something is a cow entail that it is not a tiger? The short answer is that the negations of all other species must exist inside the symbol of a cow symbolically. Most people today don't accept this idea. They say that the claim that something is a cow, and the claim that it is not a tiger, are just claims in our minds. But if this idea were taken all the way, then we must also reject the use of logical oppositions—i.e., that a cow is not a tiger—in relation to the external world. We cannot do that, because it will lead to almost a complete collapse of logic and language. Thus, we keep saying that the cow is not a tiger, but there is nothing objective about it. Hence, we don't recognize that the negation of tigers must objectively exist in the cow.

Third, when you speak about a specific cow, you also implicitly assume that it is different from other cows. This means that a symbolic representation of other cows must exist in each cow. This is the only way you can say that a claim about this cow cannot be applied to that cow because this cow is different from that cow. However, again, due to physicalist thinking, we refuse to accept that what a thing is not, cannot be part of the definition of that thing. Hence, the doctrine of each thing existing in and of itself arises, because how that thing is different from the other things (or just like those things) is in our minds.

The problem of meaning is that it involves the universal and the individual modes at a minimum—a cow is an instance of the cow. However, the universal and the individual are then defined through distinctions to mammals, tigers, and other cows. Therefore, we get three modalities of universal, individual, and contextual, and each such mode again has three further modalities. For instance, after you have distinguished a cow from a tiger and dog (which involves the contextual modality), you must say that cows, tigers, and dogs are mammals. Thus, within the symbolic representation of a cow not being a dog, there must be the idea that even a dog is a mammal. By the universal modality of a mammal, cows and dogs are identical, but by the contextual modality, they are distinct. Likewise, the distinction of a cow from other cows is the individual modality in the contextual modality. Thus, there are three modes, but each of them enters the other modes, qualifies them, and creates infinite modes.

Therefore, when we adopt non-physical thinking, then we see how contradictions can exist within the same thing, although in different modes—e.g., that the tiger is within the cow, however, the cow is asserted, and the tiger is negated. We can also see how things much bigger than the cow exist within the cow—since to know the cow, we must know that it is a mammal, animal, etc. Other individuals also exist in an individual, but in each individual, the other individuals must be present as a negation, since we somehow know that one individual is different from the other individuals. The presence of other things within each thing leads to logical contradictions unless we accept modes.

However, if we try to avoid these contradictions, then we run into a different problem. When we say that "this is not a cow", it could entail—(1) this is not a mammal, (2) this is a mammal, but it could be a tiger, horse, cat, dog, etc., and (3) something else is a cow. Which of these outcomes follow the claim that "this is not a cow"? Each of the above outcomes is possible, but because we cannot say which of them is implied, our knowledge is incomplete. Therefore, in physicalist thinking, knowledge is always either inconsistent or incomplete. It is incomplete because the negations of statements produce many possible alternatives, and we cannot determine which alternative is implied. But if we add other things within a thing, then the result of the addition is inconsistency.

All philosophies—in the West or East—are victims of these conundrums. We might say that we haven't yet understood why and how logic works, but that would be an understatement. We haven't factually realized that the existence of anything contradicts physical thinking and its associated logic. My attempt in this commentary is to transcend these limitations of physical thinking, its associated logic, and its problematic conclusions. If we have traced the source of inconsistency and incompleteness, then we can hope to solve it.

The Evolution of Vedānta

With this background, we can briefly discuss the historical evolution of Vedānta, why varied types of attempts have failed previously, and what remedies can be used. Our story begins with the question: How can opposites exist in something without creating a self-contradiction? This question arises because the world is comprised of opposites, and if these opposites have emerged from a single source, then the source must be self-contradictory. The initial answer in Vedānta to this problem is that these opposites are not always manifest. They rather exist in an unmanifest state of possibilities. But, when they are manifest, they are also separated as different places, times, and personalities. Thus, the source of everything is not everything, but the *possibility* of everything. All the contentions in Vedānta are about the nature of this undifferentiated possibility. The personalist philosopher says that the origin of everything must be a form because the formless cannot be the cause of manifest forms. The impersonalist philosopher instead makes the counterclaim that if the Absolute Truth had a form, then the various parts of this form—e.g., head and toe—would constitute many truths, and that would defeat the purpose of seeking a singular truth.

Of course, it is one thing to criticize the opponent's view, and quite another to address the issues raised by the opponent's criticism. The problem with the impersonalist view is that it cannot explain the origin of forms, while also saying that the origin is formless. In fact, Buddhism battled with this problem and concluded that because the forms are mutually contradictory, therefore, their reconciliation must lead to nothingness. Therefore, the goal of a singular truth as the original source of all forms must be abandoned. The impersonalist now says: Let's accept that there are two realities. The first reality, called Brahman, is undifferentiated and can be called the singular truth, although it is not the origin of forms. The second reality, called māyā, is differentiated and is the source of all numerous truths, or the forms observed in space and time.

The personalist responds to this conclusion by saying that two is better than nothing, but one is better than two. Therefore, we cannot accept the separation of Brahman and māyā as singular and numerous truths. We must rather say that māyā is a part of Brahman, and differentiation exists within the oneness. This diversity within oneness is conceived as the body of God: God's body parts are the diversity and God is the unity. But you might ask: What is God if not for the collection of the body parts? The answer is that God is an object, and the parts of God's body are the properties of that object. Just like a material particle has numerous properties such as mass, charge, energy, momentum, etc. which are different aspects of the particle, similarly, the singular truth has many aspects or properties. The particle is their unity, and the properties are the diversity. This doctrine, which associates numerous properties with an object is called Viśiṣṭādvaita; the object is Advaita, and the properties are Viśiṣṭa.

This conclusion, however, produces a new problem: If the various qualities of God are distinct from God, then God must be without any quality. Specifically, He cannot have a form of hands, legs, face, and torso, because these must be the qualities of God, not God. Just as the particle is devoid of all its properties like mass and energy, similarly, God must be devoid of all the qualities. This then leads to the same conclusion as Advaita: God is Brahman and His body is māyā. Whatever we call the "form of God" is māyā, not God. In fact, the form of God exists only if māyā has covered the Brahman to produce a form.

To avoid this problem, the personalist provides a counter: There are two kinds of properties—matter and soul. Brahman is the individual soul, and it is covered by matter. However, God—the object of all these properties—is never thus covered. While this solves the problem of God having a body of souls (where God is the Supreme Soul), it also creates a new problem: If the soul is the body of the Supreme Soul, then the soul's suffering must also be God's suffering. After all, the individual soul is the body of the Supreme Soul. Therefore, God may not be directly covered by māyā, but even an indirect covering is problematic since it transforms the soul's suffering into God's suffering.

To counter this challenge, the personalist now says that the individual soul and the Supreme Soul are eternally separate and different realities. This doctrine of the eternal separation of the Supreme Soul and soul is called Dvaita. That claim, however, leads to the plurality of realities, and the rejection of the singular truth—the One from which many have expanded as His parts. The pluralism leads to questions of why these different realities must interact with each other, and why the soul must be dependent upon God. In fact, if the soul is eternally separate from God, then why is devotion to God required?

The personalist philosopher now makes a very bold move. To solve the problem of why the parts of the body of God are not separate from God, He says: Each part contains all the other parts, although in a hidden form. Therefore, the numerous truths are a part of the singular truth, and the singular truth is a part of each of the numerous truths. For example, the eyes of the singular truth are His part, just like His tongue. But the tongue is hidden within the eye, and the eye is hidden within the tongue. Since every aspect is hidden in every other aspect, hence, you cannot ask what they are aspects of. After all, the thing that they are an aspect of, is within that thing. This resolves the problem of object-property separation because the object is in each property, and the properties are in the object. Now, the form of God is not māyā because the whole truth is within each of the parts. Indeed, God is not different from God's body.

Thus, you cannot say that the eyes of God are not His tongue—implying that He cannot eat with His eyes. And you cannot say that His eyes are His tongue—implying that He has only tongue and no eyes. You must rather make two conflicting claims—the eyes are the tongue and not the tongue—but this conflict is not a self-contradiction, because the eyes and the tongue are in different places, and the eyes become the tongue (or vice versa) at different times. Thus, because God has both eyes and tongue, therefore, He can both see and taste. Similarly, His eyes can manifest the tongue property and the tongue can manifest the eye property, therefore, there is no necessity to suppose that God is different from the many body parts of God's body. These aspects of God's body are manifest simultaneously as different parts of His body, and each of these body parts can transform into any other body part one after another.

The rejection of the identity of eyes and tongue is called bheda and the rejection of their separation is called abheda. These two are combined into the doctrine called Bhedābheda. Now, we can say that the soul is part of God, and God is present within the soul. Due to bheda, when the soul falls into māyā, God is not fallen. But due to abheda, the soul is not separated from God. Thus, both soul and māyā are parts of God, and yet, God is separate from both.

This resolution of the problem, however, creates a new one. The doctrine rests on the idea that the whole is inside each part, but how the whole exists inside the part is never explained. Certainly, no physical theory can explain this. But since alternative ideas about reality are absent, therefore, the Bhedābheda doctrine remains inexplicable. One way to understand the doctrine is to say that the entire body is human, and each part of the body is also human. For instance, if you see a human hand, you can deduce that it is a part of a human body, since humanness is not just the whole body, but also in the individual hand.

The impersonalist, however, exploits this analogy. He says: If the whole is present in each part, then according to the claim of soul and matter being parts of God, it follows that God is present in matter and soul too (remember that separating soul and matter from God undermines the goal of knowing a singular truth). Furthermore, if we say that the presence of God in each part of God makes those parts God, then by extension, God's presence in soul and matter must make each soul and material object God. Therefore, God cannot be considered a Supreme Person because all souls and material objects are God.

If we try to solve this problem by saying that the soul and matter are not part of God, then we end up with many separate realities, which is worse than the Oneness of the impersonalist. If instead, we say that the whole is not present in each part, then these parts become different from the singular truth, and we must now say that the individual soul and the individual material objects are māyā, not the singular truth. Whichever doctrine is employed, we either end up with impersonalism or something much inferior to impersonalism.

Impersonalism is also problematic, because if there is only one Being, then how can we be individually liberated or fallen into the material world? We can either be collectively liberated or collectively fallen. If we are collectively fallen, then we must also be collectively liberated. Therefore, I cannot be individually liberated by my effort if everyone else is not getting liberated at once. In short, there is no value in individual effort, because there is no individuality.

Seeing these difficulties, Sri Chaitanya articulated the Acintyabhedābheda doctrine which states that the singular truth must be inconceivable. This was in recognition of the fact that all doctrines had some or another issue. The issue is that we are required to make three incomprehensible statements at once: (1) the parts are in the whole, (2) the whole is in the parts, (3) the whole in the part makes some parts the whole, but other parts do not become the whole.

Each of these is a hard problem. For example, to say that the parts are in the whole, we must have some idea about the whole, but we don't. What is an ocean, if not the mere collection of the drops? Isn't the ocean merely a word used to indicate the plurality of drops by a singular noun, as if it were a singular entity? In short, isn't the ocean merely a linguistic construct when in fact there are many drops? The second claim complicates the issue further. You could say that the drops are in the ocean, but how do you say that the ocean is in the drops? That immanence of the ocean within each drop defies all intuition. Finally, how do say that some drops are the full ocean, while other drops are not the full ocean? Even if the immanence of the whole within the parts were accepted, why should it be applied selectively? Naturally, the problems magnify at each successive stage. The problem is not just that we are unable to make all these claims collectively, but that we are unable to make them individually.

The Semantic Conception of Reality

This commentary tries to solve each of the above problems individually and collectively. The cornerstone of the commentary is the change in the conception of reality from physical to semantic. For example, we should not think of the whole and part in terms of an ocean and the drops in it. We should rather think of reality in terms of concepts like cows and mammals. The mammal is the whole and the cow is its part. However, if you see a cow, you also say that it is a mammal, although you cannot reduce the mammal to the cow. Therefore, the mammal exists in the cow, and the cow exists in the mammal. However, the mammal is not equal to the cow. This is expressed by saying that— (1) the cow is a mammal, and (2) the mammal is not a cow. This is possible only if reality is described as concepts—e.g., mammal and cow. It solves the problem of why some parts (i.e., matter and the soul) contain the whole but are not the whole. They are parts of the whole, just like the cow is a part of the mammal. Since the mammal exists in the cow, therefore, the whole is not merely the collection and hence not merely a word. It is rather present within each type of mammal.

The reverse problem of why the presence of the whole in each part (in the case of God) makes the parts equal to the whole, still needs to be addressed. To solve this problem, recall how each part is defined through a distinction to the other parts. This distinction, however, can exist in three modalities—of space, time, and person. We can apply these modalities to our bodies and understand their implications. In the person modality, we would say that my hand has a 'mind' of its own. In the space modality, we would say that my hand is not my leg, but there is a leg elsewhere. In the time modality, we would say that my hand is not my leg right now, but it can become the leg. In our body, only the spatial modality is prominently found. Only occasionally, our hands are not in our control—so we say that they have their own mind. Extremely rarely can a person perform the work of the hands using the legs. But in God's body, all these modalities are simultaneously manifest. Thus, each part of God's body has a mind of its own. Each part can become the other parts. But, by distinction to the other parts, each part is also defined by what the other part is not.

The difference between the soul and God is that places, times, and personalities are 'compressed' in God—this compression is achieved through semantic abstraction—but these are 'expanded' in the world. Due to this expansion, the soul is always in a specific place and time, and this place then limits the things its body parts can do. Since the soul can move from one body to another, therefore, a distinction between soul and body is made in the case of the soul. However, since God is all the space and time, therefore, He doesn't change His body. And yet, His body is all that is possible in all places, times, and personalities. Therefore, we can say that every part of God's body is God, but we cannot make the same claim about the soul. Quite simply, the soul is localized in space and time and is, therefore, an individual. God is also an individual, but all space and time and the other souls, are merely the parts of the Supreme Person. Since the soul and God are individual persons, therefore, there is a distinction between the soul and God. But since the soul is a part of God, therefore, the soul is not *independent* of God. God, however, is *independent* of all the souls.

The whole-part relation between God and the soul can be easily understood if we say that God is the object, whereas the soul is a property of that object. The object can exist without the property, but the property cannot exist without the object. For example, you can remove some mass from a particle, and the particle is undiminished. But you cannot remove the particle from the mass. The whole-part relationship now also becomes the object-property relation.

Apart from these properties, God also exists as a purpose. This purpose exists in God, but the same purpose can also exist in each soul, without equating the soul to God. Thereby, we can say that God is 'inside' everything—as its purpose. And yet, those individual things do not become God by this immanence. Therefore, we can say that God is partially present in each of the parts, but as the whole, He is separate from each of the parts. The immanence of purpose in each thing leads us to the conclusion that God exists in everything, but everything is not God. This is because God is immanent through His purposes in different souls and material objects. Hence, the presence of God in His body parts makes all these body parts God, but the same isn't true of the soul.

The immanence of purpose, and the separation of the properties, is resolved by relations. God is the whole purpose, each thing fulfills the purpose partially, therefore, the partial purpose is related to the whole purpose, like a part to the whole. This is not a relation between two equals. It is rather the relation of an object to its properties, or the relation between the whole and the part.

The above three modalities—purpose, property, and relation—are identified in the Vedas as the aspects of existence—ānanda, *chit*, and *sat*. Hence, after we say that the singular truth must be known semantically, we must distinguish between three types of semanticism—the purpose, property, and relation.

Once we understand this simple scheme of three aspects, then we can understand how these modalities are combined infinitely. The combinations occur by dividing each mode by each of the three modes. For example, we have discussed above how the property of being a cow entails that it is a mammal, it is not a tiger, and it is not other cows. Likewise, when we speak of our purpose, we can also talk about a higher purpose, what our purpose is not, and the same purpose in the other individuals. Finally, in the context of relations, we can talk about relations that are higher than our relations, those to whom we are not related, and others who have the same relation as us. These modes are in addition to what a thing is in three modes—a universal, and individual, and relation to other individuals instantiating a universal. Through the successive divisions of modalities, infinite such modalities are produced. And these modalities then form a hierarchical tree-like structure in which there are higher, lower, and peer nodes. The higher purpose, the higher concept, and the higher relation are 'above', and constitute the wholes. The 'peer' concepts, purposes, and relations are different from a node. And the 'lower' concepts, purposes, and relations, are the parts of the 'higher' nodes. This tree-like structure is a simplified vision of reality, in which everything expands from a root through the three modalities. But the construction of this tree, how this tree violates classical logic, and yet, with modalities, how it leads to completeness, is very complicated.

This tree can expand—through new combinations. It can contract—by removing some combinations. And it can evolve—by changing the combinations. If the existence of the tree is complex, then we can imagine that the expansion, contraction, and evolution of this tree is more incomprehensible. The creation of the material world is the expansion of this tree, and its annihilation is the contraction of the tree back into its root. While the tree exists, it also evolves, and that evolution constitutes the scientific study of the material world.

With these three kinds of modalities, all the issues in Vedānta philosophy are overcome. The singular truth now has a form and is not formless. This is because the singular truth is also a concept, a purpose, and a relation. The parts exist in the whole, and the whole exists in all the parts, and this mutual innateness is due to their semantic nature. Despite this mutual innateness, the soul can fall into the material world, but by that fall, God isn't fallen; the soul's suffering is not God's suffering. Each part of God's body is fully God, so, there is no distinction between soul and body in God. Therefore, God's body cannot be called the byproduct of māyā. God is innately present in tables and chairs as their purpose, however, this innate presence of God in tables and chairs doesn't make tables and chairs God. On the other hand, certain things like deities, names of God, or books on God, embody all of God's qualities so they are God; they just seem to be material parts, but by their qualities they are whole.

All these claims have been made at different points in the evolution of Vedānta, but there is no Vedānta Sūtra doctrine currently that supports them simultaneously. In fact, when a Vedānta Sūtra doctrine makes one of these true, it also makes some other claim(s) false. If they are simultaneously accepted to be true, then the Absolute Truth becomes inconceivable due to inner contradictions. The need for a new commentary on Vedānta Sūtra arises from this problem. This commentary shows how all these claims are true at once, that truth doesn't come at the expense of other claims, and all these claims can be made collectively and individually without producing inner contradictions.

I might caution the reader that this book is not easy reading. But remember that this is not an easy problem. It has existed for thousands of years and remains unsolved. The solution is also beyond conventional models of reasoning, so don't be surprised by the existence of contradictions in a classical sense. The problem is not the philosophy or its presentation. The problem is the very nature of knowledge. As we have seen, no known scheme makes knowledge both consistent and complete. A novel approach—complicated as it seems—is necessary to address this problem. If you can grasp the problem, then the solution becomes necessary and inevitable and the journey becomes extremely rewarding. I have made attempts to simplify this for the newcomer. The following sections discuss at length the nature of the problem, the varied previously attempted solutions, and their problems, before describing the proposal. I shall examine this proposal from numerous angles—scientific, philosophical, and religious. If you can be convinced of where this book is going to take us, then the subsequent arguments that validate this description can be undertaken.

Technical Overview

Scientific Background

One of the most intriguing ideas in Vedānta is the description of reality in terms of a whole-part theory. Other systems of Vedic philosophy take a different approach to solve the same problem. Sāñkhya philosophy, for example, describes matter as objects and their properties, the senses by which these properties are observed, the mind which understands the meaning, the intellect which judges the truth, the ego which formulates intentions, and the moral sense which perceives values. And this complicated description of matter is only one of the five ontologies in Sāñkhya—the others being the soul, God, time, and karma. With multiple ontologies, the complexity arising out of their interaction explodes. How can we reduce this complexity to a much simpler idea—namely the relation between a whole and a part? Doesn't this represent an oversimplification? If so, how could it be the conclusion of all knowledge?

When I thought about this problem, I was reminded of similar attempts in modern mathematics to reduce all kinds of mathematical objects to set theory. Set theory is also a whole-part theory, in which the set is the whole, and its members—objects or sets—are the parts. Set theory is simpler compared to many advanced mathematical topics. And yet, set theory is the foundation of modern mathematics, because other mathematical objects reduce to sets.

With set theory in mind, it seems that Vedānta was doing philosophy like mathematicians do mathematics today. There are very few parallels to this style of philosophy in the West. However, this realization gave me an initial glimpse into how the parallel between the whole-part doctrines in Vedānta and set theory as the foundation of all mathematics wasn't merely serendipity. Rather, the system could be made as rigorous as set theory, logic, and mathematics.

There are, however, serious problems in mathematical set theory. The central problem is that words in a language (which can be converted into numbers) exist in multiple *modes*—such as universal and individual. For instance, the word 'barber' can denote a class of people (universal) or a specific member of the class (individual). When we try to admit both these modes in language, we end up with contradictions. Therefore, the current set theory limits itself to just one mode—the mode of individuals. Now, if this set theory is used to construct a theory of numbers, then we get incompleteness because to count three objects, we must have the concept 'three' prior, and that necessitates the universals. Therefore, we have a fundamental problem: If we use more than one mode, then we get inconsistency. If instead, we use only one mode, then we get incompleteness. This tradeoff has been shown many times in mathematics, but none more ostensibly than by Gödel's proof that number theory is necessarily incomplete because the only alternative is that the theory is inconsistent.

Now, one could imagine that perhaps set theory is a bad choice for mathematical foundations. Maybe we should seek alternative foundations for mathematics. Since set theory arose because sets were a mathematical representation of concepts, perhaps, there are other ways to conceive of concepts. But, if the same type of foundation is also employed in Vedānta, the problem must lie elsewhere. Naturally, I suspected that the problem lay with modalities. The problem wasn't the whole-part nature of reality, but the fact that this reality can be simultaneously understood in different incompatible modes. And since the root of all these problems is the existence of multiple modalities, the only solution to these problems was to step outside conventional forms of logic.

The problems of mathematical set theory convinced me that such problems would arise in Vedānta too—unless a system of modal reasoning was being used, they would necessarily lead to contradictions. If set theory is riddled with paradoxes, then there cannot be a non-modal Vedānta doctrine that is consistent and complete. So, if we find problems of contradictions in Vedānta, we need to trace them to modalities, and not spend any time trying to solve them—because there is factually no solution to the problem within current logic. Sometimes knowing what not to do, can itself be an advancement. In this case, mathematical set theory helped me understand that all systems of Vedānta—if they try to be complete—must necessarily be inconsistent in current logic.

Philosophical Problems

I had previously encountered logical contradictions in Vedānta. For example, the Bhedābheda doctrine says that the whole and part are simultaneously different and non-different. And the Acintyabhedābheda doctrine says that this simultaneous difference and non-difference is inconceivable because it cannot be logically formulated. In short, the problems of mathematical set theory, how they lead to contradictions (if multiple modes are used) have been well-known in the Vedānta system. The difference between Vedānta and mathematical set theory is one of relative emphasis. The Vedānta system is unprepared to sacrifice completeness but is prepared to admit logical inconsistencies and inconceivability. Mathematicians instead prefer incompleteness over inconsistencies; they are prepared to reject modalities if that helps avoid contradictions.

The problems of logical inconsistencies have also been shown in other traditional philosophies, such as Buddhism. One such problem concerns the logical impossibility of the concept "I". For example, if you form a set of "friends" and "non-friends", then it is not clear whether "I" am my friend (which is not possible because friends are different from me) or a non-friend (because that would entail that I'm my enemy). There are variations of this problem in other parts of Indian philosophy. For example, when we speak about self-awareness, the self-aware state comes about when we desire self-awareness. In that desire, there is a difference between the knower and the known—after all, you could not desire something that you already have. To fulfill this desire, we establish a relation between the knower and the known, which means that there is again a difference between the knower and the known, although the two are related rather than disjointed. Finally, when the knower obtains knowledge of the known, the two are non-different. Now, the difference between the knower and the known, and the relation between the two are straightforward problems, because they are involved in all perceptions. The problem arises in the final stage of self-awareness where the knower and the known are non-different.

To accommodate these contradictory ideas, the difference and non-difference of the knower and the known in knowledge, non-difference must be added, since the difference is already understood. But how can two things be both different and non-different? This is impossible in classical logic as it violates the principle of mutual exclusion: Two things must either be different or non-different. Thus, "I" becomes self-contradictory as it breaks logical principles. Here, we aren't even using set theory or a whole-part doctrine. We are only employing two modes—i.e., the knower and the known—of the same "I". We are used to thinking of each thing as one kind of thing—e.g., a knower or a known. When the same thing must be understood in many modes, our classical forms of logic don't work. When the logic doesn't work, we tend to discard the modes (in modern mathematics) and we reject logic (in Vedānta philosophy). Neither solution is fundamentally better; they are merely preferences.

The problem both in mathematical set theory and Vedānta philosophy is fundamentally one of the modalities, and how they lead to contradictions. The reality is one thing, but it must be described through mutually exclusive modes. Thus, a cow is both an individual and a universal. An observer is both a knower and the known. Everything is both a possibility and a purpose. Existence and truth are complementary modes. Truth, right, and good are different modes. How a thing looks like, and how it is used are different modalities. In a drama, an actor and a character are different modes. If we reject modes, then we can know only through one mode, and the knowledge is incomplete. If we add modes into our knowledge, then the knowledge turns self-contradictory.

The greater the number of modalities, the greater are the contradictions. And, the fewer the modalities, the more limited is the knowledge.

Thus, we can envision a spectrum of philosophical positions that range from no modalities to infinite modalities. Buddhism rejects all modalities, and it ends up with nothingness—the maximum incompleteness. Advaita accepts three modes—it can describe the soul outside matter, but not the soul in matter. Viśiṣṭādvaita adds the modality of properties to the Advaita modality of the soul, and the soul can be described both in and out of matter. But this leads to the idea that the soul must be incomplete only being the property and not an object. Similarly, God must be incomplete because He is only an object and not a property. God and the soul must therefore be mutually dependent, as they are both incomplete. Dvaita recognizes that soul and matter are different realities, so they can exist in both object and property modes. But when they know each other, then God is within the soul, and the soul is within God. Thus, knowledge breaks the doctrine of their separation. Bhedābheda says that we can accept that the soul and God are within each other, but this leads to the problem that if God is within the soul, then the soul must be God. In Acintyabhedābheda, the Absolute Truth is inconceivable, but since concepts are expressed in words, therefore, inconceivability entails the end of all words, or at least speech would never be coherent. That entails that we must also stop talking about God and the soul.

The system of zero modalities is the most incomplete because nothing at all exists. Knowledge grows as we add modalities. But each such addition in knowledge brings an ever-growing number of internal contradictions.

Since this problem is so pervasive, it must have a universal solution. That solution will not be philosophy, science, mathematics, or religion. It will be all of them, and yet none of them. It will essentially be an understanding of how knowledge can be complete with many modes, without contradictions. This idea frames the problem of a 'Scientific Interpretation of Vedānta Sūtra'. It is not regurgitating a previous idea in a new language—e.g., English. It is not using modern science to understand Vedānta philosophy. And it is not a religious philosophy. It is fundamentally solving a thus far unsolved problem. Whatever comes out as a solution must be novel, so in some sense must go past what has previously been stated—in science, philosophy, mathematics, or religion. It is for this reason that a new commentary on Vedānta Sūtra is required, not merely the translation of the previous commentaries into English. It is also for this reason that the new commentary must differ from the earlier commentaries.

Three Basic Modalities

If you have followed the argument thus far, then we can begin understanding the solution. The cornerstone of the solution is that everything in Vedic philosophy is a soul, and souls exist in three modes—*sat*, *chit*, and *ānanda*. Some soul is the whole—and is called the Supreme Soul—while other souls are parts. But every soul comprises these three modes. What are these modes? Let's understand them through the example of the problem of "I" seen previously.

"I" exists in three modes—the knower, the known, and the relation between the two. The knower is *ānanda*; it is the potentiality for desire. But since desire doesn't always exist, therefore, the soul can exist without knowing itself. Enjoyment requires something other than the enjoyer. Therefore, if the desire for enjoyment is manifest, then a schism in the soul is created—the difference between knower and known. You miss yourself, and to overcome this missing, you relate to yourself. This relation is called *sat* or awareness. It is the connection between the knower and the known. Once this connection is established, then the knower enters the known, and the known enters the knower. We call this 'knowledge', and the Vedas call it *chit*. When you see an object, the object is inside you, and yet it is outside you. Similarly, you are inside that object, and yet you are outside that object. All these modes are beyond current logic. For instance, to say that the knower and the known are identical in the ānanda stage, and yet to enjoy, they must separate, is logically contradictory. Likewise, how can the self be related to itself? Finally, when we postulate a difference between the knower and the known, how can the knower be inside the known, and the known be inside the knower? The problem is that our logic is based on physical thinking, but the soul is not physical. In physical thinking, two things are either identical or different; if they are identical, then they cannot be separated; but if they have separated, then they cannot exist within each other.

The soul defies these limitations of physical thinking. Since everything in Vedic philosophy is a soul, therefore, everything—including matter—defies this logic. To understand anything, we must begin with the nature of the soul, which means understand the three modes in which it exists and the nature of each mode. For the simplicity of our further discussion, I will call these modes emotion, relation, and cognition. Don't worry about what these words mean in English. This is a technical nomenclature, that uses English words. For those who don't know Sanskrit, it is better than ānanda-*sat-chit*. But that doesn't mean we are dealing with the mundane understanding of these words.

You can see that there is a progression in the modes—from emotion to relation to cognition. This is because emotion exists first, it leads to a relation, and then to a cognition. If there was no experience, then this gradual progression creates experience. But you can also see that in the final cognitive experience, all three modes are combined. That is, when you have a cognition, you also have a relation, and you experience an emotion. However, if you have an emotion, you need not have a relation or a cognition. This brings us to the main point: Knowledge is cognition, and it depends on a relation and an emotion. If you have no desire to know, you cannot know. If you have a desire to know, but you don't relate to the known object, again, you cannot know. So, after you have a desire, and you establish a relation, you must enter the known (to grasp the nature of the known), and the known must enter you (to represent the nature of the known). This mutual penetration is knowledge. Since cognition comes from relation and emotion, therefore, it is the fullness of the three modes. Likewise, a relation needs two modes; and emotion is only one mode. Therefore, knowledge must be described as a combination of the three modes.

Each of these three modes involves a difference and non-difference. The ānanda mode is non-difference when the potential for desire exists, but it is difference if the desire is manifest. The *sat* mode is relation between the knower and the known, but since they are the same, there is non-difference (because they are not separable) and difference (because there is a relation between the two). The *chit* mode is the knower inside the known, and the known inside the knower; due to this mutual penetration, they are neither separable nor identical. The term 'non-difference' can therefore be used for these three modes, but it doesn't mean one thing. There are factually three kinds of non-difference.

We discussed earlier that with three modes, knowledge is self-contradictory. But we can now see that even with a single mode, there is self-contradiction because each mode exists in a state of non-difference. This additional complication is due to the existence of oppositions: Everything is defined through an opposition. Thus, the knower cannot exist without a known. When the emotion, relation, and cognition are absent, then the knower and known are merged into a state of potentiality, without knowledge. But as they are separated, then knower, known, and knowledge are created collectively. As a result, we cannot speak of abstract knowledge, without a person who knows. Hence, it is possible to speak about the unmanifest state of reality in which the knower, known, and knowledge are not separated, as pure potentiality. However, this state cannot be called either the knower, or the known, or the knowledge. Neither words, nor experience, nor a reality different from the knower exists in this stage. Hence, this stage of existence cannot be known or described in words. And yet, we can postulate its existence as the basis from with everything springs.

Vedānta worsens the problem that we knew of from set theory. In set theory, a single mode will give you incomplete knowledge, but at least it won't be self-contradictory. But in Vedānta, every mode is self-contradictory. Therefore, we must distinguish between two kinds of inconsistencies—those that exist within the modes, and those that arise from their mutual combination.

The problem gets much worse when we see that there are varieties or types of each of these three modes, and these types are mutually contradictory. For example, in cognition, you have opposite types such as hot and cold, big and small, rough and smooth, bitter and sweet, etc. Normally, we keep these types separate, and say that something is either hot or cold, either bitter or sweet, etc. But the problem is that they are defined through their mutual opposition; you cannot define hot, except in distinction to cold. Hence, a new type of non-difference arises: Hot and cold are different, and yet not completely separable.

Thus, the problem of modalities gets increasingly complex upon deeper investigation: (1) the three modes of the soul are mutually contradictory, (2) each mode is self-contradictory, and (3) types of these modes are mutually contradictory, although these contradictories are also defined by each other. Since there is no respite from such contradictions, we cannot hope to solve the problem of contradictions in classical logic. We need a generic solution to these contradictions, and, therefore, let's now turn toward that generic solution.

Dominant-Subordinate

The generic solution in Vedic philosophy is that these modes go dominant and subordinate. Sometimes we observe the individuals through sense perception, without classifying them into concepts. At other times, we focus on the classification and identify the universals by defocusing from sense perception. Sometimes we decipher the meaning and sometimes we judge whether this meaning is true. Sometimes we judge if some action is right, and then we judge if it is also good. Sometimes we understand a play based on actors and sometimes based on characters. Sometimes we suppress our emotions to prioritize our duties. At other times, we prioritize cognition and suppress emotions. The modes are ever-present. But they are not equally dominant all the time.

Due to changing priorities of these modes through dominant-subordinate relationships, the conflict between the modes is resolved—the dominant mode 'rules over' the subordinate mode and suppresses its nature. The flaw in modern thinking is that we give equal priority to all these modes simultaneously. Thus, for instance, we say that if we are seeing the individual, then we cannot know the universal, because the same thing cannot both be a universal and an individual. This is a flawed argument because it assumes that individuals and universals are simultaneously perceived. They are not. While our perception is focused on sensation, it is defocused from the meaning. But when it is focused on the meaning, then it is defocused from sensation. The modes flip rapidly, so we don't realize that the priorities are changing, but the modes are never simultaneous. Our experience is consistent because of the changing priorities. Our language or reasoning is inconsistent because we don't use priorities.

The mode flipping produces change, which is experienced as time; every moment is a different mode priority. However, there are many kinds of times. The deterministic evolution of the world—i.e., what is going to happen—is the universal description of the world and constitutes the universal time; it is also identified with the God-mode description of the world. The subjective evolution of the world—i.e., who is doing what—is identified with the soul-mode description of the same world. It constitutes the soul-mode time or the personal experience of time. Finally, how things are happening—i.e., the causal mechanism—is identified as the matter-mode description of the same world. It constitutes the objective description of time. In one sense, matter-, soul-, and God- modes are mutually exclusive. In another sense, since these modes are simultaneously possible, therefore, God, matter, and soul are three descriptions of the world. And yet, what will happen is prior to who will do it, which is prior to how it will be done. Therefore, God-mode is superior to soul-mode, which is superior to the matter-mode. Someone might say that while studying matter we don't see soul or God. That's just because we are stuck in a single modality—of how things happen. If we asked other questions—i.e., who will do what, and what will happen—then we will begin seeing soul and God within a theory. The questions of what, how, and who constitute complementary modalities. Their answers also constitute different modes of God, matter, and soul.

The Absolute Truth (which is a term I will use often, and it means the singular truth) is the collection of all the modes. The innumerable modes are produced by the combination of three modes, and the three modes spring from a primordial state in which the modes are undifferentiated. Thus, a oneness divides into three, which then creates infinite variety. This variety is due to the dominant-subordinate relations between the modes. Even the material world, for instance, is described as the dominant-subordinate structure of the three modes. These modes are called *sattva*, *rajas*, and *tamas* in Sāṅkhya philosophy. What we call the 'mind' dominates in sattva; what we call the 'body' dominates in tamas; and the connection between mind and body dominates in rajas. We can simplify this terminology by saying that the body is an object, the mind is the purpose of that object, and the connection between mind and body is the control that engages the object toward a purpose. Likewise, the purpose too can be divided into three modes. The purpose in sattva is driven toward higher achievements, the purpose in rajas is driven toward the control of other living entities, and the purpose in tamas is driven toward the body's survival. In this way, all variety in Sāṅkhya philosophy is first reduced to three modes, and then these three modes are reduced to a primordial state called Pradhāna in which the distinction between the modes is unmanifest.

Thus, again, even in the case of matter, one divides into three, and three then produces infinite variety.

The three modes of material nature are reflections of the three modes of the soul that we have discussed earlier. Hence, if we understand the soul, then we can understand the nature of matter as well. The doctrines of soul, matter, and God are hence constructed in the same way. God, matter, and soul are three modes of the same reality. Each mode is in turn comprised of three modes, and the division by three continues indefinitely to create separate descriptions. As a result, we cannot say that God, soul, and matter are completely separate, just as we cannot say that they are identical. Due to modes, we must say that God, soul, and matter are non-different—as three modes of reality they are not identical, but as the modalities of the same reality, they are not different. Two things that are neither identical nor different create classical contradictions. But if we describe these things as the modes, then the contradictions cease to exist.

Alternative Philosophies

Materialism

Materialism dispenses with multiple modes by removing all concepts from the nature of reality. Without concepts, the mind cannot exist. If concepts and the mind don't exist, then knowledge cannot exist, because all knowledge involves concepts. If knowledge cannot exist, then we don't need books to understand the nature of reality. This is the position of the *nāstika* or the atheistic school of materialism in Indian philosophy. The main proponent of this philosophy—Chārvāka—argued that the pursuit of knowledge is futile because concepts don't exist. There are only individual things, and we cannot classify them into groups, categories, or classes. A concept is something that spans across multiple objects; for example, the concept 'cow' spans across many cows. But we don't see anything that spans across many cows. What we cannot see, we cannot assume exists. Hence, there is no such thing as the idea of 'cow'. There are just individual objects, and we have invented some language to describe these things similarly, but all such descriptions are our constructions. There is no reality to such concepts, and without concepts, there is no knowledge.

It is worth noting that the materialism of modern science is somewhat different. It postulates three modalities—objects, properties, and values. The same object can have many properties, the same properties can exist in other objects, and the same values can exist in different properties. Objects, properties, and values, therefore, underdetermine each other. But since they are required in a scientific theory, they must also be separate modes. Examples of objects are particles and waves. Examples of properties are kinetic, potential, and thermal energy. And examples of values are the quantities associated with a property (numbers such as real numbers, natural numbers, complex numbers, etc.). Owing to multiple modes, the description of nature can never be complete.

An example of such incompleteness is that when two particles collide, the outcome of the collision is uncertain—the particles can split and join. The properties too can be converted from one to another—e.g., energy can transform from kinetic, to potential, to thermal. Since kinetic energy can be converted into potential energy, therefore, other properties like momentum and angular momentum are not conserved. In fact, we also know that energy can be converted into mass, and vice versa, so they are only collectively conserved. In so far as a unified theory of mass and charge doesn't exist, charge is supposed to be conserved, but if a unified theory existed, then charge and energy would be interconvertible. Finally, the total value of any of these properties may be distributed between multiple particles and multiple properties in many ways. Because the number of particles is uncertain, therefore, the particles are not conserved. Since the total number of properties is uncertain, therefore, the number of properties is not conserved. The only certainty in science is that the total value is conserved. For instance, the total amount of energy is conserved, although it can be distributed across many types, distributed over numerous particles. This creates incompleteness—we cannot predict how the total energy will be distributed into multiple particles, or even how many such particles will exist.

Thus, while objects, properties, and values are used as three modes in science, only one mode—i.e., the total values of properties—is objective. Whatever is not conserved cannot be called real; reality is that which is conserved. Thus, even as theories employ three modes, only the value mode is objective. This science is necessarily incomplete because it has been made consistent.

There is another kind of materialism encountered in atomic theory, which is not well understood at present because we don't understand how nature is multimodal. In this materialism, reality exists in mutually orthogonal and complementary modes. Unlike classical physics, where you could measure all the particles simultaneously, you cannot measure all the modes at once. Thus, one mode becomes dominant at a time, and the other modes remain subordinate. Quantum theory cannot predict which mode will be dominant when, but it statistically predicts the occurrence of modes. The statistical prediction is possible due to the hierarchy in the modes. We don't get equal probabilities for each possibility, and some possibilities have a zero probability (as they lie 'in between' the orthogonal modes). In classical materialism, we could not predict the total number of particles and their properties; we just knew the total value. In quantum materialism, we know the total number of particles, their properties, and their values. But we cannot know them at once as they are different modes, which become real one after another. If we changed our view of atomic theory—from particles to modalities—then we could say that objects, properties, and values are simultaneously real, so this theory is more complete than classical physics. However, because we cannot know all the modes at once, therefore, this theory *seems* incomplete. We need a description of how the modalities manifest one by one, and then the theory would also be complete.

Idealism

Idealism takes the opposite approach to materialism. It says: Let's forget about the individuals of this world. Let's only focus on the universals, because our goal is knowledge, and we need to know this knowledge as concepts. That's a viable goal, but it means that you and I cannot separately have knowledge, because that would mean that there are two separate instances of knowledge, and we already began by saying that we cannot include individuals. This position, therefore, leads to the conclusion of solipsism: Only I exist, the world is simply my idea, and even when I see others, they are ideas within me. Due to the rejection of other things besides me, there are no individuals. There is only me, and because there is only me, we can discard the individual modality.

But there is still a problem. You can perceive two instances of red, which would require you to have two modalities—universal and individual. That would still be problematic. So, to be consistent, we must say that there aren't two instances of red; there are just two sensations, and we cannot call them red or black or yellow or anything. They are just two things, without a commonality. Philosophers call this idea "dustbowl empiricism" because your experience is a collection of data points—like particles of dust—which are not tied together into a conception of some external reality; hence there is no knowledge.

Many Western philosophers—such as Berkeley and Hume—have gone on to take these radical empiricist positions and argue that knowledge is impossible because you only have sensations, which cannot be organized into properties and objects. Without properties and objects, there can be no scientific laws. And without such laws, there can be no knowledge. Therefore, we just have experiences, but we can never convert these experiences into knowledge.

Immanuel Kant wanted to turn this problem around, and he said that the other modalities—such as properties and objects—come from *us*. The world only gives us sensations, but we add concepts (like properties and objects). But there is a problem. Since we are providing these concepts, therefore, everyone can provide their ideas in whichever way they choose. Only the sensations will be scientific, their explanations using objects and properties would be our creation. That would mean that science is possible, but it is always a personal interpretation of the world. Of course, Kant argued that to save ourselves from this subjectivity, we must say that properties and objects are universal. But that idea reinjects the universals, which are different from the individuals. The existence of universals and individuals wasn't the only problem of course. Since each observer is a separate individual, there were many 'copies' of the universal in each observer. Why should these copies of the universal be identical? Don't we have individual freedoms to interpret reality in different ways? So, Kantian universality compromised the individual freedom, and the resurrection of freedom must similarly compromise universality. Again, we can have only one of them; having both is contradictory. However, removing one of them leads to incompleteness. For instance, if there is individual freedom, then there is no universality—we cannot talk about objective knowledge. If instead there is universality, then there cannot be individual freedom. Either alternative becomes incomplete. Therefore, in practice, both modes were used by constantly revising the universals. For instance, scientists continuously invent new properties and object-types and use them in new theories, and each such theory is called a 'universal theory' until it turns out to be merely an individual perspective.

Some philosophers after Kant—e.g., Edmund Husserl—tried to solve this problem by saying that we must 'bracket' all that's coming from the external world. In short, we try to understand ourselves, because that understanding will give us the universals innate in us. In short, you pursue the object and property modalities, but you get rid of the value modality. You still cannot tell which object must have which property, so even your inner investigation of the self must remain incomplete. And by 'bracketing' the external world, you have lost the ability to test whether our innate ideas are also useful. In short, you can no longer be certain if you should be here, whether you and the world are compatible if knowledge can be acquired, and what that knowledge is good for. Martin Heidegger called this purposeless existence *dasein*— "being there". It is incomplete because there is no method to confirm whether the discovery of the dasein is actually true, and potentially everyone can make a different discovery. Now, you can get radical individuality, but there is just no universality.

There was another kind of idealism prevalent in Greek times. It argued that there exists a perfect world of ideas, called the Platonic world, and the ideas from this perfect world are reflected in this world. This meant that there was a perfect definition of a man, and some men reflected this idea perfectly, while others did not. The problem was in defining this perfect man. Greeks did not define ideality as the perfection of moral character. Instead, they reduced perfection to shape, size, and color. Therefore, tall, well-built, white men were perfect, and everyone else wasn't. The non-ideal men had to be subordinated to the ideal, which means that people with different skin tones could be enslaved. Then, the superiority of false ideals was used to propagate enslavement. This is a clear illustration of how universals negate the existence of individuals. If only tall, white, and well-built men are ideal men, then everyone else is not.

Western society continued with such false ideals for nearly two thousand years, until the dawn of Postmodernism, which rejects the pursuit of all ideals: there is no one better or worse. The rejection is correct if it is taken to mean the rejection of the false ideals of shape, size, and color. But it is flawed because it also discards the traditional moral virtues—based upon the acceptance of a higher purpose in the present life—along with the false traditional ideals. Thus, the right-wing politicians speak about the ideals, but their idealism rejects the individuality of different ideals. The left-wing politicians reject the ideals and speak about gender, race, and color diversity. They are both wrong rejecting all ideals, or applying a universal ideal onto everybody are equally useless.

Vedic philosophy also speaks of ideals, but they are identified as moral values. Those with such moral values are considered superior. However, these ideals have to be adapted to individuals and their priorities must be changed in different contexts. Therefore, when Idealism is used in Vedic philosophy, it is neither blanket universalism, nor random individualism, nor free contextual customization by everyone. The conclusion is far more nuanced—there are universal ideals, that have to be adapted to the individual's nature, which have to be adjusted based on different contexts. The domination of these three modes is variable because each of the three modes can be legitimately dominant.

Buddhism

While materialism and idealism struggle with the problem of multiple modes and the contradictions resulting from them, Buddhism says that each of these modes is self-contradictory. Thus, even if you are interested in ideas, and are prepared to reject the individuals, there is still no hope because all these ideas are defined through mutual opposites. For instance, if you say that something is a table, you mean that it is *not* a chair, house, car, bed, etc. According to Buddhism, it is fundamentally impossible to define the idea of a 'table' except through a distinction to every other idea—e.g., table, bed, house, etc. Therefore, either all these ideas are collectively defined, or nothing is defined at all. As an illustration, if you picked up a dictionary of word-meanings, you would find that words are defined by using other words. You cannot define any word by itself—i.e., there is no self-evident word. But if all the words are defined through such mutual distinctions and oppositions, then either the multitude of words exists simultaneously, or nothing at all exists. When this multitude of words exists, they exist as opposites—hot and cold, bitter and sweet, rough and smooth, etc. They are logical contraries, so you cannot call this consistent knowledge. The only consistent state is if you dissolve everything; all these contraries disappear, the contradictions go away, and nothing at all exists.

Thus, in Materialism and Idealism, there is some hope for knowledge, if you employ only one of the modes, although the knowledge will be incomplete. But in Buddhism, there is no hope for knowledge because every mode is self-contradictory. You don't just avoid contradictions by rejecting multiple modes. You must also reject even a single modality because of the contraries.

You could say that the flaw in the Buddhist argument is that even though there are opposites such as hot and cold, the same thing is never both hot and cold. So, yes, as dictionary definitions of universals, both contraries must exist simultaneously, but this doesn't mean that the same object is simultaneously those opposites. However, the Buddhist will say that you are assuming that the individual thing you are referring to as the basis for resolving this contradiction is not itself contradictory. As we have discussed earlier, the 'self' or 'I' is also self-contradictory because it is comprised of three contradictory modes.

Thus, according to Buddhism, even your claim of self-awareness is defined by an opposition between the knower and known. If you remove the known, then the knower doesn't know itself, and hence it doesn't exist. Dissolving one side of the distinction dissolves both. If the 'self' is contradictory, the individuals have the same fate as the universals—they are both mutually opposed contraries. Thus, we cannot use the separation of individuals to solve the problem of universals; you must begin by solving the problem of the individuals!

The crux of the issue in Buddhism is that there is nothing self-evident; everything is defined through opposition to something else. If we look at Western philosophy, this problem was never grasped. For instance, Descartes said that I could distrust everything in my perception, but I could not distrust my own existence. Therefore, at least my existence is completely certain to me. I am therefore not defined by a relational opposition to others. I am defined by myself. But this is because Descartes did not deconstruct the nature of the self. He merely took self-awareness as the self-evident indication of the self. When Buddhists refute this self-evident nature of the self, they conclude that there is factually no self. What we call the 'self' is the combination of two opposites, and it is as much a material construct as every other mutual opposition. The only solution is that we discard these contradictions and arrive at nothingness.

Monotheism

The journey from the material world to nothingness seems viable, but the journey from nothingness to the material world seems implausible. What causes nothingness to split into opposites? Monotheistic religions offer a solution to this problem, in which the world is created *ex-nihilo*—i.e., nothingness precedes the world and God splits this nothingness into mutual opposites.

Of course, Abrahamic religions don't have a sophisticated notion of the world as logical opposites. But in principle, that problem could be solved if Buddhist ideas were combined with Monotheism as a solution to the problems of nothingness. However, the Buddhist will still argue: The notion of 'self' or soul is self-contradictory. So, the idea of God must also be self-contradictory. How are you going to solve this problem? Unless you solve the problem, the claim that God created the world from nothing would not be acceptable, because God Himself would be defined by the existence of mutual opposites. In fact, one could argue that this opposition already exists as God and Satan.

To reinstate the existence of God, one could say that matter is not defined by mutual opposites. These opposites are semantic categories like hot and cold. But we can reject these categories and just talk about temperature as a physical property. So, the adoption of modern science becomes a solution to the problem of Buddhism because the world is no longer described by oppositions. However, if you reject these conceptual categories, then you cannot have concepts and minds, and you cannot explain conceptual knowledge. Furthermore, by rejecting these semantic categories, you have lost the ability to rationalize nothingness as the combination of opposites. So, if you say that God created the world *ex nihilo* then it follows that God created an infinite amount of energy because the world did not exist prior to God creating it. But how did God create energy from nothing? Isn't that a case of something coming out of nothing? The Monotheist can argue that God is supernatural, but this supernatural being violates the conservation of energy because He creates matter and energy. Since matter and energy are not eternal, therefore, God's existence is contrary to natural laws. Now, all religion becomes contrary to everything in science.

The problem could in principle be avoided if Monotheism discarded the *ex-nihilo* doctrine, and said that energy preexisted in God, and it was converted into the world. But postulating such a mechanism would mean that since energy in God is transformed into this world, therefore, God after creation must be reduced in energy. Just like a billiard ball transfers its energy to another billiard ball, similarly, upon creation, God must either cease to exist or even if He exists, He must be considerably diminished upon this creation. A God that is diminished by His actions of creation would not truly be called God. So, this solution is never applied, and that simply means that God's existence is contrary to the laws of nature (such as the law of conservation of energy). The *ex-nihilo* doctrine becomes the basis of conflicts between God and science.

Pantheism

The pantheistic approach tries to address the problem of conflict between God and science. It says that conservation of energy is true, and God was this energy before creation. However, when this world is created, then God simply becomes the world as all the energy is transformed from God into the world. Thus, He ceases to have a separate existence, and the world again becomes God when everything is destroyed. In other words, there is either God or the world, and these are merely two different states of energy—concentrated in God or distributed in the world. Supernatural ideas are not needed, because conservation of energy is upheld. And yet, right now, because the world is manifest, therefore, God doesn't exist. Your worship of God must be false right now.

There is still a nagging problem. How does God become the world, and how does the world become God? Clearly, there needs to be some free will or volition involved in these changes. If God has volition before creation, but then He becomes the world, then the volition must also be gone. Once the volition is gone, then the world cannot convert back to God. So, the creation of the world must be a one-time activity, and after that God doesn't exist forever. And yet, if that is indeed the case, then the worship of God becomes even more unnecessary. Earlier, God did not exist now but could exist in the future. In the new doctrine, God existed in the past but never in the present or any future.

While all this may pose some theological problems, there is no rational or logical problem in saying that this indeed happened. The new problem is that there is only energy, hence there cannot be ideas, mind, or knowledge. The addition of the mind would require a new modality, and that will create logical contradictions, and all the logical beauty of this doctrine would disappear.

Schools of Vedānta

Advaita

Advaita has a position like that of pantheism although it postulates two categories—Brahman and māyā—both of which are eternal, but their combination is not eternal. Due to the eternity of māyā, conservation of energy is true. And due to the eternity of Brahman, free will or volition also remains eternal. The living entity in this material world is said to be the combination of Brahman and māyā, and the liberated living entity is said to be Brahman without māyā. As these two are separated, māyā doesn't cease to exist. However, the experience of this māyā comes to an end. Since māyā is eternal, therefore, energy is eternally conserved, and there is no contradiction between religion and science. Since Brahman is separate from māyā, therefore, God doesn't become the world (if we say that God is Brahman), and the creation is not *ex-nihilo* (because the creation is from māyā). But you can ask: What about knowledge? We have been concerned about the nature of knowledge, and it was deemed impossible. How does the separation of Brahman and māyā address that problem? The Advaita response to this problem is that there are two kinds of knowledge. The first type of knowledge is the knowledge of this world. This knowledge is contradictory because māyā is contradictories, and these contradictories are dissolved leaving a state of nothingness. Hence, when Buddhism speaks about nothingness, it is referring to māyā and not to Brahman.

The second type of knowledge is the knowledge of Brahman, and this knowledge is not self-contradictory if we dissolve the notion of "I". Recall that the problem of contradictories is extended into the self by Buddhism. But if we dissolve the self, then contradictories don't exist. But this 'solution' raises many other questions. If there is no "I", then there is also no self-awareness, because "I" means is self-awareness. If we say that Brahman is without self-awareness because there is no "I", then how do we know that Brahman even exists? How different is Advaita, simply by postulating the existence of Brahman, when the conclusion is that there is no "I"?

Buddhism and Advaita are nearly identical doctrines because in both the doctrines the world is contradictories, and consistency is achieved when these contradictories are dissolved to produce nothingness. Similarly, in both doctrines, there is no self or "I" because "I" involves contradictories. The difference is simply that Advaita postulates that there is a Brahman beyond māyā which has the potential to become self-aware. When this self-awareness doesn't exist, then the "I" is dissolved into Brahman. And when Brahman becomes self-aware, then "I" is produced. And once this "I" is produced, then, the "I" also become ensnared in the contradictories of māyā. Hence, Advaita is slightly better in terms of being able to explain how the present world is produced.

Now, you can ask: How does Brahman become self-aware? The answer is modalities. Brahman exists as *sat*, *chit*, and ānanda, which are simply potentials or possibilities. The ānanda mode is the sense in which Brahman is different from itself—i.e., it can become different individuals or knowers. The *chit* mode is the sense in which the soul is non-different from itself—i.e., the different individuals being known. And the *sat* mode is the sense in which the knowers are connected to other knowns to create the material experience. However, since these are simply potentials, therefore, in Brahman the distinction between the different knowers, the different knowns, and the relation between these knowers and knowns doesn't exist; only the potential for such distinction exists.

Thus far, everything is good. The problem begins when we ask: How does unmanifest become manifest? If the three modes are simply possibilities, then to convert them into a reality we need a choice. This choice needs a personality, which means there must be an "I" outside

Brahman. Since Advaita has already rejected any "I" outside Brahman, it is compelled to say that the cause of the manifestation is māyā. In short, māyā causes the Brahman to divide into many selves, and then ensnares them into the material world. However, if māyā is the cause of the division of Brahman, then it must also be the cause of return to Brahman. The net result of this doctrine is that Brahman has no causality. Since we are Brahman, we have no free will to either be entangled or liberated. Both entanglement and liberation are thus dependent on the agency of māyā.

But how can māyā have any agency? And what kind of agency is that? If we say that māyā has free will and individuality, then we cannot assert that it is different from Brahman. If we say that māyā has no free will and individuality, then upon fall into matter we cannot get liberated, and if we are liberated then we cannot fall into matter. Since we are fallen right now, we cannot get liberated. After all, whatever desire for liberation we acquire is simply a desire. How can the succession of these desires lead to a desireless state? The production of desireless from desire would itself be called self-contradictory.

Thus, we can see how Advaita goes very far in addressing the issues with the other doctrines and is hence superior to them. Certainly, Materialism, Idealism, Monotheism, or Pantheism come nowhere close to Advaita. Advaita has many similarities to Buddhism, but the one difference it posits between Brahman and māyā fails to hold up to scrutiny. It only makes Brahman causeless and māyā as the origin of causality. The net result of this limitation is that Advaita cannot accurately describe the cause of the soul's fall and liberation.

Viśiṣṭādvaita

Viśiṣṭādvaita sets out to address the problem of fall and liberation. The solution is through the doctrine of God. God is also a soul, and hence, like in Advaita, He too has three modalities. But God is defined as an object, while soul and matter are His properties. Just as a particle has properties like mass, energy, momentum, etc. similarly God is an object with innumerable properties. Viśiṣṭādvaita gives the analogy of body and soul; just like the body is a property of the soul, similarly, the soul is the 'body' of God. Just as the parts of the body serve the soul, similarly, as properties of God, the soul must serve God. However, the soul may choose not to serve God, and enjoy independently. Thus, the soul falls into matter. He acquires a material body and tries to be like God—i.e., the object who then has subsidiary properties. The soul gets liberated when he gives up this mentality to be the object and remains as God's property.

Since the nature of matter is not changed in Viśiṣṭādvaita, like Advaita, it doesn't contradict the duality of matter. Likewise, since the three modes of the soul and matter are acknowledged, therefore, Viśiṣṭādvaita can explain how the "I" emerges from an unmanifest state. Thus, liberation into Brahman is not denied, however, that liberation doesn't entail the dissolution of the identity of the soul. All souls hence remain eternally individual. However, if the three modes enter an unmanifest state, then the *experience* of individuality is lost, although the individuality is not lost. Since individuality is eternal, therefore, external causes of the soul's fall into the material world are not needed. The soul can fall into matter when individuality develops, and the soul considers itself an object. Likewise, the soul can be liberated into Brahman if it dissolves its individuality. Finally, the soul can be liberated through a relation to God if it gives up the mindset of being an object and prefers to remain a property. Also, since God is a soul, hence, God is not subject to the dualities of māyā.

The term Viśiṣṭa denotes qualities or properties, and Advaita denotes the *unity* rather than *oneness*. The purpose of this unity is to connect all the diversities. God as the object of all properties is the unity, and His properties are the diversities. Therefore, Viśiṣṭādvaita means the properties of the Unity.

There is, however, one serious problem in Viśiṣṭādvaita. The problem is that when the soul enters the material world, he acts like an object rather than a property. If the soul can act as an object, then there must at least be the potential of being an object, even if this objectivity is not always visible in the liberated state. Owing to this problem, we cannot say that the soul is only a property. We must rather say that the soul can be both a property and an object. In the spiritual world, the soul is present as a property, and in the material world, a soul is an object. As an object, the soul combines with material properties (such as hot and cold, bitter and sweet, big and small) which then become the soul's properties. And as a property, the soul describes the nature of God. But if the soul can be both object and property, but only one of them is seen in the spiritual and material worlds, then the spiritual world must be as incomplete as the material world. In both worlds, the soul incompletely realizes its potential—the soul is either a property or an object and can never be both. Since both potentials can be realized, but they are only realized alternately, therefore, object and property are modalities of the soul, and they cannot be simultaneously true. It follows that if the soul has been liberated as a property of God, then it must fall as an object into matter. And if the soul has fallen as an object into matter, then it must be liberated as a property of God. Thus, neither fall nor liberation is eternal, and both situations must be experienced alternately. This is because, in each kind of world, one type of incompleteness is bargained for another.

Dvaita

The problem in Viśiṣṭādvaita can be solved if we say that the soul is not merely a property but also an object. And the property and object modalities of the soul are eternally manifest. To make this argument, we would have to change the analogy of soul and body in Viśiṣṭādvaita. We would no longer say that the soul is the body of the Supreme Soul. We would rather say that the soul is like the part of the body. To make this analogy work, we could say that God is the head of the body, whereas the soul is like the hands and legs of the body. Each part of the body—e.g., hand and leg—can be treated as an object, which then also has properties like color, shape, size, etc. And if the soul is these parts, then it exists in both object and property modes, so it doesn't have to fall into matter to realize its object modality, and the liberated state is complete.

However, now a new problem arises. If the soul is like the hand, while God is like the head, then if the soul leaves the association of God, then God must be diminished—it is as if God's hand was cut off. If, on the other hand, we say that the soul never leaves God's body, then God is never diminished, but when the soul suffers in this world, then God too must be suffering—it is as if the hand is being burnt so the pain must also be experienced by the head. This problem doesn't arise when we say that the soul is God's property because God is the object. If we remove a property from an object, the object is not changed. For example, if you take away some energy from a particle, the particle is unchanged. The problem arises if we say that we are cutting off a part of the particle. In that case, the particle would be divided into two particles. Therefore, if we say that the soul is God's property, then the object and property modes cause a problem because they make liberation temporary. If, on the other hand, we say that the soul is both object and property, then, due to the object mode, removing the soul from God would entail that God is reduced. If instead, we don't remove the part, then the soul's suffering entails God's suffering.

The Dvaita system sets out to solve this problem by saying that the soul and God are different individuals, and the soul is not part of God. Therefore, if the soul leaves God, then God is not reduced. And because the soul can leave God's association, when the soul suffers, God is not suffering with him. Similarly, matter is separate from God, and therefore, God is transcendent to matter. Now, if the soul is different from God, then, why does it need to devote itself to God? Can it not just live and enjoy independently of God? To answer this quandary, Dvaita states that God is omnipotent while the soul is not. Due to omnipotence, God is the soul's controller, and the soul is the controlled. In some sense, the soul must surrender to God because God subdues the soul by His power. Now, lest you think that God is the tyrant who rules the world by His power, Dvaita also says that even though God is omnipotent, He is also benevolent. So, His use of power is not like that of a tyrant, but like that of a benevolent ruler.

However, there is one problem in Dvaita, which is that both matter and the soul are separate from God. This contradicts Vedic statements such as *janma ādi asya yatah* which means that God is the source of everything, implying that even matter and souls have emanated from God, and both are eternal but not separate from God. He is also called *sarva kāraṇa kāraṇam* or the cause of all causes. If we say that the soul and matter are separate from Him, then God could not be the cause of matter and the soul. Finally, there are statements such as *pūrnasya purnam ādaya* which indicate that the whole is taken out of the whole, and the emanating whole refers to the material and spiritual worlds, whereas the cause of that emanation is God. If we say that matter is separate from God, then the world cannot be an emanation from God. Even as the Dvaita system solves the problem of God's suffering, it becomes inconsistent with Vedic statements because it postulates an eternal difference between the soul, matter, and God. All claims of God being the source must be discarded.

While Advaita says that there is only one reality, and Viśiṣṭādvaita says that there is a unity in diversity, Dvaita says that there are many realities without a unity. The unity is established by God's omnipotence and benevolence. Just like a king rules over others to create a cohesive society, but he is not the source of the citizens or the land on which he rules, similarly, the land and the people God rules upon are eternally real. He is just the prominent ruler. The problem here is that Vedānta is supposed to describe a singular origin. If the origin is God, then God cannot be diminished by creation. Hence, God is not just the ruler of creation, but also the original cause of the creation. His rulership of the world is established not just by His power, but by His being the creator. If you create something, then you are entitled to rule over it. In the Dvaita system, God is the ruler of the creation, but not its creator. This is because the soul and matter are eternally real, and eternally separate from Him. The ontological pluralism of Dvaita is incompatible with the Vedic claims of God being the single origin of everything, and hence it violates a fundamental principle of Vedānta.

Bhedābheda

Viśiṣṭādvaita and Dvaita set the tone for future interpretations because there are problems associated with the soul being a property of God, a part of God, and not being a property and a part of God. Regardless of which position is adopted, different kinds of problems are encountered. If the soul is a property of God, then the soul remains incomplete because he is not an object. If the soul is a part of God, then when the soul suffers, God must also suffer. If the soul is separate from God, then God cannot be the cause of the soul's origin. Given these problems, the conclusion is that the soul must be a part of God, and yet not a part of God. This simple idea is called Bhedābheda. Bheda means that the soul and God are different. Abheda means that they are non-different. This non-difference is a new logical category because it is neither different nor identical. Due to the rejection of identity, the Advaita position is rejected. And due to the rejection of absolute Dvaita, the separation of God and the soul is rejected.

Now, the contentious issue is what do we mean by different and non-different? The stock example in Bhedābheda is the whole-part relation. One such example is that of fire and spark. Bhedābheda states that because the spark came out of the fire, therefore, it was part of fire; and yet, it is now separate from it. Therefore, the spark is part of the fire, and yet not its part. The trouble with all such examples is the physicalist conception. If a spark came out of the fire, then some energy was lost by the fire. Therefore, the fire must have reduced in its intensity, and it cannot be called the same fire that existed before the spark being emitted. If fire constantly emits sparks, then it will eventually die out. So, as God creates the world, He must constantly be reduced by this creation.

Similarly, another example says that the part is like a drop of water in an ocean; the ocean is not equal to the drop, but the drop is not separate from the ocean. Again, if you remove the drop from the ocean, the ocean will reduce. Ultimately, all physical analogies of whole-part doctrine result in reductionism. The whole is nothing other than the collection of the parts. Therefore, as the parts are removed, the whole is continuously diminished in the process.

My view of this problem is that the doctrine of Bhedābheda is correct, but the examples used to illustrate this doctrine are not. The correct examples are not those of the physical whole-part relations, but *semantic* whole-part relations. Think for the moment about a mammal and a cow. A cow is a part of a mammal. But if you remove the cow from the set of mammals, then the definition of a mammal isn't changed. You can remove every type of mammal—e.g., cows, tigers, goats, horses, etc.—from the mammal, and yet, it would not change the definition of mammal. Therefore, we can see how the first problem concerning the diminishing of the whole by removing the parts is solved. If fire sparks leave the fire, then fire is reduced. But if cows are not part of mammal, then mammal is not redefined. Furthermore, we can say that a cow is a mammal, but a mammal isn't a cow. Since the cow is a mammal, therefore the two are non-different. But since the mammal isn't a cow, therefore, the two are different. So, now we get both properties needed for Bhedābheda because we changed the analogy of the whole-part doctrine from objects to concepts.

What does this mean? It means that we should stop thinking of reality in terms of objects. We must rather think of this reality as concepts. God is an idea—the original idea of knowledge. There are many parts of this knowledge, such as physics, chemistry, biology, mathematics, economics, etc. Each of these parts can be called 'knowledge' and yet they are not complete knowledge. Therefore, it would be wrong to say that biology is not knowledge. And it would also be wrong if you said that biology is complete knowledge.

Now we can apply this understanding to both Viśiṣṭādvaita and Dvaita. The idea cow is not just a part of the idea mammal, but it is produced by dividing the idea mammal into different types of mammals. Therefore, the idea cow would not exist if the mammal did not exist. In that sense, the idea cow is dependent on the idea mammal. However, the idea mammal isn't dependent on the cow. Even if all the types of mammals did not exist, the idea of mammal will still exist. Similarly, the soul is a part of God and depends on God. But God doesn't depend on the soul. Therefore, if the soul leaves God's association, it becomes incomplete, although God is not diminished by this departure. Then when the soul returns to the association of God, it regains its completeness, however, God is not enhanced. Likewise, God is the origin of all the parts, but even after emanating all the parts, God is not reduced by the emanation.

Since all concepts can be organized in a hierarchy, we can envision this like a tree, whose root is God, and its leaves are the souls. If we look at this tree from the perspective of the root, then the root is the object, and all the leaves are properties of that object. However, if we see the intermediate branches, then these are both objects and properties—properties from the perspective of the root, and objects from the perspective of the leaves connected to them.

Therefore, we can adopt both object and properties modes alternately. Since a branch is a property of the root, therefore, Viśiṣṭādvaita is true. But since the branches are also objects, therefore, Dvaita is true. Since both Viśiṣṭādvaita and Dvaita can be simultaneously true, therefore, the Bhedābheda doctrine is true. However, neither of these doctrines works in a physical sense. They only work if we use a semantic approach. But someone can say: You are using the tree analogy, which is a physical analogy. Yes, it is different from fire and ocean analogies, but it is still physical. The short answer to this problem is that this tree analogy is incomplete, and the reason is that you can say that the branches and leaves came out of the root, but you cannot say that the root is present in the leaves or branches. A better analogy would be that of a seed and fruit. The fruit comes out of the seed, but the fruit is again contained within the seed.

So, does that mean this physical analogy will now work for the doctrine? Yes and no. To make it work, we must say that the soul came out of God as the fruit came out of the seed. But then God is present inside the soul like a seed is present inside the fruit. Now you get another problem: if God is present as a seed inside the fruit, then the soul must be able to create the entire universe, just like God (as the seed) previously created all the fruits. In fact, the soul can now be the cause of the entire material creation, infinite other souls, etc. This is when this physical analogy fails, but the semantic analogy still works. When the mammal is present in a cow, the cow doesn't produce all kinds of mammals—i.e., dogs, horses, tigers, etc. Likewise, even if we say that God is present in the soul, this seed cannot be the cause of the entire creation yet again.

Acintyabhedābheda

The central problem with physical analogies is the claim that a 'cow is a mammal'. It indicates that every time we see a cow, we also see a mammal, and therefore, the mammal must be inside the cow. But how could that be, if the mammal not only transcends the individual cows but also tigers, horses, cats, etc.? Furthermore, there is also an animal inside the mammal, and a living being inside the animal, etc. All these concepts are organized hierarchically, and therefore, the higher concept transcends the lower concept. And yet, the higher concept is also immanent in each of the lower concepts. Due to transcendence, we say that a mammal is not a cow. Due to immanence, we say that a cow is a mammal. How can both ideas be true simultaneously when they are clearly contradictory? Of course, we can say that transcendence and immanence are two modes of existence, but we need a deeper understanding of this issue.

The Acintyabhedābheda doctrine clarifies the Bhedābheda doctrine. This clarification is a tripartite modality in the Absolute Truth, which are called Brahman, Paramātma, and Bhagavān. Bhagavān is transcendent; we can compare Bhagavān to the concept of mammal. Brahman is part of Bhagavān; we can compare such parts to the various types of mammals such as cows, tigers, goats, etc. Within each type of mammal, there is an immanent form of mammal, called Paramātma. Bhagavān is the whole truth, which is also transcendent; Brahman is parts of this truth, and Paramātma is the whole truth immanent in each of the parts. Since Brahman is inside Bhagavān, the diversity is inside the unity. Since Paramātma is inside diversified Brahman, unity is inside diversity. Due to these three entities, there is diversity inside unity, and unity inside diversity.

This idea is immensely important for the following reason. Suppose that the whole truth was only transcendental to all the manifest parts. To know this truth, you will have to first know all the parts and after knowing all the diversity, you could know the unity. In practice, this is impossible because none of us can know everything, and if knowing everything was the precondition to knowing the origin of everything, then the origin could never be known. Now consider the converse proposition—the whole truth is inside every part, so to know the whole truth you just must know *one* part correctly. That one part could be *you*—the knower—and if self-knowledge was obtained completely, then the origin of everything would also be automatically known. But we must remember that this knowledge of the self is not merely the self; it is the understanding of how the whole truth—i.e., Paramātma—is in the self. It is worth reminding ourselves that we are long past physical ideas of containment; the Paramātma is not *physically* in the soul; He is semantically immanent. In simple terms, knowing the self is knowing the meaning of our existence, and while this meaning is immanent in us, the meaning is not us; the meaning is immanent as Paramātma, and the meaning is transcendentally existing as Bhagavān.

The three modalities of the Absolute Truth are existence, meaning, and purpose. Many things exist; they have become manifest from a common source, but this manifestation is not a complete understanding. The fuller understanding is that the common source is the purpose immanent in the different things. Creation has a purpose immanent in each part manifested from the whole. Thus, the soul has a purpose, just as material objects have a purpose; the purpose is the same for both, so the doctrine of immanence and transcendence is not limited to the understanding of the soul; it is also the understanding of matter. Paramātma, for instance, is not just in the soul, He is also in all the material atoms because these atoms are as purposeful as the soul is purposeful. The purpose is immanent, but the purpose points to something transcendent.

This problem can also be framed in familiar terms as the problem of perception. If you are looking at an apple, then there is an apple in your mind, but the apple is also outside your mind. The apple in your mind is the picture of the apple outside, and yet this picture of the apple is a representation of the apple, not the apple itself. Because the apple is represented in our minds, it is 'inside' our mind. But because closing our eyes stops the mental picture, but doesn't destroy the apple, therefore, the apple is 'outside' the mind. The picture of the apple in the mind can be as detailed as we like—e.g., it can include shape, color, size, taste, smell, etc. So, in all practical ways, the picture in the mind can be made equivalent to the real apple outside. And yet, this picture is a projection into our minds, created by the real apple. Due to this projection, we think that what we are seeing in our mind is transparently the thing that is outside.

In the same way, the Paramātma is a *representation* of Bhagavān, like a picture of an apple is represented in our minds. The representation has all the properties of the object. And yet, it is not the object. The understanding of the Bhedābheda doctrine given by Acintyabhedābheda is that the whole divides into parts and then enters these parts as a representation. The whole is Bhagavān, the parts are Brahman, and the internal representation is Paramātma.

When this idea is applied to the soul, we can say that the soul is a symbol of meaning that was spoken by God, and this speech had a purpose. It is not enough to say that the soul is eternally existent. We must also speak about the eternal purpose of the soul's existence, and this purpose must come from God who produces the soul as His expression. The purpose is immanent in the soul, but it is also transcendent to the soul. This is just like when we say, 'the sky is blue', there is meaning in the sentence, but the sky is outside the sentence.

The problem is that our logic can deal only with physical things, and no physical thing can be both inside and outside. Therefore, this description is called inconceivable. But it is conceivable if we treat reality as meanings because the meanings can inside and outside. Thus, we say that a cow is a mammal (because a mammal is inside the cow) and a mammal is not a cow (because a mammal is outside the cow). This conceivability means that the whole, the part, and the whole in the part are three modes of existence. They are also successive stages of dividing the whole into parts and the whole entering the parts.

With a semantic conception of reality, we can speak of modes, and reality is conceivable. However, if we use the physical analogies, then the whole cannot be inside the parts, and the whole reduces to the parts. Then, only the parts are real, and the whole is an illusion. With this conclusion, knowledge is also impossible. Acintyabhedābheda indicates that reality is inconceivable under a physical whole-part doctrine. But, is that a claim that reality is inconceivable? Or is it an indictment of physical conceptions? Acintyabhedābheda can be understood in two ways—as the claim that reality is inconceivable, or as the claim that reality is not physical. In the former case rejection of inconceivability would seem to be a rejection of Acintyabhedābheda. But in the latter case, the rejection of inconceivability would be the acceptance of the reason why reality is called Acintyabhedābheda and then transcending that reason to fix the inconceivability. We can call the latter to be the project of conceiving the inconceivable.

Conceiving the Inconceivable

The Doctrine of Matter

You may have noticed that the previous interpretations of Vedānta try to solve the problem of what the soul is, how it falls into matter, and then how it gets liberated. But the soul is not the only reality; matter is also real. What is matter? In Advaita, māyā is separate from Brahman. Since Brahman is the conscious entity, māyā is unconscious, and the world is created by the combination of conscious and unconscious existence. But in subsequent interpretations of Vedānta, māyā and God are not separate. They are related as an object and its property in Viśiṣṭādvaita. They are separate objects in Dvaita, but this separation is not like that in Advaita (i.e., conscious vs. inert)—both matter and the soul are personalities. God is predominant, and matter is the predominated person. They are both separate and inseparable as in Bhedābheda, just as a part is different from the whole, and yet, the part is non-different from the whole. In short, after solving the problem of the soul's fall and liberation, these Vedānta doctrines extend the understanding of the soul to matter as well. Matter is then treated as a property, as a predominated person, or an inseparable part.

But are such extensions correct? The doctrine of the soul arises from the soul's fall and liberation. But matter never falls and is never liberated. In Advaita, matter is inert, and there is no question of fall and liberation. In other interpretations, matter is a property, a dominated person, or an inseparable part, but unlike the soul, matter is forever liberated. Thus, the doctrine of the soul cannot be extended without explaining why matter is never fallen.

Other systems of Vedic philosophy explain this by an example: God is the father, matter is the mother, and the soul is the child. The child can leave the mother and father, but the mother never leaves the father. But this example, while illustrative, doesn't clarify whether the mother is God's property, a subordinated individual, or an inseparable part. Different systems of philosophy adopt these ideas either simultaneously, or in different places alternatively.

Given the problems in Viśiṣṭādvaita and Dvaita regarding the soul's fall and liberation, it is prudent to extend the Bhedābheda doctrine even in the case of matter, rather than trying to understand matter within the Viśiṣṭādvaita and Dvaita doctrines. However, given the difference between matter and the soul, the Bhedābheda doctrine must be modified to illustrate a different kind of difference and non-difference, which is not the soul's whole-part relation.

This new doctrine is found in many places in Vedic texts, and it identifies God as Puruṣa and matter as Prakriti or Śakti. Puruṣa means the enjoyer or one who has desire and will. Prakriti is the power to fulfill this will or desire. But are these separate or inseparable? If will and power were separate, then some will could never be satisfied, and some power would never be utilized. Conversely, if they were identical, then every time there is power, the will must be present. In short, the power shall control the will, rather than being controlled by the will. Both alternatives are denied. All will can be satisfied, and all power can be utilized. So, these are not completely distinct. And yet, power can exist unutilized, but the will can never exist unfulfilled. Therefore, will is superior to power because every time there is will, the power is utilized. However, every time there is power, the will to use might not be there. In short, power serves the will, but the will doesn't serve the power. This is still a Bhedābheda doctrine, but it is not a whole-part doctrine. Rather, there are two complementary entities, which are simultaneously different and non-different. The power is feminine, and She is subordinate to the will or masculine. But this subordination is not like that of the soul which is subordinate because it is a part of God.

Therefore, we must distinguish between three flavors of Bhedābheda:

- The Puruṣa and Prakriti are different and non-different,
- The soul and the Puruṣa are different and non-different,
- The Paramātma and Bhagavān are different and non-different.

The Doctrine of Spirit

The essence of the doctrine of matter is that will may or may not be manifest; when it withdraws, the power is also withdrawn, and the creation is unmanifest. But if that were indeed the case, then why is the spiritual world always manifest? Doesn't will ever withdraw from the power? If so, this power and will must be different from the material will and power which can be withdrawn. To explain the eternity of the spiritual world and the temporariness of the material world, we either need two separate doctrines (one for matter and the other for spirit), or we must modify the will-power doctrine, in a way that explains both the spiritual eternity and the material temporariness. Naturally, a single doctrine for both matter and spirit is better than two doctrines.

Let's first consider the use of a different doctrine for the spiritual world. We could say that in the case of the spiritual world, the separation of will and power is not needed; it is needed only for the material world. If we collapse their difference and say that the will is power, and the power is will, then the eternity of the spiritual world can be explained. However, this solution would imply that the spiritual world is also static or unchanging. Everything possible would always be manifest due to will, because will and possibility are identical. This would now become the Platonic world of static universals. But this leads to the question: If the spiritual world is static, then how does this world produce pleasure? If everything is eternal, then all will is fulfilled. There is nothing left to be achieved and without the constant production of will and its fulfillment, there can be no pleasure. This state is intellectually satisfying but you cannot exist in this state eternally. You need a question, a problem, a challenge, a purpose. Problems are bad when they cannot be solved. However, the end of all problems would mean the end of life. We need a problematic life, but those problems must be solvable. In fact, ideally, one problem must lead to another problem, and the succession of problems must never end. But since every problem is solved, hence, life is an eternal process of discovery and adventure.

This is a philosophy of life, not the philosophy of knowledge or reality. And this philosophy entails that the separation of will and power is necessary not only to explain the creation and dissolution of the universe; it is also necessary to produce an eternal life of happiness. Therefore, the separation of will and power is not a defect—that causes the dissolution and creation of the universe. It is also the perfection of what we mean by living—as something that leads to happiness. Knowledge is only a means to happiness; it is not happiness itself. Happiness is the succession of solvable problems. The material world presents us with unsolved and unsolvable problems by taking from us the abilities, opportunities, and desires to solve the problems. The impersonalist hence states that we should dissolve all the problems and the quest for their solutions. The transcendentalist however says that the eternal world also has problems, however, they are successively solved, something new is discovered, which then leads to new problems. Thus, an alternative view of spiritual reality is needed. This alternative view must redefine both material and spiritual doctrines.

The alternative is that the will is a problem, and the power is its solution. Every time a problem is solved by power, a new problem is created. The problem in fact exists within the solution. Thus, the cause is present inside the effect, and the effect is present inside the cause. When the cause is a problem, then the effect of a solution is produced by the problem. When the cause is the solution, then the effect of a problem is produced by the solution. We cannot truly separate cause and effect because the cause is within the effect, and the effect is within the cause. As a result, will is the cause of power being manifest, and the manifestation of the power is the cause of the will being manifest. Every problem produces a solution, and every solution produces a new problem. Therefore, power and will are mutually the causes of each other. We can extend this idea to both material and spiritual worlds, but the joint solution would not explain why the material world is temporary while the spiritual world is not.

Matter-Spirit Combined Doctrine

This is where a modification is required. Although a solution leads to a problem, and a problem leads to a solution, these two are not *deterministically* produced. There is still a choice, which can provide different solutions to the same problem, and the solution can then be interpreted in different ways to create new problems. The difference between the material and the spiritual worlds lies in the choice of the solution to a problem, and the choice of the problem that follows the solution. Let's understand this difference in choices.

The fundamental problem with the material world is that most problems result in impractical solutions. For example, if you ask the wrong teacher for a spiritual path, he might say: You should quit everything in this world, go to the jungle and mediate. The solution may be valid, but you won't be able to execute it. Why? Because the ability and opportunity to execute the solution are absent. The ability is missing because we cannot tolerate hardships, and the opportunity is missing because we cannot find the jungles where we can survive. Even if we find such a jungle, our minds and senses are always restless. Therefore, solutions that don't account for our abilities and opportunities become useless. Since you cannot solve the problem in this way, you give up the desire to solve the problem. This is a very practical method by which desires are forced in this world: You give a solution to a problem that can never be applied. Or you provide a solution but confuse the recipient by telling them that numerous problems will arise from using the solution. Then, nobody can blame you for not providing a solution. And yet, because the solution cannot be applied, or its application will lead to additional problems, it will prevent you from using the solution. Without a solution, you will be forced to change your desires.

Now, suppose that every desire is frustrated in this way. You realize that every solution produces an unsolvable problem; or, even if some of these problems are solved, eventually you end with unsolvable problems. Once you realize that all endeavors are futile, you give up all kinds of desires. This is the nature of the material world. You try to fulfill your desires and seek answers. Material nature will mostly give you impractical answers—i.e., those for which you lack the ability and opportunity. Even if there are some practical solutions, ultimately most of them will lead you to a dead end. You attempt the solution for a while and believe in your progress, but you eventually hit a wall. The purpose of material nature is to frustrate your desires while pretending to fulfill them. Material nature is like that person who will give you 'solutions' that can never be implemented, or they will lead to more problems even if they were implemented. Ultimately, you must give up all desires. But the rejection of desires is temporary. You just feel frustrated with your failures and falsely pretend to be renounced. After some time—when you have become frustrated with the so-called renunciation—you try to engage with nature again.

The spiritual nature is different. It gives solutions that can be applied because the ability and opportunity to apply the solutions are eternal. And when these solutions are applied, whatever new problems are created are also solvable—again because the ability and opportunity to solve them is present.

Thus, material nature is described in two ways. The first description says that nature is temporary—i.e., the ability and opportunity to apply the solutions is sometimes present and sometimes absent. The second description says that the purpose of the material nature is to frustrate all our desires and make us turn toward the spiritual reality. Of these two descriptions, the purpose of frustrating our desires is a better answer, because in every situation there are good and bad answers. The good answer is that which can be applied to fulfill our desires, and the bad answer is that which will lead to frustrations. The difference is merely a choice—which question must be given which answer.

With this understanding of material nature, the distinction with spiritual nature is diminished. What is called 'material nature' is simply the frustrating answers to questions. And what is called 'spiritual nature' is satisfying answers to the questions. Even if good answers are possible, material nature will provide only frustrating answers, because it is trying to change our desires. Conversely, even if bad answers are possible in spiritual nature, they will guide you toward good answers. Thus, it becomes very hard to remain happy in the material world, and it is very hard to become unhappy in the spiritual world. Hence, one view about spiritual and material nature is that they are not different. The mechanism is simply choosing the answer to a question. If your desires are averse to the Lord, then nature will give you bad answers.

But if the desires are inclined toward the Lord, then nature will give you the good answers.

But, before we say that there is no difference with spiritual nature, along with this non-difference, there is also a difference. The difference is that in the material world, the abilities and opportunities factually appear and disappear. A few hundred years ago you could not drive a car or fly an airplane. You could enjoy horse rides and walk in a garden, which is slowly becoming impossible. Similarly, the human body and mind had much better immunity, strength, and sharpness; those abilities are now disappearing and being replaced by new kinds of abilities—e.g., to play video games on computers. The nature of the material world is that the abilities and opportunities evolve with time. The nature of the spiritual world is that the abilities and opportunities are eternal.

Thus, material and spiritual natures are non-different in the sense that the basic mechanism is the sequence of questions and answers. These two natures are different because material nature produces frustrating answers to questions and forces us to change the questions. Spiritual nature produces meaningful answers to questions and thereby produces satisfying questions and answers. For the devotee in the material world, nature only produces satisfying answers and questions, although the abilities and opportunities keep changing. Thus, the material nature will find the best answer to a problem that a devotee needs to serve the Lord. But the same nature will frustrate the non-devotees.

Thus, even though material and spiritual natures are described as Puruṣa and Prakriti, these are of two kinds. The Puruṣa in the spiritual world is factually an enjoyer, and He enjoys fulfilling His desires. The Puruṣa in the material world is also an enjoyer, but His enjoyment is austerities or self-abnegation. By this self-abnegation, the Puruṣa sets the example for others to renounce the material world. Those who don't renounce it, are bewildered by His Śakti. Thus, the Śakti and Puruṣa play complementary roles in this world: the Śakti bewilders and frustrates the soul, and the Puruṣa teaches renunciation of the world. Ultimately, both Puruṣas have a common purpose—the spiritual Puruṣa attracts the soul toward spiritual enjoyment, while the material Puruṣa pushes the soul away from material enjoyment; The former is attraction, while the latter is repulsion. Thus, they are non-different (because of the common purpose), and they are different (due to the different ways of achieving the purpose).

The Masculine-Feminine Doctrine

Thus, the doctrine of matter is revised when the doctrine of spirit is propounded. The revision is that the will and the power can be mutual causes of each other. Therefore, it is not true that the will always controls power. To the extent that the power generates a problem, it also causes the will. By changing the answers to the questions, the questions themselves are changed. Therefore, power is not a slave to will, nor is power the unconscious and acausal māyā, waiting only to be used by Brahman, as in the case of impersonalism. Her personality, individuality, choice, and control are reflected in Her ability to give different answers to a question, which then causes a change in the questions. Likewise, the masculine is a person, and His choice, personality, individuality, and control are the ability to change His questions based on the answers.

Thus, masculine and feminine are both persons. They represent questions and answers, and their choice is to ask a different question based on the answer or to answer a question in different ways. They can control each other because questions are determined by previous answers, and answers are determined by previous questions. But this mutual causality is not devoid of choice. Hence, we cannot collapse the distinction between masculine and feminine. We also cannot call one a person and the other impersonal or consider them both to be impersonal. We cannot say that one person is a slave and the other person is a master. And we cannot claim that they are independent of each other.

Once this mutual dependence and independence of the masculine and the feminine is understood, then it is modified yet again. The modification is that if the masculine and feminine are separated, then the masculine always initiates the reunion in the material creation. Similarly, when they are united, the masculine initiates the separation in the material world. Thus, in the material world, it is said that the Lord glances at His Śakti and by that glance, He expresses His desire to reunite with the Śakti. The feminine has been waiting expectantly, and She agrees with the desire. Likewise, when the masculine is fulfilled, He withdraws from the feminine, and the feminine then waits expectantly. Therefore, after stating the mutual dependence and independence of the Puruṣa and Śakti, it is further said that the masculine is superior because He initiates the separation and reunion. But the situation is reversed in the spiritual world, where the Puruṣa waits expectantly for the Śakti to initiate their union. Hence, the Lord appears if the devotee desires, and the Lord disappears if the devotee doesn't desire. In the material world, the feminine loves the fact that the masculine is independent. But in the spiritual world, the masculine loves the fact that the feminine is independent. Feminism is hence a doctrine of the spiritual world, although it is not a doctrine of the material world. When the soul enters the material world, then in the masculine body, he tries to become dominant just like the Lord of the material world. Meanwhile, the soul in the feminine body tries to become dominant just like the feminine in the spiritual world.

The Puruṣa in the material world exhibits His dominant nature. But the Puruṣa in the spiritual world exhibits His subordinate nature. For example, when Kṛṣṇa appears in this world, He plays the flute and invites the gopis to dance, but when they arrive, He acts detached and asks them to return. The gopis feel heartbroken and beg Kṛṣṇa for His love. But in the spiritual world, the dance is arranged by the gopis, and if Kṛṣṇa arrives, the gopis tell Him that He cannot participate. Kṛṣṇa then begs the gopis for participation. However, the dominant and subordinate positions of the Puruṣa in the material and spiritual world are not absolute. For example, even in the material world, where the Puruṣa is mostly dominant, some forms of Śakti—e.g., Kālī—are said to be dominant and portrayed as standing on the chest of Lord Śiva. Likewise, in the spiritual world, the Puruṣa also acts dominant by selecting to enjoy with different gopis. However, by and large, the Puruṣa is dominant in the material world, and the Śakti is dominant in the spiritual world. And yet, dominant and subordinate doesn't mean mastery and slavery. It is a role-play for enjoyment. Both masculine and feminine enjoy being dominant and subordinate alternately.

Once the equality of masculine and feminine is understood, followed by the dominant positions of masculine and feminine in the material and spiritual worlds, the doctrine is modified for the last time. The final modification says that in a primordial state, when the masculine and feminine are not separated as interdependent persons, then the combined state is Puruṣa. In this state, the Śakti remains a part of the Puruṣa as His power. However, the Puruṣa is then agitated by the Śakti from within, and as a result, Śakti separates from the Puruṣa. The doctrine is even harder, because the feminine is a part of the masculine, and yet, the feminine is the cause of the activity in the masculine. Since the Śakti is a part of Puruṣa, therefore, the Puruṣa is called superior. But since the Śakti is the cause of activity in the Puruṣa, therefore, the Śakti is called superior. If we know the nuances in these doctrines, then they are not contradictory. However, mundane ideas about domination make them confusing.

The Nature of Absolute Truth

Thus, all the problems in previous doctrines are addressed. The problem of māyā being inert and Brahman being active are rejected and accepted. The rejection is that māyā is a person and so not inert. The acceptance is that māyā is feminine, and not the efficient cause of creation or annihilation, and hence inert. The doctrine of Viśiṣṭādvaita is also accepted and rejected. The acceptance is that the Śakti is the power of the powerful and serves at the will of the powerful. Hence, She is His property. But the doctrine is rejected because the feminine is a person and remains a controller of the Puruṣa. The Doctrine of Dvaita is also accepted and rejected. The acceptance is that the masculine and the feminine are different individuals. The rejection is that because they serve each other's purpose in the spiritual world, therefore, they are not truly separable. The Bhedābheda doctrine is also rejected and accepted. The rejection is that the Śakti is not a part of the whole as the soul; She is a complementary counterpart of the Lord. The acceptance is that the Śakti is distinct and yet inseparable from the Lord. The Acintyabhedābheda is articulated in two ways. One version says that the primordial state is Puruṣa and Śakti is His part. And the other version says that the Puruṣa is activated by the Śakti—from within and not outside.

Acintyabhedābheda is therefore not yet another doctrine. When looked at through the lens of the soul, it is merely a minor extension of the Bhedābheda doctrine. But this is not the primary purpose of the doctrine. Unlike the previous doctrines which deal in the difference and non-difference between the soul, the main purpose of Acintyabhedāb-heda is to describe the difference and the non-difference between the

Lord and His Śakti. In the process, the soul-God Acintyabhedābheda is different from the God-Śakti Acintyabhedābheda. The limitation in Acintyabhedābheda is the inconceivability, which arises because reality is not described through modalities. Without modalities, all doctrines are treated as universal claims. And this universality then leads to contradictions, which leads to the conclusion that the ultimate truth is inconceivable. If modalities were adopted, then Acintyabhedābheda is also conceivable.

The conceivability is that in the primordial state, the ability to answer questions exists, just as the questions exist. However, the ability to answer the questions is not used to answer the questions. The impersonalist says that this primordial state is an answer, but the personalist says that it is a question. The reasoning for these two systems is different. The impersonalist claims that the primordial state is achieved when the answers are obtained. The problem is this: If you got the answer, then why should there be any more questions? In short, why should the world be created and destroyed again and again? If the answer exists, then how it gives rise to a question is very hard to explain. The personalist says: The primordial state is always a question. These questions can remain unanswered, but there is an internal impetus to answer them. If the question exists, then how it produces an answer is much easier. Therefore, the personalist explanation is that the Puruṣa—as the question—creates the world as an answer. The purpose of the world is to answer the question in the Puruṣa; the creation cannot become a question to be answered by the Puruṣa. Hence, the creation is always subordinate to the Puruṣa, but to the extent that the Puruṣa is impelled from within to seek an answer, the Śakti is superior.

Advaita in Vaishnavism

The conflict between Advaita and Vaishnava doctrines is very subtle. And this conflict is not absolutely upheld in all situations. There are subtle ways in which Advaita is incorporated into the Vaishnava doctrines. We can illustrate the incorporation of Advaita in Vaishnavism through the different types of experiences had by devotees. The devotee sometimes misses the Lord, and in this situation, he knows that he is different from the Lord—this is Dvaita. Then, he sometimes sees the Lord and understands he is simply a part and property of the

Lord—this is Viśiṣṭādvaita. And finally, sometimes the devotee is so overwhelmed by the devotion to the Lord that he loses his self-identity and starts acting just like the Lord—this is Advaita. Similarly, the Lord sometimes misses His devotee, and then He knows that the devotee is different from Him—this is Dvaita. Then, when He sees the devotee, He knows that the devotee is a part and a property of Him—this is Viśiṣṭādvaita. And finally, sometimes when He is overwhelmed with love, He acts just like the devotee—this is Advaita.

The understanding of Advaita thus far has been limited to that of Brahman; it is said that the soul merges into Brahman and becomes undifferentiated. Subsequent Acharyas go beyond Brahman, illustrating the nature of Vaikuṇṭha as a realm that lies beyond Brahman, and in the process, they reject the identity of the soul and the Lord. At the least, Advaita is said to be an inferior understanding of the Absolute Truth. But this is not the only understanding of Advaita. A more sophisticated view is that the soul and the Lord can take on each other's roles and moods. Normally, each actor is tied to a character. For example, the soul acts like a devotee, and the Lord acts as the master. But the actors can take on different characters. Thus, a devotee overwhelmed by the love of the Lord, forgets that he is a devotee. He starts acting just like the Lord. Similarly, the Lord, overwhelmed by the love of the devotee, forgets that He is the Lord. He takes on the role and the mood of the devotee and behaves just like the devotee. The Dvaita conception of the difference between the Lord and the devotee, the Viśiṣṭādvaita conception of the devotee as a property of the Lord, and the Bhedābheda conception of the devotee as a part of the Lord are simultaneously emasculated by one person taking on another's role. The understanding of this love revives Advaita in which the soul and the Lord are identical—in their role and mood. But they are still not to be considered identical individuals!

This new kind of Bhedābheda was demonstrated in the pastimes of Lord Chaitanya, who is Kṛṣṇa, but He takes on the role and mood of devotees. As we have discussed, the Lord has three modes of existence—role, ability, and mood. When the Lord takes on the role and mood of the devotee, then the ability to behave like the Lord is suppressed, and His opulence is not demonstrated; He just exhibits the humility and helplessness of a devotee and dances before the Lord in ecstasy. When the Lord takes on the role of a devotee, but the mood is of the Lord, then He discards His humility and helplessness; He now becomes the most fearsome critic of atheism, impersonalism, and void-ism, and destroys them like He otherwise kills demons; since He isn't actually in the role of the Lord, but only in His mood, He doesn't kill those demons; He only refutes their ideologies. When the Lord is in the mood of a devotee, but the role is of the Lord, then He accepts worship from the devotees, just like a teacher is worshipped as the Lord, thinking that the Lord is being worshipped thereby.

With this new kind of Bhedābheda, a new definition of God is obtained—He is the *chit* or the ability to be the Lord. But He may not necessarily be in the mood of the Lord (the ānanda) or the role of the Lord (the *sat*). In fact, since the mood and role can dominate the ability, even though He is the Lord, His opulence may be invisible. But since that opulence is subordinated, it can be manifest sometimes. Thus, by becoming the devotee, the Lord doesn't lose His lordship. He remains the Lord but feels and acts like a devotee. Lord Chaitanya did not teach this understanding of Himself, but because He demonstrated all these things, His followers teach them as such. The devotees also recognize that they can take on the mood and role of the Lord. When they are in the mood of the Lord, they act fearsomely against the atheists, destroying their philosophies. They don't accept humility and submissiveness; rather, just like the Lord, they consider it their job to destroy the demons. Then, when they are in the role of the Lord, they accept worship from other devotees, just like the Lord. But even as they are worshipped, they don't confuse themselves to be the Lord. But most often, they only remain as the humble servants of the Lord, constantly feeling separated from Him, considering themselves His part, and not Himself.

Since we are now splitting the modalities of the Lord into separate aspects, the devotee and the Lord can be different and non-different—although in a completely new sense. This is also Advaita, but it doesn't mean 'oneness' (because all three aspects are not identical); it rather means non-difference (because in one or more ways, the Lord and the devotee are indistinguishable). In short, the term Advaita doesn't mean *identity*. It only means *indistinguishability*.

The problem of Advaita is quite like the problem of Abheda. Most people mistake Advaita and Abheda as 'oneness'. This follows from the dualistic logical system in which if something is not Duality, then it must be Oneness. Both Dvaita and Bheda mean the same thing: There are two different things, and they must be known as different things. Dvaita is an ontological and Bheda is an epistemological claim: If there are two things, then we must know them as two things. Then, if twoness is denied in Advaita and Abheda, under the dualistic logical assumptions (arising from a physicalist worldview), non-duality is taken to mean 'oneness'. Now, Advaita becomes an ontological commitment to a single reality, and Abheda becomes an epistemological claim that we must know everything as oneness. However, this dualistic reasoning doesn't account for the difference between modalities—e.g., Being and Becoming. I can Become one thing and still Be another thing. This is possible in semantic reasoning.

The Lord can Be the Lord, and yet Become a devotee. Just like actors on a stage are one person but they act and feel like another person. This acting and feeling can make them forget that they are another person otherwise. But this is not a permanent illusion about one's identity. There is a difference between the actor and the character, and yet you cannot separate them sometimes. The distinction between the actor and the character, and yet, the inseparability of the actor and the character, is Advaita and Abheda. Such differences are impossible in physicalist thinking because in physics you cannot distinguish between an object and its role. An actor feels being himself and becoming someone else. They are neither the same nor are they separable. If you watch a performance, you can see how the actor brings his persona to the character, but it would be a mistake to apply the character back to the actor or equate the actor to the character. Thus, with a semantic view, Advaita and Abheda lose their conventional oneness claim: They both mean non-difference. Advaita is still an ontological commitment to the reality being non-different, and Abheda is still an epistemological commitment to knowing this non-different reality non-differently.

The Doctrine of Brahman

As we have seen, the Vedic system recognizes three primordial modes—*sat*, *chit*, and *ānanda*. We have previously called them the modes of relation, cognition, and emotion, and contextuality, universality, and individuality. Our cognition obtains universals—such as color, shape, size, taste, smell, meanings, etc. Our emotions individuate us from other individuals. And contextuality means giving new meanings to the universals in different contexts. Infinite variety is thus created from the three modes as the modes enter each other. Hence, creation is the process in which the universal becomes an individual and enters the instance individual of another mode. The individual then also has contextual relations to other modes. But since the mode is a universal, it is not separate from the original state of the mode. Therefore, annihilation is a process in which the mode goes from the individual and contextual state to the universal state—i.e., it 'merges' into the original state and simply exists as a universal.

Through the successive penetration of the modes within each other, a hierarchical structure is produced; in this hierarchy, the 'higher' level mode is the dominant mode, and the 'lower' level mode is the subordinate mode. Likewise, hierarchy is collapsed when the subordinate mode exits the domination of the dominant mode and goes back into the universal state. Remember that universal, individual, and contextual are simply modalities of existence. Thus, infinite instances of these three modes are just the three modes in the universal modality. This universal is also an individual, and it exists in the context of Itself. That is, the Absolute Truth is knowledge, He is a person, who knows Himself. However, this knowledge is simply what God is, not what He is not. The absence of the negative conception of knowledge means the whole exists, but the parts—and how the whole is defined in relation to these parts—do not exist.

This primordial state is called Param Brahman. However, this is not the Brahman of Advaita. This is because Śakti is within the Param Brahman, however, according to Advaita, māyā is separate from Brahman. Once the Param Brahman enters the manifest state, it divides into three personalities—Kṛṣṇa, Balarāma, and Hara. Since Kṛṣṇa is the enjoyer and the ānanda mode of Param Brahman, He represents the question to be answered. In the Param Brahman stage, the question is: "Who am I?" and the answer is "I am Kṛṣṇa—the all-attractive". In this stage, however, Kṛṣṇa is not known in relation to what He is not—i.e., His Śakti and the souls. When Param Brahman divides, then Kṛṣṇa manifests the souls, Hara manifests as His Śakti, and Balarāma as God.

If the Advaita philosopher chants the mantra OM, he refers to Brahman. But when the Vaishnava philosopher chants the mantra OM, he refers to Param Brahman. All Vedic texts and mantras employ OM. The

Advaita philosopher takes this to mean that Brahman is the primordial reality, and forms of God are manifest from Brahman. Since Brahman is separate from māyā, therefore, these forms must be the combination of Brahman and māyā. Thus, the Advaita philosopher says that the incarnations of God are Saguna Brahman—the combination of māyā and Brahman. However, the Vaishnava philosopher says that OM refers to the Param Brahman, and māyā is a part of the Absolute Truth. Therefore, when God manifests in the material world, He manifests along with His Śakti, but the form of God is not the combination of Brahman and māyā. Rather, māyā is a part of the Param Brahman and all His incarnations. Similarly, when the Vedānta Sūtra speaks about Brahman being the source of everything, the Advaita philosopher says that it is the origin of the soul, but not the origin of māyā. The Vaishnava philosopher, however, says that the origin of everything is Param Brahman; māyā or Śakti are all part of Brahman. This fundamental misunderstanding between Brahman and Param Brahman is the origin of all the problems in Vedānta. If Śaṅkarācārya had spoken about Param Brahman, and not equated it to Brahman, then successive philosophies of Viśiṣṭādvaita, Dvaita, Bhedābheda, and Acintyabhedābheda would be unnecessary. All contradictions would be reconciled in the doctrine of Param Brahman. So, in one sense, Vedānta has only progressed from Brahman to Param Brahman, passing through Viśiṣṭādvaita, Dvaita, Bhedābheda, and Acintyabhedābheda.

Aside from the confusion between Brahman and Param Brahman, Advaita also creates confusion between Brahman and Puruṣa. Factually, Brahman is that state of Puruṣa in which the Puruṣa knows Himself, but not His parts. Conversely, when the will is manifest, then Puruṣa knows Himself and His parts. Thus, we can say that in the unmanifest state, Puruṣa is Brahman—the only existent. But in the manifest state, Brahman is Puruṣa—the source of numerous other existents. The definition of Puruṣa changes from being the only existent to the source of infinitely many existents. But this change is the development of a new experience, rather than the creation of a new reality. Hence, we cannot say that Puruṣa did not exist previously, but we can say that Puruṣa did not know Himself completely, and He expands to complete His knowledge.

Once these confusions are clarified, then one can still ask: Given that the same thing can exist in a manifest or an unmanifest state, which of these states is better? Should we say that the unmanifest state is better because it is primordial? Or should we say that the manifest state is better because there is cognition, relation, and emotion—not merely the potentiality for these things?

The answer to this question is nuanced. The recombined state includes the uncombined state, but the uncombined state doesn't include the recombined state. Just because there are individual cows, you don't say that the idea cow has ceased to exist. However, it is possible that the idea cow exists, but the individual cows don't. Therefore, since the recombined includes the uncombined, therefore, it is fuller and superior to the uncombined. But this superior reality is not the primordial reality; the primordial reality is still uncombined. Thus, the central problem in Vedānta interpretation has been the confusion between the primordial reality and the superior reality. The uncombined is primordial, but it is also considered incomplete. The recombined is not primordial but it is superior and complete. We can say that the primordial reality strives toward greater completion—by desiring to know itself and this attempt at self-knowledge produces everything else. While the self-unaware state is primordial, the self-aware state is superior. Therefore, even though Brahman and Param Brahman are primordial, we still prefer the manifest personalities.

Expansions of the Absolute Truth

The Chatuśpāda Doctrine

In many places in the Vedānta Sūtra, we find a doctrine called Chatuśpāda. The term *pāda* has many meanings; in the simplest case, it means parts, but it also means aspects. The term *pada* (instead of pāda) also means words or symbols. Since we see the terms pada and pāda being used interchangeably, therefore, we nuance the meaning—there are four parts or aspects, and they are symbols of the whole. Thus, when you see a part or aspect, you don't say that it is partial. And yet, you don't say that it is the whole. When you see a drama, you don't say that the actor is not the character; but you don't say that the actor is the character. A nuanced understanding is used—the actor is the full person, but in a role, he exhibits the full personality in a certain limited way. That limited expression is partial, but it is an expression of the full actor. The actor is not partially present in the character, and yet the character is not the full actor.

The Chatuṣpāda doctrine is used in many ways in Vedic philosophy. In one way, the manifest reality is divided into four parts, aspects, or symbols. These four parts are Matter, Brahman, Vaikuṇṭha, and Goloka. Within each of these parts, there are four such aspects. The first part is the combined state of the three modalities. In the spiritual world, this primordial reality is Param Brahman and has three manifest parts—Kṛṣṇa, Balarāma, and Hara. In the material world, this primordial reality is called Param Śiva, and He has three manifest parts—Mahesh (ānanda), Viṣṇu (sat), and Śakti (chit). The Mahesh mode becomes God; the Śakti mode becomes matter, and the Viṣṇu mode becomes the soul. In Param Śiva, the God, matter, and soul modes are not manifest. They are manifest when the three aspects of Param Śiva are separated. Once these modes of God, soul, and matter are manifest, then each mode divides into three parts.

The original soul-mode manifestation is Vāsudeva. He is the Universal Soul. But since the soul also has three aspects, therefore, Vāsudeva, manifests three other forms called Kāraṇodakaśāyī (Saṅkarṣaṇa), Garbhodakaśāyi (Pradyumna), and Kṣīrodakaśāyī (Aniruddha). These three forms predominate in the three modalities of the soul. Kāraṇodakaśāyī Viṣṇu is *sat* or awareness; it is said that Kāraṇodakaśāyī "divides Himself by Himself" to create the awareness of the soul. Garbhodakaśāyi Viṣṇu is the *chit* or cognition, and He becomes the original speaker of Vedic knowledge to Brahma. Finally, Kṣīrodakaśāyī Viṣṇu is ānanda or purpose, and He exists inside everything as their purpose.

The original God-mode manifestation in the material world is Mahesh. He represents Universal Time. As a soul, He has three aspects, therefore, Mahesh manifests into three further forms called Sankar, Rudra, and Bhairava.

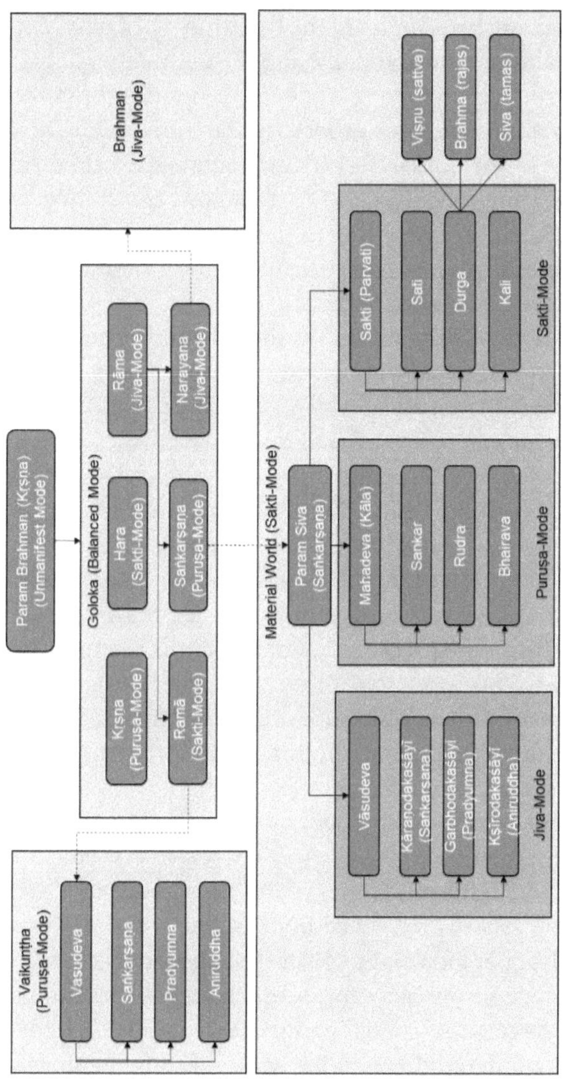

The original matter-mode manifestation is Śakti. She represents Universal Space. But, as She is also a soul, and has three aspects, therefore, Śakti manifests into three further aspects called Sati, Durga, and Kāli. Sati dominates in the universal mode, Durga in the individual mode, and Kāli in the relational mode. From Durga—who is in the individual mode—three types of universals are created: Viṣṇu, Brahma, and Śiva, and they become the sources of the three modes of nature called sattva, rajas, and tamas. And from these universals, many relational subordinates are produced. These servants of the modes (Brahma, Viṣṇu and Śiva), Who are themselves aspects of the individual (Durga), Who is as an aspect of the unmanifest (Param Śiva)—are called Āditya, Vasu, and Rudra. They constitute the 33 demigods controlling the universe. But Durga is the ultimate source of matter; Viṣṇu, Śiva, and Brahma are the intermediate sources of matter; the Āditya, Vasu, and Rudra are lower-level sources of matter.

Since Param Śiva manifests Viṣṇu and Śakti, therefore, He is called the supreme reality and is considered superior to Viṣṇu and Śakti. Since Brahma, Viṣṇu, and Śiva—as the controllers of three modes of nature—are manifest from Śakti, therefore, it is said that Śakti is the supreme reality and Śiva and Viṣṇu are subordinate to Her. Since the soul is manifest from Viṣṇu, therefore, scriptures say Viṣṇu is the only master of the soul. Finally, because Kṛṣṇa exists in the transcendent world of Goloka, it is said that He is the cause of all causes. Depending on which text you are reading, you can see these conflicting claims: sometimes Śiva is supreme, sometimes Viṣṇu is supreme, and sometimes Śakti is supreme. And those who don't understand the modal nature of reality make this 'supremacy' universal. There is indeed a supreme reality called Param Brahman or Kṛṣṇa. But because this reality is modal, and the modes enter each other and become subordinate, therefore, everything is dominant or subordinate in some or other situation. These are not contradictory doctrines. Everything becomes clear if we understand the modalities of the Absolute Truth.

In the material world, since Lord Viṣṇu is the source of the soul, therefore, the liberation of the soul is described in relation to Lord Viṣṇu. However, since Viṣṇu, Mahesh, and Śakti are manifest from Param Śiva, therefore, one could say that the soul is also originated from Param Śiva. Therefore, two descriptions of the soul's destiny are given in different Vedic texts. In the Vaishnava texts, it is said that the soul merges into Kāraṇodakaśāyī Viṣṇu. And in the Shaiva texts, it is said that the soul merges into Param Śiva. These two statements are the basis of the conflict between the Vaishnava and Shaiva systems. There is factually no contradiction between these doctrines if we understand that Kāraṇodakaśāyī Viṣṇu is a partial manifestation from the person of Param Śiva.

However, if we go deeper into other Vedic texts, we also find that there are many Viṣṇu forms manifest from Balarāma Who are transcendental to the material world. They reside in Vaikuṇṭha and are different from Kāraṇodakaśāyī Viṣṇu. Vaishnava texts clearly distinguish between Kāraṇodakaśāyī Viṣṇu who manifests the soul in the material world, Kṛṣṇa who manifests the soul in the spiritual world, and the transcendental Viṣṇu forms to whom the soul can be devoted in the Vaikuṇṭha planets. However, this distinction doesn't come out clearly in the Vaishnava philosophies. The transcendental Viṣṇu forms are present in different planets of Vaikuṇṭha and the soul can 'travel' from one planet to another because the soul is not 'bound' to any of the Viṣṇu forms. If one of these Viṣṇu forms was indeed the origin of the soul, then the soul could never go to another planet in Vaikuṇṭha. However, because the soul originates from Kṛṣṇa, he obtains the freedom to roam to all the parts of the spiritual world.

Now, based on this understanding of four aspects or Chatuśpāda, we can say that Vaikuṇṭha, Brahman, and the material world are three aspects of Goloka. From Param Brahman—which is the unmanifest stage—the first manifestation is Goloka. But this Goloka manifestation has three aspects, which are successively manifest, and these are Vaikuṇṭha, Brahman, and the material world. Vaikuṇṭha is the God aspect of Param Brahman, Brahman is the soul aspect of the same Param Brahman, and material world is the Śakti aspect of the same Param Brahman. All these aspects are alternately dominant in Goloka, but they are permanently dominant in the other aspects. Thus, in Vaikuṇṭha, the God aspect of Param Brahman is permanently dominant. In Brahman, the soul aspect of Param Brahman is permanently dominant. And in the material world, the Śakti aspect of Param Brahman is permanently dominant. Due to the permanent dominance property, they are considered relatively incomplete with respect to Goloka, where all these three modes are alternately dominant.

Thus, in Goloka, sometimes God dominates, sometimes the soul dominates, and sometimes the Śakti dominates. God often serves the devotee or acts like a devotee. God similarly serves the Śakti and acts like the Śakti. The soul and the Śakti sometimes act like God, sometimes act like each other, and sometimes serve each other. The situations in which God, soul, and Śakti act like they are God, soul, and Śakti, are hence a part of the whole truth. There are always situations in which they take each other's roles and moods and act contrary to their position. They are different, but because they take on each other's roles and moods, they are non-different. This non-difference is Advaita, but it is not oneness because there is a difference between God, soul, and Śakti as well.

Thus, Kṛṣṇa is the whole truth, Kṛṣṇa is a part of the whole truth, Kṛṣṇa has parts which are His servants, and Kṛṣṇa is also a servant of the parts. Similarly, Kṛṣṇa is transcendent to all the parts, Kṛṣṇa is the source of all parts, Kṛṣṇa is different from the parts, but the parts are not different from Him, and Kṛṣṇa is immanent in all the parts. All these positions are true, and yet, due to modalities, they are alternately true. If you deny any position, you will get contradictions. We can only assert that all these positions are true. And yet, because the universalist view of simultaneous truth also leads to contradictions, therefore, we employ a modal description. Hence, we need to avoid two kinds of pitfalls in thinking— (1) you cannot say that any of these positions are false, and (2) you cannot say that all of them are simultaneously true. Both views will create contradictions. The Acintyabhedābheda doctrine is that no position is false. But since everyone concludes that these positions must be simultaneously true, which leads to a contradiction, therefore, the result is inconceivability. Conversely, if we deny the simultaneous truth of all the positions—without making any position false—then we achieve the position of Cintyabhedābheda.

The Pañcatattva Doctrine

There are many places in the Vedic texts, where the Chatuṣpāda doctrine (the doctrine of four aspects) is updated to the Pañcatattva doctrine (the doctrine of five essences). The addition of the fifth aspect or essence is in between the unmanifest stage—called Param Brahman—and the three manifest aspects (e.g., Kṛṣṇa, Balarāma, and Hara). The doctrine goes as follows. The Param Brahman is the unmanifest; He is merely the possibility of the three aspects. However, since it is only a possibility, therefore, the self is unknown. There is no emotion, no relation, and no cognition, although the possibility of emotion, relation, and cognition exists. From this unmanifest stage, the first manifestation is the self-aware state. There is hence desire to know oneself, relation to oneself, and knowledge of oneself. In this stage, one is in love with oneself, aware of oneself, and serves oneself. This stage corresponds to the "I" that we discussed earlier; it springs from the self-unaware stage. However, in this state of "I", there is nothing other than "I". Sometimes, it is said that in this state, the three modes exist in a balanced state which means that no mode is dominant or subordinate. When the modes go dominant and subordinate, then the "I" divides into three aspects—e.g., Kṛṣṇa, Hara, and Rāma. Since Param Brahman is called Kṛṣṇa in the unmanifest stage, this manifest stage of "I" is also identified as Kṛṣṇa. And finally, the separated enjoyer aspect is also known as Kṛṣṇa. There are hence three forms of Kṛṣṇa—the unmanifest Param Brahman, the balanced manifest "I", and the "I" imbued with desires other than "I". Along with such desires, there are also things other than the self, and the power to connect the desire to things other than the self. These things to be known, and the power to know them, are manifest along with the desire to know these things. Kṛṣṇa is the desire for knowing, Balarāma is the creator for all the different things to be known, and Hara is the power that connects the desire to those things.

Thus, along with Param Brahman, and the three manifest aspects, the addition of "I" in between the unmanifest and the fully manifest leads us to the doctrine of Pañcatattva. Unlike in the Chatuśpāda doctrine, where everything was being divided into four aspects, now the division is into five aspects.

There are many illustrations of the Pañcatattva doctrine found all over Vedic texts. For example, to the four aspects of Vasudeva, Saṅkarṣaṇa, Pradyumna, and Aniruddha, a fifth aspect—called Nārāyaṇa—is added. While the previous four are called Chaturvyūha, these five are called Pañcatattva.

Similarly, in Shaivism, Param Śiva is sometimes understood as the unmanifest individual, and then also sometimes as the original "I" that creates the material universe. The "I" stage of the unmanifest Param Śiva is also called Param Śiva, but they are distinct, in the sense that when the material universe is annihilated, then the Param Śiva goes into the unmanifest mode. However, if the material universe exists, then Param Śiva also exists in the "I" mode.

Likewise, in Shaktism, Śakti has five aspects: revelation, hiding, creation, annihilation, and maintenance. The 'hiding' is the unmanifest stage of Śakti; the 'revelation' is the manifest self-aware state, which hasn't divided into further aspects; following this, the "I" state of the Śakti is divided into creation, maintenance, and annihilation as the three modes of rajas, sattva, and tamas.

In the "I" state, Param Śiva combines Puruṣa, Śakti, and soul. There are thus depictions in Shaiva and Shakta systems of an androgynous personality who is simultaneously masculine and feminine. This is the basis for the idea that the feminine was previously a part of the masculine and is created from Him.

In some depictions of Nārāyana, He is shown alone. And in other depictions of Nārāyana, He is shown along with three other aspects—Lakshmi, Seśa, and Brahma. Lakshmi is Nārāyana's Śakti-mode existence, Seśa is Nārāyana's Puruṣa-mode existence, and Brahma is Nārāyana's soul-mode existence. When He is shown alone, then He is just the "I". When Lakshmi, Seśa, and Brahma are depicted alongside, then there is "I" that is manifest in three aspects. These are not just pictures for us to see. These are scientific descriptions of reality. The entire reality is simply summarized in a picture for our understanding. But these are not physical pictures. We need philosophy to understand them.

This five-fold description of reality is employed in Gaudīya Vaishnavism, and these five aspects are called Chaitanya, Nityānanda, Advaita, Gadādhar, and Srivās. Sri Chaitanya is Param Brahman without a distinction between desire, the power to fulfill the desire, and the objects of desire. The desire, object, and power are all one. Nityānanda is the manifest stage of Param Brahman and exists as the "I". Once this "I" divides, there are three manifest aspects—Advaita is Puruṣa-mode, Gadādhar is Śakti-mode, and Srivās is soul-mode. Gaudīya Vaishnavas thus worship the Absolute Truth in five essences.

Pañcatattva in Sāṅkhya and Yoga

Such descriptions also abound in Sāṅkhya and Yoga philosophies. For example, the Yoga system describes the body as comprising of five sheaths, called ānanda-maya, vijñāna-maya, mano-maya, prāṇa-maya, and anna-maya.

In Shaiva philosophy, the ānanda-maya is further classified into five parts—rāga, vidya, kalā, kāla, and niyati. Rāga means that I can only like a few things; I cannot like everything. Vidya means I can only know a few subjects; I cannot know everything. Kalā means I am only capable of certain types of activities; I cannot perform every type of action. Kāla means I exist in a specific age and time; since I am a product of some specific age, therefore, I must live according to that age. Niyati means that I was born in a certain nation or society; since I am a product of some nation and society, therefore, I must abide by the ideologies and principles of my nationality, society, or the place of living. Thus, ānanda-maya creates our limited personality. It is the ways in which we create our material identity based on likes, abilities, knowledge, place, and time. It is a sense of "I", but it is not self-awareness; it is rather one's personality.

There is also a hierarchy within these aspects of personality. The full personality is all that you can desire. A subset of what you can desire manifests at a given time. To fulfill that temporal desire, you desire that place that can fulfill the desire. After you desire the place at a given time, then you desire to know a subset of things at that place. And once this subset of things is desired, then you desire to use a smaller subset of things in your actions. For instance, you can desire to eat Indian food, which is one of the many possible desires, but that desire manifests at a given time. Once the desire has manifest, the desire for eating becomes the desire for an Indian restaurant. Once you reach the restaurant, your desire changes and you ask for the menu. Upon seeing the menu, your desire again changes and you ask for a specific dish from the menu. Thus, from your unmanifest personality, the desire to eat manifests, which then becomes the desire for a restaurant, then it becomes the desire for the menu, and then it becomes a desire for a specific dish in the menu. Thus, the personality of desires progressively manifests into time, place, knowing, and action.

Then, vijñāna-maya is also divided into five parts. These are called Pradhāna, Prakriti, Mahattattva, Ahaṃkāra, and Buddhi. The term vijñāna means judgment, and there are five stages of judging. The fifth stage of Buddhi is the judgment of truth. The fourth stage of Ahaṃkāra is judgment is good. The third stage of Mahattattva is the judgment of right. The Prakriti stage is the formulation of preferences about truth, right, and good, based on which later judgments can be done—e.g., I will value equality over justice, or vice versa; I will value knowledge over beauty, or vice versa; I will value my job over my family, or vice versa. Once these axioms are formed, everything is judged based on these preferences. And these preferences are called Prakriti. Finally, the original stage of Pradhāna is the possibility of all such preferences; we haven't chosen them yet, but we must know the possibilities to make a choice. For example, if you did not know that equality was an option, you could not value it over justice. All these kinds of judgments are "I", but they the sense of "I" that judges.

The mano-maya represents the mind which cognizes the meanings. These meanings are also divided into five parts, which are then called thinking, feeling, willing, knowing, and acting. For example, you can say that a shooter shot an innocent person. Then, in the knowing mode, you say that the shooter was tall or short, white or black, ugly or beautiful. Then, in the thinking mode, you say that the shooter was a professional or an amateur. In the feeling mode, you say that the shooter hated, loved, or was simply careless. And in the willing mode, you judge a person's intentions—the shooter had premeditated the action, or it was an accident. These five kinds of meanings complete the understanding of any observation, and the understanding thus has five parts. This is also a sense of "I", but the self is a thinker, feeler, intender, knower, and doer. By interpreting the world as meaning, we define the self accordingly.

Then prāna-maya represents the power to do things. This power is also divided into five parts—called prāna, apāna, udāna, vyāna, and samāna. These are understood as the power of ingestion, digestion, assimilation, circulation, and excretion. A system's behavior can be explained by these five types. This is also a sense of "I", but it identifies the soul as a type of living system.

Finally, the anna-maya represents the body of 'food'. This 'food' is divided into five elements—called Earth, Water, Fire, Air, and Ether. The element called Ether is the unmanifest stage of the five elements. In the stage called Air, this Ether has manifested energy. This energy is then divided into three parts—Fire, Water, and Earth. The Fire mode of Air is called 'energy'. The Earth mode is called 'object'. And the Water mode is the 'relation' between the two. Thus, energy is not randomly distributed to every object. Rather, there are objects, a specific object is selected to receive the energy, and then energy is transferred.

Then, to measure all these things, we need some properties, these properties must have standards, and there must be an observer who applies these standards to measurement, and then observes them. The observer is divided into five parts as the five senses or jñāna-indriya. Each such indriya measures five properties—e.g., the sense of sight measures color, shape, size, distance, and direction. And each such property has its own standards. The senses are the mere possibilities of every type of perception. In this stage, they remain unmanifest. The manifestation of the sense is when a standard is selected. If your senses have selected 'big' standards, then they cannot see 'small' things, and vice versa. In the unmanifest stage, the senses of all the living entities are the same. But in the "I" stage, these senses have standards. Now, each soul has acquired a different type of sense, which can see different kinds of things.

Now, if you look at a standard—e.g., a kilogram or a meter—then it has three aspects. First, it has a property—e.g., weight or length. Second, it has a value—the value in all standards is 1. Third, the standard is also an individual object. In the same way, when senses become standards, then they divide into three aspects—objects, values, and properties. To understand this description, one should think of dreams rather than the waking experience. In a dream, experiences are produced by the senses, and each person sees different kinds of dreams. This is because they have different kinds of senses. Essentially, the sense—as a standard—divides into objects, properties, and their values. This division of the sense into three aspects causes our dreaming experience.

Once the dreaming experience is understood, then the waking experience is described in the same way. The primordial reality is created as a standard. These standards are just numbers or identities of different objects. From this identity, three further things are produced—object, value, and property. Thus, we can say that the 10th object is a table, which has the properties of shape and color, and the shape is square while the color is black. The table is the object, shape, and color are the properties, and square and black are their values. But before these objects, properties, and values, there is simply a number. Whatever originates from this number can also be described as a number. Hence, objects, properties, and values can also be understood as numbers. This description of reality as numbers (which exist in many modalities) is called Sāñkhya.

Similarly, there are five karma-indriya or the senses of actions. Each of these five indriya can do five types of things, each of these five types have their standards, objects, and values. This description is not elaborately found in the Vedic texts, but it can be gleaned and extended from the previous descriptions.

The jñāna-indriya, karma-indriya, and bhūta exist in three modes of nature—*sattva*, *rajas*, and *tamas*. Then there is a balanced state of these three modes which is called tāmasic ahamkara or "I-ness in the object mode". This is also a sense of "I", although after the previous notions of "I"—as a personality, a chooser, a knower, and a living entity—we get the identity as a body. Although the body is comprised of hands and legs, if one of these were absent, the 'body' still exists. Whatever is absent from the body (e.g., if the hand was cut-off) goes into the state of potentiality, while the other parts of the body are present. The evidence of the whole body being present is that if a part is cut-off, then the other parts continue their functions. We can contrast this to a team comprised of people; if one person leaves the team, the others share the work between them. But if your hand and legs are cut-off, then the lungs, heart, and stomach don't start doing the work of the hands or legs. This is because the missing body part still exists, although in an unmanifest state. It is as if the person has not completely left the team, but merely gone on a vacation.

A well-known illustration of this problem is the existence of 'phantom limbs'—many soldiers who return from a battle with their limbs amputated, continue to feel pain in those limbs. The reason is that the limb exists in three modes—purpose, function, and object. When the limb is amputated, the purpose and function exist; only the object-mode reality is absent. This is like a person on a team who has gone on vacation. The role and purpose exist, but the body performing that role and fulfilling the purpose is absent. But since the function and purpose exist, therefore, the other body parts don't fulfill the function and purpose of the missing part. And since the function and purpose exist, therefore, the limbs can be replaced. Sometimes even without this replacement, the limb performs its function and purpose, and hence feels the pain.

Beyond this 'body' is another body that exists in an unmanifest state. This body is a collection of successive bodies—e.g., child body, a youth body, old body, etc. All these bodies are potentialities, but different potentialities are manifest one after another. Therefore, due to this unmanifest body, we can say that the same body was a child, then become young, and then became old. Then again, since these are only potentials, we can also say that we are changing bodies, and the child body is not the same as the youth body or the old body.

Thus, we can see how our existence is divided into five sheaths, each of which is then divided into five parts, and in many cases—such as the division of the gross body—there are further five-fold subdivisions of the gross body. This is a generic method or principle of division and manifestation, and it can therefore be applied to the body, to the entire universe, and to the Absolute Truth. Therefore, Pañcatattva is a generic doctrine about five modalities.

The ānanda-maya is known as the 'unconscious' in Western psychology. The vijñāna-maya is the beginning of the conscious experience, and it is further divided into mano-maya, prāṇa-maya, and anna-maya, which are also sometimes called manas, prāṇa, and vāk, as three modes of *sattva*, *rajas*, and *tamas*. The 'unconscious' is the unmanifest stage of matter. The vijñāna-maya is the beginning of the manifestation when the person obtains a sense of conscious identity. Then, this identity is further divided into three aspects or modes.

Other Uses of Pañcatattva

This doctrine is sometimes employed in the Pañcopāsanā system as well, when five deities—Śiva, Śakti, Viṣṇu, Surya, and Iśta—are worshipped. Śiva, Śakti, and Viṣṇu are representations of God, matter, and soul. Surya represents the balanced combination of these three—the Sun god is Viṣṇu, the sunlight is Śakti, and Sun's rotation is time or Śiva. Factually, what we call the sun-globe doesn't exist as an object. It is merely a collection of potentialities. From this collection, one by one the various potentialities are selected, and these are called the aspects of the sun, represented by the 12 zodiac signs, and their succession is time. However, since these properties can be applied to every single planet—e.g., Moon or Jupiter—since they are also persons, energies, and phases, therefore, in principle, Surya is optional in the worship of five deities and could be replaced by any other planet. Nevertheless, the Sun is not replaced, and the reason is that he is considered the perfect balanced combination of Śiva, Viṣṇu, and Śakti. If one wants to worship another personality, then the fifth deity called Iśta is treated as the person being worshipped *through* the Sun. In short, you make your offering to the Sun—because he is manifest—but this offering is in turn delivered to the Iśta or the deity of your choice through the Sun. For example, those who worship Ganeśa must do so through the Sun god.

In Vedic astrology, all other planets are considered simply aspects of the Sun. Unlike the Sun in which these three aspects of Śiva, Śakti, and Viṣṇu are balanced, in other planets, these modalities are dominant and subordinate. Thus, owing to the dominant-subordinate structures, there are six other planets—Jupiter, Saturn, Mercury, Venus, Mars, and Moon—in which the modes go dominant and subordinate $(6 = 3 \times 2 \times 1)$. Hence, there are six aspects of the Sun, and together with the Sun, there are seven primary planets. Then, because the properties of these planets are further divided into dualities (such as hot and cold), therefore, two other planets—Rahu and Ketu—are added to the list. Thus, the same Pañcatattva doctrine also leads to other kinds of descriptions. In some of these descriptions, there are six aspects of a balanced reality. Then together with the balanced reality, there are seven aspects collectively. Then there are also nine aspects if we combine the dualities of the material world. Then because the Sun is the combination of Viṣṇu, Śiva, and Śakti, and Viṣṇu divides into 12 or 24 aspects, Śiva divides into 15 aspects, and Śakti divides into 8 aspects, therefore, even more complex systems of division are employed.

Vedic cosmology also describes the universe as a five-fold covering. The first such covering is the ānanda-maya, which is divided into an unmanifest, which is called the kārana, and a balanced manifest which is called mahattattva (this mahattattva is different from the same term used in other contexts). The balanced manifest then divides into six further aspects. Unlike the five-fold division in the Pañcatattva doctrine, the division, in this case, has eight parts—the unmanifest, the balanced manifest, and its six different aspects (just like the balanced manifest of the Sun has six different aspects). It might seem that this division is fundamentally different, but it is not. The first two stages are the same, and the next six stages are a variation from the three separated modes to six separated but combined modes (in dominant-subordinate states). The balanced manifest and its six imbalanced aspects constitute the seven coverings of a universe, and the unmanifest is common to all the universes. The balanced manifest is the universe's "I" state, and it springs from the common unmanifest state. Thus, all the universes are merged into the kāraṇa unmanifest state. From this state, each of the varied universes springs out as a unique "I". This "I" can be viewed as the balanced state of three modes of "I". It can also be understood as the combination of the six separated states that are imbalanced in the three modes. And finally, it can be divided into five aspects of ānanda-maya. The ānanda-maya is like the personality of the universe—there are different kinds of desires, knowledge, abilities, places, and times within each universe.

Once this ānanda-maya is produced, then there are vijñāna-maya, mano-maya, prāṇa-maya, and anna-maya divisions of the universe. All the forms of the Supreme Lord in the universe are vijñāna-maya. These forms are described variously as one, two, three, four, five, six, seven, eight, or even more. The universe is then divided into three subparts—the planets of demigods, of demons, and the hellish planets. Each of these is then divided into seven subparts. The Vedānta Sūtra speaks of these three-fold and seven-fold divisions. The planets of the demigods are in the mode of sattva, those of demons are in the mode of rajas, and the hellish planets are in the mode of tamas. They can also be called mano-maya, prāṇa-maya, and anna-maya. And yet, these are simply three aspects of the vijñāna-maya. Since these are only aspects of the Supreme Lord, therefore, the whole cosmos is understood as a Cosmic Man and the Vedānta Sūtra describes how the Lord can be understood through a cosmic form.

It is impossible to capture all the varied systems of modalities here, and I don't aim to do that. For the interested reader, I will refer you to my book *Cosmic Theogony*, which discusses this topic at greater length. My goal in the present book is to primarily illustrate how all these systems are created from a primordial unmanifest, comprising of three fundamental modalities. And this system then gives us a template of how to construct more complex modal descriptions. Even without going into further details, we can see how this modal description brings together numerous thus far disparate descriptions. These are not truly disparate; they are just developments of an unmanifest reality.

The Unity of Vedic Philosophy

When we adopt the semantic view, in one sense, we change the doctrine of Vedānta Sūtra from *achintya* to *chintya*. In another sense, this is not yet another doctrine that merely differs from the previous doctrines (or worse, contradicts them). This is a doctrine that makes every other doctrine equally true. Thus, Advaita is true because the Lord and the devotee can take on each other's moods and roles. Viśiṣṭādvaita is true because the devotee is a property that describes the object. Dvaita is true because even if the soul falls, the Lord is not fallen. Bhedābheda is true because the soul is a part of the Lord, and His Śakti is a complement of the Lord. Acintyabhedābheda is true because all these approaches cannot be reconciled in the physical view of things. And the *chintya* doctrine is true because they can be reconciled in the semantic viewpoint.

The modal view of reality helps us see how Vaishnavism, Shaivism, and Shaktism are three aspects of the same truth. In the material world, Vaishnavism is the soul-mode description of reality; Shaivism is the God-mode description of the same reality; and Shaktism is the Śakti-mode description of the same reality. As we have discussed, the God-mode defines *what* will happen, the soul-mode defines *who* will do what, and the Śakti-mode defines *how* things will happen. What, who, and how are complementary explanations of reality. The who-mode is also the *why*-mode because the soul's choices are the explanation of the soul's bondage. The Śakti-mode is also the *where*-mode since Śakti creates the variety of the material world, which is the universal space. Finally, the God-mode is also the *when*-mode because God (as Time in the material world) controls the world. Thus, if we understand these three modalities, then we get the answer to six questions—what, who, how, when, why, and where. In one sense, there are six different explanations of the same reality. In another sense, there is just one reality, which exists in three distinct modalities.

The modal description simply says that you can never answer these six questions simultaneously. You can, however, answer them alternately. If you remain fixed in the matter-mode, then soul-mode and God-mode descriptions will never be seen. If you try to add all three modes simultaneously, then you will get contradictions. Due to these problems, you either get incompleteness (you can't have all three modes simultaneously), or you get contradictions (if you use all three modes at once). If we want to get past the incompleteness and inconsistency problems, then the modal solution says that these six questions can be answered alternately, but not simultaneously. This is because the soul alternates between these modes and hence language too must alternate.

This understanding of Vedānta can also reconcile the other five systems of philosophy—i.e., Sāṅkhya, Yoga, Vaiśeṣika, Nyāya, and Mīmāṃsā. Sāṅkhya is the description of the world as mathematics, numbers, and the process of counting. Vedānta, on the other hand, is the reduction of Sāṅkhya—or number theory (and all of mathematics)—to the whole-part doctrine (i.e., set theory).

Given that there are many whole-part doctrines, therefore, we end up with many models of logic. For example, in Materialism, the whole reduces to the parts, so we get the non-contradiction and mutual exclusion of modern mathematical set theory. In Buddhism, the opposites are mutually defined, so, we must reject both non-contradiction and mutual exclusion, but we can say that these opposites combine to make the whole nothing. In Idealism, the parts are not mutually contradictory, so they can be combined in a hierarchy to produce a universalist conception of truth; however, to make this combination, oppositions must not exist; therefore, the existence of all falsities must be rejected, and nobody can ever be illusioned or have any alternative viewpoint. In Monotheism, this universal truth creates many diversities from the universal truth, but because this creation violates natural principles, therefore, the principles of non-contradiction and mutual exclusion apply to the creation, but not to God. In Advaita, non-contradiction and mutual exclusion apply to Brahman, but not to matter. They apply to Brahman because there is only one thing. And they don't apply to māyā because there are opposites in māyā. In Viśiṣṭādvaita, non-contradiction and mutual exclusion don't apply to the object, because He has contradictory properties. And they don't apply to the parts because the parts always exist in three modalities which contradict the principles of universal truth. In Dvaita, the whole and the part are different, but because each entity has modalities, therefore, each entity is self-contradictory, but collectively they are consistent. In Bhedābheda, the new category is non-difference which violates classical logic. And in Acintyabhedābheda, there are many Bhedābheda, so classical logical principles break down in numerous ways. Each of these views of reality brings a different model of reasoning. Therefore, Nyāya is contingent upon the doctrine of reality. If the notion of reality is modified, then, the attendant method of reasoning about that reality must also be changed.

Once the logic is revised, then the whole-part theory should lead to the understanding of 'atoms' in Vaiśeṣika which constitute the logical limit to the division of the whole into parts (this type of atomism is sometimes called 'logical atomism' in Western philosophy). The union of the parts with the whole forms the essence of Yoga and the analysis of the whole into parts is the essence of Mīmāṃsā. Mīmāṃsā is the description of how the whole divides into parts, and Yoga is the explanation of how despite this division the parts remain connected to the whole. If the whole-part theory is constructed correctly, then, the other five systems (Nyāya, Vaiśeṣika, Sāñkhya, Yoga, and Mīmāṃsā) become natural corollaries of Vedānta. A problem in this construction, however, makes the six systems of Vedic philosophy seem divergent and conflicting with each other. A test for the correctness of the Vedānta system is that it also makes every other philosophical system true and reconciles their apparent contradictions.

If one looks at earlier Vedānta commentaries, the doctrine of Vedānta often comes at the expense of the other five systems of philosophy, as other systems are refuted to establish a Vedānta doctrine. Since these other systems are also based on the Vedic texts—they are all considered *āstika* or theistic—the refutation of these systems entails that they cannot be considered the final truth because they contradict other Vedic texts. For example, the Sāñkhya and Yoga systems are pervasive across both śrutī and smriti. The Bhagavad-Gita describes both systems in a summary form. If a Vedānta Sūtra commentary rejects these systems, then it also rejects the Bhagavad-Gita. Similarly, other Vedic texts discuss atomism and its relation to the entire cosmos— the smallest part depends on the definition of the largest part; if we change the definition of the whole, then we must change the definition of the parts. If these ideas are rejected—by discarding Vaiśeṣika and Mīmāṃsā—then the scientific study of nature (e.g., as atomism and cosmology) becomes impossible. Similarly, just because the whole-part doctrine is contradictory to current logic, the conclusion cannot be that reality is not amenable to rational inquiry. Therefore, Vedānta doctrine cannot in principle reject the Nyāya system. Its goal should rather be to formulate the correct Nyāya, compatible with the Vedānta doctrine.

My conclusion is simple—any doctrine that rejects the other five systems cannot be considered the true Vedānta. The unity of Vedic philosophy is unquestionable. If we bring into question some part of the Vedic texts, then every other part becomes doubtful. The purpose of Vedānta Sūtra commentaries should be to establish the primacy of the whole-part theory, and how these parts exist in the modalities of will and power, without rejecting the truth of the other five systems. If this primary goal is not met, it doesn't matter what other goals are satisfied in the process. The Vedānta Sūtra states that knowledge should be acquired in such a way that the contradictions between the different texts are resolved. How can we abide by Vedānta Sūtra, if we reject the other five systems of philosophy? Therefore, the evolution of Vedānta doctrines must also endeavor to reconcile the apparent contradictions with other systems.

I'm offering these diverse examples to make a singular point—the diverse schools of philosophy are not truly disjointed. They uphold a single philosophy, which is misunderstood due to the modal nature of reality. If we adopt a semantic view of nature, then all these modalities become amenable. This modal view unites Vedānta, Sāñkhya, Mīmāṃsā, Nyāya, Vaiśeṣika, and Yoga. It reconciles diverse Vedānta doctrines and entails that none of them is false. It may not mean that they are true simultaneously. However, they can all be true alternately. There is no contradiction between the yoga systems because the devotee performs actions without the desire for results (which is karma-yoga), his actions are performed with perfect knowledge of the Absolute Truth (which is jñāna-yoga), he sees the Lord in his heart (which is aṣṭānga-yoga), and the purpose of his life is the service to the Lord (which is bhakti-yoga). Similarly, the Vaishnava, Shaiva, and Shakta traditions are aspects of a single system.

Science Without Materialism

The caveat is one—we reject physicalist, materialistic thinking in all forms. It is fundamentally opposed to Vedic philosophy; it is called *nāstika* or atheistic, and it has no place in the Vedic system. This simple caveat of rejecting all forms of physicalist, materialistic thinking segregates Vedic philosophy from modern thinking. Every other claim holds true if materialism has been rejected.

Thus, there can be an alternative non-materialistic description of matter. For example, when you desire an apple, then you are different from the apple. When you obtain an apple, then you have a relation to the apple. But when you eat the apple, you are non-different from the apple. The difference is Dvaita, the relation is Viśiṣṭādvaita, and the non-difference is Advaita. Since all three can be true, the term Bhedābheda can be applied to matter—i.e., something is simultaneously different, non-different, and related. But since we don't presently distinguish between these three modalities—that involve difference, non-difference, and relation—we end up with logical contradictions. The doctrine is now advanced to Acintyabhedābheda to say that all these three are equally true, but we cannot say so within current universalist logic. However, if we shifted the description to modalities, then the understanding is non-contradictory.

Desiring, obtaining, and eating don't happen simultaneously. They rather happen one after another, so one mode goes dominant, while the other mode goes subordinate. You desire an apple, bring it closer to your mouth, and then take a bite. Then, you desire again, bring the apple closer to the mouth and take another bite. All these are contradictory modes, but by their flipping, you desire, obtain, and eat, one by one. If we want to understand how we desire an apple, obtain an apple, and finally eat the apple, then we must revise our scientific theories to such modal forms of existence. This philosophy about the soul, God, matter, and their interrelations thus applies even to material reality.

The Structure of Vedānta Sūtra

Time and Logic

The mode-flipping produces a peculiar model of change or progression, which then changes our understanding of logic and time. The progression goes from a premise to the problem it produces, to an answer that solves the problem and becomes the new premise. This model of reasoning is not the *linear progression* from premises to a conclusion as in current logic. It is the *alternating progression* from premises to questions to answers. Thus, an answer exists, which we can call the 'premise'. But it doesn't automatically lead to a conclusion. It first gives rise to a question. The question conflicts with the premise, following which the conflict is resolved by a new answer. This new answer addresses the previous conflict, but it leads to a new problem, question, or conflict, which is then resolved again. Thus, I can say that

"I exist", which is the premise. But it can lead to the question: "Why do I exist?" This question has sent philosophers in search of the meaning of life in all ages. But there is a choice in the generation of questions from answers. For instance, after I say, "I exist", the next question may be: "How can I continue to exist or survive?" The progression from an answer to a question is not *deterministic*. In fact, because contradictory questions can arise from the same premise, therefore, it should be possible to produce answers that respond to the contradictory questions.

So, there is a fundamental difference between the current idea that logic is about *consistency* with premises and our everyday notion about 'reasoning' which alternates between answers and questions, and the basic mechanism of its progression is *conflict*. If I'm a rich man, I can ask myself different questions: "How do I become richer?" or "How do I spend my riches most effectively?" Both questions produce conflict, and I cannot just sit idle staying rich. I will rather move to answer the emerging question. The conflict is, therefore, the cause of change. Since these questions do not deterministically follow the premises, there is a choice involved in the creation of the question from the answer. And because these questions can be contradictory, and they can lead to contradictory answers, therefore, contradicting answers must be *logically* allowed; the existence of contradictions between the answers cannot be considered a *logical contradiction* because they arose in response to contradicting questions. If such contradictions are possible, then the possibility can be used to make meanings (which are defined through mutual oppositions) a reality. And since either side of the opposition can be chosen, it necessitates a role for choice. In short, an alternative view of logic enables a role for both meanings and choices.

Furthermore, because the contradictory questions take us in different 'directions', and the answers thus produced are logical opposites of other answers, we are naturally led to the conception of a 'space' in which contradictions cannot exist in the same 'place'—as that would be called self-contradiction. Two people possessing conflicting questions can, therefore, move in opposite directions, chasing conflicting answers, and this process leads naturally to a novel understanding of 'distance' and 'direction'—both must be viewed semantically rather than physically. If 'space' were defined as the domain of all possible questions and answers, then motion would be defined as the change of position in this space. Similarly, 'time' must be defined as the succession of questions and answers, or the causality that converts an answer to a question. In short, an alternative conception of logic naturally produces alternative notions of space, time, causality, and motion, in which opposite ideas are opposite 'locations' and 'directions' in space, and the movement in this space is governed by conflicting types of choices. And all this is simply a consequence of mode-flipping.

The Nature of Logical Progression

The wonder of Vedānta Sūtra is not just that it describes the process of this progression, but that it also demonstrates it through its progression from premises to questions to conclusions. Vedānta Sūtra is called nyāya-prasthāna or a logical treatise. But it is not Nyāya or logic in the sense of premise to conclusion. It is rather Nyāya in the sense of a premise to a question to a conclusion. It is therefore rationality, although it is not the Western sense of rationalism.

If we view Vedānta Sūtra through the lens of Vedānta philosophy, then we also must revise the methodology of commenting on the text. One such modification is that the text only lists the answers, but not the questions. These questions must therefore be inserted by the commentator to interpret the text correctly. Furthermore, the questions can never be repeated, such that the different answers could never contradict each other. Just as in a mathematical proof, it is acceptable to use the previously arrived conclusions as premises, but we cannot try to reprove the premise, or contradict the premise, similarly, the text must progress without repetition. Just as in a mathematical proof we cannot make leaps of inference, but must proceed step-by-step, without leaving gaps, similarly, the discussion cannot jump discontinuously from one claim to another, violating the condition of 'logical' progress. These requirements on interpretation mandate that the questions before a sūtra flow from the previous answers, without producing discontinuities, and the same conclusions cannot be proved repeatedly to avoid redundancies. This can be much harder than it seems.

The reason is that the same answer can be understood differently if the question preceding it is altered. As an illustration, the single word answer of "no" can be taken to deny any number of questions, and the meaning of "no" (i.e., what it is denying) is not apparent unless we know the question itself. So, when a conversation proceeds dialectically, the meanings become subject to the context—e.g., what was said previously, and the objection to that answer. We often find that the next question is based on not just the previous answer, but also what has been said in the entire sequence. Each sūtra is not independent of the previous sūtras. It is necessarily an incremental logical progression.

Now you might argue: Since there is a choice in inserting a question before a sūtra, therefore, such an interpretation is a personal choice. How can you call this a valid interpretation if you are inserting questions in it? The answer to this problem is that if you fix the sequence of answers, then the sequence of questions must also be fixed. The choices in interpretation begin to disappear rapidly as we elongate the sequence of questions and answers—remember that the same question and answer can never reappear, there can be no overlaps or gaps in the succession. But you might still argue: We can see that the choices in interpretations dramatically reduce as we progress, but isn't it possible that the entire sequence of questions could be changed to fit the answers differently? My response to that problem is: Yes, in principle they can be changed. However, ultimately, the interpretation must produce something consistent and complete. If this condition is not satisfied, then Vedānta Sūtra would be yet another incomplete philosophy—much like the numerous prevalent philosophies. On the other hand, if this condition is met, then even if we have alternative interpretations, their conclusion would still be the same—i.e., how do we get an alternative conception of reality that is both consistent and complete?

Therefore, the meaning of the text is not simply to be known by its textual interpretation. It must also follow from a unique methodology of logic, and the criterion of consistency and completeness. These latter imply that— (1) the six systems of Vedic philosophy must be reconciled, (2) all interpretations of Vedānta must be upheld, and (3) diverse schools of the Vedic system, such as Vaishnavism, Shaivism, and Shaktism must be simultaneously true. In short, the meaning of Vedānta—as the conclusion of all Vedic knowledge—must be compatible with the meaning of Veda (i.e., the diversified descriptions of reality). We cannot call something Vedānta if it is contradictory to Veda. If this goal is satisfied, even different interpretations of the sūtras are not a problem.

Hence, I want to refrain from the 'academic' definitions of textual interpretation, which look at a text in isolation. They only focus on Sanskrit grammar and linguistics. But, in this case, two more criteria must be added— (1) logical progression, and (2) the consistency and completeness of knowledge.

If a sūtra can be interpreted in many ways—because many interpretations are consistent with the rest of Vedic philosophy, and consistent with the Sanskrit grammar and linguistics, one such interpretation can be chosen based on the criterion that (a) the question and answer aren't repeated, (b) the question and answers don't take leaps and produce discontinuities. At the level of each sūtra, the differences thus arising can often seem rather small. But the differences accumulate and produce visible divergences over a succession of sūtras. This divergence is essential if it takes us through different modalities—e.g., how the same two things are different, non-different, and related. To deal with this one modality you need three statements that restate three different views. Then you need multiple other statements that reconcile the resulting contradictions. The divergence has a purpose—it must produce the requisite completeness.

Hierarchical vs. Cyclical

The nature of logical progression through modalities entails that you can never describe reality fully at once. You state one view and draw its conclusions. But then you find that the conclusions either conflict with previous conclusions or are necessarily incomplete. To overcome these problems, you revise the doctrine again, which is then evaluated against other inconsistencies and incompleteness yet again. This produces a cyclic type of argument because the same topics are covered, again and again, each time in a different way. This cyclic nature of the argument contradicts the book's hierarchical structure.

By a hierarchical structure, I mean that the book is divided into chapters, sections, topics, and sūtras. If we treat Vedānta Sūtra like any other text, then each chapter, section, topic, and sūtra must be devoted to a unique question or problem. Once that question or problem has been discussed, it should never be revisited, although it can be employed for subsequent arguments. Vedānta Sūtra doesn't follow this principle. Although there are four chapters, each of which has four sections, each section has a varying number of topics, and each topic has a varying number of sūtras, the argument of the text is cyclical. It discusses the same topics iteratively, constantly nuancing its position.

For example, initially, it is said that one must inquire into the nature of Brahman because it is the source of everything; later it is said that the Brahman itself originates from the Supreme Lord, as light emanates from a candle. Initially, it is said that one must aspire for liberation from the material modes, and later it is said that the devotees don't even aspire for liberation as they only aspire to please the Lord. In the beginning, it is said that the Lord is transcendent to material nature, and later it is said that He is also immanent. At first, it is said that revelation is the source of true knowledge, and later it is said that the Absolute Truth can also be directly perceived and understood rationally. In the beginning, it is said that the soul is separate from the Lord, then it is said that the soul is a part of the Lord. Initially, the Lord is distinguished from the material world, and later the material world is called His property, inseparable from Him. At some point, it is said that the Lord and the soul are qualitatively similar but quantitatively different, and later it is said the soul is both qualitatively and quantitatively different from the Lord. Initially, the Absolute Truth is described impersonally; then the same Absolute Truth is described as a masculine person; finally, the same Absolute Truth is described as masculine and feminine persons and their union. At some point, it is said that social duties must not be discarded, but later, it is said that the devotees can reject social duties if they are pleasing to the Lord. At many places, it is said that the diverse paths to spiritual progress must be rejected in favor of the devotional path, and later it is said that all these paths must be combined for attaining perfection. Initially, it is said that one must focus on the conclusion of all knowledge, and later it is said that many disciplines are important to understanding the Absolute Truth. I can go on and on with examples, but I think you understand the point.

The point is this: when we hear that X is true, then we conclude that not-X is false. We take a claim to mean that its opposite is automatically denied. But the Vedānta Sūtra doesn't take this view. It constantly revises its position to incorporate opposite ideas and reconciles them with a nuanced explanation. The previous claims are never rejected, but their opposites are accepted later. And yet, as you progress through the text, you don't find it contradictory, because the subsequent claims reconcile both the previous and the new claims. There is constant back and forth for nuancing the position to incorporate opposites. Thus, I must advise the reader: Don't conclude anything unless you have read the full text. Whatever has been said now, is likely to be updated later. If you are thinking that something is being rejected, wait until it is accepted.

If one needed a metaphor for the structure of Vedānta Sūtra, then it is like a spiral that goes outward to inward through incremental steps. At each successive step, you think you are moving one step forward, so the structure seems to be linear. This is the microstructure of the book. Over a longer interval, you see that you are going cyclically because the position is constantly revised. This is the intermediate structure of the text. And eventually, you see how the conversation goes deeper toward the center of the spiral. This inward movement is the hierarchical and macroscopic structure of the book. You find that every claim and counterclaim has been argued and reconciled, and the Absolute Truth is therefore understood as the source of every kind of contradictory idea. The successive chapters, sections, topics, and sūtras therefore can be divided into four stages—each successively more reconciled than the previous ones.

By the time you finish reading the book, you will see what I mean by logic—it is linear, cyclical, and hierarchical. This logic is also the process of life if one wants to progress toward the perfect understanding of the truth. If one has the Supreme Lord as the goal, then each stage of life is one step forward. But over time, you find yourself revisiting the same questions and problems. Finally, as you iterate over these issues and get a deeper understanding, you understand the Supreme Lord, who is the source of everything but reconciles them.

There is nothing comparable to this structure in the world today. However, this literary structure implies that the reader cannot take the hierarchical structure in the text too seriously. One should rather read the sūtras and understand the logical flow, but a chapter or section doesn't deal with exclusive topics. As we progress, the same topics will be revisited but based on the previous discussion, each time the understanding of that topic would be nuanced and enhanced. Until you finish the book, you don't know if you really have the final truth. If nothing else, this tells you to read the book from start to finish! A cursory glance at chapters or selectively picking a sūtra without the context can be erroneous. All that is said only exists as a part of this helical progression.

Chapter 1

This chapter deals with the relation between the soul, God, and nature, how the soul is entangled in matter due to its rejection of God, and how it can be liberated by devotion to God. Many methods of reviving this devotion are also described such as the meditation on the Lord in the heart, the study of the Vedic scriptures, and the understanding of the Universal Form of the Lord.

Section 1: This section begins with the prescription that the purpose of human life is to inquire into the nature of Brahman. It then prescribes the study of the scriptures as the primary method for the acquisition of the knowledge of Brahman. It describes Brahman as that which expands from itself and merges into itself. The expansion of Brahman divides the One into many, without the cessation of the One, and the cause of this expansion is the desire for pleasure. Thus, the soul is expanded from Brahman, and it is said to be different from the One, and yet never separated from the One. However, in the material existence, the soul is caught in the three modes of material nature, due to which it considers itself different from the One. To restore the connection to the One, the section prescribes liberation from the influence of matter by developing the devotion to the Absolute Truth. This constitutes the overview of the entire text, and the same themes are revisited, evaluated, and nuanced over and over.

Section 2: The discussion of the process of liberation is taken up in this section, and it is stated that the form of the Supreme Lord exists along with each soul as the Paramātma. This form of the Lord aids the liberation of the soul from material existence. The Paramātma is said to be the controller of the world, including the various demigods who control the delivery of the various kinds of karma. While the material world is different from the Paramātma, it is stated to be an expression of the Lord, like an author may express his ideas in a text. Furthermore, this expression is also said to be His property, in the sense that the Lord owns the material creation, and the creation reflects His nature. Then the text states that since the creation reflects the properties of the Paramātma, therefore, it can also be used to understand His nature. One such method of knowing the Lord is described to be the study of the universe as the Universal Form of the Lord which is not sense-perceivable but can be meditated upon. Thus, even if the soul cannot find the Lord in the heart, he can still understand the Lord through the study of His expansion as the cosmic manifestation.

Section 3: This section moves beyond the material world into the discussion of the transcendental world. This world is described as comprising many forms of the Lord, which are manifest to fulfill the different desires in the soul as well as the Lord to enjoy with the soul. The conversation then moves into how this transcendental world can be attained, and the prescription is to take the shelter of a qualified guru. Following the discussion about the qualifications of the guru, a discussion is taken up about the qualifications of the disciple. In this discussion, it is stated that those without a good moral upbringing and faith in the Lord are forbidden from the study of the scriptures. A remedy for such people is however prescribed—namely, the chanting of the names of the Lord. How the chanting of the names leads to gradual purification is then discussed.

Section 4: This section discusses how the transcendental forms of the Lord, which exist eternally in the spiritual world, incarnate in the material world. And yet, despite their presence in the material world, they are not bound by the laws of material nature. Since the Lord looks just like the other people in this world, the text states that He is identified as the Lord due to the great deeds He performs. Since the demigods also have greatness, the discussion moves into why their greatness reflects the greatness in the Lord, and hence why they must not be worshipped. A method is now prescribed for those who want to progress in the spiritual life, but do not possess devotion to the Lord: It is said that such people can study Vedic texts and elevate their understanding by reconciling the contradictions across many scriptures. As this study is perfected, then one naturally develops an attraction to the Lord, and devotion naturally springs as the byproduct of perfected knowledge. Finally, the text elaborates on how the Absolute Truth comprises the interrelated masculine and feminine aspects.

SECTION 1

Topic 1

QUESTION

What should I do?

Everyone is seeking guidance about what they must do in their lives, the purpose of their existence, and how they can achieve it. This is a natural question that arises in everyone's life, and it is the beginning of Vedānta Sūtra as well. The question emerges from the acknowledged fact of our existence.

1.1.1 (1)

अथातो ब्रह्मजिज्ञासा

athāto brahmajijñāsā

atha—now; ataḥ—therefore; brahmajijñāsā—an inquiry into Brahman.

TRANSLATION

Now, therefore, an inquiry into Brahman.

COMMENTARY

The terms 'now' and 'therefore' can be interpreted in many ways. They can refer to the fact that the reader is now in a human form of life, and therefore he must inquire into Brahman because in other species of life this inquiry is not possible. It can refer to the fact that the Vedānta Sūtra are the conclusions of the Upaniṣad, and were authored after them, so now (having read and understood the Upaniṣad) one must have concluded that Brahman is the ultimate reality, so one must inquire into its nature. It can also mean that now since you have met enlightened souls, you must begin an inquiry into Brahman. Finally, it can mean that now that you are reading the conclusion of all knowledge—namely, the Vedānta Sūtra—you must endeavor to inquire into the nature of Brahman (as opposed to other Vedic scriptures where other topics are discussed).

Topic 2

QUESTION

But why should I inquire into Brahman?

The previous sūtra stated that one should inquire into Brahman, so a skeptic can ask: Why? In other words, why is this inquiry important over the other things that I can do? Why should I focus on Brahman instead of other things?

1.1.2 (2)

जन्माद्यस्य यतः

janmādyasya yataḥ

janmādi—the birth source; asya—of this (world); yataḥ—from which.

TRANSLATION

Brahman is the birth source of this (world) from which (the world sprung).

COMMENTARY

This sūtra is exhorting the reader that the inquiry into Brahman is important because it is the birth source of everything. The term ādi can be interpreted in two ways— (1) as the origin, and (2) as one of many things (etc.). In the latter case, we would include the maintenance and dissolution of the world into the reason for the study of Brahman. I prefer to use the term ādi to denote 'original' because dissolution and maintenance will be discussed later (although including maintenance and dissolution would not be technically incorrect). The use of the term 'original' also has significance here, because there are secondary sources of the creation. For instance, Brahma is a secondary creator of the material world, who creates many kinds of life forms, after the universe of the material elements has already been formed. However, Brahma is created by the primal source. Thus, we are not interested in the secondary sources, but in the primary or original source from which the secondary sources have emanated. The purpose of Vedānta Sūtra is that primal source of everything.

Topic 3

QUESTION

How should I inquire into Brahman?

Now that the previous sūtra states that we should inquire into Brahman because it is the origin of everything, the question is: How can I know the nature of the thing from which everything originates? What methods must I use?

1.1.3 (3)

शास्त्रयोनित्वात्

śāstrayonitvāt

śastra—the scripture; yonitvāt—from being the mother (of knowledge).

TRANSLATION

From the scripture, which is the mother (of the knowledge of Brahman).

COMMENTARY

It's noteworthy that methods such as empirical observation and logical inference are not mentioned here. We will see later that this position will be revised. For now, we can say that empirical observation and logical inference employ the senses and the mind, and the origin of everything is also the origin of the senses the mind. One of the problems in scientific causality is that the cause determines the effect, but the effect doesn't determine the cause. For example, if you push a billiard ball using a cue, then you can say that the ball will move. However, if the ball is moving, then you cannot say that it was pushed by the cue; it may as well have been pushed by another ball, which was then pushed by a cue, or by a ball, which was pushed by another ball, which was pushed by the cue. In this way, there are infinite plausible explanations of an effect. This problem is known as the underdetermination of cause from the effect in Western philosophy. It implies that if the senses and the mind are effects, then we cannot know their cause from these effects. Hence, revealed knowledge given by the Vedic scriptures is the only means of knowing the original cause.

The problem of underdetermination entails that there are many possible explanations of any observation. Each explanation postulates a different cause. Given that the senses and the mind are effects, they underdetermine the cause, and many potential causes could be speculated. To avoid such speculation, and to arrive at the definitive cause, one must accept the scripture. If this cause is known, then the effects of this cause can be derived. Therefore, the origin of everything becomes the hypothesis based on which we study everything. When reason and experience are applied to this hypothesis, and everything else is explained based on the hypothesis, then reason and experience become the methods for confirming the hypothesis. The knowledge received from scripture, therefore, doesn't eliminate the use of reason and experience, except that its use is restricted to the verification of knowledge, rather than its discovery.

Topic 4

QUESTION

How can you say that by studying the scripture I will know Brahman?

The Vedic scriptures deal in many topics, such as the worship of demigods, the rituals of daily life, the narrations of the material world including cosmology, the histories of the past kingdoms, how the universe was created, the various types of species, the cycle of birth and death, etc. Therefore, how can we preclude all these topics and focus exclusively on Brahman? A related objection is that the scriptures often make seemingly contradictory claims, meant for different times, places, contexts, and persons. Which claim applies to which time, place, situation, or person is not always evident from the scripture. Therefore, one can argue that since the scripture deals with such diversities, therefore, it cannot tell us about unity. Since the scriptures cover the duality of this world and are therefore often contradictory, how do we know the Absolute Truth?

1.1.4 (4)
तत् तु समन्वयात्
tat tu samanvayāt

tat—that; tu—but; samanvayāt—on account of agreement or harmony.

TRANSLATION

But that (Brahman is known only from the scriptures), because (the understanding of Brahman) brings agreement or harmony (in the diversity).

COMMENTARY

This sūtra answers the doubt about why the study of scripture leads us to the knowledge of Brahman. The answer is that although the scriptures deal with many topics, they have a common goal, namely the understanding of Brahman. In this regard, we can envision the scriptures as a tree of knowledge. The tree has many trunks, branches, twigs, and leaves. But the tree has only one root. The leaves, branches, and trunks represent the duality and diversity of this world; however, the root from which diversity emerges is non-dual or singular. In short, the scriptures are dealing with both duality and the non-dual. However, non-dual unity is the cause of the duality and reconciles it. However, this also means that we cannot treat everything in the scripture as Absolute Truth. Some statements of scriptures are indeed like the leaves, branches, and trunks; while we accept them as true, they are not be considered the Absolute Truth. There is hence a distinction between relative and absolute truth; the latter being defined as that which reconciles the diversity and duality of the other descriptions.

The progress in knowledge, therefore, represents the path from the leaves through the twigs and trunks to the root of the tree. That root is identified as Brahman: It is both the origin of the tree as well as the destination of knowledge, although the destination is to be attained by understanding the reconciliation of the diversity. Brahman is that which harmonizes the contradictions.

Topic 5

QUESTION

You state that Brahman reconciles the oppositions and contradictions. But when you combine the oppositions and contradictions, they must mutually negate each other, and the ultimate result of reconciliation must be nothingness. How can we say that the reconciliation of contradictions and duality results in the knowledge of Absolute Truth if their combination creates nothingness?

This argument is employed in Buddhism. The argument states that the world is opposites, but to know the Absolute Truth, we must negate both oppositions. This process is also sometimes called neti-neti or not this and not that. In classical logic, the principle of mutual exclusion states that either one of the opposites must be true. Thus, if X is false, then not-X must be true. But what if both X and not-X are simultaneously true in different contexts? Since the Absolute Truth is the origin of both X and not-X, their combination must negate both X and not-X and we must end up with nothingness. If the origin of everything is nothingness, then how can this nothingness be known? After all, isn't it impossible to conceive of something that is neither X and not-X? By the fact that it reconciles the opposites, the Absolute Truth also becomes unknowable!

This point is also asserted as the claim that the source of everything cannot be grasped by words because words employ oppositions (such as hot and cold, black and white), and the source of duality must be beyond such opposites. Since the source reconciles all oppositions, and the words are representations of the opposites, therefore, the primal source cannot be expressed in terms of these oppositions. Therefore, we cannot use any word to describe Brahman, and even if some such word was employed it would just mean nothingness.

In another alternative form, the argument is presented as the distinction between forms and the formless. The forms of this world—which include the words used to describe the world—are representations of either side of duality. When this duality is reconciled, the result would be formless. Since everything has emanated from Brahman, therefore, language must have emanated from Brahman. Just as the reconciliation of words would result in something formless, similarly, the reconciliation of all duality must result in formlessness. Brahman must, therefore, be something formless, and hence it cannot be described by words, which are forms. Since the scripture is expressed in words, therefore, the descriptions must also be inadequate in describing Brahman.

1.1.5 (5)
ईक्षतेर्न अशब्दम्
īkṣaterna aśabdam

īkṣateh—seeing (thinking); na—not; aśabdam—that which cannot be expressed through words, or that which can't be spoken of (i.e., formless).

TRANSLATION
We cannot see or know that which is formless.

COMMENTARY
This sūtra accepts the argument that the formless cannot be known—and yet refutes it by providing a counterargument that if the Absolute Truth cannot be known then knowledge would be impossible. If knowledge is impossible, then the origin of everything cannot be known, and if the purpose of life is to know the origin, then this purpose cannot be fulfilled. This leads to nihilism, such that the ultimate meaning cannot be sought because there is no ultimate meaning. Or, that ultimately, the meaning is nothingness. This is indeed the path of Buddhism where ultimate reality is nothingness. Buddhism also says that reality cannot be grasped by words—which are forms—therefore there is no point in reading scripture that describes the truth in words. Buddhism also prescribes that the goal of life is to empty the mind and silence the senses.

This is the rejection of all knowledge that comes as forms. If we take away forms, then we cannot hear, see, or perceive anything. Similarly, this process applies to thought as well. Even ideas have forms. Therefore, if we remove the forms, then we cannot think either. Emptiness, nothingness, and nihilism are alternatives, but this sūtra doesn't advocate them. It just says that if we reject forms, then it would be impossible to know anything. Indirectly, this is a prelude to the subsequent conclusion that the non-dual Absolute Truth must also have a form. If we start with the premise that the Absolute Truth must be known, and then we conclude that it cannot be known, then we have ended up in a self-contradiction. This sūtra simply highlights that self-contradiction.

QUESTION

You are stating two mutually contradictory things. First, that the Absolute Truth reconciles the oppositions of this world. Second, this reconciliation of oppositions can be expressed through words, which are implicitly understood as forms and must be subject to duality. How do you reconcile this conflict?

In the previous sūtra, a proof by contradiction was presented, which is not totally satisfying. One still wants to know how the Absolute Truth can be the reconciliation of contradictions without these forms canceling each other.

1.1.6 (6)

गौणश्चेत् न आत्मशब्दात्

gauṇaścet na ātmaśabdāt

gauṇaḥ—the three gunas; cet—know; na—not; ātmaśabdāt—from the words used to describe the ātmā, i.e., the soul.

TRANSLATION

Know that the three gunas are not the words for the soul.

COMMENTARY

The previous sūtra proved the impossibility of claiming knowledge of Absolute Truth if this truth is formless. But the reader asks: How can we know something transcendent? This sūtra offers the example of the soul. The soul is beyond the material guna (modes of nature) and yet it can be known. If the material modes were canceling each other, then, anything beyond these material modes would be nothingness. But the soul is not nothingness. This is illustrative because Buddhism indeed takes the argument of nothingness all the way and says that there is no soul or God. Once the dualities are dissolved, even the self is dissolved, and there is, hence, no eternal self. This sūtra distinguishes the Vedānta doctrine from that of Buddhism by asserting that the soul is beyond the three modes of nature, and yet this transcendence is not nothingness.

Now, one can argue: Whatever you call the soul, is not beyond the three modes. That individual is only a product of the three modes of nature. So, it is important to understand what the three modes are, and how the soul is beyond these modes. The central problem is that the three modes describe the qualities, such as short or tall, dark or fair, young or old, male or female, beautiful or ugly, rich or poor, etc. But a rich person can become poor, a young person becomes old, someone beautiful can become ugly, etc. Through all these attribute transformations, the self remains unchanged, because we also claim that the *same* person who was previously rich is now poor; the same person who was previously young is now old; the same person who was previously beautiful has now become ugly. Thus, through the changing attributes ascribed to the person, the person remains unchanged. The term ātmā or 'self' pertains to this unchanging identity of the person to whom many changing attributes can be applied.

The distinction between the ātmā and the modes of nature is quite like that between an *object* and a *property*, which is often made in modern science. For example, a ball is an object and the speed of the ball is its property. The ball can move faster or slower, and the properties of the ball can change. But through this change in property, we say that the *same* ball changed its speed. The transcendence of the soul can therefore be established even within the world of the material modes—not necessarily by transcending this world. The three modes are the properties, and the object to which the properties are applied is the ātmā. These properties change over time, but the object remains unchanged.

We can extend this analogy and say that Brahman can be different from the duality of this world, and yet it can be ascribed these dual properties. In effect, Brahman is the object and the properties ascribed to this object are distinct from the object. To know Brahman, we must transcend the material attributes.

In the Bhagavad-Gita (chapter 2, verse 45), Lord Kṛṣṇa says:

trai-guṇya-viṣayā vedā
nistrai-guṇyo bhavārjuna
nirdvandvo nitya-sattva-stho
niryoga-kṣema ātmavān

The Vedas mainly deal with the subject of the three modes of material nature. Rise above these modes, O Arjuna. Be transcendental to all of them. Be free from all dualities and from all anxieties for gain and safety and be established in the Self.

The above verse recognizes that the Vedas contain information that is colored by the three modes of nature, but they also contain transcendental information. The goal of knowledge is to rise above these modes and know the self and Brahman which are transcendental. In this regard, we can note that this sūtra introduces a third category called the ātmā or the individual soul, which is different from the previous two categories—Brahman and the three guna. The impersonal interpretations reject the individuality of the ātmā. They claim that there is only one object—Brahman—and by the attachment of attributes, Brahman is perceived as the ātmā. But if that were true, then the ātmā could not be transcendental; it would be a byproduct of the three modes. The fact that it is called transcendental here means that it is not a product of three modes.

QUESTION

You have earlier referred to Brahman, and the three modes, and now you are also saying that the ātmā is transcendental to the three modes. But your statement implies that the ātmā is caught in the control of the modes. If that is the case, then how the ātmā become liberated from the three modes?

1.1.7 (7)

तन्नष्ठिस्य मोक्षोपदेशात्

tanniṣṭhasya mokṣopadeśāt

tat—to that; niṣṭhasya—of the devoted; mokṣopadeśāt—from the teaching of salvation.

TRANSLATION

From the teaching of salvation of the devoted to that (Brahman).

COMMENTARY

This sūtra states that if one wants to extricate oneself from the duality of this material world, then faith in the Absolute Truth is needed. The existence of this faith entails a distinction between the ātmā and the Absolute Truth. In the Bhagavad-Gita 7.14, Lord Kṛṣṇa makes a similar assertion as follows:

daivī hy eṣā guṇa-mayī
mama māyā duratyayā
mām eva ye prapadyante
māyām etām taranti te

This divine energy of Mine, consisting of the three modes of material nature, is difficult to overcome. But those who have surrendered unto Me can easily cross beyond it.

The previous sūtra asserted that the ātmā is beyond the three modes of nature. If the ātmā is real, then there are numerous individuals. Once we recognize that there are numerous ātmā then neither of these can be the Absolute Truth. Rather, the Absolute Truth must be separate from the ātmā. Thus, by distinguishing the ātmā from the three modes of nature, we naturally establish the distinction between the ātmā and the Absolute Truth or Brahman. This contrasts with the impersonal interpretations of Vedānta Sūtra where there are only two realities— the three modes of nature and Brahman. This sūtra alludes to the distinction between the ātmā and Brahman and states that freedom from the three modes of nature is attained for those who have faith in the Brahman.

From the previous sūtras we can see how three categories—namely, ātmā, Brahman, and guna are recognized. The ātmā was stated to be transcendental to guna, and this sūtra says that it can be liberated by devotion to Brahman. Thus, in a very few sūtras, the conclusion of Vedānta has been summarized. This devotion between ātmā and Brahman means that the term Brahman is not used here in an impersonal sense. It is rather a reference to the Supreme Lord. This will also become amply clear in the subsequent sūtras which speak about how the Lord expands into diversity and then merges it back into Himself.

QUESTION

If liberation is obtained for those who have faith in the Absolute Truth, does it mean that everyone who is without this faith does not obtain liberation?

In Vedas, four kinds of endeavors are described. These are called dharma, artha, kāma, and moksha. The first three pertain to the performance of one's mundane duties, the accumulation of wealth, and the enjoyment of life using this wealth. The Vedas state that the fourth endeavor—namely moksha or salvation from the material entanglement—is the ultimate purpose of life. The previous sūtra asserted that this salvation requires us to disentangle ourselves from the three modes of nature, but that goal cannot be achieved without faith in the Absolute Truth. Therefore, while the pursuit of dharma, artha, and kāma is described in various Vedic texts, the fourth endeavor of moksha is not possible with the knowledge of these three endeavors. Rather, since it is the fourth pursuit, its achievement would require the rejection of the first three and the acquisition of something that yields moksha. The reader is now curious: Since salvation is not achieved by the performance of the first three endeavors, should one reject the portions of Vedic texts that deal in the first three endeavors?

1.1.8 (8)
हेयत्वावचनाच्च
heyatvāvacanācca

heyatva—inferiority; avachanāt—from not being stated (by the scriptures as leading to the salvation of the soul from matter); ca—also.

TRANSLATION

From not being stated (by the scriptures as leading to the salvation of the soul), they (i.e., all other statements of the Vedas) are also considered inferior.

COMMENTARY

This sūtra confirms the claim of the question, asserting that while Vedas deal in dharma, artha, kāma, and moksha, the inquiry into Brahman pertains to moksha. It is a summary rejection of significant portions of the Vedic texts. In most religions of this world, all texts are given equal importance. But this is not the case for Vedic scriptures. Even though there are texts that describe how to live in this world, by describing marriage procedures, the rules of governing a nation, the nature of matter as created by the three modes of nature, etc., these are considered aparā vidya or inferior knowledge and must be rejected in comparison to those portions of the Veda that deal solely in transcendence.

This sūtra gives insights into how to distinguish between different scriptures. It exhorts us to neglect those scriptures that are dealing with material well-being, ascendency to higher planetary systems, different kinds of material enjoyments, the acquisition of wealth and improving life in the present world, while focusing on those scriptures where salvation is being recommended. Scriptures that deal with dharma, artha, and kāma will also keep us bound to the material world. But the scriptures about the Absolute Truth will lead us toward salvation. Therefore, a distinction between mundane and transcendental knowledge is made here. The transcendental scriptures lead to salvation, while the mundane scriptures keep a person bound to the modes of nature.

QUESTION

I understand the difference between inferior and superior knowledge, but I'm only well-versed in the inferior knowledge—i.e., the knowledge of this material world (dharma, artha, kāma). What is the nature of transcendence?

By drawing a distinction between the knowledge important for dharma, artha, and kāma vs. the knowledge necessary for moksha, the reader has understood that everything in the Vedic texts is not to be considered at the same level. He is now inquisitive about the nature of the Absolute Truth. This line of questioning implies a rejection of the mundane parts of knowledge, namely, those concerned with the material well-being and enjoyment of this world.

1.1.9 (9)
स्वाप्ययात्
svāpyayāt

svāpyayāt—from merging in one's self.

TRANSLATION

(The Brahman is known) from that which merges in itself.

COMMENTARY

To understand this sūtra, we need to discuss the process of creation and dissolution. Creation is like the emanation of trunks, branches, and leaves from a root, and dissolution is the retraction of the manifested leaves, branches, and trunks into the root. During dissolution, the element of Earth merges into Water, Water merges into Fire, Fire merges into Air, and Air merges into Ether. The Ether then merges into the mind, which then merges into the intellect, which then merges into the ego, which then merges into the mahattattva, which then merges into pradhāna. During creation, pradhāna manifests into mahattattva, which then manifests into the ego, from which other elements such as the intellect, mind, senses, besides the elements such as Ether, Air, Fire, Water, and Earth, and expand. In this hierarchy of element manifestation, the source is called sūkshma or subtle while the product is called sthūla or gross. Every sthūla element manifests from a sūkshma element. And, every sthūla element merges into something sūkshma. If this process were used indefinitely, then there must always be a higher element from which the previous element manifests. That would, in turn, lead to an infinite cascade of material elements.

This sūtra states that this process of expansion and dissolution has a natural end in the Absolute Truth. Everything expands from this Truth and merges back into this Truth; however, the Absolute Truth has not expanded from anything else. It is rather self-expanding and self-contracting. Therefore, unlike the material elements which have an origin in another element, the Absolute Truth has no such origin, as it expanded out of itself. So, here, a distinction is drawn between matter and God, namely, that the material elements have expanded from a higher element, but the Absolute Truth is self-expanding. By studying matter, we can understand how the lower element has expanded from a higher element, but to find the Absolute Truth, we must find that element that expands from itself and contracts into itself. When the Absolute Truth rests within itself, there is no world. The world is created from the Absolute Truth expanding itself. And upon dissolution, everything goes back into the Absolute Truth.

Critics of religion sometimes ask: If God created everything, then who created God? The question is rhetorical because it can be posed for any kind of theory of origin. For example, we can ask: If Big Bang created the universe, then what created the Big Bang? The answer generally offered to this kind of question is that before the Big Bang there was a Big Crunch; that there is no origin of the universe, and the universe merely expands and contracts. A similar type of claim is made in this sūtra—there is no origin to the Absolute Truth. Rather, everything expands from this Absolute Truth and collapses back into it. The two explanations differ only in one respect—namely, that God is a person, and the Big Bang is impersonal. The expansion of the person is based on His will, but the expansion of the Big Bang has thus far no known explanation.

QUESTION

You have earlier stated that Brahman is the origin of everything. You are now stating that Brahman is also the thing that manifests from itself, and therefore has no other prior origin. So, in what state was the world before it was manifest from the Absolute Truth? Where was it before it was manifest?

There is a subtle distinction between the ideas of *creation* (as found in other religious texts, where God creates the world) and that of *manifestation* which is found in Vedic texts. The problem of creation necessitates the existence of some 'stuff' from which God must create the universe. But in the idea of manifestation, God is the 'stuff' from which everything manifests. But what happens when the world is not manifest? In what shape or form does it exist? Clearly, if it is being manifest—rather than being created—it must exist eternally. But if it exists eternally, why is it sometimes manifest and sometimes unmanifest?

1.1.10 (10)
गतसिामान्यात्
gatisāmānyāt

gati—movement; sāmānyāt—from the universal undifferentiated.

TRANSLATION

From the movement of the universal undifferentiated (diversity is caused).

COMMENTARY

This sūtra states that diversity is produced from the universal and undifferentiated. The universality indicates a singular cause, and the undifferentiated indicates that it was previously undivided or One. Similarly, once the world has dissolved, it rests in the Absolute Truth. There is hence Oneness of the Absolute Truth, and the diversity rests *within* that Oneness. Oneness and diversity are therefore not mutually opposed ideas. Rather, the diversity manifests from the Oneness due to its movement and then returns to Oneness.

Therefore, even when the world disappears, it doesn't cease to exist. It remains within the Absolute Truth as a potential to manifest again. There is hence a difference between the temporariness of the phenomenal world vs. the eternity of matter. The impersonalist claims that as the phenomenal world appears and disappears, therefore, it must be an illusion; this argument is not false. The problem arises if this illusion of the phenomenal world is extended to matter. If matter is unreal, then what causes the illusion to appear or disappear?

The difference between illusion and reality is now simply this—all illusion is created by reality, but the illusion is occasionally produced although that reality is eternal. In short, we see that reality occasionally and hence call it an 'illusion'. If something is eternal, but not seen always, then how do we understand its existence? The answer is that it always exists as a possibility but is sometimes visible as a phenomenon. If it is visible, it is not 'created'. If it is invisible, it is not 'destroyed'. It is simply manifest and then unmanifest. The unmanifest state exists in the Absolute Truth, as many kinds of potentiality.

QUESTION

The śrutī primarily speaks about the Oneness of Brahman. But you are insisting that there is diversity within Brahman. This would imply that Brahman is not formless; rather just like the body has front and back, head and toe, left and right, similarly, the Brahman would have a form with many aspects. How can you justify this stance when the śruti mainly speaks about the Oneness?

1.1.11 (11)

श्रुतत्वाच्च

śrutatvācca

śrutatvāt—from being declared by the śrutī; ca—also.

TRANSLATION

(That Brahman comprises diversity) from being declared by śrutī also.

COMMENTARY

This sūtra acknowledges that Brahman has a form; there is Oneness, and diversity manifests from that Oneness. But that diversity rests in that Oneness. Unlike the seed from which the tree manifests on the supplication of soil, air, and water, there is nothing external to the Absolute Truth. However, this eternal reality is not always visible. The creation of the universe is not something coming into existence. It is something that exists eternally becoming visible.

The novelty of this sūtra is that it accepts that the Absolute Truth is not just Oneness, but that diversity exists inside that Oneness. The implication is that Absolute Truth has a form in which diversity exists within the unity. The sūtra points out that while śrutī speaks about the Oneness, it also sometimes refers to the diversity inside the unity. In short, the śrutī is not describing a formless Oneness. It is describing a Oneness that has form and the manifest diversities are the aspects of this form. The emphasis in śrutī is primarily on Oneness, which is why the sūtra states that the śrutī 'also' speak about the diversity.

Thus, this sūtra accepts both unity and diversity in Brahman—yes, the śrutī talks about Oneness, but it also talks about the diversity inside the unity. So, we don't have to take the statements about Oneness in isolation. We must rather consider them along with the statements where the Oneness is described as a form. With that form, the Oneness naturally becomes comprised of diversity.

Topic 6

QUESTION

If the Brahman is already Oneness, why does it expand into diverse forms? Since diversity is produced by the expansion of the Oneness into the many, what causes this expansion, and how should the diversity be explained?

1.1.12 (12)
आनन्दमयोऽभ्यासात्
ānandamayo'bhyāsāt

ānandamayaḥ—consists of bliss; abhyāsāt—because of habit or practice.

TRANSLATION

Because of habit or practice (of enjoyment), Brahman consists of bliss.

COMMENTARY

Here an answer to the question—how One becomes many—is given. The answer is pleasure. The cause for expansion of Brahman from One to many is the enjoyment of pleasure. The One has many aspects, but awareness of each aspect produces a different pleasure. The One is habituated to pleasure, and the aspects are separated by the desire for happiness. To obtain happiness, one must have an experience, and that experience involves a distinction between a knower and a known. Therefore, if only Oneness existed, then there cannot be happiness. Even self-experience involves a distinction between the knower and the known, although they are the same individual.

Therefore, separation from Oneness is essential to produce happiness. If Brahman is accustomed to the pursuit of happiness, then it cannot exist as Oneness; it must also separate.

In sūtra 1.1.7 (7) a distinction between the Absolute Truth and the ātmā was made. This distinction can be understood as being caused by the desire for pleasure. The One—which is Brahman—divides itself into many, and those many include the ātmā; the division creates the distinction between the knower and the known. The different knowers have different desires to know. Thus, the choice to view the known in different ways and aspects manifests. The desire for pleasure creates diverse ātmā and the diverse aspects of the Oneness.

In one sense, the One is enjoying with Itself, because there is nothing other than that One. In another sense, the One has divided into many parts—the knower and the known—by the desire for enjoyment. The diversity in the One is therefore ultimately a production of the diversity in choice and pleasure. Unless the pleasure in each aspect was different, there would be no diversity.

The diverse visions of the Oneness are a property of the ātmā, not of the Absolute Truth. The Absolute Truth is the combination of all the aspects but in the vision of each ātmā, the Oneness is perceived differently. Consider the example of a person who is a father, a husband, a friend, a brother, a son, and an employee in different relations. The person is the same, but through different relations, a different aspect of the person is revealed. The feature of being a father is not manifest in the friend relation, and the feature of being an employee is not manifest in the husband relation. Just as the person is manifest in different ways for different knowers, similarly, the One is manifest in different forms in the vision of different ātmā—who perceive the One through different relationships. This diversity attributed to the One is in the ātmā and it is also in Brahman. But in Brahman, the diversity is invisible, and in the ātmā it is visible.

It is implied here that the state of Oneness is not pleasurable because pleasure is created only by interaction with others. Since in the state of Oneness there is nothing other than One, the One expands into many to enjoy. We can infer from here that the One is not a social entity, but the many are social entities. However, these many are also expanded from the One to create society.

QUESTION

If the bliss of Brahman is attained through the division of the One into the many, then should we not say that this divided state of the Oneness is a modification of the One? In other words, the many parts of the One must come into existence when the One seeks bliss, but otherwise, it remains Oneness.

Here an argument can be made that Oneness is the fundamental state of Brahman, and the diversity is the occasional emergence of bliss. The argument would imply that diversity is not eternal but an accident of the creation of desire, resulting in the division. Of course, the argument would then beg the question—How does Brahman develop the desire for pleasure? And the answer to that question would then have to say that the desire for pleasure is a vikāra or modification of Brahman. The term vikāra can be understood as a random fluctuation, like a wave in an ocean. If the desire for happiness is a vikāra in the Brahman, then we would conclude that the One may divide into many, but this change is temporary. Whatever is temporary would become unreal, therefore, the expansions would be unreal. This argument is the extension of a similar idea in yoga philosophy where the chitta or the consciousness of the ātmā is described as an ocean in which desires emerge as occasional waves. The purpose of yoga is then said to be the termination of the vritti or modifications of the chitta. If this idea is extended to Brahman, then we must say that the desire for pleasure is a vritti or vikāra of Brahman—quite like a wave emerging in a calm ocean. We might say that the natural state of the ocean is to be calm, and without the vritti or vikāra of waves, Brahman is Oneness. Consequently, the division of the One into many must be temporary, and indeed termination of these desires (and hence the division of the One into many) must be the primordial state of Brahman. It would follow that these divisions of the One into the many must not be considered fundamental because the desires are temporary.

1.1.13 (13)

वकिारशब्दान्नेति चेत् न प्राचुर्यात्

vikāraśabdānneti cet na prācuryāt

vikāraśabdāt—from the statements of vikāra or modification; na—not; iti—thus; cet—if; na—not so; prācuryāt—from the abundance.

TRANSLATION

If it is said that from the statements of the impossibility of modification in Brahman we cannot (say that Brahman is bliss), (we say) not so, from the abundance (of bliss in Brahman).

COMMENTARY

This sūtra refutes the idea that bliss arises as a modification or vikāra in Brahman. The term ānandamayaḥ of the last sūtra cannot be interpreted as an occasional modification, because (as this sūtra clarifies), the pleasure is prachur or abundant. Abundance implies that some part of Oneness remains undivided. However, that doesn't mean that division is an aberration. Hence, the desire for pleasure is not pervasive and Oneness exists; but the desire for pleasure is also not occasional such that the division of the Oneness is incidental. Brahman can exist in an undivided form, but Brahman also exists in a differentiated form. Therefore, both the differentiated and undifferentiated forms are eternal.

If the effect is small—like the small waves in a massive ocean—then we can say that the natural state of the ocean is to be without waves. However, if the nature of the ocean is such that there are always some waves, then we cannot insist that the natural state of the ocean is to remain calm. The argument depends on the extent to which waves are found in the ocean. In this sūtra a similar argument is made—the waves of differentiation are not occasional; they are abundant. This doesn't mean that the entire ocean is turbulent. However, it means that the emergence of waves is also a natural property of the ocean.

This sūtra rejects the universality of Oneness, without completely denying that Oneness can indeed exist. Therefore, both Oneness (without differentiation) and differentiation (caused by the desire for pleasure) are permanent features of the Brahman. In fact, a more extensive argument about the fundamental nature of desire can be made as follows: If the desire for pleasure is natural, then the suspension of that desire is also a possibility. However, if the desire for pleasure is unnatural, then its emergence is problematic. So, even if we accept that the desire for pleasure is a vikāra, we would still be straddled with the problem of explaining how this modification emerges suddenly. However, if the desire for pleasure is eternal, then the suspension of this desire would be merely an aspect of desire: To not make a choice is also a choice. The suspension of choice is not the negation of choice; it is the choice of not dividing and therefore not selecting one of the divisions. Therefore, the suspension of choice is one of the applications of choice, however, the emergence of choice (if choice and differentiation are denied as being fundamental) is deeply problematic.

This nuanced understanding of choice entails that by and large there is differentiation and individuality indicated by the fact that the desire for pleasure is abundant. However, this desire is not a universal fact, and it is possible to suspend the desire and thereby dissolve the differentiation into Oneness.

QUESTION

Even if the One had pleasure originally, which then resulted in the division into many, does it not mean that now I have acquired the desire for pleasure and can, therefore, pursue my happiness without the Absolute Truth?

Here an argument about the independence of the living entity is made. The argument says that if happiness is all-pervasive, then everyone is responsible for their happiness. Therefore, each living entity doesn't have to be subordinate to the happiness of the Absolute Truth, which caused the original division. That is, everyone can pursue their happiness, and they don't have to serve the happiness of the Absolute Truth. So, the Absolute Truth created the individual beings to enjoy, but because these are now individuals, they have become free of the Absolute Truth. Due to the pervasiveness of happiness in each soul, these souls must now be entitled to pursue their separate joys and pleasures.

The individual pursuit of happiness is considered a fundamental right in modern times. Due to this, everyone becomes selfish: They think that they have a right to pursue their happiness, regardless of the happiness of others. If, however, we insist that we must please someone else in order to be happy, then the conclusion is that we must be their servants. Under this servitude, the pleasure of the master decides the pleasure of the servant. Factually, nobody wants this servitude; everyone wants to be free to pursue their happiness without having to please anyone else. Since everyone is pursuing their happiness, nobody is concerned about whether someone else is happy. Now, it depends on the individual's capacity to acquire the means for this happiness, and everyone may not be equally capable. Ideally, we expect that people achieve happiness by making others happy. But the notion that we shall become happy by pleasing others can seem very improbable: What if the other person is selfish, and they accept the happiness that we provide to them and do not reciprocate? The fear of being cheated in the process of pleasing others makes everyone wary of serving others. This then reinforces the idea that everyone is only responsible for their own happiness, and if the happiness of others were forced upon us—as the means to become happy—then our fundamental right to happiness would itself be denied (due to the possibility of being deceived in the process).

1.1.14 (14)

तद्धेतुव्यपदेशाच्च

taddhetuvyapadeśacca

tat—that (pleasure of the Brahman); hetu—the purpose, vyapa—pervasive; deśāt—from being in all the places; ca—and.

TRANSLATION

From being in all the places, that (pleasure of Brahman) is also the pervasive purpose (of everything).

COMMENTARY

This sūtra refutes the claim that everyone can pursue their separate happiness because the Absolute Truth is not only the cause of their individuality but also the purpose of their existence. In short, because the individual soul was created due to the desire for happiness in the Absolute Truth, the fulfillment of this desire is the purpose of the individual ātmā. This purpose—for which the ātmā has been created—must become the purpose of the individual and the ātmā can be happy only if this purpose is fulfilled. Thus, no ātmā can become happy by itself; it can become happy only in relation to the Absolute Truth. Therefore, ātmā's happiness must be obtained by making the Absolute

Truth happy. If the ātmā is not making the Absolute Truth happy, then it is not fulfilling its purpose, and the ātmā cannot, therefore, become happy on its own. Thus, although the ātmā is an individual, its individuality is dependent on the fulfillment of its purpose—and that purpose is the happiness of the One.

Now, you could also argue that maybe some individuals may serve the Absolute Truth, while others may become independent of the Absolute Truth. To counter this argument, the word 'pervasive' and 'in all places' is used. That is, you cannot go anywhere to seek independent happiness. The Absolute Truth is the cause of happiness or bliss in all places, and there is no place where He is not the cause. It also follows from the pervasiveness of the cause that you can be anywhere and still be blissful, in connection to the Absolute Truth, because no place is devoid of the influence of that Absolute Truth in creating the experience of bliss. Thus, nowhere is bliss possible without the Absolute Truth's bliss. And everywhere bliss is possible from the bliss of the Absolute Truth.

QUESTION

How can the individual soul become the cause of the happiness of the Absolute Truth when the Absolute Truth is the greatest while the soul is incredibly small? How can such a small entity create an effect of bliss in the greatest?

Here an argument about the incapacity of the soul is made. In the previous sūtra, it has been asserted that the ātmā is not independent and must serve the happiness of the Absolute Truth. The reader now wonders how he can serve the Absolute Truth when he's so small and incapable of making a difference to the Absolute Truth, which is the original cause of everything. Therefore, the project of fulfilling the happiness of the Absolute Truth seems unachievable.

1.1.15 (15)

मान्त्रवर्णकिमेव च गीयते

māntravarṇikameva ca gīyate

māntravarṇikam—the letters of mantras; eva—certainly; ca—also; gīyate—in singing or glorifying.

TRANSLATION

Certainly, the letters of mantras are also in the glory (of Brahman).

COMMENTARY

The answer to the question of how the individual soul can please the Absolute Truth is given here. The answer is that the soul can glorify the Absolute Truth using mantras. Since the word giyate or songs is used here, we can infer that this sūtra refers to the Sāmaveda, which comprises songs of glorification of the Absolute Truth. The Absolute Truth is infinite. However, the same Absolute Truth is represented through the symbols of the songs and names. These symbols can be grasped and known by the individual soul. Just like the universe is infinite, but the word 'universe' is finite. And this word encompasses the infinity of the universe into a finite word, similarly, the Absolute Truth is infinite, but the same Absolute Truth is finite when represented through symbols.

Implicit in this description is the idea that the Absolute Truth is both meaning and existence. The existence of the Absolute Truth cannot fit inside the soul. But the meaning of the Absolute Truth can fit within the soul. When we use the word 'universe', we haven't understood everything in the universe. And yet, by the word 'universe' we refer to the same thing. Semantically these two are identical, but physically they are different. Thus, the claim that the infinite cannot be captured by the finite is refuted. Yes, the infinite is not physically captured by the finite; but the infinite is semantically captured by the words.

QUESTION

Can we not consider these mantras as referring to the glorification of ātmā instead of the Absolute Truth? Why would we prefer the Absolute Truth?

This is a variation of the earlier question where the ātmā seeks its separate happiness rather than the happiness of the Absolute Truth. In the previous sūtra, it was stated that the Absolute Truth should be pleased by the mantra. But we can ask: Why not consider the chanting of these mantras as the source of one's liberation, rather than the pleasure of the Absolute Truth? Many mantras lead to the peacefulness of the mind, so why should we not consider the purpose of their chanting the liberation of the mind from material troubles?

1.1.16 (16)

नेतरोऽनुपपत्तेः

netaro'nupapatteh

na—not; itarah—the other, i.e., the jīvā; anupapatteh—because of the unreasonableness (or an invalid, illogical conclusion).

TRANSLATION

(The Brahman and) not the other (i.e., the individual souls are indicated here) on account of the unreasonableness (of the latter assumption).

COMMENTARY

This sūtra asserts that the mantras to be sung are not meant for the satisfaction of the ātmā. In many New Age religions, the chanting of mantras is said to quieten the mind. Indeed, the meaning of 'mantra' is itself the freedom of the mind (manah trayate iti mantra—that which frees the mind is called mantra). So, one can argue that the purpose of the mantra is the freedom of the mind from the incessant flow of thoughts and feelings, the resulting peace of mind can be considered the purpose of the mantra chanting. However, this sūtra negates such an interpretation of the mantra as being meant for the happiness and satisfaction of the self. One can then ask: But by chanting the mantra we can see that the self is satisfied. So, how can we deny this effect of mantra chanting and claim that its purpose is not the satisfaction of the self when it is practically observed? The answer is that the satisfaction from the chanting of the mantra is due to the satisfaction of the Absolute Truth and since the ātmā is a part of the Absolute Truth, the satisfaction of the Absolute Truth creates self-satisfaction. Like watering the root of the tree waters the trunks, branches, and leaves, similarly, the fact that the chanting of mantras results in the satisfaction of the self doesn't mean that the purpose of these mantras is the satisfaction of the self.

New Age religions claim that the idea of spirituality is the rediscovery of the spiritual nature of the self as different from matter. There is no dearth of people who seem to be opposed to the existence of a

Supreme Being or God as the person who must be satisfied for a person to become happy. Instead of glorifying the Lord, the New Age religions assert that religion must be freed from the conception of God, and the spiritual entity replacing God is the individual soul. Thus, spiritual practices are meant not for the satisfaction of the Absolute Truth, but the attainment of peace and satisfaction of the individual self.

This sūtra, however, states that such an endeavor is futile. If the mantras are not sung to satisfy the Absolute Truth, then words are uttered but the references of these words are incorrect. When we speak a sentence, there are two types of meanings. First, there is the conceptual meaning, or what the word or sentence states. Second, there is also a reference to the object, which the sentence describes. For instance, if we say that "John is tall", the cognitive meaning is that someone is tall, but the reference is John—a person or individual who is referred to by that statement. The *referential* component of Vedic mantras is the Absolute Truth, and the names used in glorification refer to it. If we retain the cognitive meaning, but we don't understand the reference, then the statements of glorification are false. For instance, if John is replaced by "I" in the statement, then the claims of the statement would refer to the self; but the self may not be tall. So, although the words are uttered, and their meanings are clearly understood, the statement becomes false. Salvation cannot be expected through the chanting of false utterances. The sūtra states that the glorification of the Absolute Truth cannot be applied to the individual soul. So, even if you chant the Vedic mantras thinking that they are meant for self-satisfaction, ultimately, the utterances are false because the mental intention or reference is misplaced.

Thus, it is not enough to chant the mantras. It is also necessary to mentally refer to the individual being described and glorified through the mantra. There can be some cognitive satisfaction simply by chanting the true statements; however, the truth is not just the conceptual meaning but also the reference. If the reference is missing or is misplaced toward the self, then the utterances are false. Since the meaning of the mantra cannot be truthfully applied to the self, the sūtra says that the view that the mantra refers to the self is illogical.

QUESTION

But we have previously stated that the ātmā was differentiated from the Brahman by the desire for pleasure. Once this differentiation

has occurred, then the different ātmā are just like the drops of water separated from the ocean of water. If something is said about the water in the ocean, then it must also apply to the drops of water in the ocean. Then, why can't the statements about the Absolute Truth not apply to the ātmā if the ātmā is a part of the Absolute Truth?

1.1.17 (17)

भेदव्यपदेशाच्च

bhedavyapadeśācca

bheda—difference; vyapadeśāt—because of the declaration; ca—and.

TRANSLATION

And on account of the declaration of the difference (in ātmā and Brahman).

COMMENTARY

It is true that many assertions about Brahman are also true about the ātmā. For example, the Absolute Truth is the capacity for consciousness, knowledge, and pleasure (also called sat, chit, and ānanda). The same is true of the ātmā as well. However, there are other statements about the Absolute Truth that do not apply to the ātmā. For instance, the Absolute Truth is omniscient, but the ātmā is not. The consciousness of the ātmā can be directed toward one thing at a time, but the consciousness of the Absolute Truth can be directed toward everything at once. Thus, the pleasure of the ātmā is limited to that derived from a limited awareness and knowledge at any moment, but the pleasure of the Absolute Truth is unlimited. Therefore, the ātmā and Brahman are *qualitatively* similar as they have the same capacity for awareness, knowledge, and pleasure. But the ātmā and the Absolute Truth are *quantitatively* different because the latter is omniscient and omnipotent while the former only has a limited capacity for knowledge and power. Thus, some statements about the Absolute Truth can also be applied to the ātmā; but not every statement can be used thus.

While we can say that the water in the ocean and the water in the drop have many qualitative similarities, there are also statements about the ocean—such as the "ocean is vast"—which cannot be applied to the drop of water. This similarity and difference between ātmā and Brahman have been the basis of many Vedānta Sūtra interpretations. Of special significance here is the sūtra asserting that they are not identical in all respects. Of course, the ātmā is a part of the Absolute Truth, but the part cannot be equated to the whole in all respects.

QUESTION

If the chanting of mantra must be directed to the pleasure of the Absolute Truth, aren't there other methods by which I can attain my happiness? For example, can I not detach myself from the modes of material nature using reasoning, the cultivation of knowledge, and other methods, such as austerities?

Individualism and independence are deep-seated desires in each person. We trust in our powers of sensation and reason, but we don't have faith in surrender to something other than the self. This question is prominent in today's world where people want to rely on their personal experience and mental prowess to attain their objectives. They don't want to place their faith and trust in someone or something else. There are two main reasons for this. First, there is an individual pride in each person which tells them they are self-sufficient and don't need anything else to attain their goals; surrender to something else would necessitate humility—I'm not capable of attaining my goals on my own and therefore I need to surrender. Second, there is a deep distrust of others, especially in the statements of scriptures. If the scripture says that one must chant the mantra for happiness, what guarantee exists that this process will yield the results that I'm aspiring for? Maybe this is all a fanciful imagination of some people which I must examine skeptically. The combination of pride and skepticism makes one distrust any spiritual process that demands that we put faith in something other than our powers of experience and reason. Therefore, if the scripture states that this faith is needed, then the seeker would typically make every possible attempt to avoid this reliance on faith and surrender.

1.1.18 (18)

कामाच्च नानुमानापेक्षा

kāmācca nānumānāpekṣā

kāmāt—from desiring; ca—also; na—not; anumāna—the imagination or speculative knowledge; apekṣā—expectation.

TRANSLATION

From desiring also, the imagined (thing) cannot be expected. Or, from desiring and speculation we cannot expect (to attain the Absolute Truth).

COMMENTARY

There are two possible translations of this sūtra, which are noted above. The first of these translations is quite straightforward. Why can't we attain a perfect life without pleasing Brahman? The answer is: Just by desiring, we cannot achieve the goals. We have to follow the process indicated in the Vedic texts. The second possible translation indicates that we cannot get to the Absolute Truth by speculation. Why? Because innate to that speculation is the idea that the soul is independent of the Absolute Truth, and when logical inference is based on false assumptions, then the conclusions of inference are also false.

All reasoning is based on assumptions or axioms. This is a famous critique of rationalism in Western philosophy where reason only expands upon what has already been assumed in the axioms. For example, Euclid's geometry makes five main assumptions, based on which numerous theorems can be derived; the collection of all these theorems is called Euclidean Geometry. However, these axioms are not necessarily sacrosanct. In 20th century mathematics, Euclid's fifth postulate (namely, that the shortest path between two points is a straight line) was challenged resulting in non-Euclidean geometry. While Euclid's geometry works in most practical day-to-day scenarios on Earth, there are cosmological problems where space must be considered curved—i.e., the shortest path between two points is not a straight line—to explain the bending of light. The existence of non-Euclidean geometry, however, doesn't disprove the theorems of Euclidean geometry, because these proofs are always relative to the axioms.

Mathematics is famous for formulating theories based on different axioms. Whether these theories are useful or not doesn't concern the rationalists. They aim to make assumptions and derive conclusions from them. Whether those assumptions themselves are true or not is beyond reason. Some philosophers of science then argue that these assumptions can be tested empirically. However, the issue is that the testing is relative to the domain in which you apply the theory—e.g., terrestrial vs. celestial problems for geometry. Just as Euclidean geometry is adequate for most terrestrial problems, similarly, unless we find those problems where its assumptions are invalidated, the theory would stand vindicated. The main point is that axioms or assumptions are not true or false; they are simply useful or useless relative to the problem we are trying to solve; if you are trying to build a bicycle, Newton's mechanics works fine; but if you are trying to build an atom bomb, then quantum mechanics is necessary.

Now we come to the main question that concerns us here: How do you choose the problems that are to be solved? What should you consider an important problem that has to be attacked and solved through rationality?

There is no rational prescription for picking problems. What you consider an important problem may be worthless for others. Some people are trying to solve the economic problems of a nation, while others consider earning their day-to-day livelihood an important problem. Some people wonder about the workings of nature, while others only worry about raising a happy family. In short, the problems are our *choices*. We choose a problem, and we make assumptions or axioms that are suitable to solve the chosen problem. Reason operates only when the assumptions have been made. If the chosen assumptions fail to solve the problem, we might go back to the drawing board and make new or different assumptions. Assumptions are thus never true or false; they are only good or bad relative to a chosen problem. The same assumption may be good for one problem but bad for another. Just because the assumption works in one case doesn't make it true; it must work in all cases for it to be true.

Now, we can understand this sūtra, namely, to know the Absolute Truth through reason, we must be trying to solve the ultimate problems of life. Our goal cannot be bicycles, steam engines, economic theories, or atom bombs. The goal must be to know who I am, the purpose of my existence, and the method by which it can be fulfilled. This purpose has been explained previously—i.e., satisfying the Absolute Truth. If we disregard this understanding, then we might frame some false axioms, and the result will also be false conclusions.

The implied criticism is that most people who want to know the Absolute Truth through reason, start with the wrong problem of trying to build a better mousetrap. They frame their axioms suitable to solve the better mousetrap problem. And if the mousetrap is improved, then we call the underlying assumptions as truth. Conditioned by such assumptions we now try to make inferences about the Absolute Truth. We are unprepared to change our axioms because they worked for the better mousetrap. We fail to see that to formulate new axioms, we must fundamentally change the problem. We cannot use the better mouse-trap assumptions to solve fundamentally different problems. Hence, before we try to use reasoning to know the Absolute Truth, we must change our desires toward the Absolute Truth. We must be eager to solve the ultimate problems of life, and then axioms can be rationally applied. Based on our desires we choose different problems and make different assumptions.

QUESTION

You stated at the beginning that now we must inquire into the nature of Brahman. You then distinguished Brahman from ātmā and stated that this distinction arises due to the desire for plea-sure. You then further said that the ātmā can attain freedom from the modes of nature by pleasing Brahman. What happened to the goal of knowing Brahman in this process? Haven't we shifted the goal from knowing Brahman to pleasing Brahman, and the goal of knowing has been lost in the process? How can knowing be asso-ciated with pleasing?

In the Vedic tradition, there is a contentious issue between the pursuits of knowledge and devotion. The proponents of knowledge or jñāna assert the superiority of the intellect and claim that devo-tion is inferior. This is due to the recognition that, in this material world, emotions (including desires) are the cause of the bondage of the ātmā to this world. By intelligence, we must learn to control the desires of the mind, and detach the mind from the world. But if we reject reason and inference as a process for attaining Brahman, then how can we ever hope to attain the original goal of knowing the Absolute Truth?

1.1.19 (19)
अस्मन्निनस्य च तद्योगं शास्ति
asminnasya ca tadyogaṃ śāsti

asmin—in Him; asya—of the jīvā; ca—also; tat—that; yogaṃ—union; śāsti—(śrutī) teaches.

TRANSLATION

And moreover, the scripture, teaches that the joining of this (the individual soul), with that (i.e., consisting of bliss—Brahman) results in knowledge.

COMMENTARY

This sūtra uses the term yogam or union between the ātmā and the Absolute Truth. When the ātmā is joined to the Absolute Truth, then knowledge of the Absolute Truth is attained. Therefore, after stating that the Absolute Truth must be glorified using mantras and rejecting the intellectual process of knowing the Absolute Truth, the sūtra states that the goal of knowing the Absolute Truth is not rejected by rejecting the intellectual process. Rather, by the union of the soul with the Absolute Truth, the knowledge of the Absolute Truth is attained. This represents the inversion of the process in which first we know the Absolute Truth and then we become devoted to that Absolute Truth. The previous sūtra stated that it is unreasonable to expect the knowledge of the Absolute Truth to arise without devotion. This sūtra then asserts that if devotion exists, then knowledge naturally arises. Thus, knowledge follows devotion.

Topic 7

QUESTION

To join to the Absolute Truth, I must know what the Absolute Truth is. What does this union truly mean? How to join with the Absolute Truth?

In the previous sūtra, the term yoga was used for the union with the Absolute Truth. However, before we can unite, we must know the object to be united with. This creates a circular problem—to know

Absolute Truth, we must unite with Him; but, to unite, we must know the Absolute Truth. Note that this problem doesn't arise in the case of the intellectual process because if we can know the Absolute Truth by reasoning, then we can subsequently unite with it, form a relationship to the knowledge, and meditate upon it. The previous sūtra and the one before that, however, refuted this idea of being able to know the Absolute Truth without uniting, meditating, or via a relationship. So, this creates a curiosity in the seeker: Where should I find Absolute Truth to unite with?

1.1.20 (20)
अन्तस्तद्धर्मोपदेशात्
antastaddharmopadeśāt

antaḥ—within; tat dharma—His nature; upadeśāt—from the teaching.

TRANSLATION

From the teaching of that essential nature being present within.

COMMENTARY

One possible interpretation of this sūtra is that the ātmā present within (the heart) is the Absolute Truth; indeed, this the interpretation of impersonalism. While this confusion will be clarified in the next sūtra where the distinction between two souls inhabiting the heart is described, even in this sūtra we can see that the term 'tat' indicating 'that' is used. The context reveals that this must denote the Absolute Truth because the previous sūtra spoke about union with the Absolute Truth. So, 'tat dharma' should not be interpreted as referring to the ātmā. Now, 'antah tat dharma' means that the presence of Absolute Truth as the characteristics by which the Absolute Truth is identified. It doesn't entail that the Absolute Truth is itself present, otherwise, the use of the term 'tat dharma' (or that nature) would be unnecessary. We would just state that the Absolute Truth is *in* the self. The implication is that the Absolute Truth is not present in the self, however, its distinguishing characteristics are manifest. For example, the fire spreads its influence, and by this spreading, its presence can be known everywhere, even though the fire is localized. Similarly, the presence of the Absolute Truth can be felt in the heart—like the spreading of heat from fire—although the Absolute Truth is not in the heart. So, the use of "that nature" has a nuanced use in this sūtra that cannot be equated to direct presence. As a result, this presence cannot be conveniently equated to the presence of ātma.

QUESTION

But we can interpret the above statement to refer to the ātma if we say that the ātma is not truly present in the heart, but only visible by its effects. As you have already stated, the ātma is transcendental to the three modes of nature, and the body is comprised of these three modes. So, to say that the ātma is present in the heart would entail that the ātma is somehow physically inside matter, and therefore not transcendental. Would it not be more accurate to say that the ātma is transcendental to matter but only by its effects (like the effect of heat due to fire) its presence is visible in the heart? That would imply that that which is inside—and which you are referring to as Brahman—is indeed the ātma.

In many parts of Vedic literature, it is said that the yogi must withdraw their senses from the external world and focus it upon the heart. Since consciousness spreads to the external world through the senses, it can mean that by withdrawing the senses, consciousness merges within its source. The merger is 'self-knowledge', and the yogi is atmarāma or one who enjoys within oneself. Notably, the property of consciousness is that it is aware of itself and in all forms of awareness of the world, the awareness of the self is always present. So, self-awareness precedes the awareness of the other, but if we withdraw from the awareness of the other then the other ceases to exist. We could now argue that the division of the world into knower and known is the result of the outward movement of consciousness—produced by defocusing on the self and seeking pleasure in something other than itself. If this line of reasoning is extended, one could argue that the world is manifest out of this outward movement of consciousness and it doesn't truly exist 'outside' the self. It is simply a projection of the ātma like a movie projector projects images outwardly. If therefore, the light of the projector was turned inwardly, then the projection out of the ātma would also cease to exist, and the distinction between the knower and the known—produced by the outward movement—would cease.

One could now say that by yoga we simply mean the cessation of the distinctions between the knower and the known; when the knower collapses into the known, that union can itself be called yoga. Thus, drawing the consciousness inward, defocusing on the projections, and concentrating on the self would entail detachment from the body and hence liberation from the modes of nature. The term 'tat dharma' in the previous sūtra would now be interpreted as the consciousness of the ātmā—namely, that the ātmā is not present within the heart, however, its effect (like the heat of the fire) as consciousness is seen.

1.1.21 (21)

भेदव्यपदेशाच्चान्यः

bhedavyapadeśāccānyaḥ

bheda—difference; vyapadeśāt—because of the declaration; ca—and, also; anyaḥ—is different, another, other than the jīvā or the individual soul.

TRANSLATION

And there is another one (i.e., the Lord who is different from the individual ātmā animating the body) on account of the declaration of distinction.

COMMENTARY

To refute the argument that yoga is the focusing of the consciousness on the self, this sūtra states directly that which was said indirectly in the previous sūtra—namely, the yoga is not the union with the self; it is rather with another individual who is present in the heart. This second person is generally referred to as Paramātma in the Vedic literature; He is said to be One and yet all-pervasive. The Bhagavad-Gita 13.23 describes this personality in greater clarity:

upadraṣṭānumantā ca
bhartā bhoktā maheśvaraḥ
paramātmeti cāpy ukto
dehe 'smin puruṣaḥ paraḥ

Yet in this body, there is another, a transcendental enjoyer who is the Lord, the supreme proprietor, who exists as the overseer and permitter, and who is known as the Supersoul.

This is further confirmed in the Bhagavad-Gita verse 9.4 as follows:

> mayā tatam idaṁ sarvaṁ
> jagad avyakta-mūrtinā
> mat-sthāni sarva-bhūtāni
> na cāhaṁ teṣv avasthitaḥ

By Me, in My unmanifested form, this entire universe is pervaded. All beings are in Me, but I am not in them.

This verse is important for two reasons. First, it states that the Lord pervades everything. Second, it also states that the Lord is not in those things. This is a paradoxical statement, but it can be used to understand the meaning of 'tat dharma' in the previous sūtra. Just as heat spreads from the fire and can be found in many places, but the fire is not directly present everywhere, similarly, the Lord can be One and yet spread to many different things. In fact, the standard analogy of the impersonalist—called pratibimba-vāda, or the argument of reflection—can be directly applied in this case: Just as the sun is one and yet its reflection is indicated in every pot of water, but if you break the pot, then the sun is not destroyed, similarly, the Lord is present in every heart by His qualities, although He is not in the heart. He is present by His distinguishing characteristics—e.g., heat is the characteristic of fire. The presence of the sun heats the pot, even though the sun is not within the pot of water; similarly, the presence of the Lord affects the heart, although He is not confined to the heart.

The implication is that yoga doesn't mean a merger with the self because the self is not the Absolute Truth. As already indicated, there is a difference between the ātmā and the Lord. However, if further confusion exists, then it can be stated that there are two kinds of kṣetra-jña or "knowers of the field" (the term 'field' refers to the space of the body). The ātmā is the knower of the body or limited portions of the field. However, the Paramātma knows the entire field, including the fields known by the different individual ātmā. Thus, the ātmā is a limited knower of one field, whereas the Paramātma is also omniscient.

Topic 8

QUESTION

Why should a distinction between ātmā and Paramātma be made? Can we not say that Paramātma is the all-pervasive consciousness, and ātmā is simply the experience of individuality of this consciousness? We could say that the all-pervading entity is the space in which everything exists. And the things within that space would be the experiences of consciousness. We could also say that a consciousness creates its experience and consciousness is One, but experiences are diverse. Then, by dissolving the experience, ātmā and Paramātma can become one entity—in that One, there is consciousness without experience.

Some New Age philosophers suggest that the universe is self-aware, and it is created by the production of experience within a 'field' of consciousness, but this field has no origin. It is like light, but that light doesn't emanate from a source like the sun. The ātmā can now be called an *experience* of consciousness; it exists within the universal field or space, but it is a creation of consciousness and therefore has no reality. Thus, Paramātma is the field, and ātmā is a creation of an experience in the field, and there is no origin of the field itself. Some New Age philosophers say that this 'field' can be equated to a vacuum from which objects pop out as individuals and then pop back in as energy. Thus, the all-pervading energy field transforms automatically, which manifests objects, and when the transformation is reversed then the objects disappear. This appearance and disappearance of objects can be analogically used to explain not just the creation and destruction of the universe, but also ordinary changes.

This view simplifies the ontology (the things that exist) for several reasons. First, we don't have to postulate the existence of a source—i.e., God—who manifests the field; the field is eternal. Second, we don't have to separate matter from consciousness because the field is consciousness and matter is the objects manifest within this field; hence, the problem of matter-consciousness interaction or the distinction between matter and consciousness (which in Vedic parlance we would call the distinction between ātmā and the three modes of nature) doesn't have to exist. Third, once the distinction between matter and consciousness is collapsed, then the distinction between the different individual ātmā can also be collapsed: We can say that when the experience is created, a limited notion of the knower is produced in the process, which appears to us as an individual observer. Therefore, in one swoop, we can dissolve the distinction between God, the soul, and matter, and just call it Oneness or Brahman.

1.1.22 (22)

आकाशस्तल्लिङ्गात्

ākāśastalliṅgāt

ākāśaḥ—space; tat—that Absolute Truth; liṅgāt—from procreative organ.

TRANSLATION

From the procreative organ of the Absolute Truth, the space is manifest.

COMMENTARY

This sūtra refutes the existence of light without a source of light. It asserts that the space in which everything exists is Brahman. However, this Brahman is manifest from a form or a deity. This form or deity is like the sun or fire, and Brahman is the light expanding from the sun or fire. The idea that there is all-pervading light without a sun or fire is therefore rejected. In short, we accept that there is an all-pervading space. However, we also assert that this space has an *origin* as the source of the space, and space expands from this origin.

The term liṅga can be understood as the male organ of procreation. So, this deity from which Brahman emanates as light is like the father who expands His existence like a father produces children; the source is the father, and the expanding light is His children. The Bhagavad-Gita 14.4 states this as follows:

sarva-yoniṣu kaunteya
mūrtayaḥ sambhavanti yāḥ
tāsāṁ brahma mahad yonir
ahaṁ bīja-pradaḥ pitā

It should be understood that all species of life, O son of Kunti, are made possible by birth in this material nature, and that I am the seed giving father.

In the above verse, the use of mahad-yoni is significant. Just as the term linga denotes the male procreative organ, the term yoni indicates the female procreative organ. Mahad-yoni indicates the material nature into which the seed-giving father imparts the ātmā—the 'seed' in this case is the ātmā. Notably, since the father imparts the seed, the seed previously existed inside the father, and therefore the ātmā was originally part of the seed-giving father. However, since the seed is imparted into the mahad-yoni, the seed is also separated from the father and embedded into the material nature. The material nature is inert prior to the imparting of this seed, and it expands into the world with this seed. So, the mahad-yoni (the greatest feminine sexual organ) is the kṣetra or the 'field', and the ātmā becomes the kṣetrajña or the knower of the field.

One might argue that once the ātmā has entered the material nature, and has become the kṣetrajña, it is the only kṣetrajña and hence the only one present in the heart as consciousness. This would contradict the previous sūtra which said that there is another knower—Who is omniscient—whereas the ātmā is a limited knower of the part of the field. To understand the two sūtras together, we must say that the seed-giving father not only imparts the seed but also enters the kṣetra along with the seed, as the omniscient and all-pervading entity—He is called the Paramātma or the Supreme Soul, as opposed to the ātmā. The term yoga then applies to the union between the ātmā and the Paramātma.

Hence, the all-pervading entity is Brahman, which is like light emanating from a source of light—the sun or fire. However, this light is also divided into particles—the ātmā. Notably, all three premises of the impersonal philosopher noted above are refuted in the process. First, because there is a difference between the *bīja* or seed and the *pit*ā or the father—namely, the light and the source of light—hence, there is a distinction between the soul and God. Second, because the seed is imparted into the mahad-yoni or matter, therefore, there is a difference between the ātmā and material nature. Third, since there is a difference between the father and the mother, God is different from matter.

There is a difference between the all-pervading space and the points in this space. Since the ātmā is always accompanied by the Paramātma, therefore, the points in the space can be individuated. Similarly, since the space expands from an origin, therefore, the origin can be distinguished from the rest of the points in space. There is hence no 'field of consciousness'. The 'field' is in fact comprised of points. The term ākāśa or space refers to the collection of individual points; it is not a continuum without individual ātmā. It is just collectively called the undivided Brahman, like we use the term 'space' to indicate all the locations collectively. This space of individual points has an origin, from which all the locations emanate. They were previously contained inside that origin, but they emerge from that origin. This is the significance of saying that the pitā or father distributes His seed. Therefore, although there is an all-pervading field comprised of individual points, there is an origin of the space, which constitutes the *absolute reference frame* in terms of which we measure the points.

Those familiar with relativistic conceptions of space will realize that the observer is considered different from the space: The observer becomes the origin in relation to which space is mapped. There is, however, a preexisting space as well because the conceptions of near and far are preexisting in space, not because there is an observer. The observer only adds a reference frame or the origin and the dimensional vectors to this space. Now, if we collapse the distinction between the space and the observer, then space itself must have an origin. So, there cannot be an all-pervading entity that has no origin and is without dimensional vectors because that would not be considered 'space'. In short, the idea that there is an all-pervading space brings with it the notion that there must be an origin because without that origin space itself loses meaning.

Topic 9

QUESTION

If the ātmā is injected into matter, and then becomes the kṣetra-jña, then it must also be disconnected from its source—the father imparting the seed. So, why is yoga needed when the ātmā has separated? Once separated, the ātmā must be independent of its source. Just like if a light particle has emerged from the sun, it is no longer bound to the sun. It can move independently. Yes, it can be absorbed into matter, but even if it is absorbed, it is free of its source! What would be the point of returning or maintaining a connection to the source?

We have earlier stated that Brahman is comprised of points. But if these points are independent, then the *distance* between them would become meaningless because nothing joins these points. If there is no distance between the points—i.e., a path that connects one point to another—then there cannot be space. What we call space would be a disjointed set of locations and one could not go from one location to another. Effectively, each point in space would be an island unto itself from which one cannot reach the other islands. Motion or communication would be impossible in such a space as these points are disconnected from each other, and nothing can move from one point to another.

If the points in space were ātmā, then it would follow that no ātmā can know any other ātmā. Similarly, the ātmā cannot move in this space or change its relation to other ātmā. Finally, the ātmā cannot know the source from which it emanated, as there would be no connection to this source. Each ātmā can only be considered an island unto itself, disconnected from other ātmā and the source of all ātmā. Once disconnected, the justification for yoga disappears.

In scientific terms, when we postulate the existence of space, we hypothesize two things— (1) a set of points, and (2) the metric or distance that connects these points. Once these two have been hypothesized, then we also add an observer which provides the origin and dimensional vectors for space. For the present, let us consider the metric which gives the space a structure as the proximity and distance from the origin. If the metric doesn't exist, then space has no structure, because no point is either closer or farther. We cannot order or count points in space because for ordering or counting there must be a sequence—before and after. This sequence requires a metric. If the metric doesn't exist, then there may be some points, but there is no way to know how many points there are. The metric between the points acts as the connection to the origin.

If we say that the Brahman is simply a collection of points, and if there is no connection between these points (because the points are independent), then we could not speak about the connection to the origin or the distance from the origin. In fact, we could not even speak about the path from one point to another, including the path to the source, because these points have been separated. Once we say that the separation has occurred, then the mutual knowledge of the different ātmā would be impossible, as there would be no path from one point to reach another point. If this path is voided, then no ātmā can know another ātmā or the source of their emanation. Once this knowledge has become impossible, then yoga or establishing a connection to the source—i.e., between ātmā and Paramātma—would also become impossible.

1.1.23 (23)

अत एव प्राणः

ata eva prāṇaḥ

ata eva—therefore; praṇaḥ—the prāṇa (is necessary or refers to Brahman).

TRANSLATION

Therefore, the prāṇa (is necessary or refers to Brahman).

COMMENTARY

This sūtra clarifies that even though Brahman is a collection of points—and is hence not an all-pervasive unitary oneness—there is still a connection between these individual points through the prāṇa. This prāṇa is like the path or distance between the many points, including the source from which they originate. Therefore, even if the particle of light has emanated from the sun, this particle cannot be considered independent of the sun, and the reason is that this particle is still connected to the sun through the agency called the prāṇa.

For those familiar with atomic theory, the idea that light moves from one point to another is itself a fallacy of classical mechanical thinking because the atomic particles transition from one state to another. For example, if an electron moves from one atom to another, it doesn't move between the atoms—i.e., passing through the positions in the 'space' between the atoms; the atom is at one moment in one atom and at the next moment in the other atom. So, the idea that atomic particles 'move' in space is a classical caricature of change, that has failed in atomic theory. However, a new notion of change hasn't yet emerged, and so we continue to employ the classical caricatures, even if they are incorrect.

The new notion of change is indicated here: The particles don't move to push and pull each other (called locality in modern science). Rather, the particle remotely causes a change. This agency for remote change is prāṇa; for it to cause change, there is must be a path or connection; in short, prāṇa must be able to reach the destination which has to be changed, and the path to the destination is itself the cause of change. However, nothing moves on this path; the path or connection to the other thing is itself the cause of changes. These changes can be called knowledge and action, depending on which direction we consider the path (the path that goes from A to B also goes from B to A, but the directions are different—so, there are two directions, although on the same path).

Thus, the connection between the ātmā and the Paramātma or the seed-giving father is never lost, even if the seed has been separated from the father. There is always a connection—which we can call the path to the source—which keeps the two connected. This path creates the 'distance' between the origin and the other points in space. The distance between the points and the source of space is not fixed, so the ātmā can move closer to or farther from the source. The main purpose of prāṇa is to enable the changes to the relative positions to the origin and can, therefore, be called the 'freedom' of the ātmā. Unlike the points in material space which have fixed locations, the points in Brahman are free, and that freedom is simply that these points can move in relation to the origin. By enabling this motion, prāṇa represents choice. By this choice, the soul can control its experience. In short, whether in relation to the material space or in relation to the points in the

Brahman—the cause of motion is prāṇa. And yet, regardless of how far the ātmā moves from the source, it never loses the path to the source. This path keeps the space joined together and the very reason that we can call it an all-pervading entity that doesn't have 'holes' in between.

If we delve deeper into Vedic philosophy, this structure between the source and the other points is like an inverted tree. The source of the tree is the root, and other points in space are like the trunks, branches, and leaves. The prāṇa connects the locations on the tree and therefore forms the path between the many points. Due to the existence of such paths, it is possible for one ātmā to know another ātmā and for the ātmā to know the source of all ātmā. Similarly, by changing this prāṇa, one can move closer or farther to the source. However, in no situation is the connection to the source or origin of space is lost. In short, space doesn't break apart into mutually disjointed islands, such that you can never go from one island to another. If that were the case, then each ātmā could become an island unto itself and would thereafter never need to maintain a relation to the source of ātmā. It would rather be totally independent.

Herein lies the germ of the idea in yoga philosophy that by manipulating prāṇa one can attain union with the Paramātma. The tree noted above is inverted, with the root upwards, and the leaves downward. The soul can change its distance from the source by manipulating the prāṇa; in short, it can move up or down this tree—coming nearer to the source or going farther away. The upward movement of the prāṇa takes one closer to the source, and the downward movement takes the soul farther away from the source. So, the basis of the yoga practice is the manipulation of prāṇa to move closer to the source. But even if the soul doesn't come closer, the connection to the source is never lost. Therefore, the possibility of the soul moving closer to the source is always open. There is never a point at which the soul gets disconnected from its original source.

Now, when we supplement the idea that Brahman is the space, with the idea here, that these points are joined to the source through prāṇa, we get a nuanced understanding of this space: There are many points, but the *locations* of these points relative to the source are not fixed. The points can move closer or farther from the source, so what we call 'space' doesn't have a fixed *structure*. Due to the closer or farther movement of the points, space is a dynamic entity. This is unlike the modern idea of space in which points in space have a fixed location; a point closer to the origin can never become farther, or vice versa. This is, however, not the case with Brahman. It is comprised of points that can change their relative positions, establish new paths, or destroy older paths. Through the making and breaking of paths—the creation and destruction of metric distance—the knowledge of other individuals is created or destroyed.

In the Tantra, it is said that the universes are manifest when Kāraṇodakaśāyī Viṣṇu *breathes out*—i.e., ejects the soul from His body into matter. Similarly, the destruction of the universes is compared to Kāraṇodakaśāyī Viṣṇu breathing in when the souls are absorbed back into His body. So, the soul is part of Lord Viṣṇu, but there is a difference between the whole and the part. Lord Viṣṇu is the whole and the jīvā is the part, and they are joined mutually through the prāṇa of Lord Viṣṇu. This prāṇa must be understood as the śakti of Lord Viṣṇu, which at once divides Him into many parts, and yet keeps the parts connected to the whole. In short, even though the whole is divided into parts, the parts don't get separated from the whole, because they are always connected to the whole through His śakti. Therefore, when we speak about Brahman, we must understand that it is comprised of two things—the individual jīvā and the śakti that joins this jīvā to the source. Because of the existence of this śakti which joins the jīvā to the source, Brahman is also called prāṇa in this sūtra.

Topic 10

QUESTION

You have been describing the nature of Brahman in two different ways—(a) the all-pervading whole comprising of atomic parts or ātmā, and (b) the source from which everything (i.e., these parts) emanates. You explicitly drew a distinction between the space as Brahman and the origin of this space in the previous sūtra and compared this to the emanating light and the source of that light. This implies that Brahman is not everything; there is also a source apart from it. If Brahman is not everything then what else exists apart from it?

1.1.24 (24)

ज्योतिश्चरणाभिधानात्

jyotiścaraṇābhidhānāt

jyotiḥ—the light; caraṇa—feet; abhidhānāt—from the manifestations.

TRANSLATION

From the manifestations, the light is one of the feet (of all that exists).

COMMENTARY

To understand this sūtra, we need to look at the following statements from the Chāndogya Upaniṣad 3.12.5-6 which mention the feet (pada):

Chandogya Upaniṣad 3.12-5

saiṣā catuṣpadā ṣaḍvidhā gāyatrī tadetadṛcābhyanūktam

Word-for-word meanings

Sā eṣā gāyatrī catuṣpadā—this gāyatrī has four feet [i.e., quarters]; ṣaṣvidhā—each of them sixfold; tat etat ṛcā abhyanūktam—this is stated in a Ṛk mantra.

Translation

The Gāyatrī has four quarters, each being six-fold. This is what is stated in a Ṛk mantra.

Chandogya Upaniṣad 3.12-6

tāvānasya mahimā tato jyāyāṃśca pūruṣaḥ
pādo'sya sarvā bhūtāni tripādasyāmṛtaṃ divīti

Word-for-word meanings

Tāvān—like this; asya mahima—its glory; tataḥ jyāyān ca puruṣaḥ—that [i.e., the glory] of the puruṣa is still greater; pādaḥ asya sarvā [i.e., sarvāṇi] bhūtāni—all the created entities constitute one foot [or, quarter] of him; tripād asya—[the remaining] three feet [or, quarters] of him; amṛtam divi—are in the place devoid of death.

Translation

Its glory is like this. But the glory of the puruṣa is still greater. All the created living entities (bhutani) constitute one-quarter of him. The remaining three quarters comprise the place that is devoid of death (or repeated birth and death).

The context for this śrutī is that the Gāyatri mantra is compared to the body of the living entity. The Gāyatri meter has 24 syllables, and in the above śrutī, it is said to be divided into 4 parts comprising 6 parts each. The nature of these 24 parts and what they represent in Gāyatri is an involved topic, but briefly, Gāyatri is the worship of the sun. The initial terms *bhū*, *bhuvar*, and *svar* represent the three upper planetary systems in Vedic cosmology to which the light of the sun reaches. There are 4 other planetary systems above these three (*jana*, *tapa*, *mahar*, and *satya*) that are not illuminated by the sun's light. Similarly, there are 7 planetary systems below the *bhū-loka* which are also not illuminated by the sun's light. Therefore, Gāyatri is specifically focused on the glorification of the sun, and the mantra points this out clearly. Since the sun illuminates these three planetary systems, it is sometimes referred to as Surya-Narāyanā or the incarnation of Lord Viṣṇu in the material world. The Ādityas beginning with Surya are also said to be representations of Lord Viṣṇu. The orbit of the sun is sometimes divided into 12 parts (the months) and at other times into 24 parts (the fortnights). For a discussion of the significance of these 12- and 24-fold divisions, I would refer the interested reader to my book *Cosmic Theogony*.

The main point is now made in the next śrutī which states that even this Gāyatri (representing the sun god and hence the material world) is only one-fourth of all that exists; the remaining three-quarters of existence comprises of the place that is *amrtam* or devoid of death (*mrta* represents death). In short, the place of birth and death (the material world) is one-fourth of the total existence. Also, the śrutī mentions the puruṣa and glorifies Him as someone greater than this material world, and the material world is precisely one-fourth of His full expansion; the remaining three-fourth is a realm beyond birth and death.

A brief description of the three-fourths of the existence is in order here. Throughout the Vedic texts, the living entity is described as having three aspects—*sat*, *chit*, and *ānanda*. The term *sat* represents consciousness or how we become connected or related to something other than the self. The term *chit* denotes cognition and conation—which follows the connection to something. Finally, ānanda denotes pleasure derived from cognition and conation. Hence, there is a progression from consciousness to knowledge and action to pleasure. The three parts transcendent to the material world are the domains in which these three aspects of the soul are dominant (the other two become subordinate). In the realm of Goloka, pleasure or ānanda dominates. In the realm of Vaikuṇṭha, the *chit* or the cognitive capacity and the concepts cognized by this capacity predominates. And in Brahman, the *sat* (consciousness) is dominant. Apart from these three, where there is no birth and death, is the material world, where birth and death recur. Thus, Brahman is one-fourth of the existence; another half is beyond Brahman, and one-fourth of the existence is material.

In three parts of this existence (excluding Brahman), the living entities are distinct due to the desire for pleasure. Since they are originally differentiated from Brahman, in one sense they are originally part of Brahman such that Brahman is the origin of everything. In another sense, once the differentiation has occurred, the remaining undifferentiated part is Brahman and hence it is one-fourth of the existence. Since the desire for pleasure is abundant, the differentiation is not considered temporary; otherwise, the living entities in Goloka and Vaikuṇṭha would not be considered *amrta* or beyond birth and death.

The living entities with material desire collectively constitute the form called Narāyanā when they are present within His body. He is the father of the materially embodied souls who undergo birth and death. However, because the material creation is not eternal, sometimes the ātmā exists within Narāyanā (when He breathes in), and sometimes the same living entity is embodied in matter (when He breathes out). Even within the body of Narāyanā, the living entity still has the desire for enjoyment, but enjoyment doesn't exist. Therefore, even though the soul is within Narāyanā, it is not considered liberated. In the strictest of senses, Brahman is that realm of souls liberated from matter which has transcended the body of Narāyanā and has become undifferentiated.

Finally, a few words might be said regarding the use of the term 'light' in this sūtra. Concerning Brahman, it is the agency that illuminates matter. What we mean by illumination is *differentiation*. To know something is to distinguish it from the other things. For example, in a dark room, we cannot differentiate things from one another, and hence there is no knowledge. The presence of Brahman in matter causes matter to be differentiated into *objects*. The material elements are eternal, but they are merged into the higher elements (as already discussed in the purport for 1.1.9 (9). Under the presence of the soul, these elements begin expanding from subtle to gross. This separation can be called illumination because we can know the difference between the elements. Since the presence of Brahman causes this separation, hence it can be called "light".

However, given the sūtra's context—a verse from Chāndogya Upaniṣad is mentioned referring to Gāyatri, which celebrates the sun god—and the reference to the sun god (in the material world) is then called one-fourth of all that exists, the more likely interpretation should be that "light" refers to the sun. Factually, whether we call the sun a materially embodied being who powers the universe, or we consider it the spiritual entity which helps us discriminate the things in this world, there is no contradiction in understanding. These can be regarded as different points of emphasis in relation to the same sūtra.

QUESTION

You have said that the liberation for the soul is obtained due to faith in Brahman, and by the chanting of the mantra. But now you have said that the most important of these mantras—the Gāyatri—refers to one-fourth of the existence, which is the material creation. So, previously you said that the chanting of mantra leads to liberation, but now you have said that the mantra refers to the beings in the material world. How can these mantras be suitable for liberation from the modes of nature when they pertain to the material world?

This problem was seen earlier where the reader questioned the idea that if the material world comprises the three modes of nature, then even the mantra would be these modes, as they are in the material world. How can we consider them to be the causes of liberation? To that question, the Vedānta Sūtra had responded that many parts of the Vedic scripture pertain to the three modes, but some do not. It is these parts that are considered the source of liberation.

However, now that Gāyatri has been implicated (due to reference from Chāndogya Upaniṣad) as referring to the sun in the material world, the question can be raised again—if the most important mantra is referencing the sun god, then how can we expect that other mantra will lead to transcendence?

1.1.25 (25)

छन्दोऽभधिानान्नेतचित् न तथा चेतोऽर्पणनगिदात् तथा हि दर्शनम्

chando'bhidhānānneti cet na tathā ceto'rpaṇanigadāt tathā hi darśanam

chhandas—meters like Gāyatri; abhidhānāt—from manifestations; na—not; iti—thus; cet—if; na—not; tathā—thus; ceto'rpaṇa—offering of the mind; nigadāt—from that which has left (i.e., the source of the manifestation); tathā—in the same way; hi—certainly; darśanam—it is seen.

TRANSLATION

If it is said that Brahman is not denoted by the mantra (such as Gāyatri), we reply not so, because thus i.e., by means of the meter, the offering of the mind on that—from which the manifestation has emerged (i.e., the Lord)—is stated. In the same way, the certainly it is seen (that soul dedicates to the Lord).

COMMENTARY

The impersonalist argues that everything in the material world is comprised of modes, so there cannot be a representation of transcendence in this world. But this line of argument is not without its flaws. For instance, we can now ask: If everything is material, then even the scripture being read is also material. How can the knowledge in the scripture be considered transcendent, or leading to liberation into Brahman, if everything in the world is tainted by the three modes? The argument is therefore fallacious because it denies even the validity of the scripture, and hence the source of all knowledge. Ultimately, it decries even the validity of impersonal philosophy and leads to voidism: Everything is duality and illusory, so freeing oneself from all experience must be liberation. Śri Śankarācārya battled against voidism, with the primary aim to establish the authority of the Vedic texts. In short, he aimed to say that everything else may be material, but the scripture is not material. The Vedic texts are thus said to be *apauruṣeya* or not of human origin. As the sounds are spoken by the Lord Himself, they are considered different from material nature.

However, now, one might object that not all portions of Vedic texts are transcendental. And since we have already rejected those statements, then does Gāyatri also fall into the same category? It has also been stated earlier that anything that doesn't lead to liberation from the material world must be rejected. So, this sūtra answers the question by saying that by chanting this mantra it is observed that one obtains liberation from the material world. In short, even though Gāyatri is described as praising the sun, it is not to be considered a material portion of the Vedas. The reason for this discrimination is not explained here, but in other texts such as the Śrīmad Bhāgavatam, the sun-god is called Sūrya-Nārāyana. Like Lord Nārāyana glances over material nature, and thereby experience is created, in the same way, Surya glances over the material world and makes it visible to everyone else. So, his role in the material world is like that of Nārāyana in relation to material energy (outside the universe).

QUESTION

You have said that the entirety of existence is divided into four parts, which were originally manifest from Brahman. This manifestation also includes the material world in which the souls are injected by the Lord. Thus, aren't you implying that the material world is also differentiated from Brahman? Since Brahman is all that exists, and the material world is differentiated from this Brahman, shouldn't the material world be considered a part of Brahman?

1.1.26 (26)
भूतादिपादव्यपदेशोपपत्तेश्चैवम्
bhūtādipādavyapadeśopapatteścaivam

bhūtādi—the origin of living entities; pada—foot, part; vyap-adeśa—declaration or expression; upapatteḥ—due to the proof; ca—also; evam—thus.

TRANSLATION

And thus, also the origin of the materially embodied living entities (*bhūta* = the embodied living entity, ādi = the origin of these living entities) or the existence of all material elements (*bhūta* = Earth, Water,

Fire, Air, and Ether, ādi = etc. or other such material elements of the material universe) are one foot because such a declaration can also be proven thus (using the above statements).

COMMENTARY

There can be confusion in the translation of this sūtra because *bhūtādi* has two possible interpretations. First, the term *bhūta* is used to refer to material elements such as Earth, Water, Fire, Air, and Ether; they are distinguished from the *tanmātra* and the *indriya*, and from the mind, intellect, ego, and *mahattattva*. The term ādi can now refer to 'etc.' indicating that there are many such elements. Therefore, the term *bhūtādi* would now refer to the collection of all material elements. Second, the term *bhūta* is also used to refer to the 'embodied', meaning that there is a soul which has taken birth in the material world and will eventually discard this body and take rebirth. The term ādi will now refer to the origin of these living entities. Thus, the term *bhūtādi* will refer to the origin of all the materially embodied living entities. If we take the first interpretation, then the implication is that the material world is a *pada* or part of the entire existence. If, however, we take the second interpretation, then the origin of the living entities (i.e., Brahman from where the living entity has fallen into the material existence) is one part of the entire existence from which the material world expands. In the former case, we would say that the material world is one-fourth of existence and in the latter case, we would assert that Brahman is one-fourth of all the existence. While they assert different claims, ultimately, both claims are true, because Brahman is one-fourth (after the material world and Goloka and Vaikuṇṭha are separated), and the material world is one-fourth (as already stated in the statement of Chāndogya Upaniṣad).

Of these two possible interpretations, the claim of the first was already made in 1.1.24 (24) where it was said that the material world is one-fourth of all the existence. If we take the interpretation that *bhūtādi* refers to the material elements, this sūtra would repeat the claim made previously. If instead, we take the second interpretation, the claim that Brahman is one-fourth of all the existence would be new (recall that the śrutī of Chāndogya Upaniṣad merely stated that there are three parts beyond the material world; it wasn't clearly asserted that Brahman is one part; while we had explained that Brahman which dominates in the *sat* is one part, this wasn't obvious either from the sūtra or from the śrutī of Chāndogya Upaniśad). Therefore, while both interpretations are true, we prefer the second interpretation (namely that Brahman is one-fourth of the existence) because of its novelty (the principle of logical progression due to the Vedānta Sūtra being *nyāya-prasthāna*). Therefore, if there are two interpretations, we reject one of those interpretations on the grounds of novelty.

The implication of this sūtra is that Brahman is not the only transcendent destination. While this was previously asserted (that there are three regions beyond the realm of birth and death), this sūtra states that Brahman is only one of those regions. The novelty in the earlier sūtra was that there are three regions beyond the material world. The novelty in this sūtra is that Brahman is one of those three regions. While the position of the impersonal philosopher isn't entirely incorrect—in the sense that there is an undifferentiated region beyond the material differentiation—it is ultimately false in asserting that *all* differentiation is material because there are non-material regions of differentiation too.

QUESTION

In the beginning, you said that Brahman is the source of everything. Now you are saying that Brahman is only one-fourth of everything. Previously, everything was part of Brahman. Now, Brahman is also called a part (of something which is so far unstated). Should we consider Brahman as being separate from the other three parts, or should we regard it as the source of everything?

1.1.27 (27)

उपदेशभेदान्नेति चेन् नोभयस्मन्निन् अपय् अवरिोधात्

upadeśabhedānneti cet na ubhayasminnapyavirodhāt

upadeśa—teaching; bhedāt—from the difference; na—not; iti cet—if it be said; ca—also; ena—of this; na—no; ubhayasmin—in both; api—even; avirodhāt—due to there being no contradiction.

TRANSLATION

If it be said that this is different from the teaching (i.e., that Brahman is everything) we say not so. Also, of this (i.e., that which was stated in the last sūtra—namely, that Brahman is one-fourth is not different from the teaching). In both cases (of Brahman being whole and one-fourth), there is no contradiction.

COMMENTARY

One of the sources of confusion in the Vedānta sūtra is the presence of many apparently contradictory statements, and unless they are taken collectively, there is scope for confusion. For instance, in 1.1.2 (2), it was stated that Brahman is the origin of everything. Then, in 1.1.12 (12), it was stated that this Oneness divides into many individuals because of the desire for pleasure. Now, this could be taken to mean that once the division has occurred, the Oneness no longer exists. But this assertion is refuted in 1.1.13 (13) which says that the desire for pleasure is *prachur* or abundant, but it is not absolute, which means that the undivided Oneness still exists if there is no desire for pleasure. Then, in 1.1.6 (6) it has been stated that the soul is beyond the three modes of nature, indicating that it can fall into material influence. Hence, the position in Brahman is not absolute because—(a) there are souls in the three-fourth realm which are not in Brahman, and (b) there are souls in material nature which are not in Brahman. The impersonal philosopher considers the latter of these two alternatives and he might cite 1.1.7 (7) to say that the soul can be liberated into Brahman. But in the process, he neglects other statements—such as, (a) 1.1.21 (21) which states that the ātmā is different from the Paramātma, and (b) 1.1.22 (22) which states that Paramātma is the source of ātmā and expands from there into matter. The correct understanding is that which treats all the statements as being true.

With these clarifications, we can answer the doubt—namely, whether Brahman is the origin of everything (as stated in 1.1.2 (2)) or whether Brahman is only a part (as stated in 1.1.26 (26)). The answer is that both statements are true, based on the context. As the original Oneness from which differentiation occurred due to desire, Brahman is the cause of everything. However, when the differentiation has occurred, then the undifferentiated part is one-fourth. If Brahman refers to the original Oneness, then it is the cause of everything. However, if Brahman refers to the state devoid of the desire for pleasure, then it remains as one of the four parts that are not differentiated into individuals. This resolves the contention between two conflicting ideas, namely, whether Brahman is the source of everything or whether Brahman is a part of the entire existence. Both statements are correct, based on the context—i.e., whether we look at reality before differentiation or after the differentiation has occurred.

Topic 11

QUESTION

You have stated previously that ākāśa or material space originates in a procreating organ, and this space is differentiated into many points, which are connected to the source through prāṇa. In short, that light and the source of light are never separated, even when light has emanated from the source. But this was in the context of the material creation. What does it mean for the soul?

1.1.28 (28)

पुराणस्तथानुगमात्

prāṇastathānugamāt

prāṇaḥ—the prāṇa; tathā—in the same way; anugamāt—from servitude.

TRANSLATION

In the same way, from the servitude of prāṇa (the soul is a servant).

COMMENTARY

We might recall, that a similar claim (*ata eva pranah*) was made in 1.1.23 (23), indicating that the living entity is a particle of light connected to its source through prāṇa. That statement is being referred to in this sūtra through the term *tatha* which indicates "in the same way". But we might wonder, why the same claim is made again when it has been made previously? The reason is that the previous assertion was made in the context of the material creation, wherein 1.1.22 (22) it was said that ākāśa (indicating the substrate on which the material world is sustained) is produced from a *linga* or an organ of procreation. This then led to the question of why the ātmā is not considered separated once it has been created, and the response to that was that despite being present in the material nature, the origin of space and the different points in this space are to be considered connected by prāṇa. This sūtra is, however, talking about Brahman, rather than the soul injected into material nature. And yet, it is stating that just as in the case of material nature the ātmā was connected to its source through prāṇa, similarly, even in Brahman, it is connected in the same way. Indeed, it goes on to say that the ātmā even in Brahman is a subordinate follower or servant. What is it subordinate to? That is not clarified in this sūtra. However, because of the comparison to the previous sūtra, we can infer that there is a similar connection to the source, of which Brahman is a collective emanation.

This sūtra assumes importance as the impersonal philosopher argues that because there is no differentiation in Brahman, therefore, the distinction between the ātmā and the Paramātma disappears. This sūtra refutes that claim, although in a nuanced manner. It doesn't say that there is differentiation *inside* Brahman. It rather says that Brahman (as a whole) is subordinate to the Absolute Truth (the latter is implied due to the comparison with the previous sūtra). So, the claim that because there is no differentiation in Brahman, therefore, the ātmā and the Absolute Truth have become identical is rejected, because the difference is *in between* Brahman and the Absolute Truth, and the former is a subordinate follower of the latter. Not only are they distinct, but they are also not equal (if one doubted that they could be separate domains, and the domain in which the Absolute Truth is dominant is separate from that of Brahman).

QUESTION

If prāṇa is the life force and the ātmā is the living entity, doesn't this living entity possess its separate life force independent of the Absolute Truth? Why is the life force connected to the Absolute Truth (in the material world and in Brahman)? What is the point of calling something 'living' if it doesn't have its separate life force? Without that life force, shouldn't it be considered dead?

The situation of the living entity being described here is like that of a child connected to its mother through an umbilical cord—the prāṇa being that cord. Just as the child is dependent on the mother for nutrients and life force through this umbilical cord, similarly, the soul is dependent on the Absolute Truth for its life. The term *anugamat* in the previous sūtra indicates that because of this connection, the ātmā remains subordinate to the Absolute Truth. In short, if the umbilical cord is cut, then the ātmā would be lifeless. Now, this raises the question: In what sense is the ātmā a living entity if it doesn't even have an independent life force? Just as a machine is lifeless without the power supply, shouldn't we consider the ātmā lifeless without the life force energizing it?

1.1.29 (29)

न वक्तुरात्मोपदेशादतिचेत् अध्यात्मसबन्धभूमा ह्यस्मनि्

na vakturātmopadeśāditi cet
adhyātmasambandhabhūmā hyasmin

na—not; vaktuḥ—the statement; ātmā—the self; upadeśa—teaching; iti—thus; cet—if; adhyātma—spiritual or soul; sambandha—connection, relation; bhūmā—the numerous; hi—certainly; asmin—in this (way).

TRANSLATION

If it is said that the teaching (of prāṇa) is not a statement about the self, (then we say) that the soul's connection to the numerous is certainly in this (way).

COMMENTARY

To understand this sūtra, we need to understand the role of prāṇa. The ātmā is well-known to be sat-chit-ānanda, which means it has the capacity for awareness, cognition, and pleasure. However, to create an experience, these three capacities must be combined. As an example, by directing our awareness to an apple, we can have diverse types of cognitions—such as color, smell, form, taste, etc. Similarly, corresponding to each such cognition, there can be varieties of pleasure—e.g., we can particularly enjoy the smell, tolerate the color, and dislike the shape. Likewise, each such type of pleasure, resulting from likes and dislikes, can emerge out of many different cognitions (e.g., we can enjoy clothes, books, houses, etc.) by directing our awareness to different things. What we call 'experience' is thus a combination of awareness, cognition, and pleasure.

However, each type of awareness, cognition, and pleasure *underdetermines* each other. The awareness can be directed to many different things. Following this, each such thing can be cognized in many ways. Subsequently, such cognition can lead to a variety of pleasures. To create an experience, awareness must be directed to something specific. Following this, a certain kind of cognition (e.g., taste or smell) must be selected. Following this, our desires and attitudes must be brought to bear upon that cognition. Therefore, an experience combines a specific type of awareness, a specific type of cognition, and a specific kind of pleasure. Since each aspect of experience underdetermines each other, there is a choice (of awareness, cognition, and pleasure) in the combination.

The 'field' or *kṣetra* to be known comprises many properties, to which we can relate in different ways, with different attitudes. Thus, the experience cannot be determined only by the property. For instance, we cannot say—look at John—and the rest would be automatically decided. You also must know the relation to John—e.g., whether you are looking at him as your father, son, friend, spouse, employee, etc. Similarly, you have the nature of likes and dislikes about certain types of cognition (e.g., race, height, facial features, clothes, etc.), which will decide whether you enjoy or suffer or remain neutral. The key point is that in addition to the thing being known, there is also the nature of the knower and the relationship between the knower and the known. Each of these three plays an equally important role in the construction of experience. We can call these the subjective, objective, and intersubjective components of the experience. Since they don't determine each other, their combination is a *choice*.

Prāṇa is the power of choice—or the power to combine the subjective, objective, and intersubjective—to create an experience. While the ātmā is the possibility for experience, this possibility cannot become experience without the power of choice. This sūtra (and the previous one where ātmā is said to be connected to the Absolute Truth) states that the power of choice doesn't belong to the ātmā. It belongs to the Absolute Truth and by this power the Absolute Truth places the ātmā into a combination of objective, subjective, and intersubjective, thus creating its experience. Factually, the experience of the ātmā is subordinate, because the primary *kṣetrajña* is the Absolute Truth. He knows all combinations of the above three ingredients, due to which He is omniscient and omnipresent. However, the ātmā knows a part or a specific combination of the three ingredients, which places it at a certain position in the *kṣetra*. In the material world, the *kṣetra* comprises the objective, subjective, and intersubjective, and the ātmā can roam on this field. This roaming is due to the change in prāṇa. Factually, the ātmā is not moving; the movement is of the prāṇa. The ātmā is only connected to the *kṣetra* by prāṇa—giving it a 'position' in the *kṣetra*—creating an experience. Thus, it is said that the prāṇa 'carries' the ātmā from one place to another. The ātmā is the possibility of experience, but it depends on the prāṇa to convert that possibility into an experience. In the material world, the combination comprises objects, relations to those objects, and the material desires which create pleasure, and prāṇa combines them into an experience.

When the soul is liberated, the material experience (produced from material objects, relations to these objects, and the material likes and dislikes) ceases. However, this cessation is not the end of the experience. The ātmā can still have an experience, even though it is liberated from the material world. Since the material world is missing, and the ātmā hasn't yet entered a world of differentiated living entities (i.e., Goloka and Vaikuṇṭha), the ātmā has self-experience, and this state is called Brahman. By this self-experience, the ātmā knows that it exists eternally, and its consciousness or awareness is directed toward itself. The ātmā's cognition is the cognition of the self. And its pleasure is the pleasure of enjoying oneself. This *atmarāma* state is liberation into Brahman. However, as has been noted earlier (in the description of Brahman as 'space'), even in this *atmarāma* state, the ātmā is connected to the Absolute Truth through prāṇa. Thus, there is self-knowledge, but also a relation to the Absolute Truth.

It is evident from this sūtra that the prāṇa of the Absolute Truth spreads throughout the *kṣetra* or the field to be known, thus producing experience. Just like in our body, the soul is situated in the heart, but its experience spreads in the body due to the spreading of prāṇa through the nerves and veins, similarly, the Absolute Truth is situated in one place, but due to prāṇa spreading throughout the existence, He knows everything. The ātmā can then be understood as participating in the experience of one such vein or nerve. The implication is that the ātmā is a part of the Absolute Truth for two reasons. First, the primary experiencer is the Absolute Truth and the ātmā experiences due to the

Absolute Truth's experience. Second, the power to creates this experience (by combining awareness, cognition, and pleasure) is controlled by the Absolute Truth.

The use of *bhūmā* indicates that there is a multitude or a collection of such individuals even in Brahman. However, because each ātmā is focused on self-enjoyment, it remains unaware of the existence of other ātmā and hence doesn't relate to them. This self-focused experience is advised in many scriptures where the ātmā withdraws its consciousness inward—away from the objects of the external world—and focuses it upon itself. Ideally, this focus must be upon the Absolute Truth, however, it is possible to focus it on the self. Once the awareness has been withdrawn from other individuals, they practically cease to exist for the ātmā—as far their *experience* is concerned. They haven't ceased to exist factually, but for all practical purposes, their unawareness of each other's existence entails that the differentiation between the self and the other has ceased; they consider themselves to be both knower and known. Once the knower and the known have become identical, the differentiation is experientially lost. Thus, the self-focused consciousness is said to be *undifferentiated*; it is not a factual unification of all ātmā, but a lack of observed difference. By closing our eyes the world ceases to exist in experience, similarly, by withdrawing our consciousness, the difference between the knower and the known ceases.

Since the lack of differentiation pertains to the awareness of the ātmā, not a factual Oneness of all the ātmā, the term *bhūmā* (indicating a multitude or collection) is used in this sūtra. Each ātmā is still different from the Absolute Truth and has a 'location' in the space expanded from the Absolute Truth. Thus, Brahman is sometimes called the liberated state of ātmā and at other times identified with the prāṇa (of the Absolute Truth by which He knows the ātmā).

QUESTION

You are saying that as the individual ātmā is expanded from the Absolute Truth, similarly, the individual prāṇa is expanded from the prāṇa of the Absolute Truth. What is this collective prāṇa that expands the individual prāṇa?

From the previous sūtra, the relation between ātmā and prāṇa has been explicated. The relation between ātmā and the Absolute Truth has also been explicated. We have seen that the Absolute Truth is omniscient but the ātmā is a limited knower. With such distinctions between the possibility of experience and the power of experience, it seems obvious that to be omniscient, the Absolute Truth must possess greater power than the ātmā. So, the next question becomes: What is this power of experience, which subsequently expands?

1.1.30 (30)

शास्त्रदृष्ट्या तूपदेशो वामदेववत्

śāstradṛṣṭyā tūpadeśo vāmadevavat

śāstradṛṣṭyā—through insight based on scripture or as attested by śrutī; tu—but; upadeśaḥ—instruction; vāmadevavat—like that of Vāmadeva.

TRANSLATION

The declaration (about prāṇa) is possible due to such attestations by śrutī, as in the case of Vāmadeva.

COMMENTARY

In the Tantra, Lord Śiva is said to have five faces; one of these faces is called Vāmadeva who is the representation of prāṇa. The following asserts this:

Aitareya Aranyaka 2.1.5:
> The Devas (speech, etc.) said to him (the breath): 'He is to be loved by all of us.' Because the Devas said of him, that he was to be loved (vāma) by all of them, therefore there is (the poet of the fourth Mandala of the Rig-veda, called) Vāmadeva. Therefore, people call him who is really Prāṇa (breath), Vāmadeva.

The previous sūtra asserted that prāṇa is not owned by the ātmā. This was in the context of verses that described the Brahman as prāṇa. Now, this sūtra gives another example in the context of the material world. However, there is a difference between these two descriptions. In 1.1.23 (23), it was said that the relation between ātmā and the Absolute Truth is through prāṇa because He is the seed-giving father, and

151

by this connection, the ātmā could know the Absolute Truth. In this sūtra, the knowledge of the material world is being described and the prāṇa is a form of Lord Śiva. Thus, we must understand that the same term prāṇa is used in many ways, depending on the type of experience. It always represents the combination of the three aspects of experience. However, these three aspects could pertain to the self-experience of the ātmā, the experience of the Absolute Truth, and finally, the experience of the material world.

Since Lord Śiva is the controller of the material energy, in this sūtra, prāṇa refers to the combination of the three aspects in matter, regardless of which ātmā experiences this combination. This is still called prāṇa; however, it is a material energy that produces material experience, which the soul can obtain if it applies its prāṇa given to it by Paramātma. Therefore, there are two types of combinations—(a) the combination of three aspects of matter to create an experienceable entity, and (b) the attachment of the ātmā to this entity. The former must be considered material, and the latter must be considered spiritual, although this spiritual energy has been directed toward a material combination. The former is a material choice to combine the material ingredients comprising relation, cognition, and emotion. The latter is a spiritual choice to direct the power of experience in the ātmā toward this material combination. Therefore, even though prāṇa is referred to in relation to the Absolute Truth and Vāmadeva, these two types of prāṇa factually refer to different things.

QUESTION

You are saying that the agency by which the ātmā creates its experience is not under its control; this control rests with the Absolute Truth and with Vāmadeva. But, if I'm not in control of my experience, then how can I accept or reject any spiritual process that might liberate me from the material existence? My liberation would depend on the will of the controllers of prāṇa. It would then follow that I cannot liberate myself; I must just rely on their grace.

From several sūtras, the relation between ātmā and prāṇa has been explicated and it has become clear that while the ātmā has the potentiality of experience, to have any experience, the ātmā must rely on prāṇa, which was originally described as the connection to the Absolute Truth and then as Vāmadeva. With these descriptions, it seems obvious that the ātmā is helpless in producing its own experience because the choice by which experience is created is under the control of the Absolute Truth or Vāmadeva. If the ātmā has no choice, then it is legitimate to ask how it can be held responsible for its actions? In fact, how can we say that the ātmā fell from the association of the Absolute Truth into the material world, and how can it liberate itself from the modes of nature? Since the power rests in the hands of the Absolute Truth, only He can liberate the ātmā from the clutches of material nature; the ātmā cannot do anything. This position in fact seems a straightforward denial of the free will of the soul.

1.1.31 (31)

जीवमुख्यप्राणलिङ्गान्नेति चेत् न उपासात्रैविध्यात् आश्रितत्वात् इह
तद्योगात्

jīvamukhyaprāṇaliṅgānneti cet na upāsātraividhyāt
āśritatvāt iha tadyogāt

jīvā—the ātmā; mukhya—the leader or controller; prāṇa—prāṇa; liṅgāt—that came from the progenitor; na—not; iti—thus; cet—if; na—not; upāsa—worship, meditation; traividhyāt—from the three knowledge; āśrita—taking shelter; tvāt—of Him; iha—in this way; tadyogāt—from the union with Him.

TRANSLATION

If it is said that the ātmā is not the controller of prāṇa because it came from the progenitor (the Absolute Truth), then we say no. Worship arising from the three knowledge (the three Vedas called Rig, Yajur, and Sāma), taking shelter of Him in this way, and from the union with Him (is in the soul's control).

COMMENTARY

We have discussed how the ātmā has the three potentialities for awareness, cognition, and pleasure. Of these three, the potentiality for pleasure is the controlling agency, and (generally) drives the other two. For instance, if you desire to eat tasty food, then by your awareness you will first find the relevant type of food, and then by your cognition, you will taste that food, following which the desire for pleasure will be fulfilled. The potentiality for pleasure is the ability to have desires. The fulfillment of that desire is a pleasure. Therefore, on its own, the ātmā can have desires, but these cannot be fulfilled without the power of prāṇa. The ānanda aspect of the ātmā exists as the production of desires, and the same aspect also exists as pleasure or enjoyment in the fulfilled state.

Unless the ātmā is forced by circumstances (called good or bad *karma*), it pursues its desires through its ability for awareness and cognition. However, even if the ātmā is thus forced, the desire for pleasure always exists. For instance, you might not receive tasty food due to circumstances, and you may be forced to taste unpalatable food, but the *desire* for tasty food can still exist. Thus, the ātmā doesn't have the power to acquire tasty food on its own because the fulfillment of desires requires the combination of the three agencies—i.e., the acquisition of tasty food followed by the ability (the tongue) to acquire the cognition—and this combination depends on prāṇa, which is under the control of the Absolute Truth. However, the desire for tasty food is independent of whether the tasty food can be acquired, or the tongue is capable of tasting.

Hence, there is a subtle difference between a *choice*, which as we previously noted is the power to combine the three potentialities to create an experience, and the *desire* for that experience without its fulfillment. In general, the desire arises, following which there must be the power to fulfill the desire. But even if the desire is unfulfilled, it can continue to exist in the ātmā in a latent form. With this distinction between *choice* and *desire*, we can say that the ātmā isn't free to fulfill its desires, but it is free to desire. Therefore, even if the prāṇa—or the power for fulfilling desires—is not in its control, the desire is in its control.

With this distinction, we can understand this sūtra, which denies that the soul lacks free will. The denial is that the ātmā can desire, and if by that desire it takes shelter of the Absolute Truth and develops the urges to follow the methods prescribed in the three Vedas, then it can perform yoga. It has previously been mentioned that the ātmā is liberated from the material modes by yoga. The practice of yoga requires some effort, which then needs the power of prāṇa under the control of the Absolute Truth. So, what can the ātmā do to obtain this power, to practice yoga? The answer is simply desiring. Just as the Absolute Truth is fulfilling other desires of the ātmā—in the material world—He can similarly fulfill the desire for relation to Himself if it so arises. Implicit here is the understanding that the Absolute Truth fulfills the desire of the ātmā.

In the Bhagavad-Gita 7.14, Lord Kṛṣṇa states the following:

daivī hy eṣā guṇa-mayī
mama māyā duratyayā
mām eva ye prapadyante
māyām etāṁ taranti te

This divine energy of Mine, consisting of the three modes of material nature, is difficult to overcome. But those who have surrendered unto Me can easily cross beyond it.

Similarly, in Bhagavad-Gita 10.10, Lord Kṛṣṇa states the following:

teṣāṁ satata-yuktānāṁ
bhajatāṁ prīti-pūrvakam
dadāmi buddhi-yogaṁ taṁ
yena mām upayānti te

To those who are constantly devoted and worship Me with love, I give the understanding by which they can come to Me.

BG 10.10 indicates that simply by devotion, the Lord provides the intelligence by which He can be attained. The use of *dadāmi* indicates that "I provide"; this means that the power to attain Him is not because of one's personal capacity to attain Him; rather, the power to attain Him is provided by Him. Furthermore, it is provided if someone is devotionally *yukta* or associated. Similarly, in BG 7.14, it is indicated that overcoming the material nature is very hard; however, those who are devoted to Kṛṣṇa can easily cross beyond it.

God is well-known in all religions as omniscient and omnipotent. However, whether He is also benevolent is sometimes debated—especially because the ātmā suffers in the material world as many of its desires are unfulfilled. The existence of evil leads many people to argue that God is not benevolent. However, in the above sūtras, it has been clarified that even those engaged in evil are doing so using the power of the Absolute Truth, based on His approval. This approval is based on two things—whether the ātmā desires and whether it deserves. If these two conditions are satisfied, then the Absolute Truth delegates His power. A similar kind of fulfillment is possible even in the case of yoga—provided we desire, and we become deserving. By desiring, we obtain the power to practice yoga and by the perfection of this yoga, we become deserving. Therefore, liberation from material existence would follow the same process as that which is used for the fulfillment of other (material) desires.

It is said that "man proposes, and God disposes". This sūtra also asserts the same, with one difference: The man who proposes must also be deserving for God to fulfill the man's desires. While desiring is the start, one must use this desire to become deserving of the result. The act of deserving is explained here using the term *traividya*; it indicates that one must follow the processes prescribed in the Vedas to become qualified. One cannot whimsically invent the method of transcendence. Desiring is good, and God will provide the intelligence to understand His nature and the process to attain Him, but obedience to the revealed knowledge in the Vedas is also a mandatory precondition.

SECTION 2

Topic 1

QUESTION

You are describing the path of bhakti-yoga or surrender to God. But there are other recognized systems of yoga. Since the previous sūtra said that by following the three Vedas, we perform yoga, then how can taking shelter of God be considered the primary method? Isn't there aṣṭānga-yoga, karma-yoga, jñāna-yoga, etc.? In fact, the study of the Vedic literature is considered jñāna-yoga. So, how can you assert the validity of bhakti-yoga above all else?

It is understood that books are a source of knowledge. Knowledge requires reason and logic, often argument and counterargument, and upon a long and careful analysis of the subject matter one can arrive at some reasonable conclusions. The Vedic texts themselves describe Brahman which is well-known to be the impersonal reality into which the ātmā is supposed to merge. Especially the impersonal philosophers vociferously argue that the primary method of attainment of Brahman is jñāna-yoga. How can bhakti-yoga suddenly replace it?

1.2.1 (32)

सर्वत्र प्रसदिधोपदेशात्

sarvatra prasiddhopadeśāt

sarvatra—everywhere, in every Vedantic passage i.e., in all Upaniṣad; prasiddha—the well-known; upadeśāt—from the teaching.

TRANSLATION

From the teaching being well-known or famous everywhere.

COMMENTARY

The impersonalist assumes that bhakti-yoga is inferior to jñāna-yoga. He believes that by their intellect they can grasp the nature of ultimate reality. But if the sūtras in the previous section have been understood, then it has been amply clarified that the power to think—and indeed the understanding—only comes to one if they have taken the shelter of the Lord. The assumption that the ātmā has the power to think, act, and understand is itself rejected earlier, and this is not just true for transcendence but even for material desires. The ātmā is helpless; it is entirely dependent on the grace of the Lord even in this world. Therefore, to think that one can obtain the understanding by their effort is false. Rather, the shelter of the Lord is needed to obtain intelligence. Therefore, even if one is trying to understand the meaning of the Vedas, or the understanding of Brahman—and thereby merge into the Oneness—one must still take the shelter of the Lord, because only by His grace will he get the understanding.

This is not merely an obscure or isolated aspect of the Vedānta doctrine. As this sūtra asserts, this is to be found everywhere, and is, therefore 'famous'. In short, it should be considered the purport of the Upaniṣad and Vedānta.

QUESTION

It has previously been stated that Brahman is beyond the material guna or the qualities of material nature. This is sometimes called Nir-guna-Brahman. You are talking about a personal form of Brahman which would indicate that it is imbued with qualities (and should be called Saguna-Brahman). Shouldn't these qualities be considered material, and therefore not transcendental?

1.2.2 (33)

वविक्षतिगुणोपपत्तेश्च

vivakṣitaguṇopapatteśca

vivakṣita—one who is desirous to enter; guṇa—qualities; upapatteh—because of the reasonableness; ca—and, moreover.

TRANSLATION

Moreover, this method is reasonable or suitable for one who is desirous to enter the realm of (spiritual) guna (the domain of eternal differentiation).

COMMENTARY

The root *viv* in the above sūtra means differentiation. When joined with *ikshita* it means those desirous of this differentiation. We might recall from the previous section that existence has been divided into four quarters, of which three quarters are considered beyond the realm of birth and death. Of these three, Brahman is one of the quarters where differentiation doesn't exist; however, the other two—Goloka and Vaikuṇṭha—are places with differentiation. So, the argument that only Brahman is transcendence because it is beyond the material guna has already been refuted earlier. This sūtra further asserts that the method of bhakti-yoga is especially suitable for those who are desirous of entering these differentiated realms beyond the undifferentiated Brahman.

The use of guna is contentious. It can be used as a general noun to indicate 'qualities' or as a particular noun to indicate the three modes of nature. If we take the latter meaning, then the sūtra would mean "those who are desirous of entering the material world perform bhakti-yoga", which would contradict the previous sūtra. Hence, we must translate guna as the general noun 'qualities' rather than the specific noun indicating three modes of material nature.

This raises the question that if there are qualities beyond the material world, what are those? The Vaiṣṇava Tantra describes these qualities as being six-fold: knowledge, beauty, power, wealth, heroism, and renunciation. These qualities are present even in the material world; however, they are only manifest partially. For instance, there is a knowledge of architecture, a knowledge of medicine, a knowledge of chemistry, etc., but we cannot find *knowledge itself*. Similarly, there is beauty in art, beauty in music, beauty in poetry, etc., but we cannot find *beauty itself*. And yet, despite our inability to find anything corresponding to these words, we still use the terms 'knowledge' or 'beauty' in ordinary language. What do they mean? If we say that nothing corresponds to knowledge itself and beauty itself then these words become meaningless.

If the six words mentioned above are meaningless, then we cannot use them even in the material world. Thus, it is appropriate to say that while the material world doesn't have these qualities in fullness, they are present partly, and we don't know what their fullness is. But, if someone is desirous of being acquainted with these six qualities in their fullness, he must go beyond the material world, and that quest is indicated here by the term *vivikṣhita guna*, namely, those desirous of entering the realm of qualities in their original form.

QUESTION

But why can't these qualities be attained in the present world? After all, even in this world, everyone is searching for knowledge and beauty, everyone wants to be rich, powerful, and famous, and some people renounce the world. So, if they are desiring these things, why can't they attain them here? What would be the point of transcending this world if these can be attained here?

1.2.3 (34)
अनुपपत्तेस्तु न शारीरः
anupapattestu na śārīraḥ

anupapatteḥ—not being justifiable, because of the impossibility, because of the unreasonableness, because they are not appropriate; tu—but on the other hand; na—not; śārīraḥ—the embodied, the jīvā or the soul in the material world.

TRANSLATION

On the other hand, (those qualities) are not possible (in) the embodied.

COMMENTARY

The material world is described as an inverted tree in many places in Vedic literature. The root of this tree is the fullness of everything, but the trunks, branches, and leaves are parts of this fullness. Due to the duality of material nature, these qualities also become mutually opposed. For example, there is some beauty in the forest and some beauty in the mountain; but these are different kinds of beauties. We can combine these beauties if there were a mountain with a forest on top, but that would leave out other kinds of beauties—such as that of rivers, oceans, and cities. We can conceive that some of these beauties could be combined—e.g., that there can be a small river flowing on top of the mountain, but we cannot combine a mountain with a large river or a big city. Similarly, there is some pleasure in cold and some pleasure in heat, but we cannot combine their pleasures because they will negate each other. So, we can alternately enjoy the weather of heat and then enjoy the weather of cold, but we cannot enjoy them simultaneously. This is the reason that the origin of the material world—also called Pradhāna—is described as a state in which the three modes of nature are not differentiated. In other words, the entire universe exists, but the diversities have canceled each other out. When the material world is manifest, the diversities are spread into different locations. This means that if we combine the diversities, they cancel each other, and we cannot find any diversity. On the other hand, if we see diversity, they are already in disparate or different things. So, we cannot find one thing that has all the diversity; we can only find the cancellation of all diversity or distributed differences.

As we look around this world, we find mutually irreconcilable qualities because the material world is differentiated in a way that conflicting types of properties are found in different things and cannot be combined. The combination, in fact, would produce a self-contradiction: something would have to be simultaneously large and small, hot and cold, bitter and sweet, empty and full, etc. If these things were simultaneously combined, they would cancel each other, and the combination would be nothingness. Hence, it is impossible in the material world to find something that has all the beauty, all the knowledge, all the power, all the wealth, all the fame, and all the renunciation. These must be necessarily distributed because they come in mutually opposed diversities.

Of course, the same problem exists in the case of the transcendental world as well; there are contradictory qualities. However, God is described as the person Who has all these qualities as His *aspects*. He is, for example, simultaneously the largest and the smallest, but we can perceive only one aspect of these qualities at any one time. The reason is the nature of *our* cognition: we cannot perceive something that is simultaneously the largest and the smallest. To see something very small, we must look at it very closely, but to see something very large, we must be far away from it. Since we cannot be simultaneously near and far, therefore, it is impossible for us to know if the same thing is both the smallest and the largest. To possess this knowledge, we would have to be omniscient and omnipresent, such that we can perceive all the aspects simultaneously.

So, the reason that it is impossible for the ātmā to attain these properties in the material world (or any other world) is that it is localized. It can perceive one aspect, and therefore even in relation to God, the ātmā knows God in a specific manner—e.g., as the largest or the smallest—at any given time. Indeed, the different ātmā may even disagree with each other regarding their perception—e.g., one may insist that God is the smallest and the other may claim that He is the largest. There is no way to reconcile these contradictions except if the ātmā shifts its perspective and understands the other aspect. The limited nature of the jīvā ensures that it cannot know or acquire all these properties at once.

So, there are two reasons why jīvā cannot become like God. First, in the material world, the qualities are distributed in different locations and the jīvā can only be present in one place. Second, in the spiritual world, the qualities are combined in God, however, the jīvā is still limited to observe only one aspect of this infinite diversity. In both cases, the jīvā must be omniscient to attain the fullness of the six qualities, and that is something that it can never become.

QUESTION

We see that people become knowledgeable, powerful, rich, and famous for their work. Similarly, in the Vedic texts, it is described that one can ascend to heavenly planets through austerities. Why can't that be possible for acquiring the position of God? In short, why can't we become God by our effort?

Since the world is an inverted tree, there are descriptions of how the living entity can ascend this tree, rising to higher and higher positions where they acquire greater knowledge, beauty, power, fame, wealth, and renunciation. As one rises upward, the contradictions between the diversities are reconciled, as one ascends to a position from which they can observe multiple perspectives simultaneously. If the world were flat, then one could not observe multiple aspects simultaneously, because by being in one place one could not be in other places. But, if the world is an inverted tree, then by rising upward, the diversities are incrementally reconciled. So, the question becomes: If we can ascend this inverted tree to greater and greater heights, why can't we reach the root from where everything has diversified? Then we can also become God.

1.2.4 (35)
कर्मकर्तृव्यपदेशाच्च
karmakartṛvyapadeśācca

karma—action; kartṛ—agent; vyapadeśāt—due to the teaching; ca—and.

TRANSLATION
Also, due to the teaching of action and agent (distinction).

COMMENTARY
This sūtra explains that even those who rise higher in the material world haven't acquired perfection as their *native qualities*. These qualities are due to their *karma* and there is a distinction between the actor and the result of their activities. Due to the result of activities, one obtains a higher position temporarily, but because there is a difference between the actor and the result of actions, these acquisitions are not considered permanent, as the *karma* eventually ends, and the soul falls from its previously acquired position. God is in a different position; He is called Achyuta or One who never falls from His position. Therefore, while the soul can acquire a high position by his deeds, these are necessarily temporary, and because the soul falls it cannot be compared to God.

The implication is that God did not attain His position due to hard work. His actions are not the cause of His Godliness. Rather, He acts because He is already in that position. For the soul, his higher position is due to his actions. These actions can help him rise, but by this rise, he cannot become the source of his own existence. His existence is assumed before his actions are performed. Likewise, God's existence is assumed before His actions are considered.

QUESTION

But you are accepting that one can ascend a high position by one's karma. Does this mean that we can become God temporarily by our actions?

While many people may be deterred by the idea that a position of power is temporary and would be followed by a fall from power, not everyone may be dissuaded in this way. A person might decide to enjoy these temporary pleasures, fall from that position, and then work again to regain that position. In short, there can be people who alternate between working and enjoying, and the temporariness of the position doesn't dissuade them. Even the temporary attainment of the position of God may be considered sufficiently good. After all, if they can attain it once, then they can attain it again. Like the president or a prime minister of a country can ascend to a powerful position, and then lose in the next term, only to come back again into power, similarly, one can imagine the possibility where they become God, lose it, and then acquire the position again. In short, God would not be a *person*. God would rather be a position, which anyone can attain if they have worked for it sufficiently. This is the extension of the idea of power and position in the present world where nothing is permanent; kings can lose their kingdom and win it back again. So, if God was the king of the whole world, maybe it is possible to win and lose that position based on one's effort. It might be temporary, but it would still be a fair system in which the person who works the hardest acquires the position of God.

1.2.5 (36)

शब्दवशिेषात्

śabdaviśeṣāt

śabda—they are called; viśeṣāt—because of adjectives or properties.

TRANSLATION

Because (qualities obtained by effort) are called adjectives or properties.

COMMENTARY

In this sūtra, a distinction between an object and its properties is drawn. For example, if you paint a chair red, it acquires the property of redness. However, this paint is a covering or an attribute of the object, and the object is different from that property. Similarly, if you heat water, it acquires the property of heat, but there is a difference between the heat and the water. In the same way, there is a difference between the ātmā and the qualities it acquires in the material world. This difference is described by a distinction between the soul and its body and mind. The body can be rich, powerful, famous, and beautiful, while the mind can be knowledgeable and renounced. However, since the body and the mind are the 'coverings' of the soul, they are not considered *native* properties of the soul. This difference is confirmed by the fact that the body and the mind change, and whoever is rich and powerful will either eventually die or become poor and powerless. But if one is not deterred by this proposition of losing their position and would like to acquire the position of God temporarily, this sūtra indicates that God is that person who has no distinction between the soul, the body, and the mind. The qualities being referred to are the native qualities of God. Since God is eternal, therefore, these qualities are never lost. So, not only are the qualities eternal, but they are not distinct from God. Therefore, we will not call these qualities *adjectives* of a noun; we won't say that there is a chair with the property of redness. Rather, redness is innate to that chair.

In the material world, there is a distinction between the nouns and the adjectives, and when the soul ascends to a higher position, the noun (i.e., the soul) is the same, but it acquires adjectives—e.g., power, fame, wealth, knowledge, beauty, renunciation, etc. So, we say that such and such has become powerful or famous or knowledgeable. But this use of language—i.e., associating the person with a quality—still involves a distinction between the person and the quality. The distinction is illustrated by the fact that we say that so and so *has* wealth; we don't say that so and so *is* wealth. Or, so and so *has* knowledge; we don't say that so and so *is* knowledge. The use of 'has' rather than 'is', indicates that we are distinguishing between the object and its property; the property is possessed by that object, but that object is still different from the property. In the case of God, however, the attribute 'has' is not applied. Thus, we must not say that God has knowledge; we must rather say that God is knowledge.

In short, there is no difference between God and His qualities, unlike the jīvā who can acquire these qualities but is always different from them. This is another way of saying that these qualities are the body and the mind of the jīvā and while they are attached to the jīvā as its properties, they are not the jīvā itself. On the other hand, there is no difference between God and His properties. Hence, there is no such thing as God as a soul and His body and mind. That body and mind are God. So, He is knowledge, beauty, power, fame, etc.

In the previous sūtra, it was stated that God hasn't acquired His qualities through hard work; He natively possesses these qualities. But in this sūtra, even the idea of possession is being rejected, because one could argue that even if the qualities could be possessed (and then lost) one could possess them again by hard work. God is being defined as that person Who is those qualities. Thus, a distinction between the jīvā and God is drawn here; the jīvā isn't those qualities although it can acquire them. God, on the other hand, is all those qualities.

QUESTION

But such qualities aren't mentioned in the śrutī or the Upaniṣad. If Vedānta Sūtra is the conclusion of these Upaniṣad, then how can we accept that the Supreme Person has these qualities? We only know about material qualities.

This counterexample is frequently offered by the impersonalist. The impersonalist claims that the Vedas and their divisions, such as the Upaniṣad, are the original texts, and other literature—such as the Vaiṣṇava Tantra we noted above—are later additions to the Vedic system. Most Indologists, in fact, try to date these scriptures and claim that the four Vedas are the original texts, and other things—such as the worship of Lord Viṣṇu—came much later. Since these qualities are ascribed to personal forms of God, which are then considered to be later additions to the Vedic system, therefore, it is argued that they cannot be considered as authoritative as the original texts. Since the original texts are providing descriptions of such qualities and the impersonal description is dominant in these scriptures, therefore, it must be considered secondary.

1.2.6 (37)

समृतेश्च

smṛteśca

smṛteḥ—from the smriti; ca—and, also.

TRANSLATION

From the smriti also (we know the qualities of God).

COMMENTARY

By referring to the smriti—i.e., the Purāna and Tantra—the Vedānta Sūtra clarifies that the knowledge in the śrutī is not the only source of all knowledge. If Vedānta Sūtra is considered śrutī, its reference to smriti must be considered an indication that these texts did not come 'later' as many academics currently claim. If the smriti did not exist earlier, then they could not be referenced. Factually, the entire Vedic system is considered eternal by the true practitioners, although it is divided into many aspects for differently inclined people.

In the Śrīmad Bhāgavatam, it is noted that the Vedānta Sūtra was composed after the composition of Upaniśad, Purāna, and Mahabharata. Bādarāyana who converted the oral tradition into a written one, however, was not satisfied after the composition of these works of literature as they did not explicitly glorify the personality of God and the deepest mysteries of amorous love between the soul and God were left unexplained. His guru Nārada then instructed Bādarāyana to compose the Śrīmad Bhāgavatam; since it was composed after Vedānta Sūtra, Śrīla Jīvā Goswami offers extensive justifications in the Tattva Sandarbha about why the Śrīmad Bhāgavatam must be considered a natural commentary or explanation of the Vedānta Sūtra. However, for the skeptics, who might not accept these arguments, this sūtra itself provides a reference to the smriti texts.

QUESTION

But you have previously stated that the Paramātma is also present in the heart and is a kṣetrajña like the jīvā. Doesn't His presence in the heart indicate that He has fallen into the material world and is therefore just like the jīvā?

As we can see from the previous sūtra, there is a discussion on the difference between God and the soul. This conversation has emerged especially after the previous section ended by stating that the soul must surrender and take shelter of God. The questions have therefore also shifted from the nature of Brahman or absolute reality to the difference between the soul and God. Here, the seeker is asserting that God must be considered fallen into the material nature because He is also present in the heart, just like the jīva. If the jīva can be considered fallen, then why can't God be considered fallen in the same way?

1.2.7 (38)

अर्भकौकस्त्वात् तद्व्यपदेशाच्च नेति चेत् न नचिाय्यत्वादेवं व्योमवच्च

**arbhakaukastvāt tadyapadeśācca neti cet na
nicāyyatvādevaṃ vyomavacca**

arbhak—very small; kastvāt—from going; tadyapadeśāt—a false description; ca—and also; na—not; iti—therefore; cet—if; na—not; nicāyya—the multitude or many; tvāt—Him; evam—thus, so; vyoma-vat—like the ether; ca—and.

TRANSLATION

If it is said that He (the Paramātma) is going inside a very small place (the heart) and therefore a false description (is given—that He is Supreme) we say no because He is in a multitude of places just like the all-pervasive ether.

COMMENTARY

The Lord is described as both transcendent and immanent. It is important to understand how both are true simultaneously. Consider the use of an ordinary concept such as 'cow'. The concept is transcendent to each individual cow, and it will exist even if no cow exists. However, when the cows exist, the concept 'cow' exists in each of them because of which we call them cows. Notably, if the concept did not enter each individual cow, then we could not call them cows. However, if we reduced the concept to an individual cow, then we could not call other cows by the term 'cow'. Therefore, the idea 'cow' is transcendent and immanent; as transcendent we can say that it exists when none of the cows exist; in this sense, the concept is eternal and imperishable. However, when the cows are manifest, then the concept also exists in each cow; by this incarnation of the concept inside each cow, the concept becomes immanent. The problem of transcendence and immanence is not unique to God; it is pervasive in the use of all concepts. Therefore, to understand how Paramātma is pervasive in all places, we need not focus on this as a unique theological idea; we can also examine the immanence of concepts in things to understand the problem.

This problem is that of the instantiation of a concept. There is a universal concept called 'cow', and this concept instantiates into many individual cows. Just as there is a difference between the concept 'barber' and an individual barber, similarly, there is a difference between the concept and the instance of that concept. Generally, when we start understanding concepts, we look at each individual instance; for example, if a child were to be taught about cows, then the parent will point to an instance of a cow and say— "that is a cow". It doesn't reduce the concept of 'cow' to that individual cow; however, this is how we learn about concepts: we see the instances one after another and then we generalize and start perceiving the general concept across the many instances.

So, to understand how Paramātma is in each heart, we must understand two things. First, there is a transcendent form of God called Bhagavān; He is like the concept of 'cow'. Second, this concept instantiates into each thing, when those things are created; this instantiation is Paramātma. The Bhagavān form is transcendent, and the Paramātma form is immanent. However, if all the instances were wound up—e.g., if the material world ceased to exist—then the instantiation of Bhagavān into Paramātma would cease to exist. This is quite like the fact that if dinosaurs cease to exist, then the concept 'dinosaur' still exists, however, there is no instantiation of that idea into an individual.

With this background about transcendence and immanence, we can understand this sūtra. The purport is that Bhagavān instantiates into individual things, and hence there are many instances of Paramātma, and He is present everywhere. However, the jīva is not instantiating into more than one thing at any time; therefore, there is only one instance of each jīva at any time. The reason for this difference is that Bhagavān is a general concept—He is like the idea of 'cow' which can have numerous instances. However, the jīva is a very contingent or specific concept, which can only be instantiated into one thing. As a result, Bhagavān can expand into numerous forms, with different aspects; He can also instantiate into many individuals of the same form (an example is the many deities of the Lord which are all instances of the same form). However, the jīvā cannot be present in many bodies at the same time (although it is said that by mystic perfection, a yogi can simultaneously expand into 8 bodies, but not more than that, unlike Paramātma who can have infinite expansions).

The ātmā can be likened to specific concepts, such as the Taj Mahal, the Eiffel Tower, the Pacific Ocean, or the Sistine Chapel. We call all these *proper nouns* as opposed to a cow, which is a *common noun*. There are many instances of the common noun, but there is only one instance of the proper noun. They are, however, both *nouns* that identify individuals. The difference between God and the soul is like that between common and proper nouns. The former incarnates into many forms but the latter has one instance. Hence while they are both individuals, there is a difference between the nature of these two nouns. This difference is the foundation of the distinction between the soul and God.

QUESTION

Even if we say that the ātmā is in one place and Paramātma is in many places, when the Paramātma has entered these many places, He must be enjoying or suffering like the jīvā. If the jīvā is enjoying and suffering in one place, then the Paramātma must be enjoying and suffering in many places simultaneously. The enjoyment and suffering in the world are the problems of material bondage. So, if the Paramātma is in many places, and thus subject to enjoyment and suffering in many places, then He cannot be considered liberated.

1.2.8 (39)

संभोगप्राप्तिरितिचेत् न वैशेष्यात्

saṃbhogaprāptiriti cet na vaiśeṣyāt

saṃbhogaprāpti—that it has experience of pleasure and pain; iti—thus; cet—if; na—not; vaiśeṣyāt—from the specific nature (of the Paramātma).

TRANSLATION

If it is said that (being connected with the hearts of all the individual souls due to Paramātma's omnipresence), it would also have experience of pleasure and pain, we say no, based on the specific nature of the (Paramātma).

COMMENTARY

The soul in the material world is enjoying or suffering due to material desires; if these desires are fulfilled, then pleasure is created; if they are not fulfilled, then suffering is produced. But if the desire ceases to exist, then the soul becomes equanimous to all outcomes; there is neither suffering nor enjoyment. There is still cognitive experience, but there is no emotive result because there is no desire. The soul enters the material world due to the desire for enjoyment and is hence forced to suffer when the desire is unfulfilled. However, the Paramātma doesn't enter the world for enjoyment. When the soul is spiritually advanced, then he perceives everything cognitively, but he doesn't feel sad or happy. Similarly, the Lord can perceive all that is happening, but He is not enjoying or suffering. This is because emotion is cut off from cognition. This separation between cognition and emotion is practiced by the yogis. They subject themselves to extreme austerities which produce intense suffering. But this suffering also produces the necessity to separate cognition from emotion.

Our experience arises due to a combination of outside-in and inside-out causes. The inside-out cause is desire, and the outside-in cause is karma. If desires cease to exist, then the inside-out cause ends and the generation of emotion, pleasure, and pain ceases. Then, the outside-in cause also terminates.

The position of Paramātma is like that person who has no material desires. Therefore, He doesn't enjoy or suffer, unlike the jīvā who is enjoying or suffering. Of course, by the cessation of material desires, the jīvā can also stop enjoying or suffering. By attaining this stage, the jīvā would have a similar type of experience as that of Paramātma, however, due to the previously mentioned reasons (e.g., that Paramātma is everywhere while the soul is localized) it would never become identical to Paramātma. Therefore, the claim that because the jīvā is suffering in this material world must entail that Paramātma must also suffer because they are both situated in the heart is a wrong understanding. The jīvā is influenced by material desire, but Paramātma is not thus influenced.

Topic 2

QUESTION

In many places, the Lord is described as the enjoyer of the material world. In Bhagavad-Gita 5.29, Kṛṣṇa calls Himself the enjoyer of all yajñá and austerities (bhoktāram yajñá-tapasam). In yajñá, offerings are made to the Lord for His pleasure. But you have stated that the Lord is not enjoying or suffering in this world, which would entail that He cannot be the enjoyer of yajñá and austerity. If He is not the enjoyer, then why should any yajñá be performed for Him?

1.2.9 (40)
अत्ता चराचरग्रहणात्
attā carācaragrahaṇāt

attā—the eater; carācara—the movable and immovable (i.e., the whole universe); grahaṇāt—from the acceptance (as His food or as an offering to Him).

TRANSLATION

The Lord is the eater of the movable and immovable from the acceptance of these things (if they are offered to Him).

COMMENTARY

In the Bhagavad-Gita 9.26, the Lord states that if offered with love, He accepts the offerings. Similarly, when the Lord states that He is the *bhokta* of *yajñá* and *tapasyā*, the reference is to the offerings being made by the practitioners.

> patram puspam phalam toyam
> yo me bhaktya prayacchati
> tad aham bhakty-upahrtam
> asnami prayatatmanah

If one offers Me with love and devotion a leaf, a flower, fruit a water, I will accept it.

The implication is that the Lord is not normally enjoying or suffering in the material world because He is free of material desires and has no goal to be attained. However, if He is offered something with devotion, He accepts it. The importance here must be attached to devotion; one cannot offer miseries to the Lord. Just as a person loving another person gives them those things that will please them, similarly, the meaning of loving devotion is that the offering is meant to please the Lord. Thus, those things that are displeasing to the Lord will not be accepted by Him. The acceptance or refusal rests with the Lord; He cannot be forced to accept something, unlike the living entity who is compelled by the circumstances—because he is placed in those circumstances—which may be against his desires. Thus, the jīvā is forced to accept things although he may be unwilling, and the result is displeasure. But the Lord accepts only the pleasing things, if they are offered with the intent to pleasing Him, and with the understanding of what pleases Him. If either of these conditions is not fulfilled, then the offering is not accepted by the Lord. Thus, He is not compelled to accept things; however, He does accept if something is offered devotionally.

QUESTION

You are stating that the Lord accepts if something is offered with devotion but neglects other things. But how can He selectively enjoy some offer when everything is said to be based on His approval and His supervision? How can we say that He sometimes accepts certain things (when offered with devotion) and doesn't accept (when they are evil) but still approves them anyway?

1.2.10 (41)

पुरकरणाच्च

prakaraṇācca

prakaraṇāt—from the context or the episodes; ca—also, and.

TRANSLATION

From the context (or based on the episodes) we can determine.

COMMENTARY

There is a subtle difference between approving something and wanting something. For example, children often do things that please their parents; but in many cases, they also insist on doing things that the parent doesn't approve. The parent still allows those things to happen. If the child gets hurt or unhappy because of those independent actions, the parents cannot be said to get hurt; in fact, the parent will generally say: "I told you so". In the same way, there are things that the jīvā can do for the pleasure of the Lord, and the Lord not only allows it but also accepts and enjoys it. In other cases, the jīvā does things that are independent (and not meant for the pleasure of the Lord) and the Lord still allows it (subject to the *karma* or deserving of the jīvā) but He doesn't enjoy it. This doesn't mean He is suffering because the jīvā has become disobedient.

The distinction between the two forms the attitude of the Paramātma, because in one case He approves and enjoys, and in another case, He approves (based on the *karma*) but doesn't suffer (neither does He enjoy). The distinction is that in one case He is happy, and in the other case He is neutral. While the neutral position is not as good as the one where He enjoys, it also cannot be called His suffering, because suffering would mean that it is out of His control and happening against His will. To uncover these distinctions, we must look at the emotional state of the Lord in different contexts, rather than universal statements about this state. There is a range of emotions between the extremes where the Lord is happy to when He is neutral and allows things to happen in order to fulfill the jīvā's desire. One must note in this context that if the Lord did not allow the jīvā the free will to ignore His instructions, then the love between the ātmā and Paramātma would be considered forced: We would say that the ātmā has no option other than to do what the Paramātma wants. And if there is no choice, then there can be no responsibility. Yes, there can be a perfect world in which everything is perfectly in order, but without free will. That, in turn, would entail that the ātmā cannot have its separate desires and that ultimately it is not an individual. So, the denial of free will collapses individuality; as we have noted, Oneness separates into many because of desires. If these desires are eliminated, then individuality is also lost. However, when individuality exists, all individuals are responsible for their actions. So, neither is the Lord evil because He permits the existence of free will nor is He powerless because things are happening against His will. Both types of claims are incorrect, and the distinction needs to be made based on the context, or a case-by-case basis.

Topic 3

QUESTION

If the Paramātma allows the soul to do what it desires (subject to its karma) then why does He even exist in the heart? He could stay outside, appear externally if the soul is devoted, but remain absent otherwise, and allow the soul freedom that it desires. Why should the Paramātma co-exist with the soul?

1.2.11 (42)

गुहां प्रवष्टिावात्मानौ हि तद्ददर्शनात्

guhāṃ praviṣṭāvātmānau hi taddarśanāt

guhāṃ—in the cavity (of the heart) praviṣṭau—the two who have entered; ātmānau—are the two souls (individual soul and the Supreme Soul); hi—indeed; taddarśanāt—to make that (the knowledge of the truth) visible.

TRANSLATION

The two who have entered the cavity (of the heart) are indeed the individual soul and the Supreme Soul, to make that (the knowledge) visible.

COMMENTARY

We have noted in 1.2.7 (38) that the Lord expands into an individual just as the concept 'cow' incarnates into each individual cow. Why doesn't this constitute a sufficient explanation of Paramātma's existence in the heart? Why would a seeker inquire more about the same question? The answer is that when we seek the explanation of some event, then there are several types of explanations to be offered; I will divide these into three categories—causes, reasons, and justifications. For instance, if someone with a gun shoots a person, and he is asked:

"How did the person get shot?", he might say: "because the trigger of the gun was pressed". This is the cause of the shot. But if he is asked further: "But why did *you* shoot the person?", he might say: "because I had the intention to kill". However, this still doesn't justify killing. So, if the same question is asked again, seeking to justify his action, he might say: "I was ordered to do so." In short, there are three kinds of explanations for any kind of action: objective, subjective, and intersubjective. All these three kinds of explanations can be offered.

The explanation in 1.2.7 (38) is objective: the Paramātma enters the body as it is an instance of the pure concept of a body or form—i.e., that of God's body. To this explanation, several counterarguments (such as why God doesn't suffer like the soul?) were asked and answered. But if the seeker presses for a response, a deeper reason—namely the subjective explanation—can be offered. The answer is that God wants to come along with the soul. You may ask why? The answer is given in this sūtra: The Lord comes to enlighten the soul, to give it knowledge about 'that' (meaning something beyond this world; the use of the word 'this' would have meant to provide the knowledge of the present world). The explanation indicates that the Lord has compassion for the soul; He comes as He wants to liberate the soul from the clutches of material existence.

The situation is akin to that of a child playing with fire; since the child is defiant, the mother may allow the child to do so, and doesn't need to watch (if the mother did not care for the outcome). But the mother is also compassionate; she allows the child to play with fire, and even assists the child by giving him implements to start the fire, but also keeps a close watch over the child in case he goes too far, gets burnt, and then remembers or cries for the mother to help. The mother is just nearby to immediately rescue the child if so needed.

QUESTION

Since the Paramātma is guiding the soul in both cases—i.e., when we want to enjoy the material world, and when we want to be liberated—how can we know which guidance is for which purpose? This guidance comes to us as ideas. But how can we distinguish between the idea that can liberate us from the material world and the one that is going to bind us to the material world?

This question arises in the life of all spiritual practitioners. The Paramātma simply gives us ideas to fulfill our desires. Therefore, even if we have the desire to kill somebody, Paramātma will still give us the intelligence on *how* to kill effectively (since we don't want to be caught in the act). This means that the Paramātma is supporting both good and evil desires. Now, this poses the question: How do we know which guidance is good or evil? Isn't it possible that the idea given by Paramātma is going to bind me to the material world?

1.2.12 (43)

वशिषणाच्च

viśeṣaṇācca

viśeṣaṇāt—from the distinctive qualities; ca—and.

TRANSLATION

Also from the distinctive qualities.

COMMENTARY

There are difficulties in understanding this sūtra because the meaning of 'distinctive qualities' is not apparent. We have discussed the many ways in which the ātmā and Paramātma are different; so, it is illogical to suppose that 'distinctive qualities' refers to this difference. We have also spoken about the difference between the ātmā and prakriti or the three modes of nature, and the goal of the entire text is liberation from matter; so, it is imprudent to suppose that 'distinctive qualities' refer to the difference between matter and the soul. We have also spoken about the difference between material and transcendental qualities—namely, that the transcendental qualities are knowledge, beauty, power, wealth, fame, and renunciation itself, and they are mutually reconciled in God's person, while the material qualities are just parts of these qualities and they cannot be reconciled; hence, the difference cannot refer to the distinction between God's qualities and the material qualities. We have also spoken about the differences in God's attitude toward the devotee and the non-devotee: He remains neutral to the non-devotee and favorably accepts the offerings of the devotee; He is inclined toward the devotee but not biased against the non-devotee (as He fulfills the desires of even the non-devotees). Therefore, the term 'distinctive qualities' also cannot refer to the different moods of the Lord.

If we remove all the above interpretations, because they have already been indicated previously, and don't have to be repeated (bear in mind that the Vedānta Sūtra is nyāya-prasthāna and must proceed logically), then we are compelled to use another interpretation of the term 'distinctive qualities'.

One possible understanding is that the term 'distinctive qualities' refers to the attitudes of the jīva itself. The previous sūtra mentioned that the Lord comes with the soul to save Him. But He doesn't always save Him from danger or from material entanglement. Therefore, the distinction between when He saves and when He doesn't save must be attributed to the distinctive qualities in the soul—i.e., it depends on the soul's inclination and desire. In the previous sūtra, it was mentioned that the Lord accepts if something is offered to Him lovingly. At the end of the previous section, it was also explained that even though Paramātma controls everything, the jīva can liberate Himself by taking shelter of the Paramātma. All these actions require an act of will on the part of the jīva—i.e., the jīva must endeavor by desiring the help of Paramātma. In the sūtra 1.2.10 (41) we have discussed the importance of free will, namely, that the Lord will approve even if something is dangerous to the soul. So, the Lord cannot be accused of non-compassion, because forcing the best outcome becomes contrary to the existence of free will. The implication again is that the prerogative of taking the help from Paramātma rests with the jīva, not the Paramātma.

So, the interpretation of 'distinctive qualities' can be that the jīva has different desires and attitudes; sometimes it desires surrender (when he is suffering) and then independence (especially when he is enjoying). The inspirations from the Paramātma are accordingly different. Therefore, if one wanted to truly know if the Paramātma is giving transcendental advice or simply fulfilling one's material desire, then, one can also look at one's attitudes. Am I desiring something pure and transcendental, or am I asking for material enjoyment? Is the guiding motivation underlying my desires material or spiritual?

This sūtra points towards a reflective state of the mind in which to know the truth, we don't look outward—e.g., whether some facts will confirm or deny the truth of my ideas, or whether these ideas can be proved or disproved. We rather look at our attitudes. Do I have the right attitude? Because the ideas that are coming to me may or may not be rationally or empirically confirmed; their confirmation doesn't indicate that they are spiritual, and their disconfirmation doesn't indicate that they are material (or even vice versa). The real test is the purity of the inclination or intention with which I seek answers. If my intentions are pure and transcendental, then the answers provided by Paramātma will lead me to transcendence. If they are impure, they will bind me to the material world, and I have nobody other than myself to blame. for the outcome.

Topic 4

QUESTION

Parents may sometimes abandon their children if they are consistently defiant. In such cases, even if we consider the parents of the child to be compassionate, this compassion seems to have limits. Doesn't the compassion of God have limits? Doesn't He abandon the defiant child under any circumstance?

While practicing spiritual life, a person can become dejected due to lack of progress, or very slow progress. He might realize that he hasn't entirely been dedicated to the Lord or being devoted to Him. A doubt then arises in his mind: Since I haven't been totally devoted, the Lord must have abandoned me. Since I have performed many sinful activities (sometimes called aparādha—such as by offending other devotees) the Lord has finally decided that I am irredeemable and therefore left me helpless. Now I have no hope because I have no guidance from within on how to achieve the transcendental purpose of life. I'm lost. The seeker is asking such a question: What if I'm indeed very sinful? Does that mean that the Lord will abandon me such that I have no scope for redemption?

1.2.13 (44)
अन्तर उपपत्तेः
antara upapatteḥ

antaraḥ—inside, the being inside; upapatteḥ—due to justification.

TRANSLATION

The Lord stays within because this is the justified action.

COMMENTARY

We earlier cited three explanations for a question—causes, reasons, and justifications; causes are objective, reasons are subjective, and justifications are intersubjective. The objective and subjective explanations of the Lord's presence in the heart have already been offered. We said that the Lord appears in the heart since the jīvā is an instance of the Supreme Person. Then we said that the Lord appears because He is compassionate and wants to free the soul from the clutches of material existence. But if someone insists on the same question, the third argument—the *justification*—can also be offered. Given the repeating nature of the similar statement—namely, that the Lord exists in the heart—we are compelled to ask ourselves: Why is the same thing being repeated in the same way? The answer is that different explanations are being offered.

The answer is that the Lord is duty-bound to be present in the heart. Even if the soul commits many offenses—e.g., hurting other devotees or consistently defying the instructions of the spiritual master—the Lord never abandons the soul. His compassion has a limit, and His love is not infinite; in particular, the Lord is indeed offended if other devotees and the spiritual master are offended. To hurt someone who is devoted to the Lord is indeed offensive and invites the anger of the Lord. He is not merely a passive observer; He has feelings too. But despite His feelings of anger at a defiant soul, He doesn't abandon the soul because He considers it His duty to rescue the soul. This just means that the Lord may not provide spiritual guidance to the soul, but He is ever-present lest there is a moment of repentance and realization that a change needs to be made.

This idea is important considering that in other religions the soul is eternally condemned to hell. This and the previous sūtras have been asserting that the Lord never abandons the soul. This one particularly says that the Lord is ever-present in the heart because He is duty-bound to do so. Just like we are duty-bound to protect all the parts of our body, and we never consider any part of the body a burden—even if it gives us pain—similarly, the Lord considers the soul as part of His existence, and even though He may be disenchanted with the scope for progress, He stands a watch just in case the soul changes his desire. This statement can be considered the ultimate answer to the problem of spiritual abandonment due to offenses against the Lord or His devotees. While these are real problems, the Paramātma still doesn't abandon the soul.

QUESTION

If the Paramātma is present in all living entities, why can't we worship all these living entities as if they were God? We could say that even dogs and cats have Paramātma in them, so by feeding them, we are feeding the Paramātma. In short, why can't we worship God through the other living entities?

Many people are fond of saying that "service to man is service to God". Missionary organizations, therefore, have made it a practice to provide food, clothes, education, hospitals, etc. as a method of serving God. There are of course in many cases hidden agendas underlying the missionary services: Some of them may use such offerings to 'convert' the person to a certain religion, as a way of increasing the following of that religion, etc. These conversions may then be used for political purposes or social engineering. However, even if such ulterior purposes did not exist—and 'conversion' for political or social reasons wasn't being employed—you could still say that the service of the poor and destitute was service to God because ultimately God is present in everyone.

1.2.14 (45)
स्थानादवि्यपदेशाच्च
sthānādivyapadeśacca

sthānādi—all places; vyapadeśāt—from concealments (of the object); ca—and.

TRANSLATION

And all the places (i.e., objects) are from concealments of the real object.

COMMENTARY

The contentious part of this sūtra is the use of vyapadeśāt. In other sūtras, we have translated it as 'due to the statement' or 'due to the claim'. If we apply that translation here, then the sūtra would say: "and because of the statement in all places". In reference to the previous sūtra, where the Paramātma's existence within has been justified, this sūtra would state precious little. We have expended this entire section discussing the Paramātma's existence within, how He differs from the soul, and three explanations of why He exists within. So, why should we repeat the same by asserting that "it is also said in all places". Of course, this is not an invalid translation; it would just be redundant.

Therefore, we translate vyapadeśa as the concealment of the real object. In nātya-śāstra, or the scripture on the performance of drama, this term is used to denote one of the twelve ways of expression: "to speak with the purpose of deception, is called pretext or vyapadeśa". In some contexts, the term can be used to denote 'fraud' or 'dishonesty'. What we see, is not what reality is. The implication is that even though God is everywhere, those places are the covering, a symbolic representation, or the deception of the real thing. Now, one can say that this contradicts all that we have discussed previously, so some clarification is required; we can understand the meaning by Bhagavad Gita 9.4:

> mayā tatam idaṁ sarvam
> jagad avyakta-mūrtinā
> mat-sthāni sarva-bhūtāni
> na cāhaṁ teṣv avasthitaḥ

By Me, in My unmanifested form, this entire universe is pervaded. All beings are in Me, but I am not situated in them.

Two things are important here. First, the term *avyakta-mūrtinā* which means the 'unmanifest form'; it is a form, so it is not impersonal. But it is not manifest. Now one might say: If He is not manifest, then in what way can we say that He exists? This question is answered in Bhagavad-Gita 9.29:

> samo 'haṁ sarva-bhūteṣu
> na me dveṣyo 'sti na priyaḥ
> ye bhajanti tu māṁ bhaktyā
> mayi te teṣu cāpy aham

I envy no one, nor am I partial to anyone. I am equal to all. But whoever renders service unto Me in devotion, I am also present inside them.

In short, the Lord is present everywhere, but He is not *manifest* to our vision unless there is a devotional attitude. His 'equality' toward everyone is explained by the fact that He is present everywhere, but His disposition to manifest is toward those who are devoted to Him. Therefore, all beings—such as cats and dogs—or even other humans, cannot be worshipped as God, unless they are devotees, because God is not manifest in their hearts, although He exists in an unmanifest form. He cannot accept the offering made to such beings unless He is manifest; therefore, such offerings are only to the 'covering' that hides His unmanifest form. In short, the bodies of different living entities cannot be worshipped as if they were God. This is clearly stated in Bhagavad-Gita 9.25:

> yānti deva-vratā devān
> pitṝn yānti pitṛ-vratāḥ
> bhūtāni yānti bhūtejyā
> yānti mad-yājino 'pi mām

Those who worship the demigods will take birth among the demigods; those who worship ghosts and spirits will take birth among such beings; those who worship ancestors go to the ancestors; and those who worship Me will live with Me.

This is a repudiation of the idea that if God exists everywhere, the worship of all beings must produce the same result and can be called service to God. The worship of demigods, ghosts, spirits, ancestors— and by extension, the worship of humans, animals, trees, etc.—cannot be considered God's worship.

We have explained this previously in a different way when we cited the example of the concept of cow instantiating into an individual cow. The perception of an individual cow requires us to bring to the mind the concept of cow and realize that this is an instance of that concept. But if we don't use the correct concept, then we will not see a cow. Of course, that will be a wrong perception, but it is a perception we can have. The cowness in a cow is a possibility; it can manifest itself if we perceive it correctly. But we may not perceive it correctly. In the same way, Paramātma's presence is a possibility; He exists, but He is not manifest. To convert that possibility into a reality, we need a devotional attitude. We must have a strong desire to perceive His existence. The service of those individuals where such a devotional attitude already exists can be considered the worship of God; accordingly, the service to the pure devotees of the Lord is considered the service of the Lord, because the Lord is manifest in their heart. But it cannot be extended to all beings where He is not manifest.

QUESTION

If the manifestation of the Lord in the heart is the outcome of our devotion, then how will we know where He is manifest and where He is unmanifest? In short, whose worship and service should be considered as service of God?

In the previous purport, it was said that the Lord is hidden, and the body is a deceptive covering of His existence. But if that is the case, then how can we identify in whose heart He is manifest, and where He is not manifest? This is an important practical question for those seeking self-realized devotees. How can such devotees be identified, if the body is merely a deceptive covering?

1.2.15 (46)
सुखवशिष्टाभिधानादेव च
sukhaviśiṣṭābhidhānādeva ca

sukha—bliss; viśiṣṭa—the qualities, the symptoms, the distinguishing characteristics; abhidhānāt—on account of the wealth; eva—certainly; ca—and.

TRANSLATION

And because the distinguishing characteristics of bliss are certainly manifest because of the wealth (of the presence of Paramātma in the heart).

COMMENTARY

Many people pretend to be spiritually advanced. They might speak well; they may be great scholars or have large followings. However, these are not the symptoms by which a spiritually advanced person is to be identified. A simple prescription of this advancement is described here: the existence of bliss in the heart is also manifest externally. These symptoms are sometimes called *aṣṭa-sāttvika-vikāra* or eight modifications of the body. These are: being stunned, perspiration, standing of the bodily hairs on end, faltering of the voice, trembling, fading of the body's color, tears, and devastation. As has already been indicated previously, the spiritually advanced soul is one who has the perception of God; it is not merely the acquisition of theoretical knowledge, but the realization of this knowledge as the Original Form. Since this realization requires devotion, the symptoms of advancements are also the development of an internal bliss due to the perception of the Lord in the heart. This perception then manifests through the mind and eventually through the body. Those who cannot perceive the spiritual state, or the mind can still distinguish the spiritually advanced persons through the presence of the *aṣṭa-sāttvika-vikāra*.

QUESTION

You have said that the Lord is seen by a devotional attitude. But what does a person do if he doesn't have the attitude? Can one acquire an attitude?

At the end of the last section, the surrender to the Lord was prescribed. Through the current section thus far, the nature of the Lord, His existence in the heart, and why He is present and yet absent until devotion is manifest has been described. However, the process of developing this devotion hasn't been spoken about. The seeker is now asking about the method for acquiring devotion.

1.2.16 (47)
श्रुतोपनिषत्कगत्यभिधानाच्च
śrutopaniṣatkagatyabhidhānācca

śruta—heard; upaniṣatka—Upaniṣads; gati—way, or process, or method; abhidhānāt—because of the wealth; ca—and.

TRANSLATION

And the process (of acquiring devotion) is the hearing of the Upaniṣad because they provide the wealth (of information about the Lord and the devotion toward Him; both these types of information can be considered wealth).

COMMENTARY

This sūtra indicates that if one doesn't possess the devotional attitude, then he must hear the Upaniṣad where the Lord is described. By hearing this knowledge, a devotional attitude can be developed. We must recall that the guidance to acquire the knowledge of Brahman through the study of Vedic scripture was provided in 1.1.3 (3). Subsequently, the text also discussed how the scripture discusses various topics, but their goal is to understand the nature of the Absolute Truth. Therefore, one might wonder: why is the study of Upaniṣad being prescribed again when it has already been stated at the very beginning of Vedānta Sūtra? The short answer to that is the context of this sūtra is different from that of the previous statements. Earlier, the guidance was based on the general inquiry of how one can know about Brahman. However, now, through the previous sūtras, the devotion to Paramātma has been discussed. This sūtra should, therefore, be understood not merely as a repetition of what has previously been stated, but as a further statement that the devotion to the Lord is acquired through repeated hearing from the scriptures.

Many academics study the Upaniṣad and analyze its meaning; they claim to be scholars of texts. But we cannot find the symptoms of bliss on their body, as we discussed in the previous sūtra. The meaning of this sūtra is uncovered in the context of the mention of that bliss and how it is acquired. It means that if someone hasn't developed the bliss, then he hasn't understood the Upaniṣad. They may not have a devotional attitude, or they may simply be progressing on the devotional path, although they may not have perfected it. Either way, true knowledge is understood to have been gained only if that bliss is present. This sets the benchmark for who can be considered knowledgeable in the Upaniṣad: they must have acquired the internal bliss by the perception of the Lord.

QUESTION

If we repeatedly dwell on something, we develop an attraction toward it. How can this repeated hearing not be considered indoctrination into an ideology? By repeated hearing, we change the way we look at the world. Once our mind has been altered, we are naturally bound to see the world in terms of that ideology. So, how can this repeated hearing of Upaniṣad not be considered the creation of perceptual bias, that leads to the outcome that we desire to see?

The problem of indoctrination resulting in perceptual bias is real. If we repeatedly hear about something, we begin to believe it, no matter how false it may be. This is the basis of propaganda—a lie repeated sufficiently enough times begins to be accepted as truth, just because it has been heard repeatedly. If the prescription of the process to develop devotion is to repeatedly hear about the Lord, isn't this process like the propaganda that relies on repetition?

1.2.17 (48)
अनवस्थितेरसंभवाच्च नेतरः
anavasthiterasambhavācca netaraḥ

anavasthiteḥ—not existing always; asambhavāt—from the impossibility; ca—and; na—not; itaraḥ—any other.

TRANSLATION

From the impossibility also, it cannot be any other as they are not always existing.

COMMENTARY

You can fool all people some of the time, and some of the people all the time, but not all people all the time. The same holds true of indoctrination and propaganda. It can be used to deceive many people, but eventually, most people will come to their senses. This is because all false propaganda and indoctrination have an end; it ends when facts and truths contradict their existence.

The narrations of the Lord, however, are not indoctrination because He is established in the heart, then the bliss is incomparable to anything else. The experience of bliss causes the devotee to abandon all other focuses, and the perception of the Lord becomes continuous. The experience of bliss and the persistent focus are impossible for anything else; those other things may be established in our mind and can become the lenses through which we perceive the world, however, their perception doesn't create bliss. Though stringently abiding by such beliefs, the soul is never happy; he keeps seeking something better, although he stridently claims the truth of what he believes in. In fact, if challenged about his beliefs, the person becomes angry—if this idea, which I have painfully acquired were to be taken away from me, then I would be left in utter confusion; I would have no other rock to anchor my life onto. To avoid that devastating outcome, one aggressively fights the opponents to convince himself. However, despite showing signs of external aggression and belief, such a person remains dissatisfied with their beliefs because they do not produce happiness. The perception of the Lord is not like that. It leads to bliss, the destruction of all confusion, the overcoming of anger and fear because of which the soul is completely convinced of the Lord's existence even if he is surrounded by those who may not have the same beliefs; similarly, the soul overcomes all boredom—the cause of constant distractions; he is situated in bliss. The combination of all such outcomes is impossible for anything other than the Lord.

Topic 5

QUESTION

I can understand that such attainment would be ideal. However, the process seems difficult. In the meanwhile, I have many practical problems in day-to-day life. It is said that the different demigods control the different aspects of material life—such as Kubera for wealth, Kāmadeva for marital happiness, Chandra for a peaceful mind, Surya for a strong body and health, etc. Shouldn't we worship the Lord alongside these demigods for all-round happiness of the body, mind, and soul? Your prescriptions are only meant for the soul.

1.2.18 (49)
अन्तर्यामी अधिदैवादिषु तद्धर्मव्यपदेशात्
taddharmavyapadesat antaryāmī adhidaivādiṣu taddharmavyapadeśāt

antaryāmī—the dweller within; adhidaivādiṣu—the origin of the demigods; tat—His; dharma—attributes; vyapadeśāt—being pervasively present.

TRANSLATION

The internal dweller (the Paramātma) is the origin of the demigods; His attributes and qualities are pervasively present (as the demigod's qualities).

COMMENTARY

The three modes of material nature—called sattva, rajas, and tamas—are also said to manifest into three parts called ādidaivika, ādibhautika, and ādiatmika. The ādiatmika represents the body and the mind of a person. The ādibhautika represents the other living entities with whom a person's body and mind interact. However, this interaction is controlled; it is not that anybody can interact with anybody else. These controllers—who decide who will interact with whom (or what)—are called the ādidaivika or the demigods. For example, your body is ādiatmika, food is ādibhautika, and the demigod who controls the body's access to food is ādidaivika. Therefore, the body and the mind are the subjects, the things with which we interact externally are the objects, and the demigods decide if some subject can be permitted to interact with other objects. These interactions are based on two things—our desiring and our deserving. Sometimes, the deserving overrides the desiring and delivers things that we may not desire; we may be pleasantly or unpleasantly surprised by this automatic encounter with desirable or undesirable interactions. At other times, the desiring overrides the deserving and we can choose one out of many pleasant or unpleasant outcomes. In either case, the demigods are controlling the fulfillment of desires. This sūtra further states that the Paramātma is the origin of the demigods who partially manifest His power over different things. For example, there is a controller of rain (Indra), the mind (Chandra), the body (Surya), etc. The power of their control is a partial manifestation of the Paramātma.

The implication is that even if one is worried about their mental and physical difficulties, it is best to worship the Paramātma because the demigods work under His supervision and manifest His power of control. The Paramātma has delegated these powers—as a king delegates work to ministers, but the ministers still work under the instructions and order of the king. Therefore, if the king is pleased, then the ministers will automatically do his bidding. In the Bhagavad Gita 7.16, it is stated that four kinds of pious people worship the Lord: these are called the distressed, the desirous, the curious, and the knowledgeable. Therefore, even one distressed or desirous should still worship the Lord.

> catur-vidhā bhajante māṁ
> janāḥ su-kṛtino 'rjuna
> ārto jijñāsur arthārthī
> jñānī ca bharataṛṣabha

> O best among the Bharatas, four kinds of pious men render devotional service unto Me—the distressed, the desirer of wealth, the inquisitive, and he who is searching for knowledge of the Absolute.

The sūtra indicates that the well-being of the soul—through the worship of the Paramātma takes care of the well-being of the body and mind as well.

QUESTION

But the smārta (a tradition of ritual worship prevalent in ancient India) indicates that one must perform different kinds of rituals and that is the only dharma. They are also opposed to the Upaniṣad as being the source of truth. How do we reconcile this contradiction in the different approaches?

The smārta tradition is also called Pūrva-Mīmāṁsā as it deals with the "earlier" Vedic texts, which prescribe the performance of rituals;

however, it doesn't consider the existence of gods or God, the primary knowledge. It considers the Upaniṣad as "later" texts and secondary in nature. As a result, the Vedānta system (propounded through this text) came to be also known as Uttara- Mīmāṃsā. For the Mīmāṃsā school, dharma is rituals, and social duties are of primary importance. Any philosophical doctrine of reality is secondary.

1.2.19 (50)
न च स्मार्तम् अतद्धर्माभिलापात्
na ca smārtam ataddharmābhilāpāt

na—neither; ca—also, and; smārtam—that taught by smārta brahmanas; ataddharmābhilāpāt—from qualities contrary to its nature being mentioned.

TRANSLATION

And (the Paramātma is) not that which is taught in smārta system because qualities contrary to its nature are mentioned (here).

COMMENTARY

The distinction between Mīmāṃsā and Vedānta can be illustrated through the example of *realist* and *instrumentalist* views in the philosophy of modern science. The realist believes that when an action is performed (the cause), a result (the effect) is produced. However, the connection between the cause and the effect is mediated by a law described in a theory that generally invokes many metaphysical concepts. For example, the gravitational theory postulates the existence of metaphysical ideas like mass and a gravitational force to explain the observed motion. The realist takes this causal mechanism seriously and considers it real. However, many philosophers of science—beginning with David Hume and George Berkeley—challenged these assumptions. Hume, for instance, argued that causality involves necessity (that every time the cause occurs, the effect will naturally follow), but scientific theories cannot prove necessity as they have not been tested in all possible scenarios. This problem was further established as science provided newer explanations for older phenomena. It was now realized that if older theories could be falsified, then a similar fate was imminent even for current theories. But this problem was not taken very seriously as long as there was a causal explanation. A far more damaging problem was encountered in atomic theory where one could make probabilistic predictions although there were no explanations. Many scientists now adopted an instrumentalist doctrine—that science is not about the nature of reality; it is simply an instrument that can be employed to make some predictions; these need not be all the predictions, and since the theory wasn't about the nature of reality, it could also be revised in future. The theory was simply a convenient tool to be used to build successful technologies, waiting to be changed later.

In a similar vein, the Mīmāṃsā philosopher states that the essence of life is the performance of actions; these actions produce effects, and that is enough. How the cause connects to the effects—e.g., that the actions produce results because there are demigods controlled by the Paramātma—are irrelevant to the performance of rituals and the results thus obtained. We just focus on the actions and ensure that they are performed correctly. The results will automatically follow; it is not our job to analyze why the results follow the actions, because we have no empirical method to observe what happens "behind the scenes". The Mīmāṃsā philosopher is an instrumentalist. He treats the rituals as useful methods to obtain the desired results but doesn't worry about the mechanisms that connect causes to effects. They, of course, may not deny that such causal mechanisms can exist; they are just not interested in them.

The Vedānta philosopher is, on the other hand, a realist. He is interested in how the world originated, what existed before this origination, how the soul is caught in the cause-and-effect of material nature, how it can be liberated from the cycle of birth and death, and the reality beyond this world. Owing to this focus on the nature of reality—which lies "behind the scenes"—the Vedānta system is least interested in the appearances—i.e., the performance of rituals and the obtainment of these results. He considers them temporary because all effects are eventually lost, and the actions must be performed again. He is primarily interested in the nature of reality, or that which is eternally existent.

While we might see a contradiction between Mīmāṃsā and Vedānta philosophies, they are not logically contradictory. The former is focused on action and result, while the latter on the mechanisms behind this cause and effect. Owing to this difference, the prescription of Mīmāṃsā to just be an instrumentalist and forget about the reality behind change, is rejected in Vedānta. Vedānta rejects this instrumentalist view and claims that we haven't understood the world simply because by actions we get results; we ought to know the nature of reality that underlies the phenomena because that is the eventual goal.

In that vein, the sūtra asserts that the qualities pursued by Mīmāṃsā—i.e., the action and its results—are different from those which we are discussing here. Their goal is a practical technology for solving day-to-day problems, and our interest at present is the science that makes this technology possible. Whether the Vedas described the technology before science is irrelevant to us. Ultimately, if we know the science, we can also build the technology. But, if we just know the technology, we cannot understand the science. Therefore, the pursuit of Mīmāṃsā—while practically useful—is ultimately incomplete.

QUESTION

However, you have earlier mentioned that hearing of the Upaniṣad is the path to attaining devotion. So, you are also prescribing a process, which can be called dharma. In the same way, the smārta practitioners also consider the chanting of the Vedic mantra as dharma. How can these be different?

A legitimate doubt is being raised here, namely, that the smārta Brahmins are chanting the mantra from the 'previous' sections of the Vedas, while the Vedānta system is prescribing the chanting of the verses from the 'subsequent' sections of the Vedas. Now, one may say that one is an instrumentalist and the other a realist. But for the practitioner, what difference does it make? Even the chanting of mantra by the smārta produces results. So, even if the smārta doesn't believe in the underlying realist causality, he must ultimately get the result. Vedānta may believe in the reality that causes the effects. However, ultimately, both are chanting mantras and hence both are getting their results. How can we discriminate between the Mīmāṃsā and the Vedānta if we are only looking at the outcomes of chanting instead of the phenomena vs. the reality?

1.2.20 (51)

शरीरश्च उभये'पि हि भेदेनैनमधीयते

śarīraśca ubhaye'pi hi bhedenainamadhīyate

śarīraḥ—the body; ca—also; ubhaye—both (ātmā and Paramātma); api—even; hi—certainly; bhedena—by way of difference; enam—these (the matter referred in the previous sūtra—namely rituals); adhīyate—bind or tie.

TRANSLATION

Even though both (the ātmā and Paramātma) are certainly different from the body, these (rituals) also increase the bondage to the body.

COMMENTARY

There is a problem here: Why should *ubhaye* be used, when it suffices to say that the ātmā is different from the body? The answer lies in Mīmāṃsā where the ātmā is considered eternal (and hence real), however, the system rejects (or is unconcerned) with the reality of any gods or God. By implication, the existence of Paramātma is also not accepted. By noting that even the Paramātma is different from the soul and the body, indirectly, two separate statements are being made in sūtra: (1) the bondage resulting from the performance of rituals, and (2) that there are two eternal entities in Vedānta whereas there is only one entity (the ātmā) in Mīmāṃsā. This difference is pertinent to the entire context because the purpose of yoga as described earlier is the devotion between the ātmā and Paramātma; it is not merely the performance of worldly duties.

With this clarification, we can try to understand this sūtra. The previous sūtra mentioned that the qualities of Paramātma are different than those presumed by the *smarta*; we further clarified that the goal of the *smarta* is an empirical success while the goal of the Vedānta is the pursuit of reality. However, one can argue that regardless of whether a person is a realist or not, ultimately, the results matter—e.g., salvation from the material world. If one system is chanting the 'previous' texts while the other is chanting the 'subsequent' texts, they are both chanting, and they will therefore obtain the result—i.e., salvation. So, how does the belief in some reality make a difference to the outcome?

This sūtra clarifies that the actions of the Pūrva Mīmāṃsā philosopher will bind them to the material existence. Most people work only because there is a result. This attachment to results, and performance of work under that expectation, is contrary to karma-yoga, where an aspirant is instructed to act without expectation. This detachment is necessary—while we need things for the body, the ātmā is different from the body; attachment to results doesn't lead to the realization that the ātmā is different from the body; in fact, it binds it more.

The goal of Vedānta is liberation from the cycle of action and consequence. So, there is a difference between dharma or the duties of the material world (which produce the outcomes because those outcomes must be reaped) and the dharma performed for liberation from the material world. If one keeps performing these actions, one is continuously in the cycle of action and reaction. How can that cycle be considered salvation from the material existence? The goal of Vedānta is not the pursuit of material duties, but the understanding of the transcendent reality. The mantras pertaining to this transcendent reality—i.e., the Upaniṣad—take one out of the cycle of action and reaction, and lead to salvation. Therefore, we cannot consider the 'previous' and 'subsequent' sections of the Vedas on the same level or producing the same kind of outcomes (e.g., salvation). Although both are chanted, the former pertains to the cycle of action and reaction of this world, while the latter yields freedom from this cycle.

The distinction between Mīmāṃsā and Vedānta isn't simply that one pertains to 'previous' texts while the other one to 'later' texts. The difference is not just that the former is instrumentalist while the latter is realist. The prominent difference is that the former keeps one bound to the material world through the cycle of action and reaction while the latter results in salvation from this cycle. Therefore, both are chanting the Vedas, but one is creating bondage to the cycle of cause and effect, while the other is yielding freedom from this cycle.

Topic 6

QUESTION

But how can we believe that such transcendent reality exists? It is easier to trust that which we can perceive (by our senses). The Mīmāṃsā system deals with what we can perceive—the actions and their results. On the other hand, you are describing an invisible reality. How can we believe that any such reality exists 'behind' the perceptions when perceptions are all that we can have?

This is a famous argument in Western philosophy, originally formulated by George Berkeley against the distinction between primary and secondary properties. The proponents of science claimed that certain properties (such as length, mass, speed, time, etc.—called primary properties) are real, whereas other properties (such as color, taste, smell, touch, etc.—called secondary properties) are unreal. This argument rests on the claim that the secondary properties depend on the observer, but the world must be independent of the observer. Berkeley, however, argued that the so-called primary properties are only objectification of our sensations. For example, the primary property of 'weight' is the objectification of the perceptual experience of 'heaviness'. The primary property of 'temperature' is the objectification of the perception of 'heat'. Therefore, only our perceptions are direct and real, and everything—supposedly 'behind' these perceptions—is only our theoretical construction. A similar type of argument was also advanced during Greek times by Socrates through the example of cavemen who look at shadows on the walls of the cave, but these shadows are cast by something that is behind them (they cannot see the source). How can they know that the figure of a man is created by a real man or by the hands of a shadowgraphist creating the false impression of a man? In the same vein, we can argue that Mīmāṃsā is dealing with what we can observe, while Vedānta is talking about this reality which lies behind the observation and hence remains invisible; how can we believe this reality indeed exists?

1.2.21 (52)

अदृश्यत्वादगुणको धर्मोक्तेः

adṛśyatvādiguṇako dharmokteḥ

adṛśyatvādi—invisibility; adi—the origin; guṇako—one who possesses the quality; dharmokteḥ—because of the manifestation of observable qualities.

TRANSLATION

The invisible is the origin and possessor of all the observable qualities.

COMMENTARY

All scientific theories draw a distinction between an *object* and its *property*. The property can be position or mass or speed, while the object is a particle. The particle is always invisible; however, we postulate the existence of such an invisible entity to give a realist interpretation to science—namely that there is something to which the properties are bound; this particle is the 'possessor' of the properties; thus, for instance, we say that the particle has mass or speed or position. In classical physics, two such types of objects are used, namely, particle and field. The main difference is that the particle has a definite position (i.e., is in one location) while the field doesn't have a position (because it is spread everywhere). We could talk about the position within a field, but we could not attach a position to the field itself. Therefore, it was understood that certain types of objects can only have certain types of properties. This fact has created many problems in atomic theory because the atoms—which we like to think are particles—seem to be simultaneously present in more than one place, thus exhibiting the property that we would normally associate with fields. However, there cannot be two objects underlying the same property because then we could not say that the object is the possessor of the property. The point is that of the distinction between an object and a property; the object is the invisible entity to which the visible properties are attached, as nouns and adjectives.

So, if we argue that since the object is invisible, and its existence is therefore suspect, and only the visible properties must be considered, then the result is the collapse of realism because we would be preoccupied with the study of properties, and not know what lies 'behind' these properties, which ties them together. Once we lose the reality of the object, then how the properties hang together would also be lost. We could still speak about 'property atoms'—e.g., a unit of mass or speed—but we could not tie these two properties together because the agency of the object that tied them doesn't exist. This idea is sometimes called 'dustbowl empiricism' where the universe is the dustbowl of properties; there are merely atoms of properties, but nothing ties them together, and therefore this 'dust' doesn't accumulate into objects. There is also a more serious issue, namely, that we cannot formulate the laws of change if we take away the objects. For instance, we could not say that the particle is moving *because* it has mass. After all, the speed of motion and the mass are two unrelated properties as the object which tied them together no longer exists. So, the rejection of the invisible leads to a complete collapse of science. This might be news to many people, who think that science deals only in what can be observed; this is not true. Science also postulates the existence of invisible things—e.g., particles—which tie all the visible properties together and it is due to the postulate about the invisible that we are even able to formulate predictive natural laws.

Returning to the sūtra, a similar point is made here: The invisible objects (the ātmā and Paramātma) tie together the material properties. They are akin to the 'objects' of science, which possess material properties. As a result, we can say that the ātmā 'has' a body, or the ātmā 'has' thoughts, etc. If these objects are taken out of the equation—as the Mīmāṃsā philosopher argues—then we are left with 'dustbowl empiricism'; we will have properties, but we cannot tie them together. Without the agency that binds these properties, we cannot explain why some taste is tied to some smell or some color is tied to some form; once we lose this property binding, all predictive causality would be lost.

Another distinctive point in this sūtra is that the objects tying the properties together are ātmā or the Paramātma. There is no 'particle' or 'wave' as in the case of material science. This is a rejection of material 'objects' that tie the properties together. The claim is that there are material properties, but they come together because of the soul. This is very important because it entails that all the material properties such as taste, smell, touch, form, color, etc. are not 'together' into an object because of some material object (such as a particle or a wave). These are together due to the existence of the invisible objects of ātmā and Paramātma. There is hence a subtle but important difference between the notion of invisible objects in the case of modern science and Vedānta: Science postulates the invisible material objects, e.g., particle and wave. Vedānta Sūtra instead states that there are no such material objects; the object in question is the ātmā or the Paramātma. If these don't exist, then material properties cannot come together to form bodies; the world would be a dustbowl of properties.

Now, we can answer the question of whether the object that ties together these properties is ātmā or Paramātma. This question should be answered from the perspective of the Mīmāṃsā philosopher, who accepts the ātmā, but not the Paramātma. The context also indicates that the difference between the performance of material duties and transcendence is in regard to the Paramātma. The 'invisible' should, therefore, be understood as the Paramātma; He is called avyakta-murti or the invisible form. We can also say that for the ātma the existence of the self is not in doubt; this could also be asserted based on the Cartesian dictum that "I think therefore I am". When we talk about 'invisible' in material science, the question is different than for someone who accepts the ātma.

Therefore, the implication is that the Paramātma binds the properties together. Vedic texts describe the Paramātma as a manifestation of the mode of sattva-guna (unlike Brahma who represents rajo-guna and Śiva who represents tamo-guna). Furthermore, the Paramātma 'maintains' the world, Brahma 'creates' it, and Śiva 'destroys' it. These descriptions can be understood through this sūtra. The creation, maintenance, and destruction pertain to the body. The material properties are eternal; however, they are instantiated, combined or dissociated. While they are associated, the Paramātma is the 'maintainer' Who keeps everything together. In short, the fact that I have a body is because the Paramātma is the object who is holding the material properties together.

However, this raises a difficult issue: If the Paramātma is holding the world together, and He is the object underlying the phenomena, then the laws of nature must also apply to the Paramātma. In short, He would become implicated in the process of our actions. This is where we must invoke the understanding of the previous sūtra where the Paramātma is holding things together on behalf of the soul; He accompanies the soul to fulfill its desires. Therefore, if the body is like a chariot, then the seat, wheels, axle, reins, etc. of the chariot are held together by the Paramātma, and the soul becomes the passenger in the chariot. The Paramātma drives this chariot according to the desiring and the deserving, and therefore only the ātma is implicated in the cycle of cause and effect.

The main takeaway from this sūtra is that we cannot claim that the gods or God—in this case the Paramātma—don't exist because we cannot observe them. If this view is adopted, then the object that holds things together will disappear. If the ātma is the cause of this binding, then the implication would be that the ātma is well-versed in the understanding of material nature because it is orchestrating the body.

This is obviously not true, because most of us are not aware of how the body works. The only reasonable position is that someone else is orchestrating this machine on which the ātmā is only a temporary passenger.

QUESTION

It was quite acceptable when you said that the Paramātma is the *kṣetrajña* or knower of the *kṣetra* or the field because there was an implicit difference between the knower and the known. Owing to this difference, we could say that the Paramātma is transcendent to the matter. However, by saying that the Paramātma is the object that binds together the material properties, you have broken that distinction. It now seems that the Lord has acquired material properties. How can we consider the Lord transcendental when He is being attached to material properties? Wasn't the purpose of Vedānta Sūtra to describe how the Lord is different from the material properties or transcendent to them?

In modern science, the distinction between an object and a property is *logical.* There is no mechanism by which we 'connect' an object to a property. Therefore, if we say that an object has a property, it is implied that the object and the property are connected, however, because the nature of this connection is not clarified, it is natural to suppose that if an object has a material property, then it has become material. In earlier sūtras, the difference between the Lord and the material guna was described, and it was stated that the Lord has no material guna. However, now, we have stated that the Lord possesses these material gunas. This produces a contradiction between the two statements.

1.2.22 (53)
वशिषणभेदव्यपदेशाभ्यां नेतरौ
viśeṣaṇabhedavyapadeśābhyāṃ netarau

viśeṣaṇa—adjectives or qualities; bheda—difference; vyapadeśābhyām—on account of the hiding or covering; na—not; itarau—the other two.

TRANSLATION

The other two (the ātmā and Paramātma) are different from the adjectives or qualities (of the object) because (the latter) are coverings (of the former).

COMMENTARY

There are two distinct ways in which the word 'property' is used: (a) in the scientific sense, the property controls the object, and (b) in the ordinary sense the object controls the property. Take for example the claim that I own this house, this house is mine, and therefore I control the house. The house is my *property* and I am not controlled by the house; rather, I am the controller of the house. However, in the scientific sense, when we ascribe a property to an object, the property becomes the object's controller. For example, a particle moves in a gravitational field due to its mass. The mass is the property, and the particle is the object. But the object is not in control of the mass: i.e., the object cannot decide whether the mass should exert a force or not. The mass acts independently of the particle, according to the laws of gravitation, and that force then pushes the particle. In short, the mass drives the particle's dynamics. If the same situation was applied to the ordinary ownership of properties, then we would say that the acquisition or ownership of the house is forcing me to do things (that I would not otherwise do). That would, however, bring to question the premise of ownership: Do I possess the house, or does the house possess me?

It is true that the Lord is the *kṣetrajña* or the knower of the *kṣetra* or the field. It is also true that the *kṣetra* is a property of the *kṣetrajña*. However, unlike the scientific properties, which control the object, in this case, the object controls the properties. In scientific theories, the causality of motion is in the property (such as mass) and the particle is causally inert. In the case of Vedānta, the material properties are inert, and the object has the causality of motion. In short, the world is moving not because there is some mass that is attracted by other masses due to gravitational force, and the objects (e.g., particles) are dragged by this force. The world is moving because the observable properties (like taste, touch, smell, sound, sight) are inert, but they are pushed by the will of the Lord. The claim that matter is a property of the Lord presents a problem if matter drags the Lord. But it doesn't present a problem if the Lord drags matter.

With this understanding, we can say that this sūtra reiterates the difference between the Paramātma and matter, *after* we have asserted that matter is His property. We cited the fact that the Lord holds the world like a particle that holds diverse properties such as speed, mass, energy, momentum, etc. This was necessary to explicate the idea that there are no 'material objects'; that the world doesn't hang together due to matter itself; it rather hangs together because of the presence of the Paramātma. He is, therefore, the object underlying the properties. But this also invokes the counter-image of the object being controlled by the property. We should thus understand that the term 'property' can be used in two ways—I can possess the house, or I can be possessed by the house.

The Lord has been called the possessor (of the material qualities) previously; if its true meaning wasn't clear before, it has been clarified here. As an illustration, if you go to meet a friend at his house, you can see that he lives inside a house. However, because the house covers the friend doesn't mean it controls him, or that he is bound by the house. The friend can walk out of the house if he wants, and he would still be the owner of the house and the house would still be his property. The problem arises if we think in physical terms—the house is large, and the friend is small. Since he is living inside the house, therefore, he must have come under its control. This idea of the covering controlling the covered is prominent in material science—where the covering (e.g., mass) controls the covered (e.g., the particle). This idea is also prominent in the case of the ātmā—the soul comes under the control over the material covering. However, if the term property is understood in a different sense, the problem doesn't arise. The owner is different from the house; the owner possesses the house as his personal property, but the house doesn't possess the owner.

In this case, both ātmā and Paramātma are different from matter. However, Paramātma controls matter while the ātmā is controlled by matter. The Lord indirectly controls the ātmā through the material energy: He controls matter, which controls the ātmā. The liberation from this control has been noted earlier: devotion to the Lord frees one from material control. On a related note, this sūtra could have been translated as: "The two (ātmā and Paramātma) are different because the material qualities cover (the ātmā)". The covering of the ātmā by the material modes and the transcendence of the Lord have been stated previously. However, positing this transcendence also entails that matter must be working independently because the soul and Paramātma are transcendent. To solve that problem, we must say that the soul and Paramātma are the objects, which control the properties. However, the soul can also be controlled by the properties. Just like mass is the controller of particles, similarly, under the material influence, the soul becomes just like a material particle controlled by the material properties. Its liberation is when it comes out of this control.

QUESTION

You have said that the Lord controls matter, although He is different from matter. This presents the classic mind-body problem in the case of God, where God and matter seem to be different like the 'mind' and 'body', and yet the mind somehow controls the body. How should we understand this interaction and control by God? How does the Lord cause the material energy to work?

1.2.23 (54)

रूपोपन्यासाच्च

rūpopanyāsācca

rūpa—form; upanyāsāt—from a fictional reality; ca—and, also.

TRANSLATION

(The Paramātma) gives the world a form, from a fictional reality.

COMMENTARY

A contentious term here is *upanyāsāt*. Generally, fictional literature—such as novels, dramas, stories, etc.—are called *upanyāsa*. However, the word could also mean "as has been narrated". The latter translation would bring to question: Where has it been narrated? Clearly, the control of the material world by the Lord has not been described previously. However, it is possible to invoke statements from other Upaniṣad to describe this control. I have preferred the 'fictional' translation here because of two reasons. First, it doesn't require us to invoke other texts, and we can rely on the present text itself. Second, there is indeed real meaning to the term 'fictional' here, as will become apparent shortly. Notably, the fiction exists, but its meaning is imaginary. It is, therefore, a concoction and hence it is not true; and yet, its existence is factual. The claim is therefore that the Lord is orchestrating a fictional story by His control.

Presently, let's turn to the word rūpa which means form or structure. Again, there are two possible interpretations of this term. First, we can say that the material world is a formless substance, and the Lord gives it form. Second, we can say that the material ingredients themselves have form, although the Lord provides an additional form to these ingredients. The primordial material reality is called Pradhāna in Sāñkhya philosophy and it is indeed formless. However, this formlessness arises because the three modes of nature—sattva, rajas, and tamas—are in a 'balanced' state. Diversity begins when these modes are separated, and then one mode becomes dominant over the other modes. All variety follows from this dominant-subordinate structure between the modes because sattva can subordinate the mode rajas, but rajas can also then subordinate (another instance) of sattva. This dominant-subordinate pattern produces a tree-like structure in which the root is formless, but by distinction, it produces three trunks of sattva, rajas, and tamas, which then divide into three parts, and the process continues indefinitely. This leads to the question: What are the three modes? And how are the many instances of these modes produced?

To answer these questions, we must distinguish between the universals and the individuals. The three modes are universals, but there are only three of them. Since these modes proliferate in many things, the modes must also be replicated many times, to produce the dominant-subordinate structure. The universals are described in Sāñkhya as 24 elements—5 gross elements, 5 tanmātra, 5 knowledge senses, 5 working senses, mind, intellect, ego, and mahattattva. Once these universals are created, numerous instances of these universals must be combined to produce individual objects. For instance, the purple color can be produced by a combination of the instances of red and blue. Once the individuals are created, then they can also be collected into systems and societies where each individual interacts with some other individuals.

Accordingly, rūpa or form can be seen in three ways. First, it can pertain to the 24 elements of Sāñkhya. Second, it can pertain to the instantiation and combination of these elements into individual things.

Third, many types of instances of the universals enter causal relations with each other to produce different structures. Due to the first two, rūpa is individual things that we can perceive and conceive by the senses and the mind. Due to the third, rūpa is the creation of roles in a society into which the individual objects participate.

The Lord's control of matter can then be described as these three processes. The first process is the creation of the universals, which is called Śakti. The second process is the combination of these universals into individual objects, which is caused by three forms of Lord Viṣṇu—(1) Kāraṇodakaśāyī Viṣṇu creates the individual desires, (2) Garbhodakaśāyi Viṣṇu creates the individual roles, and (3) Kṣīrodakaśāyī Viṣṇu creates the individual bodies. The third process is that Śiva creates the universal society in which the individual bodies and roles are combined. Together, these constitute five kinds of rūpa. The universals are rūpa as they are pure concepts. The individuals are rūpa because the universals are combined in a particular manner to create a form. The roles are rūpa because they organize different individuals into a social order. The evolution of this society is also rūpa because it follows a cyclical and hierarchical pattern. As the creator of all these forms, the Lord is the controller of the world.

Now, one might argue: If the Lord is the creator of everything, and the Lord is eternal, why is His creation called fictional? The short answer is that the universals, individuals, roles, society, and the resulting drama are not fictional. The same types of things are produced again and again. The same kinds of roles are created over and over. Due to this repetition, they are eternal; they only become manifest and unmanifest. The fictional aspect is that a certain soul becomes a certain type of individual, then plays a certain role, at a certain place and time. This mapping of the soul to the body to the role to the place and to the time is not eternal. Hence the universe is called an upanyāsa or fictional story.

The term 'real' pertains to the eternally existent, although it may be manifest or unmanifest. The bodies, roles, places, and times are eternal and real in this sense. But their combination with a soul is not eternal. The difference with the spiritual world is simply that this mapping between the soul, body, role, place, and time is eternal in the spiritual world. Thus, a different actor can play the same character in this world, so actors are not tied to characters. However, each actor is a different character in the spiritual world. If the actor and the character are tightly connected, then we don't consider their behavior a 'drama'. What they do is their eternal role, not just a temporary role upon a stage. Thus, both the soul and the forms are eternal. However, the forms of the soul are not eternal in the material world. These forms are eternal in the spiritual world.

Topic 7

QUESTION

You have said earlier that the Paramātma is invisible, and yet He is the object underlying the material properties. Then, in the previous sūtra, you said that He gives the world its form. Does this suggest that since this visible form is produced by Him, we could consider this form as His representation?

We are inclined toward the things that we can see. If we cannot see the Paramātma, it is much harder to understand Him. In such a situation, can the understanding of the external world—which can be observed and analyzed—be considered a suitable substitute for loving devotion to Paramātma?

1.2.24 (55)
वैश्वानरःसाधारणशब्दवशिषात्
vaiśvānaraḥ sādhāraṇaśabdaviśeṣāt

vaiśvānaraḥ—Cosmic Man; sādhāraṇa śabda—common word; viśeṣāt—because of the qualities.

TRANSLATION

Because of its qualities, the ordinary word for (the universe) is Vaiśvānara.

COMMENTARY

Etymologically, Vaiśvānara is comprised of two parts—*visva*, meaning the universe or the creation, and *nara*, meaning the man. Therefore, Vaiśvānara can be translated as the Cosmic Man. The sūtra confirms that if one is unable to meditate on the Paramātma within, then he can understand the nature of the Lord by the study of the external world—provided, through this study, we can conceive of the universe as a body. This form is sometimes called the Virāta Rūpa or the Gigantic Form in the Purāna. The different parts of His body comprise the different Loka or planetary systems; the head is the place of Brahma while the feet are the hellish planets. Now, one might ask: What would be the point of such an understanding? The short answer is that it makes you see the universe as an interconnected whole in which the different parts are not independent of each other. Just like the hand feeds the stomach, and the stomach gives strength to the hands, similarly, there is interdependence between all the parts. This interdependence is described in the Bhagavad-Gita where the demigods and the humans are interdependent—the humans by offering sacrifices to the demigods, and the demigods by providing the daily necessities such as water, sunshine, air, etc. to the humans. By seeing the universe as a body, we begin to understand that we are just parts of the whole (which is quite evident even now), but these parts also must work cohesively (which is not very apparent right now). The cohesion among the different parts—which we might call 'cooperation' within the material universe—can curtail the evil that bedevils everyone: Namely, the tendency to be envious, selfish, and uncooperative. One realizes that their existence depends on serving someone else because they too are being served; without this mutual service, their existence is impossible. Ultimately, one must serve the Lord, but if one finds that the Lord is invisible, even the understanding that one must serve the demigods (which have been described as the manifestations of the Lord previously) can be progress.

In this ongoing discussion, many methods to attain transcendence are being successively described. At the beginning of Vedānta Sūtra, it was stated that the study of the scriptures—provided they are devoid of the three modes of nature—is the process for transcendence. The previous section ended by stating that surrender to the Paramātma is the method for transcendence. Then the chanting of the Upaniśad was prescribed, along with a distinction between Mīmāmsā and Vedānta (i.e., the worship of demigods was rejected). Now, if the seeker is feeling helpless in all these ways, then, another method is being permitted—namely, that of meditating on the Universal Form of the Lord (and thereby indirectly meditating on the presence of demigods in this world).

Modern science also studies the cosmos, although it can only understand the visible part—which is now said to be only 4% of all that exists. The invisible parts are called 'dark', although the nature of this 'darkness' is hypothesized in contrary ways—the 'dark energy' causes expansion, and the 'dark matter' causes contraction. In Vedic cosmology, this 'darkness' is ascribed to the fact that our vision is confined to a limited part of *bhū-loka*, some parts of *svarga-loka* (e.g., the planets such as the sun and the moon, although planets like Rahu and Ketu are not visible), going up to the *Dhruva Loka* or the polestar. The four planetary systems above this—namely, the *jana, tapa, mahar,* and *satya-loka*—are not visible to us. Similarly, the lower seven planetary systems, and below which like the 27 hells, are also invisible. Large parts of *bhu-loka*, including the other parts of *Jambudvīpa*, and the other six 'islands', are also invisible.

If we compare what is visible vs. invisible in Vedic cosmology, the visible part is much less than 4%. In short, we don't know the structure of the universe if we rely on the visible part. But by adopting the understanding of the Universal Form, we can obtain a fuller understanding of the creation, and how each part of this universe is interdependent on the other parts. Finally, we must also understand that certain places in the material universe—such as *Sveta-Dvīpa*—are described to be the residence of Paramātma, and they are included as part of the Universal Form. So, not only are we observing the existence of higher and lower beings, but also understanding how they are under Paramātma's control. This true picture of the cosmos, therefore, also leads to cosmic theism.

There is a growing interest in Vedic cosmology among people today. Counterarguments against this study say—our goal is to transcend the world, and everything produced from the three modes of nature. How can the study of cosmology be considered a route to transcendence? By implication, how can it be regarded as being of any relevance to the person aiming for transcendence? The answer to this question is provided in this sūtra, and the answer is that it is very hard to understand the Lord because He is invisible. In fact, as we discussed earlier because He is invisible, it is even harder to trust that He exists. However, the universe—at least some parts of it—are still visible to us.

Based on this visibility, we can gain some trust in the existence of the other parts, which we cannot see. If faith is reposed in these descriptions, and the person meditates on this Universal Form, the process can lead to transcendence.

QUESTION

My question is only partially answered by the previous response. Since we have previously talked about the surrender and devotion to the Lord, does this study or meditation on the cosmos constitute an adequate substitute for that devotion to the Lord? Can the scientific study of the world be considered a substitute for the devotion to the Lord, which was described previously?

As described in the Bhagavad-Gita, Lord Kṛṣṇa displayed the Universal Form to Arjuna, but he did not like it very much; he requested Kṛṣṇa to return to His normal human form with which Arjuna was more acquainted. However, Kṛṣṇa had to display this form to convince Arjuna that He is indeed the lord and master of the universe. This immense display of power is often required to convince an ordinary person about the greatness of God. Since the form of the Lord looks just like our forms, many people may underestimate His nature, or even disbelieve His existence. Therefore, an ostensible display of power changes the seeker's perspective: He can see that the Lord is not an ordinary mortal. It can be a preparation for surrender—after all, we are naturally inclined to surrender only when we see the other person is extremely powerful. But does this preparation also constitute a substitute for the devotion to the Lord?

1.2.25 (56)
समर्यमाणमनुमानं स्यादिति
smaryamāṇamanumānaṁ syāditi

smaryamāṇam—meditation; anumānam—imaginary, indicatory, or something from which we can draw an inference; syāt—perhaps; iti—because, thus.

TRANSLATION

Because that (cosmic form of the Lord) is only an imaginary or indicatory mark, one may perhaps meditate upon it (but it is not the conclusion).

COMMENTARY

Here it is clarified that the meditation on the Universal Form is neither necessary nor sufficient. But to the extent that the alternatives can seem harder to some people, this meditation is not decried or rejected as a useless process.

The Vedas progress gradually toward the conclusion. For instance, in the Bhagavad-Gita, Lord Kṛṣṇa initially gives a materialistic argument to Arjuna— "if you win this battle, you will enjoy the earth; but if you lose the battle, you will still enjoy in the heavenly planets". It is only gradually that the discussion proceeds into many forms of yoga, including karma-yoga and jñāna-yoga, before the final instruction of surrender to Kṛṣṇa. In the same vein, we have discussed how the 'earlier' portions of Vedas deal with rituals, and the later portions of the Vedas are the conclusion of the Vedas. Likewise, in the Purāna, such as the Śrīmad Bhāgavatam, the initial goal of devotion is described, but subsequently, the text moves into the discussion of material nature (in the 3rd Canto), followed by the discussion of cosmology (in the 5th canto). It is only later that Kṛṣṇa's pastimes with the gopis—which are considered the pinnacle of the love of God—are described. The Ācāryas have therefore recommended gradual step-by-step progress, rather than 'jumping' to the conclusion quickly.

This sūtra should, therefore, be looked at pragmatically. In principle, the love of God is supreme. However, in practice, to attain that love of God, one must progress slowly. Those who have progressed in earlier lives can skip the meditation on the Universal Form. But for the new initiates, such a process can be useful. Therefore, the prescription is not definitive; this is indicated using the term *syat*, which means 'perhaps' or 'maybe'. The decision is finally left to the practitioner, hoping that he can estimate his state of progress correctly.

The reason for this ambivalence is also described in this sūtra; the Universal Form is called 'imaginary' or 'indicative' or 'something from which we can draw inferences'. To understand this predilection, we can draw parallels from how society is compared to an organism, which is described as having four parts—the Brahmanas are the head, the Kshatriyas are the hands, the Vaishyas are the belly, and the Sudras are the legs—but this 'body' or 'organism' is not a living person. Society is ruled by powerful people, who can organize and structure it. But this structure is only an indication of the intent in the controller or ruler. The societal structure doesn't become a conscious being by this process. In the same vein, organizations and institutions today are widely viewed as organisms and persons—with rights and duties—although they are not conscious beings. The meditation on the Universal Form should be viewed in the same light; the Paramātma is the controller, however, He is invisible. And yet, if we can understand the cosmic structure, and give the Paramātma a 'position' in this structure, at least we can see that He is the supreme controller in relation to the other beings. We may not have a face-to-face encounter with the Lord; however, at least we have understood His 'position' regarding other beings.

For example, if you understand an organizational structure in which the CEO is at the top, different department heads are under his supervision, and so on, then you can attribute many actions to the people you don't see. Thus, you could say— "the department head ordered this work to be done". You may have never met the department head, but you can still know that he exists. Organizational structures are not conscious beings; however, the different parts of the structure are interdependent like parts of the body. In that sense, they are collectively compared to an 'organism' even though they are non-conscious. The universe is similarly a large organization with many layers of governance. It is, collectively speaking, a diverse society comprised of many types of living entities. This society or organization is the Universal Form. Its parts constitute the living places or occupations in the universe. The individuals occupying these roles are controlled by Paramātma, but the Universal Form is not alive.

QUESTION

By calling the Universal Form 'imaginary' aren't you delegitimizing the meditation on this form? The world has already been called 'fictional' in a previous sūtra. All these descriptions seem to indicate that we must only consider meditation upon the true Lord to be the One established within the heart.

The proponents of many religions are often seen arguing with each other about whose method is superior. The proponents of jñāna-yoga claim that bhakti-yoga is inferior because it involves 'emotion' which is inferior to 'reason'. The practitioners of bhakti-yoga might claim that the Vedic knowledge has a divine origin, and to have faith in this knowledge, one must have faith in the teacher—i.e., the Lord—who provided this knowledge. Such arguments are generally pointless. Just like to reach a destination you might first walk, then catch a taxi to a train station, then take a train to the airport, and then catch a flight that takes you to the destination, similarly, different methods can and must be employed at different stages of the spiritual journey. Yes, the airplane may take one to the destination, but to reach the airport, one needs to walk, take a taxi, and then catch a train. Therefore, just because the final leg of the journey involves catching a flight doesn't mean that other steps aren't needed. However, if one says that the preliminary steps are not going to take you to the destination, then, a natural doubt arises: Are we rejecting this process?

1.2.26 (57)

शब्दादभिभ्योऽन्तःप्रतिष्ठानाच्च नेति चेत् न तथा
दृष्ट्युपदेशात् असंभवात् पुरुषमपि चैनमधीयते

**śabdādibhyo'ntaḥ pratiṣṭhānācca neti cet na tathā
dṛṣṭyupadeśāt asambhavāt puruṣamapi cainamadhīyate**

śabdādibhyaḥ—many descriptions; antaḥ—within; pratiṣṭhānāt—from the established (i.e., the Lord who is situated within the heart); ca—and; na—not; iti cet—if it is said; na—not so; tathā—in the same way; dṛṣṭyupadeśāt—based on the instructions to see; asambhavāt—from the impossibility; puruṣam—the person; api—even; ca—and; inam—in this way; adhīyate—in remembering.

TRANSLATION

If it is said that by many descriptions or words, that which is established within is not known, (we say) not so. In the same way, based on the instructions to see, even though the Puruṣa is impossible to see, in this way also is seen.

COMMENTARY

One of the specialties of Vedānta Sūtra is that it defies a simple interpretation. We have seen many examples of this before: The Brahman is Oneness, but it is also comprised of the individual ātmā; the ātmā is part of the Paramātma and yet he is to be considered separate from the Lord; the Vedas are a source of truth, however, not everything in the Vedas can be considered Absolute Truth; matter is originally formless and is then given a form by the Lord but we cannot consider the form produced by the Lord as He Himself, etc. As we proceed through the discussion, we always find that the answer is very subtle: it is neither of the two extremes that deny the opposites, but something more nuanced. In this case, the contentious issue is whether the Puruṣa is inside or also the Universal Form, and the answer is that neither position can be rejected. They must rather be understood as different stages of the same understanding.

QUESTION

The term 'Puruṣa' is generally taken to mean not just a person, but also a controller. The Universal Form seems to possess a form like a person, but He cannot be called the controller of the universe because you have previously said that the Paramātma is the origin of the ādidaivika or the controllers. So, in what way should the Universal Form be considered a Puruṣa if He is not a controller?

The term Puruṣa has many meanings; it can represent 'male' or 'man', and it also means 'dominator' or 'controller'. We have discussed previously that the controller is Paramātma who is hidden in the heart; He is also the source of all the demigods. The Universal Form cannot, therefore, be called the controller. And yet, if He not called a controller, then how can we consider Him a Puruṣa?

1.2.27 (58)
अत एव न देवता भूतं च
ata eva na devatā bhūtaṁ ca

ata eva—for the same reasons; na—(is) not; devatā—the controller; bhūtaṁ—the living entities or the embodied souls; ca—and.

TRANSLATION

And for this reason (the Universal Form) is not the controller of the soul.

COMMENTARY

The sūtra accepts that the Universal Form is not the controller. But this view must also be nuanced with details. In this regard, we can compare the Universal Form to the idea of a Vāstu Puruṣa prominently employed in Vedic systems of architecture. The land, and the construction upon it, are compared to a person, with head, hands, legs, belly, etc. The properties of these parts of the body become the defining method for placing different functional parts of the house in different parts of the Vāstu Puruṣa body. For example, some parts dominate in the element fire, so, the kitchen must be kept in that part. In the same way, time is also divided into different phases and has different characteristics. Thus, the musical ragas are suited for certain times. So, the place and time are 'rulers' as they have functional properties—they prescribe what type of activity must be performed at which place and time. Similarly, the Vāstu Puruṣa is a controller—different parts of His body represent the places in which different types of activities are performed. There is hence a place for the sun, the moon, the other planets, the stars, the demigods, the demons, the humans, etc. The Universal Form is the functional design of the universe, and it is neither fictional nor arbitrary. But in another sense, the design is different from the designer.

When a car is manufactured, the design constitutes the system architecture for the car—e.g., how long and wide it will be, whether the engine will be in the front or the back, whether the car is a two-seater or a four-seater, the space for luggage or goods that must be provided, etc. This architecture is not random or whimsical; it is produced by a designer's intention to produce a certain type of car. In fact, once the system architecture has been produced, it dictates where people will sit, and how many of them can sit, how much luggage can be carried, etc. So, the architecture itself 'controls' many things. But the architecture is not the person who designed the car. In the same way, there is a person who designs the car, and then there is a design that controls the other things.

Similarly, the Universal Form is and is not a controller. He is a controller because different parts of the universe are meant for different kinds of roles, pleasures, cognitions, and activities; the places in the universe determine what is possible or impossible at that place, and the universe is not *uniform*. Because of the design, the Universal Form can be called a controller. But because the design is not the designer, the Universal Form is not the controller. The structure of the universe is like a body, but the Lord is the soul of that body. We cannot say that this body is our creation, or that it doesn't exist, or that any part of the body can do anything. On the other hand, we also cannot say that the body is identical to the soul. The body exists because of the soul; so, it is a representation of the qualities of the soul; however, it is not the soul itself.

QUESTION

The idea that the Universal Form is itself a representation of the Lord is like that of Pantheism, which identifies God with the universe. Pantheism rejects a transcendental God who created the universe but stands apart from it. By supporting such an idea, aren't you delegitimizing a transcendental God?

If we only accept the transcendental form of the Lord, then we can be accused of delegitimizing the meditation on the Universal Form. However, if we accept the Universal Form, we can be accused of supporting pantheism and rejecting a transcendental Lord. The question about the first delegitimization has been asked before; the seeker is now asking about the second problem.

1.2.28 (59)

साक्षादप्यविरोधं जैमिनिः

sākṣādapyavirodhaṃ jaiminiḥ

sākṣāt—the visible; api—also; avirodhaṃ—no difficulty; jaiminiḥ—(so says) Jaimini.

TRANSLATION

Jaimini (says that there is) no difficulty in also (accepting) the visible (as a form of God as opposed to the invisible or the transcendental form of the Lord).

COMMENTARY

The sage Jaimini was a disciple of Bādarāyana and the founder of the Mīmāṃsā school. He is well-known for his treatise entitled the Pūrva Mīmāṃsā Sutras, also called Karma-Mīmāṃsā. We have already discussed the differences between Mīmāṃsā and Vedānta; in particular, both accept the eternality of the soul; however, Mīmāṃsā rejects the existence of the invisible gods or God. The focus of Mīmāṃsā was on what can be sensually perceived and practically used. The sūtra mentions his name and quotes him saying that the Universal Form is apparent (sākṣāt) because it represents the structure of the universe. This should not be considered the delegitimization of a transcendental Lord; it can rather be used by those who cannot accept a transcendental Lord and would be more comfortable in accepting the universe itself as the form of God. This is an indirect reference to atheists who don't accept a transcendental form of God or a God who creates the universe but stands apart from it. Jaimini has been quoted here because the Mīmāṃsā system doesn't accept the existence of God, although they still accept that we can think of God as the Universal Form.

QUESTION

However, the main problem remains; you have said that the Universe is controlled and given form by the Lord. Yes, we can study this form, and we are indirectly understanding the creation of the Lord. However, the Pantheists will still say that there is no separate God apart from the universe. There is God, but He transforms into the universe. So, once the universe is manifest, there is no separate God. And God, therefore, exists only when there is no universe. How will you address the resulting problem that God did not *create* the universe, but God *became* the universe—which eventually results in Pantheism?

We have previously said that the Universal Form is the *design* and the Paramātma is the *designer*. However, the pantheist can argue that there is no designer separate from the design; rather the designer itself became the design. We can compare this to the existence of a seed from which a tree grows; once the tree has grown, the seed ceases to exist. In fact, since the tree may produce other seeds, we can say that the original seed produced many designers, which remain in potential form but eventually convert themselves into a tree. So, this cycle of the designer becoming the design repeats itself many times, and hence a single seed can then lead to the production of many seeds—i.e., different living entities—who are constantly transforming themselves into the trees (namely, the mind and body), and there is no seed left once the tree has grown.

1.2.29 (60)

अभवि्यक्तेरति्याश्मरथ्यः

abhivyakterityasmarathyah

abhivyakteḥ—duetoexpression;iti—so;āśmarathyaḥ—Āśmarathya.

TRANSLATION

On account of the expression, so says Āśmarathya.

COMMENTARY

This sūtra states that the universe is the *abhivyakti* or expression of the Lord. Like thoughts can exist in our minds, and we express them into words, similarly, the universe exists inside the Lord and is then expressed outwardly. We cannot say that the speaker becomes the speech, and this example of the seed becoming the tree (and disappearing thereafter) is unsustainable due to the eternality of the soul. The same soul reincarnates into multiple bodies. So, we cannot say that the seed manifests into the tree, and then it ceases to exist. We must rather say that the seed manifests into a tree, and it remains; in fact, it can manifest into different trees one after another. The seed is therefore never destroyed. In the same way, the universe is an expression of the Lord, but it cannot be equated or identified with the Lord. This can be understood based on the similarity between the ātmā and the Paramātma; the ātmā undergoes reincarnation and manifests different bodies as its expression. Since it is not destroyed by the expression, the Paramātma is also not reduced to the creation.

Thus, the designer can never be the design because the same designer can produce many designs. We have compared the universe to a house owned by the person who lives in it. The person inside the house is different from the house, and yet, the house represents his qualities. For instance, the house of a devotee would be decorated by pictures of the Lord, but the house of a materialist would be decorated by portraits of himself, his family, or ancestors. The house of a poor man may be spartan, but that of a rich man would be opulent and full of many assets. The house of an academic would contain books, that of a musician musical instruments, and that of a sportsperson sports gear. A person with classical tastes will live in an ornately designed house, whereas one with modern tastes will live in a house with simple functional designs. So, we can understand the person from their expressions. These things are a 'reflection' of the person who owns and creates them, but those things are not the owner.

In the same way, the sage Āśmarathya is being quoted as saying that the universe is the *abhivyakti*—the articulation of thoughts into words—of the Lord. Yes, the words are separate from the person who speaks them. However, by hearing those words, we can know the person's thoughts. In the same way, the Lord can be understood by this external manifestation of His person.

QUESTION

If we call the universe an expression (abhivyakti) of the Lord, as you have compared it to the expression of the mind into speech, doesn't it follow that we would be preoccupied with the perception of the senses? We have discussed that many parts of the universe are not perceivable by the senses. So, on one hand, we cannot perceive the Universal Form by our senses, and on the other hand, it is an expression of the Lord. How do we reconcile these positions?

1.2.30 (61)

अनुसमृतेर्बादरिः

anusmṛterbādariḥ

anusmṛteḥ—for the sake of meditation; bādariḥ—(so says) the sage Bādari.

TRANSLATION

The sage Bādari says that (Vaiśvānara) is for meditation.

COMMENTARY

Since in the previous sūtra the Universal Form was compared to a verbal expression of the thoughts in the mind, one might conclude that the Universal Form must be seen through the senses—after all, the words are heard by the ear. This sūtra rejects this idea. It quotes sage Bādri as saying that this Universal Form is for meditation or mental remembrance. It is an indirect statement that we cannot observe the Universal Form by senses. This is also directly confirmed by the fact that many parts of the Universal Form (such as the lower planetary systems, the many parts of *Jambudvīpa*, many of the higher planetary systems above the polestar) are not sense perceivable. Therefore, even though there is a difference between the designer and the design, we cannot assume that this design is completely sense perceivable. The use of *abhivyakti* or expression in the previous sūtra is meant to indicate a difference between a design and a designer; it is not meant to indicate that the expression (or the design) is entirely sense perceivable (like it would be if that expression was audible speech).

This sūtra also confirms that this design can be understood mentally. In short, to meditate upon the Universal Form, we need to employ the mind, rather than the senses. This fact is illustrative for those who draw 'models' of the Vedic universe and having constructed the model, they think that it represents the universe in its sense perceivable form. They neglect the fact that many parts of the universe cannot be perceived by the senses. So, how can a model in which we perceive these parts by our senses be a representation of those parts? A classic example of such confusion is to treat the flatness of the bhū-mandala as the literal flatness of the earth, thereby producing contradictions with observations. This sūtra answers this point—we must see the form mentally, rather than sensually. It is thus a *mental model* of the universe, not a *sensual model*.

Let's understand this idea through an example from modern science. Take the Standard Model of particle physics for illustration. It is typically drawn as a set of 16 boxes stacked on top of each other into four rows. There are 6 quarks, 6 leptons, and 4 bosons. The picture of the Standard Model is a mental model; it is how we organize things in our minds, but it doesn't represent any facts about the perceivable world. There are no boxes with 6 quarks, 6 leptons, and 4 bosons in the real world. Similarly, take the Periodic Table of chemical elements as another example. It is a classification method that divides elements into alkali, alkaline, lanthanides, actinides, metals, metalloids, noble gases, etc. This is also a mental model of the world of chemical elements.

However, you will not find a stacking of a hundred-odd boxes representing elements anywhere. And yet, we consider the periodic table very 'real'. It is 'real' if you use the periodic table for understanding; it is unreal if you use it for sense perception. In such mental models, something is 'above' and something is 'below'. Something is to the 'left' and something is to the 'right'. This above, below, left, and right has nothing to do with sense perception. Just because Hydrogen and Helium are shown to be at the same 'level' in the periodic table doesn't mean that we will observe Hydrogen and Helium at the same height if we perceive sensually.

In the same way, the Universal Form is for mental understanding. It is not a description of the sensual world, but a conceptual description of reality. Therefore, it should not be confused with empirical measurements of modern science (e.g., that the bhū-mandala is not sensually flat—just like Hydrogen and Helium at the same level in the mental model doesn't mean that they are at the same 'height'). It follows that the Lord's expression of the universe is in the form of a mental model; it should not be confused with sense perception.

QUESTION

But previously we compared the creation to the design of a designer and said that the designer is different from the design. In the case of ordinary designs—e.g., the design of a car—we can understand the design through sense perception. Are we now suggesting that there are many types of designs, some of which are sense perceivable while others may not be sense perceivable?

1.2.31 (62)
संपत्तेरिति जैमनिःतथा हि दर्शयति
saṃpatteriti jaiminiḥ tathā hi darśayati

saṃpatteḥ—because of the changing nature; iti—thus, so; jaiminiḥ—(says) Jaimini; tathā—in this way; hi—because; darśayati—can be seen.

TRANSLATION

Because of the changing nature (of the visible world), one must (mentally) perceive (the Universal Form of the Lord)—so says the sage Jaimini.

COMMENTARY

We have compared the Universal Form to society as an organism. When society is compared to an organism, the Brahmanas are higher than the Kshatriyas, who are higher than the Vaisyas, who are higher than the Sudras. But if we see with our eyes, we will not find the Brahmanas standing at a greater height than the Kshatriyas. This point has been illustrated in the previous sūtra where we spoke about mental models. The present sūtra makes another point: that from a sense perception view, things are always changing. For instance, particles are created, destroyed, or moved. But from the perspective of the mental model, they are fixed in a position (in the model). Thus, the Kshatriya may climb a mountain and be present at a greater height than the Brahmana; but by changing his location in this way, the Kshatriya doesn't become a 'higher' role than the Brahmana. So, if we see society by our senses, then we will observe people moving around, doing their work, etc. but we will never see the hands, the legs, the belly, or the mouth of the society. This means that there is a difference between mental models and sense perception, as we have said before.

Now, one may argue that in some cases, we don't see such a difference. For example, there is a similarity between the design of a house comprising a kitchen, bedroom, dining room, living room, study, toilets, etc., and the physical structure of the house. Similarly, there is a correspondence between the design of the car and the structure of the car. Normally when we understand models, we view them as pictures of the physical world—or physical models. But there are also mental models where no such correspondence can be found. So, how can we understand the difference between these two kinds of models?

Underlying the two types of models, are different notions about space. In the physical space—where we draw physical models—'height' has a physical meaning. But there is another space in which we draw the mental models; in this model, there can be many kinds of distances. For example, if we draw the tree of life, and show tigers and jaguars close by, we are not indicating that they are always found close to each other; we are rather indicating that they belong to the cat family. Likewise, if we draw an organizational structure, and show that the CEO is above the department heads, it doesn't mean that the department heads cannot walk up in a building and the CEO cannot walk down; this hierarchy represents a functional structure. We can speak about emotional proximity: e.g., that someone is 'close' because we are emotionally attached to them, whereas some other people are emotionally 'distant' from others.

The tigers and jaguars can run around, but the conceptual distance doesn't change. The CEO and the department heads can walk up and down, but it doesn't change their position in the organization. The emotionally close ones can go to another country, without changing their emotional proximity. While the world keeps changing in many ways, the models persist. To depict this persistence—in the face of a changing world—we need alternative notions of space. The models drawn in these spaces have nothing to do with the physical space in which things seem to move and change. So, if someone is wondering why we need such mental models, the answer is that we want to understand a changing world in an unchanging way. We might note in this regard that even the heavenly bodies are moving; and yet, the Universal Form is fixed. This sūtra states that we are picturing a changing world using an unchanging model.

In modern science, only the laws of nature are unchanging. Thus, as time passes, the bodies move, but the laws governing that motion don't change. But in this case, we are introducing a new category of reality—namely, many types of mental models—which are also unchanging. There is considerable similarity between the scientific theories or laws and such mental models. The difference is that we don't treat such laws as things that exist; they are just formulae that govern and control the world, but they are nowhere to be found. In the case of the Universal Form, however, we are stating that the mental models are real. They are expressions of the Lord; however, we should not confuse them with physical designs—e.g., the architecture of a house or the design of a car. While the house and car design represent the physical models and can be called the expressions of the creator, we are speaking about a more sophisticated idea.

QUESTION

Your proposals seem quite like the difference between phenomena and reality in Western philosophy. The phenomena are what is apparent to us (which you have called the 'physical' world) but there is an underlying reality (of which we draw mental models). You are

suggesting that the Universal Form is reality rather than phenomena, even though it is to be considered material and imaginary (because it not truly a person). Would you agree with this?

1.2.32 (63)

आमनन्ति चैनमस्मिन्

āmananti cainamasmin

āmananti—(they) teach; ca—also, and; enam—this; asmin—in this.

TRANSLATION

Also, they (the scriptures) teach this (the Universal Form) in this (way).

COMMENTARY

As we come to the end of this section, the description of the Vaiśvānara is being summarized by saying that the scriptural references to the Universal Form (i.e., the descriptions of Vedic cosmology) are to be understood as mental models upon which we can meditate upon, but cannot sensually perceive.

The distinction between phenomena and reality is illustrative. The indication is that the phenomena are not 'real'—as they are changing. The transcendental form of the Paramātma is eternal and unchanging. In between the eternal but transcendental form of the Paramātma, and the changing world of phenomena, there is something unchanging—namely the nature of material reality from which these phenomena are constructed, and which we understand through science and philosophy by drawing mental models for our understanding. Just as in science we say that the laws of nature are unchanging, similarly, there is a 'form' of the world produced by the Paramātma that is unchanging. The descriptions of cosmology should be understood as that unchanging reality. Even though it is material, it is quasi-eternal (in so far as the universe is temporary and is repeatedly created and destroyed). This type of meditation is not the loving devotion to the Lord and is not a substitute for it. But to the extent that we find it hard to understand the form of the Lord relative to the moving bodies of the present world, the unchanging material reality can be a stepping stone toward that deeper understanding. Specifically, the scriptural descriptions should not be confused with the sensual perception of the world. It is rather a mental model by which the universe can be understood. It can be meditated upon because simply the distinction between the material phenomena and the material reality can be quite illustrative before we speak about the transcendental reality (and the transcendental phenomena arising from that reality).

SECTION 3

Topic 1

QUESTION

You have thus far spoken about the origin of the soul (from the Supreme Lord), the difference between ātmā and Paramātma, and that the ātmā, Brahman, and Paramātma are beyond the material world. You have also said that the Paramātma is the controller of the material world through the demigods. I would now like to know about the origin of the material world.

1.3.1 (64)

दद्युभ्वाद्यायतनं स्वशब्दात्

dyubhvādyāyatanaṃ svaśabdāt

dyu—space, sky; bhu—earth, or the entire universe; ādi—the origin; ayatanam—the abode or the resting place; sva—own; śabdāt—from the saying.

TRANSLATION

From the saying, the origin and resting place of space and the universe is His abode.

COMMENTARY

This verse can be translated in two ways, one of which is given above. The other translation can be: "The heaven, the earth, etc. are considered His own abode". Such a translation would be inconsistent with the previous statements where the Lord's abode has been said to transcend the material world, and with the subsequent verses where only the liberated (from the material world) can attain this abode, and many methods of making advancement (which are valid methods of moving within the material world) are rejected as being capable of yielding such a possibility. Even if we say that there is a form of the Lord within this universe, and the place is called Sveta-Dvīpa, it is still a specific place; it cannot be identified with heaven, earth, or other places in the universe. We could also say that since the Lord is in the heart of each living entity—as Paramātma—thus He can also be found in all places, including heaven, earth, and all the other places where the living entities are found; however, such a statement would be redundant because His pervasiveness in this form has been noted many times before; what would be the point of repeating it again? Therefore, the translations which identify heaven, earth, etc. as the abode of the Lord should be rejected given all the problems that follow from it. Now that we eliminate the alternative translation, we can try to understand this sūtra.

We have previously discussed that the material world is one-quarter of the entire existence; even in this quarter, the Lord injects the soul into the material energy, and the soul remains connected to the Lord even in the material world—both due to prāṇa as well as due to the presence of Paramātma. In fact, the very notion that the jīva has 'fallen' into the material world when understood physically—as if he has 'entered' the body like a person is inside a house—is misleading because the jīva is always transcendent to the material nature. The 'fall' into the material existence should be understood as the change of its experience: its *focus* has been diverted into the material nature. The expansion of the material world is, therefore, the expansion of the substrate of the material experience, and the consciousness of the jīva is directed to this substrate by the influence of a material prāṇa (different from the prāṇa that connects the jīva to the Lord). The soul is said to be 'carried' to different bodies by this prāṇa; however, this should not be understood as physical transport. It should be seen as the changing focus or awareness of the soul. In short, we can say that a material prāṇa 'connects' the jīva to the material substrate. If this connection changes, then without movement, the jīva's experience changes.

In the same way, the material substrate must also be seen as expanding from the Lord's abode. This expansion is sometimes called māyā, or that which is *not*. We have noted previously that the Oneness differentiates to become many due to desire. The expansion of the material world should also be understood as the expansion due to a certain type of desire—which we can call the 'material desire'. The term 'māyā' should be understood as being defined in relation to the Lord; the material world is all that the Lord is *not*. The negations, however, don't have an independent existence. Even to say that something is 'not red', we must postulate the existence of 'red'. If we say something is 'not a table', we must assume that there is something called 'table'. Thus, we can understand that the material world is the negation of the Lord, but these negations are possible only when the assertion already exists; if some assertion did not exist, then the negation would also not be possible. Hence, the material world, as the negation of the Lord, has a root in the Lord. Unlike the jīvā which has emerged out of His body, the material energy is separated from the Lord; and yet, the material energy is completely dependent on the Lord, just as the negation depends on the assertion. Therefore, the material world has no independent existence. And yet, the Lord stands apart from the material world.

However, we must distinguish between two distinct concepts of origin. First, we use the term 'origin' in a substantive sense: The Lord originated the world, so the world was previously existing within the Lord; since other types of origins are from within His person, this origin must also be from within His self. Second, we can use the term 'origin' in a scientific sense: the material world is all that the Lord is not, but since the negations must have an 'origin' in the assertions, therefore, the Lord is the origin of the material world. Since the material energy is His negation, therefore, it is called *apara* or inferior when the Lord is called *par*ā or superior. This is because the negation depends on the assertion. However, these two concepts about origin present contradictions. For example, if the material energy is a negation of the Lord by the second concept, then how can it exist within the Lord by the first concept? Doesn't the existence of the negation of the Lord within the Lord present a self-contradiction?

The answer is that the Lord is the original qualities of knowledge, beauty, power, wealth, fame, and renunciation, but these are not mutually contradictory. Their subdivisions, however, can be mutually contradictory. For example, if color is the whole, then black and white are its parts. Black and white exist inside color, but in this state, they do not create a contradiction. It is only when color is divided into black and white, a mutual contradiction is produced. But this division also produces a space in which black and white are in distinct locations. They are like the branches of a tree whose root is color. Since color is not self-contradictory, therefore, the origin is not self-contradictory. Since black and white are in different locations, therefore, they are not self-contradictory. Thus, contradictions are resolved in many ways. First, contradictory concepts are reconciled into a more abstract concept (just like black and white are reconciled in color). Second, if they are not reconciled, they exist in different locations. Third, if they exist in the same location, they are separated by time.

The material and spiritual worlds are present different possibilities in different regions of space. The Lord advents in different forms—with different desires—to control these worlds. In the material world, this form is called Param Śiva (also called Shambhu), and the Brahma Samhita compares this form to milk turning into yogurt. The forms of the Lord in the spiritual world are engaged in the enjoyment of pleasure, but the form in the material world is engaged in austerity. There is pleasure in austerity too—you can enjoy exercising, working, etc. So, the Lord is not suffering in the material world. However, His pleasure takes an opposite form than the pleasure in the spiritual world. This austerity is said to cause the Lord to 'sweat', and the material energy exits His body through the pores on the skin; then it forms the Kārana Ocean, or the Causal Ocean, in which the Lord lies; He then glances at this material energy, and the jīvā is injected into the Causal Ocean through His glance. In short, the material energy has exited His body through the pores on His body, and the jīvā has entered the material energy—not physically—but simply by getting absorbed in the perception of this energy through His glance. Therefore, the Lord is both the substantive cause of the material world—because the material energy exits His body as His sweat resulting from austerity. And He is also the seed-giving father, although the soul doesn't physically exit His body (like the material energy). The soul is only absorbed in the perception of the material energy.

The process by which the senses perceive the world is described in the Bhagavad-Gita, where it is said that the yogi withdraws His senses like the tortoise draws its limbs inwards. This means that while perceiving the world, the senses are drawn outwardly. In modern science, we think that light enters our eyes and creates an impression in the brain. However, in Sāñkhya and Yoga philosophy, the senses are moving outward. Due to this outward movement, it is possible to control the senses and choose to not see something. Such control is impossible in the scientific description because, by the time you see, the light has already entered the senses. In the same way, the perception of the material energy—through the Lord's glance—must be considered the outward movement of the Lord's senses, rather than a physical detachment of the sense from the Lord's body. The injection of the soul into the material energy is like the senses moving outward into the perceived objects. Therefore, the jīvā—like the glance of the Lord—is never truly 'detached' from the Lord. And yet, its awareness is focused on the experience of the material energy produced by austerity.

Therefore, the Lord is the origin of the material world in both the substantive and the scientific sense: the material energy is His negations, which have emerged out of His own body. As negations, the energy is 'separated' from the Lord, and yet since the negation has no independent existence, the Lord is still the resting ground for them. Likewise, the energy has separated from His body when the Lord changed His nature from enjoyment to austerity, therefore, the Lord can also be called the substantive origin of the material world.

QUESTION

If the Lord is the origin of the material world, and the jīvā has entered the material energy by the agency of the Lord, then how can the jīvā return to the abode of the Lord? Would that return not be contrary to the Lord's will?

1.3.2 (65)

मुक्तोपसृप्यव्यपदेशात्

muktopasṛpyavyapadeśāt

mukta-upasṛpya—to be attained by the liberated; vyapadeśāt—because of the material covering, or because of the declaration.

TRANSLATION

Because of the declaration (in the scriptures) or because of the material covering (of consciousness), (His abode) is attained by the liberated.

COMMENTARY

The sūtra states that even though the Lord has created the material world, and the soul is in the material world due to this creation, the soul can still return to the abode of the Lord, and this return would not be contrary to the Lord's will. This return is called mukti or liberation. The contentious issue is what mukti really means, because it must explain why the soul entered the material world, to begin with. Since the Lord is the cause of the material world, the soul is not the sole cause of his entry into the world. At the least, the Lord is the creator of the material opportunity, and the soul uses this opportunity. Similarly, since opportunity exists even if an individual soul is liberated, therefore, the individual soul is not the complete cause of the opportunity. Rather, we must consider the desires of the other souls as well. But ultimately, each soul's material journey is caused only by their desire, not the Lord's will.

The next problem is the point at which the soul is considered liberated. For example, if some soul develops the desire to be liberated, does it mean he is immediately liberated? Or, must he wait for death before liberation? If the soul is liberated without leaving the material body, then presence in the material world isn't bondage. In many religions, liberation only comes at the point of death, but in Vedic texts, a person in the material body can also be liberated. Such a person is called jivanmukta, and even Śri Śankarācārya, who otherwise taught liberation as merger into Brahman (which only happens when the bodily individuality is lost) accepted liberation during one's lifetime. This presents a contradiction in the impersonal view, because if liberation is the dissolution of the material identity, then as long as the soul is in the material body, the identity is not dissolved. So, how can a person be called jivanmukta with the body?

The correct answer to this problem is that the soul's fall is due to his desire, and the liberation is also due to a change in his desire. However, this liberation is not a desireless state, because that would entail the dissolution of the body, and would be possible only after death. For someone to be liberated in this body, liberation must be understood as a change in desire—which creates individuality, and therefore entails a body—and yet that desire is not material.

If the jīvā has developed loving devotion toward the Lord, then he is considered jivanmukta and 'mukti' is freedom from material desire rather than from the material world. In Gaudīya Vaiṣṇavism, the aspiration for mukti as the merger into Brahman, or the liberation from the cycle of birth and death, are both rejected. The aspiration is only to turn one's consciousness toward the Lord. Thus, Śri Chaitanya emphasizes the following in His Śikṣāṣṭakam:

> na dhanam na janam na sundarim
> kavitam va jagad-isha kamaye
> mama janmani janmanishvare
> bhavatad bhaktir ahaituki twayi

O, almighty Lord, I have no desire to accumulate wealth, nor do I desire beautiful women, nor do I want any number of followers. I only want Your causeless devotional service birth after birth.

The rejection of wealth and beautiful women must be understood as the rejection of the material pleasures of the gross material body. The rejection of many followers must be understood as the rejection of the pleasures of the subtle body (mind, intellect, ego, and mahattattva). Finally, the statement about 'birth after birth' entails that there is also a rejection of the liberation from the cycle of birth and death. The devotee is only desirous of the 'causeless devotional service'. The meaning of 'causeless' is that it springs naturally from the soul's ānanda potency, and it desires nothing but the happiness of the Lord (excluding even liberation from the cycle of birth and death—which entails that material suffering is acceptable). This is a radical concept of liberation, that goes beyond the concept of jivanmukta which is liberation within the present body, without scope for rebirth; the jivanmukta is not expected to be reborn. In Śri Chaitanya's description, even rebirth is acceptable if there is devotion.

The soul's fall into material nature is not physical. The soul is still with the Lord; as the Lord glances at the material energy, the soul's consciousness is diverted into material nature. But just like the Lord's eyes don't get detached from His body due to this glance, similarly, the soul doesn't get detached from the Lord. The soul's fall is the misunderstanding about the purpose of the material world—the soul thinks that this world is for his enjoyment when the fact is that it is meant to be Param Śiva's austerity. The world can also be the pleasure of the Lord—in the transcendental sense. But it is never the pleasure of the soul. If this understanding of purpose is revised, then the soul is liberated. The soul doesn't have to forego the material experience, only the misunderstanding that the world is meant for his enjoyment. Thus, we can distinguish between two kinds of liberation. First, it is the entry into the spiritual world, which the Lord has created for His pleasure; the soul also enjoys in this spiritual world. Second, it is a development of the same devotion in the material world by which the devotee engages everything in the material world in the service of the Lord.

Entry into the abode of the Lord has no relation to the exit from the material world, the discarding of the material body, or the freedom from the cycle of birth and death. Yes, in many cases, the jīva who has developed a devotion to the Lord will never be born again. But that would also entail that the jīva is not in the Lord's abode while in the body; He can only attain the Lord's abode after the death of this body. In the deepest conception about this attainment, the soul can exist in the Lord's abode even if he is living in the material world.

QUESTION

You are saying that the soul's fall is due to his desire. But others say that the soul's fall is due to ignorance. The desire is an emotive state, and ignorance is a cognitive state. Accordingly, the proponent of 'desire is the cause of fall' can argue for liberation by devotion. However, the proponent of 'ignorance is the cause of fall' argues that knowledge is the cause of liberation. You have yourself said that the study of Vedic scriptures leads us to liberation. Therefore, it seems that you support both the fall by ignorance and fall by desire. Which of these two positions must be considered the real cause of the soul's fall?

1.3.3 (66)

नानुमानम् अतच्छब्दात्

nānumānam atacchabdāt

na—not; anumānam—what is imagined or inferred; atat-śabdāt—not from the scriptures.

TRANSLATION

Not (attained) by imagination (or) even the study of scriptures.

COMMENTARY

In 1.1.3 (3) it was stated that the śāstra or the scriptures are the right sources of knowledge about the Absolute Truth. This sūtra, however, states that the study of the śāstra itself doesn't lead to entry into the Lord's abode. In this regard, we might reference the following statement by Śri Śankarācārya:

> bhaja govindaṁ bhaja govindaṁ
> govindaṁ bhaja mūḍha-mate
> samprāpte sannihite kāle
> nahi nahi rakṣati ḍukṛṅkaraṇe

> Worship Govinda, worship Govinda,
> Worship Govinda, oh fool!
> At the time of your death,
> Rules of grammar will not save you.

As a classic example, many Indologists and Western scholars have studied the scriptures and translated them into English and other languages. However, despite this study, they have no faith in the truth of the scriptures, and they haven't developed devotion to the Lord. Therefore, despite studying the scriptures, they cannot be liberated. If the qualification for liberation was merely the study of the scriptures, then Indologists and Western scholars who have no devotion to the Lord would automatically be considered liberated from material existence, and hence qualified to enter the abode of the Lord. This is not an admonishment of the study of scriptures; it is only a statement that theoretical understanding residing in the mind and intellect is not enough. To enter the Lord's abode, one must also develop devotion to the Lord. If the scholar of Vedic texts is averse to the Lord—which most of the Indologists and Western scholars are—their study of scripture is a veritable waste of effort and time.

Yes, once we understand, we may begin to like it. But understanding may not lead to liking. Many people go to colleges to study courses;

they may even do well in the exams and obtain good grades, but they hate the subject they are studying and dislike the educational process. They have naturally developed a good understanding of the subject under study, but they have not developed a liking for the subject. On the other hand, many people may have a natural like for some subject, and even if they are unable to go to college, they may study the subject on their own, and obtain a good understanding. Therefore, we can accept that understanding doesn't always lead to liking but liking always leads to understanding (given enough time and opportunity). In that sense, the study of the scripture is inadequate, because one may not develop the devotion.

QUESTION

You have said that the jīvā and the Lord are connected by the prāṇa. Thus, yogis state that by controlling the prāṇa one can transcend the material world and enter the Lord's abode. The practice of yoga and prāṇayāma are quite popular. They are presented as secular practices, which can be adopted by a person of any religion. Are these the appropriate methods of transcendence?

1.3.4 (67)

पुराणभृच्च

prāṇabhṛcca

prāṇa—the five airs; bhṛta—carried (by prāṇa); ca—also (na—not).

TRANSLATION

(Nor) by the support of the prāṇa (i.e., the practice of prāṇayāma).

COMMENTARY

There can be some contentions in the translation of this sūtra because the meaning of *pranābhṛta* is "carried by the prāṇa". This term can be treated as a noun or a verb. If it is treated as a noun, then it represents the soul (as the soul's consciousness is carried from one body to another due to prāṇa). However, if it is treated as a verb, it represents a process by which one can enter the abode of the Lord. Suppose we treat *pranābhṛta* as the noun; the sūtra would then state, "the soul also cannot enter the abode of the Lord", which would make the entire Vedānta Sūtra doctrine pointless. Therefore, I have treated it as a verb. Under this translation, the sūtra reads: "the soul cannot enter the abode of the Lord by the effect of prāṇa". This is not problematic, but it must be understood.

We have previously noted that the attention of the soul is diverted from one part of the material world to another due to prāṇa. By controlling prāṇa, one may also divert their attention toward other things. However, this method is rejected for entry into the Lord's abode. The reason is that the prāṇa by which we control the body and the mind is also material in nature. It is not the prāṇa by which the soul is connected to the Lord. Therefore, even though the process of prāṇa manipulation is useful in advancing to better bodies in this world, this method is not enough for entry into the Lord's abode. This should, however, not be considered a rejection of the aṣṭāṅga-yoga system, because the system comprises of eight stages, and control of prāṇa—called prāṇayāma—is the 4th stage. The 4th stage is control of the material prāṇa. Following this, the crucial 7th stage of dhāraṇā or fixation of the attention on the Lord must follow. The 7th stage involves the prāṇa that connects the jīvā to the Paramātma; it is a different kind of prāṇa which exists in the spiritual world, and indeed in Brahman, as we have discussed previously. Therefore, merely the control of the material prāṇa is inadequate; it can help control the mind and the body and prepare it for focus on the Lord. But despite this control, the Lord is not easily found even in the heart of the yogis. The cessation of thoughts and enjoyment doesn't entail the development of devotion to the Lord. Vedic texts describe many yogis who have succumbed to material enjoyment after thousands of years of such practice—when they are enticed by heavenly damsels for sex. Such yogis have obtained mastery of the material body and the mind, but they haven't developed devotion to the Lord. Hence, despite their control of the body and the mind, their consciousness is still not diverted toward the Lord. Since it is still focused toward matter, the yogis may fall when the opportunity presents itself.

Many people say that yoga is secular, and it has hence become an alternative to other religious practices—which explicitly accept a transcendental God. Secularism merely indicates that there are many ways to approach God, and the soul may adopt one of the many methods. However, ultimately, the purpose of any spiritual practice is to develop devotion to the Supreme Lord. If yoga is practiced with the aim to develop loving devotion, as is recommended in the Bhaga-vad-Gita, where the ascetic withdraws the senses inwards and focuses the awareness on the Paramātma in the heart, the process is legitimate. However, if the process is without loving devotion to the Lord, then it must be considered atheistic—although more advanced than current materialism. Atheism is the aversion to the Lord, and everyone who practices yoga without devotion to the Lord is atheistic. Āsana and prāṇayāma are not spiritual processes; they are mechanical changes to the gross and subtle bodies. The key to spiritualism is the change in the consciousness that connects the jīvā to the Lord.

We noted above a difference between the prāṇa by which the soul controls the body and the mind, and the prāṇa that connects the jīvā to the Lord. In general, prāṇa is the connection between the knower and the known. If the Lord is the known, the connection is still called 'prāṇa' even though the nature of this connection and the process of observation (of the Lord) are different from that of matter. The prāṇa that carries the jīvā's consciousness in the material world is controlled by other types of material agencies, such as guna, karma, and time. Even when the soul moves to another body, the previous body and mind are left behind, but the guna and karma move with the soul caused by time.

In this regard, we must understand that there are many kinds of material prāṇa. There is a type of prāṇa that works under the control of guna and karma. Due to this prāṇa, the body continues to work even when we don't exercise volition. Then there is a prāṇa by which the soul accepts or rejects the desires automatically created due to guna. Then there is another prāṇa by which the demigods and ultimately the Paramātma control the delivery of karma. In short, there is a prāṇa which is inferior to guna and karma, and there is a prāṇa that is supe-rior to guna and karma but under the control of different entities—the prāṇa superior to guna is in control of the jīvā and the prāṇa superior to karma is in the control of the Paramātma (as well as the demigods). Finally, there is a prāṇa which directs our consciousness toward the Lord. This prāṇa works under the control of the devotional energy of the Lord and without such devotion, this prāṇa cannot be activated. This sūtra only refers to the inferior forms of prāṇa—which are used to control the gross, subtle, and causal bodies—and the spiritual prāṇa under the devotional practice isn't referenced.

QUESTION

It seems from your statements that no process—either involving the discipline of the body or the mind—is adequate for attaining the abode of the Lord. These processes are merely an adjustment of the mind, senses, or the prāṇa. The true cause of change must happen in the desires of the soul. However, how can we be led to such changes if none of the practices can lead one toward it?

1.3.5 (68)

भेदव्यपदेशात्

bhedavyapadeśāt

bheda—the difference; vyapadeśāt—from the covering of vision.

TRANSLATION

From the covering of vision (of the Lord), the difference (of the jīvā).

COMMENTARY

Both terms—*bheda* and *vyapadeśāt*—are contentious here. The term *bheda* means difference, but the difference between which two things? Does this difference refer to that between the jīvā and the Lord? If so, it has already been stated many times earlier. Does it refer to the difference between jīvā and the three modes of nature? That too has been stated earlier. Does it refer to the difference between Prakriti and the Lord? That too has been noted earlier (the Lord is transcendental to the three modes of nature). If all these differences have already been noted, and cannot be repeated, then what does *bheda* refer to?

To understand this sūtra, we need to carefully analyze the origin of the jīvā's entry into the material world. In 1.1.12 (12) we discussed that the Oneness becomes differentiated due to desire for pleasure. We have discussed earlier that the ānanda aspect of the jīvā is the capacity to enjoy; the capacity always exists; however, the pleasure may not always exist. Enjoyment is preceded by desire, and it is the fulfillment of desire. If things go according to our desire, then we enjoy; if they are against our desires, then we suffer. The root cause of differentiation of the jīvā from the Oneness is desire; in the case of the material world, it must be understood as material desire. But, what do we mean by material desire? How is it different from other kinds of desires? Since the desire of devotion to the Lord has been noted as yielding liberation from the material world, we can surmise that 'material desire' is the opposite of devotion.

The jīva has also been described as always being connected to the Lord through the prāṇa; by this connection, we described how the jīva must be understood as a part of His body. Just like in our present body, the prāṇa flows from the heart to the different parts of the body, and this expansion of the prāṇa then makes us conscious of the entire body, in the same way, if the Lord is understood as the Supreme Soul, then jīva can be described as a part of the Lord's body; the Supreme Soul can be considered the 'heart' and the jīva is then the different parts of the body connected to the heart through the prāṇa. The entire body is spiritual; however, the Supreme Soul is the 'heart' while the individual souls are the different parts of the spiritual body connected to the heart through prāṇa; this prāṇa makes the Lord aware of the existence of the soul. And yet, the soul cannot be identified with the Lord because of the difference between the body's heart and the other parts of the body connected to the heart.

The different parts of the body serve each other—e.g., the hand feeds the stomach, and the stomach energizes the hands—and they ultimately serve the soul. In the same way, the jīva must serve the other jīva, but ultimately the Supreme Soul. It has previously been described that the Absolute Truth reconciles the diversities and we compared this to the root of the tree. The Supreme Soul is the root, from which the prāṇa expands like many branches of the tree—stretching over the body and covering all the parts—connecting the body to the soul. In this case, the jīva and the Supreme Soul are simultaneously connected and yet different. By service to each other, and ultimately by service to the Supreme Soul, the jīva is liberated from material existence and is situated as part of the Oneness, which has many parts (like in the body). This process of liberation achieved through devotion to the Lord has been described previously.

So, now, we have two facts to consider. First, the soul is always connected to the Supreme Soul. Second, it has entered the material world because of something called 'material desire', which must be understood as being opposed to devotion. By putting these two facts together, we can understand what we mean by 'material desire': It is the desire to be independent of the Lord; rather than being situated as part of the Oneness, it is the need to be a separate individual; rather than serving as part of the Oneness, and the heart of that Oneness, it is the need to be independent and different from parts and from the heart.

However, we have also discussed how the jīva is simply the potentiality of enjoyment; it can have desires, but it cannot fulfill the desires on its own. As we noted in the previous sūtra, the soul can control the prāṇa that controls the guna. However, it cannot control the prāṇa that controls the karma. Therefore, Paramātma facilitates the fulfillment of the desire in the material world. However, if the desire is to become independent of the Lord, it can never be fulfilled because the jīva doesn't have its own power of fulfillment—it must always rely on the prāṇa that delivers *karma* which is under the control of the Paramātma. Thus, the attainment of independence is ultimately futile; the jīva must realize that it depends on the Supreme Soul's goodwill to even fulfill its material desires of enjoyment, but the desire for independence cannot be fulfilled. To the extent that the jīva harbors this desire, it must exist in the material world where the *illusion* of independence is created when the Lord becomes invisible to the soul. Because the Lord is invisible to the jīva, the jīva can imagine that the Lord doesn't exist and that it is free to enjoy independently, rather than serve others, and ultimately serve the Lord. When the explicit desire to see the Lord is developed, the desire for independence must be given up; the jīva can be liberated from the cultures of material existence if the material desire is overcome.

In 1.3.1 (64) we discussed how the material world is the negation of the Lord. But we had described this negation cognitively ("not red", "not table", etc.). We can now describe the same negation emotively: the jīva develops a 'distance' to the Lord by becoming averse to Him; the 'distance' here is 'emotional distance'. Both ordinary and scientific uses of the term 'origin' can be understood in this context. Substantively, the 'origin' represents the thing we are averse to (i.e., the Lord), and māyā represents this emotional rejection of devotion to the Lord. Scientifically, we also use the term 'origin' to measure the distance from a chosen center (of some coordinate system). In this case, the Lord is described as the origin, and both types of meanings can be applied.

There is a sense in which the jīvā emotionally negates the Lord, and there is a sense in which the jīvā moves 'away' from the Lord; the 'distance' between the jīvā and the Lord grows. The cause of distancing is the desire for independence.

The emotional distancing is the primary source of the separation—as has been noted in 1.1.12 (12). Thus, when the material world originates in the Lord, we must understand this origination primarily in the emotional sense, and secondarily in the material sense. As space is defined by the distance from the origin, similarly, the material space is to be primordially understood as the distance from the Lord. Thus, the term *bheda* used in this sūtra must be understood as the difference between the jīvā and the Lord; however, this difference has already been noted. What wasn't described is that this difference is unbridgeable due to which any process of spiritual progress—such as jñāna-yoga or aṣtān-ga-yoga—doesn't take one into the Lord's abode unless the emotional attitude is changed. Therefore, even if one is studying scriptures, one must do it devotionally. Even if one is performing meditation, one must focus on the Lord. The term *bheda* hence refers to the aversion toward the service of the Lord. It points to the aspiration to become free of His control, or equal to Him, and not to be devoted to Him. This desire makes every other effort futile.

Similarly, the term *vyapadeśāt* is contentious. We have previously translated it as— (1) statement, claim, or declaration, (2) the covering, hiding, or misrepresentation. Both translations are appropriate here. Based on the first, we can say that "it is declared that the jīvā has aversion to the Lord". Alternatively, *vyapadeśāt* can also mean that "the jīvā's aversion hides the Lord (from its vision)". The Lord doesn't appear before the jīvā, and the jīvā cannot forcefully enter the Lord's abode if there is an aversion in the jīvā. The Lord is present everywhere; He is not absent even from this world. However, He is still invisible due to the presence of material desire in the soul. No process of transcendence—whether the reading of scripture, analysis, and discussion, or meditative practices—can deliver the results if this aversion remains unchanged.

Even though the reading of scriptures and chanting of its mantras has been advised previously, we must distinguish between the cognitive and the emotional aspects of the soul. The cognitive aspect is called *chit*, and it represents the capacity to understand and do things.

However, it is different from the emotional aspect called ānanda, which represents the desire and capacity to enjoy. If we read the scriptures without faith and devotion or chant the mantra without such devotion, the processes don't have an effect. On the other hand, the reading of scripture is not necessary. The gopis of Vṛndāvana, for example, did not study scriptures; when Uddhava approached them with the philosophical understanding of the Absolute Truth, they rejected it, and only desired to know about the Lord's well-being. Thus, every process can work when devotion is employed, and no process will work without the presence of devotion.

QUESTION

But what is the guarantee that the jīvā will aspire for devotion to the Lord and will be able to enter His abode? How can we trust this process?

There is natural skepticism in everyone because we have been cheated in love in this life or in our previous lives. The idea that love is reciprocated is touted in romantic novels, but true love is very hard to find. On the other hand, the process of love involves many sacrifices—e.g., to develop an attachment to the Lord, one must give up attachment to this world. In short, one would have to sacrifice the worldly possibility of love, in order to develop the love of the Lord. So, the seeker may question the process itself: What if I'm cheated in the process of love, and I sacrifice everything, and yet do not obtain the result?

1.3.6 (69)

पुरकरणात्

prakaraṇāt

prakaraṇāt—from the episodes, descriptions, pastimes (in the scriptures).

TRANSLATION

From the many episodes and pastimes (of devotees in the scriptures).

COMMENTARY

There is no panacea for doubt when it comes to devotion. Doubts can pertain to the nature of reality, and they can be discussed rationally or empirically. Devotion doesn't come under this category. We can explain the nature of the Absolute Truth through philosophical argument. But we cannot make anyone *like* the Absolute Truth by arguments. Such liking may automatically develop in some when the understanding is gained. But it may also not develop in others even with an understanding. Also, it is said that the progress in understanding depends on devotion; with devotion, the understanding advances; without devotion, the understanding remains preliminary. In short, reason can destroy doubts about what the Absolute Truth is. But the destruction of doubts is not devotion. One may know that the Lord is the origin of everything, but that doesn't mean that one will necessarily love the Lord or have trust in the Lord.

The panacea for such doubts is assurances given in the scriptures. For example, in the Bhagavad-Gita 18.66, Lord Kṛṣṇa assures Arjuna that He should not worry (*mā śucaḥ*) that surrender to Him will lead to any suffering.

sarva-dharmān parityajya
mām ekaṁ śaraṇaṁ vraja
ahaṁ tvāṁ sarva-pāpebhyo
mokṣayiṣyāmi mā śucaḥ

Abandon all varieties of religion and just surrender unto Me. I shall deliver you from all sinful reactions. Do not fear.

The best panacea for doubts is the association of pure devotees because this devotion is infectious. They have surrendered to the Lord and found bliss in their devotion. If one is unable to find such devotees, then the pastimes of the devotees described in the scriptures can be used to understand the nature of devotion. Such pastimes often contain elaborate prayers to the Lord, where His glories are sung, and His affection toward the devotees is described. Devotion can only be acquired by experiencing the devotion; it cannot be acquired by logic and reasoning. However, to the extent that rational doubts prevent us from developing devotion, a philosophical understanding is necessary.

QUESTION

But why can't the Lord become kind to the soul and appear before it? Since the Lord is said to be magnanimous, He can demonstrate this magnanimity and appear before the jīvā despite its doubts or aversion. Just like a mother or father forcibly love the child, why can't the Lord do the same with the averse jīvā?

1.3.7 (70)

स्थित्यदनाभ्याम् च

sthityadanābhyām ca

sthiti—fixed; adana—food, act of eating; abhyām—the two; ca—also.

TRANSLATION

(The Lord is already present with the soul) on account of the two (living entities) one of which silently observes even as the other eats (enjoys).

COMMENTARY

Many people practicing spiritual life become frustrated with the process. They claim that they have been studying the scriptures, following rules and regulations, controlling the body and the mind, etc. And yet, they don't seem to find the bliss that must come with the devotion to the Lord. Then they blame the Lord for being too discerning or unkind, for not appearing before them, showing them some 'signs' of His presence, or demonstrating kindness in other ways. As we have discussed in the previous sūtra, the processes of reading, understanding, or even practicing (by the body and mind) are not adequate. They are merely cognitive and conative changes, and they cannot produce the ultimate result unless one develops devotion. This devotion cannot be acquired by any process; however, if the devotion exists, then all processes help its advancement. Factually, even though many people perform spiritual processes, they harbor alternative material aspirations, rather than unconditional love to the Lord. Their main aim may be to become happy in this life, to improve the condition of the world, to initiate many disciples and be known as a spiritual leader, etc. All these desires are hindrances to spiritual progress; every process will work if there is a latent desire to unconditionally love the Lord. Similarly, no process—even the reading of scripture and chanting of mantra—will work if the desire is to pursue alternative goals rather than the devotion to the Lord. Lord Kṛṣṇa states in the Bhagavad-Gita 4.11 His reciprocal approach to love.

ye yathā māṁ prapadyante
tāṁs tathaiva bhajāmy aham

 As they surrender to me, I am devoted to them in the same way.

 The term *prapadyante* means 'surrender', and the term *bhajāmy aham* indicates the Lord 'worships' the jīvā in the same way. The root *bhaj* indicates devotion, and the Lord ascribes to Himself that devotional reciprocation in accordance with the way in which the soul surrenders to the Lord. The cause of the Lord not appearing is thus the lack of devotional attitude in the soul.

 But, if one goes further, and argues that the Lord should be the bigger person in the devotional relationship, and must initiate the devotional inclination, then this has already been confirmed by the presence of the Paramātma in the heart. As we have discussed earlier, the Lord comes with the soul due to three motives—causes, reasons, and justifications. The cause of the Lord's presence is that He delivers the good and bad results of his actions, the reason is that the Lord is attached to the soul, and the justification is that He considers it His duty to liberate the soul. The magnanimity of the Lord is not in question because He is already present in the heart as the silent observer and approver of the soul's desires for independent enjoyment. The desire for independence can only be fulfilled if the soul had the power to create a world for himself; in short, he should become a creator just like the Lord. The soul aspires for such independence where it creates its own world and becomes its master. This illusory type of enjoyment is facilitated by the Lord. So, He cannot be faulted for lack of progress in the spiritual life; the responsibility rests entirely with the soul.

Topic 2

QUESTION

You have stated that the Lord is the origin and the basis of the material world. He has been called transcendent to the material world. What is the nature of this transcendence, and how does it differ from material existence?

1.3.8 (71)

भूमा संप्रसादादध्युपदेशात्

bhūmā samprasādādadhyupadeśāt

bhūmā—the multitude, collection, assembly, world; samprasādāt-adhi—from beyond the state of deep sleep; upadeśāt—from of the teaching.

TRANSLATION

From the teaching, the bhūmā is from beyond the state of deep sleep.

COMMENTARY

The term bhūmā represents the plurality of individuals. It is not merely the Supreme Person we call "God" but a 'world' that exists in relation to God. We can call it 'Godhead'. This is also evident from the previous topic, which stated that the abode of the Lord is the origin of the material world. This sūtra continues the discussion and calls this 'abode' bhūmā or a world in which God exists with His devotees. In relation to the material world, it is described as being beyond the state of deep sleep; in the Yoga philosophy, there are four states of conscious experience— (1) vaikharī or waking state, (2) madhyamā or dreaming state, (3) paśyanti or deep sleep state, and (4) parā or transcendent state. The bhūmā or the transcendent reality is here described as the fourth state.

During the waking state, the soul acquires experiences of the five gross elements—namely, Earth, Water, Fire, Air, and Ether. When these elements interact, they produce a representation of the world, which the senses, the mind, the intellect, and the ego interact with to create an experience. During the dreaming state, this bodily interaction with the world is absent; however, the senses, the mind, the intellect, and the ego are still active. These senses and the mind are not just perceivers of the world; they can also create this world. During the waking experience, the perception of the world is dominant, and therefore, the waking state is identified with the five gross elements. It is not that the subtle elements are absent; it is just that these five elements are the dominant cause of the experience. However, when we enter the dreaming stage, the senses and the mind become creators of the experience. In this state, we can understand the mind and senses better than during the waking experience, and hence the dreaming stage is identified with the working of the senses, the mind, the intellect, the ego, and morality. The dreaming state is said to be superior to the waking state because during dreaming we can realize that experience is not limited to the gross body. Therefore, if one was identifying with this body, then dreaming indicates that this body is not the cause of experience, because such experiences can also exist during dreaming. The movement of the senses, the mind, the intellect, the and ego stops during the deep sleep state, but the unconscious—called the kārana sarīra—remains active. This activity involves the integration of the waking and dreaming experience into the formation of deep-seated beliefs, fears, wishes, and relationships. It is sometimes said that what we learn during the waking state needs deep sleep to be assimilated.

Beyond these three kinds of activities, there is also the activity of the soul. This activity originates in the automatic springing of desire for enjoyment. While the previous three are described as material, the fourth state—namely, the activity of the soul—is considered transcendental to matter. This sūtra states that the abode of the Lord also involves activities, but they are in the fourth state of experience—i.e., they are produced by the soul, and not by matter.

QUESTION

By calling transcendence the fourth state of consciousness, you are only distinguishing it from different types of matter. It can also be construed as a negative definition—the transcendent state is *not* these three states. But how do we understand the transcendent state in a positive sense—what it is?

1.3.9 (72)
धर्मोपपत्तेश्च
dharmopapatteśca

dharma—nature; upapatteḥ—cause, justification, evidence; ca—and.

TRANSLATION

And (its) nature is (self)-causation, (self)-justification, (self)-evidence.

COMMENTARY

In logic, *upapatti* is used in various ways to indicate causation, evidence, justification, substantiation, and the rationale underlying a law. The transcendent state is here described as something whose very nature is causation, justification, and rationale. This can be understood in contrast to the previous sūtra where the previous three types of material experiences were noted; all these experiences involve matter. The material elements such as Earth, Water, Fire, Air, Ether, mind, intellect, ego, and morality are not automatically activated; they are activated by the presence of prāṇa. The prāṇa is also not automatically active in the material world; it is animated by guna and karma. Finally, guna and karma are also not automatically causal; they are activated by the influence of time. This time—which causes all changes—is the representation of the Lord, called Saṅkarṣaṇa. Time automatically animates the material world, however, the jīva can reject the animations of guna. The jīva cannot reject the animations caused by karma. Thus, we cannot control what will happen to us, but we can control how we respond to it. This 'response' to the automatic animation due to time is the ability in the jīva to reject the automatically arising desires. For instance, if someone slaps you, your mind would automatically develop a fight or flight response. This inclination is automatically produced by one's guna (some people may want to fight while others will try to escape) under the influence of time. The jīva can reject such automatically created impulses.

But we must now ask: What is the cause of the jīva making a certain type of choice? And the answer is that there is no external cause. The nature or dharma of the transcendent reality is that it is self-caused, or spontaneous. Therefore, as we seek deeper forms of causality, we progress from the body to the senses, to the mind, intellect, ego, and morality, into the unconscious guna and karma, which are animated by time, and finally to the jīva who chooses a response. This choice cannot be pushed further back to anything other than the soul; the choice is self-caused, self-justified, and the jīva is the only cause of such a choice.

So, the transcendent reality is the ultimate *upapatti*—the cause, reason, and justification—for all experiences. Within this self-justified and self-initiated causation, the Lord has greater power to control, greater capacity to enjoy, and greater ability for cognition, compared to the jīva. Hence, the jīva is subordinate to the Lord. However, both the jīva and Lord have self-causation. In short, both the soul and the Lord have free will by which they can change things. The transcendent reality is being described as that which has self-causation; in contrast, the material reality is without self-causation or spontaneous action and must, therefore, be animated by either the will of the soul or that of the Lord.

Topic 3

QUESTION

You have previously said that the Lord is the origin of the material world. Now, we have also talked about the Lord's abode, and you described it as bhūmā, entailing that there are many living entities. Is the Lord also the origin of these liberated living entities, like in the case of the material world?

The impersonalist philosophers sometimes accept the Lord's worship as a stepping stone into the impersonal Brahman; they call the forms of the Lord Saguna-Brahman as opposed to the Nirguna-Brahman; the implication is that the Saguna feature of the Lord is temporary in this material world: He appears in a form to liberate the living entity, but thereafter merges into Brahman. The seeker is asking whether this differentiation (as previously indicated by bhūmā) must also be considered another 'world', just like the material world?

1.3.10 (73)

अक्षरमम्बरान्तधृतेः

akṣaramambarāntadhṛteḥ

akṣaram—the Imperishable; ambara-anta—to the end of space; dhṛteḥ—supports.

TRANSLATION

The Imperishable supports (everything) till the end of space.

COMMENTARY

We have earlier discussed the four quarters of existence. All these collectively constitute everything that exists, although they are divided into different domains. In this sūtra, by using the term *ambara-anta*, or the end of space, an indirect reference to the hierarchy between these domains is being made. The material world is at the bottom of this hierarchy; Brahman is above the material world; the Vaikuṇṭha planets are above the Brahman, and Goloka is above the Vaikuṇṭha planets. Each of these places is differentiated into individuals, and accordingly, each of these places involves a 'distance' between the Lord and the jīva; if this distance did not exist, the jīva would be identical to the Lord.

We have previously discussed how the jīva is averse to the Lord, and its 'distance' from the Lord is based on the emotional aloofness produced by aversion. But in the three-quarters of liberated realms, the jīva are not averse to the Lord. So, how are they still different from the Lord, rather than identical with Him? To understand the differentiation, we must distinguish between different kinds of desires. There is a type of desire in which the jīva loves the Lord and wants to serve Him personally. Due to the attitude of service, the jīva considers himself different from the Lord, and yet he wants to see Him face to face. This desire is devotion but accompanied by a *boldness*—I'm qualified to serve the Lord. To serve, I must be different from Him, and yet close to Him. There is another kind of desire in which the jīva loves the Lord but is shy; he keeps a distance from the Lord since he considers himself unqualified to meet the Lord face-to-face. Such a soul prefers to serve the other devotees of the Lord. This 'distance' to the Lord is however only cognitive; the jīva stays out of sight, and this cognitive separation intensifies the emotional separation and brings him emotionally closer to the Lord. In fact, the shy devotee is emotionally dearer to the Lord than the bold devotee. There is also a third type of desire in which the jīva recognizes that the Lord is Supreme, and He is not averse to the Lord, but His appreciation is silent and distant. The jīva doesn't want to be independent but he also doesn't want to come close to the Lord. In this case, the jīva is both cognitively and emotionally distant, although not averse to the Lord.

These three types of desires correspond to the three-quarters of existence that we have discussed previously. The devotion conditioned by shyness constitutes the place called Goloka. The devotion conditioned by boldness constitutes the place called Vaikuṇṭha. The devotion of silent appreciation is called Brahman. And apart from these three—the fourth quarter of existence—the material world, is the place where the jīva has the desire for independence.

In Goloka, the jīva has the greatest emotional connection to the Lord, exacerbated by the cognitive distance (in this world, distance makes the hearts go fonder). In Vaikuṇṭha, the jīva is cognitively close, but the emotional connect is reduced (in this world, familiarity breeds contempt). In Brahman, both cognitive and emotional distances are greater, as the jīva doesn't want to serve the Lord personally, and he doesn't miss the Lord because of not serving Him. The jīva is content appreciating the Lord from a distance. And in the material world, the jīva is averse to the Lord. Therefore, based on the emotional distancing, we can construct the space of the four quarters of existence: Goloka is closest in emotional distance, Vaikuṇṭha is slightly farther, Brahman is even farther, and the material world is the farthest. In this sūtra, it is stated that the Lord supports everything up to the farthest end of space. This 'farthest end' should be understood as the material existence, and it is most detached from the Lord.

The main point is that even the transcendent realm is differentiated like the material realm. It can be described as multiple 'worlds' in which the same Lord is the Supreme Person, although based on the cognitive and emotional distancing, He is understood in different ways. Thus, we should not think that the material world is differentiated, and transcendence is undifferentiated. The statements about Oneness should rather be understood as the unity in purpose, being parts of a Whole, and being interrelated rather than independent.

QUESTION

You have previously said that the Lord is the controller of the material world, and the demigods are subordinate to Him. Does this

kind of rulership or control of the other living entities exist even in the transcendent world?

Everyone in the material world resents having a boss, but everybody wants to be the boss. The impersonal viewpoint envisions the dissolution of this boss mentality by suggesting that we are all one, so there is no boss because there is no difference between us. But if we get past that idea, and acknowledge the existence of individuals, there is also the conception of an egalitarian society in which people live in a communion comprised of equals where nobody is anyone else's boss. Modern ideas of democracy have emerged from the attempt to dismantle the permanence of bosses; however, given that there would be anarchy in the material world if there were no boss, we still envision the existence of a temporary boss—e.g., a democratically elected leader—who can be replaced by someone else if he acted too bossy. So, one can surmise that the existence of bosses was a necessary evil in this material world, and a transcendent world must therefore be perfectly egalitarian—because everyone is well-behaved, so there is no need for a boss. In short, if we cannot merge with God to become God, then at least we can still aspire to become equal to God. God may remain the first among equals, but he could not wield power over the others.

1.3.11 (74)

सा च प्रशासनात्

sā ca praśāsanāt

sā—this (the previous sūtra); ca—and, also; praśāsanāt—from rulership.

TRANSLATION

From the rulership, also this (the Lord is the origin and supporter).

COMMENTARY

The sūtra rejects all egalitarian ideas—which often follow when the impersonal oneness is rejected. It states that the Lord is the ruler apart from being the origin and the supporter of all existence. The term *praśāsana* means 'administration'. It has been noted that in the material world, the Lord has administrators in the demigods—each responsible for various departments of the worldly control—and the Lord presides over them. Accordingly, there is a hierarchy in this control structure: there isn't one ruler who controls everything. Rather, He delegates the power of control successively through a hierarchy of controllers. Now, if one thought that this was unique to the material world, the implication here is that the hierarchy applies even to the spiritual world. In short, not only is there one Supreme Controller, there are also subordinate controllers under the supervision of the Supreme Controller. The souls, therefore, work under the supervision of 'senior' or 'superior' souls, and the society isn't egalitarian.

QUESTION

What is the necessity for supervision or rulership when everyone is liberated? Since the jīvā is freed from aversion to the Lord, and hence aversion to other living entities, they would naturally cooperate with each other. With this natural cooperation, there should be no need for a supervisor or ruler.

1.3.12 (75)

अन्यभावव्यावृत्तेश्च

anyabhāvavyāvṛtteśca

anya—another; bhāva—nature; vyāvṛtteḥ—due to diversity; ca—and.

TRANSLATION

Due to diversity (of opinions) and different natures (of the souls).

COMMENTARY

The emergence of a cooperative mindset doesn't entail the dissolution of variety and diverse opinions. Just because everyone is liberated doesn't mean they will perfectly agree with each other on everything. They may maintain diverse viewpoints, and still, one viewpoint must win over the others. The hierarchy enables the existence of diversity, and yet a choice among the diverse viewpoints can be made. The cooperation is simply that those individuals whose viewpoints were overruled will not harbor resentment. They will rather respect the opinion of a superior living entity, even if they disagree with it.

Topic 4

QUESTION

Why should different liberated souls have different opinions and natures? Aren't we discussing the nature of the Absolute Truth which must be considered universal, and hence its perception must also be the cognition of the universal? How could we regard such diverse opinions of the Absolute Truth?

1.3.13 (76)
ईक्षतिकिर्मव्यपदेशात् सः
īkṣatikarmavyapadeśāt saḥ

īkṣati—seeing; karma—acting; vyapadeśāt—because of the appearance, or because of the description, or because of representation; saḥ—He.

TRANSLATION

Because He is seen and acts in many ways (in relation to different jīvā).

COMMENTARY

We have discussed earlier how all the quarters of existence are substantively expanded from the Lord. We have also seen how the jīvā adopts different emotional attitudes toward the Lord (here we are discussing only the favorable attitudes). Finally, we have noted that the 'space' of the different domains of existence is defined in relation to the 'origin' in the Lord—i.e., different positions in the creation are different places in relation to Him. Accordingly, from the viewpoint of each jīvā, the same Absolute Truth is perceived differently.

Topic 5

QUESTION

You earlier stated that the Absolute Truth is Oneness, which reconciles the diversity. The diversity was the parts of the whole, like the branches of the trees. Now, you are also stating that whole or the root itself—which was earlier said to be Oneness—can be understood in diverse ways. Then, why would we consider this diversity as Oneness, when it presents itself in diverse ways?

1.3.14 (77)

दहर उत्तरेभ्यः

dahara uttarebhyaḥ

daharaḥ—child or small; uttarebhyaḥ—due to being subsequent.

TRANSLATION

Due to being subsequent, (the soul) is small or the child (of the One).

COMMENTARY

In the previous sūtra, it was stated that the Lord is seen and acts in different ways in relation to the different jīvā. This leads to the doubt that even the Absolute Truth is not the *universal truth*, because each jīvā can have a different conception of the Absolute Truth. This doubt rests on the notion that the universal truth is an idea, and everyone must have the same idea. In Vedic philosophy, however, the Absolute Truth is a person, and everyone can know the same person differently. If the Absolute Truth is only an idea, then the knowledge of this Absolute Truth must also be the universal truth. If on the other hand, the Absolute Truth is a person, then this person can be known by different individuals in different ways. This is not to say that the Absolute Truth is not an idea; He is also the original ideas of knowledge, beauty, power, wealth, fame, and renunciation. But everyone need not have a perfect understanding of all these principles. For example, many devotees of the Lord may not see His power; they may merely see His beauty. Likewise, they may not consider the Lord as the completeness of all knowledge; they may think of Him merely as a child, or a handsome young man. Thus, everyone is allowed a different conception of the Absolute Truth, if they all pertain to the same Absolute Truth.

This problem comes up frequently in the clashes between different religions. The monotheist says that there is only one God, and under the notion of Absolute Truth being the universal truth, he asserts that everyone must have a common conception of God. The Vedic system rejects this idea. There is an Absolute Truth, which is also an idea, however, that idea may be partially or fully understood by different souls. The full understanding is better, but even a partial understanding is not bad if it pertains to the Personality of God. Thus, even the demons who think of the Lord's qualities in an angry mood attain liberation. You just need to be a sufficiently angry demon to always think of the Lord.

This sūtra says that the individual jīvā is subsequent to the Lord. With each jīvā, there is a different idea of God, but the idea has a common *reference*. Just as one person might say that John is a father, while the other person says that John is an employee, similarly, different jīvā can describe the Lord in different ways, but there is no fault if they refer to the Absolute Truth. The many forms of the Lord don't entail many Gods, but the personalized understanding of each soul. Across these souls, the Absolute Truth isn't the universal truth. There are individual truths in each jīvā which are partial understandings of the Absolute Truth. They are not considered *falsity* if they refer to the Absolute Truth.

Thus, you can say that God is kind, and you can say that God is cruel. You can say that He is the oldest, and you can say that He is just born. He can be called most loving, or the most fearsome. He can be attached or detached. Whatever we can think of, God can be assigned that quality. This is the meaning of Absolute Truth—He is the origin of all words and hence all ideas. Each soul can worship the Lord based on a different idea of the Absolute Truth. They create personalized and relativized truths, but because they are all attributed to the Absolute Truth, they constitute a partial understanding of the whole. This understanding is not false, and it is also not the whole truth. If there were no diversity, then there would be no difference between the soul knowing God, and God knowing Himself. But if there was no unity, then we could never say that we know the truth. Thus, there are two notions about truth—the reference and the meaning. Monotheists confuse these two; they believe that if there is one God, then He must be understood in the same way. The Vedic system accepts the universality of the reference but rejects the universality of meaning.

QUESTION

In our earlier discussion, it was implied that there are many individual jīvā. However, the jīva was also described as the potentiality for sat, chit, and ānanda, and it followed that the soul can desire, perceive, and form relations. But now we are explicitly stating that these individuals are also different from each other—they have different viewpoints and desires. So, they aren't merely different individuals of the same type, but different types of individuals.

Things in the world are distinguished based on many modalities. For example, you can say that two things are different because one is a table and the other is a chair. Or, you can say that two things are different because they are two separate instances of a chair. The preliminary understanding of individuality is that there are different things. But a more advanced understanding is that some of these things are also different or similar types of things. This leads to the question: Should we say that all souls are basically similar types of persons? Or, should we say that they are different types of individuals?

1.3.15 (78)

गतशिब्दाभ्यां तथा हि दृष्टं लिङ्गं च

gatiśabdābhyāṃ tathā hi dṛṣṭaṃ liṅgaṃ ca

gati—view, conception; śabdābhyām—from the statements; tathā hi—likewise; dṛṣṭaṃ—it is seen; liṅgam—the forms; ca—and.

TRANSLATION

Just like different meanings can be derived from the same statement, similarly, the different forms are seen (from the same Absolute Truth).

COMMENTARY

Here a comparison is being made to the relation between statements and their meanings. The same statement can be interpreted in many ways. A well-known example of such interpretation is the statement: "I saw a man on a hill with a telescope". This statement has at least four different meanings:

- I saw a man using a telescope. The man was on a hill.
- I saw a man. I was on the hill, looking through a telescope.
- I saw a man. The man was on a hill and had a telescope.
- I was on the hill. I saw a man. The man had a telescope.

Meanings are determined in three different ways. First, they depend on the words themselves—a different set of words would constitute a different statement and therefore a different meaning. Second, the meaning is decided by the context—the place, time, and the roles of the people who are exchanging these words. Third, the meaning is decided by the intention of the person speaking it. In this process, the intention is the highest: we begin by the desire to say something. The context comes next: we judge which context requires the meaning to be expressed in which way. Finally, the combination of the intention and the context is converted into words. When the listener hears these words, he can obviously perceive the words (provided he can hear). He can also—in most cases—understand the context if enough information about the context is available. This context requires us to know what was said before and after, the place in which it was said, and the relation between the speaker and the listener. The words are objective, and the context is intersubjective. But the intention is subjective and depends on a person's goals and objectives. Many people take this to imply that the real meaning underlying a statement is unknowable.

Intentions are knowable by the perception of emotions—normally through tones and pitches. For example, the statement "I hate you" can mean many things based on the tone: (1) if said quietly, the statement means the person indeed hates the other person, (2) if said angrily, the statement entails that there is actually love, but it is not being fulfilled, (3) if said jokingly, the statement entails that there is no hate, but the speaker has been embarrassed and since they are unable to respond appropriately, they jokingly state their hatred.

This sūtra states that the fact that the Absolute Truth is interpreted differently is based on the relation to the jīvā and the jīvā's emotional state. In one sense, all the souls are the same because they are capable of emotion, relation, and cognition. In another sense, they have different desires, relations, and viewpoints. Factually, there is no contradiction in these two statements. Normally, the preliminary understanding is of the capacity, and the advanced understanding is due to the outcomes of that capacity. The fact that the jīva is differentiated from Oneness due to desire, entails that everyone has a different desire. So, they see the Lord in a different way because they want to see Him differently. This perception of the Lord is a subjective interpretation of the jīva.

QUESTION

If you say that the different perception of the Lord is their subjective experience, then doesn't it follow that these subjective perceptions are like hallucinations, and there is no objective existence to them? It would mean that the diverse forms and activities of the Lord are merely in my experience?

There is a prominent school of philosophy—called Idealism—which is contrasted against Realism. Idealism emerged out of the problems of interpretation. Given that everyone can have a different view of the world, philosophers claimed that there is no objective reality. This leads to the ridiculous position of solipsism in which only I exist, and everyone else is just my idea. To do a little better than solipsism, the Idealist philosopher says that there is an objective but meaningless world, to which we attribute meaning and purpose. In short, the existence of the world is objective, but the meaning and purpose are subjective. If you accept either of these positions, you are dangerously close to claiming that everyone has their own personalized hallucinations, and your truth is no better than mine. It then follows that nobody can claim to know the truth.

1.3.16 (79)

धृतेश्च महमि्नोऽस्यास्मिन्निनुपलब्धेः

dhṛteśca mahimno'syāsminnupalabdheḥ

dhṛteḥ—supporting; ca—moreover; asya mahimnaḥ—of His greatness or diversity; asmin—in the Lord; upalabdheḥ—being seen.

TRANSLATION

Moreover, His greatness (i.e., diversity) is seen to be supported in the Lord.

COMMENTARY

This sūtra can be understood through an example. A man reveals his romantic side in relation to his wife, his compassionate side toward his children, his bossy side toward his servants, and his friendly side toward his compatriots. When a friend meets the man, he doesn't say that I met a 'part' of the man; the man is fully there; and yet, the friend will not see his romantic side or the bossy side. All these aspects of a person are simply potentialities. They are present, but they are not always revealed. The potentiality is converted into a vision and action through a relation. If the relation changes, the same person is seen differently, and he acts differently. In the same way, the Lord is innumerable potentialities, aspects, and personalities. However, in different relationships, He manifests a different side of His person. Therefore, when we see the Lord as Kṛṣṇa we should not say that Rāma is not present in this form. We must understand that Rāma is also a potentiality that is latent in Him; however, based on the relationship, the Rāma aspect of the Absolute Truth is not manifest.

The situation can be contrasted with the idea of five blind men seeing different parts of the elephant. They don't know that they are seeing an elephant. They just claim to see a trunk, a tail, a stomach, ears, or legs. And they think that these parts are the whole truth. The correction for the blind men is simply that these are aspects of the elephant. The difference between the ignorant and the enlightened soul is that the ignorant soul thinks that different visions are different things, and the enlightened soul knows that there is only one thing to be known, which has innumerable aspects. The ignorant soul thinks that the many forms of God must be different persons. But the enlightened soul knows that they are the same person, although manifesting only a certain aspect.

The difference between meaning and reference is relevant here. The five blind men think that the legs, the tail, the trunk, the belly, and the ears are both the meaning and the reference. But the man with vision knows that the reference is the elephant while the meanings are the legs, tail, trunk, belly, and ears. The souls with diverse opinions about the Lord are not like blind men seeing parts of the elephant, who think that these are factually different things. They are rather like the wife, child, friend, and employee of a person, who see the same person, and yet, only an aspect of their full personality is revealed.

Now, in some relationships, many aspects of a person can be

revealed. For instance, married couples can have many types of diverse relations; they can have romantic love for each other; they can be friends; they can pamper each other like a parent pampers a child, and sometimes they may even boss over each other (with the other person happily accepting their bossiness). Based on this example, we can distinguish between relations in which many aspects of a person are revealed vs. those relations where only one aspect may be revealed. Accordingly, there is a relation in which the complete form of the Lord is known—i.e., all His aspects are understood. There are also relations in which fewer or only one aspect of the Lord may be seen. These various forms are called Bhagavān-svayam (God in fullness), aṁsa (part of the full), kalā (part of the part), and puruṣa (part of the part of the part). So, when we speak about diverse relations, we must understand that some relations are *superior* to others because they reveal more personality aspects of a person than the others.

Therefore, the argument that if we have diverse opinions then we cannot be talking about the Absolute Truth is wrong. It is a caricature extended from the perception of the five blind men to the spiritual realm. This type of understanding should be rejected. We must rather say that whether the Lord appears as Vāmana or Narsimha or Kṛṣṇa, the exact same Absolute Truth has appeared, although only a certain aspect of the Absolute Truth is manifest. Therefore, there aren't many Gods. There are simply many descriptions of the same God relativized to the person who interacts with the Lord in a different way.

The description of reality as potentiality applies even to the material world and is found in atomic theory. However, atomic theory is not well understood because we look at the world like blind men seeing an elephant. For example, when we observe the atoms, we think that they are like the leg, the tail, the belly, the trunk, and the ears of the elephant, which is correct. The problem is that the blind men think that these are independent individual things, rather than *aspects* of the elephant. In short, you see parts, and you think that there is no whole other than the parts. Since we don't understand the whole, we don't even think that when we see the legs of the elephant, we are seeing the elephant, although in a certain limited way. The correct conception of reality is that the part of the whole is an *aspect* of the whole, not separate from the whole. The aspect is not equal to the whole, and it is not separated from the whole.

When reality is described through aspects, then we find many kinds of aspects. The legs, the seat, the backrest, and the armrest are some of the aspects of a chair. Similarly, the 'garden chair' and the 'study chair' are different aspects of the same thing. Likewise, shape, size, and color are different aspects of the chair. These aspects constitute the different modalities of perceiving the chair. You can enter the physical modality and see the chair as the aspects of legs, seat, backrest, armrest, etc. Then you can enter the sensual modality and see the same chair as color, shape, size, etc. And then you can enter the mental modality and see the same thing as a garden chair or a study chair. Then you can enter the intellectual mentality and see this as a hallucination or reality. There are many such modalities in our perception, and each modality is comprised of many sub- and sub-sub-modalities. All these modalities are aspects of the whole, but they are not at the same level. The physical modality is lower than the sensual modality, the sensual modality is lower than the mental modality, which is lower than the intellectual modality, etc. The hierarchy between the modalities is the key differentiator from the physicalist view. In the physicalist view, a part of the whole is like a leg or a backrest of the chair, but in the hierarchical viewpoint, these parts are many different types of aspects of the whole. The first step in knowing reality is to transition from blind men to men who can see. Then transition to thinking, judging, intending, moralizing, and so forth.

Each modality is a partial understanding of the Lord. However, as we rise in the hierarchy, the understanding gets better. Thus, the Lord's toes are a modality of the Lord, just like His hands. But the full Lord is also modal, and He appears as a child, father, friend, master, lover, etc. The blind man thinks that these are different, but the enlightened soul understands that the same Lord manifests Himself in different aspects through different kinds of relations.

Now, if someone says that these modes are simply our hallucinatory perception, then this sūtra denies that claim. The feet and hands are aspects of the Lord; they can exist in our perception, but they also exist in the Lord. Likewise, the father and the child aspects of the Lord can also exist in our perception and in the Lord. So, the claim that these perceptions are hallucinations is rejected.

QUESTION

You previously noted that the different understandings of the Absolute Truth are like the different meanings of a sentence. That led to the view that these meanings are private conceptions of the Lord held by the jīvā and don't have an objective existence. But now you are saying that these meanings of the sentence are within the sentence itself. In fact, you are saying that these meanings are parts of the sentence or partial understandings of the sentence.

1.3.17 (80)

पुरसदिधेशच

prasiddheśca

prasiddheḥ—due to being well-known or famous; ca—also

TRANSLATION

And (the diverse forms of the Lord are) due to His being famous.

COMMENTARY

We have earlier discussed the six qualities of the Lord, namely, knowledge, beauty, renunciation, power, wealth, and fame. The Lord is knowledge itself, the original idea. The idea, however, is only one aspect of the Lord. The other aspect is that He is a person. When the idea and the individual are combined, we say that the Lord is the embodiment of the idea or a symbol of the idea. The idea is, in fact, not separate from the symbol. These two aspects are the śabda-brahman and artha-brahman, or word and meaning, aspects of the same thing. The artha is the meaning, and the śabda is the instance of that meaning.

The Absolute Truth is also beautiful, and this beauty has two aspects: the symbol is beautiful, and the meaning is beautiful. The Lord looks beautiful and His thoughts are beautiful. The meaning and the symbol are cognitive, and the beauty is emotive. So, knowledge and beauty are related and yet distinct.

As the original idea, the Absolute Truth is self-evident and independent. He doesn't need anything to rationalize, justify, explain, or cause His existence. This self-evidentiary nature of the Absolute Truth is also a modality, due to which we say that the Lord is not just a person, but also the Original Person. As a result, we make three claims about the Lord—(1) there is the idea of knowledge, (2) there is a symbol of this idea, and (3) this symbol and idea are the original thing from which everything else has expanded or manifest.

As He expands into other things, this creation becomes His wealth. All the creation in the four quarters is His property or wealth, and He is the object underlying that property. We have earlier discussed the attribute and ownership meanings of property; these two meanings are also the modalities of the Lord's creation. Due to the attribute mode, we can say that the creation is simply an attribute of the Lord, like weight or size is an attribute of a table, and the two cannot be separated. However, due to the ownership mode, we can say that the property is different from the Lord, and the Lord owns the creation. Thus, when the creation ends, the Lord is not minimized. However, when the creation exists, knowing the creation is tantamount to knowing aspects of the Lord.

Once the wealth of the creation has expanded from the Lord, He also exercises control over His wealth. This control is called His power. Finally, He also enters this creation in many forms to enjoy it, like one may live in one's house, drive one's car, wear one's clothes, etc. This entry into the creation is called His fame. If we think of the creation as His ownership, then we can say that to enjoy different kinds of owned properties, He takes many different forms. However, when we say that these properties are simply His attributes—like mass is an attribute of a particle—the understanding is more nuanced: the mass was previously in the particle, and now the particle is present within the mass. Thus, by knowing anything, we can know the source from which it emanated.

The Lord's renunciation aspect is that He is outside of everything. And His fame aspect is that He is present inside everything. He also has the controller aspect, all the things are simply His aspects, the source of this diversity is the individual who embodies the idea of knowledge, which is also beautiful. Thus, to know the Lord as these six attributes is to know the entire existence.

The jīvā is also a manifestation of the Lord, and the Lord enters the jīvā. Since the Lord is knowledge, therefore, by this entry the jīvā acquires an understanding of the Lord. However, since the jīvā is a part or aspect of the Lord, the understanding of the Lord is different in each jīvā. Thus, the part is inside the whole, and a partial understanding of the whole is inside each part. This partial understanding is the Lord's fame. However, this partial knowledge is also a part of the full knowledge. So, it is not merely a hallucination in the jīvā. It is also present in the Lord. The difference is in the reference of this partial understanding. In the material world, the parts are considered independent things. And under spiritual realization, these parts are aspects of the Lord. The understanding may be partial, but the reference of that understanding is full.

QUESTION

So, the implication seems to be that the diverse perceptions of the Lord are not merely subjective interpretations of the Lord by the jīvā. They are also objectively present, and hence they cannot be treated as personal creations. Why couldn't the Lord allow the jīvā to create its own subjective creations?

It is possible to make arguments for and against subjectivity. If the argument is for subjectivity, then it might say that due to subjectivity I'm seeing a hallucination that doesn't really exist. If the argument is against subjectivity, then it might say that if I'm not free to interpret reality as I like, then I have no free will. The former argument was previously made. The latter is made here.

1.3.18 (81)

इतरपरामर्शात् स इति चेत् न असमभवात्

itaraparāmarśāt sa iti cet na asambhavāt

itara—the other, or the individual soul; parāmarśāt—because of the judgment, or the opinion, or the viewpoint, or the reference; saḥ—He (the Lord); iti cet—if it be said; na—no; asambhavāt—on account of impossibility.

TRANSLATION

If it is said that the Lord is simply the opinion or judgment or viewpoint of the individual soul, (we say) no, on account of the impossibility.

COMMENTARY

We have discussed earlier that the jīvā is only a potentiality. It has the capacity to desire, relate, know, and act, but it cannot fulfill its desires. This means that the jīvā has senses to perceive and act, but it depends on the Lord to obtain the objects of sensation and action. Thus, when the jīvā obtains an experience, that experience is not his creation. The experience is always the result of the Lord fulfilling the desire of the jīvā. In the same way, when the soul desires to perceive the Lord, the Lord appears by His grace. This experience is not the creation of the jīvā. It is the soul's desire being fulfilled by the Lord.

This constitutes the resolution of two contradictory arguments—for and against free will. If the Lord is objectively present, then someone can say that there is no free will: The Lord is forcing a vision upon us. If, on the other hand, we freely create an understanding of the Lord, then one can argue that this understanding is a subjective opinion and not objective truth. However, if the soul can only desire (and not create the opinion) and the Lord appears to fulfill that desire, then both arguments can be simultaneously refuted: The Lord is objectively present and not a subjective creation, and yet, He has appeared in a form that was previously desired by the jīvā. So, there is free will, and yet there is objectivity. The object appears based on the desire, to fulfill the desire.

The 'impossibility' refers to the inability in the jīvā to fulfill its desires. This is true in the material world, and it is true in the realm of liberated souls as well. In both cases, the Lord fulfills the jīvā's desires. In the material realm, this fulfillment is subject to a condition—namely, that the jīvā deserves fulfillment based on its karma. However, in the realm of the liberated soul, this requirement of deserving is removed; there is only desire and its fulfillment.

QUESTION

You have previously said that the jīvā is subsequent to the Lord. You have also now said that the Lord appears in many forms (objectively) to fulfill the jīvā's desires. Therefore, it would follow that these different forms of the Lord are also subsequent to the Original Form? In short, the various forms of the Lord would not be eternal, but they would appear based on the changing desires of the soul. So, if a soul develops a new desire, then the Lord will also manifest in a new form to fulfill that desire, which did not exist earlier.

1.3.19 (82)
उत्तराच्चेत् आविर्भूतस्वरूपस्तु
uttarāccet āvirbhūtasvarūpastu

uttarāt—from the subsequence; cet—although; āvirbhūta—manifest; svarūpaḥ—the form; astu—present.

TRANSLATION

Although manifest subsequently, these forms are eternally present.

COMMENTARY

In the previous sūtra, it was said that the Lord fulfills the soul's desires. Therefore, one can argue that the Lord's forms that fulfill these desires are created after the soul's desires, and these forms could not be preexisting. This sūtra rejects this contention. Yes, the Lord appears in a different form to fulfill the jīva's desire, but these forms are preexisting. To understand this better, let's consider the example of a hallucination when we see a rope as a snake. The association of the snake with the rope is a hallucination. However, that doesn't mean that the idea of a snake is a creation of the person hallucinating. Factually, the idea preexisted our perception, and therefore, the experience of the snake is real. However, the reference of experience—namely, that *this* thing is a snake—is false. Therefore, even when the soul is hallucinating, the experience is real, and only the reference of that experience is false. Now, we can extend this argument to diversified notions about God. All these notions are preexisting, and the soul is not the creator of these notions. Its free will is simply in choosing a notion. When God fulfills the soul's desire, the Lord's form is not created.

It has already been said that the Lord is objectively present (and not merely a subjective hallucination). However, it may now be argued that this objective presence is temporary, and the Lord merely appears in a certain form to fulfill the jīva's desire, and if that desire disappears then the Lord's form also disappears. Such a situation would amount to the Lord taking on a temporary role to fulfill the jīva's desire, which would be akin to serving the jīva for his happiness. Buddhists have a notion called Pratītyasamutpāda which means an apparent codependent arising. It states that the subject and the object are co-created, so if the observer disappears then the observed also disappears. If this idea were applied to the Lord, then it would follow that the Lord takes on a form only when the jīva desires, and then gives up that form when the jīva doesn't desire. This sūtra refutes this idea and states that all the forms are always manifest.

However, it was previously said that the jīva is subsequent to the Lord, and the other forms of the Lord—beyond the Original One—are also subsequent. So, one can wrongly interpret this idea to say that the different perceptions are created just-in-time for the soul's experience. The correct way to understand these forms is that they present opportunities for the jīva to serve the Lord. The opportunities are eternal, but the desire may not be eternal. In short, the Lord has manifested in all the ways in which the jīva can ever desire. There is no possibility of pleasure that cannot be fulfilled. So, we shouldn't think that there is some desire that was previously not considered by the Lord as a possibility, and when this desire arises the Lord comes to the jīva to supply it. Rather, we must understand that all the desires have previously been anticipated and the method of fulfilling them is already existing. The jīva doesn't create a form of the Lord; however, the jīva can approach a certain form of the Lord.

QUESTION

If all the forms of the Lord are already manifest, and the jīva has the desire for a different form, how does the jīva attain the vision of that form?

1.3.20 (83)

अन्यार्थश्च परामर्शः

anyārthaśca parāmarśaḥ

anyārthaḥ—for a different purpose; ca—and; parāmarśaḥ—pulling, drawing, seizing.

TRANSLATION

And (the soul) can pull, draw, or seize (a form) for a different purpose.

COMMENTARY

The different forms of the Lord are eternally situated in their own planets in the space beyond the material world. These planets and their ruling forms are never created or destroyed. But the jīvā can enter one of these planets if it so desires. It has already been stated that the jīvā enters the Lord's abode based on loving devotion. So, if the nature of the jīvā's devotion changes, it can enter a different planet, and see a different form of the Lord and serve Him differently. This is effectively the jīvā roaming through the spiritual world.

The main purport of this sūtra is that free will doesn't end when the jīvā enters the spiritual realm. This free will is the basis on which the jīvā is differentiated from the Lord. But the implication of such differentiation is also that the 'distance' between the Lord and the jīvā is not fixed. The jīvā can come closer or move farther; it can also go back to the material world after being liberated, although the chance of such a thing happening is extremely remote (due to which it is said that once liberated the jīvā 'never' falls). However, more importantly, the implication of free will is that the jīvā can change its liking or how it wants to enjoy. The Lord is simultaneously enjoying in all the possible ways, and the jīvā can enjoy with the Lord in different forms one after another. Another implication is that there can be natural curiosity in the jīvā to know the different forms of the Lord and he may want to see the different pastimes of the Lord. To entertain such possibilities, the jīvā must roam in the spiritual world. If the jīvā has decided that he prefers a certain form of the Lord and would like to serve Him exclusively, then his position would be fixed. If such a decision hasn't been made, it can be made after reaching the spiritual world. Finally, it also means that spiritual development doesn't end with the exit from the material world. The jīvā can constantly develop spiritually—i.e., change the extent of its devotion toward the Lord. In all these ways, the spiritual world is just like the material world—i.e., one can see different visions and act differently.

QUESTION

But what happens if the jīvā is not able to decide which form he prefers? You have described that there are as many forms as there are possible desires, and all these forms are eternally existent. So, should we not study all the forms before we decide which of the forms we prefer? But if the forms are infinite, then how can we ever make an informed choice about a specific form?

Some people have a problem with choice. After all, there are infinite options to choose from. How can we decide which alternative to choose unless we understand all the options? If we are hasty and we choose without understanding all the alternatives, then won't there be doubts in our heart that we may not have made a perfect choice? With such doubts, how can we devote ourselves to the Lord? On the other hand, the alternatives are so huge that we cannot hope to know everything—in this case all the forms of the Lord. So, given this limitation, how can we choose a specific form of the Lord over the others?

1.3.21 (84)

अल्पश्रुतेरिति चेत् तदुक्तम्

alpaśruteriti cet taduktam

alpa—smallness; śruteḥ—because it is heard, or because the śrutī states; iti cet—if it be said; tat—that; uktam—has been explained (in the last sūtra).

TRANSLATION

If it is said that on account of the scriptural declaration of the smallness (of the jīvā) (we cannot decide) (we say that) has already been explained.

COMMENTARY

If someone considers choice a burden, and fears that he might choose the wrong alternative, then the answer to that has been given in the last sūtra where it was stated that the jīvā can choose a different alternative. The problem can seem real to some people because in the impersonal philosophy the choice is simple—remain entangled in the material world or attain liberation from the material world. When the choice is presented in this binary way, it seems that liberation would be preferred. However, if liberation leads to entry into three-quarters of existence, as opposed to one-quarter of the entire material existence (which comprises innumerable universes), then the problem of choice becomes worse with liberation. If we could not fathom the entirety of the material creation (or even the entirety of a single universe), then how can we fathom the realm of the liberated living entities which is three times bigger? And if we cannot fathom the entirety of the spiritual creation, then how do we choose?

In Western philosophy, this is called the problem of Buridan's Ass. The story goes that there was an ass who had hay and water before it but could not decide whether to chew the hay or drink the water first. Unable to decide, the ass remained both hungry and thirsty. If we were like Buridan's Ass, then if we go to a grocery store looking for cereal, and we find hundreds of brands of cereal (which we cannot perfectly compare), we don't try to compare them. We pick the first one that satisfies our needs, although there may be other brands that could satisfy us more. Unless we are dissatisfied with a cereal brand, we keep picking the same brand every time—because it has worked before.

In the same way, there may be infinite possibilities, but we don't analyze everything before we make a choice. We rather pick the one that satisfies us, and we settle with that choice. Unless there is dissatisfaction with the choice, there will never be a change. So, this problem of infinite choice, resulting in decision paralysis, is not a real problem. Every living entity has a natural desire toward some form of the Lord. This preference is not based on an analysis of every other form— maybe that one is better than this one. It is an intuitive desire by which the jīvā chooses a form of the Lord and serves Him eternally because there is no dissatisfaction. If, however, one is still insistent that he may want to change his mind later on, and if the possibility was eliminated after the first choice then the person would feel 'stuck' forever, the answer has already been given—you can change the choice; this is not a type of bondage or captivity.

Topic 6

QUESTION

I am still not convinced. If you say that there is an intuitive desire for a specific form of the Lord, then I don't have any intuition. I'm in the material world, and I have little understanding of what transcendence is. If I cannot choose a form of the Lord, then what will I

meditate upon? And without such a choice, how will I develop devotion by which I can enter the Lord's abode?

1.3.22 (85)

अनुकृतेस्तस्य च

anukṛtestasya ca

anukṛteḥ—due to acting according to instruction; tasya—them; ca—also.

TRANSLATION

(You can) also (develop devotion to a form of the Lord) by following their (the pure devotees of the Lord) instructions.

COMMENTARY

We have discussed in the earlier sūtra that devotion to the Lord is not attained by theoretical knowledge, reading of scriptures, or even bodily and mental exercises, although if these things are performed with devotion they lead to advancement. But this begs the question: How will I develop devotion if not for these processes? We briefly discussed the method for this earlier—the association with the devotees who can impart this devotion. However, this sūtra states something different—it is by following the instructions of such devotees.

One might wonder how following the instructions of a devotee leads to devotion. The answer is that devotion is an emotional state, and it is acquired from a devotee when we become emotionally attached to the devotee. For example, if we associate with an angry person, we also become anxious. If we are with a happy person, the association gradually makes us happy. Similarly, if we associate with a devotee, we can also acquire their mood. These moods are infectious, but they are not transferred cognitively as the words are. The transfer of moods happens only when we are emotionally attached to a person. Thus, for example, a doctor in a hospital sees so many people suffering but he or she may not become sad by their suffering, because they are not emotionally attached to them. On the other hand, we are easily affected by the sadness or happiness of those whom we love. In the same way, a deep emotional attachment to the spiritual master makes a person qualified to receive a devotional attitude. Now, one may ask: How do you get emotionally attached to the devotee? The answer to that question is stated in this sūtra—namely, *anukriti*, or doing and acting as instructed. Thus, by following the instructions of the advanced devotee, one develops an attachment to them. Through that attachment, we acquire a devotional attitude. And with that devotional attitude, we can see the Lord.

The 'acceptance' of a guru is called 'initiation'. Many people confuse this process with a ritual. However, in the Chaitanya Charitāmṛta, this process is called the acquisition of a bhakti-lata-bīja or the 'seed' of the devotional creeper, which is obtained by the grace of the guru or the spiritual master. The 'initiation' is not a ritual; far from it, it is the development of an emotional attachment by which one begins following the instructions. So, the 'acceptance' of a guru is implicit in obeying the instructions of the spiritual master. However, one must be careful in distinguishing between ordinary people—who can speak the knowledge but have no devotion—and a genuine guru who has devotion. The qualification for devotion is not academic learning, the ability to chant mantras, the number of followers, or his standing in the material world. There is simply one qualification—he does everything with a devotional mood. If one obeys the instructions of an ordinary person, they may get attached to such a 'guru', but they cannot impart the devotional mood, because they don't have it themselves. So, the qualification of being a guru is the possession of pure devotion. The term *tasya* refers to such devotees; not the ordinary charlatan so-called 'guru'.

QUESTION

But how will I identify a genuine devotee? What are the symptoms of such devotees? How can we distinguish a devotee from other non-devotees?

1.3.23 (86)

अपि च स्मर्यते

api ca smaryate

api ca—moreover; smaryate—in the smriti.

TRANSLATION

Moreover, (the symptoms of pure devotees) are described in smriti.

COMMENTARY

The sūtra doesn't go into details about the qualifications of the guru but merely states that one must consult the smriti. Herein, we can understand the importance of smriti in addition to the śrutī—the śrutī gives information about the Absolute Truth, but the processes of attaining this (such as the surrender to a guru, the qualifications of guru, etc.) are described in the smriti. Therefore, the śrutī provides knowledge of the Absolute Truth, and the smriti describes the practical processes and methods for the realization of this knowledge.

Topic 7

QUESTION

But despite the description of the qualifications in the smriti, there are still many difficulties in identifying a guru. The reason for such difficulties is that we can only observe a person's actions but not understand the extent of their spiritual realization. We may see that a person is austere, pious, renounced, etc. But how can we know that such a person is also a devotee of the Lord?

1.3.24 (87)
शब्दादेव प्रमतिः
śabdādeva pramitaḥ

śabdāt—from the word; eva—certainly; pramitaḥ—measured.

TRANSLATION

(We can) measure (the guru) certainly based on the words.

COMMENTARY

We have earlier discussed three kinds of meanings used for understanding: objective, intersubjective, and subjective. The objective meaning is evident from the words and the grammar. The intersubjective meaning depends on the context between the speaker and the listener, the sequence of questions and answers, etc. And the subjective meaning comes to us from the mood, style, or the way it is spoken. When the spoken words are converted into written text, the words remain intact, and the context may also be preserved (unless something is taken out of context). However, the mood, style, and the way it is spoken are lost. Therefore, the written text is never as accurate as the spoken word.

Owing to this fact, most people prefer to see a person talking live, rather than reading a book. The power in a speech contains not just the words, but also the emotions behind it. The intonation or emphasis on different sounds can often change the meaning. We can go back to any number of powerful speeches and try to read them in their edited form; you can see that these two are just not the same. Therefore, considerable emphasis has been laid in the Vedic system on 'hearing' from the right person. It is not merely the objective meaning arising out of words and grammar; it is also not merely the context in which these things are spoken; it is also the way of speaking that delivers meaning.

Many people can memorize the sūtra and statements from the scriptures; they may also present them scholarly. But unless the speaker is convinced through realization, and by putting that teaching into practice in their own life, they cannot change anyone's life. The conviction is not apart from the words, but it is present only in the words of a person who has realized that knowledge. Of course, a person who only knows the truth theoretically is better than one who doesn't know the truth or is convinced of falsities. Thus, speaking convincingly is not a substitute for speaking the truth. Scriptures do not begin with the qualification of a guru. They begin with the nature of the Absolute Truth. Once that question is settled, and what is to be said is decided, the next question is about who is convinced of this truth vs. who just knows it theoretically. The questions of Absolute Truth have been settled previously, and this sūtra is only speaking about the qualification of the person who has realized this truth.

QUESTION

But what if a person is unable to find a suitable spiritual master or guru who can guide him toward spiritual progress? Should the

person just keep waiting for the guru to come around? Or should one do something else?

This question is prominent today due to a shortage of spiritually advanced people. Many who claim to be gurus have been corrupted by greed, power, lust, and fame. They are often involved in illicit sexual activities, drug abuse, the accumulation of wealth, improper use of power, lying, cheating, and other more heinous crimes such as murder. So, someone who seemed spiritually advanced may later be revealed to be a cheater. As many cheaters are exposed, people lose faith in the spiritual path. Even those who continue the process, suffer from the trauma of having been cheated and find it harder to believe that the process might work for them. Can we get out of this destructive stage?

1.3.25 (88)

हृदयपेक्षया तु मनुष्याधिकारत्वात्

hṛdyapekṣayā tu manuṣyādhikāratvāt

hṛdi—in the heart; apekṣayā—in comparison to; tu—but; manuṣya—the human being; adhikāratvāt—from having the entitlement.

TRANSLATION

But in comparison to (the problems) one can take shelter of (the Lord) in the heart, (because spirituality) is the entitlement of every human being.

COMMENTARY

In this sūtra, the term *manuṣyādhikāratvāt* is used, which means "due to human rights". The United Nations defines human rights as follows: "Human rights include the right to life and liberty, freedom from slavery and torture, freedom of opinion and expression, the right to work and education, and many more. Everyone is entitled to these rights, without discrimination." This declaration of human rights doesn't mean they are going to be fulfilled. For example, we can say that we have a right to work and education, but so many people are jobless and uneducated. The governments may try to reduce joblessness and improve education, but they cannot guarantee these "rights". A fundamental right is one that can never be denied. The encounter with a suitable guru doesn't count as one of the fundamental rights. In fact, it is said that one meets a suitable guru only due to great fortune, as a result of pious activities. So, if one hasn't performed these pious activities, their encounter with a suitable guru is unlikely. In fact, because of one's impiety, one may meet a cheating guru.

What is one supposed to do if they haven't been pious, or have met cheating gurus, or cannot find a suitable guru despite their efforts (subject to the judgment by the words as was prescribed in the previous sūtra)? This sūtra recommends that one must take shelter of the Lord and seek His guidance. Specifically, the guidance is to be sought from the Lord situated in the heart. The ability to take shelter of the Lord in the heart is every human's birthright, because it can never be denied, regardless of one's personal situation, the ability to find the right guru, etc. So, life and liberty, education and work, freedom of opinion and expression, freedom from slavery and torture, are not "rights" guaranteed by nature and the Lord. These are merely human concoctions, which we believe will help us form a just and equitable society. And yet, nobody can guarantee these rights because a person's life is controlled by their past karma. Under such a situation, one must focus on "duties" rather than "rights". If there is confusion about what my duty is, then we have a "right" to consult the Lord in the heart. This is the only fundamental and inalienable right that we can claim.

In this regard, we can also note that this sūtra talks about "human rights", which means taking shelter of the Lord as a guru in the heart is unique to humans. The animals don't seek a guru. So, there is no question of how to identify the right guru, and what to do when the right guru is not found. The animals might consult the Lord in the heart to save their life and limb. But that is not the purpose of the guru. In the same way, those humans who take shelter of the Lord to save their life and limb are not considered 'humans' here. This is a specific comment about what to do if one is unable to find a suitable guru. This means previous efforts to find and learn from a guru have been made.

The encounter with a suitable guru is a matter of *bhāgya* or good fortune produced by good actions in the past. Therefore, not everyone is entitled to a guru, at least not a good one. Many are also entitled to cheating gurus. However, the soul's surrender to the Lord in the heart is not subject to good fortune. The surrender to the Lord in the heart for spiritual guidance is an inalienable right in the human body. We should use this "right" to consult the Lord.

Topic 8

QUESTION

Does this mean that only humans can make spiritual progress, and this progress is impossible in any other form of life? I'm asking this because it seems possible that one's spiritual journey may remain incomplete in one life. How can a person keep progressing in spiritual endeavors in other bodies?

1.3.26 (89)

तदुपर्यपि बादरायणःसंभवात्

taduparyapi bādarāyaṇaḥ sambhavāt

tadupari—above them, i.e., living beings higher than humans; api—also; bādarāyaṇaḥ—Bādarāyaṇa opines; sambhavāt—because (it is) possible.

TRANSLATION

Also (beings) above them (the humans) (are entitled for surrender to the Lord) on account of the possibility (of it) according to Bādarāyana.

COMMENTARY

In Vedic cosmology, human beings are described to exist on the bhū-loka; notably, there are many kinds of humans—some more advanced than the others. However, all of them have been stated as having the "right" to surrender. Above the bhū-loka, are six other planetary systems, namely, bhuvar, svarga, jana, tapa, and satya. The living entities in svarga are called ādidaivika and they have been earlier described as being expansions of the Paramātma. The Lord entrusts them with important responsibilities to manage the universe given that they are obedient to the Lord. In the realms beyond svarga are ascetics and sages, who are naturally inclined toward the worship of the Lord. In fact, in Vedic cosmology, the bhū, bhuvar, and svarga-loka are periodically destroyed, but the upper four planetary systems—and the living entities in them—remain. In this sūtra, all these living entities above the humans are said to be qualified to surrender to the Lord. In short, if one has progressed from a lower planetary system to a higher one, due to the dint of their pious activities, but hasn't yet completed the process of spiritual advancement, they can continue it from their new positions. Notably, this hasn't been stated about the lower planetary systems; therefore, implicitly, spiritual progress has been denied to them.

This sūtra quotes the possibility of even the higher living entities advancing in the spiritual life to Bādarāyana, who is the author of Vedānta Sūtra. One might wonder: Why is Bādarāyana referring to himself in the third person by saying that "this is the opinion of Bādarāyana"? The other statements by him are not being referenced in this way. So, why this one? One answer is that Bādarāyana appears at the end of every Dvapara-yuga and divides the Vedas into four parts. In a day of Brahma, there are 1000 chatur-yugī, so Bādarāyana appears 1000 times in a day of Brahma. The person appearing as Bādarāyana is different each time, but he is always performing the same duty of dividing the Vedas and is hence referred to as Veda Vyas or Bādarāyana. It is possible that the name 'Bādarāyana' used here refers to a person from a previous age.

QUESTION

But isn't it said that the demigods are engaged in material enjoyments of heaven? And these enjoyments are contrary to spiritual advancement?

1.3.27 (90)

वरिोधः:करमणीति चेत् न अनेकप्रतपित्तेर्दर्शनात् ॥ २७ ॥

virodhaḥ karmaṇīti cet na anekapratipatterdarśanāt || 27 ||

virodhaḥ—contradiction; karmaṇi—to actions; iti cet—if it is said; na—not; aneka—many; pratipatteḥ—statements; darśanāt—from the philosophies.

TRANSLATION

If it is said that the actions (of the demigods) are contrary (to the surrender to the Lord), (we say) no because we find many statements from philosophies (which permit a process of gradual progression from lower to higher).

COMMENTARY

In the Bhagavad-Gita 7.16, Lord Kṛṣṇa states the following:

catur-vidhā bhajante māṁ
janāḥ su-kṛtino 'rjuna
ārto jijñāsur arthārthī
jñānī ca bharatarṣabha

O best among the Bhāratas, four kinds of pious men render devotional service unto Me – the distressed, the desirous of wealth, the inquisitive, and those searching for knowledge of the Absolute.

Generally, most people come to religion due to suffering—mental or physical. The poor and destitute are suffering physically and they worship the Lord for relief. Many rich and powerful also turn to religion due to suffering—although the suffering may be mental. However, those who are situated in a position that is relatively free of bodily and mental suffering are generally not inclined toward devotion to the Lord. Therefore, in general, it is understood that the practice of devotion is harder in other planetary systems because there are many incentives for enjoyment. The demigods are especially in a situation of great power, and their enjoyment generally prevents them from surrender to the Lord; they are not disobedient to the Lord, but they are busy enjoying their position of power and the luxuries of the heavens. Therefore, if someone argues that their position is not suitable for spiritual advancement it is correct.

However, we must note that the previous sūtra used the term *sambhavāt* indicating the possibility of seeking the Lord as one's guru or spiritual master. The sūtra did not say that the higher beings are necessarily devoted to the Lord in this way. Indeed, it is often stated that the guru of the demigods is Brihaspati. He is also identified with the planet Jupiter, and its positive influence indicates the inclination toward knowledge. However, this may or may not be spiritual knowledge of the kind being discussed here—namely transcendence from the material world. Thus, just like humans have a possibility of surrendering to the Lord in the heart, and seeking His guidance as a guru, similarly, the possibility also exists for the demigods. The demigods are after all very pious, and favorable to Lord Viṣṇu, so they can accept surrender to the Paramātma. On the other hand, the animals are too ignorant, and the demons in the lower planetary systems are explicitly averse to Lord Viṣṇu, which makes this surrender impossible. Therefore, we must distinguish between the suitability of the heavens for spiritual progress and the possibility of such progress. The heavens are not suitable, but it is still possible for a person to advance spiritually as opposed to animals or the demons for whom even such a possibility doesn't exist.

Similarly, this sūtra also indicates the existence of many philosophical positions about spiritual progress. One can, for instance, perform karma-yoga in which the actions of mundane duties are performed, but the results of this action are offered to the Lord. Similarly, one can pursue jñāna-yoga with the understanding that there are many stages of knowledge and the top-most stage is the understanding of the Lord. The aṣṭānga-yoga system can be practiced with the aim that once the preliminary stages of āsana and prāṇayāma have been crossed, one will turn one's consciousness toward the Paramātma in the heart. These are described as jñāna-karma-miśra bhakti or devotion "mixed" with the processes of jñāna and karma. The possibility of such mixing entails that these processes are not mutually exclusive. Notably, the sūtra is not recommending such an approach, but just pointing to the possibility of its existence.

So, the allurements for enjoyments make the devotion to the Lord difficult; nevertheless, the possibility of such devotion always exists. This sūtra should be understood in the context of the previous sūtras where it was said that one generally approaches a guru but if one is unable to find a guru then the Lord in the heart can be a guru. This is a possibility for humans and demigods.

QUESTION

But you have previously stated that for enlightenment one must

listen to the words of the advanced devotees. You have also stated at the beginning that the scripture must be considered the source of Absolute Truth, implying that other methods—such as jñāna or speculation and karma or activities followed by their results—are unsuitable as the source of the Absolute Truth. However, now you are saying that all processes can be mixed as they are described in the scriptures, and therefore they should all be considered valid. How do we reconcile the contradiction between the previous and the present statements?

1.3.28 (91)
शब्द इति चेत् न अतःप्रभवात् प्रत्यक्षानुमानाभ्याम्
śabda iti cet na ataḥ prabhavāt pratyakṣānumānābhyām

śabde—in regard to the words (Vedic texts); iti cet—if it be said; na—no; ataḥ—from these (words); prabhavāt—because of the creation; pratyakṣa-anumānābhyām—the methods of direct perception and reasoning.

TRANSLATION

If it is said that (only the) words (of devotees and scriptures are valid), (then we say) no because from these words have emerged the methods of direct perception and inference (or empirical and rational knowledge).

COMMENTARY

In the previous sūtra, the term *darśanāt* was employed, indicating many philosophical positions. However, etymologically, the term indicates "seeing". When taken together with śabda or scripture, used in this sūtra, we can understand this as "seeing through the lens of the scripture". Specifically, this sūtra states that the processes of jñāna and karma are not contrary to the process of bhakti, and we should not consider them as being mutually exclusive. Rather, these processes can be combined or mixed (as was stated in the previous sūtra). This sūtra also asserts that the methods of direct perception and inference (which constitute the basis of karma and jñāna) should be understood as having emerged or manifested or being created from the śabda or scriptures. This is a very profound statement, and to understand it we need to digress a little.

Perception involves the acts of distinguishing and ordering. By distinguishing I mean there is more than one thing, and by ordering, we mean that something is more important or preferred over the other. For example, if you see a cow grazing in a field, you must be able to distinguish the cow from the field; without such distinction, there is no ability to identify that there is an individual cow separate from the field. To make such distinctions, one must possess the concepts of 'cow' and 'field' a priori. If we don't have these concepts, then our visual field will only have colors. To aggregate these colors into objects, we must have the concepts of cow and field. In fact, we must also have the concept of color, white, green, shape, etc. Otherwise, we will not be able to say that there are some properties (color and shape) with values (white and round), which belong to a 'cow' or a 'field'. The perception of a cow in a field arises when one already has a certain number of concepts. If you have never seen a computer before, and you are asked to search for a computer, you will not be able to identify such a thing even if it was right in front of you because you don't have the concept of a 'computer'. Therefore, to perceive things, we need concepts.

If a distinction between a cow and a field has been made, there must also be an ordering of these objects—e.g., that the cow is foreground and the field is background (or vice versa, based on what you are focusing on). This ordering is a function of our choices: we can focus upon either the cow or the field.

Similarly, reasoning also needs preexisting concepts. We call these assumptions or axioms which we take for granted as being true. Using these concepts, we can construct more sophisticated concepts through combination. In fact, logic in some forms is understood trivially as the ability to mutate the simplest of concepts to arrive at more complex concepts; therefore, from the premise of accepted axioms, we can use logic to prove more complex theorems.

Therefore, to use reasoning and observation, one must have some basic ideas. From these ideas, we can acquire more ideas. The child, therefore, cannot be born a 'blank slate', as John Locke claimed (suggesting that the world is objective properties). As George Berkeley argued, the so-called 'primary' physical properties are mere objectifications of subjective experience. Therefore, according to Berkeley, there is no objective reality apart from subjective experience. Then, David Hume took this a step further to say that doing science necessitated laws, and in forming a law we had to invoke a necessity—namely, that the effect necessarily followed the cause—and this necessity could never be established because we had no way of knowing what's happening in reality. Immanuel Kant, in his *Critique of Pure Reason*, claims that he was "woken from his slumber" by Hume's critique of science, and went on to argue that we don't acquire ideas from the external world in order to create science, laws, an objective reality, etc. Rather, all these ideas are innately present within us.

This notion of preexisting ideas is explained in Sāṅkhya philosophy as the superiority of the mind and intellect over the senses and the objects, not just because the mind controls the senses and their objects but also because the senses and their objects 'emerge' from the mind. The mind itself emerges from the intellect, which comes from the ego, which follows from the mahattattva. The 25 elements of Sāṅkhya are then equated to the 25 consonants of Sanskrit in many Tantra texts. The 16 vowels and 8 semi-vowels are similarly compared to deeper forms of material energy (which are different from the Sāñkhya elements). These 49 letters, along with three other conjunct consonants (क्ष्, त्र, ज्ञ) which are separated representations of the three modes of nature and are to be combined as Prakriti, constitute the 50 alphabets of Sanskrit. The separation of material energy into these forms is attributed to a sound representation of eternal reality—called Śabda Brahman. The Śabda Brahman symbolizes the primordial concepts that we can know, use, enjoy, and relate to, and the world takes a form pursuant to the native capacities of the soul to relate, know, act, and enjoy. Thus, matter is modeled after the nature of the soul or consciousness.

Hence, we can understand the claim that "from these words have emerged the methods of direct perception and inference" in two ways. First, based on the analysis of ordinary experience—which has been carried out in Western philosophy—we can note that some primordial ideas must exist before we can even perceive. Second, based on the descriptions in Sāñkhya and Tantra, we can elucidate this hierarchy from the most primordial ideas to the manifest world that we can relate to, perceive, use, and enjoy. These primordial ideas are the śabda or the eternal truths about the nature of the soul and God; they represent a detailing of what we mean by soul and God in terms of the myriad abilities to perceive, conceive, judge, act, connect and enjoy. The term śabda also denotes the 'scripture' as the explanation of a transcendental reality. These two uses of the term śabda—namely, the primordial symbolic representation of Brahman and the scripture which explains the nature of this Brahman—are closely related in the sense that both explain the nature of the soul and God. The Śabda Brahman is the more fundamental reality and the scriptures are verbose and detailed descriptions of the same reality. This sūtra emphasizes the first meaning—namely, that even our direct perception and imagination or inference have ultimately emerged from the primordial reality. Therefore, if we keep the understanding of the scriptures in view, then this manifest world of thoughts and perceptions can be seen through the lens of the scripture.

We must emphasize here that direct perception and inference are not taken as independent methods of attaining knowledge. Rather, the claim is subtler—*if* you take the śabda for granted, then you can use it to confirm the understanding by observation and reasoning. In short, reasoning and observation are used to validate and confirm the śabda, rather than to discover the nature of reality. There is a subtle but important difference between 'discovery' and 'verification'. Faith in the śabda is needed for discovery, but reason and observation can be used for verification. So, there is no fundamental contradiction between reason, observation, and scriptures, provided scriptures have been accepted. If one has understood the scriptural knowledge, then its application to day-to-day life (through reason and observation) will only confirm the scriptural truth. Hence, even those who engage in other methods—such as karma and jñāna—are still to be considered progressing in their spiritual understanding, although this understanding comes through confirmation by reason and observation.

Implicit faith in the Lord as the source of knowledge is essential, otherwise, one would never put their faith in the scriptures. The faith in scripture is itself the faith in the Lord: only if you trust a teacher, would you trust their books. If trust is placed in the books, implicit trust is placed in the teacher as well. In fact, many times to understand the books, a spiritual aspirant can approach a guru. If such a guru is unavailable, one can approach the Lord in the heart. So, by this sūtra we can see why faith and devotion in the Lord are not contrary to the practices of jñāna and karma—provided faith is reposed in the Lord.

QUESTION

However, by allowing the possibility of jñāna and karma along with devotion to the Lord, aren't we compromising the exclusivity of devotion itself? By saying that bhakti can be mixed with other processes—as these have been described in the scriptures—aren't we saying that purity of devotion (and the rejection of the other processes such as jñāna and karma) is unnecessary?

Many devotees argue that if we are relying on reason and observation, then in some sense we are trying to confirm the knowledge of the scripture by our senses and the mind, and therefore our faith in the Lord is not perfect because we are unable to accept the truth of the scripture as they are. Our need to confirm the truth by other methods—experience and reason—indicates our lack of faith. So, this mixing of jñāna and karma with bhakti can be construed as lacking faith in the scripture or the words of the Lord. In short, if we were perfect devotees, free of jñāna and karma, then we must blindly accept the scripture.

1.3.29 (92)

अत एव च नत्यित्वम्

ata eva ca nityatvam

ata-eva—from this very reason; ca—also; nityatvam—the persistence.

TRANSLATION

From this ability (to mix karma and jñāna with bhakti) also follows the persistence (of the devotion in the scripture and toward the Lord).

COMMENTARY

In the previous sūtra, we discussed that when faith in the scripture and devotion in the Lord has been reposed (by acceptance of scriptures and the Lord as the teacher in the heart), then there is no contradiction between reason, observation, and scripture. However, one may argue that this continuous process of asking questions, and the need to understand things based on reasoning indicates a lack of faith. This sūtra refutes this argument and states that our continuous inquiries from the scriptures, guru, and the Lord in the heart, are an indication that our faith in these methods of getting knowledge is intact.

The term *nityatvam* can be understood in many ways; it can indicate eternity; it can also indicate continuity or persistence. The latter meaning clarifies this sūtra much better than the former, given the context of previous sūtras. The claim is that even if we ask repeated questions, expressing our doubts, and seeking clarification, we should not be considered a non-devotee. Similarly, if we learn something from the scripture, the guru, or the Lord, and we put it to test by applying it in day-to-day life, it is not the rejection of faith. Implicitly, a distinction is drawn between 'faith' and 'blind faith'. Blind faith is the uncritical acceptance of whatever is said or taught. Under it, we listen to something, but we don't ask further questions, and we don't try to test its truth. On the other hand, faith means that we try to examine the teaching using observation and reason, and every time a doubt arises, we will go back to scripture, the guru, and the Lord to overcome the doubt. So, one who is testing the teaching should not be considered unfaithful, and his devotion should not be doubted. In short, we reject the blind acceptance of the teaching and encourage rational and empirical verification; these are not symptoms of lacking faith in the Lord.

In this regard, we must note that Vaiṣṇava Ācāryas have indeed rejected bhakti mixed with jñāna and karma. Śri Rupa Goswami writes in the Bhakti-rasāmṛta-sindhu, that bhakti free from jñāna and karma is the highest.

anyabhilasita-sunyam jñāna-karmadyanavrtam
anukulyena krsnanusilanam bhaktir-uttama

That which is free from other desires, that which is not covered by jñāna and karma, and that which is the favorable following of Lord Kṛṣṇa is called supreme (or superior) bhakti.

However, such bhakti is attained after the destruction of all doubts when perfect knowledge has been realized through direct experience, and there is no more need for testing the teachings of the scripture or the inspiration of the Lord. We should not confuse the rejection of testing after realization with the progressive stage of bhakti where the soul is still developing an understanding. Yes, in the ultimate state, when all doubts are destroyed, the tests of knowledge end. However, while doubts exist, and tests are being performed, they should not be considered unfaithfulness in the guru, the Lord, or the scripture.

QUESTION

But you have earlier said that the transcendent realm is the three quarters beyond the world of birth and death, and the material world is the place of repeated birth and death. On this basis, a distinction between the material and the transcendent realms was drawn. But now you are saying that the transcendent truth can also be confirmed or verified in the world of birth and death?

1.3.30 (93)
समाननामरूपत्वाच्चावृत्तावप्यविरोधो दर्शनात् स्मृतेश्च
samānanāmarūpatvāccāvṛttāvapyavirodho darśanāt smṛteśca

samāna-nāmarūpatvāt—because of the similar names and forms; ca—and; āvṛttau—in the revolving of the world cycles; api—even; avirodhaḥ—no contradiction; darśanāt—from the śrutī; smṛteḥ—the smriti; ca—and.

TRANSLATION

And on account of the sameness of names and forms in every fresh cycle, there is no contradiction (to the confirmation of eternal knowledge) even in the revolving of the world cycles, as is seen from the śrutī and the smriti.

COMMENTARY

Here, the terms *nāma* and *rūpa* are used; they respectively mean names and forms. Rūpa indicates the bodily forms or species of life, such as cow, horse, lion, dog, cat, etc. These species are not always manifest. Of late, due to environmental degradation, millions of species are becoming extinct. However, this sūtra states that they will appear again with the cycles of time. In short, the idea of the species is eternal, but its manifestation as an individual of that species is temporary. In the same way, nāma indicates the name by which we identify someone. These names can pertain to an individual or to the role of a person. For instance, we call the same person 'John' or the 'President'. Notably, John may not be President in every cycle of time, but the President will still appear. In this regard, we can note that the names of demigods such as Indra, Surya, Chandra, Yama, etc. are quite like we call someone "Mr. President". The person who occupies this role can, however, change. Since these roles are recreated, therefore, they are conceptually eternal; nobody occupies the position of Indra permanently. However, the meaning of the term Indra—i.e., the duties that this role is expected to perform—remains intact. So, because these names and forms reappear, again and again, we must consider them conceptually eternal.

We have previously spoken about three components of our experience—subjective, objective, and intersubjective. The rūpa or bodies are objective. The nāma or roles are intersubjective. However, the person occupying the body and the role is subjective. The person who takes a body and roles doesn't repeat the same body and role in the different cycles; if this were the case, then the soul could never be liberated from the cycle of birth and death. So, there is a temporary aspect to the world—namely, that the soul changes its body and role. And there is a permanent aspect to the world—namely, the bodies and the roles reappear. This reappearance entails that the body and the role are conceptual.

The implication of this eternity is that the species we find in the material world (cats, dogs, fishes, birds, etc.) exist in the spiritual world as well. Similarly, the roles of this world such as Indra, Chandra, Surya, etc. exist even in the spiritual world (they may be called by different names). Due to the absence of the time cycles, however, these are never created and destroyed. Their conceptual eternity is therefore also their existential eternity. Similarly, because there is no birth and death, once a person has occupied a role and a body, they never have to change that role and body. So, the eternity of the role and the body is indirectly implied by the lack of birth and death. In short, the diversity in this world is conceptually eternal and is also manifest in the eternal realm. This diversity appears and disappears in this world, but due to the repeating cycle of appearance and disappearance, the roles and the species are conceptually eternal. This eternity is similar but not identical to that in the spiritual realm.

The contention of this sūtra is that this conceptual eternity is itself the eternal transcendental knowledge. So, just because the soul is changing bodies doesn't entail that everything in the material world is temporary. This world is also reflecting the eternity through the reappearance of names and forms in every cycle of time. Therefore, it should not be supposed that the eternal truth cannot be understood from the temporary world. If we limit our focus to certain periods of time and specific places, then the cycles of time indicate change. But if we broaden the understanding through scriptures, then the same roles and species are eternal. So, the focus on the testing of knowledge obtained through scriptures or the Lord in this world is legitimate and such tests should not be considered contrary to scriptures because we are obtaining the concepts to understand from these scriptures and checking if these concepts are true.

QUESTION

But if the demigods have such powerful positions, and a life relatively free of difficulties, then why aren't they advancing in spiritual life? Why is it said that the demigods fall from their position and are born again on earth?

1.3.31 (94)

मध्वादिष्विसम्भवादनधकिारं जैमनििः

madhvādiṣvasambhavādanadhikāraṃ jaiminiḥ

madhvādiṣu—In Madhu Vidya etc.; asambhavāt—on account of the impossibility; anadhikāraṃ—disqualification; jaiminiḥ—Jaimini (is of opinion).

TRANSLATION

On account of being in Madhu Vidya, the demigods are disqualified (from spiritual life) because of the impossibility (of practicing Madhu Vidya and spiritual life simultaneously), such is the opinion of the sage Jaimini.

COMMENTARY

Madhu Vidya refers to the drinking of the intoxicant called Soma.

The nature of any intoxicant is that it makes you fearless, daring, and confident. Intoxicants also give rise to a higher level of creativity. At the level of the body, this creativity manifests in elaborate sexual activity. At the level of the mind, the same creativity manifests in fantastic visions resulting from auditory and visual stimulations, and these stimulations then get mixed in various ways. It is said that upon drinking Soma one feels so confident that he considers himself as powerful as ten thousand elephants. In this regard, we can note that the body can be made extremely strong and powerful, provided the person is emotionally strong. Most illnesses arise due to emotional weakness, which damages the immune system and brings other diseases. So, if one becomes emotionally strong and is freed from fear, then their body automatically becomes stronger. Therefore, Soma is also said to be something that nourishes the body and makes it stronger. But the cause of this strength is not that Soma is an exemplary type of nutrient. The real cause is that it destroys the fear within a person.

All of us are gripped by fear within; even the demigods are afraid that they will one day be replaced by someone else. This fear is exacerbated due to circumstances incompatible with our emotional nature. For instance, a naturally peaceful person will avoid conflicting situations, but if he is thrown into conflicting situations, he would become naturally fearful. On the other hand, the person who enjoys conflict will become morose if he is unable to engage in aggression with others; such people will get naturally excited and energized by the possibility of conflict. So, there is a natural fear in the heart, and it gets exacerbated by the situation. People take intoxicants to overcome this fear.

The devotee of the Lord is also often gripped by this fear in the material world, but he takes shelter of the Lord and seeks His protection from within the heart. As soon as the love of the Lord appears in the heart, one feels fearless. The love of the Lord is therefore the most powerful type of intoxicant.

Thus, there are two methods by which to overcome fear—the use of intoxicants which make one feel very powerful, and the devotion to the Lord. If one is accustomed to intoxicants, then the love of the Lord takes a backseat. The disqualification of the demigods is their drinking of Soma, which makes it impossible for them to love the Lord because fear is being mitigated by the intoxicant. So, even though there is a possibility they can surrender to the Lord and seek His shelter, they generally do not do so. They rather use Soma to feel strong. It is only when they lose battles against the demons, they seek help from Lord Viṣṇu, but once having regained their position they go back to enjoying. This is quite like a person who worships the Lord when in difficulty but forgets the Lord as soon as the difficulty is mitigated and starts enjoying again.

The demigods are being portrayed in a bad light here. One could conclude from this that the demigods are no better than us. After all, they are just enjoying an intoxicant! We must caution against this hasty conclusion, because this view is attributed to Jaimini—who, as we have seen, disregarded the existence of demigods and God. If someone argued against Mīmāṃsā by citing other Vedic scriptures where the demigods are said to be in a superior position, their counterargument would be— "Oh, their superiority is just due to drinking Soma". This is not truly the position of Vedānta Sūtra, which will become clearer in the subsequent sūtras. This is the explanation of why the demigods are not being liberated from the material world despite their superior position, and this somewhat derogatory view of demigods is attributed to Jaimini.

QUESTION

So according to Jaimini, the demigods are no better than human beings. As we are conditioned to forget the Lord, likewise the demigods are prone to neglect the Lord. Hence, they are not exemplars of devotion to the Lord?

1.3.32 (95)
ज्योतिषि भावाच्च
jyotiṣi bhāvācca

jyotiṣi—as mere spheres of light, or as mere astrological entities; bhāvāt—because (they are used) in the sense; ca—also.

TRANSLATION

(Jaimini further states that the demigods are) mere spheres of light or astrological entities; after all, (their names are) also used in this sense.

COMMENTARY

The view of Jaimini is continued in this sūtra. According to him, the demigods simply don't exist. The world is controlled by the movement of planets or the spheres of light, and we have artificially personalized nature by calling these spheres of light demigods like Surya, Chandra, Brihaspati, etc. But since nobody can see these demigods, all such demigods don't exist. Again, we shouldn't get carried away by this viewpoint, because the next sūtra refutes it, and because this view is attributed to the atheistic philosophy of Jaimini.

Now, a question arises: Why discuss the demigods at all, if they must be portrayed in a poor light? The answer is that the demigods were introduced into the discussion by the question of whether any beings other than humans are qualified to pursue a spiritual life. The answer to that question is that there are indeed beings who have performed austerities and situated in sattva-guna as opposed to humans who are largely in rajo-guna and the demons below who are largely in tamo-guna. So, from a material perspective, the demigods are higher. They are also higher because sattva-guna is closer to transcendence than rajo-guna and tamo-guna. However, this material superiority shouldn't be taken to imply spiritual superiority. Normally when we see people in positions of greater power, we are inclined to respect them. A devotee of the Lord may be poor and destitute, and he would not be as much respected according to social customs. The position of demigods is also similar—they have performed austerities and practiced sense control due to which they have superior positions in the administration of the universe. According to social customs, they are respectable. But this respect for demigods in society should be taken with a pinch of salt when discussing the extent of their spiritual advancement. This is not to say that the demigods are atheistic or opposed to the Lord like demons. However, it is also not to be presumed that their superior material position automatically entails that they are also spiritually advanced. So, the discussion about their intoxication is simply to reveal the other perspective, so that one can form a balanced opinion about their position. A derogatory view of the demigods has been presented—but it is a view from a spiritual viewpoint.

QUESTION

However, you have previously said that the demigods are ādid-aivika and work under the supervision of the Paramātma. If we accept Jaimini's opinion that the demigods simply don't exist, then how shall we reconcile it with your previous statements about them being the controllers of the material world?

1.3.33 (96)
भावं तु वादरायणःअस्तिहि
bhāvaṃ tu vādarāyaṇaḥ asti hi

bhāvaṃ—the existence (of demigods); tu—but; vādarāyaṇaḥ—Badarayana (maintains); asti—does exist; hi—because.

TRANSLATION

But Bādarāyana accepts the existence (of demigods) because they exist.

COMMENTARY

The controversy created by the previous two sūtras is finally put to rest by saying that even though Jaimini believes that the demigods don't exist because we cannot observe them, Bādarāyana maintains that their existence is real.

In 1.3.30 (93) it was stated that the transcendent reality of names and forms is also visible in the material world in the different cycles of time, and we had identified these names as Indra, Chandra, Surya, etc. But the Mīmāṃsā philosopher could argue: if you are claiming that a transcendent reality can be confirmed in this world by reason and observation, then I cannot see such demigods through my senses. So, your claim that a transcendent reality exists, and can be confirmed by our observation to reaffirm our faith in its existence, must be rejected. And since we cannot confirm the existence of such a reality through reason and experience, then any attempt to ask repeated questions or test the knowledge through practical application must also be rejected. The only recourse for the transcendentalist is blind faith in such claims, and if someone wants to have such blind faith, then why even engage in a discussion? After all, the discussion is supposed to be carried out using reason and observation, and if the claims cannot be confirmed by reason and experience, then there is no point in any discussion. Your belief in gods or God is simply blind faith.

We have seen how the Mīmāṃsā philosopher is an instrumentalist rather than a realist. Modern science is very close to the Mīmāṃsā position although it doesn't accept the existence of a soul, karma, or even choice. But it is quite possible to turn modern science in a New Age movement, which accepts the existence of a soul, karma, and choice, and yet remains atheistic. This is an important point because many people are enamored by the onset of such New Age movements, which advocate the existence of a soul, choice, and even karma, and they think that this is significant progress toward a spiritual understanding. They may not realize how dangerously close it is to blatant atheism. A person involved in gross materialistic activities, who accepts the reality of demigods and God, should be considered far superior to the New Age movements. The worship of demigods is not the ultimate destination, but one who worships the demigods recognizes the existence of a higher authority even in this world. Their devotion to the demigods is superior to one who believes that such demigods and God don't exist, although he accepts the soul, choice, and karma.

Topic 9

QUESTION

You have earlier stated that humans are qualified to take shelter of the Lord in the heart (in case they cannot find a suitable guru). But some so many people are guided by their material desires, even when they claim to be guided by the Lord. Similarly, if the real guru is to be judged by their words (conviction), but many humans may not be so perceptive to understand the real meaning. So, in what way are all humans qualified for spiritual progress if they don't have the qualification to either find a real guru or accept Lord's guidance in the heart?

1.3.34 (97)
शुगस्य तदनादरश्रवणात् तदादरवणात् सूच्यते हि
śugasya tadanādaraśravaṇāt tadādravaṇāt sūcyate hi

śuk—grief; asya—his; tat-anādaraśravaṇāt—from hearing the insult; tat—that (about him); ādravaṇāt—owing to his approaching in a not humble manner (ādrava—not liquid or melted); sūcyate—is referred to; hi—because.

TRANSLATION

He was in grief on hearing insulting words about him because he did not approach in a humble manner—this can be referred to (as a counterexample).

COMMENTARY

In the earlier sections, the qualifications of a guru were discussed. In this section, the qualifications of the disciple are being discussed. In Bhagavad-Gita 4.34, Lord Kṛṣṇa states the qualification of a disciple approaching a guru:

tad viddhi praṇipātena
paripraśnena sevayā
upadekṣyanti te jñānaṁ
jñāninas tattva-darśinaḥ

To know that (the Absolute Truth) fall before (a spiritual master), ask him questions submissively, and render him service. They can teach the knowledge because they have seen the truth.

The first such qualification is that one must be extremely humble; one must ask questions submissively, and one must render service to the guru. If these conditions are not satisfied, then the guru is not obliged to teach the knowledge. Therefore, not every human is qualified to learn from a guru; they must be submissive and deeply inquisitive, and prepared to serve the guru to learn.

This sūtra cites a counterexample from Chāndogya Upaniṣad where King Janasruti approached a teacher Raivaka in a not so humble manner. The specific term used here is ādrava which means in a non-liquid or non-melted manner. It can be contrasted to Lord Kṛṣṇa's use of *pra-nipatena* in relation to the guru which means prostration at someone's feet in a very humble manner. Instead of offering his humility, the King offered Raivaka some material goods—a necklace, a chariot, and some cows—and asked him to impart spiritual knowledge. Looking at his arrogant attitude, Raivaka was greatly displeased and called the King a "Sūdra" or a man unqualified for spiritual knowledge. Raivaka returned all the gifts the King had brought and refused to impart him knowledge.

QUESTION

What did the King then do? Did he approach the Lord in his heart? Did he approach another spiritual master? Was he able to obtain knowledge?

1.3.35 (98)

क्षत्रयियत्वगतेश्चोत्तरत्र चैत्ररथेन लङ्गात्

kṣatriyatvagateścottaratra caitrarathena liṅgāt

kṣatriyatva-gateḥ—having the nature of a Kshatriya; ca—and; uttaratra—subsequently; caitrarathena liṅgāt—by exhibiting signs like Chaitraratha.

TRANSLATION

(Despite him) having the nature of a Kshatriya (i.e., pride and arrogance), subsequently (he) exhibited the signs like that of Chaitraratha (i.e., humility).

COMMENTARY

The story of King Janaśruti continues from the previous sūtra. The Kshatriyas are naturally very proud and do not submit to anyone easily. Yet, despite this natural pride in him, and the insult that caused him grief, the Chāndogya Upaniṣad describes that the King came back a second time to Raivaka. This time, he was much humbler and offered his daughter in marriage to Raivaka. A daughter is especially very dear to a father, so if a father is offering his daughter in marriage, his seriousness should be accepted. Looking at the King's changed attitude, Raivaka agreed to impart the knowledge to the King. In this context, a comparison between Janaśruti and Chaitraratha is made. Chaitraratha was a Gandharva, who demonstrated great arrogance to Arjuna, considering him to be a mere human. Then, Arjuna defeated Chaitraratha in a battle and was about to behead him. Chaitraratha and his wife begged Arjuna to spare his life, and Arjuna demonstrating his compassion let Chaitraratha go free. The comparison with Chaitraratha is appropriate as he was initially proud and arrogant and fought against Arjuna and later begged for his mercy. The implication of the previous sūtra was that if a person is arrogant, then the guru must reject him. But if he becomes humble, he should be imparted knowledge.

QUESTION

In the story of Janaśruti and Raivaka, since Raivaka calls Janaśruti a "Sūdra", and then rejects him as a disciple, does it mean that the Sūdra cannot be accepted as disciples? You have earlier said that spiritual knowledge is appropriate for all human beings. But now you are saying that it may not be meant for the Sūdra. Doesn't this create a contradiction with the earlier claim?

1.3.36 (99)

संस्कारपरामर्शात् तदभावाभिलापाच्च

saṁskāraparāmarśāt tadabhāvābhilāpacca

saṁskāra-parāmarśāt—from purificatory ceremonies and morality being mentioned; tat-abhāva-abhilāpāt—from its absence being declared; ca—and.

TRANSLATION

Because purificatory ceremonies and moral character are mentioned (in the twice-born) and because their absence is declared (in the case of the Sūdra).

COMMENTARY

There are two meanings of saṁskāra, one generic and the other specific. The generic meaning is that while growing up, a child is taught moral values, good behavior, dignity and respect toward others, cultivation of the mind, cleanliness, pure habits, regulated living, the importance of austerity, etc. In this generic meaning, saṃskāra indicates the latent impressions on the psyche that are formed during childhood. Childhood is a formative time during which the mind, intellect, and body are developed. Whatever happens during childhood leaves a lasting impression. Thus, the generic meaning of saṃskāra is ethical and moral upbringing". The children are impressionable; they gather ideas quickly from their surroundings. These are typically obtained from parents, teachers, and friends. Therefore, a good family upbringing and association are important during childhood. These leave impressions which last a lifetime.

The second, more specific, meaning of saṃskāra is the performance of a ritual. In the Vedic custom, a pūjā is performed invoking the Lord's blessings before beginning anything important. This pūjā has two purposes—(1) remembering the Lord before starting anything new, and (2) seeking His blessings to remove any defects that remain in our actions despite our best efforts. Such rituals include the ceremony of marriage, the ritual of impregnation, childbirth, the beginning of solid food by the child (different from mother's milk), the first introduction to reading and writing, the beginning of formal education, and the completion of education whereby the guru grants a sanctified thread to be worn by the disciple used for chanting the Gāyatri mantra three times a day.

Take the example of Garbhādhāna or the impregnation ceremony. The husband and wife are not expected to engage in indiscriminate sex for enjoyment. Sex is primarily meant for conceiving the child. And if the husband and wife desire to have a child, they perform a ceremony and seek the blessings of the Lord. The entire family is invited to this ceremony, and through it, everyone comes to know that the couple will now engage in sex. Sex is therefore not a private matter or something that two people do, unknown to everyone else. It is rather publicly declared that a couple is now seeking a child, and hence they will indulge in sex. If one wants to have more children, this ceremony is performed for every child. Therefore, every instance of sex is preceded by a ceremony of conception, and through such ceremonies, life is regulated.

In this degraded age, a moral upbringing, seeking the shelter of the Lord, and asking for His blessings to remove any remaining defects despite our best efforts, have mostly disappeared. There is still in some cases a residual sacrament of wearing a thread, even if these people don't chant the Gāyatri mantra three times a day. It is just a physical adornment used by some people to call themselves "Brahmana" as opposed to those who don't wear such threads. As a result, the term saṃskāra has come to symbolize those with a thread.

We should, however, understand saṃskāra in a broader sense— beginning with a moral upbringing and seeking the benediction of the Lord at every stage of life, along with the purificatory ceremonies that are performed to regulate enjoyment in life. The thread comes at the culmination of the education, but there is much more that precedes and follows the wearing of the thread.

With this background, the Sūdra are those people who do not abide by this system. They don't have a good moral upbringing, and they don't invoke the Lord's blessings at important stages in their life. Thus, a person who has sex without declaring the intention of conception is to be considered a Sūdra. Similarly, those who have sex with contraception are to be considered Sūdra.

In an earlier sūtra, Raivaka insults Janaśruti as Sūdra because he did not show the respect that a disciple must toward the guru. There are many such Sūdra spiritualists at present who despite their ignorance about the truth, a misfortune which distances them from good teachers, and laziness to study books, remain extremely arrogant. When a genuine teacher approaches them despite their misfortune, instead of showing humility and gratitude, they simply challenge and criticize the teacher. Their hubris indicates a lack of moral upbringing, and such people are not considered civilized in the Vedic system.

Raivaka could see that Janaśruti was a king. After all, who but a king can offer such wealth? But the fact that the king thought that he can buy knowledge in exchange for some of his wealth indicated his depraved mindset. It is an indirect statement that even the kings can behave like Sūdra and they should, therefore, be considered Sūdra. Conversely, when his behavior changed, and he returned humbly, Raivaka granted him knowledge, which again indicates that correct behavior and mindset are the basis of deciding who a Sūdra is.

The essence of this sūtra is that not all humans can be granted spiritual knowledge. There is a basic threshold of moral character and faith in the Lord that is a prerequisite for this knowledge. Furthermore, the prospective disciple must also demonstrate humility instead of arrogance. Those lacking in all these basic qualifications should not be granted spiritual knowledge. The upper three classes in society, namely, the Brahmana, Kshatriya, and Vaisya are expected to have these qualities to varying degrees, with the Brahmana possessing them to the highest level. Similarly, the Sūdra are those who don't possess such qualities. Therefore, they are disqualified from being taught Vedic knowledge.

QUESTION

You are stating that a guru cannot blindly accept disciples. Rather, the guru must evaluate the suitability of a person based on their moral character and faith in the Lord before deciding to impart them spiritual knowledge?

1.3.37 (100)
तदभावनिर्धारणे च प्रवृत्तेः
tadabhāvanirdhāraṇe ca pravṛtteḥ

tadabhāva—the absence of that (namely, the qualities of a Sūdra); nirdhāraṇe—in the ascertainment; ca—and; pravṛtteḥ—from inclination.

TRANSLATION

In the ascertainment of the absence of that (the existence of good qualities and lack of faith in the Lord—i.e., the qualities of a Sūdra) and based on their inclinations (a guru can impart knowledge to a prospective disciple).

COMMENTARY

In the previous sūtra, the action of Raivaka was clarified and justified—namely, why he called Janaśruti a Sūdra and later accepted him as his disciple. This position is now being generalized for all the prospective teachers and their disciples. In the process, the sūtra states that not only must one not have the qualities of the Sūdra, but one must also have the *pravritti* or inclination and tendency toward this knowledge. What do inclination and tendency mean? It indicates that a person—once having acquired such knowledge—will not abandon it. He has a natural inclination and tendency toward practicing this knowledge, and the guru is assured that the disciple will not acquire this knowledge and then either misuse it, or abandon it, and thereby become a bad example for others who might be seeking such knowledge in the future.

Many people join spiritual practices and take initiation from a guru. But it may often be done on the spur of the moment. As time passes, their natural disinclination becomes obvious. The person now abandons the spiritual path and takes to other activities that are totally counterproductive to this path. They may also try to use this knowledge for their own material advancement. Or, sometimes, they may totally abandon the path and engage in activities that prompt others to wonder—If this man could do such things after so many years of spiritual practice, then is there something wrong with the practice itself?

The sūtra holds the guru responsible for preventing such outcomes. He is expected to judge the disciple not only from the present demonstration of good qualities such as humility and submissive inquiry, but also the long-term prospect of a person being able to continue the practice in such a path. This further constrains the process of spiritual initiation—One should not initiate just because a person is demonstrating good qualities right now. Rather, the guru must also judge a person's nature and estimate whether he would be able to sustain this practice over his lifetime. Sometimes people approach a guru because they are distressed; their temporary suffering draws them toward a guru, but their real inclination is quite different. So, the reasons for which someone approaches a guru must be judged by the guru and a decision must be made as to their suitability to impart the knowledge based on their true inclinations.

QUESTION

It is sometimes said that the śrutī—e.g., the Upaniṣad—are harder to understand for the common people, and they are therefore recommended or allowed only for the most advanced people. It is also said that the smriti—such as the Ramayana, Mahabharata, and the Purāna—can be studied even by the less intelligent or less qualified people. So, when you speak about the disqualification of a disciple, does it pertain only to the śrutī or also to the smriti?

1.3.38 (101)

श्रवणाध्ययनार्थप्रतिषेधात् स्मृतेश्च

śravaṇādhyayanārthapratiṣedhāt smṛteśca

śravaṇa-adhyayana-artha-pratiṣedhāt—because of the prohibition of hearing, studying, and interpreting; smṛteḥ—the smriti; ca—also.

TRANSLATION

Because of the prohibition from hearing, studying, and interpreting the smriti (those lacking in moral character and faith in the Lord) as well.

COMMENTARY

The distinction between śrutī and smriti is not as hard and fast as is sometimes made out to be. For example, the Bhagavad-Gita is a Upaniṣad and can, therefore, be called śruti. However, because Bhagavad-Gita is a part of Mahabharata, and the latter is considered smriti, therefore, the Bhagavad-Gita is also called smriti. In the same vein, it is argued that śrutī is what was heard from the Lord, while smriti is produced by enlightened souls. If we take that distinction, then the above description of Raivaka and Janaśruti cannot be considered the speech of the Lord; it is clearly a narration of events like those in the Purāna. By that measure, Chāndogya Upaniṣad must be considered a smriti rather than śrutī. Owing to these objections, sometimes the Upaniṣads are treated as smriti rather than śrutī. But the problem is not limited to the Upaniṣad. There are numerous conversations between the Lord and His devotees found all over the Vedic literature; The Bhagavad-Gita is an example of Lord Kṛṣṇa instructing Arjuna; since it is spoken by the Lord, it must be considered śrutī. Likewise, there are many such conversations between the Lord and His devotees in the Purāna and the Tantra. So, by the claim that śrutī is spoken by the Lord, the Tantra and Purāna must also be classified as śrutī and the scope of smriti is practically limited. A classic example of this problem is that Sāṅkhya philosophy is spoken by Lord Kapila to mother Devahūti in the Śrīmad Bhāgavatam. As an incarnation of Lord Viṣṇu, His words must be considered śrutī, and Sāṅkhya philosophy (which is classified as one of the six schools of philosophy under the smriti category) must now be considered śrutī instead of smriti.

Now, some historians say that only the four Vedas are śrutī. But Vedic texts describe how the four Vedas are created from the four heads of Brahma. If śrutī is only spoken by the Lord, then the four Vedas are spoken by Brahma. So, by that measure, the four Vedas cannot be called śrutī. Furthermore, the division of the Veda into four parts is a creation of Brahma, after he received the knowledge from Lord Viṣṇu. So, the four-fold division of knowledge is due to Brahma, and not due to the Lord who spoke the knowledge to Brahma. If śrutī is only Lord's speech, then we cannot consider even the four Vedas śrutī.

The bottom line is that no definition of śrutī and smriti works correctly. Words of the Lord are found in the smriti, and narrations of advanced preceptors are found in the śrutī. Any method of classification based on history, grouping, and literary style is useless. The terms śrutī and smriti are used heuristically, which means by and large the śrutī will contain direct information from the Lord, and smriti will contain its understanding and interpretation by the advanced preceptors. However, these are not mutually exclusive categories. Ultimately, the term 'Veda' means knowledge or to know. It comprises several types of knowledge, some of which are mundane, and others are transcendental. The 'earlier' parts of the Veda, which comprise the mantras for the worship of demigods, and which formed the basis of Pūrva Mīmāṃsā, are generally mundane knowledge. Conversely, the 'later' part of the Vedas, such as the Vedānta Sūtra, constitute transcendental knowledge. So, even if we look at the accepted chronology of the texts, the progression isn't always from the transcendental to mundane; is it often also in the reverse order. Given all these difficulties, we must not consider śrutī and smriti as being fundamentally different. The Mahabharata for example describes the Purāna as the fifth Veda. We must rather view them as taking a seeker to different levels of spiritual advancement. The context reveals which scripture is meant for which purpose.

With the inability to clearly separate śrutī and smriti, it is no surprise that this sūtra states that those without a good moral character, faith in the Lord, and the long-term inclination to pursue and practice this knowledge, should also not be taught the smriti. In short, there are some prerequisites for all disciples, and those not meeting the qualification should not be imparted this knowledge. This sūtra explicitly forbids hearing, studying, and interpreting. These are progressive stages—one begins by hearing, then studies them himself, and then may author an interpretation. The implication is that if one can hear, then he will start studying, and eventually author an interpretation. As interpretations by the unqualified proliferate, it would become impossible to distinguish between the true understanding and the concocted ideologies. The knowledge will therefore eventually get corrupted and misunderstood.

We can understand from here that such corruptions have occurred many times in history, so this statement is made with the benefit of hindsight. As Lord Kṛṣṇa states in the Bhagavad-Gita, He appears in every age to re-establish the knowledge when it has declined, and we should assume that despite this forbidding of hearing, studying, and interpreting by the unqualified, such things happen; as a result, the understanding declines, and the Lord then appears again to reestablish it. So, even as this sūtra cautions against teaching the knowledge to the unqualified, we can assume that such things happen anyway.

Topic 10

QUESTION

You have sent me into a great dilemma by stating that those without a good moral character and faith in the Lord should not be imparted spiritual knowledge, because most people would be disqualified by this predilection. Especially in today's time, most people don't have a good moral character and they don't have faith in the Lord. The implication for them is that they are all disqualified from this knowledge. If that is so, then how can they become qualified if we close the doors to real knowledge for them? The only hope for liberating such a person is to have them acquire this knowledge, although they may still reject it due to their nature. But if we close the doors to this knowledge by precluding them, then what hope exists for such unfortunate people?

1.3.39 (102)

कम्पनात्

kampanāt

kampanāt—from the vibrations.

TRANSLATION

(Spiritual knowledge can be obtained) from the vibrations.

COMMENTARY

To understand this sūtra, we can recall the life story of Sage Valmiki who was a hunter in a forest prior to becoming a sage. Once, upon a chance meeting with Nārada Muni, he was advised to give up his hunting and purify himself of his sinful actions. But due to the accumulated effects of his actions, he had lost all good moral character and faith in the Lord. He could not even chant the names of the Lord. So, Nārada advised him to chant "Mara" instead of "Rāma". "Mara" means "to kill" and given Valmiki's proclivities at that time, he could easily chant this word. When "Mara" is repeated again and again, it produces the same sound as "Rāma". So, even though the mental state of the chanter is to utter "Mara", over the course of time the sound purified him, and he became the great sage Valmiki who composed the epic Ramayana, which is considered a smriti. This sūtra similarly suggests that even if someone is unqualified to hear, study, and interpret, they can still just utter the sounds as "vibrations".

The Śrīmad Bhāgavatam narrates a similar story about Ajāmila, who was born a Brahmana but then abandoned all his good qualities, including his wife, and started living with a prostitute. Once some sages came to Ajāmila's house and seeing the prostitute pregnant with Ajāmila's child, asked Ajāmila to name the child Nārāyana. When this child was born, Ajāmila became deeply attached to his son, and would constantly call him "Nārāyana". At the time of death, the servants of Yama came to take him to hell, and out of fear and desperation, Ajāmila again called out for his son "Nārāyana". No sooner than this name was uttered, the servants of Lord Nārāyana arrived on the scene and saved Ajāmila from going to hell; he was in fact taken to Vaikuṇṭha. Ajāmila had no understanding of the meaning of Nārāyana; he wasn't calling out for Lord Nārāyana, but the sound vibration was enough to save him from the gravest danger.

In the previous sūtra the hearing, studying, and interpreting of scriptures has been forbidden for unfaithful or sinful people. All these activities involve the mind. Hearing involves the attempt to understand, which means giving the sound an interpretation. Studying involves the correlation of the acquired meaning with the ideas previously acquired, checking if they are consistent or inconsistent, and in case of inconsistencies, seek alternative meanings. Finally, interpretations are the reconciliation of some apparent contradictions and clarifying the understanding of each scripture by explaining the meaning.

The unfaithful regard the scripture with disdain, and never even try to understand them. If they happen to study something, any encounter with a contradiction reinforces their disdain. Hence, they never progress into the study phase where these contradictions are reconciled. Then, without such reconciliation, people begin authoring commentaries based on their limited understanding. Such misrepresentations abound today due to the reading, studying, and interpreting by scholars and academics who had no faith in the scripture or the Lord. In short, the unqualified are forbidden from using their minds.

Then, in this sūtra, such unqualified people are permitted to engage in "vibrations". Notably, we need not use our minds to understand these vibrations. We can simply listen to these sounds attentively, and there is no need to understand what they mean. This can make an unqualified person qualified.

The normal course prescribed for a spiritual aspirant is that they acquire knowledge, and then put that knowledge into practice. But if the aspirant is disqualified from acquiring knowledge, then this sūtra states that they can still "vibrate" some sounds. What are these sounds? In the above examples of Valmiki and Ajāmila, they are the sounds of the names of the Lord. The difference is that in the case of scripture, one needs to grasp the meaning, but in the case of chanting the names of the Lord, the understanding of meaning is unnecessary. Without understanding the meaning, one can still reap the benefits. In this regard, we can note that the Kali-Santārana Upaniṣad mentions that the chanting of the names of Hari is the only process for transcendence in Kali-yuga where most people have little faith in the scripture and the Lord and don't have a good moral character. If one is sincere about chanting the names of the Lord, then they can eventually come to the point of developing an understanding.

Topic 11

QUESTION

You previously said that one must worship the Lord in devotion and surrender to Him. For this surrender, one must have some knowledge, which we discussed can be tested through reason and observation, and upon such confirmation, we can repose faith in the Lord and then surrender to Him. But if knowledge itself is being precluded for such a person, then how can vibrating the names of the Lord lead to the ability to acquire the knowledge? Should it not be considered the uttering of some mumbo-jumbo, which we ourselves don't understand? How can mumbo-jumbo lead to perfect knowledge?

1.3.40 (103)

ज्योतिर्दिर्शनात्

jyotirdarśanāt

jyotiḥ—light; darśanāt—from seeing.

TRANSLATION

From seeing the light (by the performance of vibrations).

COMMENTARY

The previous sūtra said that if someone chants the names of the Lord then they will become qualified for receiving spiritual knowledge. And this sūtra reinforces that understanding—the changing of the names of the Lord is light. When the names of the Lord are heard, then attentive hearing is the reception of light, by which the nature of the self is understood. Similarly, when the names of the Lord are uttered attentively, then those names become the light by which everything else is demystified. The utterance of the names is now like a torch that illuminates things in a dark room. As the saying, 'knowledge is light, ignorance is darkness', this sūtra indicates that by the chanting of the Lord's names we get enlightened in two ways: (a) to see the nature of the self, and (b) to perceive the nature of reality. But we have to chant to experience this.

We earlier noted that to see a 'cow', we must possess the concept of 'cow', because only then can we discriminate the cow from the field it is grazing in. We had concluded that there must be some basic set of innate concepts using which we must acquire new concepts, but we ended the discussion on the note that this indicated concepts must be logically prior to the external things. Now we are faced with a different question: How do I acquire a concept of which I have no understanding yet? I need this concept to discriminate it from other things, and if I don't have it then even if I see those things right in front of me, I would still not be able to understand their presence. Just like a person who doesn't know what a cow is, won't see a cow even if it were in front of him. In the same way, without the understanding of the Lord in some form, we cannot understand the scriptures. Books use words, but the meaning of these words has to be realized by experience. If these meanings are wrong, then all subsequent understanding is also incorrect. This sūtra recommends that such an understanding can be obtained through sound vibrations; as an example, those trying to understand the nature of Brahman are advised to vibrate the sound 'OM'. This sound is the *name* by which Brahman is called, and by repeating the sound, we get the meaning. Using those meanings, we understand scriptures. In short, if you don't know the meaning, don't go consulting a dictionary! Rather, chant the names of the Lord, and then those meanings will be seen.

In this regard, we can recall that all concepts are universals, but they are also instantiated as individuals. So, an individual cow is an instance of the universal concept 'cow', and to create this instance, the individual must associate with the universal. Once the concept is instantiated, it exists both inside the instance (as the immanent meaning) and outside (as the transcendent concept). In the same way, if we chant the name 'Kṛṣṇa', then Kṛṣṇa is both outside and inside the name. The name contains the meaning like the individual cow contains the concept cow. If we repeat this name, the mind can acquire the meaning. If the meaning is acquired, then it becomes the 'light' by which we can discriminate. Just like knowing the meaning of 'cow' helps us see the 'cow', similarly, by knowing the meaning of 'Kṛṣṇa' we can see Kṛṣṇa. Without this meaning, even if Kṛṣṇa was right in front of us, we won't be able to see Him.

So, 'light' means the concepts by which we discriminate, distinguish, organize, etc. It is called 'light' in comparison to ordinary light for the ocular vision, which helps us distinguish things. The claim of the previous sūtra was that by chanting some sounds, we can acquire the meaning. The claim of this sūtra is that by acquiring these meanings we can begin to understand the scriptures—the word is now understood. With even a preliminary understanding, we can start reading the scripture, and follow the rest of the process of analyzing, testing, accepting a guru or seeking the Lord's guidance. If one has no faith in the Lord, because he has no understanding of the Lord, then reading scriptures would not help, because these scriptures will merely refer to Him by a name. To understand the meaning of that name, we must repeat that name, and by this repetition, we will also acquire the meaning automatically, and once such a meaning has been acquired, it will then enable us to read scriptures.

Topic 12

QUESTION

If the meaning is already in the sound, then a single utterance must reveal the meaning to us. Why do we have to repeat this sound again and again? Also, if this process were extended to the rest of the language, then why would anyone ever need a dictionary or translation? We can just hear the sounds, and since they contain the meanings, we should have no problem in understanding the spoken words. In fact, if such meanings were innate, then even by reading the scriptures we will automatically acquire the meanings the first time, and we would never be disqualified due to our moral character or lack of faith. So, how you reconcile the immanence of meaning with the repeated chanting?

1.3.41 (104)
आकाशोऽर्थान्तरत्वादिव्यपदेशात्
ākāśo'rthāntaratvādivyapadeśāt

ākāśaḥ—the space (whose property is sound); artha—the meaning; antaratva—because it is different; ādi—the origin; vyapadeśāt—from the hiding.

TRANSLATION

From the hiding of the origin, a difference between sound and meaning.

COMMENTARY

To understand this sūtra, we need to recall our previous discussion about the universals and individuals. My body has hands, legs, head, chest, belly, fingers, etc. and all of these are universals because your body has them too. These universals are organized in a hierarchy. For example, the higher-level universal for us is 'human'. Inside this universal, a lower-level universal is the 'hand'. Inside this is another lower-level universal, the 'finger', inside which is another lower-level universal of 'nail'. But, when an individual body is created, all these universals are instantiated. Thus, we acquire a personal hand, leg, belly, head, chest, fingers, etc. The instantiation is rooted in the soul, but from this soul—who is an individual—the individuality expands to instantiate the different parts of the body. As we have discussed earlier, this individuality originates in the ānanda potency of the soul and is understood as 'desire'. Just like there is a hierarchical tree of universals, similarly, there is a hierarchy of desires, which expand from the soul into the subtle body and then into the gross body, and then from this gross body into products of this body such as speech. Every part of our body, therefore, has desire; it's not that desire only exists in the heart or the mind; it is expanded all over the body. Thus, our tongue, skin, eyes, genitals, legs, and hands, all have desires. The mind can control these senses because the mind has a higher-level desire, and the soul can control the mind as it has an even higher-level desire. Thus, in summary, the body and its products (such as speech) are the combinations of the cognitive and the emotional—the cognitive is the universal, and emotional desires create an individual instance.

Now, when we chant the name of the Lord, we are creating an instance of the universal, and this instantiation involves a desire. However, this instantiation can occur at many levels—from the deepest level of the soul's desire to an intellectual, mental, sensual, or gross material level. A person without devotion to the Lord doesn't have the higher-level desires of the soul, intellect, or mind. So, he has no attraction for chanting. Nevertheless, if he chants, there is an instance as a gross sound, due to some desire. If there were no desire to chant, even this gross sound would not be produced. So, for one who has no deeper level desires, the chanting is recommended because at least we can instantiate the name of the Lord using the lowest level desire of the body. If this process is continued, then the desires rise—from the body to the senses, to the mind, to the intellect, and eventually to the soul. Accordingly, the same universal—i.e., the Lord—can be perceived at many levels. The grossest perception of the Lord is the sound vibrated by the tongue, but this doesn't lead to a sensual or mental understanding. The sensual understanding comes when the desire expands from the body to the senses. Now, the tongue can 'vibrate' the sound without producing anything audible. Similarly, when the desire expands from the senses to the mind, then one can chant in the mind, without the tongue. So, the meaning appears in the mind because the desire expands into the mind.

Ultimately, the universal is very subtle; as we have discussed earlier, the universal is the combination of knowledge, beauty, power, wealth, fame, and renunciation. By our senses, we can hear words, but we cannot understand the meaning. By our mind, we can grasp some meaning, but we don't know if it is knowledge. By the intellect we judge something to be true—and hence knowledge—but it is in a specific field, such as physics, psychology, economics, etc. We have no clue about what 'knowledge itself' means. This can only be grasped by the soul. Therefore, even though the universal manifests as the sound which we can hear, the universal is not the gross material vibration.

This sūtra states that the sound—which manifests in the ether—is different from the meaning. Why? Because the universal is innate in the sound, but we cannot perceive that innateness, even though it is present within the sound. But if we persist with the chanting, then the innateness is also perceived. This is because the perception depends on the acquisition of the concepts: If we don't have the concept, then we cannot perceive it. Thus, through desire, we chant, and by chanting we acquire the ability to perceive, and then a greater desire. This cyclical process of desiring, chanting, and perceiving leads to perfection.

Topic 13

QUESTION

You seem to be indicating that there isn't one kind of meaning—e.g., that we understand through the mind. Rather, this meaning deepens through the development of desire, and while the ultimate meaning is transcendent, it can appear, manifest, or be represented (as through sound) even at the gross material level. How many such levels of understandings can be obtained? You have indicated the gross material sound and the understanding at the level of the mind or intellect by which we can understand the scriptures if the desire develops from the gross body into the mind. Are there deeper forms of understanding the Lord, that go beyond the representations of the body and mind?

1.3.42 (105)

सुषुप्तयुत्करान्तयोर्भेदेन

suṣuptyutkrāntyorbhedena

suṣupti—deep sleep; utkrāntyoḥ—death; bhedena—there is a difference.

TRANSLATION

There is a difference between deep sleep and death (or transcendence).

COMMENTARY

In the previous sūtra, a difference between the gross material sound (as the property of ether) and the meaning (which resides in the mind) was made. In this sūtra, a further distinction between the deep sleep and transcendent states is being made. Collectively, these are called vaikharī, madhyamā, paśyanti, and parā. The gross material sound is vaikharī; the mental and sensual meaning is madhyamā, the deep sleep state is called paśyanti, and the soul is parā. These are also identified as waking, dreaming, deep sleep, and transcendent states of experience. Since the distinction between word and meaning (i.e., vaikharī and madhyamā was drawn in the previous sūtra), this sūtra states a further difference between the states of deep sleep (paśyanti) and transcendence (parā).

Each of these four states is described in Vedic texts as a 'space' that possesses 'sound'. However, the nature of the space and the sound changes successively. At the level of vaikharī, the 'sound' is objective information; at the level of madhyamā, the sound is meaning, judgments, intentions, and morals. At the causal material level of paśyanti, the sound is the unconscious material identity or personality. And at the spiritual level of parā, the sound indicates the nature of the Lord, relation to the Lord, and devotion to the Lord. The implication is that there is a process of purification by which first the body is purified, followed by the sensations, thoughts, judgments, intentions, and morals, followed by the unconscious material personality, following which the soul perceives the Lord through its spiritual cognitive, emotional, and relational abilities. If there is some purification of the mind and the senses (which have been called a 'good moral character' or saṃskāra earlier), and if there is some faith in the Lord (which exists at the unconscious level, called the deep sleep state here), then the aspirant is entitled to scriptural study, and acquiring spiritual knowledge. If deeper imprints are missing, then one can chant such that the body, the senses, the mind, the intellect, and the unconscious can be gradually purified.

QUESTION

But the Lord is the Absolute Truth, and the origin of everything else, and the sound of His name is just one of the parts of the material manifestation. How can the whole truth be represented by a name in the universe? Doesn't this create a contradiction where the whole is represented inside the whole?

1.3.43 (106)

पत्यादिशब्देभ्यः

patyādiśabdebhyaḥ

pat—falls, descends; adi—the origin; sabdebhyah—by the sound.

TRANSLATION

The original form of the Lord descends or incarnates by the sound.

COMMENTARY

There are some difficulties in translating this sūtra which arise when we try to dissect the word *patyādi*. One possible dissection is *pati* + *adi* which would render this sūtra as indicating "He is called by names such as *pati* or husband". The other possible dissection is *pat* indicating a fall or descent, *adi* indicating from the origin, and *sabdebhyah* now indicates "as sound". This would render the sūtra as "the original form of the Lord descends as sound". Which of these two translations must be used for understanding this sūtra?

If we interpret this sūtra based on *pati* + *adi* then the inference would be that *pati* is a name of the Lord, which can lead to spiritual understanding. But a closer look at the prevalent names of the Lord in the scriptures reveals that the name *pati* is never used in isolation as a name of the Lord. The Lord has names such as Lakshmīpati (the husband of Lakshmi), Umāpati (the husband of Uma), Dwarakapati (the ruler of Dwaraka), Bhūpati (the Lord of the earth), Kailaśpati (the ruler of Kailash), Pashupati (the ruler of all animals), Kamalāpati (the husband of Kamala or Lakshmi), Prajapati (the ruler of all the population), etc. The Lord is indeed the *pati* or master. However, He is never called *pati* in isolation; whenever the husband or master is spoken of, the wife or the servant is necessarily mentioned, and the Lord takes a form suitable for that role.

Therefore, we translate this sūtra as "the Lord incarnates as His name". We have earlier said that the name is a 'sound representation' of the Lord; the Lord is immanent in the sound, and yet transcendent to the sound. His appearance in His creation is like the word 'universe' is a part of the universe, and yet represents the entire universe. The sound is a part and yet the meaning is the whole. Thus, He is physically a part, but semantically the whole. Here it is noted that the name of the Lord is an incarnation of the Lord within the creation.

SECTION 4

Topic 1

QUESTION

You have stated that the Lord incarnates or descends as His name and by vibrating this name we can purify our senses and our mind. However, in our previous discussion, you had said that the material world was related to the Lord as the house is related to an owner, or the design is related to the designer. You explicitly forbade the idea that the designer becomes the design. And yet, now, you are saying that a part of the design is the designer because the sound vibration is a material entity, and we consider this an incarnation of the Lord. How do we reconcile the contradiction between the material world being a separate entity from the Lord, and yet the Lord incarnating in this world? In fact, since the Lord is said not to have a material body, His incarnations in the material world are sometimes called forms only meant for our imagination.

1.4.1 (107)

आनुमानकिमप्येकेषामिति चेत् न शरीररूपकवन्यिसतगृहीतेःदर्शयति च

ānumānikamapyekeṣāmiti cet na śarīrarūpakavinyastagṛhīteḥ
darśayati ca

ānumānikam—that which is imagined; api—also; ekeṣām—as an individual; iti cet—if it be said; na—no; śarīra-rūpaka—in the form of a body; vinyasta—has descended; gṛhīteḥ—for capturing; darśayati—seeing; ca—and.

TRANSLATION

If it is said that what appears as an individual is also imagination, (then we say) no; (the Lord) descends in a bodily form for our capturing and seeing.

COMMENTARY

There is a subtle difference between saying that the Lord is reflected in His creation like an artist's personality is seen in his works and the idea that the art is itself the artist. When we spoke about the connection between the Lord and the material energy, we treated this energy as His property. Like the owner lives in the house, but doesn't become the house, similarly, the Lord remains separate from the material energy. However, in the previous few sūtras, we shifted our position by saying that the Lord incarnates as His sound vibration.

This question is part of a larger problem of religious symbolism in the philosophy of religion. Although we grant that the material world is comprised of three modes, and these modes must be transcended, it is also recognized that certain things in this world—e.g., the process by which transcendence must be attained, which involves the use of material ingredients—must be transcendent. If the process of transcendence—e.g., the chanting of mantra—is tainted by the material modes, then there would be no hope for attaining transcendence.

Now, we have discussed this problem earlier in the context of the Vedas. We noted that if everything in this world is material, then even the Vedas must be material. After all, they are printed using ink and paper, and although prior to this printing, they existed in an oral form, even that sound is material. If these sounds are considered mundane, then they cannot lead to transcendence. We also discussed how Śrī Śaṅkarācārya established the divinity of the Vedas—stating that there is at least one thing (i.e., the Vedas) that is transcendental (with respect to those parts which lead to liberation). He, therefore, opened the door to religious symbolism in which religious texts are symbols of truth. But he did not cross the chasm: If Vedic scriptures can represent truth, then why can't other things—e.g., deities and names of the Lord—also represent this truth? What is so sacrosanct about the words written on paper with ink that the same meaning cannot be embodied in other ways? Why should we consider the scripture to have a divine origin, and other things such as deities or pictures or names of the Lord—which are also described in the scriptures—to not be of divine origin? The problem lay in the rejection of demigod worship in Śrī Śaṅkarācārya's philosophy. If these forms are rejected for transcendence, then all forms—including those of the transcendent Lord—must be rejected.

Śrī Śaṅkarācārya did not distinguish between the demigods and God. His philosophy accepted the divinity of Vedic texts but rejected all other forms. But we can see that even scripture is a form—and is often worshipped on par with the deities. By drawing a distinction between scripture and deities, which is artificial, and then not making a distinction between demigods and God, he condoned the idea that the incarnations of the Lord must also be just like the demigods—they appear to teach us knowledge, but they are not transcendent. With the introduction of the Lord's names as His incarnation, the door opens to treating many such names and forms as the Lord's incarnations as well.

This distinction requires us to induct the ability of an artist to draw his self-portraits, in addition to other things (such as landscapes) that he might paint. The self-portrait is also an expression of the artist, and therefore on par with the other works of art. And yet, the self-portrait is also a complete representation of the artist. Therefore, there is no contradiction in saying that the world is an artist's expression, and the idea that the artist is in that creation—provided we admit the ability of the artist to draw his self-portraits as works of art. Of course, the artist is in the painting even when a landscape is painted, but the artist is hidden in the painting. He or she becomes visible in a self-portrait. Hence, there is a distinction between worldly landscapes and self-portraits. The form of the self-portrait resembles the form of the artist even without a deeper look.

In so far as we admit the reality of everything else that is perceived, such self-portraits must also be real. Just as the landscape is not imaginary, similarly the self-portrait is also not imaginary. We have only augmented our previous notion of the Lord as the artist by saying that He can also paint His self-portrait. So, the claim that such forms of the Lord are imaginary is automatically rejected based on the reality of other works of art that are considered real. It does, however, lead to the question of why the artist would paint a self-portrait. The answer to this question is given in this sūtra—for those who can only see the works of art and not the artist, the self-portrait is a vision of the artist.

QUESTION

But we can argue that if the Lord has become visible or perceivable to our senses, then His body must be comprised of the five material elements such as Earth, Water, Fire, Air, and Ether. If the Lord takes on a material body, then how can He be considered transcendental to the nature of material reality?

1.4.2 (108)

सूक्ष्मं तु तदर्हत्वात्

sūkṣmaṃ tu tadarhatvāt

sūkṣmaṃ—subtle; tu—but; tat—that (He, the Lord); arhatvāt—from being deserving, celebrated, or praised.

TRANSLATION

But He (the Lord) is celebrated as the subtle (cause) (of the visible).

COMMENTARY

In 1.2.29 (60), the material world was called Lord's *abhivyakti*, or expression, like a person expresses thoughts in their mind. The speech objectifies the meanings in the mind so that others can perceive them (using their senses). This objectification is called 'sound' in the ether; it is the reality that exists before we perceive sound. Similarly, the other elements such as Air, Fire, Water, and Earth are the objectification of touch, sight, taste, and smell; they are the reality that exists before our senses interact with them to produce the sensations of touch, sight, taste, and smell. However, this is only one aspect of objectification; if this all that existed, then we could not say that a book objectifies knowledge, that a painting or musical composition objectifies beauty, that a person represents the idea of power, etc. After all, we are only seeing taste, touch, sight, sound, and smell; how could we perceive 'knowledge', 'beauty', 'power', etc. in the same representation? The answer is that there are many layers of gross and subtle realities in every representation. However, they are perceived through separate types of senses: The gross reality is perceived by the five senses, and the subtle reality by the mind. Thus, the mind is decoding knowledge, beauty, power, etc., just as the five senses are decoding taste, touch, smell, sight, and sound.

The term sthūla indicates 'gross' and the term sūkshma indicates 'subtle'. They are related as words and meanings. The meaning is present in the words, but it is only perceived by the mind. Furthermore, we don't speak the word and then worry about the meaning. We rather determine the meaning, and then use the word to express it. Therefore, the meaning is the cause of the word. In the same way, the sound of the Lord's name is caused by the Lord (meaning).

The fact that the pure and transcendental meanings can be expressed in this world produces a conundrum. When the Lord incarnates in this world, His presence is temporary—He is visible for some time, and invisible after that. This prompts people to think that because the Lord disappears from the world, and because truth can never cease to exist, therefore, this form must be false. This confusion is a byproduct of two distinct meanings of *sat* and *asat*. The term asat means that which is (1) temporary and (2) false. Conversely, sat means that which is (1) eternal and (2) true. Since the Lord's incarnations are not eternally manifest (in this world), should we say that they are temporary or false?

We can compare this problem to the existence of Vedic knowledge. The knowledge of the Vedas is true, but it is not always manifest. In the present age, for example, several Vedic scriptures have been lost. Lord Kṛṣṇa states that He appears repeatedly (as incarnations) to resurrect this knowledge. So, we must distinguish between *truth* and *eternity*. The distinction is that the meaning is eternal, but its manifestation can be occasional or temporary. Therefore, what we call sat should pertain to the meaning, rather than to the expression. Just because some portions of the Vedas are now lost, doesn't mean they have become asat or false. They are still eternally true, but they are invisible now.

A fiction book exists for a few years, and its meanings are false. The Vedic texts can also exist temporarily, but their meanings are true and eternal. Therefore, if we apply *sat* to meaning, then eternity is truth and truth is eternal, and the two meanings of *sat* are identical. However, if we apply *sat* to the expression of meaning, then the two meanings of *sat*—i.e., eternity and truth—are not identical because the truth is only expressed temporarily through a book. The Lord's appearance in this world must be understood in the same way—He manifests temporarily although the meaning being manifest is eternal. The temporariness refers to the manifestation and not to the meaning. The meaning is still true and eternal; however, the meaning's manifestation is temporary, but not false.

This requires us to distinguish between *existence* and *truth*. In modern logic, truth is proven if existence is proven. The proof of existence, therefore, becomes the proof of truth, and proof and truth are equated. This is, however, a misleading premise of modern logic. If I think that "the sky is green", then the thought exists in my mind, but it is false. So, false things can exist, just like true things can exist. Since they can exist, their existence can be proven. And yet this proof doesn't indicate their truth. So, the term *asat* indicates temporary existence. It doesn't necessarily indicate falsity. Under this temporary existence, there can be fictions that are false and knowledge that is true. So, both the truth and the false can be temporarily manifest; regarding the form of the Lord, the terms *sat* can be applied because the meaning is true, and the term *asat* can be applied because the meaning is temporarily manifest in our vision. The fact that the world exists temporarily should not be interpreted as indicating everything is false; it should rather indicate that everything is temporary. However, underlying this temporary expression, there can sometimes be eternal truth.

This sūtra states that the Lord is the *sūkshma* cause of the visible. In short, He is the eternal meaning, which is temporarily expressed through words. The Lord is the eternal form of knowledge, beauty, power, wealth, fame, and renunciation. This form can become visible to our senses if the Lord manifests.

QUESTION

When the soul accepts a material body, he is said to be caught in the material world. Why should that entanglement in matter not be applied to the Lord when He accepts a body just like the other beings? After all, there are some laws of nature, which must apply to anybody present in this world. And if these laws start applying to the Lord, must He not also be under nature's control?

1.4.3 (109)

तदधीनत्वादर्थवत्

tadadhīnatvādarthavat

tat—His (the Lord); adhīnatvāt—from being dependent; arthavat—just like meaning.

TRANSLATION

From being manifest from the Lord, the manifestation is dependent on the Lord just like meaning (is dependent on the speaker of that meaning).

COMMENTARY

The soul is caught in the material body due to guna and karma. The guna are the soul's desires, which need to be fulfilled by the body; to the extent that the body fulfills these desires, the soul remains attached to the body, and doesn't want to leave it. But even if the soul wanted to leave the body, he cannot until he has reaped all the consequences of past karma. These two conditions of the soul's bondage don't apply to the Lord. The Lord is innately blissful, and He doesn't need a material body to fulfill His desires. Similarly, the actions of the Lord do not produce any consequences or karma. Therefore, unlike the soul who is bound due to guna and karma, the Lord is not bound in either way.

But one might still say: If I mix sugar with milk, then I will get sweet milk, rather than salty milk. To the extent that these are laws of nature, the Lord also cannot produce salty milk by mixing milk and sugar, so He must be bound by the laws of nature. This is indeed true; the Lord cannot produce salty milk by mixing sugar and milk. However, this is not bondage. Unlike the soul, whose access to sweet milk is restricted by their guna and karma, the Lord is not restricted in this way. We may not enjoy sweet milk, or we may not have access to the ingredients to produce sweet milk. The Lord is not restricted in either of these two ways. This doesn't mean that the Lord violates the laws of nature; He still follows the natural law according to which the mixing of milk and sugar produces sweet milk. But He cannot be prevented from drinking sweet milk due to karma, and He cannot be compelled to drink sweet milk due to guna.

There is a difference between descriptive and prescriptive laws. The descriptive laws pertain to the production of sweet milk by mixing milk and sugar. The prescriptive laws pertain to the consequences of actions or karma and the near impossibility to control desires caused by one's guna. The Lord is bound by descriptive laws, but He is not bound by the prescriptive laws.

The previous sūtra used the term *arhat* and this sūtra uses the term *artha*; the former indicates transcendence and the latter indicates the meaning. The Lord is both *artha* and *arhat*: He is the meaning, which is also transcendent.

QUESTION

But if the Lord is not compelled to come to the world, then why does He appear? You have stated that He is independent of the world, He is the meaning and purpose of its existence, and He is not bound by nature's laws. You have also said that the material world is unlike His nature, and the living entities here are averse to Him. So, why does He take the trouble of manifesting if there is no compelling force that is pushing Him towards manifesting Himself?

1.4.4 (110)

ज्ञेयत्वावचनाच्च

jñeyatvāvacanācca

jñeyatvā—knowability; vacanāt—through the words; ca—and.

TRANSLATION

And (the Lord appears) so that He can be known by His words.

COMMENTARY

In the Bhagavad-Gita, Lord Kṛṣṇa states that whenever there is a decline of religion and a rise in irreligion, He manifests to reestablish the principles of religion, protect the devotees, and destroy the demonic living entities. His actions of protecting the devotees and destroying the demonic living entities involve the display of His heroism or 'greatness'. This will come up for discussion shortly in a subsequent sūtra. In this sūtra, only the purpose of reestablishing the principles of religion is noted. It is further noted that He speaks so that He can be known through His words; in short, He speaks about Himself.

QUESTION

But isn't it said that the Vedas are His speech? If He has already explained His nature through the Vedas, then shouldn't we just

study the Vedas? Why does the Lord appear when His words are already recorded in the Vedas?

1.4.5 (111)

वदतीति चेत् न प्राज्ञो हि प्रकरणात्

vadatīti cet na prājño hi prakaraṇāt

vadati—(someone) says; iti cet—if in this way; na—no; prājñaḥ—intelligent; hi—for; prakaraṇāt—from the treatise, books, passages.

TRANSLATION

If it is said that (the Lord) is already known from the Vedic texts, then (we say) no (because these texts) are meant only for the most intelligent.

COMMENTARY

The question arises: Why should the Lord speak about the nature of religion by appearing again and again when the Vedic texts are already present? The short answer is that the existence of these texts is not always enough; there must also be intelligent people who can understand and present the true essence of Vedic knowledge. This essence is preserved through the guru-disciple succession. But if this succession is broken, then false conceptions of religion are produced. In fact, demonic people now use religion for political, economic, and sociological aims. He appears to establish the essence, purpose, and the core ideas around which all other ideas must be organized and understood.

Knowledge has an innate hierarchy—from core to context. But what is core and what is context keeps changing with time. During a spiritual era, the core idea of human life is to attain transcendence from material existence, and God becomes the center around which everything else is organized. During a materialistic era, the core idea is to obtain unrestricted enjoyment, and sense enjoyment becomes the center around which everything else is organized. The Vedic system comprises many texts with different cores and contexts. The texts on medicine, for example, focus on the body, with some references to the mind, little attention to the soul, and almost no reference to demigods or God. If you are looking at the veins on a leaf, you cannot see the whole tree, let alone the forest. This focus on different areas is deliberate—sometimes you need to see the leaf instead of the full forest. But these differing areas of emphasis can also produce confusions—maybe the leaf is more important than the forest?

The existence of various texts doesn't tell us how they must be organized—from most important to less important to least important. The intellect produces this hierarchy, and whatever is ordered first becomes the basis on which the importance of the subsequent things is judged. So, the decline of intelligence means that we lose the ability to understand the difference between core and context; different people start treating the context as the core, and they might even consider the core irrelevant or false. So, the Lord appears to establish the difference between the core and the context of knowledge within the Vedas.

QUESTION

But if the main problem is that people are less intelligent to understand which part of the Veda is more important, then could this not be established by some intelligent person? Why would the Lord need to appear Himself?

1.4.6 (112)

तरयाणामेव चैवमुपन्यासःपरश्नश्च

trayāṇāmeva caivamupanyāsaḥ praśnaśca

trayāṇām—of three; eva—really; ca—and; evaṃ—thus; upanyāsaḥ—introduction or hint or stories; praśnaḥ—question, doubt; ca—and;

TRANSLATION

And (the Lord appears) really to display the pastimes of the three (quarters of existence) (for those) who might have doubts (about its existence).

COMMENTARY

After saying that the Lord appears to speak about Himself, and then stating that the Lord defines the core and the context of knowledge, this sūtra establishes the final point, namely, that ultimately the Lord appears to display (within the material world) the nature of the three-quarters of existence beyond the material world. The Vedas contain theoretical knowledge of the nature of Absolute Truth, exhorting the living entity to transcend the material world. But unless we say what the transcendental world looks like, how will people be attracted? Freedom from material suffering may not be an adequate justification for many people to pursue transcendence. Furthermore, many people may cynically believe that the present life here is all that is ever possible, and whether we like it or not, there is no better type of life. So, the Lord's appearance is also to provide a hint or indication of the nature of transcendence. These hints are available through the Lord's pastimes with His devotees in the world.

QUESTION

But His pastimes seem like ordinary human activities in many cases. How can anyone understand that He is also the Supreme Being by such pastimes?

1.4.7 (113)
महद्वच्च
mahadvacca

mahadvat—like greatness; ca—and.

TRANSLATION

(He) also (acts in) great ways or demonstrates (His) greatness.

COMMENTARY

Many people might argue that the pastimes the Lord displays in a human-like form indicate that He is just a human. To counter this argument, this sūtra states that the Lord also demonstrates His greatness to convince people that He is not a mere mortal. In the Bhagavad-Gita, for example, Lord Kṛṣṇa displays His universal form to convince Arjuna of His greatness. We earlier noted that the Lord also protects the devotees and destroys the demonic. This constitutes His heroism and shows that He is not merely a mortal. His pastimes are often imbued with the sweetness of love, affection, and personal relationships. But that should not mislead anyone to think that He is an ordinary mortal. We should look at the other side of His pastimes which are humanly impossible. For instance, Lord Kṛṣṇa lifted the Govardhan mountain even as a child, which is an activity humanly impossible for anyone to perform. By demonstrating such activities, the Lord not only protects the devotees and destroys the demons, but for those who might have doubts, He clarifies His greatness.

Topic 2

QUESTION

It is sometimes said that "God is great". However, greatness can also be found in this world. There are many people who have attained great things in this world. So, if greatness is the measure by which we detect the presence of God (because His pastimes seem like those of an ordinary mortal), then by that measure, should we not consider other great people as incarnations of God?

1.4.8 (114)

चमसवदवशिेषात्

camasavadaviśeṣāt

camasavat—like a spoon; aviśeṣāt—from nothing special (about them).

TRANSLATION

(Others are) like spoons; from there being nothing special (about them)

COMMENTARY

The term *camasvat* in this sūtra follows the term *mahadvat* in the previous sūtra. Since *mahadvat* is "like greatness", *chamasvat* should be understood as "like insignificant". If we make a contrast to greatness, we must ask: What is greatness? Greatness is often measured by the magnitude of what one achieves, and how difficult it was to achieve;

thus, for instance, walking is not very difficult, so if someone is able to walk a mile, we would not consider it great. However, if someone walks the entire earth, then the action would be called 'great'. But, if one has lost their legs, then winning a walking race for the physically challenged would be considered great. Greatness is, therefore, relative to the difficulty. If one is born in a poor family and has no access to wealth or education, but still manages to achieve success, then their achievement is considered great. All stories of heroism are based on the basic theme that a hero overcomes difficulties and comes out victorious against them. The stories of heroes, therefore, become inspirational narrations for common people—they motivate us to overcome the obstacles in life and come out victorious by such struggle.

However, nothing is difficult for the Lord. He has no challenges and He doesn't become a hero by overcoming obstacles. The idea that "God is great" is a materialistic conception of God. When He demonstrates His greatness, by performing deeds that would be impossible for others, He isn't the hero who has overcome difficulties. These deeds are considered great from our perspective; they are ordinary for the Lord. But to the extent that we are impressed by such things, the Lord performs them, to convince us that He is not a mortal.

For example, when Lord Rama constructed a bridge to Lanka over the ocean, ordinary people might consider this action great, and they may then compare it to modern engineering marvels where humans have also constructed long bridges over the sea. But the Lord's greatness doesn't lie in the construction of the bridge; it lies in the fact that the stones from which the bridge was made were floating in the water simply by writing His name on the stones. So, people can make great bridges across the ocean, but they cannot match the greatness of the Lord who has the mystical power to have large boulders float in water simply by the power of His name. Similarly, after the bridge was constructed, the Lord gave credit to the monkeys who wrote His name and threw the boulders into the ocean. So, the Lord is not impressed by such feats.

Likewise, some people lift weights to demonstrate their strength, and we see them huffing and puffing as they lift the weights for a few moments. But Lord Kṛṣṇa held the Govardhan mountain on His little finger continuously for seven days without huffing and puffing. After He put the mountain down, He gave the credit for this lifting to the cowherd boys supporting the mountain by their cattle staffs! The Lord's greatness is not just that He performs deeds that nobody else can, but also that He is not enamored by these great acts. Any ordinary mortal would feel proud of their achievements and brag about them. But the Lord does far greater things, and yet He is not impressed by them. Therefore, the Lord's deeds should not be compared to those of the ordinary heroes; in this sūtra, the deeds of other heroes are dismissed as "just like spoons".

QUESTION

But it is sometimes said that everything great in this world is the Lord Himself. For example, in the Bhagavad-Gita, the Lord states that He is the taste of water, the light of the sun and the moon, the power in men, etc. So, doesn't this indicate that everything we consider great can be worshipped as the Lord? In effect, we would not need to chant the names or the Lord or worship His incarnations, if we only consider all such heroic greatness as the Lord Himself.

1.4.9 (115)

ज्योतरुपक्रमा तु तथा ह्यधीयत एके

jyotirupakramā tu tathā hyadhīyata eke

jyotirupa—heavenly bodies like the sun and the moon; kramā—method or simile; tu—but; tathā—so; hi—because; adhīyata—remembering; eke—by some.

TRANSLATION

Heavenly bodies (like the sun and the moon) (are not the Lord) but it is said so because (they are) similes or methods (for) remembering by some.

COMMENTARY

The world is an expansion of the Lord and previously existed within Him. Since it has expanded from the Lord, therefore, everything is His part. However, it has been described previously that these parts are the properties or the wealth of the Lord. Certain things in the world—such as the light of the sun and the moon, or the power in men, etc.—are attributed to the Lord, not because the Lord is those things but because by thinking in this way, we can always remember the Lord. For instance, every time we drink water and relish its sweet pure taste, we can remember the Lord as that sweetness. Likewise, when we see powerful people, we can think of the Lord and consider His presence in their power. In this way, the presence of great things in this world can be a reminder of the Lord, and meditating in this way can be considered a method of remembering the Lord. However, all the powerful people, or light and water, should not be considered the Lord Himself. The use of the term *tu* (but) indicates that heavenly bodies are not the Lord. Similarly, the use of *tatha* (in this way) indicates that they are spoken of as the Lord. Finally, the use of *hi* (because) indicates that there is a reason for speaking in this way, which is then clarified using *krama* (method) and *adhīyata* (for remembering) and *eke* (by some people).

QUESTION

So, you are supporting those who think of the Lord in terms of the greatness manifest in this world, even though this greatness is not the Lord?

1.4.10 (116)

कल्पनोपदेशाच्च मध्वादिवदविरोधः

kalpanopadeśācca madhvādivadavirodhaḥ

kalpanopadeśāt—from the instruction for imagination; ca—and; madhvādivat—just like honey etc.; avirodhaḥ—no incongruity.

TRANSLATION

And from the instruction for imagination, there is no incongruity (if one consider them great), just like honey (is seen as a representation of the moon).

COMMENTARY

When someone is wealthy, we say that he has Lakshmi (the goddess of wealth). A powerful king is sometimes called Bhagavān (the Supreme Lord, who possesses everything). Fruits and vegetables are sometimes called soma or the moon because they give strength and nourishment. And fire is sometimes worshipped as the sun. This doesn't mean that coins are themselves Lakshmi, or the king is the Supreme Lord, or that fruits and vegetables are the moon, or that the fire is the sun. It only means that they have some of the qualities that are fully present in the deities. Just like biology may be called 'knowledge' although it is not knowledge itself (because there are other areas of knowledge), similarly, there are partial representations of qualities in different things, and by these qualities, we can think of the origin which has these qualities in full. The partial presence is helpful because it spiritualizes our thinking. For instance, if we call money Lakshmi, we will be careful not to waste it. We will also not be proud of owning money; we will consider it the grace of Lakshmi. So, there are many advantages in this type of thinking because it makes us treat the world around us with respect, as it has originated in the Lord. The greatness of this world can remind us of the Lord, and it is hence a method of meditation. This sūtra states that if we think of the Lord while seeing the greatness in this world—e.g., knowledge, beauty, power, wealth, fame, renunciation—there is no incongruity in such meditation, as it reminds us of the Lord's presence.

Topic 3

QUESTION

Once we start thinking of the great things in this world as deserving of our respect, we also start worshipping them. For example, even if vegetables and fruits are not the moon, by worshiping the moon we can obtain vegetables and fruits. Even if the intellect is not the sun, by worshiping the sun we can obtain intellect. Since you have indicated that all such great things are manifestations of the Lord, is it appropriate to worship all these great things themselves?

1.4.11 (117)

न संख्योपसंग्रहादपि नानाभावादतिरेकाच्च

na saṃkhyopasaṃgrahādapi nānābhāvādatirekācca

na—not; sāṅkhya—the elements of Sāṅkhya philosophy; upasaṁ—worship; grahād—the planets; api—even if; nānā—many; abhāvāt—on account of the absence; atirekāt—on account of doubtful excess; ca—and.

TRANSLATION

Do not worship the planets (for obtaining) the elements of Sāṅkhya, even if there are many kinds of absence or if the abundance seems doubtful.

COMMENTARY

The 24 elements of Sāṅkhya philosophy form our gross and subtle bodies. Due to karma delivered by the planets, which are studied in astrology, the gross and subtle bodies are hurt or benefitted. If one is undergoing difficult times in their life, astrologers often advise their clients to worship these planets for alleviating the suffering. Similarly, even if someone has abundant pleasure, due to greed, they may worship these planets to expand that pleasure. Many people think that these planets and their demigods are the causes of the various kinds of material well-being, and since these planets are the representations of the Lord by which we can think of Him, it is alright to worship these planets.

In the previous sūtra, we noted that the material world around us should be treated with respect because it is a manifestation of the Lord. However, the previous sūtra also clarified that this respect is only for our thinking about the Lord or meditation upon Him. Now, one can argue that if we are thinking of these planets as the greatness of God in this world, then why not worship these planets because they are delivering us greatness through such worship?

This sūtra clarifies this confusion by stating that these representations of greatness in the material world should not be worshipped because they are not the Lord Himself. In this regard, we can recall our previous comparison with the artist and the work of art. If we respect the artist, then we treat his works of art with respect. We may even praise the work of art, with the understanding that it has been created by the artist, and such praise reminds us of the artist through the work of art. However, we should not worship the work of art; the work of art is only a reminder of the greatness of the artist. Similarly, material nature is not to be worshipped, although it manifests the Lord's greatness.

The previous sūtra stated that there is no incongruity in treating the greatness of the material world as a representation of the Lord. But in this sūtra, the worship of the representations of greatness is rejected. We say that a cow is a mammal, but the mammal isn't a cow. The cow can help us understand the nature of the mammal, but that doesn't reduce the mammal to the cow. Similarly, everything in the world can help us understand the nature of the Lord. But all these things are not the Lord. People worship the demigods either when they are suffering or when they are greedy. Hence this sūtra notes two conditions—"due to absence" and "when abundance is doubtful"—and rejects both cases.

QUESTION

But the same type of argument could be advanced in relation to the soul and the body—if the soul is rejuvenated, then the body and the mind don't need a separate rejuvenation. However, in practice, we do feed the body and lead a healthy lifestyle, nourish the mind by knowledge and loving relationships, apart from making spiritual advancement for the soul. So, even if the demigods are subordinates to the Lord and feeding the root feed the trunks and branches, in practice, we do feed the body and mind apart from the soul. By this practical application, doesn't it entail that we can worship the demigods even with the understanding that they are for the body and mind, and not for the soul?

1.4.12 (118)
पुराणादयो वाक्यशेषात्
prāṇādayo vākyaśeṣāt

prāṇa—the vital force; adayaḥ—the origin; vāk—the sound or words; aśeṣāt—not the residue, or completely.

TRANSLATION
The prāṇa is the complete cause or origin of the sound or words.

COMMENTARY

There are several interpretive difficulties in understanding this sūtra. First, should the term *adayah* be interpreted as "the origin" or as "etc."? Second, should *vākyaśeṣāt* be dissected as *vāk* + *aśeṣāt* or as *vākya* + *śeṣāt*? The first dissection would mean "the complete sound" and the second dissection would mean "the statement about the residue". Accordingly, we can enumerate the following four potential translations based on the above two alternatives:

- The vital force etc. are the residue of the words
- The vital force etc. are the complete word
- The vital force is the origin of the residue of the words
- The vital force is the complete origin of the words

To choose between these translations, I will use the tripartite distinction between *manas*, *prāṇa*, and *vāk*, found at numerous places in the Vedic texts. The term manas represents the meaning or the mind. The term vāk represents the sound representation of this meaning or the expression of meaning into words. And prāṇa is the agency by which meaning is converted into words.

The residue of words can refer to manas rather than prāṇa. For instance, even if do not remember the exact words spoken by someone, we can remember the meanings of those words. But, if we remember the words, then we also remember the meaning. Therefore, if the words are present, then the meaning is also present. But if the words are absent, then the meanings can still be present. Therefore, the meaning is the residue of the sound. If we attach 'residue' to prāṇa, then we will produce a contradiction with ordinary experience.

Then, we can discuss whether *adayah* refers to "the origin" or "etc.". By treating *adayah* as "etc." we get "the vital force etc. are the complete word", which is patently false because the prāṇa can exist even when the words are not expressed. When the soul moves to a new body, it is carried by prāṇa, even as the gross body is left behind. The power to speak exists, but the speech doesn't exist; the prāṇa is the power by which we can speak, and the words are the outcome of that power. Therefore, we can eliminate three of the four alternatives. We are now left with: "the prāṇa is the complete origin of the words".

This translation is consistent with the distinction between manas, prāṇa, and vāk, where the power of prāṇa causes the expression of manas or meaning into vāk or words. Thus, if the prāṇa is weak, the mind may have thoughts, but we cannot speak or express our thoughts in proper words. If the prāṇa is disturbed, then we may have thoughts, but their expression would be garbled, and people won't be able to understand what we are saying. In this way, we can distinguish between prāṇa or power and vāk or the use of that power.

The tripartite distinction between manas, prāṇa, and vāk, is a generic template for constructing a hierarchy. Thus, when you hear someone speak, the sound is converted into meaning. But once you have understood what is being said, you also want to know if it is true. The judgment of truth is a deeper level of meaning, for which the meaning in the mind is the 'sound'. Then, to judge the person's intentions behind telling the truth or lying, the truth or falsity are the 'sound' and the intention or purpose behind it are the meaning. Likewise, to understand one's values from their intentions, one needs another layer of meaning; now, the intention is the word, and the value is the meaning.

The elements of Sāñkhya form a hierarchy, with many levels of meaning. Each of these levels is vāk relative to the higher level, and manas relative to the lower level of meaning. Thus, for instance, the 'meaning' of being evil expands into the 'word' that deception is justified because it is in my self-interest, and becomes a new level of meaning, which then expands into a lower level 'word' of developing an intention to cheat others, which then expands into a careful crafting of an argument that seems logical and consistent but is aimed to deceive others, this argument is then expressed into mental meanings, which are then expressed into words. At each level, there is some 'sound', which is a symbolic expression of the deeper level 'meaning'. This expansion of meaning into words is caused by prāṇa—as the power of expression. Similarly, the words are converted into deeper meanings by prāṇa—as the power of assimilation.

The hierarchy of words/meanings constitutes a tree, in which the nodes at the various levels of the hierarchy are connected to each other due to prāṇa. Owing to prāṇa, this tree expands during expression, and contracts during assimilation. If prāṇa disappears, then expression and assimilation end.

Now, with this background, we can understand the meaning of

this sūtra, which is that the elements of Sāṅkhya are expanded due to prāṇa. So, the greatness we see in this world is the expression, but the power underlying this greatness is prāṇa. We have previously noted that there are many kinds of prāṇa of which two are most important in this context. The first prāṇa helps the soul to reject the automatically arising desires. And the second prāṇa is used by the Paramātma to deliver the results of actions, or karma. By the first prāṇa, we can desire. But this desire cannot be fulfilled unless Paramātma uses His power. This is indicated in Bhagavad-Gita 7.8 when Lord Kṛṣṇa says that He is *pauruṣaṁ nṛṣu* or the power in men, and in 7.10 that He is *tejas tejasvinām* or the strength in the strong. So, the elements of Sāṅkhya are the perceivable appearances of greatness—e.g., that someone has a sharp mind or intellect, someone has a strong and beautiful body, etc.—but, ultimately, all this is a result of Paramātma delegating His power to fulfill the desires of the jīvā. Therefore, we should not attribute the display of power to the demigods, because such attribution would be false; the real attribution is to the Lord who controls prāṇa by which karma is delivered and the person seems powerful and great.

The role of prāṇa and its control by Paramātma has been noted earlier. So, we can ask: Why is that being repeated here? The short answer is that the explicit connection between the symbols of greatness and the power that creates that symbol wasn't made earlier. Therefore, one can be confused that if someone is demonstrating power, then he must also have the power, and can be considered the greater person. The demigods are not just subordinate to the Lord, and not just displaying a part of the greatness that the Lord can display. They are rather helpless without the support of the Lord. Their only qualification is that they have good karma and they have the desire or guna to enjoy in a certain way. They don't have the power to even fulfill their own desires, so how can they fulfill our desires (if the goal of worship is to fulfill some desires)? They are mere passengers in a chariot that moves very gloriously and gives the illusion that the person sitting in the chariot is the cause of that movement when the fact is that the Lord is moving that chariot by deploying His power.

QUESTION

If the Lord is the all-powerful controller and deploys His power to create the appearance of the powerful, then why do some people

worship the demigods? Shouldn't they realize that the power under-lying the appearance of the powerful is owned by someone else that they cannot see in this greatness?

This is an argument from popularity: If many people accept something to be true, then it must be true. One such example is the prestige of modern science. Although there are many conceptual, logical, and experimental problems in modern science, its prestige—and wide acceptance by many people—leads to the question: If science was wrong then why would so many people accept it? The seeker here is asking the same type of question—if demigod worship is so bad, then why are so many people doing it? Shouldn't the wide prevalence of such rituals and worship indicate that there is indeed some truth in it?

1.4.13 (119)

ज्योतिषिकेषामसत्यन्ने

jyotiṣaikeṣāmasatyanne

jyotiṣ—astrology, the luminaries; ekeṣām—of some; asati—unchaste or unfaithful (wife); anne—for food.

TRANSLATION

Some unchaste or unfaithful (people) (worship) the luminaries for food.

COMMENTARY

The conjunct *asatyanne* used in this sūtra can be dissected in two ways—(1) *asatya + anne,* or (2) *asati + anne.* The former would mean "false food" or "false enjoyment", if *asatya* or falsehood is attached to food or enjoyment. This translation would indicate that the food or enjoyment is itself false or doesn't exist. It takes us toward the notion that the things that we eat, or the pleasure we enjoy in this world, aren't real. It is a short step from here to say that the world is an illusion. To avoid this conclusion, we have noted earlier that *sat* can indicate both truth and eternity. Food and pleasure are not false, although they are fleeting. So, if we use *asatya + anne,* the sūtra would translate as "some (people) worship the luminaries for temporary food (or pleasure)". This kind of resigned agreement to the actions of common people doesn't befit the speaker of the Vedānta Sūtra. Therefore, we prefer to use *asati* + *anne*, and apply the term *asati* to *ekesam*, which then means "some unchaste men".

In all legitimate worships of demigods in the Vedic system, Lord Viṣṇu is worshipped. A mound of rice may be placed at the center, and through a mantra, the presence of Lord Viṣṇu is invoked. The other demigods may be represented by mounds of rice surrounding the center, and mantras are chanted to invoke the presence of these demigods. In other cases, Lord Viṣṇu may be substituted by Lord Śiva as the controller of the material energy. In the Śrīmad Bhāgavatam, it is described that King Daksha performed a yajñá but did not deliberately make an offering to Lord Śiva to insult Him. Sati, Lord Śiva's wife, and the daughter of Daksha was present in that yajñá and pained by the humiliation of Her husband, immolated Herself. Lord Śiva then ordered the destruction of the yajñá because the demigods are never worshipped without the presence of either Lord Śiva or Lord Viṣṇu or both. In this sūtra, people who worship the demigods alone are called *asati*. This has a two-fold meaning. First, it means 'unchaste', and second, it also means someone who is unlike Sati. The term 'unchaste' indicates a wife who has a husband but desires other men. We can conclude that such offerings are never legitimate Vedic sacrifices.

Topic 4

QUESTION

I understand that most people worship the demigods to get something from them. But can't we worship them simply because they are glorious? We may not ask them for benedictions to improve our lives, and by not desiring any benefits, we can remain unselfish. But could we still worship them because they are glorious individuals, not because we want something from them?

This is a sophisticated argument for demigod worship that equates devotion to the Lord with the devotion to demigods. An impersonalist can argue that the goal of life is liberation from material existence, so there is no point in getting entangled in various types of rituals which then lead to karma and then rebirth. Therefore, worshipping demigods to get a good material life is pointless. However, to the extent that these demigods are representing the qualities of greatness in this world (even if partially), they can be worshipped as the path to liberation. In fact, one could argue that any demigod can be worshipped because there is no fundamental difference between the worship of the Lord and those of the demigods. This type of impersonalism applies the principle of *bhakti* to the demigods and states that the forms of God and demigods are equally good because we are not asking them for benedictions anyway. We are just worshipping them for their qualities, and that unselfish devotion, when applied to the demigods, is as good as when it is for the Supreme Lord.

1.4.14 (120)

कारणत्वेन चाकाशादिषु यथाव्यपदष्टिोक्तेः

kāraṇatvena cākāśādiṣu yathāvyapadiṣṭokteḥ

kāraṇatvena—as the cause; ca—and; ākāśādiṣu—the origin of space; yathā—just as; vyapa—pervading; diṣ—directions; ukteḥ—it is stated.

TRANSLATION

Just as He is the cause and origin of space, similarly, it is stated that (He) pervades in all the directions.

COMMENTARY

The previous sūtra rejected the principle of selfish worship—e.g., for obtaining food. But if someone argues that the demigods can be worshiped unselfishly, quite like we glorify the Lord for His qualities (rather than asking Him for benedictions), then the counterargument would have to say that the Lord is the creator of the qualities that we consider glorious in the demigods. Since all these glories are encompassed in the 24 elements of Sāṅkhya, the Lord should be described as the creator of these elements, and hence all the greatness. This is what this sūtra does, although the meaning is not immediately evident unless we understand the precise nature of 'space', 'place' and 'direction'. So, before concluding that this sūtra refutes the unselfish bhakti to demigods, let's understand why the Lord is the creator of all the glories attributed to demigods.

The contentious term in this sūtra is *vyapadiṣ*. Readers can recall that we have translated *vyapadeśa* in three ways earlier—(a) a statement, (b) the hiding or covering of the truth, and (c) as pervading in all places. There is an important difference between *vyapadiś* and *vyapadeśa*, but we will return to this difference shortly. Let's apply the above three possible translations of *vyapadeśa* to this sūtra and understand the meanings that result from their application.

Suppose we say that *vyapadeśa* refers to "the hiding of the object". The sūtra will then say that "the cause or origin of space is hidden". This conclusion was noted in 1.2.14 (45): "And all the places (i.e., objects) are concealments of the real object". Suppose we say that *vyapadeśa* refers to a true statement or assertion. Then the sūtra will say that "it is stated that He is the cause or origin of space". This too was previously stated in 1.3.1 (64): "It is said that the origin and resting place of the space and the universe is His abode". This translation would also produce a duplication of meaning between *vyapadeśa* and *ukteh*; the former means "statement", and the latter "saying", and their combination would produce a meaningless repetition "statement is stated". If we apply the third meaning of "pervading in all places", then this too has is noted in 1.1.14 (14): "And because He is the cause of it (i.e., of bliss) and it is pervasive in all places". By the criterion of not duplicating claims, we reject these translations.

Now, we can note the difference between *vyapadeśa* and *vyapadiś*. The term *deśa* means a 'place', and the term *diś* indicates a 'direction'. This difference would cause no change to the first two meanings, namely, "a true statement", or "the hidden object". But it will result in a difference in the third meaning. Like *vyapadeśa* indicates "pervading in all places", *vyapadiś* would indicate "pervading in all directions". This is unique and has not been said before, so from a logical viewpoint, it can be acceptable. However, we may still wonder: if "all the places" are noted earlier, doesn't this include "all the directions"? The resolution to this problem is that the previous application of "all the places" in 1.1.14 (14) was in relation to the individuality that emerges from the desire for pleasure. The Lord accompanies the soul everywhere, so as the cause of all bliss, and by accompanying the soul, He can be said to be all-pervading. The term *vyapadiś* must, therefore, refer to something other than the soul. In this context, the only other thing that we can speak of in terms of place and direction is the material world, so *vyapadiś* must pertain to the 'directions' in space.

We have spoken of three kinds of spaces—universals, individuals, and relations. The universal 'cow' combines with an individual to create an individual cow. Similarly, the universal 'field' combines with an individual to create an individual field. The individual cow and the individual field are then placed in mutual relation to say that "the cow is grazing in the field". The relation between the cow and the field is established by the demigods owing to karma—the cow gets to eat the grass because of its karma. The power for delivering the karma is under the control of the Paramātma, and the demigods are subordinate departments which deliver different kinds of karma, which has been discussed previously. Therefore, the space of directions can refer either to the space of universals or of individuals (and not to the space of relations).

From a logical standpoint, we must speak about the universals before the individuals. After all, there is no sense in talking about an individual cow, if we don't know what 'cow' means. Therefore, because the individuals follow the universals, universals must be spoken of first, and this sūtra must be understood as indicating the directions of space when these pertain to the universals. Moreover, we will see the description of the individuals in the next sūtra.

Now, we can see what "pervading in all directions" means. We are speaking about a conceptual space, which is organized like an inverted tree from root to leaves. The root represents the highest-level or the most abstract concept, while the branches and leaves constitute parts of the root and the lower-level concepts. As an example, tigers and leopards belong to the cat family; the cat family belongs to mammals; the mammals belong to the animal family; and the animals are one branch of all forms of life (trees, birds, fishes, being separate). Thus, a tiger is both a lower-level concept and a part of the highest-level concept. In the tree structure, everything is both a dimension and a value—it is a dimension when we look 'downward' (from the root toward the leaves), and it is a value when we look 'upward' (from the leaves toward the root). Thus, all trunks, branches, twigs, and leaves of this tree are dimensions; it is an infinite-dimensional space because the concepts are practically infinite. The concepts of animal, mammal, and cat are present even within the tiger. So, as these branches are diversified from the root, the source becomes all-pervading. Thus, "pervading in all directions" refers to the root being present in all the leaves.

Once these universals are created, they can also be instantiated into individuals. The demigods are perfect or ideal instances of these concepts. Relative to them, lower individuals are imperfect or non-ideal instances of such concepts. However, as we saw above, before we speak about the ideal or non-ideal instance, we must speak about the concept or universal, which is then instantiated into an individual. Thus, someone can say that I created the perfect computer. But before this perfect computer was created, the idea of computing—e.g., as a Turing Machine—was theoretically constructed. Before steam locomotives were created, the theoretical model of a steam engine was produced.

The perfect instance of an idea embodies all the elements or aspects of that idea. An imperfect idea, on the other hand, implements that idea partially. So, the credit of a person who instantiates this idea perfectly lies in copying the idea completely, perfectly, and honestly. In the same way, the Lord is the creator of all the elements, and the credit of the demigods is that they are representing these elements perfectly, without removing anything or contaminating them in any way. They can be called 'pure' in this sense, but it is only an instance of the purity that was created by the Lord. Just as the disciple who perfectly repeats the words of his spiritual master can be credited for not changing the knowledge imparted by the guru, but he cannot be credited for the knowledge itself, in the same way, the Lord must get the credit for the greatness.

This sūtra says that just as the Lord is the origin, He is also the expansion in many directions. As the origin, He is the highest-level idea, and we have discussed this before—the Lord is ideas of knowledge, beauty, power, wealth, fame, and renunciation. There are many subparts of these higher-level ideas, which pervade this world. The demigods are instances of these parts. So, each demigod only embodies one type of idea, whereas the Lord embodies all the ideas together. Nevertheless, if someone was to argue that we can worship these ideas one by one, rather than all in the combined form, then this sūtra states that the Lord is not just the original idea, but the cause of all the ideas, whereas each demigod is the perfect instance of one of these ideas. Therefore, whether we want to see all these ideas in combination, or whether we want to understand them separately, their greatness only belongs to the Lord.

QUESTION

But I can only understand these great qualities by looking at their great instantiations. For example, if I have never seen an individual cow, how can understand the concept of 'cowness'? Similarly, if I have not seen cats and dogs, then how can I understand that a 'mammal' is a higher-level concept? In the same way, before I understand the highest-level idea, should I not understand lower-level ideas? How can we understand the highest-level idea if we don't gradually proceed upwards passing through all the lower-level ideas?

We can see a progression from worshiping demigods for material benefits, to worshiping demigods unselfishly because they represent some form of greatness, to now arguing helplessness to understand the Lord without worshiping the demigods, as demigod worship may be easier on our understanding.

1.4.15 (121)
समाकर्षात्
samākarṣāt

sama—similar; ākrṣāt—from the attraction.

TRANSLATION

From the attraction of the similar.

COMMENTARY

The author of Vedānta Sūtra has offered counterarguments against the worship of demigods on matters of principle—e.g., that they are not powerful, that they are not the origins of the greatness or the glory you seek, and that such worship will entangle you in the cycle of birth and death. But if someone claims that they are helpless in understanding the Supreme Lord, and find it is easier to understand the demigods, the author can at best be resigned to the seeker's tendency and say that—"similar things attract each other"—indicating that if you are expressing helplessness in understanding the Lord and find the understanding of the demigods much easier, then this attraction to the demigods cannot be justified on principle, although it can be attributed to your nature.

It is an indirect rejection of the seeker's question by saying that he is not attracted to the Lord, because if he were, then he would seek Him. If he changes his nature, then by the principle of similar things attracting each other, he would be attracted to the Lord. The process of such advancement has also been noted earlier—namely, that if you are not qualified to understand the scripture, then you can still chant the names of the Lord. In Bhagavad-Gita, Lord Kṛṣṇa states that those who worship the demigods go to the planet of the demigods. And in 1.3.31 (94), it was said that the demigods are disqualified from spiritual pursuits due to their intoxicating habits. So, the gradual upliftment from human life to the life of demigods in the onward journey toward the Lord's abode has been rejected previously. But if the seeker still expresses helplessness in pursuing the direct path, then the teacher can only express their resignation.

However, this resignation is also an indication of a path forward. The indication is that we don't have to pass through a theoretical or conceptual understanding of greatness, one step at a time. We can rather leapfrog this hierarchy and jump to the highest level—if we develop an attraction for it. Now, one can argue: How can I be attracted to something if I don't know what it is? In this argument, the intellectual understanding precedes the devotion. But even if we were to know something, the attempt at knowledge is long and difficult. How would one persist on such a path unless they had a strong desire for achieving the goal? That strong desire to know the Lord is indication of one's devotion to the Lord. If this devotion doesn't exist, then knowledge is never obtained because the seeker quickly abandons the path due to difficulties. On the other hand, if the seeker persists through the difficulties, their persistence purifies the soul of materialistic desires, and the truth is now seen uncontaminated by our desires for the truth to be something. Therefore, devotion must exist to acquire knowledge, and sincerity is essential to succeed even in the path of knowledge. Ultimately, devotion leads to persistence, purification, and knowledge. Therefore, the Absolute Truth is not known other than through pure devotion.

The claim that "similar things attract each other" needs some explanation. In this case, we are not speaking about the universals, but the individuals. Specifically, a person's individual nature attracts them to similar other things. To understand this idea better, we need to go beyond Sāṅkhya, which deals with the universals and consider the Vaiśeṣika system which deals in the individuals. The individual instances of the Sāṅkhya elements are called 'atoms'. For example, there is a universal called the 'element' of 'earth' which indicates a class of things, and then there are individual 'atoms' of earth, which are members of this class. In modern science, the term 'atom' and 'element' are used interchangeably—the element Hydrogen, for example, is an atom of Hydrogen. In the Vedic system, however, there is a demarcation between the atoms or individuals and the elements or the universals. This system of demarcating the universals from the individuals carried forward into Greek metaphysics, which identified four elements—Earth, Water, Fire, and Air—as 'substances', and for a while, there was no conception of atoms. Atomism was introduced in Greek philosophy by Democritus, and after that, the atoms of Earth, Water, Fire, and Air, were spoken of. The distinction between the element and the atom was however dropped in physical sciences subsequently due to the rejection of universals as materially real things. Thus, only individuals were recognized, and universals remained non-material (although theoretical) entities. This is part of the larger project to banish the reality of the mind from physical sciences.

Once we understand that the universals are different from the individuals, we need to ask: How are these individuals created? We have seen that the soul differentiates itself from Brahman due to desire. A similar principle is employed for material individuation as well; the desire is also called guna and constitutes the causal body of the soul. Based on this causal body, the subtle and gross bodies are produced by instantiating the universals into the individuals.

Thus, every atom of an element is produced due to some desire, and it is because of this desire that the elements are attracted to each other. For example, each of us has an atom of the universal element called ghrāna or the sense of smell. Similarly, there are atoms of the element earth. These two atoms are attracted to each other—if the guna or the desire in them are compatible or 'similar'. Thus, the senses of smell in different people are attracted to different kinds of smells, and this attraction is the cause of their interaction. As a result of this interaction, a sensation of smell is produced, which then fulfills the desire of smell. Whether the sense of smell deserves to interact with the objects of smell is due to karma, but whether the sense of smell will desire that smell is due to guna. Similarly, the enjoyment or suffering after inter-action is due to guna.

So, to know the Lord, our past karma can bring us in contact with teachers who can impart this knowledge. There are also compassionate teachers who take the trouble to educate people who might otherwise be undeserving of this knowledge due to their bad karma. Thus, the problem of bad karma can be overcome by a teacher's compassion. However, eventually, one must have the guna or desire toward the Lord to undertake the journey of understanding. The fact is that most people are not just unfortunate to not get good teachers, but also lazy to not pursue this understanding even if the teacher is prepared. This laziness is not due to karma, but due to guna. If we have the appropri-ate guna, then we will be naturally attracted toward the understanding of the Absolute Truth. This is the meaning of "similar things attract each other"—we must become similar to the Lord to desire Him. This is the only goal of human life.

Topic 5

QUESTION

I understand your point about knowledge not being achievable without devotion. Since you have earlier noted that this devotion is itself developed through the chanting of the names of the Lord, I want to understand this better. Why the emphasis on chanting? Aren't there other methods for devotion such as deity worship, which have been practiced for ages in the Vedic system?

1.4.16 (122)

जगद्वाचित्वात्

jagadvācitvāt

jagat—the world, or all that is visible; vācitvāt—from the speech-like.

TRANSLATION

The world or all that has become visible is from the speech-like.

COMMENTARY

Western philosophers have argued that when we perceive the world—e.g., a red apple—then the redness, sweetness, and roundness of the apple is only in our senses and the mind. The world itself is not red, round, and sweet. It is comprised of primary properties—such as length, mass, charge, momentum, energy, etc.—which are completely unlike our sense perception. This then gives rise to the question of how these properties become sense perceptions, thoughts, judgments, intentions, morals, and desires. This problem has come to be known as the mind-body divide in Western philosophy, and so far, it has no resolution. While we can identify certain parts of the body and brain, which, when stimulated, produce sensations and thoughts, we cannot explain how the physical properties of the world are creating subjective experiences.

In Vedic philosophy, this problem is addressed by describing the world as word and meaning; the meaning is logically prior, and the word embodies this meaning and expands from that meaning. The distinction between word and meaning is a template, which recurs over several levels in a hierarchy. Thus, if the external world is words, then the senses are the meaning; if the sensations are the word, then thoughts are the meaning; if thoughts are the words, then judgments are the meaning; if judgments are the word, then the intention is the meaning; and if intentions are the word, then moral values are the meaning.

Thus, everything is treated both as a word and a meaning, depending on which tier in the hierarchy it is being spoken of. For example, when the apple is seen as red, round, and sweet, then the external world is the symbol of these ideas. These symbols are objective, and therefore red, round, and sweet is also objective—hence, you can claim that the 'apple is red' is a true statement (not merely our imagination or hallucination). However, to understand the symbol, we need an interpreter, which in this case are the senses. Therefore, the senses interact with the symbols of red, round, and sweet, and produce the sensations corresponding to these words. Thus, everything from our body to our senses, mind, intellect, ego, and moral sense are 'vibrations' that encode meanings. We have earlier discussed three broad classifications of this meaning into gross, subtle, and causal bodies, and how the soul is beyond these bodies. We can also say that the soul is the meaning of these three bodies. The soul is also a symbol whose meaning is God. God, however, is His own symbol and meaning, and the distinction between words and meanings ceases to exist within God.

This sūtra summarizes this understanding by stating that the entire *jagat* or the reality that can be perceived (by the senses, mind, intellect, etc.) is like sound. Therefore, whether we are thinking about the Lord, or whether we are doing deity worship, or whether we are chanting the Lord's names, ultimately, everything is a sound or a symbol of meaning. The Lord can be worshipped by offering Him a fruit, flower, water, or leaf (Bhagavad-Gita 9.26), and these are also symbols. Just because they are different from the words we speak and hear shouldn't confuse us about what we mean by 'sound' or *vāk*. Sometimes, *vāk* is used to just indicate the spoken word. But in the ultimate sense, every-thing is sound. When we hear the names of the Lord, we hear the mean-ing of our existence. Therefore, the chanting of the names of the Lord is the simplest *complete* method of realizing our own nature. It doesn't require regulations, unlike deity worship where cleanliness is import-ant. One cannot do deity worship while eating, bathing, walking, or working; but one can always chant the names of the Lord during any type of activity. Therefore, the chanting is recommended. It is not a rejection of deity worship, but a preference for chanting.

QUESTION

Many people might argue that by chanting the names, and medi-tating on the sound, one *becomes* the meaning denoted by the sound. Thus, for example, it is argued that by chanting the mantra OM, one becomes Brahman. In the same way, by chanting the names of the Lord, does one become the Lord?

In the Vedic texts, five kinds of liberation are described, beyond the liberation of Brahman. These are called *sālokya* (on the same planet), *sārūpya* (having the same form), *sāyujya* (merger into the Lord's form), *sāmīpya* (similarity and proximity to God), and *sārsti* (having the same opulence as God). In these forms of liberation, the jīvā becomes very similar to the Lord, and because the jīvā can be like the Lord, many people confuse this with the notion that the jīvā has become the Lord. Thus, they might practice devotion to become the Lord.

1.4.17 (123)

जीवमुख्यप्राणलिङ्गान्नेति चेत् तद्व्याख्यातम्

jīvamukhyaprāṇaliṅgānneti cet tadvyākhyātam

jīva-mukhyaprāṇa-liṅgāt—from the jīvā being the master of the body of prāṇa; na—not; iti cet—if it is said; tat—that; vyākhyātam—has already been explained.

TRANSLATION

If it is said that (liberation is obtained) from the jīvā being the master of the body of prāṇa, (then) we say no, (because) that has already been explained.

COMMENTARY

Sometimes the child of a king may want to sit on the king's throne to just experience how it feels like to sit on the throne. The king is not envious of his child and allows him to sit on the throne. In the same way, sometimes the jīvā might think: "How does the Lord feel to have so much power, wealth, knowledge, beauty, fame, and renunciation?" When such a desire arises, then the Lord is kind enough to give the jīvā an understanding of His own nature, by giving him a form, power, knowledge, wealth, etc. just like He has it. But just as a child wanting to sit on his father's throne is doing so playfully, and doesn't want to displace the king, similarly, the Lord grants this position because the child is devoted to the Lord and is free from the desire to replace Him. By sitting on the king's throne, the child doesn't become the king, although he playfully pretends to be just like the king, and this playfulness between the Lord and His devotees is called liberation in the various forms. There is an implicit understanding in the child that he is not the king but is occupying the throne because the king loves his child and would give anything to him.

In the same way, the jīvā in the liberated state understands that he is acting just like the Lord, by the grace of the Lord. This sūtra states that even if one attains a position like the Lord, the real power behind the position is still under the Lord's control. This is true not only in the material universe but also in the spiritual world. Even if the jīvā occupies a position just like the Lord, there is still a difference between the jīvā and the Lord, because the jīvā is desiring and the Lord is fulfilling the jīvā's desire. This fulfillment doesn't mean that the jīvā has become the Lord. Rather, the jīvā has desired to be like the Lord, and due to his devotion, the Lord has fulfilled that desire. The greatness exhibited by the forms of the jīvā acting as the Lord cannot be attributed to the jīvā. The greatness is rather like that which is exhibited by the demigods in which the Lord fulfills the desire of the demigods based on their karma. The difference in the case of liberation is that the Lord grants such desires due to the jīvā's devotion.

So, as one chants the names of the Lord, and becomes devoted to Him, he may develop the curiosity—I can understand what the Lord is, but I want to have the first-hand experience of what the Lord feels to be the Lord. If this desire is present without envy of the Lord and is intended only playfully, the Lord can even fulfill the jīvā's desire to be just like Him. This fulfillment should not be confused with the idea that "I have become God". One should rather understand that the Lord is kind enough to fulfill my desire to be like Him, and the real power that enables this position is the power of the Lord, not mine.

QUESTION

So, what happens to a person who has no devotion to the Lord, but may have some (intellectual type of) interest in transcendence or spirituality?

1.4.18 (124)

अन्यार्थं तु जैमिनिःप्रश्नव्याख्यानाभ्यामपि चैवमेके

anyārthaṃ tu jaiminiḥ praśnavyākhyānābhyāmapi caivameke

anyārtham—for another goal (different from the devotion to the Lord); tu—but; jaiminiḥ—Jaimini; praśnavyākhyānābhyām—because of the question and elucidation; api ca—moreover; evam—thus; eke—some.

TRANSLATION

Some (people), like Jaimini, with other goals (not devotion to the Lord), (believe that transcendence) can also be achieved by questions and answers.

COMMENTARY

We have discussed earlier that the Mīmāṃsā philosophers did not believe in the existence of God or demigods, although they treated the soul as an eternal entity, and considered the Vedas to be true. This truth was predicated on the claim that the instructions for the performance of rituals work. If something works, then it must be considered true, unless someone else can come up with another description of how things work. The Mīmāṃsā philosophers also believed that the meaning of each text is self-evident because the meaning is in the sound itself. The Sanskrit language in their view is not an ordinary spoken language where the connection between the word and the meaning is made largely by speaker and listener conventions. The Mīmāṃsā philosophers held that the sounds of letters in the Sanskrit language is itself meaningful. This idea has been confirmed through phonosemantic studies in languages such as English, which show that sound is itself the denotation of meaning. For example, the sound 'str' as found in words like strip, strap, street, straight, etc. denotes something thin and elongated. Empirical studies on dictionaries have classified the words based on these phonemes and found that each phoneme has a couple of different meanings, but the association between the phoneme and the meaning is not arbitrary. So, the claim is that the meaning of the text is in the sound or how it is spoken, and if we want to find the complete truth in the Vedas, then we must discover this meaning through the analysis of the sound.

But how do we find the relation between sound and meaning? Mīmāṃsā philosophers provided rules for interpreting the texts, but ultimately, the criterion for truth is practical—it must work. So, if we are confused by what something means, then we can test whether it works. The act of testing involves asking a question, and the result of that testing provides an answer. This method can be applied to the verification of ritual practices—e.g., perform them and see if you get the results. If you get the results, then you have understood the meaning of the text. Over time, as we develop a deeper understanding of texts, we can also formulate rules by which texts must be interpreted. But these rules are gleaned by the study of many texts, seeing what works, and then formulating the rules by which we can show that the meaning is indeed verifiable.

Jaimini has been quoted here because he did not believe in the existence of God, and correspondingly rejected devotion to the Lord. But he still accepted the authority of the Vedas. So, if there are people who believe in the truth of the Vedas, but don't want to devote themselves to the Lord, then they can try to glean the truth of the Vedas by linguistic analysis or empirical testing. This view is attributed to Jaimini, not explicitly endorsed by the author, nor is it rejected by the author. We can recall that at the beginning of the Vedānta Sūtra, the scriptures were described as the source of knowledge, and reason and observation (as methods of discovery) were rejected. But we also noted that scriptures are open to rational analysis and empirical confirmation, and anyone who asks questions and seeks answers should not be considered faithless if they are prepared to accept the source of knowledge. The Mīmāṃsā philosopher is one who considers the Vedas to be true, and yet not spoken by the Lord. In one sense, he has faith in the scripture, and yet, he doesn't have faith in the Lord speaking it. The knowledge of Absolute Truth is therefore in the Vedas, although this truth is not provided by a person. If you reject the existence of a person, then you are left with impersonal semantics and you can analyze these meanings by asking questions and answers until you think you have arrived at the truth.

It is sometimes said that Bhagavān takes many forms, and the books about Him are also representations of His person. So, if one has faith in the book, but doesn't consider these books a 'revelation' by the Lord, then he can simply study the books, analyze their meanings, and test their truth. This is a scientific literary-semantic analysis to obtain an understanding of the Absolute Truth. Indologists also carry out such study of Vedic texts. However, they do not believe that these texts are true. They don't make an attempt to understand the descriptions as they are found across different texts—instead of accepting that the same knowledge is presented in different ways in different texts, they claim that this knowledge has evolved over time, and they try to date these texts. If the truth of these texts is not accepted, they are never put into practice or tested. They simply remain things of historical and archeological interest. Such study of texts is, therefore, worse than the Mīmāṃsā approach, which accepts the texts as true, tries to understand their meaning, and puts them into practice.

Topic 6

QUESTION

But we have discussed that the different Vedic texts may not always be consistent, or one text may not provide the complete information about a subject. How does one deal with the problem of inconsistency (of various texts) and the incompleteness (of individual texts) to obtain complete truth?

1.4.19 (125)

वाक्यान्वयात्

vākyānvayāt

vākya-anvayāt—from the logical connection of passages.

TRANSLATION

(Vedic texts should be understood) from their logical connections.

COMMENTARY

This sūtra should be understood as indicating that the different Vedic texts are not contradictory, although each text may be individually incomplete. The differences between the texts may be due to the differences in the questions of the seekers—as in the previous sūtra the phrase 'question-and-answer' was employed. They may be different based on the context of the presentation, the place, or the time. If we do not find the complete truth in one place, then we can consult other texts. But as we consult other texts, we may start coming across differences or contradictions. And yet, these differences are still logically connected because they are answers in response to different questions. The truth lies in the reconciliation of these apparently contradictory claims. In the beginning of the Vedānta Sūtra, it was discussed that the Vedic texts are contradictory, and it was advised that we should consider only those parts of the texts which are pertaining to transcendence (and neglect others). It was also said that the Absolute Truth is that which reconciles the diversity, whereupon that unification was described, and faith in that Absolute Truth led to liberation. If, however, one wants to return to the study of the texts, without explicit devotion to the Lord, this sūtra states that you must now study the texts in a way that the inconsistency and incompleteness of individual texts is resolved. In short, if you see an inconsistency, understand that a deeper level of truth will reconcile this conflict. And if you find something incomplete, look at other texts until you find the corresponding information that completes it. The texts are logically connected to each other, so they must also be understood collectively.

QUESTION

But how will we know that we have obtained the truth by this study?

A standard problem in all empirical and rational approaches to knowledge is that we never know if we have obtained the complete truth. Even if our knowledge works in many cases, we don't know if it will work in all the cases. Owing to this fact, the empirical and rational methods are known to be forever incomplete—the ideas can be falsified in the future, but they cannot be confirmed to be true (as potential falsifiability always exists). Similarly, if we take to analyzing texts and understanding their meaning, what is the guarantee that we have obtained the complete truth? Isn't it entirely possible that what we know now may be an incomplete understanding, which could be updated later?

1.4.20 (126)

परतज्ञिआसदि्धेर्लङि्गमाश्मरथ्यः

pratijñāsiddherliṅgamāśmarathyaḥ

pratijñā—knowledge of everything, or certain knowledge; siddheḥ—on the fulfillment; liṅgam—indicatory mark; āśmarathyaḥ—Āsmarathya.

TRANSLATION

On knowing everything indicatory marks (appear), (says) Āsmarathya.

COMMENTARY

The term *pratijñā* has many meanings. In the simplest form, it should be considered as a 'promise'. But if we dissect *pratijñā* = *prati* + *jñā*, *prati* can mean 'toward' or 'in relation to' such as in *pratispardhā* or competition. And sometimes, *pratijñā* is also used to indicate 'certain knowledge'. For instance, in Bhagavad-Gita 9.31, Lord Kṛṣṇa says to Arjuna: *kaunteya pratijānīhi na me bhaktaḥ praṇaśyati* which means "O son of Kunti, know with certainty that my devotee is never vanquished". The interpretation of *pratijñā* as 'promise' is inappropriate in this context because the sūtra would be translated as "on fulfillment of the promise indicatory marks are visible" and no promise has been referred to thus far. It is possible to translate *prati* as "in relation to knowledge" or "toward knowledge", but the sūtra would then be translated as "as one approaches knowledge or tries to learn, indicatory marks appear". This translation is consistent with Sanskrit, but such a claim has no confirmation in the Vedic texts. Therefore, I have preferred to translate *pratijñā* as "certain knowledge".

This sūtra sidesteps traditional methods of knowledge by empirical and rational methods—which seek confirmation in the external world. It states that the confirmation lies in the knower, and when certain knowledge is attained, the indicatory marks appear in the knower. What are these marks? They are not described in this sūtra, but it is assumed that the listener already knows.

The basic indicatory mark of knowledge is freedom from fear and hope—resulting in detachment. This is an emotional state, rather than an intellectual state. If we are not sure that our knowledge is true, then there will be fear in the heart—we are unsure if something is true and could be falsified later. On the other hand, if it has been falsified, then we search for truth under the hope that it will be confirmed. But even if it is confirmed, the fear remains because it could be falsified in the future. Thus, one oscillates between fear and hope—the hope arises from the excitement that we may find the full truth and the fear from the despair that we may not find the full truth, and whatever seems true right now may be demonstrated to be false at a later time. However, this sūtra states that if truth has been obtained, then these hopes and fears will be destroyed. This confirmation is not based on empirical and rational demonstrations. Rather, when the truth has been obtained, a new emotional state of peace, satisfaction, contentment, along with freedom from fear and hope is established.

So, even though the Mīmāṃsā philosophers are not devotees, they are not complete materialists either. They understand that the purpose of knowledge is freedom from the suffering in this world, caused by hope leading to hard work, which then becomes futile, leading to despair, and the seeker then goes in search of another truth under hope. If one wants to be free from the cycle of hope and fear—which we can call 'liberation' or 'salvation'—then the symptoms of knowledge must appear in us rather than in empirical confirmation in the external world, or rational agreement through argument and discussion. It is an introspective view of the knowledge by which one obtains salvation.

QUESTION

If we allow this intrinsic confirmation of the truth, then everyone will likely pretend or claim to know the truth. They might feign contentment, satisfaction, etc. How can one know that this method will naturally lead to the truth?

1.4.21 (127)

उत्क्रमष्यित एवंभावादतियौडुलोमिः

utkramiṣyata evaṃbhāvādityauḍulomiḥ

utkram—automatically arising or springing; iṣyataḥ—desires; evaṃ bhāvāt—such emotional states; iti—thus; auḍulomiḥ—(the sage) Audulomi.

TRANSLATION

Such emotional states (e.g., of contentment, satisfaction) automatically arise like desires (are automatically created), thus says the sage Audulomi.

COMMENTARY

The term *utkramiṣyataḥ* is significant in this sūtra. The meaning of *utkram* is random, unpredictable, impulsive, etc. The meaning of *iṣyataḥ* is desires. The sūtra states that just like desires automatically arise in the heart, similarly, the symptoms of having perfect knowledge—namely, the emotional states of contentment and satisfaction also arise automatically. So, there is a difference between a person feigning the satisfaction, and the person in whom these arise automatically. The difference is that the pretender tries to look contented, while the person who has truly attained the knowledge is naturally contented. Those who feign such contentment, however, cannot always remain satisfied. They will eventually become dissatisfied, which would be seen in their pursuits.

Spiritual advancement is different from mental or intellectual development because when something is known mentally or intellectually, it doesn't exist permanently. We keep forgetting it, and then we must keep reminding ourselves about its truth. However, when something has been perfectly realized, then the soul never forgets about it and doesn't need to be reminded of its truth. All doubts are therefore destroyed by the perfect realization. And thereafter, the recollection of knowledge automatically springs in the heart. Therefore, in the Bhakti-rasāmṛta-sindhu (1.2.234) we find the following statement:

atah śrī-kṛṣṇa-nāmādi
na bhaved grāhyam indriyaiḥ
sevonmukhe hi jihvādau
svayam eva sphuraty adaḥ

Therefore, the names etc. of Śri Kṛṣṇa cannot be grasped by the senses. But certainly, as one becomes inclined to serve with the tongue, these (i.e., the names etc.) automatically spring.

The relevant term here is *sphurati* which means springing forth with a quivering, vibration, etc. A similar term *utkram* is used here, which indicates automatically arising or springing without an effort, and the comparison to desires is drawn, indicating that the springing forth is just like the arising of desires. The main point is that as we start the process of learning, we try to understand and assimilate the knowledge, and we need to constantly remind ourselves of its truth. But, as one reaches perfection, the truth automatically springs in the heart. The knowledge is innate in the soul, but the soul must be awakened. Like a diamond when polished naturally starts shining, similarly, when the soul is purified of the contamination of ignorance, it becomes a spout of truth.

QUESTION

But how can someone—who hasn't reached such a state—know if a person claiming to have reached such a state has indeed attained perfection in knowledge? Many teachers may look peaceful and content, but it is not clear if that is just an acquired habit, or deceitful presentation, or something that is deeply internal, which is springing forth naturally and automatically. In short, how can someone distinguish between a realized soul and a charlatan?

1.4.22 (128)

अवस्थितिरिति काशकृत्स्नः

avasthiteriti kāśakrtsnah

avasthiteh—firm, fixed; iti—thus; kāśakrtsnah—Kāśakritsna.

TRANSLATION

Because they are firm and fixed, so says Kāśakritsna.

COMMENTARY

A similar question was asked previously in the context of the selection of a guru but that was in the context of knowing whether a person has become a devotee of the Lord. The answer to that question was that a self-realized person can be known from his words; these words are not merely flowery speech, but something that will transform your life by germinating the seed of God's love in the heart. In this sūtra, we are not speaking about the devotees of the Lord. We are rather considering those people who study the scriptures and analyze their meaning. Their conviction is naturally much less than those of the devotees because the happiness, contentment, and conviction in a devotee are much higher. However, even those who don't have an infallible conviction can still be highly convinced. Their words may not convince others, but we can see that at least they are themselves fixed in their pursuit and path. When the understanding reaches a point of maturity, a person will not fall back into the states of ignorance indicated by fear and hope. Such a person is technically said to be situated in the mode of undeviating *sattva-guna* or the mode of goodness. He may not have an experiential vision, but he has progressed in his knowledge to a point where he is fully convinced of its truth and will never deviate.

Topic 7

QUESTION

But it is hard to detect if someone is going to deviate. So many times, we trust a person who seems fixed in their knowledge, but we eventually find that they have deviated. Isn't there a better criterion for judging such a person?

1.4.23 (129)

परकृतश्िच परतज्ञिआदृष्टान्तानुपरोधात्

prakṛtiśca pratijñādṛṣṭāntānuparodhāt

prakṛtiḥ—material nature; ca—also; pratijñā—full knowledge; dṛṣṭānta—illustration; anuparodhāt—not injuring or being contradictory.

TRANSLATION

(They) also have full knowledge of the material nature and can illustrate and demonstrate it (for you) without producing any contradiction.

COMMENTARY

Most of us tend to think that a person advanced in religion knows about the transcendental world. Since we don't have direct experience of that world, many people are frequently cheated in the process, as they start trusting a person who fakes their advancement. While there are methods to detect such impersonation, such as checking if a person is fixed in the path or not, or whether they display symptoms of inner bliss, or whether their words are transforming our lives, many of these are subject to deception as well. This sūtra, therefore, guides the seeker to check a claimant's understanding of the material world. This is not to say that one who has perfect knowledge of the material world would necessarily have a perfect understanding of the spiritual world as well. It is to say that one who understands the spiritual world will also understand the material world. Therefore, material knowledge doesn't entail spiritual knowledge. But spiritual knowledge entails perfect material knowledge.

This criterion can be applied both to individuals and to religious systems. Anyone who claims to be spiritually advanced but cannot explain the material world is a pretender. Similarly, any religion that cannot explain the material world, or provides false explanations, should be rejected. So, this sūtra is prescribing a sniff test, in which one doesn't have to accept a religion as indicating the truth if they do not have a full understanding of the material world.

QUESTION

But how can the perfection of knowledge of the material world be related to the understanding of the transcendental world? We have spoken of how the material world reflects the Lord, like a painting is expressed by an artist. We also spoke of how the Lord incarnates in this world. We have spoken about the Universal Form of the Lord as something suitable for meditation. But all these were meant to glean the understanding of the Lord from material nature, not indicate expertise in the study of material nature. Now you are saying that a spiritualist is also advanced in material knowledge and that this expertise is a test of their advancement. How do we reconcile these varying viewpoints?

1.4.24 (130)
अभिध्योपदेशाच्च
abhidhyopadeśācca

abhidhya—longing for; upadeśāt—on account of the teaching; ca—also.

TRANSLATION

The teaching (of the material world) also leads to longing for (the Lord).

COMMENTARY

The study of material nature through modern science has made many people atheists. But science is itself deeply flawed. First, there is no explanation of perception, or how we experience color, taste, smell, touch, etc. which arises because modern science draws a distinction between the physical properties and the perceived qualities. Second, if such qualities are rejected, then the concepts are also rejected; in fact, both sensations and concepts are merely in the mind, and therefore unreal, and hence meanings become unreal. If meanings cannot be understood, then how can science explain the existence of meaningful objects—e.g., books, music, works of art, or even claim the possibility of knowledge—which is always expressed through symbols of meaning?

Third, if we cannot understand meanings, then how will we judge? These judgments come to us in three ways—like truth, right, and good. The existence of a sentence doesn't tell us its truth (in modern science truth is judged by existence). So, even truth cannot be judged without meanings. Then, we also incorporate judgments of good (e.g., what is pleasing or displeasing) and right (i.e., something that is my duty or not, based upon my roles and responsibilities). If we cannot judge the truth, then the judgments of right and good are also excluded. Therefore, we can never formulate laws of choice and consequence, because we fundamentally don't have a conception of right and good. No action can be called right or wrong because it is just the motion of particles. Likewise, no such motion can be good or bad, because we cannot explain the difference between enjoyment and suffering based upon such particle motions.

The atheism of modern science is founded on ignorance. It is not just ignorance about the soul and God. It is also the ignorance about sense perception, the understanding of meaning, and the abilities to judge truth, right, and good. The real understanding of nature is that which allows us to incorporate sensations, meanings, and judgments of truth, right, and good. On the other hand, if sensations, meanings, and judgments are understood, then we can understand choices, and how the choices should ideally be made (because the non-ideal choices reduce the freedom to make choices). That scientific understanding of reality would not be contrary to the existence of the soul and God.

The Bhagavad-Gita states that the process by which the body changes at death is the same as the process by which it is changing right now. So, the body is not 'growing' (from childhood to youth) and not 'declining' (from youth to old age). Rather, the connection between the soul and the body is changing every moment. Just as one can wear different clothes, and then abandon them, similarly, the change of the body is the soul picking different kinds of clothes. Thus, the change of body must be described as the selection of a dress, rather than one dress evolving into another dress. If you remove the shirt and pants and wear denim and t-shirts, the shirt and pants haven't evolved into denim and t-shirt. Rather, the person has changed his clothes. This view of change entails that the wardrobe of clothes preexists the selection of a dress. The clothes are not created or destroyed. Rather, when something is worn, it is visible, and when it is removed, it goes back into the wardrobe and remains invisible. Even this invisible piece of clothing, however, exists as a *possibility*. What we call 'matter' is, therefore, a possibility hidden in a wardrobe. The laws of science should be able to describe how this possibility becomes an experience.

The key point is that theism is not a superimposition of the ideas of the soul and God on the unchanged substrate of atheistic scientific ideas. Rather, theism entails a change to all scientific notions about the nature of matter, causality, and laws. If the paradigm of change is the motion of billiard balls, then the laws of nature are deterministic. But if the paradigm of change is wearing and discarding of clothes, then the causality of this change will involve many new ideas—e.g., that we desire certain clothes and we deserve certain clothes. This desiring and deserving leads to the selection of some clothes, and the laws of nature should explain how this causal mechanism of desiring and deserving evolves. This kind of description, in turn, requires us to introduce several things that have been left out of modern science—from perception to concepts to judgments of truth, right, and good—and the laws of nature would now be based on these judgments. For instance, the right action leads to happiness, and the wrong action leads to suffering. To define right and wrong, we must have a 'role' in addition to a body, and to define good and bad, we must introduce an individual whose desires result in the experience of pleasure and pain.

Meanings necessitate a change in our conceptions about space—from a box to a tree. The conversion of meanings into things requires a distinction between universals and individuals. Their combination enters roles, which define right and wrong. If we understand that the cycle of birth and death is due to our right and wrong actions, then we can speak of transcendence. Once we understand that our suffering or enjoyment is dependent on the demigods delivering the results of our past actions—under the supervision of the Paramātma—then we can see that nature is administered by personalities and it is not impersonal. With the foundations of personalism, we can speak about transcendental persons, who are not compelled to change their dress due to natural laws.

Thus, material knowledge doesn't lead to atheism. Modern science is atheistic because it is false. It studies parts of our experience and neglects the senses, mind, intellect, happiness, and the relation between choice and consequence. Based on a limited investigation, it formulates a false understanding of space, time, causality, and laws of nature. And due to its economic power arising from modern technology, it pushes atheism by destroying all dissenting voices. If these ideas are corrected, then the knowledge of the material world would naturally lead to the understanding of the Supreme Person beyond this world.

This viewpoint is confirmed in this sūtra by stating that the understanding of material nature leads to a longing for the Lord. In numerous Vedic texts, such as the Śrīmad Bhāgavatam, and other Purāṇa, the material world and the cosmic structure are described alongside the devotion to the Lord. Thus, the idea that knowledge of the material world is opposed to transcendental understanding is false. A true understanding of matter leads to devotion to God.

QUESTION

If the study of scriptures without devotion leads to devotion, then can the reverse be said—i.e., that those who are devotees, also understand the material world (even if they have not spent extensive efforts in the scriptural study)?

1.4.25 (131)
साक्षाच्चोभयाम्नानात्

sākṣaccobhayāmnānāt

sākṣāt—direct; ca—and; ubhayām—both; nānāt—the diversities.

TRANSLATION

(The devotees) obtain direct experience of both (spiritual and material worlds) and the many kinds of diversities (present in these kinds of worlds).

COMMENTARY

The term *sākṣāt* indicates 'directly'. It is different from *pratyakṣa* which means phenomena. The meaning of *sākṣāt* is the understanding of reality as it is different from phenomena. All phenomena are mediated by the senses, mind, intellect, etc. But *sākṣāt* indicates perception by the soul or knowing things as they are. The term *ubhayām* indicates both the material and the spiritual worlds, and along with *sākṣāt* it means the direct (and unmediated by the senses, mind, or the intellect) perception of both material and spiritual reality. Finally, the term *nānāt* indicates that both material and spiritual worlds are diverse. The impersonalist believes that the material world is diverse, but the spiritual reality must be undivided. This is a wrong understanding as indicated in this sūtra. The existence of unity doesn't imply the absence of diversity. The Lord is the unity and the different parts expanded from this unity are the diversity. If one has understood the unity, then the nature of the diversity is also understood because we can see that the unity has a form of knowledge, beauty, fame, wealth, power, and renunciation; the unity also has a desire and the capacity for relationships. Due to His desire, the unity expands into diversity, His qualities are divided into their parts, and He relates to all these parts.

The study of diversity perplexes us about the nature of unity—we wonder how all this diversity can expand from one thing. And a naïve and simplistic view of this unity is that all the diversity must be destroyed when the unity is attained. The correct understanding is that all this diversity exists within the unity; the unity is knowledge, and the diversity is the many kinds of knowledge; the unity is beauty, and the diversity is the many types of beauty. It is not easy to understand unity since it is comprised of all contradictory qualities. But if one can understand the unity, then the understanding of the diversity is automatic. Therefore, one who has understood the Supreme Lord understands both material and spiritual diversity manifested from the Lord.

QUESTION

You have mentioned that the devotees know both the spiritual and the material worlds. What is their understanding of how these are produced?

1.4.26 (132)

आत्मकृतेःपरिणामात्

ātmakṛteḥ pariṇāmāt

ātmakṛteḥ—done by the self, on the self; pariṇāmāt—as results.

TRANSLATION

(The worlds are produced) as the results of the Self acting on the Self.

COMMENTARY

The Absolute Truth is the combination of two things—the will and the power to fulfill that will. If He was only will, He could desire, but those desires would never be fulfilled without the power. If He was only power, it will lie inert, and never produce anything, because there is no will to use the power. These two aspects of the Absolute Truth—namely, will and the power—are identified as masculine and feminine aspects of the same reality. The will is called Puruṣa and the power is called Śakti. These are two aspects of the same reality, and yet they are neither separable nor are they identical. They are simply two complementary ways of understanding the Absolute Truth.

When there is power, the possessor of the power is enticed to use it, and that enticement is will. The presence of power thus creates the will. And once the will is created, then the power which produced the will is used by the will. Thus, the feminine aspect of the Absolute Truth agitates the masculine aspect to create a will in the masculine aspect. The masculine aspect then uses the feminine aspect as its power to fulfill the will. The feminine aspect is both the cause of the creation of the will and the agency that fulfills the will. And yet, because the power serves under the control of the will, the masculine is said to be superior. Factually, these considerations about which is superior to the other are pointless. The feminine is superior because She agitates the masculine. And the masculine is superior because He uses the feminine to fulfill His desires.

The term ātmakṛteh or Self acting on the Self refers to this dynamic between the two aspects of the Absolute Truth. When the feminine Self agitates the masculine Self, She acts on Him to create a desire. Then, when the masculine Self is agitated, He uses the feminine Self to fulfill that desire. The fulfillment of the desire produces pleasure, and the creation is the process by which the desire is fulfilled. The fulfillment of desire requires the combination of will and power, and the combination creates the world as a byproduct, as indicated by the term *pariṇāmāt*. Thus, two aspects of the Absolute Truth, which are inseparable, act upon each other as if they were separate. Then they unite to produce an effect, which becomes the agency by which enjoyment is produced. This separation and union of the two aspects of the Absolute Truth produce the world as a result. The situation is loosely compared to the mating of a male and a female, who then produce a child as a result. The creation is the child of this Absolute Truth because it has expanded out of the Absolute Truth. However, this creation was previously within the Absolute Truth, so even though it has emerged from the Absolute Truth, it remains a part of that Absolute Truth. This is unlike the products of worldly sexual activity, in which the children are separated from their parents. Therefore, the divine masculine-feminine intercourse should not be confused with the materialistic male-female sexual activity.

This process can also be understood as the interaction between possibility and choice. If you go to a shopping mall, and you see some goods to buy, you naturally get the desire to buy them. The goods exist as a possibility for enjoyment, and they create a desire in the buyer to procure these goods. But as soon as this desire is fulfilled, the desire automatically expands to explore more possibilities. With the expansion of desire, the possibility also expands, which then leads to more desire, more possibility, and the process continues indefinitely. The initial cause of the desire is the feminine, which entices the masculine with a desire. But once that desire has been triggered, it not only seeks the feminine but also expands in new ways, which then causes the feminine to expand. In an earlier sūtra, it was noted that the cause of the One becoming many is a desire for pleasure. This sūtra develops that understanding and states that the many are produced due to the expansion of the One when It acts upon Itself.

In the case of the material creation, the desire is triggered by the feminine energy of the Lord, and the Lord then enjoys with this energy. But after a long period, the desire for enjoyment contracts, and the feminine energy also contracts accordingly, until the entire creation collapses back into the Absolute Truth. In this collapsed state, there is the potential for desire, and the potential to fulfill that desire, but both potentials remain dormant. They are activated again when the desire is produced, and the universe expands again. This expansion and contraction produce a cyclic change of creation, sustenance, and annihilation of the material universes, and while the Absolute Truth is eternal, the manifest universes are temporary. The material world is therefore sometimes considered non-different from the Absolute Truth, and sometimes called an illusion. In the case of the spiritual world, the desire for enjoyment never contracts, and the masculine never disengages with the feminine, and the feminine never stops agitating the masculine. The spiritual world is thus eternal, and unlike the material creation, it is neither created nor annihilated. Owing to this, the spiritual world is always described as being non-different from the Absolute Truth, and never termed as an illusion (like the material universe).

QUESTION

If the creation is the result of the separation and union of the masculine and feminine aspects of the Absolute Truth, then what is the nature of the soul? Should the soul be described as masculine desire, or the feminine power to fulfill the desire? Is the soul known as the enjoyer puruṣa or the enjoyed śakti?

1.4.27 (133)
योनश्चि हि गीयते
yoniśca hi gīyate

yoniḥ—the feminine; ca—and; hi—because; gīyate—sings in praise.

TRANSLATION

(The soul) is also feminine because (she) sings in praise (of the Lord).

COMMENTARY

In an earlier sūtra, it was stated that the Lord is the *linga* or the masculine genital that injects the soul into material nature; from that claim we would tend to think that the soul is part of the masculine but gets injected in the feminine. In this sūtra, the soul is described as feminine because she is devoted to the Lord. By that devotion, the soul attracts the Lord, and the Lord then uses the soul for His pleasure, and the soul enjoys being used for the Lord's pleasure. These two sūtras create confusion—is the soul masculine or feminine?

The answer to this question lies in the process by which the masculine and the feminine expand. As we have noted in the purport of the last sūtra, the feminine agitates the masculine to produce a desire in the masculine. The soul is this agitation in the masculine and is created as a desire in Him. But this desire enters the feminine, and the desire to enjoy in the masculine becomes the desire to fulfill the desire in the feminine. The entry of the masculine's desire into the feminine is called the masculine injecting the feminine with His 'seed' or *bīja*. This 'seed' is the soul. In a simple sense, the masculine is the father and the feminine is the mother. And the soul produced out of their interaction is neither the mother nor the father. The soul is not the father, because it cannot create more children. And the soul is not the mother because the soul cannot agitate the masculine to create more children. Therefore, before we answer the question of whether the soul is masculine and feminine, we must understand that the soul is neither the mother nor the father. And yet, because the soul originates in the masculine, he is sometimes called masculine. Similarly, since the soul is the desire to fulfill the masculine as part of the mother, so she is feminine.

Even though the soul originates in the father, it cannot become the enjoyer of the mother, imagining that it was created as the desire to enjoy with the mother. Likewise, even though the soul enters the mother with the desire to fulfill the masculine, the soul is not the mother to enjoy with the father.

Therefore, in one sense, the soul is both masculine and feminine—the soul originates as the desire in the masculine and enters the feminine to fulfill that desire. And yet, in another sense, the soul is neither the father nor the mother. So, even if the soul takes a male or female form, it is incapable of creating a soul—which the real father and mother are. Finally, even after the soul is created as a desire, it has no capacity to fulfill the desire. Since the soul cannot fulfill its own desires, therefore, it must serve the masculine's desires, as part of the feminine. If the soul accepts this position, then it becomes the enjoyer who enjoys by fulfilling the feminine who is trying to fulfill the masculine. Thus, by serving the feminine in this way, the soul is satisfied, the feminine is satisfied, and the masculine is satisfied. The satisfaction of the masculine fulfills the purpose of the soul's existence because the original desire is being fulfilled.

The separation of the soul from the masculine doesn't entail that the soul is an independent enjoyer. However, when the soul develops the illusion of being an enjoyer—as a father or a mother—then it falls into the material world. Even in this world, the soul cannot fulfill its own desires. But the soul develops the illusion that the real father doesn't exist, and therefore an incestuous relation to the mother is possible. The mother is not interested in incest. Therefore, she treats the soul as Her child, and this makes the soul very angry and frustrated. The soul tries to obtain power over material nature, trying to impress the mother to be its consort. But all such attempts are always frustrated, because the mother always steals this power and makes the soul a helpless child.

Topic 8

QUESTION

The description of the Absolute Truth as will and the power to fulfill that will—which you have called masculine and feminine—explains how the Absolute Truth is simultaneously one and yet expands into many by its action upon itself. I can now understand how the One becomes many due to desire for pleasure, and how the soul is simultaneously a part of the masculine and yet considered feminine. Is this the supreme understanding of the Absolute Truth?

1.4.28 (134)

एतेन सर्वे व्याख्याता व्याख्याताः

etena sarve vyākhyātā vyākhyātāḥ

etena—thus; sarve—all; vyākhyātā—explainer; vyākhyātāḥ—explains.

TRANSLATION

In this way, the explainer explains everything.

COMMENTARY

Here, the term *vyākhyātā* or the explainer should be understood as the Supreme Lord, and the *vyākhyātāḥ* or the explanation should be understood as the expansion from the Supreme Lord. The explanation is the combination of the Lord's will and His power, so the explanation is both masculine and feminine. However, this explanation is the manifestation by the Absolute Truth acting upon itself. The Vedas are said to be the Lord's speech, and the material manifestation has been called His 'expression'. So, why does the Lord speak, and why does He expand from One to many? The answer is that He as the explainer explains Himself, and that explanation is the manifest world. The explanation has expanded from the explainer, and it describes the explainer. The explainer is the cause, and the explanation is the effect, but the effect describes or explains the cause. So, by this explanation, we can understand the explainer, provided it is understood that the explanation came from an explainer.

If one begins with the explainer, then one can easily understand the explanation. But even if one begins with the explanation, one can find the explainer, because the explanation is about the explainer. So, the explanation and the explainer are not identical, and yet, one can be known from the other. The explanation of everything is that the Absolute Truth is One but has masculine and feminine aspects; the masculine is the will, and the feminine is the power to satisfy that will. The power and the powerful cannot be separated, and yet they are also distinct. By this distinction, the Absolute Truth acts upon Itself and the One becomes many. The simultaneous unity and the distinctness of the masculine and feminine principles is the explanation of all other explanations.

The many interpretations of Vedānta Sūtra, such as Advaita, Dvaita, Viśiṣṭādvaita, Bhedābheda, etc. all deal with the relation between the soul and God. The Advaita system says that the soul and God are identical. The Viśiṣṭādvaita school states that diversity is part of the unity. The Dvaita system states that the Lord and the soul are distinct. The Bhedābheda system says that the soul is separate from the Lord but also dependent on the Lord; due to this dependence, it cannot be considered separate (i.e., independent); and yet because the soul is not identical to the Lord, therefore they are separate.

All these interpretations take off from the fundamental problem that Śrī Śaṅkarācārya created by identifying the soul with Brahman; this is a problem because we could not explain how that One divides into many. The impersonal doctrine that māyā covers the soul has been explicitly rejected above because the Self acts upon the Self. It is not māyā that is acting upon the soul. It is rather the desire in the soul, which māyā fulfills. Therefore, māyā is not responsible for the soul's fall into matter. It is rather the soul who desires the fall, and māyā fulfills it. For the soul to have a desire, it must have personality. The fall into māyā entails the preexistence of a person, and if there is a pre-existing person, then how individuality was produced from Oneness becomes a problem. The personalist interpretations of Vedānta Sūtra are a solution to that problem.

Śrī Chaitanya's philosophy differs from all previous Ācāryas in one significant respect—it is not preoccupied with the relation between the soul and God. It is rather preoccupied with the nature of the Absolute Truth as comprised of masculine and feminine aspects, which are simultaneously different and yet inseparable. This description of the oneness and difference in the Absolute Truth is called Acintyabhedābheda. The non-difference in Bhedābheda is about the relation between soul and God, and not the aspects of the Absolute Truth.

This grand shift in Vedānta is not understood if Acintyabhedābheda is presented as the relation between the soul and God when it is the relation between the two aspects of the Absolute Truth. The addition of inconceivability to the preexisting doctrine of Bhedābheda doesn't produce new clarity; in fact, it leads to more confusion—if it is inconceivable, then how do we understand it, and how can something inconceivable be considered a view on Vedānta Sūtra which is supposed to be clarifying the nature of reality through logic?

To understand Śrī Chaitanya's philosophy, we need to sidestep the relation between the soul and God, and look at the Purāna, Itihāsa, and Tantra scriptures, where there are pervasive descriptions of couples, such as Lakshmi-Nārāyana, Sita-Rama, Radha-Kṛṣṇa, Śakti-Śiva, etc. They are one, and yet they are different. The soul is always subordinate to these couples, and emphasis should, therefore, be laid on the understanding of these couples rather than the relation between the soul and the Lord. The doctrine of Acintyabhedābheda pertains to the unity and distinction in the couple, rather than to the relation between God and the soul. Once this type of Bhedābheda is understood, then the relation between the soul and God is automatically clarified as a corollary. The soul originates in the father, so he is part of the father, but then the soul becomes part of the mother, and hence separate from the father. But since the mother is inseparable from the father, the soul is not totally detached from the father. And yet, he is also not identical to the father. So, a new kind of Bhedābheda doctrine related to the soul results from the focus on the Bhedābheda in the Divine Couple. This understanding of Vedānta Sūtra dissolves the distinction between śrutī and smriti. Whereas in śrutī that One Absolute Truth is emphasized, in the smriti the same Absolute Truth is described as comprising of two inseparable aspects. The Vedānta Sūtra, when understood in this way, becomes the doctrine of unity across diverse Vedic scriptures.

Chapter 2

Having undertaken an overview of the summary of the Vedas, this chapter starts addressing many common philosophical objections to these descriptions. These include the discussion of the problem of evil, the cause of the soul's fall in the world, how the soul creates karma by choosing evil over good, and how these choices arise due to the envious nature of the soul. The simultaneous existence of good and evil entails that classical logic is inadequate to understand the Absolute Truth, but when they are combined in the Lord, they enhance the sweetness of His nature, which is then relished by the Lord's devotees.

Section 1: This section discusses the nature of the soul, why the soul falls into the material world, how the responsibility of the fall rests on the soul (rather than the Lord), and yet despite this fall, the soul's original purpose of serving the Lord is never lost even when the soul is fallen. The connection between the soul and the Lord comes up yet again. Especially important is the fact that the soul is a part of the Lord, however, when the soul falls into matter, the Lord is not considered fallen. Although the soul falls due to his own desires, he might often attribute the fall to the Lord's will (in what is called the problem of 'evil'). The section discusses how evil is also created by the Lord, but evil is not prescribed by the Lord. Therefore, the responsibility of choosing the evil rests with the soul. Finally, the section discusses how evil exists in the Lord, but it makes the goodness of the Lord sweeter. Thus, lying, stealing, and deception are part of the Absolute Truth, but they enhance the Lord's goodness.

Section 2: This section discusses the nature of dharma or duties and how the neglect of duties produces karma. As one goes through different stages of good and bad karma, the section advises one to remain detached from the results of previous actions and continue performing one's duties. The fall of the soul is again discussed and attributed to the enviousness in the soul against the greatness of the Lord, and his attempt to try to become just like the Lord. How the negation of the Lord leads to conflicts and competition in society is discussed. These conflicts lead to suffering and make society unstable. However, when the Lord's supremacy is recognized, then competition is replaced by cooperation, and society becomes stable again. This leads to the understanding that the soul falls into the material world due to its selfishness of prioritizing himself and seeking his interest over the collective happiness of all beings.

Section 3: This section discusses how the understanding of the Absolute Truth violates the conditions of classical logic such as non-contradiction and mutual exclusion. For example, things are supposed to be either hot or cold, but the Absolute Truth must contain both these alternatives simultaneously as the source of these contrarian opposites. Similarly, because the Absolute Truth contains the opposites, therefore, the principle of mutual exclusion cannot be applied to Him. However, the violation of these logical principles doesn't entail the impossibility of understanding the Absolute Truth because these opposites manifest one by one, or if they are manifest at once, then one of these qualities remains dominant while the other qualities are subordinated. The section then discusses several ways in which a person can become qualified for spiritual emancipation. Finally, the section discusses many ways in which a person becomes disqualified for spiritual emancipation—e.g., by neglecting the basic rules of living associated with the body. Many forms of deceptive religious activities are discussed and rejected as being unfavorable to transcendence.

Section 4: This section discusses how the practices of jñāna-yoga and aṣṭāṅga-yoga can be employed in conjunction with bhakti-yoga, although without devotion these methods do not lead to liberation. An extensive discussion about the nature of matter and how it is controlled by prāṇa follows, which then leads to the discussion of how demigods deliver the consequences of actions, or karma. While the worship of demigods was previously rejected—as the means for obtaining better results for enjoyment—the worship of demigods that improves a person's ability to perform their duties or dharma is recommended. Thus, the power of demigods as the providers of good and bad results is distinguished from the power that makes a person more capable of handling the situations being produced due to the good and bad results. While the former disqualifies a person for transcendence, the latter becomes an assistance.

SECTION 1

Topic 1

QUESTION

In many smriti the Lord is known as the Supreme Person, and His Śakti is subordinate to Him. If we now say that the Śakti is inseparable from Him (although not identical to Him) don't we create a contradiction with the claim that the Lord is supreme and His Śakti is subordinate to the Supreme Person?

In most Vaiṣṇava and Shaiva scriptures, Lord Viṣṇu or Lord Śiva are described as the Supreme Person (of the spiritual and material worlds).

2.1.1 (135)

स्मृत्यनवकाशदोषप्रसङ्ग इति चेत् न अन्यस्मृत्यनवकाशदोषप्रसङ्गात्

smṛtyanavakāśadoṣaprasaṅga iti cet na
anyasmṛtyanavakāśadoṣaprasaṅgāt

smṛti-anavakāśa-doṣaprasaṅgaḥ—the defect of having no scope for (some) smṛti; iti cet—if it be said; na—no; anyasmṛti-anavakāśa-doṣaprasaṅgāt—from the defect of leaving no scope for other smritis.

TRANSLATION

If it be said that (by calling the Lord and His energy inseparable) there would be a defect of leaving no scope for some smṛti (which describe the masculine as the supreme), we say no, (on the contrary, the rejection of this separation will) create the defect of leaving no scope for other smṛti (which describe the masculine and feminine as two aspects of the same Absolute Truth).

COMMENTARY

Apart from the Vaiṣṇava and Shaiva scriptures, there are also scriptures on the supremacy of the Śakti. Together, these three constitute the three main types of personalism—Vaishnavism, Shaivism, and Shaktism. Therefore, the masculine forms of the Lord are accepted alongside the feminine forms as being supreme. Furthermore, even in Vaiṣṇava scriptures, the names of the Lord are almost always preceded using Śri which indicates His energy. Thus, Vaishnavism doesn't speak about Lord Viṣṇu alone. He is rather referenced as Sri Viṣṇu. The different descriptions are differences of emphasis. As noted earlier, the feminine is supreme because She agitates the masculine to enjoy. And the masculine is supreme because He uses the feminine to enjoy. The feminine is the cause of desire in the masculine, and the masculine is the cause of activity in the feminine. Due to this mutual causality, both masculine and feminine are controllers of the other, and in different contexts they are said to be supreme. There is no discrepancy in these descriptions if the context is understood.

QUESTION

Isn't the doctrine of a single universal Brahman better than the doctrine of that Absolute Truth comprising of a masculine and a feminine aspect?

The doctrine of two distinct but inseparable aspects of the Absolute Truth is certainly more complex than the one that posits an undivided Brahman. This separation but inseparability is hard to understand although we can see that there is a distinction between the will and the power of fulfilling the will. Could there not be a third doctrine that makes this conclusion simpler? On the other hand, if there isn't a third doctrine, doesn't the doctrine of Oneness seem to be superior to the doctrine where that Oneness has two distinct aspects?

2.1.2 (136)

इतरेषां चानुपलब्धेः

itareṣāṃ cānupalabdheḥ

itareṣāṃ—of the others; ca—also; anupalabdheḥ—non-perception.

TRANSLATION

Anything else also cannot be known, perceived, or is non-existent.

COMMENTARY

The use of *itareṣāṃ* can be understood either as referring to the Oneness of the Brahman, or some third doctrine (which hasn't been mentioned). If it refers to a third doctrine, then *anupalabdheḥ* would simply indicate that no such thing has been mentioned in the scriptures, or that it is never known, etc. If, however, *itareṣāṃ* refers to the Oneness, then *anupalabdheḥ* would indicate that this Oneness cannot be known or perceived. We have explained the reason for this before—the masculine is the potential for desire, and the feminine is the potential for activity. When they are united, there is the potential for desire but there is no desire. Similarly, there is potential for activity but there is no activity. Without desire and activity, the Oneness must remain unknowable. Even self-knowledge involves the union of the desire to know the self and the power by which the self can be known. The Self acting on the Self produces this self-knowledge and it activates both the desire and the power simultaneously. If these are not activated, the Oneness exists as an unknowable possibility.

Topic 2

QUESTION

But haven't we spoken about yoga as the union between the jīvā and the Lord, indicating that they are somehow combined or unified. In the same way, can we not say that the masculine and the feminine are united into Oneness?

2.1.3 (137)

एतेन योगःपरत्युक्तः

etena yogaḥ pratyuktaḥ

etena—by this; yogaḥ—yoga philosophy; pratyuktaḥ—is (also) refuted.

TRANSLATION

By this (claim of Oneness), the yoga philosophy is also refuted.

COMMENTARY

The impersonal philosophers claim that yoga is the union of the ātmā and Paramātma. The assumption in this claim is that the jīvā has its own power and capacity to know, and when it knows itself, then the distinction between the self and the other is understood as being illusory, and the individuality of the ātmā is thereby lost. One now realizes that he is identical to Paramātma.

But what if the jīvā has the will to know but no power to know? And the distinction between will and power itself entails that even if one knows oneself, it is only with the power that is coming from somewhere else? When the power of knowledge belongs to the Lord, then the correct use of that power is knowing the Lord. When the jīvā is absorbed in the consciousness of the Lord, then it loses even self-consciousness, just like a person absorbed in the perception of an attractive external object loses the sense of one's present condition. It is not to say that the individual merges into the object of perception; it is only to say that one's awareness is directed from self-interest to the nature of the observed object. If the Lord is that object of observation, and He remains aware of Himself, while the soul becomes absorbed in the awareness of the Lord, then their awareness is united—they are both perceiving the same thing. There can be an identity of awareness and purpose, without the identity of the individuals. If two people have the same beliefs, knowledge, purpose, and thoughts, then their experiences are identical, but they are not identical. The meaning of yoga is using the Lord's power to understand the Lord. The power acts under the will, and if the will is directed toward the Lord, then it is identical to the Lord's will.

Yoga involves experience. It is not the cessation of all experience. The jīvā only has the power to know itself, but this self is one of the numerous selves. As a result, the self-knowledge of the jīvā is also incomplete knowledge, because in knowing oneself, the jīvā only knows a small fraction of everything that exists. However, if the jīvā seeks the purpose of its existence, and connects this purpose to the Lord, then by this union, the diversity is connected to that unity, without dissolving the diversity into the unity. The impersonalist argues that the soul is a drop of ocean, and it should merge back into the ocean, without explaining how the drop of the ocean came out of the ocean in the first place. The cause of the soul's separateness is the desire in the Lord to enjoy. So, when the soul wants to merge into the Lord, his desire is opposed to the Lord's desire, and it defeats the reason why they were separated for seeking pleasure.

Topic 3

QUESTION

But haven't you said that the Lord is transcendent to material nature, which implies that there is a difference between the Lord and material nature? Doesn't that seem contrary to the claim that the Lord and His power are inseparable? How does this inseparability compare to the Lord being different from material nature? How will we reconcile these two seemingly contradictory claims?

2.1.4 (138)

न वलिक्षणत्वादस्य तथात्वं च शब्दात्

na vilakṣaṇatvādasya tathātvaṃ ca śabdāt

na—not; vilakṣaṇatvāt—from contrary nature; asya—of this (world); tathā—in the same way; tvam—you (the soul); ca—also; śab-dāt—it is said.

TRANSLATION

(The Lord) is not from the contrary nature of this world; in the same way, you are also (not of a contrary nature to the Lord); so it is stated.

COMMENTARY

The transcendence of the Lord doesn't entail the separateness of the Lord from material nature. The meaning of transcendence is that the Lord is never bound by the laws of material nature—i.e., action and consequence—which cause repeated birth and death. Since the soul is bound by these laws, to motivate his liberation it is said that the soul is transcendent to matter. Most people take this to mean that the soul must get out of the material body, and therefore death must be the precondition to liberation. However, that view of transcendence would also mean that a liberated person cannot exist in the material world, or if the Lord appeared in this world, then He would also be bound by the laws of choice and consequence. The notion of transcendence where one must get out of the material world to be liberated from the laws of matter is false.

Within the material world, there are two kinds of causality—material causality and efficient causality—and both have separate laws. A law of material causality is that salt can be dissolved in water. A law of efficient causality is whether I will be dissolving salt into water. The laws of material causation can remain true, but they may not apply to us. Thus, salt will still dissolve into water, but I may not be the one dissolving salt into water. In simple terms, my choices are not forced by my previous actions. When the Lord appears in the material world, the laws of material causation remain true, but the laws of efficient causation are not. Similarly, the soul can also exist in the material world, and not be affected by the laws of choice and consequence. Thus, the separation of the soul and the Lord is not necessary to say that they are transcendent.

This distinction between the Lord and the soul arises because the soul is acting contrary to the Lord's will, while material energy is still acting according to the Lord's will. Therefore, there is a perfect union between the Lord and material nature. However, because the soul's will is contrary to the Lord's will, therefore, the soul is contrary to material nature as well. Material nature is still serving the Lord, but the soul is trying to satisfy itself. The Lord has allowed the soul to satisfy itself, within the constraints of previously created karma. If the soul's will is identical to the Lord's will, then karma is never produced. And without karma, the soul is never impeded by the laws of efficient causality. Thus, the terms 'bondage' and 'liberation' are applied to the soul when the soul is disobedient to the Lord's desires. The Lord is never bound in this way. Ultimately, both the soul and the Lord are transcendent to matter, but they don't need to be separated from matter to demonstrate their transcendence.

QUESTION

If material nature is working according to the will of the Lord, why isn't it obvious to the soul? Why does the soul consider itself the doer? For example, when I eat food, I believe that I am the cause of my eating; I do not consider the Lord to be the cause of my eating. Therefore, in all such practical ways, the Lord's actions are hidden from the soul. Why should they be so hidden?

2.1.5 (139)
अभिमानिवि्यपदेशस्तु वशिेषानुगतभि्याम्
abhimānivyapadeśastu viśeṣānugatibhyām

abhimānivyapadeśaḥ—due to the covering of arrogance or pride; tu—but; viśeṣa—the property; anugatibhyām—being an obedient follower.

TRANSLATION

Because of the covering of pride or arrogance, (the soul) gets the property of being a follower (of material nature, i.e., comes under its full control).

COMMENTARY

In Bhagavad-Gita 3.27, Lord Kṛṣṇa states the following:

prakṛteḥ kriyamāṇāni
guṇaiḥ karmāṇi sarvaśaḥ
ahaṅkāra-vimūḍhātmā
kartāham iti manyate

The spirit soul bewildered by the false ego thinks himself the doer (of its actions) when (in fact) these actions are enacted by prakriti (or material nature) due to the collective guna and karma.

The term *ahaṅkāra* used in the above verse and the term *abhimāna* used in this sūtra indicate the same thing—the false pride of "I am the doer".

The Bhagavad-Gita, however, goes a step further in calling this causation the result of collective guna and karma. Let's consider the example of a buyer purchasing some fruits from a vendor. The buyer has the desire or guna to eat fruits, so this desire to eat fruits is the cause of the purchase. Likewise, the vendor also has a desire or guna to sell fruits, so the vendor's desire is also a cause. Then, the buyer has some money due to their karma, so this karma is also a cause. Finally, the vendor has some karma due to which he has acquired fruits to sell, so his karma is also a cause. Thus, two pairs of guna and karma are involved in each transaction. Sometimes, a buyer may be forced to buy against his wishes, and a vendor may be forced to sell against his wishes. But what is force? Each person will do unpleasant things to avoid a greater unpleasantness. That preference for one unpleasantness over another is guna. Thus, even if it seems that we are doing something against our desire, there is desire which is causing it. Hence, there is no action without a pair of guna and karma.

This is a simple example, but it quickly gets very complicated if we realize that the fruit seller exists only because there is a large market of buyers of fruits. And this market exists because there is a choice of many types of fruits, so there must be many sellers. In short, the guna and karma of the souls are fulfilled collectively by creating a market of buyers and sellers. Their guna and karma are their individual material qualities, but their fulfillment is collective.

The prakriti or material nature is described here as the cause of this collective fulfillment. It is not the causality of modern science in which one particle pushes another without any desiring or deserving. But, the introduction of desiring and deserving can lead to a misunderstanding that because I am desiring, therefore, I am the cause of my actions. This notion of "I am the doer" is rejected here. The desires in us are automatically produced by the guna. We don't have control over the production of these desires, but we can reject these automatically created desires. When we reject them, the desires cease to exist, and in that case, we can say that we prevented something from happening. But we can still not say that we were the cause or the doer of anything. The prakriti is still the cause of when things happen, but we can refuse to take part in them. By that refusal we retain our free will, but we are not the doer of the actions.

The desires are different from the soul, but all desires produce the experience of absence—desire means that someone is missing something. That someone can be me, or it may not be me. When the soul rejects these desires, he says—I am not missing this, so it cannot be my desire. On the other hand, when the soul accepts these desires, then he agrees—I am indeed missing this. Thus, the desire is a negative identity of the soul: It represents what I am not.

When this negative identity is created, it must be compensated by a positive identity. That positive identity is called 'pride' or *ahaṅkāra*. If we lose our pride, then we also lose our desire. For example, if a woman insults a man, then he will stop desiring her. This is not because the desire is gone, but because the desire is a negative identity, and it cannot exist without a positive identity. When a person undergoes depression or anxiety, their pride is undermined, and since the positive material identity ceases to exist, therefore, desires also disappear. Whatever seemed pleasing previously seems tasteless now. However, depression and anxiety are not due to freedom from desires. They are rather situations in which a person's pride, ego, or self-respect is destroyed.

Ahaṅkāra is necessary for any desire to exist, and it exists even for the devotee. The devotee feels great pride in being the servant of the Lord. Due to this pride, he accepts all the desires to serve the Lord. And then he also thinks—I am the servant of the Lord, and I am serving the Lord, and he feels happy due to this pride. Factually, even while serving the Lord, the soul is not the cause of his actions. Those actions are still carried out by the Lord's Śakti. However, since *ahaṅkāra* must exist for desire to exist, therefore, even the devotee must have an *ahaṅkāra* or pride. It is just that the nature of pride is different.

This sūtra uses the term *anugatibhyām*, which means being the obedient servant or follower. When the pride is in one's being a master, then the soul becomes a servant of the material nature. But when the pride is in being the servant of the Lord, then the soul not only fulfills the desire of being a servant but out of this servitude to the Lord, it often acts as the Lord's master. Thus, if one pursues the pride of mastery, then the desires are frustrated. But if one pursues the pride of servitude, then both mastery and servitude are fulfilled.

QUESTION

Many people say that this material world is a dream. Just like in a bad dream we might feel that we have been imprisoned by some

enemies and we are being tortured, and we might suffer, but factually we haven't been imprisoned. In the same way, the soul is not truly bound by the material world.

In the previous sūtra, it was said that the idea that the soul is the doer of all the actions is an illusion because these actions are carried out by the material nature. The skeptics like to take this idea further and claim that if the idea that I'm a doer is an illusion, then the entire experience must be an illusion.

2.1.6 (140)

दृश्यते तु

dṛśyate tu

dṛśyate—is seen; tu—but.

TRANSLATION

(Even if you call it a dream) it is still experienced.

COMMENTARY

This sūtra doesn't confirm or deny whether the world is an illusion. It just says—even if you think it is an illusion, you are still experiencing it. So, you are suffering and enjoying in a way that is beyond your control. You cannot deny that you are suffering or enjoying, because even in a dream you suffer and enjoy. And because you are suffering, you cannot claim that you are in control (because you do not want to suffer). So, if your suffering is out of your control, then how can you say that I'm the cause of my pleasure? Wouldn't it be more appropriate to say that both pleasure and suffering are out of my control?

It is a commonly seen fact that when people enjoy their lives, or are successful, then they claim to be the doers. Only when they start suffering, fail in their lives, or lose control over what they can and cannot do, then they claim that the world must be an illusion. So, this is a sour grapes mentality: If I cannot get what I want, then it must be that even getting something is illusory. However, these claims about illusion or not don't change anything in the real world, because you keep suffering, and it remains out of your control. Calling something illusory only works if you can get out of the illusion. So, if this world were an illusion, then why can't the person calling it an illusion wake up? Why can't he just put an end to his suffering by realizing that everything is an illusion? Since this is practically undoable, these claims are armchair philosophizing.

QUESTION

But the point of calling it a dream is to then say that it is self-created, and the suffering is self-inflicted. Just like a spider might emanate a web from itself, and then feel that it is caught inside that web. In the same way, the world we see is a projection from within, like the web of a spider. So, then we can say that the material world is not dragging us like a menial servant. Rather, we have created the web of hallucinations in which we have now become caught.

2.1.7 (141)
असदतिति चेत् न परतषिधमात्रत्वात्
asaditi cet na pratiṣedhamātratvāt

asat—non-existent; iti cet—if it be said; na—no; pratiṣedhamātrat-vāt—from it being merely a restraint.

TRANSLATION

If it is said that (the world) doesn't exist (as it is self-created), (we say) no; (after all, even in the example of a spider), there is restraint (e.g., the web).

COMMENTARY

The main problem in calling the world a dream or hallucination is still the same as when it is considered real: Why isn't this dream or hallucination perfect and pleasing? If we are creating our dream or hallucination, then we must have created it perfectly, such that we were always enjoying this dream, rather than suffering in it. Why would we create a dream and suffer because of it? Since we don't want to suffer, but we are forced to suffer, we cannot claim that we are creating this suffering; if it acts against our will, then it is not caused by us.

The term *pratiṣedha* has many meanings. It can mean a restriction that is preventing us to attain our goals. It can mean something that is forbidden (due to laws or regulations). Basically, *siddhi* means attainment, and if *prati* precedes *siddhi* then it is something that prevents that attainment. Everyone wants to attain enjoyment and pleasure; so, this pleasure is the goal that we would like to attain. But the material world is preventing this attainment. So, there is no point in the semantics of whether the world is cognitively an illusion, and whether it is created by the self. These cognitive positions about the reality of the world don't change the fact that we want to enjoy, and we are suffering.

QUESTION

I don't deny that we are suffering, or that it is against or will. However, if the world is produced as the web of a spider from the spider itself, then the spider can potentially withdraw the web and then become free of the web.

2.1.8 (142)
अपीतौ तद्वत्प्रसङ्गादसमञ्जसम्
apītau tadvatprasaṅgādasamañjasam

apītau—by deflating or absorbing; tadvat—like that (it was previously created); prasaṅgāt—the episodic world of events; asamañjasam—creates a doubt.

TRANSLATION

(The claim that we can become free of the world) by deflating or absorbing the episodic world of events just like (it was previously created) creates a doubt (about why it was produced to cause the soul's suffering in the first place).

COMMENTARY

Just as the seeker is persisting on the argument that the world is an illusion or hallucination produced by the soul, the author of the Vedānta Sūtra is also persisting on his original argument that you cannot claim yourself to be the creator of the world if you are caught in the web and suffering because of it. In this sūtra, the specific claim that if we call this world a self-created illusion, then we can also withdraw it ourselves, begs the question of why this illusion was created in the first place. Why would anyone tie themselves into ropes? Moreover, why would anyone make this argument and not merely withdraw the web of illusions? After all, if the world is an illusion, then the argument about the world being an illusion must also be an illusion. Why perpetuate the illusion by making such arguments if you can simply withdraw the illusion? Arguments about illusion must end in the claimant shutting up permanently.

QUESTION

We can say that this emanation of the world from ourselves was a mistake. We did not know that we will be caught in the web created by ourselves, and by mistake we created it. Now we want to correct this mistake by withdrawing it back. Can we not be prone to mistakes and then aspire to correct them?

2.1.9 (143)

न तु दृष्टान्तभावात्

na tu dṛṣṭāntabhāvāt

na—not; tu—but; dṛṣṭānta-bhāvāt—the feelings caused by the events.

TRANSLATION

But you cannot (explain) the feelings caused by the events.

COMMENTARY

The argument about a person making a mistake rests on their ignorance about the nature of reality. A child can play with fire, and then say that he did not know that the fire will burn him and that ignorance about the nature of the fire caused the burn. However, this argument is acceptable only if the child isn't the creator of the fire. If the child created the fire out of himself, then he must have known what it can do. Whatever exists in the effect, must exist in the cause. So, the fact that the fire will burn the child would have existed as the intention to self-burn, if the child is the self-creator of the fire that burns him. So, the argument from ignorance or mistake cannot be applied if we also keep calling the world our self-creation. If we create something, we know its nature, and we also know how to control it. We cannot claim to create a monster out of ourselves and then say that we did not know that it would be a monster that swallows the creator. The act of self-creation entails a full understanding of the action.

The term *bhāvāt* has many potential meanings. It can mean 'existence', in which case the purport of this sūtra would be that "you cannot explain the fact that the existence of events (which cause your suffering) is based on a mistake when you are the creator of the world". It can also mean 'nature', in which case, the purport of this sūtra would be that "you cannot explain the nature of the events of this world (i.e., that they cause suffering) based on a mistake when you are the creator of the world". Finally, it can also mean 'feelings' or 'emotions' such as pain and suffering, which would make the same meaning even more direct, and there would be no need to import the notion of suffering from the previous sūtra. Owing to this directness, I have preferred this translation.

QUESTION

But in many religions of this world, the fall of the soul into the material world is attributed to his own mistake. For example, Adam and Eve fall from heaven because of a mistake, and if they correct the mistake then they can return to heaven. Isn't this path of self-correction open in your viewpoint?

2.1.10 (144)

सॢवपक्ॢषदोषाच्ॢच

svapakṣadoṣācca

svapakṣa-doṣāt—due to faults in one's view; ca—also.

TRANSLATION

(The fall into material world is) also due to faults in one's view.

COMMENTARY

The existence of the fault in the soul is not denied; in fact, this sūtra accepts that the fall is due to the faults in the soul. However, the use of *ca* indicates that this is not the only cause. In particular, the soul cannot say that he made a mistake, and due to that mistake, he created a world out of himself, in which he was then caught, and now wants to be liberated. The mistake entails that the soul is not the creator or the controller of the world, nor does he have full knowledge of the world. He thought that he could enjoy in the world, and his mistake arose out of a misunderstanding of the true nature of the world.

If the soul is not the creator, then the world must be created by someone else—i.e., the Lord. So, its existence cannot be called a hallucination or imagination. Such a world must truly exist objectively, and hence the events of the world must be objective, and the suffering caused by them must be real too. So, by saying that the fault in the soul is *also* the cause, it is implied that it is only one of the causes; the Lord is the other cause of the creation; in fact, He is the creator and the controller, and therefore fully knows the nature of the material world. He may advise—as in some religions—to avoid committing the mistakes that can lead to a fall. But if the soul ignores this advice, then the world is not created by this neglect; only the fall into the world is due to this neglect.

QUESTION

If you are accepting that the soul has fallen due to a mistake of his own, then how did this mistake arise? If we say that the mistake is always innate, then the soul cannot get liberated. If on the other hand, we say that the mistake was caused by an external source, then why should the soul suffer for it?

If one says that the evil is in the soul, and he falls due to his own mistake, and God is only fulfilling the wishes of the soul, then we are led to the question: If the evil is in the soul, and the soul is eternal, then evil must also be eternal. If the soul is eternally evil, then how can he get liberated from this world?

2.1.11 (145)

तर्कापरतषि्ठानादपि; अन्यथानुमेयमिति चेत् एवमप्यनिर्मोक्षपरसङ्गः

**tarkāpratiṣṭhānādapi; anyathānumeyamiti cet
evamapyanirmokṣaprasaṅgaḥ**

tarka-pratiṣṭhānāt—by reasoning we cannot establish; api—also;

anyathā—otherwise; anumeyam—should be inferred; iti cet—if it be said; evam—so; api—even; anirmokṣa-prasaṅgaḥ—there will be outcome of no liberation.

TRANSLATION

If it be said that we should be able to infer (the cause of fall down) otherwise we also (cannot practice the process of liberation) (we say that) by reasoning we cannot establish (the cause for the fall down), and even (if we tried to do) so, that will not lead us to liberation (from material existence).

COMMENTARY

It has been stated in the previous sūtra that the fault lies in the soul, although the soul alone isn't the cause of material experience. The desire of fall is attributed to the soul, but the facilitation and fulfillment of this desire is due to the Lord and His Śakti. And yet, none of these causes are permanent. If the fall was due to God, then why will God try to liberate the soul after the fall? Similarly, if the soul was inherently and eternally evil, then its liberation would be impossible. Thus, after placing the responsibility of the fall with the soul, the sūtra states that the origin of the fall cannot be traced, and moreover, such questions do not lead to liberation. The focus should be on liberation rather than figuring out what might have led to the fall. By trying to guess the cause of the fall we will never come to any conclusion, and the time that could be spent in the process of liberation would be wasted in a meaningless investigation. In short, there should be no attempt to rationalize or justify or explain the fall.

Topic 4

QUESTION

Some people say that the evil stands apart from God, almost on an equal footing as God, and has the power to delude the soul. This evil is sometimes called Satan. So, God and Satan are pulling the soul in different directions.

2.1.12 (146)

एतेन शष्टिटापरग्रिहा अपि व्याख्याताः

etena śiṣṭāparigrahā api vyākhyātāḥ

etena—by this (i.e., holding the soul responsible for his fall); śiṣṭāparigrahāḥ—not accepted by the wise; api—also; vyākhyātāḥ—are explained.

TRANSLATION

In this way (i.e., holding the soul responsible for his fall) (other ideas which are) not accepted by the wise are also explained.

COMMENTARY

In some religions, such as Christianity, the problem of fall is partially attributed to the existence of Satan, who deludes the soul. Satan is considered a fallen angel and can never be liberated from this evil. However, the soul can be liberated if he becomes obedient to God. By postulating the existence of Satan, the problem of evil is confined into *one* individual: The evil exists in Satan, and by that, it can spread to others, but others are not inherently evil; they are rather tempted and deluded by Satan. But that again begs the question: If Satan is deluding the soul, then why is the soul suffering rather than Satan who deluded the soul? Why is God punishing the soul instead of Satan? Moreover, if Satan is a fallen angel, then how did he fall, and why can't he ever be liberated?

This sūtra states that such ideas—which attribute a fall to someone other than the soul, in trying to partially reduce the soul's responsibility—are not accepted by the wise. However, if one insists that the soul can get deluded by the influence of others, they too are fallen in the same way as the other souls. There is no eternally fallen agent like Satan who causes the fall because that doesn't minimize the soul's responsibility of being tempted by Satan. On the other hand, the postulates of a fallen soul who can never be liberated are not accepted by the wise. Liberation is open to everyone if only they are interested in it.

Topic 5

QUESTION

You have previously said that even if the soul enters the world, he doesn't lose the connection to the Lord. So, it is sometimes said that the soul is never truly separated from the Lord and hence should not be considered 'fallen' into the world. This fall is only the experience of enjoyment or suffering of this world when the consciousness of the soul is directed toward the world.

2.1.13 (147)
भोक्त्रापत्तेरविभागश्चेत् स्याल्लोकवत्
bhoktrāpatteravibhāgaścet syāllokavat

bhoktrāpatteḥ—the fault of being the enjoyer; avibhāgaḥ—non-distinction; cet—if it be said; syāt—possible; lokavat—just like in this world.

TRANSLATION

If it is said that the fault of being the enjoyer is non-distinction (from the Lord—as He is also enjoying), (we say), that is possible as in this world.

COMMENTARY

There are two prominent theories of causation—local and non-local. The local theory of causation states that two objects must be in close proximity to each other in order for an object to affect another object. A classic example of such causation is the collision of two billiard balls, in which the balls must contact each other before either ball pushes or is pushed. In the non-local theory of causation, two objects can be far apart and yet can exert an influence on each other; a classic example of such causation is the idea of a gravitational force.

In the same vein, one can say that the soul is 'fallen' into the material world and has therefore contacted it like a billiard ball contacting another such ball. We can also say that the soul is not physically 'fallen' into the world but is remotely connected to the world just as in the case of gravitational force.

In the previous sūtra, we have said that the soul is connected to the Lord through prāṇa. We also said that the soul connects to the material world through prāṇa. When the soul moves to a different body, the prāṇa 'carries' the soul to that body, thereby establishing a connection to a new body. We also described that when the Lord glances over the material energy to inject the soul, the glance is like the senses moving outward to perceive an object, but the senses don't get disconnected to the Lord through such a glance. Therefore, the soul is always connected to the Lord even in this material world. Only the consciousness of the soul is directed toward the material world, just as in the case of remote causation, in which an object contacts another object remotely.

But should we say that this turning of consciousness away from the Lord into the material energy is not a 'fall'? Factually, both positions can be argued for. Because the soul turns his consciousness away from the Lord into the material energy, he can be called 'fallen'. And because the soul hasn't lost the connection to the Lord, therefore, he can be called 'not fallen'. If we understand how the soul is connected to both the Lord and the material energy simultaneously, either the connection to the material energy can be used to call it a 'fall', or the connection to the Lord can be employed to call it 'not a fall'. It doesn't change the fact that the soul is entangled in the laws of material nature, even though the soul is transcendent to material nature. This entanglement is essentially the consciousness of the soul evolving from one experience to another.

Therefore, this sūtra uses the term *syat* or possibility of saying that the soul is not fallen, even though it has been clearly stated earlier that the soul is entangled in the material world. Depending on whether the connection to the material world or the Lord is emphasized, either position can be argued for.

Topic 6

QUESTION

If the soul is always connected to the Lord, then why is the fall of the soul into the material world not considered the fall of the Lord? Shouldn't we say that a part of the Lord has fallen therefore the Lord must also be fallen?

2.1.14 (148)

तदनन्यत्वमारम्भणशब्दादिभ्यः

tadananyatvamārambhaṇaśabdādibhyaḥ

tad—its (the soul's); ananyatvam—non-difference; ārambhaṇa—origin or beginning; śabdādibhyaḥ—just like the origination of words.

TRANSLATION

The non-difference of the soul (from the Lord is asserted) due to origination or beginning, just like the words (are spoken by a speaker).

COMMENTARY

The material world has previously been called the Lord's 'expression' and compared to speech. In this sūtra, the soul is also compared to the Lord's speech. The speech is separate from the speaker, and yet, it is always connected to the speaker because the speaker is the cause, origin, or beginning of speech. We have earlier spoken of the triad of *manas-prāṇa-vāk*, in which *manas* is the meaning, *vāk* is the speech, and *prāṇa* is the connection between the two. Very simply, the meaning resides in the speaker, and through prāṇa, it is expressed as speech. Once the speech has been expressed, the spoken words can be twisted or interpreted in many ways. But these twisted meanings are not the real explanation of why the speaker spoke those words. To understand the meaning, we must reference the speaker's intentions because those intentions were the cause of the speech. In the same way, the soul is an expression of the Lord, and the Lord created that expression for a certain purpose or intention. However, once the expression was created, it is open to misinterpretation. When such misinterpretations are applied, then because of the difference between the intended meaning and the interpreted meaning, the soul and the Lord become separate. However, despite such misinterpretation, the origin of the speech is still the Lord, so the speech must always be attributed to Him.

In short, the disconnection between the soul and the Lord is due to the disparity in the intended and interpreted meanings. The Lord intended the soul for a certain purpose, but the soul interpreted its existence differently. As the speaker of the word, the Lord is still connected to the word. But because the meaning has been altered, the Lord has become disconnected from the soul. Therefore, the fall of the soul must not be attributed to the Lord; this fall is like the misinterpretation of the meaning of the word, and its variance from the intended meaning is due to the soul's free will, not the Lord's intention.

QUESTION

When the words are separated from the speaker, can we ever truly know the meaning that the speaker intended? On the other hand, if the meaning is never available after the words are separated, then how can one know what the meaning was, or should be, since the words have already been separated?

2.1.15 (149)
भावे चोपलब्धेः
bhāve copalabdheḥ

bhāve—in the intentions, meanings, purpose, or desires; ca—also; upalabdheḥ—are available, present, experienceable, or obtainable.

TRANSLATION

(The meaning is) also perceivable in the intentions (of the words).

COMMENTARY

When we hear a sentence, our ears only process the sounds of the words. But the mind is capable of understanding three kinds of meanings—(1) the dictionary meanings and grammatical structures, (2) the nature of the context in which these words are spoken, and (3) the intention of speaking based on the understanding of the speaker. The sounds are universal—i.e., the same for everyone. The dictionary meanings and grammar structures are native to the speakers of a certain language. The context of speaking is further limited to a few people who might have been in that situation. And the intention or personality of the speaker is unique to that speaker. Thus, to understand meanings, we go from the universal, to the social-cultural, to the contextual, and finally to the individual. Each such transition is not easy, but such transitions are possible. The bigger question is: are these transitions simply our interpretations? This sūtra refutes this claim. It says that the meaning is present in the words.

We have discussed this idea before while considering the three modalities of nature. When we see an individual cow, which is a symbol of the idea of cow, the idea cow is present in the individual cow. Likewise, the words are expressions of the meanings, and meanings are present within them. All these arguments are being made to establish a simple idea—that the soul is a symbol, this symbol can be interpreted, but the symbol also has an innate meaning.

The expression of meaning begins with an intention, which is then used to produce a structure, which is then populated by individual words. This three-tier model of meaning expression can be seen in the process of making a chair. The chair's designer begins with the intention to make a chair; the intention leads to a design; and finally, the design is converted into an object using pieces of wood. We can see the pieces of wood. If we move our attention away from the individual pieces and look at the collection of these pieces, we can also see the structure or interrelations between the parts. However, we don't conclude that something is a chair unless we believe that it was meant to be a chair.

Materialists abhor the idea of design in nature. They claim that given enough time, even a monkey hitting the keys of a typewriter can produce the complete works of Shakespeare. And the debate then shifts to asking how fast the monkey is typing, and how long has the monkey been typing. There are no clear answers to this problem because the rate of typing can change with time, and the duration for which the monkey has been typing is only knowable when something meaningful starts to come out of that typing. Materialists neglect the fact that for something to be called living, it must be able to perceive and understand its environment, and that involves representing the outside world within. That representation entails that some molecules within a living entity are symbols of the external world. If *some* molecules could be symbols, why not all molecules? In short, why would some nature be meaningful, and the rest of nature be meaningless? There is no other way to explain this problem unless we say that all nature is meaningful. And if there is meaning, then there must be purpose, because that meaning and purpose causes the expression.

Thus, material objects like books, art, music, scientific theories, legal documents, etc. have both a meaning and a purpose. Even tables and chairs are symbols of ideas. So, why should we not consider atoms and molecules to also be symbols of ideas? The atomic particles are phonemes, they are combined into complex sentences using grammatical structures, and this structure has an underlying intention. The world is not meaningless, and not purposeless.

This sūtra claims that the intended meaning exists in the spoken words objectively, not merely in the mind of the speaker. The mind is a 'sense', which is capable of producing and absorbing meanings; when the words are spoken, even the meanings are objectified along with the words. However, to understand these objective meanings, the minds of the speaker and the listener must be similar. If the speaker and the listener have very different minds, then the listener will not grasp the objectively present meaning. He will then try to *interpret* the words according to his own mind and arrive at a different meaning. So, the claim that once the words have become separated from the speaker then we cannot know the true intended meaning of the speaker is rejected here.

QUESTION

But why does the soul misinterpret the intended meaning? What is the cause of its turning away from the true meaning toward a false meaning?

2.1.16 (150)

सत्त्वाच्चापरस्य

sattvāccāparasya

sattvāt—from the truth; ca—also; aparasya—aversion, inferiority.

TRANSLATION

Also (the fall is) from the aversion to the truth.

COMMENTARY

It is not easy to live in the presence of greatness, because that greatness makes us feel inferior. The devotees of the Lord see the Lord's greatness and they feel protected by this greatness; they are naturally inclined to serve the Lord because He is so great. However, the soul can also develop a sense of inferiority looking at the greatness of the

Lord. We have discussed previously how every desire is accompanied by pride. The pride can be that I am a servant of the Lord, or it can be that I am myself the enjoyer. If there is pride in being the servant of the Lord, His greatness reinforces the devotee's pride. But if the pride in being the Lord's servant is lost, then the soul develops an aversion to the Lord due to his own sense of inferiority. When this aversion develops, then the soul reinterprets his existence, creating his own purpose as the pursuit of superiority. This false interpretation 'covers' the original meaning; the original meaning is hidden, and the false interpretation is accepted as the truth.

We can see many common occurrences of this type of phenomenon in the present day. When we contact a person far superior to us, there is a natural tendency in many people to challenge their superiority. Unable to accept that someone is better than us, we try to put them down, insult them, humiliate them, or point out their faults. We also try to demonstrate our superiority by arguments or achievements. This outward projection of our greatness is caused by an innate sense of inferiority. The greater the sense of inferiority and self-loathing in a person, the greater is the outward projection. Thus, people who feel innately inferior try to project their power, wealth, beauty, knowledge, etc. seeking the attention of others. The slightest of inconveniences in demonstration makes such a person angry and the feeling of self-loathing returns.

The true devotee of the Lord is free from the sense of inferiority. He takes pride in the fact that he is a servant of the Lord. But many spiritualists don't have this sense of pride in being a servant. They may be seeking salvation, but they don't like to call themselves the servants of the Lord. They rather use terms like 'spiritual but not religious' or a 'seeker' instead of calling themselves servants of the Lord. These are symptoms of an inferiority within the person, and an aversion to the Lord. So long as it exists, there can be no salvation.

QUESTION

Some philosophers say that a sentence doesn't have an objective meaning. Rather, the meaning must be derived from the context in which that sentence is being used. The same sentence used in a different context can, therefore, have a different meaning. In the same way, if the soul is like the speech of the Lord, then we cannot

say that it has an original intended purpose. Rather, we must say that this purpose changes from one context to another, just like the same words being used in different contexts have different intended meanings.

2.1.17 (151)

असद्व्यपदेशान्नेति चेत् न धर्मान्तरेण वाक्यशेषात्

asadvyapadeśānneti cet na dharmāntareṇa vākyaśeṣāt

asat-vyapadeśāt—due to covering by false (ideas, pride); na—not; iti cet—if it be said; na—no; dharmāntareṇa—by change in the person's duties; vākyaśeṣāt—(the original meaning) from the sentence that remains.

TRANSLATION

If it is said that (the fall of the soul is) not due to a false covering (of the original intention), (we say) no (because) by changing the contextual duties (the original meaning) of the sentence can be known from that which remains.

COMMENTARY

The intended purpose of a kitchen knife is to cut vegetables. However, the knife can also sometimes be used as a weapon. The use as a weapon doesn't undermine the fact that the knife was originally produced for cutting vegetables. In the same way, the original intended purpose of the soul is to serve the Lord. This service is always performed through a relationship with the Lord. But when the soul enters the material world, he also enters other temporary relationships such as father, mother, son, daughter, wife, husband, friend etc. in relation to other persons. In these relations he performs his duties quite like the knife may sometimes be used as a weapon. These duties are called dharma, but they are different from the sanātana-dharma or the eternal duty in relation to the Lord. This sūtra asserts that just because one's duties change (*dharmāntaran*) in this world, doesn't mean that the original duty ceases to exist.

Some philosophers of language claim that the words don't have intrinsic meaning because the same words could be used in different contexts to indicate different things. It is true that the words under-determine the meaning. But it has also been asserted that the words won't come into existence unless there was a meaning. So, even though the same word may be used in different contexts, in each such context there is also a different intended meaning. The contextual use of words doesn't take away the fact that the speaker intends to say something to a listener. The context rather determines what is appropriate or right and can be justified based on a person's roles and duties. So, the intentions underlying the words always exist, although some of these intentions may be wrong—e.g., meant to cheat or lie—and incompatible with one's duties.

Whether the speech is right or wrong is a separate question from what is being meant in that speech. Only when we can determine the meaning, can we decide whether it is right or wrong. So, by rejecting the existence of inherent meaning, and then using the context to decide what is being meant, we remove the possibility of determining whether the thing being said is right or wrong, whether it should have been said or not, and whether it was a person's duty to say such things or not. Instrumentalists have had such a view of language and they think that speech is meant to get a job done. Thus, speech may be used to command, instruct, cajole, insult, inquire, or answer, and that gets some work done. The meaning of the words is the work that gets done; this liberates the quest for meaning from the pursuit of intentions and reduces meaning to the observation of facts and changes that result from getting some work done. But what if someone disobeys the command or instruction, and does something contrary to what was intended? By the criterion of measuring the meaning by the effects it produces, we would say that the meaning was the effects. In short, we will lose the ability to judge whether the words were true or false, right or wrong, and good or bad. Words would become akin to billiard balls that push some objects to produce some effects, and just like the billiard ball carries no meaning but can produce some effects, similarly, words too will be judged by their effects. This would entail the collapse of meaning and judgment.

Therefore, the context should not be used to decipher the meaning. It should rather be used to determine whether the actions are right or wrong.

QUESTION

You are saying that the use of the same word in different ways in different contexts is an aberration? By the example of a kitchen knife being used for cutting vegetables, you are indicating that each thing has a unique intended purpose and, thus, any other type of usage must be regarded as an aberration?

2.1.18 (152)
युक्तेःशब्दान्तराच्च
yukteḥ śabdāntarācca

yukteḥ—to be used (plural, indicating many different uses); śabdāntarāt—from the differences in the words; ca—and.

TRANSLATION

Different words (should) also (be put to) different uses.

COMMENTARY

A chair can sometimes be used as a table, and at other times as a ladder. Yes, such a usage gets a job done, but we would typically use the chair as a table or a ladder only if we did not have the table or a ladder. If we had the ladder, we would *prefer* to use the ladder rather than a chair. Similarly, we might also use a chair as a ladder if we don't need a ladder frequently. If we needed to use a ladder more frequently, we will acquire a ladder because it is more suited for the job. Thus, an expert workman would have many types of tools in his toolbox ideally suited for different kinds of activities. An amateur, on the other hand, may try to get the same things done inefficiently with fewer tools. But if the amateur needs to do expert work, then he must procure the best tools.

This sūtra is therefore prescriptive—it is saying that ideally, you need to have different tools for different jobs. Each tool is meant for producing a different effect, and it should be employed for that purpose. While other tools may seem to also get the job done in many cases, they are inefficient for the purpose, and may also not get the job done perfectly. The implication is that each person is suited for a certain type of activity, and they should ideally be engaged in that type of work. They might be able to do other things imperfectly because they haven't been crafted for that purpose. Just like the chair will ideally work as a chair, but non-ideally can substitute an ideal ladder, in the same way, each soul has a unique purpose in relation to the Lord. When it is employed in other ways, it does the job imperfectly and can therefore never be satisfied.

QUESTION

But many philosophers say that all souls are identical to each other; they have the same capacity for cognition, emotion, and relation. They are compared to drops of water in an ocean of water. But you are saying that each soul is different—not only as an individual drop of water—but also that this drop must be put to a different use because it is ideally meant to be used so?

2.1.19 (153)

पटवच्च

paṭavacca

paṭavat—like cloth; ca—and.

TRANSLATION

(You can) also (think of the soul) as cloth.

COMMENTARY

Sometimes all it takes to change our understanding is the change in the analogy. If we think of the soul as a drop of water, then all the souls seem identical. But if we think of the soul as cloth, then we can also see that it can be crafted into different types of clothes—such as shirts, trousers, hats, socks, underwear, etc. As a cloth, all the souls are identical. But as different clothes they are different. So, we should not think of the different souls as mere pieces of cloth which can alternately be used as a shirt, trousers, underwear, etc. We should rather think that this piece of cloth has already been crafted into a specific type of garment and hence it is meant for a different kind of purpose. Yes, the shirt can sometimes be wrapped around the waist, and trouser can also be used to cover the chest. But these are not the ideal purposes of the shirt and the trouser. The shirt and the trousers have been created for different purposes.

We can, therefore, make a distinction between two kinds of individualities. The first individuality refers to a different identity—like a different drop of water. The second individuality refers to a different type of object—like a different kind of garment. In the previous sūtra, the first type of individuality has been indicated—namely, that the soul is an individual, and this individuality emerges because of the desire for enjoyment. In this sūtra, a further distinction is made by stating that each such individual is also a different type of individual. In short, they are not merely different persons, but they also have different *personalities*. Each such personality is ideally suited for a different kind of role and purpose, and this personality, therefore, constitutes its intended purpose.

QUESTION

You seem to be indicating that the soul's personality is innate and eternal. If each soul has a unique personality, then how is this personality created?

2.1.20 (154)
यथा च प्राणादिः
yathā ca prāṇādiḥ

yathā—just as; ca—also; prāṇādiḥ—the origin in the prāṇa.

TRANSLATION

Just as (the soul) has its origin (in the Lord) through prāṇa, also (the personality of the soul is created in the same way).

COMMENTARY

In 1.1.22 (22) it was stated that Brahman is to be identified as a 'space' and the Lord is its origin. Then in 1.1.23 (23) it was stated that Brahman is also called prāṇa. Then in 1.1.24 (24), Brahman was compared to light. In the purports, we noted that these three sūtras taken together indicate that locations in the space called Brahman are the different individual souls, while prāṇa is the connection from the origin to each individual soul, which can also be called the 'distance' from the origin to different points in the 'space' called Brahman. This idea is understood by stating that Brahman is like the rays of light emanating from the source of light—i.e., the Lord. Brahman is hence also called Brahmajyoti. This Jyoti or light is not without a source; in short, there is a source of light in the Lord, and the soul is the particle of light that emanates from this source.

These sūtras are being referred again by the term *yatha prāṇādiḥ*, indicating 'just as the soul is connected to the source via prāṇa'. The use of the term *ca* or 'also' indicates that the unique personality referred to in the previous sūtra (by comparing each soul to a garment crafted from cloth) is also due to the same reason. In short, the different locations in Brahman are not just individual persons, but also different types with unique personalities. Just as in the body, the prāṇa spreads to many parts of the body such as hands, legs, stomach, head, etc. and each of these has a different function and a type, similarly, the souls emanating from the Lord (and connected to Him via prāṇa) have different personalities. The identity of the soul is not merely a unique individuality but also a different personality. As individuals, these souls are unique persons. But as differing personalities, they are also different from the other persons. Just like a chair and a table are not just two different things, but also two different *types* of things, and each such thing is ideally suited for a different kind of purpose, similarly, the unique purpose of the soul is based on its unique persona.

We have noted earlier that 'space' in Vedic philosophy is semantic. There is a type of space in which individual locations are different concepts. There is another type of space in which different locations are different roles. And there is another space in which different locations are different emotions. These three types of spaces constitute the three aspects of the soul, namely, *sat* (the role), *chit* (the concept), and ānanda (the pleasure). The role defines the duties of the person; the concept describes how those duties are fulfilled, and the pleasure describes how the fulfillment of duties results in different types of happiness. We have also discussed how the three aspects of the soul often conflict: what you desire may be incompatible with what you are capable of, and what you are capable of may not be available in your present role. And yet, the experience is the combination of these three components. When there is a conflict between three aspects, and yet the three must be combined, the combination is produced by creating a dominant-subordinate structure. For instance, some people will remain focused on fulfilling their desires, and if they don't have the ability and opportunity, they will try to attain those first to fulfill their desires. Others may just accept whatever is possible within the current ability and role. As these three potentialities can be organized in a hierarchy, the dominant-subordinate structure produces many kinds of personalities. Prāṇa is the choice of creating such combinations by producing a dominant-subordinate hierarchy.

Therefore, prāṇa is described as both a connection to the origin, as well as the cause of the individual personality. The individual particles of 'light' are not identical to each other, nor are they 'merged' into a single 'field'. They remain, individuals because they have an inner form caused due to the prāṇa. The prāṇa being spoken of here should be considered spiritual rather than material. It is the agency by which a soul can create his experiences (including the experience of self-existence). This agency has been given to the soul by the Lord, and it was intended to produce a certain type of experience—i.e., a specific dominant-subordinate structure—which would then create a unique personality. So, the personality of the soul is God-given, and it cannot be changed. However, this same personality can be adapted to different situations just like a chair may also be used as a ladder. Such uses, however, don't fulfill the soul, as they are contrary to his innate and predefined nature, and the soul remains unhappy. It is only when the native personality is reinvigorated that the soul becomes happy.

Topic 7

QUESTION

It would have been easier to understand the fall if the soul did not have an innate personality. Now that you are saying that the soul has an innate personality, by which is it meant to be devoted to the Lord, how does he go against his innate nature? Doesn't this make the cause of the fall harder to understand?

2.1.21 (155)

इतरव्यपदेशाद्धितिाकरणादिदोषप्रसक्तिः

itaravyapadeśāddhitākaraṇādidoṣaprasaktiḥ

itara—the other (the Lord); vyapadeśāt—from the covering; dhita—bestowed; akaraṇādi—causeless origin; doṣa-prasaktiḥ—imbued with faults.

TRANSLATION

Due to the covering of the Lord, which has a causeless origin, the soul becomes bestowed (into material nature) and imbued with many faults.

COMMENTARY

The question of fall is again brought up, this time in the context of the claim that the soul has an innate personality. If a fall occurs, then the soul must go against his own nature. It is not because of extraneous factors, and therefore the responsibility of the fall still rests on the soul (as has been asserted before). However, one is again perplexed: Why would someone go against their own nature? The sūtra repeats the previous answer—namely, that we cannot find the origin because it is causeless (i.e., not caused by external factors). However, it augments that answer by the claim that the fall is because the soul turns away from the Lord. Just as we might have a natural love for someone, but we might occasionally turn away to look at other people, similarly, the soul too has a love for the Lord, but due to unexplainable reasons, he sometimes looks away. The moment he looks away, and forgets the Lord even for a moment, he falls.

Devotion to the Lord is exclusive and continuous. One cannot maintain multiple simultaneous affections that cause us to forget the love of the Lord. Even if we love others, that love is due to their attachment to the Lord. So, even in the love of others, the Lord is constantly remembered. The moment one starts loving someone else directly—and forgets that this love is due to the connection to the Lord—the Lord exits our consciousness and we become focused on the other person. This forgetfulness of the Lord then results in the fall. The implication is that the devotees in the spiritual world do not forget the Lord even for a moment. Their remembrance is continuous and unwavering. But even if the soul forgets the Lord and falls, the Lord still remembers to rescue him.

QUESTION

Doesn't it sound excessive that a moment's fault of forgetting the Lord leads to the fall? It entails that the soul is not allowed to commit mistakes, or the consequences of that mistake are dire. Why can't the situation be more permissive where the soul can occasionally either love or forget the Lord?

2.1.22 (156)
अधिकं तु भेदनर्दिेशात्
adhikaṃ tu bhedanirdeśāt

adhikaṃ—excessive; tu—but; bheda-nirdeśāt—on account of the instructions about the difference (between matter and spirit, or soul the Lord).

TRANSLATION

(The situation may be called) excessive, but, the difference (between matter and spirit, or soul and the Lord) has already been instructed (and known).

COMMENTARY

Here a simple definition of matter and spirit is being provided: The spirit is the remembrance of the Lord, and matter is the forgetfulness of the Lord. The spiritual world is called yoga-māyā or the idea that "I am not the Lord, but I'm His servant, I'm connected to Him". The material world is called mahā-māyā or the idea that "There is no Lord, and I am independent". In both cases, the term māyā means "that which is not". In the spiritual world, the soul realizes that he is not the Lord, but is connected to the Lord. In the material world, the soul forgets the existence of the Lord and considers himself independent. When matter and spirit are demarcated in this way, then a moment's forgetfulness of the Lord naturally entails material existence. We may call this 'excessive', but the difference between matter and spirit is clearly described in this way.

The qualification of entry into the spiritual world is described here. It is not membership of an institution, taking initiation from some guru, or even some service to the Lord. If a moment's forgetfulness leads to falling into the material world, then the qualification of entry into the spiritual world is unceasing remembrance of the Lord. In fact, the moment we remember the Lord, we are already in the spiritual world. And the moment we forget the Lord we are immediately in the material world. As we have said previously, the soul doesn't physically fall into matter. Only its consciousness is directed toward matter. Similarly, consciousness can also be directed toward the Lord. The moment it is directed toward the Lord, the soul is in the spiritual realm, and the moment it is directed toward its own enjoyment, the soul is in the material realm.

QUESTION

But some people might call the Lord hard-hearted because He banishes the soul from the spiritual world just because the soul has forgotten the Lord.

2.1.23 (157)

अश्मादिवच्च तदनुपपत्तिः

aśmādivacca tadanupapattiḥ

aśmādivat—like stone etc.; ca—also; tadanupapattiḥ—its untenability.

TRANSLATION

(The claim that the Lord is) like a stone is also untenable.

COMMENTARY

There is a saying: Heads I win, tails you lose. If the Lord was to never allow the soul to leave the spiritual world and let him enjoy his independence, the Lord would be called hard-hearted as He doesn't give the soul freedom. If, on the other hand, the Lord allows the soul to immediately leave the world as soon as he desires independence, the Lord may again be called hard-hearted. Such arguments are untenable because the Lord is not 'punishing' the soul by abandoning him. He accompanies the soul and waits for the soul to turn toward Him. Many people turn toward God when they are suffering and ask for His grace. But as soon as the suffering is over, they again forget the Lord. This is an indication that despite suffering, the soul is not inclined to return to the Lord. Despite seeing how everyone is suffering in this world and experiencing such suffering directly, the soul still thinks that he can enjoy independently. Even if this enjoyment comes along with some suffering, if there is some enjoyment, people are prepared to tolerate a lot of suffering. This continued neglect of the Lord indicates that the soul indeed carries a desire for independence. So, not allowing the soul independence as soon as he develops such a desire would be tyrannical, rather than immediately allowing him the freedom and waiting for his return. If the Lord was hard-hearted, He would not accompany the soul in the material world as Paramātma in the heart who enables the enjoyment.

Topic 8

QUESTION

You say that the Lord is very kind, and He appears in the material world to take the soul back to the spiritual world. But isn't He also very powerful, who can forcibly change the circumstances in a way that the soul can return to His place? We have seen that kind and compassionate parents sometimes force the child against his wishes to do what is right and avoid what will hurt him. So, why can't the Lord forcibly take the soul to the spiritual world? The Lord can show some miracles to the soul to attract Him if He wants the soul to return.

2.1.24 (158)

उपसंहारदर्शनान्नेति चेत् न क्षीरवद्धि

upasaṃhāradarśanānneti cet na kṣīravaddhi

upasaṃhāra—the act of drawing closer; darśanāt—from being seen; na—not; iti cet—if it be said; na—not; kṣīravat—like milk; hi—since.

TRANSLATION

If it is said that the Lord is not drawing the soul closer by becoming visible to him (e.g., through miracles etc.) (we say) no, because (He is) just like milk.

COMMENTARY

The problem of evil generates much debate in the philosophy of religion. This problem has been indirectly brought up previously. For instance, earlier it was asked about why the Lord accepts things offered with devotion, but doesn't accept other things (which are not offered with devotion) although they are still done under His supervision? And the answer was that there is a difference between wanting something and approving something (reluctantly). The Lord accepts what He wants, but He approves other things (if the soul wants). Subsequently, it was asked: If the soul has evil in this world, and the Lord created the soul, then the evil must be in the soul. To that, the answer was that the Lord created the soul to serve Him, but the soul felt inferior in this position and wanted to become independent of the Lord's service to overcome this inferiority. In the previous sūtra, there was an attack on the kindness of the Lord by stating that since He allows the soul to enter the material world, He is unkind; the response to that was that the Lord also comes along to save the soul. Now, a different kind of critique is offered: If the Lord is this kind, then why doesn't He demonstrate His presence to the soul by becoming visible to the soul?

To counter this argument, the author compares the Lord to milk, which is the source for innumerable kinds of foods—cream, buttermilk, yogurt, cheese, butter, clarified butter, cottage cheese, etc. Sometimes, the material world is compared to yogurt, while the spiritual world is compared to milk. Now, the point is that when we see varied transformations of milk, we don't see the milk, although these are transformations of milk. We think that the milk has disappeared, and a transformation has appeared. In the same way, even the material creation is an emanation from the Lord, but it has been transformed. The capacity to transform the milk into many kinds of preparations means that the Lord behaves in relation to the soul just as the soul wants to relate to the Lord.

If the soul wants to be devoted to the Lord, then the Lord becomes sweet. But if the soul wants to compete with the Lord's greatness, then the Lord is prepared to compete. We cannot compete with a greater person and then expect them to be defeated by us despite their greatness. Therefore, the Lord's transformation into a competitor means that the soul will always be defeated. This is not a fault in the Lord. It is based on the soul's desire to compete.

We can also say that milk is sweet, while yogurt is sour. The sweetness is love, and sourness is competition. It leads to disunity, disharmony, clashes, and conflict. The unity that was previously present in milk is now missing. The lack of unity, however, arises because we have rejected the unifying entity—the Lord. However, if the Lord is understood as the unifying agency, then the same world can be transformed back into milk, and oppositions will not entail contradictions; they will simply indicate two complementary sides of the same thing. Just like a coin has head and tail, and yet these are simply two sides of the same coin, in the same way, there are opposites, but there can be unity if each side is viewed as denoting a complementary aspect of the same reality.

Therefore, the argument should not be that the Lord has disappeared from our vision, and He is not appearing in our vision to attract us back to the spiritual reality. The argument should rather be that *we* have decided to reject the presence of the Lord, thereby creating disunity and disharmony, which then leads to conflict and suffering. This suffering is our creation, not the Lord's.

QUESTION

Does the presence of conflict and disharmony in this world indicate that the Lord is absent from this world, or is He present even in this world?

2.1.25 (159)
देवादविदपि लोके
devādivadapi loke

devādivat—like the demigods and higher living beings; api—also; loke—in their respective planets or places in the world.

TRANSLATION

Like the demigods and other higher living beings who are situated in higher planetary systems, (the Lord) also (is situated in His place).

COMMENTARY

In the normal course of things, yogurt doesn't transform back into milk. However, in this case, the material world can become the spiritual world if the presence of the Lord is acknowledged. This sūtra states that the Lord exists even in this world, although we compete for superiority. Despite the conflict in the material world, the world doesn't fall apart, and it won't fall apart, because the Lord is keeping it composed and organized in His role as a *maintainer*. In short, there is conflict and disharmony due to the soul's desire for superiority. However, there is no anarchy because the Lord still preserves the universe. Conflicts, therefore, do not entail the absence of the Lord. On the other hand, we should see why the conflicts do not result in the complete destruction of the universe. In this sūtra, the Lord's presence in the universe is compared to the presence of the many demigods. Each demigod occupies a different planet, and the Lord too has His own planet within the universe, which is called śveta-dvīpa. This planet is said to be the residence of the Paramātma or Kṣīrodakaśāyī Viṣṇu.

Even though the existence of the Lord in the heart has been stated earlier, most people are not inward-looking. They like to think that if God exists, then there must be a place of His residence. If the residence is beyond the material world, then His existence is suspect. So, both answers are dissatisfying in some respect— (1) that God exists beyond the world and is therefore invisible, and (2) God exists in each person's heart but is still invisible to most of the people. Since we cannot see the Lord beyond the world or in the heart, someone can say that the Lord doesn't exist in the world. This type of question is being answered here by saying that the Lord is not just existing beyond the material world, and not just in each person's heart. He is also present on a planet within the material universe, just like the planets of the other demigods. While the other demigods perform the administration of the different departments in the universe, the Lord prevents the world from falling apart. We might note in this regard that the different departments in a government or a company compete for power. The head of the government or the CEO in a government resolves their conflicts by balancing their respective powers. If the head of the government or the CEO of the company is absent, the government and the company will fall apart due to internal competition between the departments. Similarly, the Lord gives greater and lesser powers to different demigods to balance them. He also punishes the tyrants and rewards the cooperative. Through all these actions, the Lord maintains and preserves the world of competitors, although this competition is never eliminated due to the tendencies in the soul.

Topic 9

QUESTION

You have earlier indicated that the duality of this world must be rejected, and only the unity must be accepted. You are now stating that this duality need not be rejected because it is complementary aspects of the Lord, which seem to be conflicting due to our vision lacking the unifying cause. How should we understand the rejection of duality and the acceptance of complementarity?

2.1.26 (160)

कृत्स्नप्रसक्तिर्निरवयवत्वशब्दकोपोवा

kṛtsnaprasaktirniravayavatvaśabdakopovā

kṛtsna-prasaktiḥ—devotion to the whole; niravayava—without parts; tvaśabda—many scriptural statements; kopovā—against the prevalent.

TRANSLATION

The devotion to a whole without parts is against the scriptural statements.

COMMENTARY

In the previous sūtras, it has been argued that the suffering of the material world is our creation, and it exists despite the Lord's attempts at unification. It has also been stated that these so-called conflicts of this world are factually non-existent. Just like a coin has a head and tail, or a person has a back and front, similarly, these opposites are reconciled in the Lord. However, if we don't see the Lord, then we think that these oppositions are irreconcilable, and hence one side of the opposition must be true. Then, we compete in ensuring that one side of the coin wins, but the fact is that it cannot exist without the other side. The Lord ensures that the balance between the sides is restored, but as each side occasionally wins or loses, we tend to consider the material world as a place of suffering because we are not constantly winning. The cause of this distress is that we are capable of being one side only; only the Lord is capable of being opposites. So, when we compare the world to ourselves, we think that only one side of the coin must be real or true, while the other side must be unreal or false. The devotee instead compares the world to the Lord, not to themselves. He can see that these opposites are simply different facets of the Lord, and they seem opposed to each other because of our comparing the world to ourselves.

This sūtra goes on to state that there is no point in thinking of a coin by rejecting the head and tail of the coin. There is no point in thinking of a person who doesn't have a front and a back, head and feet, a left and a right, etc. We must rather understand both the unity and the diversity. The diversity cannot be rejected, although the unity must be prioritized. The earlier rejection of the duality is merely to indicate that there is a unity beyond this diversity. Once we understand that, then we can understand how this diversity is parts of the unity. Like the head and the tail are parts of a coin, or the head and the feet are parts of the body, similarly, the duality is aspects and parts of the Lord. So, simply the study of unity is not enough. We must also see how the diversity is part of that unity, has expanded from it, and is also reconciled within it.

QUESTION

The simultaneous study of unity and diversity is interesting because you previously rejected the importance of diversity in favor of unity. Since we had said that we should reject the scriptures that deal in duality, and only focus on those scriptures that deal with the unity, does it mean that we can go back to studying all the scriptures—even those that are dealing in the duality?

2.1.27 (161)

श्रुतेस्तु शब्दमूलत्वात्

śrutestu śabdamūlatvāt

śruteḥ—the scriptural texts; tu—but; śabdamūlatvāt—on account of the sound having a common root (in the Lord).

TRANSLATION

The diverse scriptures (both dealing in the study of duality and non-duality) are but (the diverse manifestations of) a common root (in the Lord).

COMMENTARY

The term *mūla* means a 'root', and the term *mūlatvāt* means 'from just like a root'. When the speaker of the scriptures—i.e., the Lord—is the root, then the scriptures are like shoots. Some of these scriptures may make conflicting statements, and followers of these scriptures may sometimes argue with each other claiming the superiority of their scripture or their viewpoint. Previously it was said that we must reject the scriptures that are dealing in duality, and only focus on the transcendent unity. But now it is also being stated that these scriptures—which can seem mutually contradictory—must be understood as words of the Lord. They are diversified just like shoots are diversified from the root. The ultimate goal of all the scriptures is to reach the root, the shoots must not be understood as being false; they too are of divine origin and parts of the Lord.

This claim is important because Vedic philosophy is often accused of presenting conflicting points of view. For instance, there are personalist and impersonalist views. Within personalism, there are differences between Shaivism, Shaktism, and Vaishnavism. The personalist and impersonalist views are only interpretations of Vedānta—one of the six schools of theistic philosophy; schools like Mīmāṃsā don't accept the existence of a God or demigods. Meanwhile, other schools such as Sāṅkhya deal with the nature of the material universals, Vaiśeṣika deals with the nature of material individuals or atoms, Nyāya deals with the process by which the world of individuals evolves (e.g., through a succession of questions and answers), and Yoga deals with the understanding of how this diversity can be understood as being related to a single unity.

Owing to the multitude of doctrines, most modern academic students conclude that all these ideas must have existed at various times and these scriptures must have been written at different times. They date the written copies of these texts or examine the points in time at which one philosophy dominated over the others, thereby concluding that these have indeed evolved over time. But in this sūtra such attempts have been rejected. All these philosophies are branches of a common root; they can aid in the understanding of the root, and they are reconciled if the root is understood. Just as the understanding of head and tail helps us understand the coin better—i.e., something that has opposite sides—similarly, these scriptures should be viewed as leading us to the root.

QUESTION

But why create so many scriptures when only one truth is important? Yes, we can say that the diversity expands from the unity, and both must be studied. But doesn't the explication of this diversity create numerous confusions? In particular, as you have said, they can bind the soul into the material world unless the transcendent portions of these texts are emphasized. So, why even create those Vedic texts that can then mislead the soul into meaningless pursuits?

2.1.28 (162)
आत्मनि चैवं विचित्राश्च हि
ātmani caivaṃ vicitrāśca hi

ātmani—in the individual soul; ca—also; evaṃ—thus; vicitrāḥ—diverse; ca—also; hi—because.

TRANSLATION

The diversities are also found in the individual soul in the same way because (they exist in the Lord) also.

COMMENTARY

Although the goal of the Vedic texts is attaining the understanding of the root from which everything has emanated, not everyone is interested in the conclusion. We find people interested in mathematics, physics, economics, psychology, etc. although everyone seeks to find the meaning of their lives. Even the study of diverse subjects is ultimately the quest for oneself through these diverse subjects; if we understand these subjects, we think we have partly understood ourselves. So, in one sense, there are many partial and diverse ways of understanding the self, and in another sense, there is a complete understanding of the self. All these partial and complete types of pursuits are present in the different souls because the souls are also diverse with material and spiritual personalities. This sūtra states that all these diversities are created for people with diverse interests, such that they can gradually progress from the shoots to the root. Each scripture may emphasize one aspect of reality, but they do not reject the truth of other realities. For instance, even scriptures devoted to Vaishnavism mention Lord Śiva and His Śakti as the masters of the material world. This was earlier indicated in the sūtra 1.4.19 (125) by the 'connected nature of the scriptural passages' implying that even if one sees apparent conflicts, one should only accept the interpretation that resolves their apparent conflict.

One might wonder: What is the need to propound theories about the material world if such theories can be created by humans? Shouldn't the scripture be exclusively devoted to the transcendence that we cannot perceive? The short answer to that question is that the theories produced through our speculation are not guaranteed to converge into a coherent understanding. At the present, not only are there diverse irreconcilable theories within each department of knowledge (e.g., physics), but most of the departments (such as physics, psychology, and philosophy) don't even read each other's works or attempt to formulate a shared understanding of the truth. They are quite content working in isolation, making conflicting claims. A system that doesn't even aim for unity cannot hope to achieve the goal of unity and explain how that unity expanded into the observable diversity. The Vedic descriptions are substitutes for these endeavors since the reader can progress from one aspect to another and obtain greater levels of unity in their knowledge. In short, you traverse from the leaves to the twigs, to the branches, to the trunks, and finally to the root. Your interest in the leaves is not contradictory to the understanding of the root, although limiting oneself to that leaf is not recommended. By stating that the scriptures have a common root, it is implied that one can find the unity by studying them. Meanwhile, those who are directly interested in the diversity, rather than the unity, can still study these scriptures according to their differing natures. Such studies will not be futile in the quest for the nature of the complete reality.

QUESTION

Many people claim that the diverse fields of inquiry can never be reconciled. They are necessarily limited models of reality that have been created for our own understanding and we should not even demand their consistency. Accordingly, we should not aim for the quest of the ultimate truth, as there is no guaranteed method for attaining such a truth by attempts of reconciliation.

2.1.29 (163)

स्वपक्षदोषाच्च

svapakṣadoṣācca

svapakṣa—one's own opinion; doṣāt—on account of the faults; ca—also.

TRANSLATION

On account of faults in one's own opinion also (should be rejected).

COMMENTARY

All modern attempts at knowledge are beset with the dilemma between consistency and completeness. This dilemma arises due to duality, which is then presented as contradictions between the opposites. Owing to this duality, if you study one side of the opposition, you can have consistency within your viewpoint, but your views will necessarily be incomplete because they do not incorporate the other side of the opposition. If, on the other hand, you try to reconcile these opposites without the understanding of the Lord in whom these opposites are reconciled, then your attempts at reconciliation will fail—i.e., they will lead to contradictions. If we avoid the contradictions, then our understanding is always incomplete. So, due to duality, the pursuit of consistency results in incompleteness, and the pursuit of completeness results in inconsistency. The person who argues against the attempt to unify the diverse areas of study has understood that they are indeed dealing in dualities, and they are prepared to sacrifice completeness in favor of some internal consistencies within their fields. They are worried that if they tried to unify, they would have to throw away the assumptions that contradict the other fields, leaving them with nothing.

But we must also realize that any incomplete description is also necessarily false. For instance, in physics, light was initially described by Newton as corpuscles, which turned out to be false when interference phenomena were detected and led to the idea that light is a wave. This wave theory was also found false with the discovery of black-body radiation which entails that light is absorbed or emitted as particles. Today, two incongruous ideas—namely, wave and particle—are employed to describe the nature of light, which means that unless you induct both your theory is incomplete, and if you use only one, then your theory is necessarily false (i.e., incompatible with the facts). The point is that you cannot claim the truth of a theory unless you have reconciled these contradictions, and all seemingly consistent theories are all potentially false.

So, the person who argues for keeping separate fields of consistency must face not just the problem of incompleteness, but also the problem of potential falsity. Similarly, the person who argues for completeness must face the problem of inconsistencies between the dualities. The solution to the latter problem has been described—if you use the scriptures to study the diverse fields, you will find the unity in the diversity. You will not only understand the diversities but also how they exist inside the unity. Therefore, the argument of the person who rejects such unification is also rejected here on the grounds that their approach will neither lead to completeness nor even to an incomplete truth.

Topic 10

QUESTION

But even if we study the diverse scriptures, we may keep seeing the contradictions in them, and we may never be able to resolve these contradictions. What is the guarantee that we will come to a

complete understanding? Isn't it possible that we are forever lost in conflictual ideas in diverse scriptures?

2.1.30 (164)
सर्वोपेता च तद्दर्शनात्
sarvopetā ca taddarśanāt

sarvopetā—having everything; ca—also; tat-darśanāt—from seeing that.

TRANSLATION

(Full knowledge is) also (attained) from seeing that which has everything.

COMMENTARY

Every area of scientific inquiry is based on the formulation of models. For example, the motion of planets in the solar system is based on the model of a stone tied to a rope being rotated around a center. Similarly, the model of light is based on the idea of vibrating strings or water waves. Each area of human inquiry creates an understanding of the world based on a model, and these models are often conflicting, which leads to conflict between the theories. To reconcile these contradictions, we need a model that contains all the diversities.

This sūtra asserts that the Absolute Truth is that model. What does this mean in a practical sense? It means that we must think of everything as persons, which exist in complementary ways. Material nature is therefore not impersonal. It should also be understood as a person. But what do we mean by a person? The answer is that a person has three aspects—cognition, relation, and emotion—and material nature should also be described in terms of these three modes. Then, because the Absolute Truth can expand, similarly, material nature also expands from a root into trunks, branches, and leaves. Thus, matter is also organized as a hierarchy of relations, cognitions, and emotions. Then, each of these relations, cognitions, and emotions comes in various flavors. For instance, cognition has six aspects of knowledge, beauty, power, wealth, fame, and renunciation. Thus, all the expansions also have all these qualities. Finally, the cause of all these changes is that the feminine creates a desire in the masculine, and the masculine then uses the power of the feminine to fulfill the desire.

So, by the model, we mean that nature is not moving linearly; it is rather a dialectical movement from questions to answers to questions. This dialectic involves three aspects of a person, each of which is organized into a hierarchy, and this hierarchy is produced by the mixing of the three aspects. Thus, clues about the nature of the Absolute Truth give us the model by which we can understand how diversity is created, and how it can be reconciled. We cannot speculate our way to such an answer; we must rather understand the nature of the Absolute Truth, which can then result in the unifying understanding.

QUESTION

The central problem seems to be that most people like to think of the Absolute Truth impersonally, rather than personally. Thus, for instance, the world must be governed by laws, rather than by a person. The origin for everything must be something without will or consciousness, and the world must exist without a purpose. Or, that life arises late in the evolution of the material world. You are saying that we must begin in understanding personalities and their interactions and that the material world would be explained in the same way?

2.1.31 (165)

वकिरणत्वान्नेति चेत् तदुक्तम्

vikaraṇatvānneti cet taduktam

vikaraṇatvāt—as if from something devoid of instruments (of perception and action); na—not; iti cet—if it be said; tat—that; uktam—has been explained.

TRANSLATION

If it is said that (everything is produced) as if from something devoid of instruments (i.e., senses), (we say) no, and that has already been explained.

COMMENTARY

This sūtra is the summary rejection of impersonalism and voidism. In voidism, the ultimate truth is the reconciliation of opposites, and that reconciliation leads to nothingness, because the opposites cancel each other. In impersonalism, the opposites are not present in the Absolute Truth; they are instead the attributes of material energy, which can either be regarded as real or as illusory, but since the opposites are missing from the Absolute Truth, ultimately (even if we regard the material energy as being real), all the opposites are unreal.

This sūtra says that we should not think of the Absolute Truth in terms of impersonalism and voidism. We should rather think of the Absolute Truth as a person with senses. When there are senses, there is a cognitive capacity and a desire for pleasure. To fulfill this desire, there must be diversity, and the senses are used to create the diversity and then enjoy with the diversity. And since the diversity is created by a personality, that person is also the Supreme Being.

Of course, this understanding has been stated at the end of the first chapter. So why is it being repeated? The answer is that the previous description pertained to *everything* and the present description pertains to *anything*. Impersonalism and voidism reject personalism when it comes to the ultimate reality, and if personalities are rejected in an absolute sense, they must also be rejected in a relative sense. For instance, the world must be governed by impersonal laws rather than personal administration. The personalist acknowledges the reality of personalities in an absolute sense. But with that acceptance, we should also acknowledge the reality of personalities in a relative sense. For instance, we must now say that the world is controlled by persons; the lawfulness in nature is because these persons behave in a regulated manner, rather than randomly. The judgment of right and wrong, the delivery of results of pleasure or suffering, are all under the supervision of persons. The understanding of the laws of nature simply means understanding the person who implements the orderly behavior that we consider a law. This orderly nature is the personality of the person and the law prevails because a soul administers the law.

So, personalism is not merely a theory about the nature of the absolute reality. It also entails a different understanding of how ordinary phenomena must be modeled in terms personalism. Every time we face problems in understanding something, we can resolve them by thinking in terms of persons.

For example, the wave-particle duality in atomic theory can be understood if we say that the 'particle' is a symbol of meaning, with contextual relations to other particles which we call the 'field'. The complete description of a cow involves saying two things—(1) that there is a particle called cow, and (2) there is a field that defines how this cow is not a tiger, it is a mammal, and it is not other cows. In classical physics, each physical particle could exist by itself. But now, because reality is symbols, therefore, the symbols are only defined through a distinction to other symbols. The field entails the inseparability of the cow from everything else. So, the quantum is observed as a particle, and it is indeed an individual thing. However, this individual thing is not a classical particle; it is rather a symbol of meaning defined in relation to other such symbols. Finally, something being a cow, and not being a tiger are complementary descriptions of the same thing; therefore, they cannot be applied simultaneously. Indeed, we might sometimes contrast the cow to a tiger, and say that the cow is gentle, and the tiger is fierce. Then we may contrast the cow to the horse, and say that the cow is slow, and the horse is fast. Then we may contrast the cow to a goat, and say that the cow's milk is thick, while the goat's milk is thinner. In this way, different properties of the cow are revealed in contrast to other animals. However, since all these contrasts are not simultaneous, therefore, all the properties of the cow are not known at once. We rather know the same thing in different ways—one after another—because these qualities are *modes* of the cow.

The remaining question is—what is the order of these contrasts? Do we know the cow in contrast to the horse before we know the cow in contrast to the goat? The answer to that question is that these contrasts are sequenced due to our desiring and deserving. The properties of the cow in relation to the goat, horse, tiger, etc. constitute the *chit*. The desiring constitutes the ānanda, and the deserving constitutes the *sat*. Current physics describes the *chit* or cognition as meaningless particles. If we enhanced this understanding as cognition and conation, then the same world would be known as symbols of meaning. And then we can talk about how these symbols are sequenced through desiring and deserving. Thus, if we model the atomic world using the principles of persons, then we can solve one of the most perplexing problems of modern time.

The same principle can be applied to any area of inquiry, such as biology, psychology, sociology, economics, etc. We can use the understanding of the Absolute Truth to understand anything else. Thus, when everything or the Absolute Truth is known, then anything or the individual relative truths are automatically known. These are not two separate kinds of knowledge. Only those who do not know the Absolute Truth find a difference between the Absolute and the Relative truths. If the Absolute Truth is known, everything is known. In fact, everything is known consistently and through the same model.

Topic 11

QUESTION

Whenever we speak about senses (of perception and action), we also speak about the objects of these senses. For example, for the sense of smell, the smell is an object. The senses are drawn toward their objects, and the purpose of these senses is to interact with these objects. In the case of the Lord, who is described to have senses, where are the objects of these senses—i.e., their purposes?

2.1.32 (166)
न परयोजनवत्तवात्
na prayojanavattvāt

na—not; prayojanavattvāt—as if on account of having needs or wants.

TRANSLATION

(The senses of the Lord) are not as if driven by needs or wants.

COMMENTARY

If you are unhappy, then you want your friends because they can make you happy. You expect them to lift you up, say cheerful things, so that the enjoyment will dissipate your unhappiness. But if you are already happy, when you meet a friend, you share your happiness, and try to make them happy. You are not expecting anything from them; you are rather expressing your happiness. There is hence a difference between needing and sharing. Our senses are needy; they contact the material objects to overcome the incompleteness. But the Lord's senses are not needy; and yet, they are used to express His happiness. Thus, in the material world, we use our power to acquire objects of the senses so that the unhappiness of desiring can be overcome. However, in the spiritual world, the power is used to express or expand a person's happiness. This expression makes others happier, and they then express their delight, producing an unending cycle of happiness and its expression. In the material world, everyone is needy, and when they take some objects of happiness, then someone else becomes unhappy. So, our quest for the objects of the senses to find happiness should not be compared to the expression of objects due to happiness. The search for happiness in the external world is the *prayojana* or the purpose of material causality and it drives our senses towards their objects. But the expression of inner happiness is the *prayojana* or the purpose of spiritual causality and it produces the objects of the senses for the happiness of the Lord.

QUESTION

Since you are distinguishing between material and spiritual causality, in both cases the senses are being employed, but for different purposes. Does this mean that the spiritual world is in some ways quite like the material world in that in both places there are senses, objects, and their mutual interactions?

2.1.33 (167)

लोकवत्तु लीलाकैवल्यम्

lokavattu līlākaivalyam

lokavat—as in this world; tu—but; līlākaivalyam—liberated pastimes.

TRANSLATION

(The spiritual world is) just like this world, but it is liberated pastimes.

COMMENTARY

After denouncing impersonalism and voidism, this sūtra clearly states that the transcendent world is just like this world—i.e., there are persons with desires, they have senses, which then interact with the sense objects. The use of the term *tu* or 'but' followed by *līlākaivalyam* or 'liberated pastimes' indicates a difference between the present world and the spiritual world. The use of *kaivalyam* or liberation means that we are free from the hankering of material desire, which is produced from an inner unhappiness and sense of incompleteness, and to overcome that unhappiness we try to use others for our happiness. When this hankering of desire arising from inner incompleteness is overcome, then a new type of desire is produced, which *expresses* the inner happiness. Now, the soul becomes interested in making others happy rather than becoming happy. Since everyone is trying to please everyone else, and nobody is in need for happiness arising from internal distress, the result is unending joy. The activities of this spiritual world are *līlā* or pastimes just like the social interactions in this world. However, they are not caused by selfishness to satisfy one's own senses. Rather, the senses are satisfied through satisfying others' senses.

Topic 12

QUESTION

You seem to be implying that even the material world is a *līlā* or pastime of the Lord. Isn't it harsh and cruel to say that the world in which the souls are suffering life after life is merely an enjoyable pastime for the Supreme Lord?

2.1.34 (168)
वैषम्यनैर्घृण्ये न सापेक्षत्वात् तथा हि दर्शयति
vaiṣamyanairghṛnye na sāpekṣatvāt tathā hi darśayati

aiṣamyanairghṛnye—partiality and cruelty; na—not; sāpekṣatvāt—on account of the selfish view; tathā—so; hi—indeed; darśayati—perceives.

TRANSLATION

(The Lord's pastime in this world is) not on account of partiality and cruelty, (but) on account of the selfish viewpoint (the soul) indeed perceives it so.

COMMENTARY

In 2.1.23 (157) the claim that the Lord is just like stone or hard-hearted because He banishes the soul from the spiritual world was rejected. It was explained that the soul turns away from the Lord, but the Lord still accompanies Him into the material world as Paramātma to bring the soul back. However, one can still argue: while I'm suffering, the Lord is not suffering, so He must be cruel. Implicit in this argument is the demand that the Lord must also suffer when the soul is suffering; after all, the soul won't complain that the Lord is not enjoying when the soul is enjoying. The intent of coming to the material world was due to the inferiority relative to the Lord, and the desire to be like Him. But if the soul is unable to attain the same position as the Lord, then he can complain that the Lord is cruel that He makes us suffer while He continues enjoying.

This sūtra rejects the conclusion that the Lord is cruel but acknowledges that due to the soul's selfish attitude he indeed sees the Lord as cruel.

Psychologists recognize a Narcissistic Personality Disorder in which a person humiliates others in order to feel superior to them; however, when they are shown to be in the wrong, they refuse to accept responsibility for their actions, while arguing and fighting with the person who pointed out their faults, ultimately trying to turn the tables in order to prove that their accuser is at fault. Their basic inner insecurity prevents them from accepting that they are ever wrong. They always try to shift the blame to someone else. Most often, these blames are shifted to the people who are kindest and gentlest toward them. A narcissist believes that such people who are caring for them will not be able to retaliate, and their attempts at shifting the blame would be successful. Their inner crisis is so severe that they consider any criticism as fundamentally undermining their self-love, and they are unable to accept their mistakes.

The soul who considers the Lord unkind and cruel is a prime example of a person suffering from a Narcissistic Personality Disorder. This narcissism, or the need to love oneself unconditionally, while refusing to accept any fault and then blaming others for one's unhappiness, is referred to here as *sāpekṣatvāt* (being situated on one's own side, or considering only one's own viewpoint). Acceptance of mistakes leads to guilt, which then leads to corrections. But if the person is so weak that they cannot accept the mistake, then they inevitably resort to blaming the people who are kindest and gentlest towards them. Such blaming doesn't solve any problem; it just pushes the kind and gentle people away, leaving no one to blame. In the same way, by blaming the Lord, the soul increases his distance to the Lord, and gradually becomes atheistic. When the Lord no longer exists for the soul, the soul is left with no one to blame. Ultimately, by pushing the Lord away, the soul is forced to accept responsibility. So, the right approach would be to accept responsibility from the start.

QUESTION

But many people ask: Why do bad things happen to good people? They say that they have been good all their life and done all their duties. They even have faith in the Lord. And yet, bad things have happened to them. If these bad things are happening, then what is the point of being good or doing good deeds? The world seems not to care about our good or bad natures. And if there is no morality in this world, then how can we repose our faith in the Lord?

2.1.35 (169)
न कर्मावभिागादिति चेत् न अनादित्वात्
na karmāvibhāgāditi cet na anāditvāt

na—not; karma—actions; avibhāgāt—due to lack of distinction; iti cet—if it be said; na—no; anāditvāt—because of (karma) being without a beginning.

TRANSLATION

If it is said that there is no distinction between (good and bad) actions, (we say) no, because karma is going on since time immemorial.

COMMENTARY

While we have indicated the role of karma in the purports to the previous sūtra, this is first instance of the use of this term in Vedānta Sūtra. Karma is responsible for what happens to us; how we react to it is based on our guna. Everyone is situated in some role in their life, which demands the performance of duties, which are called dharma. Ideally, one must perform their duties without expectation of results; "doing as a matter of duty" is called karma-yoga because by such performance one does not produce karma. However, in this material world, we always perform our duties expecting some results. When dharma is performed with the desire for happiness, then good karma is created. But what is 'good'? It is whatever we like. If a person is lazy, then good karma will allow him to live a lazy life. If, however, a person is hardworking, then good karma will give him many opportunities to work. So, karma doesn't have an absolute meaning; the meaning of karma—i.e., good or bad—is relative to our guna. When our duties go against our nature or guna, then we tend to neglect them, or perform them reluctantly, or perform them with bitterness. This negative intentional state then produces bad karma. Accordingly, the actions of a person are classified into three categories—*sukarma* or good karma, *vikarma* or bad karma, and *akarma* or no karma. Once sukarma and vikarma have been created, they lie latent or unmanifest; they gradually become manifest through the course of one's life, and indeed, over the course of numerous lives.

The time of birth fixes the type of karma that will manifest over our lifetime. This is the basis of astrology, by which we can predict what will happen to us; however, we still cannot predict how we will react to it. Even though a person has guna or a material nature, which predetermines one's reactions to situations, the guna can be controlled by the soul if it rejects the automatically produced reactions due to guna. The time of birth that fixes the karma that will manifest over our lifetime is called *prārabdha*. As time passes in this life, both good and bad karma are manifest according to the dashā of planets. The karma that is manifesting right now is called *kriyamāna*. And the karma that is still in store for future lifetimes is called *sañcita*. So, if you have performed good or bad deeds, the results are not immediately seen, because the karma of the lifetime was fixed at the time of birth—called prārabdha. Similarly, if you perform bad deeds, the results will not manifest immediately; you can keep enjoying the results of prārabdha even as you perform bad deeds. The results of our actions are stored in the repository called sañcita. Based on a person's guna, one gets a certain type of body—e.g., human, dog, cow, bird, tree, fish, etc. And a small part of the sañcita then becomes the prārabdha for a given lifetime.

Once we understand this science of action and consequence, then we can see how doing good things may not immediately lead to good outcomes; it is because of previous bad actions, that in turn defined the prārabdha, that our life may continue to be full of difficulties. However, this doesn't mean that there is no consequence of our actions. All these actions are getting accumulated in the sañcita and will produce their effects over successive lifetimes. Nature has a perfect system of morality, and every action produces a consequence. But we must understand the science of this action and consequence, and not assume that good actions must immediately produce good outcomes. This sūtra specifically states that the cycle of action and reaction has no beginning. The karma we are reaping right now could have come from any of the previous lives. So, instead of thinking that there is no consequence of our actions, we must understand that our suffering is due to bad karma produced in earlier lives.

QUESTION

But many people will say that they are not willingly doing bad actions; rather, circumstances are forcing them to do so. For example, if a man is born very poor, is abandoned by his parents, and then falls into bad company, which then indoctrinates him into crime, should we not blame the circumstances? If these circumstances are produced due to previous bad karma, and the bad circumstances then lead him into further bad action, then he is perpetually caught in the cycle of bad action, bad consequence, and then more bad action. It seems that bad action then predestines him to eternal suffering due to karma.

2.1.36 (170)
उपपद्यते चाप्युपलभ्यते च
upapadyate cāpyupalabhyate ca

upapadyate—is produced; ca—and; api—also; upalabhyate—is reaped; ca—also.

TRANSLATION

(The consequences of actions, or karma) are being produced just as they are being reaped (the same action both produces and reaps karma).

COMMENTARY

The sūtra refutes the claim that one must necessarily be caught in an eternal cycle of bad actions leading to bad circumstances which then lead to more bad actions. Every bad circumstance offers us an opportunity to act in an appropriate way; it may not be the best thing we want, and it is also possible that we may not be able to do the ideal thing. But if it is the best thing that could be done in that situation, then performing those actions will lead to good karma. Dharma or duty is not universal; it is always contextual. We cannot change what happens to us, but we can change how we respond to it. So, even if we are in a bad situation, we still have the choice to change our response to it. It may not be easy, but who can we blame for a bad situation if we are creating these situations through our actions? Every action is partially governed by the situation and partially governed by our response to the situation. The situation is due to the reaping of past karma, and the response creates new karma.

Topic 13

QUESTION

So how can a person become free of the suffering caused due to karma?

2.1.37 (171)

सर्वधर्मोपपत्तेश्च

sarvadharmopapatteśca

sarva-dharma-upapatteḥ—caused by the doing of all duties; ca—also.

TRANSLATION

(The freedom from karma) can also be gotten by doing all our duties.

COMMENTARY

In the previous sūtra it was stated that karma is simultaneously being reaped and created, and in this sūtra, the reason for the creation of karma is being explained. The reason is that we don't perform all our duties. Why? Because there is always contention between different duties. Sometimes we neglect our family because we are driven by the greed to earn more money at the workplace, and sometimes we neglect the workplace because we are too attached to enjoying with the family. Contentions between different duties drag us in different directions, and to prioritize one duty over another we ask ourselves: What type of work will produce better results for me? We don't realize that karma entails a destiny about what will come to us, and by greater or lesser effort we cannot change that outcome. We rather become enamored by the possibility of better results by the performance of one type of activity and we neglect other duties. If we realize that karma fixes what results we will get, then we will perform our duties in a detached manner, and the side effect of that detachment is that we will perform all our duties. Of course, sometimes some duty takes precedence over others, and that is part of understanding dharma. So, the ask is not to perform all the duties simultaneously (because that isn't possible). The ask is not to neglect a duty, by balancing different duties. And the cause of karma is that we are driven by greed and neglect some duties.

The performance of duties without the expectation of results, and the performance of all the duties, are just two ways of expressing the same idea. To perform all the duties, we must be detached from the results—e.g., that I'm spending time away from some work, which might produce better outcomes for me. And by getting detached we can perform all the duties. The detachment from the expectation of results is called karma-yoga, and the same idea is explained here differently—performance of all duties is also karma-yoga.

Note the use of *ca* or 'also' in this sūtra. The performance of all the duties is not the only way for obtaining freedom from karma. Specifically, how can a person become detached from the results of our actions unless they realize that they are not this body, and the present life is one of many lives lived before and after? The cultivation of knowledge or jñāna-yoga helps in detachment, and therefore, the performance of all the duties. Similarly, even if we cultivate knowledge, there are latent unconscious tendencies, which force a person to behave in pre-determined ways. How does one gain control over the mind and make it free of these unconscious productions of desires? This is where the practice of aṣṭāṅga-yoga can be useful, which teaches one to control the body followed by the mind, and then focus one's consciousness in the heart. But how can one keep oneself focused on one thing unless he is enjoying the experience? Ultimately the desire for enjoyment will drag the person somewhere else. Thus, the practice of bhakti-yoga is important to make life pleasurable so that the mind can be detached from other mundane desires and their push-pull. Thus, the implication is that karma-yoga is one of the ways, and it doesn't stand alone. To properly practice karma-yoga, one must have cultivated detachment which comes due to the acquisition of knowledge. This knowledge is made practical by the control of the body and mind. And this control is persistent only through devotion to the Lord. If this devotion exists, then all other things—i.e., control of the body and mind, the realization of knowledge, and the detached performance of duties become automatic. On the other hand, if one doesn't have devotion, then a person can begin by doing all the duties to gradually develop detachment, which will then assist in knowledge, which will then lead to control over the body and the mind, which will then lead to devotion.

SECTION 2

Topic 1

QUESTION

But how do we know what all the duties we need to perform are? Most of the duties we perform seem to be artificially created by social circumstances, and they change from one culture and society to another. For example, the laws of behavior are different in different countries. Thus, many people argue that these so-called duties are mere social constructions; there is nothing fundamental about them, and we can create whatever duties we deem fit for us.

2.2.1 (172)

रचनानुपपत्तेश्च नानुमान

racanānupapatteśca nānumānam

racanānupapatteḥ—due to the absurdity of fabrication; ca—and; na—not; anumānam—that which is imagined.

TRANSLATION

It is absurd to say that our duties are fabricated, and (we must know) that these duties cannot be (concocted) based on our imagination (or inference).

COMMENTARY

When materialism is born, meaning, choice, and morality die. The materialist in physical sciences claims that meanings don't exist; then the materialist in the mind sciences claims that choice is an illusion; and finally, the materialist in the social sciences claims that morality is our creation. But all three claims are false. Our bodies are symbols of meaning: the meaning is a universal type or concept. These symbols are instantiated from the universal idea due to our choices or desires. And these symbols are then placed in different roles, contexts, situations, or circumstances due to karma, where we can reap the results of good or bad actions in the past. These situations create our roles, and each role comes with a different duty, responsibility, and morality. The violation of that morality produces karma, which then changes our circumstances.

The materialist claims that we are randomly born rich or poor, that our birth in a specific society or to a specific type of mother and father is random, and that we can collectively concoct our duties based on what we like. The fundamental question that the materialist never answers is this: Why is someone rich while another person is poor? Why is someone healthy while the other person is sick? Why is someone enjoying, while others are suffering? Even most religions are unable to answer these questions correctly because they don't realize that we are enjoying or suffering due to the results of our past actions. These results are produced because there was a duty and responsibility that we fulfilled or neglected. And these duties are defined by our role in society. We may not see this role as an object, because it exists as relationships, and the causality of choice and consequence operates based on these relationships. So, the claim that our duties are simply our imaginative constructions is rejected here.

QUESTION

But aren't there practical difficulties in deciding our roles and duties? How do we know or decide what type of role and duty one must accept?

2.2.2 (173)

परवृत्तेश्च

pravṛtteśca

pravṛtteḥ—based on the tendency; ca—also.

TRANSLATION

(The duties can) also (be decided) based on (a person's) tendencies.

COMMENTARY

It has been noted above that a person must perform all their duties. But what if those duties are very hard to perform? What if the person is simply not inclined toward certain types of duties, or is incapable of doing them? For example, to become a philosopher, one must have the necessary intellect for analyzing things, must have the patience to not be disturbed by arguments and counterarguments, and must be able to think about not just what is true, but also what is right and good. A soldier cannot be expected to indulge in intellectual arguments; he must rather get the opportunity to engage in physical contact, aggression, and engagement of chivalry for a greater good. Those who are physically and mentally weak and cannot endure the hardships of battle or the rigor of intellectual discussion, but can still build strong human relationships, can engage in business and trade. And those who are incapable in all these ways can position themselves as workers who assist the other types of people.

This classification of people based on their respective tendencies is called the Varna System of social organization. The type of role accepted by a person is not based on their birth into a certain class or to certain types of parents. It is determined by their own ability to perform all the expected duties, because the non-performance of such duties leads to adverse karma and one cannot cite their inability or disinclination as the causes of this neglect. For example, a person who is emotionally weak should not become a ruler or leader in society. The basic qualification for a leader is that they are fearless and can do what is right regardless of the adverse consequences that follow— even including their death. Unfortunately, at present people become leaders even if their hearts and minds are gripped by fear and insecurity about their position. They aim not to do the right thing; they aim to protect their position of leadership or power. By neglecting their duties, they are constantly producing bad karma, which will then lead to suffering in their future lives. This sūtra advises people to accept only those roles and responsibilities that are compatible with their tendencies—i.e., their abilities to do what is required, and their inclination to do it.

So, if one wants to become free of the effects of bad karma, then one must not accept roles in society that they cannot fulfill completely. Their acceptance of such roles not only creates problems for others, but for themselves too.

QUESTION

You say that one's roles and duties should be defined by their ability and inclination, but we can see that so many people who are qualified by their ability and inclination don't get the appropriate roles in society. On the other hand, the unqualified people often ascend the roles that they are unqualified for. We can understand that the unqualified people will incur bad karma, but what about those people who are qualified but don't get appropriate roles? Isn't the principle that one gets the role if they are qualified inapplicable here?

2.2.3 (174)
पयोऽम्बुवच्चेत् तत्रापि
payo'mbuvaccet tatrāpi

payo'mbuvat—like milk and water; cet—if it be said; tatra—there; api—even.

TRANSLATION

If it is said (that a person doesn't get a role according to their tendencies), even there (one must be) like (the mixture of) milk and water.

COMMENTARY

The three aspects of the soul—emotion, cognition, and relation—manifest into desire, ability in the body, and opportunities. The soul is only born with desires, but due to opportunities afforded by their circumstances, they develop the body of abilities. Therefore, the body is a consequence of both guna and karma—we develop the abilities based on what we like to do, and what we can do (under the circumstances). However, since karma can be both good or bad, sometimes due to good karma (and guna) we obtain good abilities, but due to bad karma we don't get the appropriate opportunities. Conversely, due to bad karma (or guna) we don't obtain the necessary abilities, but due to good karma we get opportunities we aren't suited for. All these discrepancies are produced because guna and karma don't work in lockstep. The ideal situation is that the unqualified must not accept the roles for which they are unqualified.

When a conflict between our ability, desire, and opportunity is produced, there are two ways in which we can respond. First, we can get frustrated and angry that we are qualified and yet not receiving our due; under this anger and frustration, we would tend to neglect even the duties that are currently available to us, and that would then result in adverse karma. Second, we can accept our fate, and use our abilities to the best extent possible under the given circumstances; in short, we don't become angry and frustrated by the situation and don't neglect the responsibilities that are presently available to us. We can continue to perform our duties in whatever role we have received, even if it is not appropriate for our abilities, and inconsistent with our tendencies.

The term 'milk' represents our desires or pleasure. And the term 'water' represents the dilution of the milk. The mixture of milk and water represents the unfulfilled or partially fulfilled desires. If there is a little bit of milk and a lot of water, the mixture will taste like water— i.e., something that we don't want. If there is a lot of milk and a little bit of water, then the mixture will taste like milk—i.e., we will be mostly satisfied with the outcome. The mixture represents a compromise; if we cannot get the perfect thing we want, we can work with whatever we have received, but also control our emotions—i.e., not get angry and frustrated with the situation, and not neglect the current duties. If our duties are performed in this detached manner, then gradually the bad karma will come to an end, and no bad karma would have been created in this time. Thus, by being patient in difficult times, we can transcend the effects of karma.

QUESTION

It is so difficult to live like this; how can a person remain in a situation that is contrary to his nature, where he is unable to act according to his nature?

2.2.4 (175)

व्यतिरिकानवस्थतिश्चानपेक्षत्वात्

vyatirekānavasthiteścānapeksatvāt

vyatireka—separation; na—not; avasthiteḥ—being situated; ca—and; anapeksatvāt—due to becoming impartial (toward the good or bad of this world).

TRANSLATION

Be situated (in the understanding of being) non-separate (from the Lord) due to becoming impartial (toward the good and bad of the present world).

COMMENTARY

Many things have been said in the previous sūtras one by one. First, it was said that one's suffering is because of one's bad karma. Second, it was said that bad karma is created due to neglect of duties. Third, if one objects that this neglect arises because the duties are contrary to one's nature, it was said that one can choose their duties based on their nature so that they can avoid bad karma. Fourth, if one argues that I'm not able to find the duty compatible to my nature despite my best efforts, the previous sūtra stated that one must learn to compromise. Finally, if one expresses their helplessness is practicing this compromise with the material world, this sūtra states that one must consider himself non-separate from the Lord because by this a person can be impartial or neutral (i.e., neither averse nor attached) to the events occurring in this world.

This is an indication that karma-yoga is very difficult to practice because as we face adversities in this world, it is very difficult to remain detached. If one reacts impulsively and neglects their duties or does something not allowed by their duties, then they are further implicated in the consequences of karma. So, after propounding the theory of karma, material entanglement, and possible ways to get disentangled, the Vedānta Sūtra arrives at the original conclusion of remaining devoted to the Lord and considering oneself non-separate from Him. Non-separate means: (1) we are not identical to the Lord, and (2) we are not separated from Him. We are rather the parts—which are neither equal to the whole nor are they separate from the whole. When one is situated in this understanding, then he automatically becomes detached from this world. Therefore, karma-yoga cannot be practiced without devotion to the Lord.

QUESTION

What are the symptoms of a person who has obtained detachment from this world due to developing devotion and attachment to the Lord?

2.2.5 (176)

अन्यत्राभावाच्च न तृणादवित्

anyatrābhāvacca na trnadivat

anyatra—elsewhere; abhāvāt—because of absence; ca—and; na—not; trnadivat—even as grass etc.

TRANSLATION

(Such a person doesn't go) elsewhere due the absence (of luxuries) and (he is) not (disturbed) even if (he is treated) like grass etc. (i.e., stepped upon).

COMMENTARY

Previously the symptoms of devotees have been described by stating several things: (1) they develop bodily symptoms of divine happiness, (2) by their words they can change the life of other materialistically inclined people. In this sūtra, another such symptom is described: such devotees are undisturbed by worldly difficulties; they don't run away from a situation even if there are difficulties, and they are not deterred even if they are mistreated by others. In short, they are emotionally resilient to difficulties and humiliation. They are free from fear, and remain steadfast in their duties, performing them to the best of their abilities, and considering themselves the servants of the Lord.

Many people think that devotion to the Lord is very easy. They claim that the devotees abandon their worldly duties, they do not take the trouble of acquiring knowledge, they don't perform the austerities necessary for purification, etc. Their quick acceptance of the Lord's shelter entails that they are emotionally weak. This sūtra refutes such misconceptions. It states that contrary to these ideas of weakness, the devotees of the Lord are stronger than everyone else in the face of difficulties. Even sages who have practiced yoga for thousands of years are unable to handle humiliation; if treated badly, they become angry and curse others. Intellectuals are especially arrogant; they consider themselves superior as they have thought through things much more than others. However, this knowledge also makes them incapable of handling difficulties. They live in their cocoon of ideas, where they feel superior to everyone else by imagining that they have conquered the mysteries of the world by their mind. But what if someone doesn't care about their learning and erudition? Similarly, people who are righteous about their duties cannot accept mistreatment after having performed their duties; they expect to be respected for doing their job. If society rejects them with disrespect—after they have performed their duties—they tend to become extremely unhappy and perhaps rebellious. This sūtra states that the devotees of the Lord are so strong that they are not disturbed even if treated like blades of grasses—stepped upon by others.

We have discussed earlier how living entities in this world are suffering from fear and shame. This shame is then covered by false pride and one projects this false pride outward to overcome the innate sense of inferiority. The practices of karma, jñāna, and yoga help one progress in the control of the mind and senses, but they are often the avenues for expressing pride that covers the inferiority. Thus, people who perform great deeds, acquire a great deal of knowledge, or mystical powers due to yoga, seem happy because the pride covers their inferiority. But these achievements are not everlasting. As soon as the achievements are gone or ineffective, the pride is shattered, and the innate sense of fear and insecurity rears its ugly head again. Only the devotees of the Lord can overcome the deepest levels of fear and insecurity, and while they may seem externally meek and obliging, they are internally free from all fears.

QUESTION

But why should one tolerate disrespect at the hands of others—e.g., being treated as blades of grass and trampled upon? Isn't it our fundamental right to protect our dignity? How can you justify meekness against mistreatment?

2.2.6 (177)
अभ्युपगमेऽप्यर्थाभावात्
abhyupagame'pyarthābhāvat

abhyupagame—accepting; api—even; arthābhāvāt—because of the absence of any purpose.

TRANSLATION

Even though (it is a duty of ordinary people to defend their dignity) (the devotees) accept (the material suffering) because (the principles of defending one's dignity do not apply to those) devoid of (mundane) aspirations.

COMMENTARY

Defending our dignity, or leading a life of dignity, are often stated to be fundamental rights of a person. Tolerating injustice, on the other hand, is considered a weakness, and one is urged to retaliate against any oppression. But this sūtra states that all these conceptions of dignity and fundamental rights are based on mundane aspirations or goals. The fact is that due to karma, one's rights and aspirations may be frequently stepped on anyway, despite our best efforts. Since many 'fundamental rights' are violated due to karma, we cannot consider them inviolable rights. But to the extent that normal people fight to defend their rights is because they are attached to their bodies and positions in society and seek enjoyment. The devotee has no such aspirations. He is satisfied in the devotion to the Lord, and he understands that both material suffering and pleasure are fleeting. If a person is so devoid of material aspirations, even the commonly stated rights and conceptions of justice do not apply to them.

QUESTION

But if someone is so meek and helpless, then how can he defend the position of the Lord or of His devotees? Materialistic people will consider him foolish as he tolerates all difficulties, so won't he condone the attacks on the Lord and His devotees because he has accepted a meek position in society?

2.2.7 (178)

पुरुषाश्मवदिति चेत् तथापि

puruṣāśmavaditi cet tathāpi

puruṣa-aśma-vat—like a rock; iti cet—if it be said; tathāpi—even though.

TRANSLATION

If it is said (that a meek person would tolerate insults to the Lord) (we say) even though (they tolerate personal insults) (they become) just like men made up of stone (if there is any insult to the Lord or His devotees).

COMMENTARY

The meekness of the devotee of the Lord should not be considered his weakness. While he is prepared to tolerate all kinds of personal difficulties and insults, he becomes just like a stone or a rock when the Lord is attacked. The devotee is meek like a sheep on account of personal difficulties, but he is also ferocious like a lion on account of the devotees and the Lord. They may not stand up for their personal rights or against personal injury, but they will always defend the Lord and His devotees like a stone is used to injure others. This shows that they are factually not weak or helpless. They just tolerate the material difficulties as they don't want to waste their time trying to correct others when it comes to their personal well-being. Their lack of goals pertains to this mundane world, not to the devotion toward the Lord or His devotees.

Many people accuse devotees of insulting atheists or materialists; they say that a spiritualist must remain polite and humble. This politeness and humility is a standard practice in academic circles where atheists constantly attack devotion to the Lord, and devotees are—owing to their humility—not expected to attack them. This sūtra rejects such humility; the devotee is humble, but he is not spineless. He is devoted to the Lord, and like a servant protects his master, similarly, the devotee fights on behalf of the Lord. Of course, the Lord is not in need of such defense. His material energy can easily punish the atheists. But the devotee out of love behaves as if the Lord needs protection like a helpless child. These are not symptoms of a devotee trying to win a mundane battle to establish his own superiority. They are rather the symptoms of the love of the Lord. When the devotee becomes ferocious in defending the Lord, the Lord also relishes the mood of a helpless child being defended by a protective parent. Therefore, hidden under the façade of external aggression, there is no personal ambition. There is only unflinching love toward the Lord, and the devotee doesn't shy from aggression on the pretext that devotees must be tolerant.

QUESTION

But even the atheists are souls, and as such they are parts of the Lord. Shouldn't the devotee consider them as parts of the Lord's body and thereby not attack them? By such attacks, isn't the devotee attacking the Lord?

2.2.8 (179)

अङ्गतिवानुपपत्तेश्च

aṅgitvānupapatteśca

aṅgitva—the position of (the soul) being a part (of the Lord); anupapatteḥ—owing to the inapplicability or an illogical conclusion; ca—and.

TRANSLATION

(The use of the argument that) the soul is part of the Lord (so any punishment to the soul must also be a punishment to the Lord) is illogical.

COMMENTARY

A kitchen knife may be intended for cutting vegetables, but if it is being used as a weapon, then it must be considered a weapon. The intended use of an object cannot be considered the reason for treating it as such when it is not being used in that way. In the same way, the soul is intended to be a servant of the Lord, and that intended use always remains a possibility (like a kitchen knife can always be used to cut vegetables). But if the soul takes an alternative course, then we cannot make the argument that since the intended purpose was to be a part of the Lord, therefore, the soul should be treated *as if* he is part of the Lord. The intention and the ability don't exhaust the free will of the soul. When the soul changes the intention and engages in another possibility, then the intended possibility is subordinated, and the soul is technically not a part of the Lord.

In short, we should clarify that the soul is not physically a part of the Lord. He carries a portion of the properties of the Lord (the capacity for knowledge, beauty, power, wealth, fame, and renunciation). The soul has a portion of the desires the Lord has (i.e., to express one's happiness and become happy by the happiness of others). And the soul is a part of the system or organization supervised by the Lord—whether in the spiritual or the material worlds. But if the capacities of the soul are employed for another purpose (e.g., his own enjoyment) then the soul is intentionally detached from the Lord, although he continues to have the potential to return to the service of the Lord. In this regard, we can note that every object reveals different properties in relation to different things. The same person behaves differently as a boss, husband, father, subordinate, child, etc. When the soul contacts the material energy, his behavior as the controller of this energy is markedly different from the behavior as the child of the Lord. Just because the soul is supposed to be a child of the Lord doesn't entail that he should be treated as a child even if he is acting like a boss. In particular, the child disowns responsibility for his actions, being subordinate to the parents, and the parents assume responsibility for the child. But this is not true for the boss; the boss must assume responsibility for his actions. Hence, this sūtra asserts that this logic of the soul being a part of the Lord when he is not acting according to the nature of the part is illogical and inapplicable.

QUESTION

But the Lord is also said to be omniscient because He is present everywhere as Paramātma. You have previously said (in sūtra 1.2.8 (39)) that the Paramātma doesn't suffer along with the soul because He has a different nature—i.e., He doesn't desire material enjoyment, so His consciousness is drawn away from the material world. Doesn't this imply that the Lord is not omniscient because He doesn't know about the type of suffering the soul undergoes? If on the other hand, He knows the suffering, shouldn't He also be suffering?

2.2.9 (180)
अन्यथानुमितौ च ज्ञशक्तिवियोगात्
anyathānumitau ca jñaśaktiviyogāt

anyathā—otherwise; anumitau—if it be inferred; ca—even; jñaśakti-viyogāt—owing to the absence of the power of knowledge.

TRANSLATION

Even if it is inferred otherwise (that the Lord is omnipresent, so He must be suffering) (we say no) due to the absence of the knowledge energy.

COMMENTARY

In sūtra 1.2.8 (39) the objection was brought up that since the Paramātma is present everywhere He must be suffering just like the soul; in fact, the soul is only in one place but the Paramātma is everywhere; so He must be suffering far more than the soul. The response to that question was that Paramātma has a different nature—i.e., He doesn't have desires about the material world, so He doesn't suffer or enjoy, because His consciousness is withdrawn. The same point is repeated here but also elaborated to counter the argument that if the Lord doesn't suffer like the soul, then He must also not be omniscient.

To understand this elaboration, we must note that the Lord is said to have three kinds of energies, which are described in Śvetāśvatara Upaniṣad 6.8.

parāsya śaktir vividhaiva śrūyate
svābhāvikī jñāna-bala-kriyā ca

The energies of the Lord are said to be numerous; they can be classified into three categories called jñāna, bala, and kriyā.

The *bala* of the Lord is the energy that creates desire in the Lord; as we have seen previously, the Lord's Śakti agitates Him and produces a desire. This agitation is called *bala* or the power of will. Once this will is created, the *kriyā-śakti* fulfills the Lord's desires by creating what He has willed. Finally, with the *jñāna-śakti* the Lord knows what has been created; this knowing fulfills the previously created desire, and that fulfillment produces the pleasure in Him.

This sūtra makes a technical point that the jñāna-śakti is missing in the material world. However, the bala and the kriyā-śakti are still active. Therefore, the world is working according to the will of the Lord, and all the actions of the kriyā-śakti are performed under this will. However, the Lord is not observing this world like the soul due to the absence of the jñāna-śakti. So, He wills, and things happen according to the will, but because He never observes the results produced due to this desire, His desire doesn't produce pleasure or pain. He is still omniscient because He has willed, and this will is never violated. So, He doesn't have to double-check through the jñāna-śakti whether the will has been fulfilled. In fact, He is not interested in the material world, so He keeps His consciousness or the jñāna-śakti away from the observation of the world.

It has also been said earlier that there are two birds in each body: one bird (the soul) eats the fruits, while the other bird (the Paramātma) watches. We might wonder: What is He watching? The short answer is that the Paramātma watches the soul who is eating, but He doesn't eat Himself. As we have noted earlier, the soul and Paramātma are connected through prāṇa. The soul and material energy are also connected through another prāṇa. But the Lord is not connected to the material energy by this prāṇa. In short, there are two different kinds of jñāna-śakti involved here. The soul's jñāna-śakti is attached to the material energy, but the Lord's jñāna-śakti is attached to the soul. So, the Lord knows what is happening to the soul, but He is not experiencing the material energy, because His jñāna-śakti in relation to the material world is absent. He can see that the soul is suffering, but He is not suffering just like the soul.

QUESTION

If the Lord doesn't observe the world because of the absence of jñāna-śakti, then why can't the soul do the same? Can he not withdraw his consciousness when there is suffering, and then use it again when there is enjoyment? That way, he can selectively enjoy the pleasures but avoid all the suffering.

2.2.10 (181)

वपिरतषिधाच्चासमञ्जसम्

vipratiṣedhāccāsamañjasam

vipratiṣedhāt—due to conflicts; ca—also; asamañjasam—being disturbed.

TRANSLATION

(The soul is) also disturbed by conflicts.

COMMENTARY

Whenever we are faced with conflicts, there is a natural fight-or-flight response. When a person's courage dominates, then there is a tendency to fight. But when fear dominates, then there is a tendency for flight. The confusion is whether to fight or to flight. If one flies away from a situation, he naturally feels inferior, and he cannot keep escaping without hating himself. Sometimes, to restore self-confidence, the person also fights. There is always hope in a person that if he fights, he will win, and then prove himself to be superior. But there is also fear in the person that if they fight, they might be vanquished. So, even a person who flies away from a situation hopes to come back and fight again. And even a person who is fighting is always gripped by the fear that they may be vanquished. The soul is gripped by the tendencies of hope and fear.

The fear is caused by tamo-guna and hope is caused rajo-guna. The mode of sattva-guna represents detachment—i.e., freedom from both fight and flight—which gives one the ability to endure difficulties without fear, and without hope for winning and becoming dominant again. If one becomes detached, then he can withdraw his jñāna-śakti. The yogi is advised to withdraw their senses from the world just like a tortoise draws its limbs inward into its shell. The cessation of jñāna-śakti represents this withdrawal of the senses. But if the person is gripped by fight or flight, then he cannot withdraw the senses. He must remain on high alert—either due to hope or due to fear. In this state of high alert, the senses and the jñāna-śakti are always drawn outwardly.

Scientists describe our nervous systems as being comprised of the sympathetic and parasympathetic systems; the sympathetic system represents the fight-or-flight response, which is conditioned by rajo-guna and tamo-guna. The parasympathetic system represents the relaxation and is conditioned by sattva-guna. The yogi activates their parasympathetic nervous system and becomes relaxed from the tendency of fight and flight by the control of breath. This is a mechanical process by which one gets situated into sattva-guna and free from rajo-guna and tamo-guna. The suffering of the soul is due to the fight and flight tendencies, which keep the soul anxious and disturbed. Under their influence, the soul cannot relax and hence cannot become detached from the world.

Topic 2

QUESTION

But what is the root cause of these conflicts? Why can't the soul get out of these conflicts, become detached, and then become free of suffering?

2.2.11 (182)

महद्दीर्घवद्वा ह्रस्वपरिमण्डलाभ्याम्

mahaddīrghavadvā hrasvaparimaṇḍalābhyām

mahat-dīrgha-vat—just like greatness and bigness; vā—moving; hrasva—atomic; parimaṇḍalābhyām—by surrounding or engulfing it.

TRANSLATION

Just like something big surrounds something small and makes it move.

COMMENTARY

The term *vipratiṣedhāt* used in the previous sūtra can also be translated as "due to restrictions or bondage". In this sūtra, *parimaṇḍalābhyām* can be understood as that restriction or bondage that surrounds the soul. However, all these are somewhat superficial meanings, because it isn't clear what is small and what is big, why the big surrounds the small, and causes it to move. Are these metaphors or is there a deeper meaning underlying these sūtras?

Let's begin by asking: what is big and small? In modern science, we think that the universe is big, and the atoms are small. But big and small in Vedic philosophy have a different meaning: they indicate the biggest and the smallest things we can conceive of. Atomism is not based on what we can perceive by the senses, but what we can conceive. Thus, if you can mentally analyze something into smaller and smaller parts, then the smallest thing you can conceive is called the 'atom'. It is not an infinitesimal point; it must be the idea that you can understand. Similarly, the entire material creation is called mahattattva and is the biggest material thing we can conceive of. However, mahattattva isn't physical bigness. It is rather the principles of greatness. These big and small conceptions cover the soul. Under the conception of bigness, the soul conceives of the greatest personality that he can be, and under the idea of smallness, the soul conceives the smallest personality that he can be. We have discussed earlier how the soul enters the material world under the influence of inferiority relative to the Lord. The Lord's devotee knows that he is very small and insignificant, but he feels delighted by the greatness of the Lord. The non-devotee, on the other hand, realizes that he is small, but feels angry at the greatness of the Lord. So, the origin of the material existence is the sense of smallness (which is present even within the devotee) compounded by jealousy and fear of the big.

This sense of smallness, coupled with the jealousy and fear, is called māyā or that which is *not*. The soul is covered by the sense that he is not beautiful, knowledgeable, powerful, famous, wealthy, or renounced. But immediately from this sense of inferiority springs the idea of greatness—namely, that even though I am not great, I *want* to be great. This idea of greatness is called mahattattva. It covers our inferiority and gives rise to ideas about how we can be great. But even if we developed some ideas of greatness, we will not be able to do anything if we keep thinking that I'm not even great enough to pursue greatness. To overcome this problem, from mahattattva springs ahamkāra or false pride: I don't just have ideas of greatness, but I'm also great (in terms of one or more of the ideas of greatness). At least, I'm entitled and deserving of this greatness. So, I may not have this greatness in full, but I'm great enough to pursue greatness. Once this sense of greatness or entitlement arises, then the intellect or buddhi springs from the false pride: since I'm entitled, I'm now going to construct plans and methods for becoming great. From this buddhi springs the mind, which starts conceiving of all the external things that will imply our greatness. From this mind spring the senses, which add sense perceptions to the meanings by the mind. From these sense perceptions spring the objective world. This process of gradual development of material nature from the innate sense of insecurity and smallness to the external world is called Sāñkhya.

The conflict described in the previous sūtra is between the innate smallness and the superficial covering of greatness that arises from the smallness. No matter how great we become, the inferiority never goes away; the more you achieve, the more you want to achieve because you never stop feeling small despite your achievements. The desire to achieve more leads to fear (as it reinforces the idea that we are incomplete) and hope (because we believe that if we have come so far in greatness then we can hope to become even greater).

With this understanding, we can see that the different ideas, namely—(1) the soul is caught in conflicts, (2) the soul is covered by the idea of greatness, (3) the soul is itself conditioned by the idea of smallness, (4) the conflict is between inferiority and greatness, and (5) this conflict keeps the soul engaged in the world, are all deeply intertwined. The hope and fear we spoke of in the previous sūtra are connected to the greatness and smallness in this sūtra.

Topic 3

QUESTION

But just a few sūtras ago you stated that the cause of suffering is karma, and you confirmed that this karma is going on since time immemorial. I had understood that the fall of the soul in the material world happens because of the soul's aversion to the Lord, but the suffering was only due to karma, which arose due to neglect of duties. Now you are stating that the soul is always suffering because there is a conflict between the sense of bigness and smallness? Which of these two things should be considered the cause of suffering?

2.2.12 (183)

उभयथापि न कर्मातस्तदभावः

ubhayathāpi na karmātastadabhāvaḥ

ubhayathāpi—in either case; na—is not; karma—activity; ataḥ—therefore; tat-abhāvaḥ—negation of that.

TRANSLATION

In either case (whether you consider the cause of suffering as karma or not), it is (ultimately) not karma; therefore, it is the negation of that (the Lord).

COMMENTARY

There are two causes of suffering—one external and the other internal. The external cause of suffering is due to karma because it puts us in situations contrary to our desires. But the internal cause of suffering is the incessant desires which can never be fulfilled. In fact, even the neglect of duties arises because we have desires, which are produced because we are trying to overcome the sense of inferiority in us. Therefore, it is not wrong to say that karma is the external cause of suffering. But ultimately, even this karma is produced due to internal desires. So, after stating that the soul is suffering incessantly due to karma (in response to the question about why bad things happen to good people), this sūtra says that karma is not the ultimate cause. Rather, the negation of that (i.e., the Lord and His service) is the ultimate cause of suffering. As we have discussed earlier, this negation appears as māyā or the idea that "I am not that". This māyā is also referred to here as *tat-abhāvaḥ* or the absence of "that".

QUESTION

How does the absence of the Lord lead to suffering in this world?

2.2.13 (184)

समवायाभ्युपगमाच्च साम्याद् अनवस्थितेः

samavāyābhyupagamācca sāmyād anavasthiteḥ

samavāya—collection; abhyupagamāt—from the agreement;

ca—also; sāmyāt—harmony or stability; anavasthiteḥ—in the unstable.

TRANSLATION

Because (the Lord's presence brings) agreement or cooperation in a collection (of individuals), also (the Lord's presence brings) stability in instability.

COMMENTARY

Several times before we have spoken of the Lord as being the unity in the diversity. There are three such kinds of unity—of purpose, of origin, and of control. The unity of purpose arises due to the Lord's ānanda: when He is the person to be pleased, there is unity of purpose. The unity of origin arises due to the Lord's *chit*: when He is the origin, all diversities of this world are reconciled in the singular origin. The unity of control arises due to the Lord's *sat*: when the Lord is the ruler or controller, everyone is subordinated to His control. The unity spoken of earlier was prominently in the sense of *chit*: The Lord is the common origin from which the diversity springs, and this has been expressed in various ways by stating that Brahman is beyond the diversity, the world is the expression of the Lord, and even the soul is compared to the Lord's speech. In this sūtra, the unities due to ānanda and *sat* are being referred to.

The unity of ānanda is the unity of purpose. When this unity is present, then there is cooperation between the different individuals; everyone has a common goal—namely, the pleasure of the Lord—and nobody has an individual goal (namely, their own satisfaction). When the individual goals are dissolved, and a common goal is established, then cooperation between individuals naturally follows. Similarly, the unity of *sat* is the unity of control. When this unity is present, then there is a central command authority under whose supervision everything is done. Just like societies have kings, and organizations have CEOs, and these leadership roles bring about unity in the society, similarly, the presence of the Lord and obedience to His command brings about unity.

When the unity of purpose and control are removed, we are just left with the unity of origin. We can speak about the fact that all this diversity has originated from a common source, but it doesn't help to bring a unity, because we can still claim to have different purposes and refuse to accept any control authority. Then, everyone would work for themselves, and society would be engulfed by anarchy. To create cooperation, rulers and politicians have used religion since time immemorial: the king was supposed to be the representation of God on earth; similarly, the acceptance of a common God was the incentive to bring about political unity in disturbed times. This is not to rationalize the wars of religion, or how kings have misused religion to establish their rule. It is only to say that the principle of unity exists only when there is a common control and a shared purpose. If this unity is removed in principle—by dissolving the existence of God—then the world would be thrown into chaos; everyone will fight with the other person considering themselves independent and autonomous, neglecting the collective interest. To avoid such outcomes, some societies collectivize by claiming that everyone must work for the government, although the government is not itself under a moral or spiritual principle. That then leads to even greater atrocities and chaos than acknowledging individuality. The real answer to these problems is the recognition that society has a common purpose and control. When this purpose and control is established, then competition gives way to cooperation, and instability gives way to stability. Similarly, when the Lord is removed from the picture, then suffering ensues because everybody acts in their interest; they don't acknowledge their duties, and by the neglect of duties adverse karma is produced, which then leads to constant suffering. Likewise, when nobody is cooperating, then everyone's desires will remain unfulfilled. These unfulfilled desires will then exacerbate our inner insecurities, and thereby lead to greater unhappiness in society. So, everything hinges on the presence of unity as it brings cooperation and stability in the world.

QUESTION

It is seen that when there is cooperation and stability in a society, the society also becomes long-lived. On the other hand, competition and lack of central control lead to instability, which then leads to temporariness. Does this mean that the eternity of the spiritual world is due to the presence of the Lord?

2.2.14 (185)
नतियमेव च भावात्
nityameva ca bhāvāt

nityam-eva—certainly eternal; ca—also; bhāvāt—because of the existence (of the Lord).

TRANSLATION
The existence of the Lord also makes the (spiritual world) eternal.

COMMENTARY
The soul and the Lord have already been said to be eternal. Similarly, the material energy is also eternal, being a consort of the Lord. However, the material world created by this energy—namely, bodies, planets, universes—are temporary, while the spiritual world is eternal. This difference is now attributed to the presence of the Lord as the common purpose and controller of existence. History shows that civilizations continue to exist if there is a powerful ruler who brings order in society, and the people have a sense of affiliation to that nation, society, and ruler. If the ruler becomes weak or corrupt or goes missing, alternative rulers spring up, and the society loses its affiliation to that country or civilization. The longevity of a society therefore depends on the effectiveness of the ruler, under whose command the rest of society operates. If this ruler is eternal, and everyone is devoted to the ruler, the society also will become eternal. Thus, the spiritual world is eternal because of the Lord's presence.

QUESTION
But in modern society it is believed that while the universe has a common material origin, there cannot be a common purpose and central control. Everybody is different, and they want to be able to choose their purpose and ruler according to their nature. The argument goes that given that there cannot be a common purpose, a common control will inevitably lead to conflicts. So, allowing different purposes and controllers is the method of getting stability.

2.2.15 (186)
रूपादमित्तत्वाच्च वपिर्ययो दर्शनात्
rūpādimattvācca viparyayo darśanāt

rūpādi—form etc.; mat—(differing) opinions or beliefs; tvāt—from just like; ca—also; viparyayaḥ—conflicts or oppositions; darśanāt—as it is seen.

TRANSLATION

From the existence of multiple opinions or beliefs just like diversified forms also (arise) conflicts and oppositions as it is seen (in the world).

COMMENTARY

People may organize themselves into groups, organizations, societies, cultures, or religions, based on a shared purpose and control, but they will continue to fight with other groups, organizations, societies, cultures, and religions based on their differing opinions. The diversity of this world naturally leads to oppositions and conflicts—unless there is a shared purpose and control. If there is a shared purpose, then we can understand that all the diversity can be employed for a common goal—i.e., serving the Supreme Lord. But even with a shared purpose, unless the Lord is considered the ruler and controller of the world, many different leaders will spring up and claim that there should be a common purpose, but *their* purpose is that common purpose. The Lord should thus be considered the common origin of diversity, the common purpose to be served by the diversity, and the common controller who creates order.

In this sūtra, the different opinions or beliefs are compared to forms etc. (including things like color, size, etc.). Thus, ideas too have the properties perceived by the senses, which is why we identify ideological positions by colors such as red, blue, and green; we say that thinking is sharp or dull; we attribute lightness and darkness to ideas; ideas are called big and small, etc. These are not merely metaphorical ways of speaking; the ideas too have shapes, colors, sizes, besides sensations such as hard and soft, hot and color, bitter and sweet. The meanings in our mind are classified into six categories—knowledge, beauty, power, wealth, fame, and renunciation—and each of these is further divided into different forms of knowledge, beauty, etc. These forms have different shapes, sizes, colors, taste, hardness, etc. For instance, mathematics and physics are called 'hard sciences', and in our minds, we think of them as having angular shapes. Likewise, economics and sociology are considered 'soft sciences', and in our minds, we think of them as having oblong shapes.

Since ideas have different forms, they are incompatible with other such ideas, unless we know how to fit them together in complementary ways just like filling up the pieces of a jigsaw puzzle. To complete this jigsaw puzzle, two things are essential—(1) we must be convinced that this diversity is actually parts of a single larger picture and must be used to construct that picture, and (2) there must be somebody who puts the pieces together into that picture. If everyone believes that there isn't a single picture, or if there is nobody to put the pieces together, then the pieces of the puzzle remain incompatible.

QUESTION

The impersonalist argues that this world is temporary, and because it is comprised of duality, we can expect clashes and conflicts. To get away from these conflicts, we must dissolve the individuality of separate purposes, and the existence of a central controller who organizes a diversified society. By removing the need for a shared purpose and common control, all the diversity will be ultimately collapsed into a common origin—the Brahman—and this Brahman can be considered the origin of the temporary material diversity.

2.2.16 (187)

उभयथा च दोषात्

ubhayathā ca doṣāt

ubhayathā—because of the two; ca—also; doṣāt—from existence of faults.

TRANSLATION

Because of the two (the rejection of a common control and shared purpose) from the existence of faults (the impersonalist viewpoint is also faulty).

COMMENTARY

Here the impersonalist view is criticized on the ground that it recognizes a common origin in Brahman but doesn't consider that Brahman to be the shared purpose of existence, and the central controller of diversity. To avoid acknowledging the shared purpose and common control, the impersonalist dissolves the diversity into a unity, and the existence of a world comprised of diversified qualities, different individuals, who perform different roles, also disappears. By considering this to be the ultimate reality, the impersonalist is ignorant of a transcendental world in which the Lord is not merely the origin, but also the purpose and controller. There is a stable, cooperative, and eternal society due to the presence and recognition of the Lord. Of course, the Lord also exists in the material world, but His presence is not accepted by everyone. So, everyone considers themselves free to do whatever they want, competing with others, disregarding their responsibilities, and breaking laws. The impersonalist thinks that the solution to the problems of the material world is dissolving all the diversity. No doubt, this is *a* solution, but it is not the *only* solution.

QUESTION

Are you rejecting the impersonalist viewpoint as a legitimate solution?

2.2.17 (188)

अपरग्रिहाच्चात्यन्तमनपेक्षा

aparigrahāccātyantamanapekṣā

aparigrahāt—because it is not accepted (by the devotees); ca—also; atyantam—in the ultimate analysis; anapekṣā—cannot be used for comparison.

TRANSLATION

Also, because it is not accepted (by the devotees), in the ultimate analysis (the impersonalist's viewpoint) cannot be used for comparison.

COMMENTARY

The previous sūtra said that impersonalist view is faulty but did not completely reject it because the undivided Brahman indeed exists. So, in this sūtra, it is said that in the ultimate analysis—after analyzing all the pros and cons—we can reject the impersonal viewpoint. The Absolute Truth has three aspects—*sat*, *chit*, and ānanda. The *chit* creates different objects, bodies, planets, etc. which are diversified from a root. The *sat* creates the roles in which these objects are organized into a hierarchical structure, at the root of which lies a ruler who controls the world. And ānanda creates diverse kinds of pleasures, desires, and wills, which are all subparts of the pleasure, desire, and will of the source of diversity. The impersonalist negates the roles of individuals organized in a hierarchy, and how these individuals serve at the pleasure of the common source, the Lord. Having gotten rid of a common ruler and a shared purpose, he then collapses the diverse objects into a single unified existence devoid of diversity. And when this diversity has been rejected, the impersonalist calls this the ultimate truth. This raises a fundamental question: Why should *sat* and ānanda exist if they must be rejected? And why should *chit* be capable of producing diversity when all this diversity must be rejected? The impersonalist incorrectly attributes the problem to diversity, rather than the absence of common control and shared purpose. With a shared purpose and common control, the same diversity is the cause of an eternal, stable, peaceful, and delightful society.

The rejection of impersonalism is not the rejection of Brahman. Most people tend to incorrectly equate these two ideas. As has been discussed earlier, even Brahman is particles of light originating from a source of light. The flaw in impersonalism is recognizing this light and rejecting the source of light. As light seems diffused and you cannot see small particles of light, similarly, the impersonalist supposes that the light is the ultimate undivided reality. If, instead, it was recognized that even Brahman is small particles of light, then we would have to accept that this light has an origin. Once that origin is recognized, then we can see that He is also the purpose because the diversity emerges from Him due to His desire for pleasure. And since He is the creator of this diversity, He becomes its controller, using the creation for His enjoyment. All these conclusions follow naturally when we realize that light is not an undivided unity; it is rather comprised of small particles of light that seem undifferentiated.

So, the impersonalist view is a limited caricature of the whole truth; the devotees of the Lord don't accept it because it rejects the source of light, the reason why the source emits this light, and how the source then controls the manifestation. The Vedānta Sūtra recommends the rejection of this view.

Topic 4

QUESTION

You have said that without a shared purpose and a common controller there will be clashes and conflicts in society, which will lead to instability. But the materialist doesn't consider this a problem. He rather claims that conflicts between individuals lead to natural selection in which the unfit are eliminated, and the fit survive. Therefore, conflict and clash are not a bad thing for the materialist. They would claim that it is the very means for making progress.

2.2.18 (189)
समुदाय उभयहेतुकेऽपि तदप्राप्तिः
samudāya ubhayahetuke'pi tadaprāptiḥ

samudāye—in the collection; ubhaya-hetuke—in both reasons; api—even; tat-aprāptiḥ—that is not achieved.

TRANSLATION

Even in the collection, that (unity) is not achieved in both reasons.

COMMENTARY

Groups of people are formed only when there is a shared purpose and a visionary leader. If there is no shared purpose, and if there is no leader, people will not even come together. Sometimes, people may come together because of a shared purpose, although a leader has not yet emerged; the leader is selected later. Similarly, sometimes, there can be a visionary leader who then defines a purpose, that is adopted by everyone. Thus, if there is a vision but not a leader, a group can still be created. Similarly, if there is a leader, but not a vision, the group can be formed. The missing components are added subsequently. However, if both a shared mission and a common leader are missing, the group is never formed. This sūtra asserts that if both the shared purpose and a common leader are missing, we cannot even speak about the formation of a group. Unless a group is formed, we cannot speak about selection and evolution.

Modern science studies the world as material objects and claims that these objects aggregate to form complex systems due to natural forces. However, every such interaction due to natural forces is indeterministic. Take for example the collision of two billiard balls. The laws of physics say that the total energy and momentum remain conserved before and after the collision. However, this conservation of energy and momentum is achievable in innumerable ways: (1) all the energy can be transferred to ball A or ball B, (2) the energy can be distributed in many ways between the two balls, and (3) each of the balls can be blown into smaller pieces, each possessing a different amount of energy. The total number of possibilities resulting from the same laws is so vast that we can never predict what will happen. Now, we have three possible alternatives. First, we can say that our laws are complete, but nature is indeterministic. Second, we can say that our laws are incomplete, although nature is not indeterministic. Third, we can say that our laws are wrong as they cannot predict the outcomes. Scientists today take the first route; they say that nature is indeterministic, thus allowing 'random mutations' which cause objects to aggregate. The right answer is that the laws are incomplete and wrong. Specifically, our notion that matter aggregates due to forces of nature is itself flawed.

In Vedic philosophy, three causes of material aggregation are recognized. First, there are the objects or particles which aggregate. Second, the aggregation is due to a structure, in which each object is accorded a different role in the collection. Third, this structure is created due to a purpose or goal. For example, if you are constructing a chair, the construction begins with the purpose. It is then exemplified into a structure, which we call the design of the chair. And finally, this design is then converted into an actual chair by using wood blocks. The wood blocks don't aggregate without a preexisting structure. And the structure cannot exist unless there is a purpose. So, what scientists call 'random collections' are not random; they are occurring because of the existence of deeper forms of reality, which we refuse to acknowledge. What scientists call force fields are not forces at all; they are forms of space in which objects are organized. And these forms are produced due to an objective intention.

In everyday life, this structure is visible through the functional divisions in society—e.g., that an organization has many functional parts, or a government is divided into functional departments, etc. And this functional division appears because there is a purpose—e.g., people aggregate into an organization due to a shared purpose, and then they organize themselves into various functional departments. If there is no purpose, then there can be no structure, and without this structure, there cannot be aggregation of individual parts. The functional structure is the mechanism of control, and the goal to be fulfilled by that functional organization is the purpose for which the structure exists.

If we take out the purpose and the structure, then there cannot be any aggregation of parts. This is what the sūtra states. There must be some purpose, which then leads to some structure, to organize the world. It is quite possible that the purpose is not shared, and according to different purposes, different structures are created, which then compete and clash with each other leading to conflicts. But the claim that nature is without purpose and without controller entails that there will be never be a stable arrangement of bodies, societies, ecosystems, and organizations. So, the claim that nature randomly aggregates into larger systems is a flawed idea because the laws on the basis of which we arrive at this conclusion are predictively incomplete, but rather than accepting that our theories and laws are flawed, we transfer the randomness to nature. These are shortcomings of our understanding of nature, not of nature itself.

QUESTION

Some philosophers accept the reality of structure, without acknowledging the existence of a shared purpose and a central controller. For example, Buddhists advocate the idea of Pratītyasa-mutpāda or co-dependent origination in which two opposites simultaneously manifest from nothingness as mutual opposites. Each opposite becomes the reason or the justification for the other, so they are mutually justified, but we cannot trace this origin to a First Cause. As these opposites appear, structure is created, but there is

no central controller or a shared purpose for its causation. Therefore, Buddhists don't accept the existence of a God or a soul, but they thus explain the order in nature naturally.

2.2.19 (190)

इतरेतरप्रत्ययत्वादिति चेत् न उत्पत्तिमात्रनिमित्तत्वात्

itaretarapratyayatvāditi cet na utpattimātranimittatvāt

itaretara—mutual; pratyayatvāt—from as if proof, definition; iti cet—if it be said; na—no; utpatta-mātra—merely produced; nimittat-vāt—from being symptoms.

TRANSLATION

If it is said that from as if mutual proofs or justifications (of opposites) (we say) no (because) they are merely produced as symptoms (of the real cause).

COMMENTARY

A classic illustration of the thesis of Pratītyasamutpāda is the yin-yang duality, which is depicted by two parts of a circle—one black and another white—with a part of the black being white, and a part of the white being black. Each part, therefore, contains its own opposite, even as the opposites are said to be complementary. If these opposites are collapsed, then their mutual opposition results in nothingness. Hence, they are said to spring from nothingness and can dissolve back into nothingness. When they exist, they justify the existence of their opposite, and hence the opposites emerge and dissolve simultaneously. This idea is not entirely new; it exists in the Vedic description of the world as duality: the world is comprised of opposites such as hot and cold, bitter and sweet, rough and smooth, and these opposites are defined mutually. However, this mutuality of the opposites is only a partial description of nature. For instance, hot and cold are opposites within the sensation of touch; bitter and sweet are opposites within the sensation of taste, etc. We can normally perceive the existence of hot vs. cold, bitter vs. sweet, but we don't perceive the existence of touch or smell, or taste. We just use them as invisible concepts that cannot be perceived, although they are properties in terms of which we perceive.

These properties are both transcendent and immanent. For example, black and white are both colors, so color is immanent in both black and white. However, since there are other colors—e.g., red, green, blue—therefore, color is beyond black and white. Thus, color exists in both black and white, and yet, color is neither black nor white. Since color is inside black, and white is a type of color, therefore, white is also inside black. Similarly, since color is inside white, and black is a type of color, therefore, black is also inside white. If the transcendent property of color did not exist, then black and white will also not exist. And if the immanent property of color (within black and white) did not exist, then black and white would remain logical opposites, but not definitionally interrelated because the common property of color—which is immanent in both—would not exist. Therefore, the claim that two opposites are mutually defined is only a superficial understanding. The deeper reason for this mutuality is that properties such as color are both transcendent and immanent.

Now, by the above argument, we would say that the property of color is immanent in shades of color, but not in flavors of taste. Similarly, the property of taste would be immanent in flavors of taste but not in the colors. This is factually wrong. Some colors produce sensations of sweetness—e.g., lavender. Likewise, other colors produce the sensation of bitterness—e.g., brown.

This is the point at which we must recognize that these concepts are arranged in a hierarchy, and emanate from a root like trunks, branches, twigs, and leaves. The root of this tree is the Original Idea which exists as the form of knowledge, beauty, power, wealth, fame, and renunciation. This form is sometimes called Bhagavān in Vedic philosophy, because He is full of all the qualities (i.e., everything is in Him), and He is transcendent to everything. Similarly, the immanent form of these properties is called Paramātma, and it exists inside everything. Thus, the Lord is both immanent and transcendent; inside everything and outside everything. Due to the immanence of the Lord, everything is inside everything else, because the whole truth exists inside all partial truths.

These partial truths are visible to us, but the complete immanent truth remains invisible. Lord Kṛṣṇa calls this invisible form avyakta-mūrti. But from this invisible form, anything can be manifest, so nothing is truly separated from anything else. Thus, tastes can appear within colors, and colors can appear within tastes. The Buddhist claim that the structure in this world is visible as mutual oppositions is true. However, the claim that these opposites are mutually defined on their own is incorrect. The reason for this interrelatedness is the immanent form of the Lord. As the transcendent form, He manifests all the opposites, and as the immanent form, He interconnects everything. Thus, it is said that everything is inside the Lord, and the Lord is inside everything. This inside and outside is not a unique property of the Lord; it is rather a pervasive property of all concepts. It's just that ordinary concepts are immanent only in a few objects, but the Original Idea is immanent in everything. Therefore, when we speak about conceptual oppositions, we can relate colors like black and white, tastes like bitter and sweet, but we cannot connect everything to everything, unless we say that there is an original idea which is immanent in everything, because everything is a partial manifestation of the transcendent Being.

QUESTION

If everything is inside everything, then why isn't this visible? When we see a table, we don't see a chair in the same thing. Due to the mutual exclusion of these things, we believe that these are separate material objects. But you are saying that because the Lord is immanent in everything, everything is inside everything else. And yet, why don't see everything inside everything else?

2.2.20 (191)

उत्तरोत्पादे च पूर्वनिरोधात्

uttarotpāde ca pūrvanirodhāt

uttarotpāde—in the time of the production of the subsequent thing; ca—also; purva-nirodhāt—because the antecedent one has been forbidden.

TRANSLATION

Because in the time of the production of the subsequent thing, the previous thing has also been forbidden.

COMMENTARY

All things in the material world are built out of the three modes of nature—sattva, rajas, and tamas. In the primordial state of prakriti, these modes are said to be in 'balance', and this state is called śuddha-sattva. As an example, the mode of tamas represents inertia, the mode of rajas represents activity, and the mode of sattva represents knowledge. When tamas or rajas are present, then knowledge is absent, and whether one is lazy or active, both are under ignorance. The lazy person remains inert under ignorance, and the active person works very hard under ignorance. The lazy person produces no results, while the active person produces adverse results. When sattva is present, then knowledge is gained, but there is no activity. So, knowledge is not being applied to produce something useful. The balanced combination of these modes represents knowledge that leads to activity, but without losing stability. The person is not hyperactive or endeavoring very hard. At the same time, he is also not lazy. Everything is done with understanding, deliberately, and at due pace. The combination of the three modes doesn't result in nothingness; it rather results in a pure state that is devoid of the separated influence of the three modes.

So, what is separation? When the soul is injected into the material energy, based on the soul's choices, the three modes become dominant and subordinate. For example, when tamas dominates, and sattva is subordinated, and rajas is further subordinated, then due to tamas the person remains lazy, due to subordinate sattva he indulges in armchair philosophy, and due to rajas, he produces books on this armchair philosophy. Similarly, if sattva dominates, and tamas is subordinate, and rajas is further subordinate, then due to sattva there is pursuit of knowledge, but due to tamas this pursuit describes nature as being dull and meaningless particles, and due to rajas, these particles will be moved by some force. If the order of rajas and tamas is flipped, then a philosopher will say that there is only change and particles are the epiphenomena of this change. Thus, we can psychoanalyze the author from the theories they have produced.

The variety of the world is due to the repeating dominant-subordinate structure of the three modes, and it exists in a tree-like structure—the root is śuddha-sattva, the three modes are the trunks, each of these trunks is divided into three parts by each mode, and this process continues indefinitely. If we count the instances of sattva, rajas and tamas in anything, by and large, everything has the combination of the three modes in equal proportion. The objects are different only due to the hierarchy or the dominant-subordinate structure of the three modes. Therefore, to change one thing into another, we don't need new material 'stuff'. We just need to change the hierarchy of the modes.

The modes organized in one specific hierarchy constitute one branch of the tree; other hierarchies represent other branches. In one sense, each branch is merely a transformation of another branch in which the components of a branch are rearranged in a different order. In another sense, each of these branches are unique, individual things. Due to the first reason, everything is inside everything else in a potential form—you could transform it into anything else if you changed the hierarchy of the modes. But as soon as you make that transformation, the present thing will become unmanifest and rest as a potential.

This is what this sūtra states succinctly: everything exists in everything else, but the moment one thing manifests, the other thing is hidden. This hidden form is the world resting in a potential state, so, we cannot perceive it because it is indeed not manifest. But if we understand the science of material transformation, then we can convert anything to anything else. While material scientists may be excited by the possibility of creating gold out of sand, this knowledge has been previously used for transforming oneself into a better person.

QUESTION

Generally, we say that if something exists, then it must be observable. But you are saying that even the possibilities—which cannot be observed—are existing. And everything is inside everything else as a potential or possibility. How can we justify a stance in which the non-observable is considered real?

2.2.21 (192)
असति प्रतिज्ञोपरोधो यौगपद्यमन्यथा
asati pratijñoparodho yaugapadyamanyathā

asati—in the non-existence; pratijña-uparodhaḥ—obstruction of the possibility; yaugapadyam—simultaneity; anyathā—otherwise.

TRANSLATION

In the non-existence there is obstruction of possibility. Otherwise, we must say that (all possibilities) must exist simultaneously.

COMMENTARY

There can be some contention regarding the translation of *prati-jña* used here. The root *jña* means knowledge or to know. The root *prati* indicates towards or against. Thus, in combination, *pratijña* has many meanings, based on the context. It can mean a 'promise' which is toward a reality (fulfilled by the promise) and not yet a reality (because it is still a promise). It can mean a 'possibility', which is toward a reality and not yet a reality. It can also mean a 'claim' which hasn't yet been proven, so it is toward a reality and not yet a reality. It can mean 'the thing to be known, which is not yet known'. I have translated *prati-jña* as possibility here, based on the context of the previous discussion.

There are two ways to measure reality. First, we can say that the thing that exists is all that we can see. Second, we can also say that the thing that exists is produced by the negation of all the other things that it could have been. Generally, when we measure the world as matter, we employ the first method—we measure the properties of an object and we say that such and such exists. However, if we measure the world as information, we employ the second method—we say that the total information contained in something is equal to the number of choices that had to be made to eliminate all the alternative possibilities. The second method of measuring existence is now standard practice in many areas of modern science in the last couple of centuries, starting with the introduction of the statistical mechanical description of thermodynamic phenomena. In classical mechanics, reality is described as everything it is. In thermodynamics, the opposite method—i.e., everything it is not—was found to be suitable.

To describe the information contained in a system, we construe all the possible states of the system, which is called its 'entropy'. The information in the system is then said to be inversely proportional to the entropy—i.e., if the possibilities are too many, then the information encoded in the system must have had to remove all these alternatives to create something definite; the larger the number of possibilities to eliminate, the greater the information needed. Therefore, if we only describe the world as material things, then reality would be all that we can see. But if we describe the same world as information, then reality would be all that is possible, and what we can observe would be created by the elimination of all except one potentiality to create something definite.

In Indian philosophy, the Vaiśeṣika system is known to have introduced abhāva or absence as a category of knowledge. For example, when you conclude something is a cow, you also conclude that it is not a dog, not a horse, not a tiger, etc. In Western philosophy, the negative method of proof has been called reductio ad absurdum, or that the contrary postulate leads to a contradiction. But despite these prevalent methods, the underlying metaphysics for why this method is so useful isn't understood, because we tend to think that parts are the primordial reality and the whole is constructed from the combination of the parts. If we invert this idea and say that the whole is the reality, and the parts are produced by negating portions of the whole, then the part would be defined only after we consider the whole. In short, we would have to first consider all the possibilities, and then how they are eliminated to create an observation.

The Vedic metaphysics follows this inverted system, in which the root is the whole truth, and the parts are produced from this whole (as branches emanating from the root) through successive but partial negations of the whole. The process of this negation is called māyā or that which is not. Māyā 'covers' the Absolute Truth (in the vision of the soul, not in the vision of the Lord) and creates partial truths. Therefore, we cannot understand a table just by looking at its observable properties. We must understand this object in relation to the complete set of possibilities—i.e., the whole truth—and how it fits as a part of that whole. Just because we don't see the whole truth doesn't entail it doesn't exist. In fact, this invisible reality is the basis on which to understand the visible. Thus, every part must be understood only in relation to the full truth.

This point is made in this sūtra by asserting that if we claim that the alternative possibilities don't exist, then we would have to conclude that they are impossible. On the other hand, if we say that they exist, then we would have to acknowledge that all the possibilities are eternally and simultaneously true.

QUESTION

Since you are saying that the whole truth exists inside all the partial truths, can we not just negate all these partial truths and we will get the whole truth? After all, these partial truths are negations of the whole truth, so by negating the negation, we will obtain the whole truth. Many philosophers call this the method of negation—that by denying everything we obtain the truth.

2.2.22 (193)

प्रतिसंख्याप्रतिसंख्यानिरोधाप्राप्तिःअवच्छेदात्

pratisaṃkhyāpratisaṃkhyānirodhāprāptiḥ avicchedāt

pratisaṃkhyā—the countable; apratisaṃkhyā—the uncountable; nirodha-aprāptiḥ—not obtainable by negation; avicchedāt—owing to inseparability.

TRANSLATION

The uncountable cannot be obtained by negating the countable, because (the countable) is inseparable (from the uncountable).

COMMENTARY

To understand this sūtra, we must understand what we mean by countable and uncountable. Countable means all those things that can be numbered as 1, 2, 3, 4, etc. This numbering is infinite, but it is still possible to individually count them; hence, in mathematics, this is called a countable infinity. The universe is comprised of such countably infinite things, if we look at the universe at any given moment of time; i.e., if we take a snapshot of the universe at any given moment, then we can enumerate the things in the universe one by one. However, because the universe is changing continuously, the things that appear at any given time, may not appear at another moment in time. The things that appear in the universe at a moment in time are a subset of all the possible things that could appear. Therefore, if the set of all possible things is N, then the manifest things at a moment would be a subset of N. In fact, as time elapses, each moment would create a different subset of all the possibilities. This set of all subsets (of the set of all the possibilities) is exponentially larger than N—and denoted as

2N. It is also sometimes called uncountable infinity, which represents all the states of the universe through time. Thus, there are two kinds of space—(1) the countably infinite space of all possibilities, and (2) an uncountably infinite space of all the subsets of all the possibilities, as they appear in time.

The significance of the uncountably infinite space is that we can draw the evolution of the universe as a trajectory in this space. Each point on this trajectory would represent the state of the entire universe at a given moment. And, in principle, the trajectory would cover the entire space over the lifetime of the universe. With these two spaces, we would say that the universe is uncountably infinite, however, at any given moment, it appears to us as countably infinite. This countable infinity is all the manifest things, but the uncountable infinity is all those things that the universe could be but is not at the present moment. The uncountably infinite space would constitute the 'entropy' of the universe, and the information encoded in the universe at any moment in time would be defined relative to all the states that the universe hasn't taken currently.

If we count all the currently existing objects, we will get a countably infinite reality. But that isn't the reality. The reality is that which can be observed any time in the past, present, or future. This reality—as we said—is uncountably infinite. So, the method of negating what we currently see to understand reality is flawed, because reality is exponentially larger than this negated observation. The fact that both these realities are infinite shouldn't entail that they are similar because the uncountable reality is qualitatively different than the countable reality. The uncountable reality is what the universe can ever be, and the countable reality is all that the universe is presently. The countable reality is created by negating the information in the uncountable reality. We can say that time chooses one point in the uncountable space to create the universe at any moment, but the universe is factually the entire space, not just a point.

This understanding of countable and uncountable can help us understand this sūtra. The countable is a point in the uncountable space, so by negating that countable we will only obtain a point in the uncountable space, not the entire space. If, however, this is wrongly taken to mean that the countable and uncountable are different things, then, that conclusion is also rejected by stating that these two are inseparable. Essentially, what is visible at any given time is not separate from that which exists timelessly. And yet, what exists timelessly manifests what is visible in time. To understand that timeless reality, we must observe all that will manifest over time. The method of negation must be rejected because it doesn't give us that timeless truth. Only the method of seeing everything over the duration of the universe gives us the timeless reality.

The conclusion is that if we see an object right now, it is not merely defined in relation to the other objects that we can see right now. Instead, everything that can be presently seen, is defined in relation to those things that have been visible in the past and will exist in the future. Just as we cannot separate a specific state in space from the other states, similarly, we cannot separate all these states collectively from the states at any time in the past or the future. It is hard enough to know all the states at present to fully know the state of an individual object. If these states are collectively defined in relation to past and future states, then the problem is much worse. However, this much worse problem also gives us an insight into how the universe evolves. It is not due to the actions in the individual objects; it is rather the collective state selection of the entire universe. Thus, the evolution of the universe is independent of any individual actor. This evolution is deterministic, because of the order of states in the uncountable space, and the ordering of states within each such state (from the uncountable space) creates a predetermined sequence of events. However, this determinism is different from that in classical physics, where when a state is visible, the previous states are gone. In the determinism described here, every state exists in relation to every other state, and each state is created by negation of other states. There are two kinds of negations—of distinct locations in space and time.

Apart from the space and time distinctions, there is also the distinction of observers. The observer is not predetermined, even though the events in space and time are determined. Therefore, what will happen—in space and time—is fixed, but who will do it is not fixed. As a result, we get three kinds of complementary descriptions—of space, of time, and of persons. As we have discussed earlier, these are the Śakti-mode, the God-mode, and the soul-mode descriptions of the same observation; they constitute the how, the what, and the who. The determinism of the universe is predictively complete, but it is explanatorily incomplete. That explanation requires the observers. Thus, two modes of space and time suffice to say what will happen, but the third mode of persons is necessary to explain who will do what. These three modes provide the complete prediction and explanation of everything—which is the goal of science.

QUESTION

You are saying that the material world can never be completely known. What is then the point of this knowledge if it takes the life-time of the universe to know everything? How can anyone exist for such a long period of time?

2.2.23 (194)
उभयथा च दोषात्
ubhayathā ca doṣāt

ubhayathā—in either case; ca—also; doṣāt—because of faults.

TRANSLATION

In either case (you can) also see faults.

COMMENTARY

If the world was completely knowable in an instant, then the universe would be static, and nothing would ever change. One would argue: What is the point in living in this world when we know every-thing in the future? Then, there would be no point in any action because actions would not change anything. If, on the other hand, the world is known only when it is lived through experience, then someone can argue: If the world is never fully known in finite time, then what is the point of even attempting to know anything? Either way, one can claim there is a fault, so there is no point in explaining either alternative. The argument against change is the argument against the existence of time. There is a timeless reality called Brahman in which only the self is known. Nobody ever knows anyone else, the different things that they are capable of, or what the others are capable of. Neither space nor time exists in the Brahman. Although there are many individual persons, they are never known. Only the self—as devoid of all space and time distinctions—is known. This knowledge of the self is eternal, and yet, it is incomplete. On the other hand, the complete truth is all that is ever possible, and it is completely known over time. It can mean I never know everything since it manifests over time. But it can also mean that life is a constant process of discovery of novelties. If this process of discovery is pleasurable, then there should be no problem with the novelty.

QUESTION

You have earlier said that the Lord is the origin of space, from which the rest of space expands. You are now saying that the Lord is also the whole space in which all the possibilities pre-exist as potentials to be known. How can we reconcile these two ideas about the origin and the complete space?

2.2.24 (195)
आकाशे चावशिषात्
ākāśe cāviśeṣāt

ākāśe—in case of space; ca—and; aviśeṣāt—due to being no difference.

TRANSLATION

Also due to there being no difference between (the origin) and the space.

COMMENTARY

The difference between origin and the rest of the space arises in a physical conception of space, in which the origin is only one point in space. But, if we view space as a domain of concepts organized hierarchically as a tree, then the higher concepts contain the lower concepts. For example, Alsatians and Pomeranians are breeds of dogs, which are part of mammals, which are part of animals. When space is understood conceptually, then the trunks, branches, twigs, and leaves are all emanations from the root, and they are contained inside the root, although they may not always be visible. The expansion of the root into the visible tree is making the possibility manifest, and this manifestation requires higher-level concepts to be manifest before the lower-level concepts. For instance, the idea of a dog must be manifest before the Alsatian or the Pomeranian are manifest. So, the root is the collection of all the possibilities in unmanifest form, and the tree is the same possibilities in a manifest form. Hence, there is no difference between the origin and the rest of space—if we are speaking about the possibilities that preexisted their manifestation because the origin contains everything as a potential from which the manifest world expands.

QUESTION

If everything already exists in the Lord, then why is it not manifest simultaneously? Why are different aspects being revealed at different times?

2.2.25 (196)

अनुस्मृतेश्च

anusmṛteśca

anusmṛteḥ—the memory of a small part; ca—also.

TRANSLATION

(You can understand this) also as the recollection of parts of memory.

COMMENTARY

The Lord is the fullness of all possibilities, but even He doesn't know everything about Himself all the time. Rather, all these possibilities are like long-term memory which are recollected one by one; when they are recollected, they are manifest in His experience, and that manifestation then becomes the world. More accurately, His capacity for desire is infinite, and His Śakti fulfills that desire. However, the Lord doesn't desire everything simultaneously. His desires are sequenced, and that sequence appears as time; as these desires are fulfilled by the Lord's Śakti, the world is manifest and unmanifest. By comparing this process of manifestation to recollection of memories, two questions are being addressed here. First, the existence of all possibilities is compared to memory; even though we have memories, we aren't always remembering them; and yet, just because we don't recall something right now doesn't mean we don't know. Therefore, the fact that the Lord remembers one thing at a time doesn't entail that He is not omniscient; He knows everything because it exists as His memory, and yet He isn't conscious of everything simultaneously. Second, when the memory is recalled, a new experience is created, and the succession of these experiences constitutes time. The awareness of the Lord therefore simply scans His memories and that recollection becomes His experience.

This analogy is slightly misleading because memory is different from the soul. The memory is unconscious, and the experience is conscious. This is where we can recall the discussion about each part being defined in relation to all the other parts—including those parts in the future and the past. Therefore, in one sense, knowing something right now is knowing the past and the future, because the past and the future are embedded in the present by a negation. In another sense, knowing something right now is not knowing what is in the past and the future. If only the latter meaning is adopted, it seems that God is not omniscient about the past and the future. If, to overcome this problem, we say that everything is known at once, then it entails an eternal but static world. The knowledge by distinction to past and future solves both these problems. The Lord is fully omniscient because in knowing the present, He also knows the past and the future, although the past and the future are currently unmanifest. Thus, His experience is evolving, and yet His knowledge is eternal. The knowledge is knowing everything that is everywhere and everywhen. But experience is here and now. These claims are not contradictory because the experience here and now is not knowledge; the knowledge is its relation to everything else including all the past and future experiences, and all parts of these experiences.

The use of the term *anusmṛteḥ* is significant here because it comprises of two parts—*anu* or atomic, and *smriti* or memory. As we have discussed, the space of all possibilities is uncountable, and what manifests at a given time is a point in that space. This point is the 'atom' of recollection out of the entire space of *smriti* or memory. Thus, for us, the universe seems infinite, but for the Lord it is only an atom. These atoms are uncountable which means that there is no limit or end to the memories of the Lord, and hence time never ceases.

QUESTION

Does that mean that even if something is not visible to us, it continues to exist in the Lord as a pre-existing memory which can be later recalled?

2.2.26 (197)

नासतोऽदृष्टत्वात्

nāsataḥ adṛṣṭatvāt

na—not; asataḥ—non-existent; adṛṣṭatvāt—from not being seen.

TRANSLATION

(Something) from not being visible has not become non-existent.

COMMENTARY

The universe is temporary for us, but it is eternal for the Lord. Impersonalist philosophy is based on the idea that because the world is temporary, therefore it has no reality; it just appears as an illusion to us. This sūtra directly contradicts this belief by stating that even if something is destroyed, it hasn't become non-existent. It has just gone out of our vision because this vision was created by the Lord's recollection of His memory. The world seems temporal and changing because the Lord's awareness moves through His memory, and this movement makes the world manifest or unmanifest. This awareness is called *sat* but the substrate on which it moves is called *chit*. The cause of this movement is His desire for pleasure or ānanda. Thus, the Lord recollects or understands Himself driven by His desire for self-knowledge resulting in pleasure. As His consciousness scans His memory, the world is manifest. When the consciousness moves to another memory, the experience corresponding to the previous memory disappears, but the memory is not destroyed. The impersonalist claims that because bodies, societies, and civilizations are created and destroyed, therefore, everything is unreal as it ceases to exist eventually. Reality must only be that which exists eternally, and Brahman is thus real because it is eternal. In this sūtra, it is stated that even the material world is eternal.

Therefore, although the world appears and disappears it doesn't become non-existent. Brahman is the knower and it never appears or disappears, in the sense that one never ceases to be aware of one's own existence. But going in and out of awareness is not the criterion for measuring reality. If I turn my head away from something and stop seeing it, the fact that my experience of that thing has ended doesn't entail that the thing has ceased to exist. In the same way, the changes we see are the effects of the Lord's moving awareness.

QUESTION

If the material world is eternal, then there should be no reason for happiness when something is created, or lamentation when it is destroyed. Then, why are people becoming happy on seeing, and lamenting on destruction?

2.2.27 (198)

उदासीनानाम् अपि चैवं सदिधिः

udāsīnānām api caivaṃ siddhiḥ

udāsīnānām—those who are detached or indifferent (to this world); api—even; ca—and; evam—thus; siddhiḥ—attainment of perfection.

TRANSLATION

Even those who are detached or indifferent (to this world) can also attain perfection (liberation from the laws of matter) by this understanding.

COMMENTARY

Most people are excited by the achievement of things that they haven't seen before, and they lament the loss of things they have achieved. They may not realize that the things we have achieved have been previously achieved by innumerable people, which were subsequently lost, and then achieved again. There is no novelty in this material world; we have been rich and poor, beautiful and ugly, powerful and weak, intelligent and stupid, and respected and ill-treated innumerable times. Whatever is achieved is lost, and whatever is lost is achieved again. If one understands that this cycle of loss and achievement repeats innumerable times, then one becomes detached. For example, we might think that the creation of modern technology such as airplanes, telephones, televisions, etc. are great advancements of our time, which did not exist before. And we get enamored by the progress of technology as it seems to bring new things. But one who is knowledgeable realizes that all this has existed before; it periodically manifests and unmanifests; if we are seeing something today, it will certainly be lost; and if something has been lost, it will certainly be achieved again. So, there is no permanent gain and no permanent loss. One who has attained this realization becomes detached from the events of this world. He is neither delighted on an achievement nor suffers due to a loss. Such a person, who has transcended the effects of material gain and loss is said to have achieved perfection because he loses all desire for material achievements.

Topic 5

QUESTION

But if both material and spiritual worlds are eternal realities, and they are both manifested by the Lord, then what is the harm in being attached to the material world? How can we prefer the spiritual reality over the material reality, when both realities are eternal, and both are created by the Lord?

2.2.28 (199)

नाभावःउपलब्धेः

nābhāvaḥ upalabdheḥ

na—not; abhāvaḥ—unmanifest; upalabdheḥ—experienceable.

TRANSLATION

The unmanifest is not experienceable.

COMMENTARY

In the spiritual world, there is night and day; the Lord wakes up in the morning and goes to play with His friends, grazing His cows. In the evening He returns home and talks about His escapades during the day with His father and mother. But in the night, He escapes from the home of His parents to dance with His girlfriends. Due to the passing of day and night, we say that the Lord's experiences are manifest and unmanifest—sometimes He is playing with His friends, then talking to His parents, and then dancing with His girlfriends. However, this doesn't mean that when He is not talking to His parents, friends, or girlfriends, they must disappear. They exist simultaneously, but they meet the Lord one after another. This meeting and separation constitute the evolution in time. However, this spiritual time is different from material time in which people die such that you cannot talk to them the next morning like you were doing previously. The eternity of the spiritual world is not static. It essentially means that nobody dies, and nobody is born. The evolution of the material world is birth and death. So, we cannot equate these two kinds of times.

The previous sūtras said that even in the material world, if something has been destroyed, the potentiality for that thing has not ceased, and it is manifest again and again. In short, the dinosaurs disappear, and the dinosaurs appear. The disappearance of dinosaurs from our experience doesn't mean that the species did not exist previously or would not exist in the future. So, the material world is eternal in that sense. However, this eternity of the material world is different from the eternity of the spiritual world because in the spiritual world nothing ever dies. Hence, this sūtra says that what has become unmanifest has gone out of our experience. The reverse is not necessarily true. For instance, something that has gone out of our experience is not necessarily unmanifest. Thus, even in this world, we can stop reading a book, and that doesn't mean that the book has disappeared. However, if the book is burnt, then we must necessarily stop reading it. In the spiritual world, all change is because of choice—just like we stop reading a book. In the material world, changes are both due to our choices and forced due to time—i.e., the book can be burnt, and we can stop reading the book. In this sūtra, the burning of the book is referred to. The content of the book—i.e., the ideas in it—are not burnt when the book is burnt. That content will again manifest, but it is not visible right now.

QUESTION

But someone can argue that even if the dinosaurs are not visible right now, we could still experience them during dreams. Since these

things become visible during dreams, they are testimony not only to the fact that they are eternal but also the fact that they can be manifest to us at any point in time. How then can we say that certain things are not available to us at certain times?

2.2.29 (200)

वैधर्म्याच्च न स्वप्नादिवत्

vaidharmyācca na svapnādivat

vaidharmyāt—due to the difference of (material and spiritual) nature; ca—and; na—is not; svapnādivat—just like dreams etc.

TRANSLATION

There is a difference between (material and spiritual) natures, and (the spiritual world) is not like the dreaming state (in the material world).

COMMENTARY

The dreaming state is considered superior to the waking state because in the dreaming state we can see things that we will not see during the waking state. How do we see such things? Are they merely 'creations' of the mind? All perception in Vedic philosophy is perception of a preexisting reality. It may exist as our memory, or it may exist as an external possibility, or even a manifest reality. Our mind and the senses merely 'roam' in this space of possibilities, and through this contact experience is created. So, the cause of experience is the roaming of the senses and the mind. But what causes the roaming? As we have seen earlier, there are two causes—guna or desiring, and karma or deserving. Sometimes when we have an intense desire to solve a problem, we might see a solution to the problem in our dreams, although we could not see it during waking. Similarly, due to karma, we might have good or bad experiences during dreams. The guna and the karma themselves manifest under the influence of time. So, the dreaming experience is as much subject to the influence of time as the waking experience. Just because we can see dinosaurs in dreams should not mean that we can see anything or everything that is possible. Just as waking experiences are subject to the influence of time, similarly, the dreams are too. The difference is that dreaming enables us with a much wider contact with possibilities because our senses and the mind directly contact the possibilities, unmediated by the body. While the body is present in one place—e.g., sleeping on the bed—the mind and the senses can roam far and wide. In one sense, this shows how we are not bound to the body, and the understanding of dreams can lead to spiritual progress. But in another sense, the laws of converting the possibility to reality are the same whether in the case of waking or dreaming.

In simple terms, if our karma doesn't allow it, then we cannot enter heavenly planets during dreams, and enjoy just like demigods. So, even in dreams, we are bound by our karma. The spiritual world is not like that because there is no bondage of karma. Thus, we are not forced to have bad experiences, like we are forced to have bad dreams in this world. And we are not prevented from having good experiences—e.g., that of entry into heavenly planets—like we are prevented due to karma in this lifetime. In the spiritual world, everything is always accessible, everything is always pleasing, and nothing is forced. Therefore, the spiritual world cannot be compared to the materialistic dreams.

QUESTION

If we can see things during dreams that we cannot see during waking, and you are acknowledging that material reality is eternal like spiritual reality, then what is the main difference between the material and the spiritual realities?

2.2.30 (201)
न भावःउनुपलब्धेः
na bhāvaḥ anupalabdheḥ

na—not; bhāvaḥ—existence; anupalabdheḥ—not experienced.

TRANSLATION
All that exists (i.e., is possible) is never inexperienceable.

COMMENTARY
In the last but one sūtra it was stated: *nābhāvaḥ upalabdheḥ*, or that

which doesn't exist cannot be experienced. In sūtra, the reverse statement is being made: *na bhāvaḥ anupalabdheḥ*, or that which exists can never be inaccessible to experience. The former statement pertained to the material world, and the present statement is about the spiritual world. The sūtra indicates that everything in the spiritual world is always knowable. It doesn't mean that everyone knows everything in the spiritual world. It only means that anyone can know anything if they so desire. The *upalabdhi* is availability and is not forced.

The existence of this possibility also entails that someone always knows something that others do not know, and collectively all individuals know everything. One only needs to develop the right type of relationship to the Lord to know His various aspects. The Lord is always revealed to different devotees in different ways, and one who has the desire and the suitable relation to the Lord can know Him in that manner. This point has also been made a little differently earlier where it was said that there are innumerable forms of the Lord according to desire and relationship of the soul to the Lord. In this sūtra, the converse point is also made, namely, that every aspect of the Lord is always manifest to some devotee. The situation is thus incomparable to the material world.

QUESTION

But the same argument could also be applied to dreams, namely, that different people can dream different mutually exclusive things, and therefore, we can say that even the material reality is always manifest to someone.

2.2.31 (202)

कषणकित्वाच्च

kṣaṇikatvācca

kṣaṇikatvāt—on account of the momentariness; ca—also.

TRANSLATION

(We cannot say that the spiritual reality is like a dream) also because (the dreams) are momentary (and the spiritual experience is not momentary).

COMMENTARY

The material world is produced due to the combination of guna or desiring, and karma or deserving. We may desire good things to happen to us, but they may not happen due to bad karma. Similarly, we do not desire bad things to happen to us, but they will happen due to bad karma. Even if our desires are stable, our karma is temporary, and since our experiences are caused by karma, all these experiences are temporary. Even if we are enjoying a dream, it will not continue permanently. And even if we have something good during waking experience, it will not continue to exist permanently due to karma. So, even though the material energy is eternal, our karma is not eternal. The temporariness of karma creates temporary experiences. If this karma is dissolved, then we are just left with guna or desires. Now, karma doesn't restrain what we can or cannot experience. As soon as we desire something, there is no inhibition in achieving it. So, if our desire remains stable, then the experience also remains stable. We cannot be forced out of some experience due to bad karma. Thus, the material and the spiritual worlds are both eternal, but the material experience is not eternal. The spiritual experience, on the other hand, can always be eternal.

QUESTION

Are you saying that temporariness is the main problem of the material world because we are compelled to change our position due to karma?

2.2.32 (203)

सर्वथानुपपत्तेश्च

sarvathānupapatteśca

sarvathā—in every possible way; anupapatteḥ—inappropriate; ca—and.

TRANSLATION

And (the comparison of the spiritual world to material dreams) is inappropriate in every possible way.

COMMENTARY

Multiple arguments refuting the comparison of the spiritual world to materialistic dreams have been made in the previous sūtras. First, we are forced to suffer even in dreams due to our karma. Second, we are restricted from pleasures during dreams in the material world. Third, whatever pleasure is obtained in the material world through dreams is temporary. Conversely, in the spiritual world, the soul is not forced to suffer; the soul is not restricted from any pleasure; and whatever is obtained can be obtained eternally. Thus, it is not one argument against this comparison; there are multiple arguments against it.

Topic 6

QUESTION

You have said that the Absolute Truth is all the possibilities that will manifest in the world. What if someone has a desire that is outside this possibility? Since the Absolute Truth doesn't have this possibility, it can never be fulfilled. So, how can we say that freedom from material world leads to happiness?

2.2.33 (204)
नैकस्मन्निन् असंभवात्
naikasminn asaṃbhavāt

na—not; ekasmin—in one; asaṃbhavāt—on account of the impossibility.

TRANSLATION

Nothing is impossible in the One (the Absolute Truth).

COMMENTARY

It is one thing to say that the Absolute Truth is all the possibilities that will manifest. It is quite another to say that nothing is impossible in Absolute Truth. One can argue that I'm not satisfied with everything possible; I want something that is impossible, or outside the collection of all possibilities. If I develop such a desire, how can that be fulfilled if the Absolute Truth is only the possible things? This sūtra states that whatever you can desire is already there in the Absolute Truth. The Absolute Truth is not just all the possibilities that can be realized, but nothing is impossible in the Absolute Truth. Essentially, by 'possibility' we don't mean a realm restricted by laws or conditions. For example, a scientist can say that anything is possible if it doesn't violate the laws of logic, mathematics, and physics. But what if someone has a desire for something that violates these laws? You might want a car that runs without fuel, or a time-machine that takes you into the past, etc. Are these in the realm of possibility or not? The sūtra states that nothing is impossible in the Absolute Truth.

QUESTION

If everything that can be desired is also possible in the Absolute Truth, does that mean that every soul can desire any of these possibilities?

2.2.34 (205)
एवं चात्माकार्त्स्नयम्
evaṃ cātmākārtsnyam

evam—thus; ca—also; ātmā—the soul; akārtsnyam—incompleteness, or non-fullness.

TRANSLATION

(Just as the fullness of the Absolute Truth implies the existence of all possibilities) in the same way the incompleteness of the soul also (implies that the soul cannot desire everything that is possible in the Absolute Truth).

COMMENTARY

Everything in the Lord can be liked by someone, but everything in the Lord will not be liked by everyone. Just as there are opposite kinds of smells, tastes, colors, forms, etc. similarly there are also opposite kinds of likes and dislikes. If the soul desires, then he can experience the opposite natures of the Lord. But that doesn't mean that soul will desire all such opposite natures. Thus, for instance, some devotees are attracted to the childhood pastimes of the Lord, but they don't like the fearsome, commanding, and intimidating features of the Lord. Conversely, some like the Lord to be powerful and fearsome, and don't like His pastimes as a child where He remains dependent on His parents. Every soul is attracted in a different way to the Lord, and while the Lord can fulfill all desires, it doesn't mean that every soul is attracted to all aspects of the Lord. The existence of desire entails the existence of a personality that chooses or prefers some aspects over others. Since the soul is small and incomplete, it will always be attracted only to some aspects of the Lord, not to all His aspects. Thus, the varied forms of the Lord are not opposed to monotheism. Rather, monotheism is restrictive as it says that the Lord is always known in one way. We should understand that the soul wants to know one of the many personality features of the Lord and prefers to be involved only in some pastimes.

QUESTION

If the soul cannot desire every possibility, does that mean he is bound to always live in a certain limited understanding of the Absolute Truth?

2.2.35 (206)

न च पर्यायादप्यवरोधःविकारादभिृयः

na ca paryāyādapyavirodhaḥ vikārādibhyaḥ

na ca—neither; paryāyāt—approach from (a different view); api—even; avirodhaḥ—no hindrance; vikārādibhyaḥ—on account of change etc.

TRANSLATION

Neither is an alternative approach (always occurring); (nor) even is there a hindrance to (a soul) changing (their understanding of the Lord).

COMMENTARY

We have previously discussed that the soul has an innate nature based on how it was intended to serve the Lord. And yet, the soul sometimes foregoes this intended nature of serving the Lord and tries to become independent. This independence indicates that there is always potential for change even in the spiritual world, because whether in the spiritual or the material worlds, the soul retains its free will. But such changes are not frequent because the soul has an innate nature, and although it can change its nature, this is a rare event. So, the intended nature of the soul should not be considered as being contrary to the existence of free will—i.e., that the soul is permanently bound to have a fixed personality. Conversely, we should also not assume that because such changes can occur due to the soul's free will, they must be occurring frequently. In short, the existence of free will does not entail whimsical experimentation.

QUESTION

So, can we say that by and large, the soul and the Lord are situated in a fixed relationship that is typically not expected to change, although in principle it can change if the soul develops an alternative desire toward the Lord?

2.2.36 (207)

अन्त्यावस्थतिश्चोभयनति्यत्वादवशिेषः

antyāvasthiteścobhayanityatvādaviśeṣaḥ

antya-avasthiteḥ—ultimately situated; ca—and; ubhaya-nityat-vāt—from the two in an eternal (relationship); aviśeṣaḥ—due to inseparability.

TRANSLATION

From the two (the soul and the Lord) being ultimately situated in an eternal relationship due to their inseparability.

COMMENTARY

There are many relationships in this world, but they are temporary. The relationship between the soul and the Lord is eternal, and this eternity is attributed to their inseparability—the Lord is the whole and the soul is the part. The part can never be separated from the whole, and yet the part is never equal to the whole. Therefore, the soul can never become the Lord, but even if it tries to pretend to have become the Lord, the relationship between the soul and the Lord is never broken. This is the reason that the term *antya-avasthiteḥ* is used in this sūtra, which indicates the ultimate position. And this ultimate position is also described as being *nityavat* and *aviśeṣaḥ* or eternal and inseparable. We might wonder why this claim is being made again, when the same types of claims have been made previously. The reason is the context, where the seeker was asking the question about whether the soul can change its relation to the Lord and know the Lord in one of many possible ways. Such a change was not forbidden, and yet it wasn't considered typical. In that context, we can again say that the soul and the Lord are in a mutual and eternal relationship.

Topic 7

QUESTION

If the soul is situated in such an eternal relationship to the Lord, can he fall into the material world? Can this relationship be forgotten or suspended?

2.2.37 (208)

पत्युःअसामञ्जस्यात्

patyuḥ asāmañjasyāt

patyuḥ—the fall; asāmañjasyāt—from being very doubtful or unlikely.

TRANSLATION

(If the soul is situated in an eternal relationship to the Lord) the fall (into the material world) is very doubtful or unlikely or unconventional.

COMMENTARY

The relationship between the soul and the Lord is so sweet that the fall into the material world is very unlikely. The basis of love is that each person is seeking the happiness of the loved one. Under such a situation, both sides—the soul and the Lord—willingly compromise and bend to each other's desires. Due to this loving relationship, the discrepancy in their relation is very unlikely.

QUESTION

But you are not completely ruling out the possibility of the soul's fall? You are saying that this is very unconventional, but there is still a possibility?

2.2.38 (209)

संबन्धानुपपत्तेश्च

saṃbandhānupapatteśca

saṃbandha-anupapatteḥ—adversity in the relation; ca—also.

TRANSLATION

Adversity in the relationship also (can result in a fall).

COMMENTARY

This sūtra affirms that the fall is always a possibility; the relation between the soul and the Lord is based on love, but love can never be forced. Even though the fall has been called unconventional in the last sūtra, this sūtra states that any insufficiency or adversity in the relationship can result in a fall.

QUESTION

But what can lead to such an adversity that the soul leaves the Lord?

2.2.39 (210)

अधष्षिठानानुपपत्तेश्च

adhiṣṭhānānupapatteśca

adhiṣṭhāna-anupapatteḥ—rulership being impossible; ca—and.

TRANSLATION

(The fall can occur when the soul tries to be the Lord) because rulership (of the soul over the Lord) is impossible.

COMMENTARY

In several previous purports we have noted the sense of inferiority in the soul, and how the soul tries to overcome this inferiority by trying to become the Lord. This is the first sūtra, however, where this desire in the soul to become the Lord—rather than remain a servant—is explicitly noted. We have discussed how the soul has the power of will but doesn't have the power to fulfill the will. Thus, the soul depends on the Lord's Śakti to fulfill his desires. The Lord's Śakti, however, is only serving the Lord, so it cannot become the Śakti for the soul, especially if the soul is trying to be a competitor to the Lord. Thus, the soul's attempt at rulership (over the Lord or His Śakti) is deemed impossible.

Nevertheless, if the desire for rulership arises, then the soul falls into the material world. He is granted independence, but that independence comes with a responsibility. Accordingly, the laws of choice and responsibility are framed, and if the soul follows these laws, then he enjoys independently. However, the nature of the material world is that the soul easily forgets that he is bound by these laws. While enjoying, he thinks that he has become the master, and the laws of choice and responsibility do not apply to him. That in turn leads to suffering. In contrast, in the spiritual world, there is only choice and no responsibility. Whatever is done in devotion to the Lord has no consequence. Thus, the soul doesn't love the Lord so that the Lord will love him. And the Lord doesn't love the soul because the soul is loving Him. These cause-and-effect relations cease to exist. The soul spontaneously loves the Lord, and the Lord spontaneously loves the soul. The material world is different—everything is based on cause and effect. Therefore, if you have loved, then you will be loved. If you have not loved, then you will not be loved. Hence, independence comes at the cost of responsibility, but independence is also possible. Except that this is not domination or control over the Lord. That domination is rejected here.

QUESTION

But can't such discrepancies in the mutual relationship arise due to inadvertent circumstances? The soul may be just trying to serve

the Lord, but he may fail in serving appropriately. How can such discrepancies result in a fall?

2.2.40 (211)

करणवच्चेत् न भोगादभिभ्यः

karaṇavaccet na bhogādibhyaḥ

karaṇavat—as an instrument; cet—if it be said; na—no; bhogādibhyaḥ—because of the desire for enjoyment.

TRANSLATION

If it is said that (the fall is due to discrepancy) as an instrument (i.e., mistake in serving the Lord) (we say) no; (the fall is) because of the desire for enjoyment (by becoming the master or ruler, as already stated in the previous sūtra).

COMMENTARY

Here, the fall is attributed not to a mistake but an aversion toward the Lord, which leads to the desire for independent mastery and enjoyment.

The soul has three aspects—cognition, emotion, and relation. The cognition is achieved through the mind, senses, and the body, and these are the *karana* or the instruments. The senses of action, the intellect, and morality are also the instruments. But there is a difference between a *karana* and a *kārana*—the former is the instrumental cause, and the latter is the intentional cause. Sometimes we might make mistakes even though we have good intentions. If the *kārana* or the emotional state is not flawed—e.g., due to revulsion to the Lord—then the mistakes of *karana* or the instrumental cause are disregarded. The Lord is extremely forgiving of mistakes made by the soul if the intentional and emotional state is devotional, and the soul is trying to serve the Lord rather than pretending to be His master. The rules and regulations of devotional life are not hard and fast. They are prescribed to overcome pride, disrespect, disregard, and laziness. Those who are already devoted need not follow such rules. But even those who are following such rules may make mistakes despite their best intentions. The Lord is sāra-grāhī or the seeker of the essences. He doesn't consider the mistakes of the *karana* seriously because He understands the *kārana*. This sūtra states that any discrepancy in the actions of the soul do not lead to a fall. It is only the emotional state, which, if changed, can result into a fall.

This sūtra hints at the possibility of mistakes even in the spiritual world. These mistakes can arise if the devotee doesn't read the mood of the Lord correctly. For example, the Lord might say: "I love you so much, that I cannot live without you", and He is expecting a banter in response: "Is that so? All your promises in the past have been broken. So, why don't you prove your love?". That response will be a segue into a pastime where the Lord will beg incessantly for forgiveness and concessions, while the devotee will pretend to be abstruse. But after much begging, the mood of the Lord can change, and He then wants to be accepted. In that situation, the devotee should also acquiesce. However, the devotee may not read the Lord's mood correctly, and stay abstruse. This is a discrepancy in the loving exchange. However, this is a discrepancy in understanding the Lord's mood, and not enviousness to become the Lord's master. While such mistakes can occur, these are not the cause of the soul's fall.

Advancement in spiritual life is not just knowing the Lord philosophically; of course, one must know the philosophy. But advancement means being able to grasp the changing moods of the Lord. An advanced devotee reads the Lord's moods correctly, and that ability to understand the Lord leads to intimate relationships. If that understanding is limited, then the Lord also keeps a distance from the devotee, saying what He means, rather than saying things that are contrary to what He intends. But in advanced stages, the discrepancies between words and meanings become prominent. These discrepancies between what is said and what is meant can lead to misunderstandings. However, such mistakes are tolerated by both parties, and not the cause of a break in their love.

QUESTION

But how can we know the difference between aversion and mistakes? After all, a discrepancy can be attributed to a deliberate neglect or to an inadvertent mistake. How can we say that it was indeed a deliberate neglect?

2.2.41 (212)
अन्तवत्त्वमसर्वज्ञता वा
antavattvamsarvajñatā vā

antavat—being limited; tvam—you; sarvajñatā—omniscience; vā—the revered one.

TRANSLATION

You are limited, but the revered one (the Lord) is omniscient.

COMMENTARY

We normally associate knowledge with cognition, but our emotional state can also be known. Common examples of the emotional manifestation include the rising of the blood pressure on anger, the calming of the body on happiness, etc. But, in general, decoding the emotional state is harder than decoding the cognitive state. For example, to understand the anger from a person's speech is harder than understanding the meaning of the words. Thus, one can argue that some bad action is caused due to a sincere mistake rather than a deliberate dereliction of duty. But this difficulty pertains to ordinary people who see the body and try to infer the mental and the intentional state. The problem doesn't apply to the Lord who can perceive all the levels of reality from gross to subtle. In this regard, we must note that even emotions have forms. When the soul has a different desire or intention, it changes form. Under different kinds of emotional states, the soul's form changes. We may not perceive these subtle forms because we are conditioned only to sense perception, and even mental forms are not easily perceived by us, then what to speak about the spiritual forms.

The Lord is, however, not limited in this way. He can see when the soul has changed its form due to a different desire. The notion that certain things are 'private' to us is ultimately false; there is nothing private; everything is deciphered from the forms, but externally, these forms are *known* and internally these forms are *experienced*. There is hence a difference between being angry and knowing that someone is angry. But it is always possible to know the emotional state. The omniscience of the Lord pertains to this ability to know everyone's emotional state from the change in their forms. Even in this world, the ability to read people's emotions through their body language is considered an art and not easily understood by most people. Even those who can decipher emotions from bodily forms may not always be correct in their determination. Such faults are thus outcomes of our limited understanding of the relation between emotion and forms. The Lord is not constrained by such limitations; He is not prone to make mistakes in understanding the soul's real intentions.

Topic 8

QUESTION

Does the aversion to the Lord suddenly arise out of nowhere even within a devotee? Can we say that someone suddenly becomes a non-devotee?

2.2.42 (213)

उत्पत्त्यसंभवात्

utpattyasambhavāt

utpatti-asambhavāt—owing to the impossibility of genesis.

TRANSLATION

It is impossible to postulate a genesis (out of no previous existence).

COMMENTARY

Throughout Vedic philosophy we can find the idea that everything that exists in a manifest form previously existed in an unmanifest form. We never find the notion of genesis out of nothingness. Even when the Lord creates the universe, it is an expansion out of Himself, not ex nihilo creation. Therefore, if something is emerging within the soul, it must preexist in the soul. Accordingly, even the aversion toward the Lord must have a preexistence in the soul. We cannot claim that this aversion suddenly springs out of nothing. Such a claim would in fact support ex nihilo creation. Thus, by rejecting the notion of genesis, the sūtra indicates that the aversion doesn't emerge out of nothingness.

We have extensively discussed the theory of modes, which exist in dominant and subordinate states. Aversion to the Lord exists innately in all souls, but it becomes dominant in some souls and remains subordinate in others. When it becomes dominant, we cannot say that it emerged out of nothing. And when it is subordinated, we cannot say that it has disappeared permanently. Thus, a soul who has been liberated hasn't lost the ability to fall again. And the soul who has fallen has not lost the ability to be liberated. The aversion to the self also exists within the Lord. This self-averse form of the Lord is known as Param Śiva and He indulges in self-abnegation. Similarly, if the soul becomes averse to the Lord, he falls into the material world ruled by Param Śiva.

Thus, the rejection of the Lord is within each soul because self-rejection is also within the Lord. The Lord is not always enjoying. He is also sometimes guilty about that enjoyment. That guilty form of the Lord is Param Śiva. He indulges in austerities and denies Himself pleasure. The difference between the soul and the Lord is simply that the soul can alternate between different modes of self-enjoyment, self-abnegation, and serving the Lord. The Lord, however, is simultaneously in all these modes. Thus, when the soul becomes averse to the Lord, then he enters a realm in which the Lord is averse to Himself. In this state too, the soul is only serving the Lord, although in a different mood. Thus, the soul never goes out of the Lord's service. However, in the material world, the soul must undergo austerities if he wants to enjoy. While performing these austerities, the soul is directly a part of Param Śiva by acting just like Him. And while enjoying, the soul serves Param Śiva by becoming His negation. Thus, many souls, who enjoy austerities, can permanently remain servants of Param Śiva, and that state of austerity is also considered to be their liberation. Other souls, who don't like austerity, tend to suffer because they desire pleasure, however, this pleasure cannot be obtained unless austerities are performed.

Thus, the so-called 'evil' exists in everything because it also exists in the Lord. It appears as Lord's self-abnegation. Thus, the Lord is not just an enjoyer. He is also austere, where He denies His own pleasure and enjoys that austerity. Finally, the Lord is also self-satisfied, where He is neither enjoying nor performing austerities. These states of enjoyment, austerity, and satisfaction are different moods of the Lord. In the Goloka realm, the Lord is the enjoyer. In the Vaikuṇṭha, He is satisfied. And in the material world, He is austere. These are simply different moods of the Lord. Nevertheless, the enjoying state of the Lord is considered superior to His satisfied state, which is considered superior to His austere state. Accordingly, the soul also participates in these varied moods of the Lord by enjoying with Him, being satisfied with Him, or assisting His austerity. In no situation is the soul contrary to the Lord. The soul is factually always the Lord's servant. But the soul may be serving austerity when he wants to enjoy. And this discrepancy leads to suffering in the material world.

QUESTION

Since the Lord is said to be the cause of all causes, can we say that this aversion is in some way created by the Lord's actions or by an agency?

2.2.43 (214)
न च कर्तुःकरणम्
na ca kartuḥ karaṇam

na ca—nor; kartuḥ—from the action; karaṇam—the instrument.

TRANSLATION
Nor (is the aversion) created by an action or instrument.

COMMENTARY
While the previous sūtra clarified that the soul's rejection of the Lord is caused by the soul itself, the seeker is still asking the same question by presenting alternative mechanisms of such fall. Maybe the rejection of the Lord is caused due to an action (of either the Lord or a soul) or something other than these two (e.g., the energy of the Lord, which acts as His instrument)? It was previously said that some mistakes can occur in our actions, and maybe once these mistakes occur, then the Lord becomes unhappy even though the soul did not intend to make Him unhappy, and seeing this unfavorable response to the soul's sincerity, maybe the soul also becomes averse to the Lord? Similarly, since the Lord's energy fulfills the soul's desires, perhaps some shortfall in this fulfillment creates an aversion? Finally, the energy also creates desires in the soul, thus, maybe the Lord's energy is the cause of the soul's aversion?

This sūtra rejects all such alternative mechanisms for the fall. It says that no action or instrument is the cause of this fall. Coupled with the previous sūtra, which said that the cause of the fall is within the soul, this is a rejection of any external causation. In short, the fall must be attributed to the soul alone. Even though the Lord has the mood for self-abnegation, and correspondingly His Śakti also aids in this self-abnegation by creating a world where the soul enjoys by forgetting the Lord's pleasure, the existence of the Lord's moods and His Śakti's assistance of that mood are not the causes of the soul's rejection.

People sometimes argue that if the soul has evil, and God created the soul, then the evil must originate in God. Then, why should the soul be considered responsible if God created this evil in the soul? If, on the other hand, God is not the creator of the evil, then how can evil exist in the world? In monotheistic philosophies, this problem is solved by postulating a Satan opposed to God, who tempts the soul and creates evil in him. This hardly solves the problem, because Satan is created by God, and is a 'fallen angel'. If Satan could fall and then cause others to fall, then the cause of all that fall must be in God who created an angel who then had the tendency to fall. Thus, the problem is only one step removed from God by the postulate of Satan, not truly solved by it.

The answer to that problem is that what we call evil is not truly evil in the Lord. The Lord's self-abnegation is the Lord's austerity. He is not punishing others; He is punishing Himself. In fact, as Param Śiva performs austerities, He also sets the example of how one must live austerely. Nevertheless, the Lord created the soul with the ability to reject Him. If this ability were not created, then free will would lose its meaning. The Lord would be called a master who created the soul as His slave. The slave has no choice whether to serve or leave the master. By creating the ability to reject the Lord, the Lord created not a slave, but a person with free will. The existence of free will, however, doesn't entail that the Lord supports or causes its misuse. The soul is entitled to reject the Lord due to its free will, but the soul is not entitled to interfere with the free will of others. In fact, even the Lord does not consider Himself entitled to interfere with the other's free will. Then, how can the soul be entitled to this interference?

The problem of evil is simply this—both the soul and the Lord have free will, the Lord created this free will in the soul, but the Lord doesn't misuse His free will and yet the soul does. The Lord cannot be faulted for free will in the soul, so how can He be faulted for the soul's misuse of that free will? The misuse of free will arises if the soul compares himself to the Lord, finds himself lacking, and tries to overcome this inferiority by dominating others. The Lord doesn't force anybody to love Him, and yet, the Lord's devotees love the Lord out of their own free will. Since the soul is not loved in the same way by other souls, his envy causes him to try to force that love out of others. In short, the soul tries to bend others to his will. Once free will is misused in this way, it creates karma, and the person is entrapped in the recurring cycle of suffering. At that point he again says: God made me perform all this evil, but that is not true.

QUESTION

But you have said that the enlightened soul already has perfect knowledge about the material and the spiritual worlds, so he must know the nature of the material world. Doesn't this knowledge control his negative attitudes?

2.2.44 (215)

वज्ज्ञानादभिावे वा तदप्रतषिधः

vijñānādibhāve vā tadapratiṣedhaḥ

vijñānādibhāve—in the existence of the realized knowledge etc.; vā—moving or going; tat-apratiṣedhaḥ—no restrictions due to that.

TRANSLATION

In the existence of realized knowledge etc., there are no restriction of moving or going (against the Lord).

COMMENTARY

The impersonalists make an argument about ignorance, claiming that the soul falls because he comes under the influence of māyā. In this sūtra, this claim is rejected. The soul is fully enlightened at the time of fall; ignorance doesn't come before the fall; ignorance is the consequence of the fall. The fall is rather a deliberate desire in the soul, which has no external cause, is not influenced by the will of the Lord, and cannot be said to be sprouting out of nowhere.

The only legitimate argument is that God did not make me God, so that I could be capable of creating souls, who would then be subordinate to me. But even if God had made the souls as god, who could then create more souls, those souls who are created by the second-order god, would have the same complaint! They would now say: God was compassionate in creating second-order gods. But these second-order gods did not create souls equal to themselves. Then the problem of evil would propagate back to God—namely, that He did not create second-order gods such that they would in turn create third-order gods, and everyone would eventually be god. But even if God created other gods capable of creating more such gods, then every new generation of god would complain: what good is being god if we have no subordinate souls? We are simply god in name, and we have no rulership over anyone else!

So, the argument that God did not make the soul god, is ultimately nonsense. If some of these souls are god, then God still receives the blame of partiality. If each one of these souls are god, then everyone complains incessantly. And both these situations are no better than just one God. The conclusion is that there is no situation better than the one that we are presently in. The only alternative is: I don't mind if God is unfair, if only He is unfair in my favor.

QUESTION

You are rejecting many potential causes of the fall—external circumstances, the will of the Lord or His agency, spontaneous generation, and the unsolicited covering of ignorance. Then what is the true cause for the soul's fall? How can he go from being a devotee to suddenly having an aversion to the Lord?

2.2.45 (216)
वपि्रतषिधाच्च
vipratiṣedhācca

vipratiṣedhāt—because of contradictions; ca—also.

TRANSLATION

(The fall) is also caused by the presence of contradictions (in the soul).

COMMENTARY

The soul has three aspects—*sat*, *chit*, and *ānanda*. In the material world, these manifest as opportunities, abilities, and desires, and they are generally contradictory. Thus, we might desire something, but we don't have an opportunity to get it. Or, we may get an opportunity, but we don't have the ability to use that opportunity. Conversely, the opportunities presented to us are contrary to our desires. Or, the opportunities may be contrary to our abilities. In all these ways, the soul suffers due to contradictions between ability, opportunity, and desire. These contradictions also lead to compromises. For example, if our desire is not fulfilled in the current opportunities, then we may change our desires to enjoy whatever is available in the present opportunity. Or, if we don't have the ability to get what we want, then we try to get what we can. Conversely, if our desire is very strong, then we will keep seeking the opportunity that can fulfill our desires. Or, if we don't have the necessary abilities right now, we might try to enhance our abilities to get what we deeply desire. Thus, sometimes, desires subordinate the opportunity and ability and push the person toward obtaining the appropriate opportunity and ability. At other times, the opportunity or ability may subordinate the desire, and force us to like what we can get. Thus, due to the contradiction between ability, desire, and opportunity, there is a constant tussle between the three factors that create experience about which goes dominant, and which others are subordinated. Each such dominant-subordinate relation represents a *choice* as well as a *compromise*. Basically, the soul resolves the conflicts in his experience by making some compromise. Once that compromise has been made, the soul feels peaceful again, until the next conflict arises, which then necessitates a new compromise, and so forth.

However, when the soul enters the spiritual world, these conflicts or contradiction between ability, desire, and opportunity ends. The soul is perfectly capable of doing what he desires, and he gets the opportunity to use those abilities. Everything is driven by desires, and the ability and opportunity are fulfilled according to those desires. There is hence no need for compromises. The nature of choice is now altered—from making compromises to desiring.

But, if you could desire anything, what would you desire? Remember that desiring also involves prioritizing: If I'm both hungry and thirsty, should I eat before I drink, or should I drink before I eat? The end of conflict between ability, opportunity, and desire, doesn't mean the end of conflicts themselves; these conflicts now appear within the desires themselves. In the material world, the locus for all decisions is the self: we decide based on what we like, or what will be good for us. In the spiritual world, the Lord is the locus for all decisions: the soul decides what is good based on what the Lord will like. There can be discrepancies in this understanding—one might think that the Lord will like something, but He might not. But that doesn't cause a fall because this is not a discrepancy of love, but a shortfall in understanding the Lord's nature. The fall is caused if the locus of decision-making shifts from the Lord to the soul: the soul starts deciding what is good for him, rather than what is the Lord's liking.

The conflict is within the soul—should I prioritize myself or the Lord? And there is a range of responses to this question ranging from always thinking of the Lord to sometimes thinking of oneself and sometimes thinking of the Lord, to always thinking of oneself. Depending on the type of response, the soul can be in the different spiritual realms or the different material existences. The devotees of the Lord, therefore, reject the aspiration of liberation from the material world because it involves some level of thinking about oneself. They are rather content with staying in the material world life after life *if* that pleases the Lord. Not everyone in the spiritual world is necessarily always thinking of the Lord; they are sometimes also thinking about their welfare. The material world is just the limiting extreme where the soul rarely remembers the Lord, and even if he does remember the Lord, it is only for getting a better life for himself.

Modern thinking has been developed upon the idea that change follows logical reasoning, and logical reasoning follows the principles of consistency. Thus, even the soul is understood in some religions as a rational being. He has some premises—which could be internal or external—and he arrives at the conclusions. This line of thinking doesn't recognize that in the material world, the internal and external premises are not always consistent, and giving one premise priority over another itself requires a compromise. But even if there was no conflict externally, there are always internal conflicts—we too have many desires, and they cannot be fulfilled at once. To fulfill each of them, we must prioritize and compromise—e.g., let's do this one first before we do others. Therefore, conflict is the basic principle of reasoning. It is not that consistent reasoning is impossible; however, that consistent reasoning depends on premises being consistent. If the premises are contradictory, then reasoning cannot lead to a conclusion. Therefore, the initial step in reasoning is resolving conflicts. The focus of any problem solving is conflict resolution through compromises.

The soul also has innate desires for love of the Lord and independence from the Lord. Each of these desires can be dominant or subordinate. This dominant-subordinate pattern of desires is the soul's choice. The Lord has created the soul to be able to choose. But the Lord doesn't choose for the soul. And the soul is conflicted. If the soul could only desire one thing, then the Lord would be accused of limiting the soul to one desire. If the soul is capable of many desires, then it must make choices and compromises. Thus, these inner conflicts in the soul are described to be the cause of the soul's fall in this sūtra.

SECTION 3

Topic 1

QUESTION

If the conflict is within the soul, then why doesn't the soul split apart into different individuals? Doesn't the existence of inner contradictions imply something that is logically contradictory and cannot be self-consistent? For example, hot and cold cannot exist in the same place due to self-contradiction. Then, why should the soul remain self-contradictory due to conflicting desires?

2.3.1 (217)

न वियत् अश्रुतेः

na viyat aśruteḥ

na—not; viyat—going apart; aśruteḥ—not stated by śrutī.

TRANSLATION

(The soul) does not split apart, as this is not accepted by śrutī.

COMMENTARY

The idea that objects in this world must only have one kind of property is an illusion of the physical world. All material objects have many properties—often contradictory—which are manifest in different situations. For example, we can say that a cow is normally gentle, but she can be aggressive if her calf is in danger. So, the properties of being gentle and aggressive are in the cow, but they are visible in different situations. It is pointless to say that since the cow is gentle, her aggression should split the cow into two parts: one gentle and the other aggressive. Both properties exist in the cow, but they are manifest alternately. We cannot collapse these differences to create a self-contradiction since these properties are manifest in different places, times, and situations.

In the same way, the soul is capable of contradictory desires—sometimes being active, and at other times being inactive, sometimes being gregarious and at other times being silent, sometimes being bold and at other times being shy. Each person is capable of all such desires, but their relative proportions vary. Thus, the cow is mostly gentle and only occasionally aggressive. The tiger, on the other hand, is mostly aggressive and occasionally gentle. That doesn't entail the absence of aggression in the cow or the absence of gentleness in the tiger. All such properties exist in contrast to their opposites. However, the gentleness can subordinate aggression or vice versa. That subordination makes some qualities invisible, but they are not absent. Thus, contradictions exist in everything, and this creates inner contradictions, which then lead to dominant-subordinate conditions. The soul makes a choice of what is dominant or subordinate.

QUESTION

But then you are accepting that the soul cannot be understood logically because it can have mutually contradictory desires, at least one after another?

2.3.2 (218)
अस्ति तु
asti tu

asti—there is; tu—but, of course.

TRANSLATION

But, of course, such is the case (the soul not being logically consistent).

COMMENTARY

Classical notions of logic entail that given a premise there must be only one conclusion, or at least, the conclusions must be mutually consistent. The premise of the existence of the soul, however, doesn't entail such consistency because contradictory desires can be produced from the same premise. We have noted this problem at the beginning where we said that the premise of my existence can lead to diverse questions: "Why do I exist?" or "How can I continue to exist?" Troubled by the problems of life, some people develop a stronger desire to fight their problems while others resign to end their lives. Thus, the same premise leads to mutually inconsistent conclusions. Hence, the soul cannot be studied using logical consistency. We have seen earlier how "I" is riddled with problems of mutual exclusion and non-contradiction. For instance, if we classify all the individuals into two groups—friends and non-friends—then it is not clear whether I'm my friend (because friends must be different from me) or non-friend (because how could I be my enemy?). Regarding the self, we are compelled to conclude that I am neither my friend nor my non-friend.

Thus, due to the production of conflicting desires, we must say that the soul is *both* these desires. And due to being separate from the material opposites (such as friends and non-friends) we must say that it is *neither* of these opposites. The use of both and neither is contrary to classical conceptions of logic because if something is not-X then it must be X, and it cannot both be X and not-X. The soul cannot be studied using classical logical categories.

QUESTION

Shouldn't we say that this inner contradiction is due to the influence of the material modes? The reason is that the material world is the experience of conflict and contradiction. If we say that the soul is itself contradictory, then aren't we imputing the contradictions of this world back onto the soul itself?

2.3.3 (219)

गौणी असंभवात्

gaunī asambhavāt

gauṇī—mixed up with guna; asambhavāt—due to the impossibility.

TRANSLATION

(The conclusion of being) mixed up with guna is impossible.

COMMENTARY

Material nature exists in three modes of sattva, rajas, and tamas. But the soul also exists in the three modes of sat, chit, and ānanda. Just as the three modes mix over and over to produce a tree-like hierarchical structure, similarly, the modes of the soul also mix over and over to create his personality of desires, a body of senses, mind, intellect, ego, and morality, and diverse types of relations in which the soul is superior in some roles and inferior in other roles.

Therefore, the claim that if there are some contradictions, then they must be due to material modes is ignorant of the fact that the soul is also in three modes. The material nature is the Lord's Śakti, and a person. The three modes of sattva, rajas, and tamas are reflections of the sat-chit-ānanda in the Lord's Śakti. The problem in impersonalism is that it considers the soul to be living and material energy to be dead. Thus, Brahman is alive and māyā is dead. This is an utterly false caricature because material nature is the Lord's Śakti.

The three modes of nature are universal, individual, and relational. In the spiritual world, the universal mode dominates over the relational mode, which dominates over the individual mode. Therefore, the Absolute Truth is dominant, everything is defined in relation to Him, and the individual soul remains subordinate. In the material world this prioritization is inverted. Now, the individual mode dominates, the relational mode is subordinate, and the universal mode is further subordinate. Therefore, every soul thinks that he is the master of the universe, everything is defined in relation to him, and whatever universal truth exists—e.g., in case of modern science—must be used in his service.

The problem is not the qualities of nature, but their prioritization or the dominant-subordinate structure. Thus, the material world becomes the spiritual world for the devotees, and the spiritual world becomes the material world for the materialist. The qualities in both worlds are the same. But the ordering of these qualities is completely opposed in these two worlds. Therefore, the claim that the qualities are only due to the material world is false. Qualities exist in the spiritual world too, but their hierarchy is inverted in matter.

QUESTION

We don't see a rational and logical person saying self-contradictory things. How can we say that a soul, purified of material influences, is conflicted?

2.3.4 (220)

शब्दाच्च

śabdācca

śabdāt—from their words; ca—also.

TRANSLATION

(We can know the conflicts in a soul) from their words as well (i.e., they will say contradictory things).

COMMENTARY

The Vedas are the primary examples of conflicting ideas, as there are many mutually contradictory ideas described in the Vedas. Thus, the Lord is both transcendent and immanent, the material world is His part and yet separate from Him, and the Lord exists in many moods, forms, and relationships.

The term śabdāt can refer both to the words of spiritually realized souls, or to the Vedic scriptures. Since these scriptures are spoken by the Lord and His devotees, the contradictions exist in the Lord Himself, but they manifest in different times, places, and contexts. The soul is similarly capable of many kinds of desires, and different levels of advancement. Thus, the different kinds of scriptures are meant for people with different mentalities and desires. For those who desire material enjoyment, a restricted form of enjoyment through rituals is prescribed. For those who want to renounce these enjoyments, the path of knowledge and detachment is prescribed. Those who want to change the quality of their enjoyment are advised in modifying their minds and bodies. And those who want to enjoy in the association of the Lord are prescribed devotion.

The unity underlying this diversity is that each of these processes uplifts the soul toward devotion to the Lord, but the stages of this upliftment may be mutually contradictory. Thus, the Vedas describe both *pravritti* and *nivritti*, which encourage practitioners to engage in their duties or renounce their duties. A self-realized teacher may advise one disciple to go out and work, take care of their family, perform their social duties, etc. because he is not yet prepared for renunciation; even if he was advised to sit in one place and meditate, he would keep thinking about what he is missing. Only a person who has indulged in these activities and realized their futility can be advised renunciation because he can then withdraw the mind and senses from worldly engagements. A person who cannot control his sexual urges may be advised to have multiple marriages, while a person who has transcended such urges may be advised to renounce. The conflicting statements are meant to achieve the same purpose, ultimately, although they are intended for people who have different levels of spiritual progress, and hence prescribe different paths of progress for them.

The Lord Himself has contradictory desires—in Goloka He desire to enjoy with others, in Vaikuṇṭha He remains self-satisfied, and in the material world He engages in austerity. Some forms of the Lord are angry, while other forms are humorous. These are simply manifestation of the different desires in the Lord, and He enjoys in innumerable ways by fulfilling His desires. Thus, contradictions appear in the Lord, and they appear in all the souls. The extent of contradictions in us is nowhere near the extent of contradictions in the Lord because we are limited to a few places, times, and situations. Since the Lord is manifest in everything, therefore, the variety is both contradictory, and yet it has a single source. If we can understand the existence of contradictions within us, then by extension we can imagine their existence in the Lord as well.

QUESTION

We can understand that when a single truth manifests into many individuals, and they are placed in different situations or contexts, then different paths may be prescribed, and contradictory statements can be made. But shouldn't the Absolute Truth from which everything originates be logically consistent? How can we understand an Absolute Truth that is also self-contradictory?

2.3.5 (221)

सयाच्चैकस्य ब्रह्मशब्दवत्

syāccaikasya brahmaśabdavat

syāt—is possible; ca—and; ekasya—of the same; brahmaśabdavat—like śabda-brahman (manifests conflicting meanings).

TRANSLATION

Just like śabda-brahman is manifest (as conflicting meanings) from the same source, (similarly), it is possible (for a pure soul to say conflicting things).

COMMENTARY

The ideas of self-consistency are based on physical notions of reality. When we think about concepts, however, both cows and tigers are part of mammals. The cow is gentle, and the tiger is aggressive, and yet, they are both mammals, and they are part of mammals. Since they are parts of mammal, therefore, contradictory things come out of the same truth. But someone might say that we only know about cows and tigers, never about mammals. For such people we can say that the mammal is also within the cow and the tiger. Thus, there is diversity inside the unity, and unity inside the diversity. There are opposites, but because they are not manifest simultaneously, there is no contradiction. These contradictory opposites are potentialities in the Absolute Truth, and then are manifested as partial expressions of this Absolute Truth. When they are manifest, we think they are opposites and don't see their unitary source.

This sūtra gives the example of śabda-brahmān, which is a sound representation of Brahman. Since it is the origin of all words, therefore, many contradictory words are produced from Brahman. Thus, śabda-brahmān is not without contradictions because it is the origin of all the words, whose meanings are mutually contradictory. The words are also not formless; therefore, the source of all words cannot be formless. Each word is a unique form, and the origin of these forms is the speaker of these words. The speaker must have an organ of speech, which can also represent the knowledge of all the parts of His body. Thus, śabda- brahmān is all the words, and the speaker of śabda- brahmān provides the description of Himself. Therefore, śabda- brahmān is a representation of the Lord. This representation is all the mutually contradictory words. Therefore, the source or the speaker of śabda-brahmān must have these contradictions. Therefore, we cannot understand the source using logical consistency.

We might note here in addition that these forms are semantic, rather than physical. Left and right, top and bottom, front and back, are not merely physical sides; they are also conflicting meanings, and this conflict is illustrated by the fact that if something doesn't have a top, then it also won't have a bottom. If something doesn't have a front, then it also won't have a back. These are mutually opposed, and they are only defined in the presence of the other. The Absolute Truth combines these opposites, so it is outside conventional logic.

QUESTION

You keep saying that the Absolute Truth is outside conventional logic, but how are we to understand this new type of logic? What new logical principles must be adopted, and which older logical principles must be discarded?

2.3.6 (222)

पुरतज्ञिआहानरिव्यतरिकाच्छब्देभ्यः

pratijñāhāniravyatirekācchabdebhyaḥ

pratijñā-ahānih—non-contradiction; avyatirekāt—from the non-exclusion; śabdebhyaḥ—the words.

TRANSLATION

From the non-exclusion of the words, there is no contradiction.

COMMENTARY

Our conventional understanding of the world is based on the idea that X and not-X are non-contradictory and mutually exclusive. So, if X is true, then not-X must be false, and at least one of these must be true. This sūtra accepts non-contradiction but rejects mutual exclusion. In fact, mutual exclusion is replaced by *avyatirekā* or non-exclusion. To understand this position, think of the head and the tail of a coin. Only one head will be seen at any time. However, the mere presence of a head entails the existence of a tail, although both are not seen simultaneously. Therefore, since either head or tail are seen, therefore, there is non-contradiction. However, since the existence of either entails the existence of the opposite, therefore, there is non-exclusion. The non-contradiction pertains to our experience, and the non-exclusion pertains to existence. Hence, both opposites exist and are mutually defined, but only one of them is seen at any given moment, in a specific situation. The basic point is that all reality has a form, and we can see only one aspect of the form. Just like we see one of the two faces of the coin, or one of the six faces of a die, similarly, the existence of forms entails that everything is not seen at once. However, seeing any aspect entails the existence of the other aspects as these are mutually defined.

Thus, when the scriptures or the advanced souls speak of different aspects at different times or in different contexts, we should not presume contradiction. We should rather say that when one claim was made, the opposite one automatically entailed—just like seeing the head of the coin entails that the tail also exists. In short, assertions don't entail the negation of their opposites. Rather, the assertion entails that the opposite is true but in a different context.

Mutual exclusion is commonly used in *reductio ad absurdum* proofs, where, the mere truth of X entails the falsity of not-X. This problem arises because logic doesn't have the distinction of space, time, and persons, and logical truth is supposed to be Universal Truth. The Vedic conception of truth is not universalist; it is rather absolutist. What is the difference? When we speak about Universal Truth, then relative truth is not true; it is just what you and I think and because you and I think differently, therefore, at least one of us must be thinking falsities. It is possible that both of us are under illusion; but at least, one of us must be under illusion. Now, the problem with logic is that whatever is false also cannot exist. Thus, if the sky is blue, then a red sky cannot exist. This leads to a serious problem—the person who is thinking falsities cannot exist—if only true things exist. So, if someone says that the sky is red, he must not exist. But, of course, we can see the existence of those who don't agree with us. By the universalist notion of logic, only one of us must exist. Since I cannot deny my existence, therefore, I must say that whoever disagrees with me cannot exist. Thus, universalist conceptions of truth lead to obvious problems.

However, when we speak about the Absolute Truth, then relative truth is not false; it is only a *part* of the whole truth. Each such partial truth also has three further aspects—objective, subjective, and relational. For example, in seeing a snake, there is an objective snake, I must be there to see the snake, and I must see it correctly as snake. Relative truth is when the objective, subjective, and relational are consistent. That is, there is a snake, I am present near the snake to see it, and I see it as a snake. Relative falsity is when either there is no snake, or I am not present to see the snake, or I don't see it as a snake. However, seeing the snake—when it is seen perfectly (i.e., there is a snake, I was there to see it, and I saw it correctly)—is not Absolute Truth. It is only relative truth. The relative truth is different from relative falsity; relative truth is not falsity.

Thus, in the universalist conception of truth, all relative knowledge is false. But in the absolutist conception of truth, all relative knowledge is partial.

The implication of this partial knowledge is that it doesn't exclude its opposites. Thus, if I see a snake, then someone else can see a rope. I may see the snake and the rope at different places or times. And two people can see snake and rope simultaneously at different places. If one of these—the time, place, or person—is different, then there is no contradiction in different seeing. And the absence of such contradiction precludes mutual exclusion in the universalist sense; we can say that seeing a rope doesn't exclude the seeing of a snake, and this seeing of the snake is not a falsity if seeing the rope is true. Since all these truths emerge from the Absolute Truth, the existence of such contradictory knowledge is not actually contradictory because perception involves the distinctions of place, time, and person, and the Absolute Truth is all the perception, but that perception is divided across many places, times, and persons.

As we have discussed earlier, the Absolute Truth exists in three modes—place, time, and person; the Śakti-mode is the place-mode; the God-mode is the time-mode, and the soul-mode is the person mode. Through the combination of these modes, infinite relative truths are created. But when they are uncombined, then the same truth is called Absolute Truth. The uncombined is the whole truth, and the combinations are the parts of the whole truth. Hence, partial, or relative truth is created with the Absolute Truth as diversity. This diversity is non-contradictory due to different place, time, and person. But it is also non-exclusive because one place, time, and person entails others.

Impersonal philosophers misinterpret this diversity by saying that since all such truths are possible, therefore, whatever anyone sees must be truth. This is again a wrong position. There are both relative truths and relative falsities. The Absolute Truth is never false, and the Universal Truth is always false. So, the recognition of the falsity of Universal Truth doesn't entail that every relative experience now becomes truth. You can see a snake when there is a rope. That seeing is relative falsity, not relative truth, and certainly not Absolute Truth. Thus, the rejection of Universal Truth is not the rejection of Absolute Truth, and the rejection of Universal Truth doesn't make every relative lie a truth.

QUESTION

Won't the rejection of mutual exclusion as a logical principle lead to many faults? For example, we say that "you can't have your cake and eat it too" because eating the cake and having it are mutually exclusive alternatives.

2.3.7 (223)
यावद्वकिारं तु वभिागो लोकवत्
yāvadvikāraṃ tu vibhāgo lokavat

yāvat-vikāram—whatever faults; tu—but; vibhāgaḥ—separateness; lokavat—as in the world.

TRANSLATION

Whatever faults (we impute on these words) are but due to the (idea of) separateness (of opposite claims) just as in the material world.

COMMENTARY

The previous sūtra rejected the application of mutual exclusion to the Absolute Truth, but this sūtra accepts its application to the material world. The result of this principle is change: if you are given some cake, and you eat it, then the cake no longer exists. In short, eating the cake would entail a change as the cake ceases to exist. In contrast, we can envision the spiritual world as a place where you can eat the cake and the cake also remains intact. Your eating therefore doesn't end the existence of the cake, and hence everything is eternal.

There are two kinds of eternity we can envision. First, everything remains static and unchanged, and in this state, there are no activities—e.g., you cannot eat anything. Second, you can envision a world where there are continuous activities—e.g., you can eat cakes—and yet everything is eternal. The impersonalist argues for the first type of eternity, and the personalist for the second type of eternity. The first type of eternity is static, and it implies the absence of change because change would—under the material world logic—entail birth and death. The second type of eternity is dynamic, and activities are constantly being performed, their results are being enjoyed, and yet the world is eternal. This eternity is impossible with mutual exclusion, but it is possible if we agree upon non-exclusion as the logical principle— as stated in the last sūtra.

In this world, change occurs when a cause becomes an effect, and then ceases to exist. That cessation of the cause, after the effect has been created, is called mutual exclusion. This mutual exclusion is false in many cases. For example, we can use a block of wood as a chair or as a table; while using it as a table, we can say that the table exists, but we cannot say that the chair doesn't exist. Rather, the same thing can be used as table and chair one after another. However, there are situations in this world when things are *destroyed,* and they cannot be said to exist anymore. The eating of the cake is its destruction. If you burn wood, then the wood ceases to exist and is replaced by ash. From this ash you cannot get the wood immediately, although over time, the ash will mix into soil, will be consumed by a seed, become a tree, and then wood again.

This so-called irreversible change is different from the reversible change. For instance, I can act as a father at home and employee at work, and such changes are reversible. But when I die, the change is irreversible. If all changes were reversible—as in the spiritual world—then non-exclusion would hold, and mutual exclusion would always be false. If some changes are reversible, as in the case of me shuttling between father and employee roles, then sometimes non-exclusion is true, and sometimes mutual-exclusion is true. But whenever the change is irreversible, then mutual exclusion is true and non-exclusion is false. This sūtra says whatever cases of mutual exclusion we see are unique to the material world. By this, the phenomenon of birth and death is indicated.

It is not truly mutual exclusion, because those who have died will be born again, and they could be born in the same species, in the same gender, and even potentially at the same place. Even if they are born in another species, gender, or place, they can return to the same species, gender, and place later. Thus, birth and death can be reversible, as the soul goes through 8,400,000 species. As he passes through these species, he cannot say that being in a dog body excludes his being in a cat body. However, these changes are not obtained at will. Thus, I can go to work and come back at home at will. But I cannot become cat and dog at will. That gives rise to the idea of irreversibility, but over a longer time, it is not. If the soul is in the material world, and undergoing cyclic changes, everything is reversible, although not at our will. Only liberation from the material existence is irreversible, but as we have seen earlier, a liberated soul can also fall into the material world, so it is also not considered irreversible.

Thus, we can ask: Is there anything irreversible and mutually exclusive? The short answer is no. Everything is always possible, and hence always reversible. This reversibility entails non-exclusion. The difference is simply that in the spiritual world, this reversibility is obtained at will, and in the material world, it is not obtained at will. The absence of change at will makes us think that the world is irreversible—e.g., that time goes linearly forward—but that is not true. Therefore, the apparent lack of reversibility is an outcome of our inability to control our lives with our will, and to the extent that we can control it things are reversible, and when we can't control it seems irreversible. This irreversibility is an apparent phenomenon observable in the material world.

Topic 2

QUESTION

You have said earlier that the possibilities are eternal, and that the possibilities are also contradictory. Above, you have also said that these contradictory possibilities cannot be realized at once, which means that the possibilities are manifest one by one. What is the process of this manifestation?

2.3.8 (224)

एतेन मातरिश्वा व्याख्यातः

etena mātariśvā vyākhyātaḥ

etena—by this; mātariśvā—air; vyākhyātaḥ—is explained.

TRANSLATION

By this (conflicting separations) (the emergence of) air is explained.

COMMENTARY

Beginning with this sūtra, the emergence of successive realities will be explained one by one. The existence of possibilities defines a 'space' which is also called ākāśa or ether. This ether is a tree-like structure, which means that locations in this space are like branches of a tree. From every branch, twigs and leaves can grow. The emanation of these twigs and branches is the successive elements such as air, fire, water, and earth which manifest one by one. Notably, all these elements are present in the ether, just as a cow is present in mammal. And yet, the cow is invisible in the meaning of mammal. The manifestation of the cow from the mammal involves the subdivision of the mammal into parts. When the subdivision has occurred, then the mammal is also inside the cow. In the same way, the ether contains all the elements, and when an element manifests from the ether, then it also contains the ether. Therefore, space is the container of everything, and space is inside everything. The first such element is described here—it is called 'air'. The property of air is touch, which leads to the sensations of pressure, heat, roughness, etc. The property of ether is sound, which leads to tone, pitch, form, etc. The successive elements carry the property of the previous element and they also modify these properties by adding new properties. Thus, for instance, everything that can be touched can also be heard. However, everything that can be heard is not necessarily touchable. This simply means that the possibility of a thing exists as a sound, but when it begins to manifest into perceivable things, the first such perception is touch. If you can talk about the possibility, it has already manifest partially—i.e., as a sound. If you can feel the effect of that possibility as heat, roughness, or pressure, then it has manifest as air. The manifestation of vision or sight follows next.

Topic 3

QUESTION

But I can talk about anything, and yet it doesn't become manifest as touch. What explains the fact that the possibilities do not always become real?

2.3.9 (225)
असंभवस्तु सतःअनुपपत्तेः
asaṃbhavastu satah anupapatteh

asaṃbhavah—that which has not become possible; tu—but; satah—eternal; anupapatteh—as it not attainable.

TRANSLATION

That which is not possible is also eternal, but it is not (always) attainable.

COMMENTARY

All the possibilities are not always manifest due to the nature of time. Time in Vedic philosophy is classified into several *yuga* or ages, and different kinds of phenomena manifest during these ages. This doesn't mean that these possibilities are temporary; they are still considered eternal, but a distinction between unmanifest, about to manifest, and manifest is made to describe how the world transitions from unmanifest to about to manifest and certain things become possible at that time. For instance, the modern world of technology emerged out of the age of Enlightenment in Europe where the human powers of reasoning and observation were used to formulate laws of nature. The age of Enlightenment itself arose out of the Protestant movement, which then arose out of the disenchantment with the corruption of the Catholic Church.

The previous stage creates the conditions for the manifestation of the next stage, and these conditions are called the 'about to manifest' stage. From the about to manifest, emerges the manifest. History is studied as the succession of these manifests, but a closer inspection of history also indicates how the conditions that manifest subsequently were building up and preparing for the advent of the next stage. In many cases, we can see that everything that lies prior does not decide the future, and many such prior trends die or are weakened, and the stronger trend determines the future. The selection of which trend becomes stronger or weaker is the function of time. Time makes some trends stronger even if they were weak, and it weakens other trends even if they were strong. We can attribute these changes in the strength of trends to different actors, but the absence of such actors would not have prevented them; these actors would only have been replaced by other such actors. Thus, history or events is predetermined, but the actors and their participation in different trends is not. The manifestation of the unmanifest entails that the future exists in the past and is produced by the past, whereas the past exists in the present and hides it. There are many possible futures hidden in the present, but one such future would be selected by time, while others will remain hidden. Whatever remains hidden will eventually manifest, although at a different point in time.

The life of the universe is the realization of all the possibilities within the universe, and the size of the universe is all those possibilities. Thus, the size of the universe and the life of the universe are directly related to each other in the sense that in the lifetime of the universe, all possibilities must be manifest. As have noted earlier, the space of all possibilities is uncountable and the manifestation at a moment is countable. The countable emerges from the uncountable, and therefore everything manifest at one moment can be counted—although it is infinite. The succession of these countable states is itself uncountable. The term *asaṃbhavaḥ* or that which has not happened indicates that uncountable. Like the space of real numbers—which are uncountable—it is also eternal, but not always visible. Conversely, *anupatteh*—which is the countable—indicates the manifest. The discussion of countable and uncountable occurred earlier. So, why is the same topic of manifest and unmanifest being revisited now?

The answer is that we have now spoken of how the countable and the uncountable are defined mutually such that even if they are contradictory meanings, their successive existence is not contradictory, and their simultaneous existence is not excluded. Since successive existence is not contradictory, therefore, a society that was earlier barbaric can later become civilized. And since their simultaneous existence is not excluded, therefore, a civilized society may exist in conflict with another barbaric society. The meaning of non-exclusion is simply that it is not necessary for a civilized society to exist in a conflict with a barbaric society. And the meaning of non-contradiction is that there is no logical condition that prevents barbarians to become civilized. Thus, the evolution of the same thing and the conflict with another opposite thing are both possibilities—neither are these possibilities precluded, nor are the logically necessary. Generally, in the universalist logic, denying something means confirming its opposite. Both the preclusion and necessity of outcomes is rejected here. This goes to say that logic doesn't contradict choices. Logic is the enabling of choices. Logic also decides consequences of choices, but that is not discussed here. At the present, we are only discussing how logic can never preclude choices.

When civilization can emerge out of a barbaric society, then we must say that the seed of civilization existed within them but was not manifest. This seed of the future exists in everything, and the past exists in everything as a seed. We all have seeds of many kinds of futures; the question is simply: Which seed are we going to water? Logic allows the choice of watering different seeds.

Thus, although terms like countable and uncountable—which are found in modern mathematics too—we previously used, the temptation to say that these things about numbers being talked about in modern mathematics are the same as those in the past, are untenable. Current number theories uphold mutual exclusion, which means that if 2 were true, then -2 must be false. In short, a barbaric society cannot become civilized, because 2 cannot become -2. If you found a single theorem that demonstrated how a sequence of logical steps could convert 2 into -2, then everything in modern mathematics would collapse. To prevent that outcome, mathematicians choose consistency over completeness. They choose the impossibility of some barbarians becoming civilized.

Such transformations are modal in nature. The change begins with desire, which is a mode. The desire for change doesn't contradict the reality. This desire then leads to contact with the opposite—namely, those from whom civilization can be learned. Then after it is learned, then it is put into practice. That practice is the sequence of steps of reasoning. However, now we are dealing with two contradictions— the contradiction between desire and reality, and the contradiction between two realities (e.g., of barbarianism vs. civilization). The first contradiction pushes for a change, and the second one prevents a change. The person or society caught in these contradictions is also conflicted—which contradiction should be preferred? If the first contradiction is preferred, then barbarians become civilized due to logic— they are trying to overcome the first contradiction. Notably, they could have also preferred the second contradiction and remained uncivilized. Therefore, logic enables choices, rather than preclude them.

Here we can see a preliminary insight into how completeness can be obtained—it begins in the acceptance of non-exclusion. This acceptance forms the seed of the Bhedābheda doctrine, which is also called non-difference. Exclusion would have entailed a difference and non-exclusion is non-difference. This sūtra explains how non-difference comes about—the opposing things are not manifest in the same place, time, and person. If we combine this claim with those in the previous sūtras, then we can see how the existence of possibilities is so intimately tied to the problems of modern logic and mathematics.

Topic 4

QUESTION

You said that air manifests from space, and we can feel pressure, heat, roughness, etc. But we cannot still see the things that create such sensations? What is the cause of the world becoming visible as we experience the effects?

2.3.10 (226)
तेजोऽतःतथा ह्याह
tejo'taḥ tathā hyāha

tejaḥ—fire; ataḥ—therefore; tathā—so; hi—verily; āha—emerges.

TRANSLATION

The element fire therefore verily emerges from this (air).

COMMENTARY

Western science has believed that everything that exerts a pressure must be visible, but here it is described that we may not see those things which exert a pressure. This idea is important in modern cosmology where 'dark' energy and 'dark' matter are postulated to explain the pressure. They are 'dark' because they don't emit light, and we cannot see them. And yet, their presence exerts a pressure that can be measured. This dark reality is the element of air, which has not yet manifested into fire. Therefore, it cannot be seen, and yet it can exert pressure. Modern science struggles with a reality that can exert pressure but cannot be seen, so, we can infer that it is limited to the gross element of fire. This element of fire is described in atomic theory as electricity or electrons, and light or photons. When this light is present, then air is present intrinsically, therefore, with electricity we can push things—e.g., drive the machines. But the problem is that light and electricity are not the cause of motion. The motion is caused by air, and not by fire. But since we don't understand air, and air exists in fire, therefore, we assume that electricity must cause the fan to move. Factually, it is not electricity but the air present within that electricity. The electricity is the element of fire, and the cause of motion is the air in the electricity.

Another problem in atomic theory is that heat and light are combined into a single theory of radiation. This is a problem because heat is perceived by the sense of touch, and light is perceived by the sense of seeing. These are separate senses and separate elements, so there cannot be a common theory because sometimes heat may be present although light is absent. Similarly, sometimes, light may be present, but heat may be low. A practical example is that sometimes there is no sun, but the day is very hot because there is also no wind. If heat was caused by the sun, then the absence of the sun should entail a cool day. But that is not always true. We see is that a sunny day can be cool if there is wind. And a dark day can be hot if there is no wind. This is because heat and light are attributed to different elements of air and fire. Heat isn't light, although light can be heat. Modern physics combines these two assuming that since there is heat whenever there is light, therefore, heat must exist due to radiation.

A further problem in cosmology is the notion of Cosmic Background Radiation, which is said to be 40 K. What we measure is heat, but we interpret this to be radiation or light—because atomic theory equates heat with light. As more and more such equivalences are drawn, the confusions become endless.

Atomic theory has many conceptual problems about the nature of reality—namely, that reality is conceptual and not physical, that the meanings of conceptual reality are only defined through distinctions to other concepts, etc. However, all these conceptual problems are today accepted on the premise that the theory *works*. What is that working? Well, electricity can push fans and motor cars. Since it is working, therefore technology is possible, and so we accept the truth of the theory. Then, we face a new problem: this pushing is possible even when you cannot see the thing that is pushing. To explain that, we would have to modify the theory in a very practical sense—the push is not due to the electromagnetic forces postulated in atomic theory. The push is due to air, which cannot be seen, but its presence can be perceived due to pressure.

Hence, the theory is not just flawed in the sense of conceptual problems, but also in a practical sense that the things we see, and which are supposed to be pushing, are not actually pushing. The cause of that push is something that we haven't yet understood in atomic theory because it cannot be seen.

When most people come across the theory of five elements, they often roll their eyes. They think that modern science has changed the understanding of matter and all these ideas are false. On the contrary, science hasn't shown anything wrong with Vedic philosophy, but Vedic philosophy can show many things wrong in modern science. These mistakes are both conceptual and empirical, and hence these ideas remain important for scientific development.

Topic 5

QUESTION

What is the next manifestation after the manifestation of vision?

2.3.11 (227)

आप:

āpaḥ

āpaḥ—water.

TRANSLATION

(The next element emerging from fire is called) water.

COMMENTARY

The element of water brings the property of taste or flavor. Everything that can be tasted, can also be seen, can also be touched, and can also be spoken of. Thus, when water exists, the previous elements of fire, air, and ether also exist. The ordinary water that we drink is a combination of water, fire, air, and ether. For example, when we boil water, it becomes hot. However, this heat is not due to the water; it is due to the presence of air. Similarly, the fact that we can see water isn't because of water; it is due to the presence of fire. The element water should not be confused with ordinary water; the element is responsible only for taste, although ordinary water also can be seen, touched, and talked about.

Present day computers carry information through electricity and light. The computer works through electricity, but the information coming into the computer can be due to light. However, we cannot carry taste and smell through electricity or light. Therefore, if you are having a videoconference on a computer, then you can see others and hear them. With virtual reality techniques, you can also feel the push and pull. But you cannot get the taste and smell. According to modern atomic theory, taste and smell are due to the molecular structure, and this structure is caused due to the electromagnetic forces. If taste and smell were due to the molecular structure, then it should be possible to encode the information about this structure into light, transfer the light, and then convert the molecular structure back into smell and taste at the receiver. But this can never be achieved because the elements of water and earth—which carry taste and smell—are not just the element of fire. Water and earth emerge out of fire, however, in the fire element, water and earth are not manifest.

The problem with atomic theory is that it observes things that have taste and smell. But this observation is limited to the study of the molecular structure. Since everything that has taste and smell also has form, color, and structure, therefore, scientists infer that the taste and the smell must be due to the atomic structure. This is a false conclusion. Taste and smell are not perceivable in fire. Hence, we cannot conclude that molecular structure causes taste and smell. The practical result of this problem is that computers that run on electricity and light cannot transfer the taste and the smell, although we can see, touch, and hear.

We can conclude that present atomic theory is limited to the fire element. The more subtle elements such as Ether and Air are not understood because they cannot be seen. And the more gross elements of Earth and Water are not understood because fire doesn't manifest taste and smell. Modern Western science is highly visual—all its explanations are based on what we can *see*. But what we can see is not all that we can perceive. So, science attempts to reduce all perception to the models obtained by seeing. Thus, space is described as a box because that is what we see. The push and pull of air are attributed to the properties of fire—e.g., the 'charge' of particles—when it is due to air. The taste and the smell are not even explained. Thus, by reducing the properties of the five elements to the properties of one element—namely, fire—a hugely problematic theory is produced. And people enamored by modern science think that this explanation of matter is far superior to the theory of five elements.

It is commonly observed that even those who accept the authority of Vedic knowledge, are unable to understand these five elements. For example, they continue to think that space is a box. That the planets must be moving due to gravitational force. That light actually 'travels' in space, or that this movement is the cause of heat. They have carried forward numerous caricatures of reality in modern science and they try to interpret the Vedic descriptions according to these presuppositions. A little careful thought would show that these two systems cannot be reconciled. And it is because modern science is totally false. Science is a long way away from studying the five elements instead of one. Then it is even farther away from combining these five elements into a single theory rather than many disparate theories. This combination is possible only when we say that reality is symbolic. But acknowledging that symbolism entails throwing away conventional logic and mathematics. We have seen the problems of logic above, but as a result, all subsequent ideas like the nature of numbers and the notion of space and time in geometry must be changed.

Topic 6

QUESTION

What follows the manifestation of water (and its associated taste)?

2.3.12 (228)

पृथिवि अधकिाररूपशब्दान्तरेभ्यः

pṛthivī adhikārarūpaśabdāntarebhyaḥ

pṛthivī—earth; adhikāra—position, office, section; rūpa—form, color, etc.; śabdāntarebhyaḥ—within the sound.

TRANSLATION

(The next element emerging from water is called) earth; it (was previously) situated (as a part) within sound, form, color, etc.

COMMENTARY

A fundamental aspect of the Vedic doctrine of causality is that everything that manifests as experience was previously present within the cause. Thus, even though air, fire, water, and earth manifest successively from ether, these are not 'creations' out of nothing; they were previously unmanifest or hidden inside the cause. In this sūtra, this claim is made explicitly by stating that earth was situated inside sound, form, color, etc. The property of earth is smell, and while everything that can be spoken of, or touched, or seen, or tasted, need not have smell, the smell is intrinsically hidden inside those things. The smell cannot be perceived, but we cannot say that it doesn't have the smell. Thus, when a person talks in a crude language, we say that his speech is "bitter". Even when you don't smell, you can say that "this person stinks". And without tasting, you can say that a person is "sweet". There is no sense perception corresponding to these claims, but the mind doesn't depend on the sense perceptions. The mind decodes these unmanifest realities even when the senses cannot. Therefore, the mind is the sense that is superior to all the five senses, because it can perform the job of all the five senses—although in understanding, not in sensation.

Likewise, it is seen that when you smell tasty food, then your mouth starts watering, and there is naturally a taste on the tongue. From this taste, there is naturally fire produced in the gastric system, and the body naturally warms up. Therefore, if someone was feeling cold, the mere smell of tasty food can make them feel warm. Likewise, someone's speech can make you feel cold, just as some speech can make you feel warm. How the subtle manifests into gross, and the gross carries the subtle is a very sophisticated science. But this science is available to all of us through ordinary perceptions and experiences. If we can analyze these experiences, we may be able to accept Vedic descriptions.

Much of the damage in the public perception of these theories was caused by the Greeks in the West and the Chinese in the East. The Greeks discarded the Ether, and only accepted Earth, Water, Fire, and Air as four elements. There was no understanding of how the grosser elements exist inside the subtler elements, and the subtler elements exist inside the grosser elements. There was no understanding of how these elements are related to the five sensations. And, there was no understanding of how the mind perceives all five of them. Thus, a caricature of this theory was presented, debated, and eventually rejected. The Chinese had some understanding of how one element can be created from another. But to fit the theory in their understanding, they modified the elements. Ether and Air—the two subtle elements which are hard to understand—were replaced by Wood and Metal, keeping only Fire, Water, and Earth. If we try to explain the Vedic descriptions, many people may start recalling the older Greek and Chinese ideas, which would be worse than modern science.

Topic 7

QUESTION

How does one element exist inside the other even as it is unmanifest?

2.3.13 (229)

तदभिध्यानादेव तु तल्लिङ्गात् सः

tadabhidhyānādeva tu talliṅgāt saḥ

tadat-abhidhyānāt—because of the purpose being reflected internally; eva—certainly; tu—but; talliṅgāt—from His senses; saḥ—He.

TRANSLATION

Because the purpose reflected internally (in the elements) is but certainly Him caused by His senses (from which the material elements emanate).

COMMENTARY

In the previous sūtra it was stated that the elements are inside the other elements. This sūtra states that this embedded nature of the elements is because the Lord is embedded inside the elements as their purpose, as this purpose has emanated from His senses. The elements are Prakriti and they exist as pure possibility. The Puruṣa is the will and activates this possibility to become reality. The body of the Puruṣa is the many types of desires, and His senses are the desires for sense enjoyment. Therefore, the purpose underlying the creation is the fulfillment of the Lord's desire. This Puruṣa or the will is the efficient cause of the creation while the Prakriti or the possibilities are the material cause; the created elements combine the possibility with the will to produce a reality.

If the will has manifested from the Lord's sense of hearing, then the manifested element is ether. If the will has manifested from the Lord's sense of touch, then the manifested element is air. Similarly, the wills manifested from the Lord's sense of sight, taste, and smell manifest the elements of fire, water, and earth. But each of the Lord's senses is capable of every other function. Thus, His sense of taste can produce the desire of sight; His sense of touch can have the desire for smell; and His sense of hearing can have the desire for seeing. The reason for this is that all desire arises in the mind, and depending on the type of desire, it is simply manifest through the senses. Thus, if a person can control their mind, then they can also control their senses. The desire in primordial form becomes the desiring for hearing, then it advances into touching, then it develops into seeing, then it progresses into tasting, and finally into smelling. Similarly, the elements also manifest from the subtle element due to the development of desire. But the possibility of everything exists in the ether; to see a specific property, the desire for that possibility must convert it into reality.

The desire created in the mind can transform into desire of any of the senses, and accordingly the element that fulfills that desire can also become the element corresponding to any of those senses. The progressive manifestation of the elements is simply the development of desire that converts one element into another. This is the seed of a material science in which anything can be created simply from space by the application of desire. We might think that space is empty, but it is the possibility of becoming anything we desire. Our desires are fulfilled due to the presence of karma, but one who understands this science can create anything out of space; it will seem magical to others, but it is not magical; this is also a science in which possibility develops due to desire.

Topic 8

QUESTION

If the Lord can create through desire, can He also destroy by desire?

2.3.14 (230)
वपिर्ययेण तु क्रमोऽतःउपपद्यते च
viparyayeṇa tu kramo'taḥ upapadyate ca

viparyayeṇa—in the reverse order; tu—indeed; kramaḥ—order; ataḥ—from that; upapadyate—in the order of creation; ca—and.

TRANSLATION

And (the destruction) occurs indeed in the reverse order from that in the creation (i.e., the elements dissolving back into previous elements).

COMMENTARY

An element exists in a certain form only if there is a purpose or desire to sustain it. If the desire is withdrawn, then it collapses back into the previous possibility. Thus, by withdrawing the desire for enjoyment, the Puruṣa also withdraws the Prakriti from the manifest into the unmanifest form. Thus, earth dissolves back into water, the water into fire, the fire into air, and everything goes back into ether. The ether itself goes back into the mind, the mind collapses into the capacity for judgment, which has three parts—the judgment of truth in the intellect, the judgment of good in the ego, and the judgment of right in the moral sense or mahattattva. These judgments then collapse back into the axioms or assumptions about truth, right, and good, which are called Prakriti.

Each person has a unique Prakriti, which means that they carry varied notions of truth, right, and good. In modern society, for example, the perceptions of the five senses are considered true; we may have different ideas and beliefs in the mind, but these are not considered true. Therefore, if you speak about something that people cannot perceive by the five senses, then they will say: "maybe that is your opinion, but it cannot be true". In modern science, even these opinions are considered unreal, because there are only molecules. Likewise, people think that goodness is only the enjoyment of the five senses. If you are giving people food, clothing, and shelter, then it is good. But if you are teaching people about the nature of the soul, then it is a delusion. Right and wrong are also based on the five senses, and it is believed that these only exist as social customs. Thus, each government is free to create laws of right and wrong, ignoring dharma and karma. Thus, eating cows is legal in some societies, but eating dogs is not. In other societies, eating anything is legal.

Ultimately, these ideas about truth, right, and good emerge from the Pradhāna which is the unmanifest reality. The meaning of unmanifest is that truth, right, and good are not separated. Therefore, truth is right, and right is good. In the manifest world, truth, right, and good are separated. Thus, truth is not required to lead to right action, and right action is not required to lead to happiness. Thus, a scientist can be immoral or unhappy, and his morality and happiness are not a criterion to decide if he knows the truth. This separation of truth, right, and good is called Prakriti, and it creates problematic ideas about how truth, right, and good must be judged—i.e., that these can be independent.

Modern society has been adopting such systems with vigor. At the dawn of the modern age, two such separations were carried out— (1) the separation of church and state, and (2) the separation of body and mind. The former separation says that right and good are separate things; the state will decide what is right, and the church can decide what is good. The latter separation says that scientists will decide what is true, but each person can decide what is good for them. This is a classic example of extreme separation of Prakriti. Formerly, there were separations, but modern society has taken them to extremes. Thus, as time elapses, sometimes Prakriti is more separated, and at other times it is less separated. The universe originates in the unseparated state of Pradhāna.

During creation, Pradhāna creates Prakriti, which creates mahat-tattva, ego, and intellect, which produce the mind, which manifests the senses, which produce the sensations, which create the five gross elements. Within these five elements, Earth comes from Water, Water from Fire, Fire from Air, and Air from Ether. During annihilation, they collapse back in the reverse order. Finally, everything rests in the unmanifest Pradhāna, which is the unseparated state.

Topic 9

QUESTION

In the material creation, we also spoke about the manifestation of the four aspects of the internal organs—namely, mind, intellect, ego, and mahattattva. Aren't these elements also being differentiated from the Lord's senses?

2.3.15 (231)

अन्तरा वज्ज्ञानमनसी क्रमेण तल्लङि्गादतिचेत् न अवशिषात्

antarā vijñānamanasī kramena tallingāditi cet na aviśeṣāt

antarā—the internal organs; vijñānamanasī—intellect and the mind; kramena—in the order; tallingāt—owing to separate senses for that; iti cet—if it be said; na—not so; aviśeṣāt—on account of non-difference.

TRANSLATION

If it is said that the internal organs such as the mind and intellect should manifest in order due to having separate sense organs for that, (then we say) no, (because) there is no difference (between these senses in the Lord).

COMMENTARY

The *antaha-karan* or the internal instrument is divided into four parts in the living entities according to both Sāñkhya and Yoga systems. These four parts are called manas or mind, buddhi or intellect, aham-kara or ego, and mahattattva or morality. The mind generates mean-ings, the intellect judges if these meanings are true, the ego judges if these meanings are good, and the morality judges if these meanings are right. Since the meanings generated by our mind can be false, bad, and wrong, therefore, there is a difference between these four senses. But if the mind is purified, then everything it thinks is always true, good, and right, and this separation of thinking from judgment becomes unneces-sary. The Lord's mind is also purified in the sense that it is not subject to the judgments of truth, right, and good. Rather, whatever appears in His mind is the very definition of truth, right, and good. Thus, His thoughts are always true; His desires are always good; and His actions are always right. Therefore, the *antaha-karan* of ordinary living enti-ties is divided into four parts, due to the separation of meaning, and its truth, rightness, and goodness. But as a person becomes spiritually advanced, these differences are dissolved. Ultimately, there is only the mind, and there is no need to judge if it also true, right, and good. The Lord is said to have such a pure mind; His *antaha-karan* is only one.

Therefore, the primordial reality should be understood as true meaning, the desire for this meaning, and the action of creating true meaning. This meaning has six forms, as we have discussed earlier—knowledge, beauty, power, wealth, fame, and renunciation. But, among these six categories, knowledge is the most fundamental, and other categories spring from knowledge. Thus, the Absolute Truth is some-times also called *jnanam-advayam* or non-dual knowledge (our knowl-edge is imbued with dual opposites). Ultimately, the 'mind' of the Lord is inseparable from His intellect, ego, and morality, because the meanings, desires, and actions are always true, good, and right. This distinction is made in the material elements for the souls whose minds are contaminated by selfish desires, producing illusory thoughts, and engaging and unsuitable actions. The separation is a facility for the living entity to perform judgments about what they think, desire, and do, and these instruments of judgment are therefore pathways to understanding the Lord as truth, right, and good.

Topic 10

QUESTION

If the Lord manifests the world as truth, right, and good, then how does it become false, wrong, and bad? How can something good turn into evil? How can something true turn into falsity? How can right turn into wrong?

2.3.16 (232)

चराचरव्यपाश्रयस्तु स्यात् तद्व्यपदेशो भाक्तःतद्भावभावितिवात्

carācaravyapāśrayastu syāt tadvyapadeśo bhāktaḥ tadbhāvabhāvitvāt

carācara—the moving and stationary; vyapāśrayaḥ—the shelter of the all-pervading; tu—but; syāt—may be; tadvyapadeśaḥ—pervading in all of that; bhāktaḥ—the enjoyer; tadbhāva-bhāvitvāt—it becomes due to the absence.

TRANSLATION

The Lord may be (the creator of) the moving and stationary, the shelter for the all-pervading (Brahman), present pervasively (as Paramātma), and their enjoyer (as Bhagavān), but (the world) manifests due to His absence.

COMMENTARY

We indulge in inappropriate actions due to selfish desires. Our conceptions of truth are impersonalized to detach truth from the Supreme Person. Our notions of right and wrong are socially constructed to avoid the idea that our actions are being judged by the Lord. Therefore, although the Lord creates the world through His mind, we think it is disconnected from the Lord. We forget that He is the shelter of Brahman as the light emanates from a source. We forget that He is the original meaning that incarnates inside every created thing. We forget that He has created the world for His enjoyment, and we consider that it exists for our pleasure. When our desires turn away from the Lord, the purpose underlying the creation is not seen. We then invent ourselves as the purpose of our existence, and we lie, cheat, deceive, and disown our duties because we don't see that the truth, right, and good are defined in relation to the Lord.

The truth, right, and good are three distinct realities but they have been mentioned as inseparable in the previous sūtra. This simply means that when the Lord creates the world, then everything that exists is true (falsities don't exist), every action is pure (wrongs don't exist), and all desires are based on love (selfishness doesn't exist). However, the living entity separates the inseparable reality and creates his conception of truth, right, and good, in relation to himself, rather than in relation to the Lord. The separation of truth, right, and good is the rejection that only the presence of the Lord unifies them; anything that is devoid of the understanding of the Lord may be partially true, partially right, or partially good; but it cannot be completely true, right, and good.

The separation of truth, right, and good is caused by māyā which stands for the rejection of the Lord's existence. When our vision is covered by this illusion, then we don't see how truth, right, and good cannot exist separately. A classic example of this separation in modern times is the differences between physical, social, and mind sciences. The physical sciences study the nature of truth, but they have no idea that this truth must be tied to morality. The social sciences speak of social roles and responsibilities, but they have no knowledge of how there are laws of choice and responsibility. Finally, the mind sciences aspire to create happiness, but they have no idea of how happiness is produced. Thus, because of māyā we tend to separate truth, right, and good, and everyone pursues their conception independently, while everyone rejects the Lord.

The cause of the separation of truth, right, and good is the absence of the Lord. He is not truly absent. But the soul thinks that He doesn't exist. The soul's Prakriti is a byproduct of the extent to which the soul thinks that the Lord is absent. Thus, some people will accept kindness, justice, equality as inviolable principles, but they may not accept their origin in God. Others may reject all these ideas and claim that might is right. In short, if you have the power, then you create your own definitions of what is right and wrong. As atheism grows, there are as many definitions of truth, right, and good as there are people. And since nobody can agree with anyone else, the atheists fight with each other.

This fighting, competition, enviousness, and hurting the others is the primary form of evil in this world. It is not created by the Lord. It is rather created by the soul under the delusion that the Lord—the principle of unity—doesn't exist. Thus, the Lord can't be accused of creating lies, wrongs, and suffering. These are rather created by the soul when he rejects the Lord's existence.

Topic 11

QUESTION

But you have earlier said the soul is not the creator of anything, that all creation is carried out by the Lord and His Śakti. So, how can we now attribute the creation of lies, evil, and wrongs to the soul? Even if we say that the evil is created by the separation, then the separation is not caused by the soul.

2.3.17 (233)

नात्मा आश्रुतेर्नत्यियत्वाच्च ताभ्यः

nātmā āśruternityatvācca tābhyaḥ

na—not; ātmā—soul; āśruteḥ—not being (so) mentioned by scriptures; nityatvāt—from being eternal; ca—also; tābhyaḥ—practiced by them (souls).

TRANSLATION

The soul is not (the creator of evil) as it is not mentioned by scriptures; from (such things) being eternal also; the soul is accustomed to them (the evil).

COMMENTARY

If you cook food for someone, then you can say that they are the cause of the cooking, even though they are not the cooks. In the same way, the world is created by the Lord and His Śakti, but it remains about to manifest. The soul is the cause of the manifestation. Therefore, the soul is the cause of evil, and he is not the cause of evil. In the previous sūtra, it was said that the division of nature occurs due to the Lord's absence, but He is not factually absent. His absence is only in the soul's imagination. But we have also said earlier that the material world is created due to the Lord's self-abnegation. We can now draw a distinction between these two kinds of creations. The creation by the Lord is the unmanifest becoming about to manifest, but it is manifest by the soul. The conversion from about to manifest to manifest is due to karma and guna, which are controlled by the Lord. But these occur because the soul desires and has karma to be reaped as the consequences of actions due to his past desires. Therefore, ultimately, the Lord is the cook, but He cooks based on the souls' desires.

We have spoken about the separation of truth, right, and good, but this is not the only kind of separation. The separation occurs many times over. For example, truthfulness, kindness, cleanliness, and sacrifice are generally understood to be moral principles in every society. But they are reconciled only in the Lord. When the Lord is absent, then these principles are also separated.

The result of this separation is that we often see contradictions between these principles. For example, we can show kindness to others and sacrifice for them, but we may also demand kindness and sacrifice from them. We can say that criminals do not deserve kindness, because they treat others unkindly. Or, we can say that to correct the mistakes of criminals, they must be shown kindness. Thus, if we punish the criminals, then we are demonstrating the principle of truthfulness, but we are not showing kindness. Conversely, if we don't punish them, then we are showing kindness, but not demonstrating truthfulness. By the virtue of truth, a criminal must be punished, and by the virtue of kindness, he must not be punished. Which of these virtues must be upheld?

Thus, morality is simply virtues, which can be dominant or subordinate. One could argue that for a petty criminal, we can show more kindness than truthfulness because he has just begun his crimes, and he can be corrected. But the reverse argument can also be made—if we don't teach this guy a lesson right now, then he will grow into a more hardened criminal. Finally, one could say that such severe punishments are the main cause of hardening a criminal. Thus, we can go on arguing endlessly because we don't know the nature of the person. Thus, the basic principle of morality in Vedic philosophy is tit-for-tat. No criminal goes unpunished, regardless of the severity of their actions. If they are further hardened by their crimes, then nature punishes them even more. However, compassion is also shown by educating the person in right and wrong.

The Lord sets the example of how truthfulness and kindness are resolved. He punishes the demons, but He also imparts the principles of dharma. Thus, compassion is applied to education, and truthfulness to the consequences of one's action. But when these principles are detached from the Lord, then how the Lord employs them is forgotten. We then think that these principles are universal, and that universality then produces conflicts and contradictions. The conclusion is that no doctrine based on principles or ideas works. It is only the person who embodies all these qualities that knows how to apply them. Therefore, to apply morality, we must study the Lord's actions via His pastimes.

Topic 12

QUESTION

If the soul is creating the separation between truth, right, and good, then how can the soul know what is simultaneously truth, right, and good?

2.3.18 (234)
ज्ञोऽत एव
jño'ta eva

jñaḥ—knowledge, or intelligence; ata eva—for this very reason.

TRANSLATION

Knowledge or intelligence is to be used for this very reason (i.e., understanding what is simultaneously true, right, and good).

COMMENTARY

In this sūtra, the symptoms of a truly intelligent and knowledgeable person are described. The symptom is that he is simultaneously able to judge what is truth, right, and good. We have previously said that the intellect judges the truth, the ego judges the good, and the moral sense judges the morality. These are collectively being called 'intelligence' here, which basically indicates the power of judgment. Every judgment must be performed *relative* to some assumptions. For instance, if you believe that the sky is blue, then anyone who makes the statement 'the sky is green' would be deemed false. Similarly, if you consider truthfulness as a moral virtue, any liar, no matter what his intentions are (good or bad) would be considered immoral. If you consider intoxication a form of suffering, then any intoxicated person would be considered unhappy.

In short, every judgment requires us to have preformed ideas, beliefs, or axioms. Therefore, intelligence, judgment, and knowledge are tightly interrelated ideas. Based on your beliefs—or what you accept to be true—you judge the truth, rightness, or goodness of other things. The act of drawing comparisons between your beliefs and the facts you are judging is intelligence. But intelligence is simply an instrument of determining truth, good, or right; it can produce results only if there are preformed beliefs. Within this context, we can see that to judge something that is true, right, and good, we must understand the Lord who is simultaneously true, right, and good. If we don't have such a belief about something that is true, right, and good, then we will have several fragmented and potentially incorrect judgments of truth, right and good. Thus, knowledge or intelligence simply entails an understanding of the Lord.

Topic 13

QUESTION

But what happens if we are unable to understand what is simultaneously true, right, and good, and we keep considering or viewing them separately?

2.3.19 (235)

उत्क्रान्तिगत्यागतीनाम्

utkrāntigatyāgatīnām

utkrānti-gati-āgatīnām—dying, going, and coming.

TRANSLATION

(The cycle of) dying, going (to another place), and coming (being born).

COMMENTARY

In every life we seek the nature of truth, right, and good, although the understanding of truth and right is most prominent in the human form of life. In the human life, we can also understand that there are several grades of happiness—e.g., from the sense pleasures, to mental and intellectual happiness, to the quest for eternal happiness, finally leading to the understanding of the self and the Lord. The pinnacle of this understanding is that there is something that is simultaneously true, right, and good, which reconciles all the contradictions. If we don't arrive at this understanding, our journey of discovery must continue. This journey is called repeated death, transport to another place, and rebirth into another body. Thus, the discovery of truth, right, and good isn't necessarily a single life endeavor. It is, in fact, the cause of birth and death, because if we have developed some misconceptions, then they can be corrected only by contrary experiences, and such experiences may require other types of bodies, environments, interactions, etc. The understanding of the Absolute Truth is the only purpose of repeated birth and death, and thus the Vedānta Sūtra began with the assertion that now, therefore, we must inquire into Brahman.

QUESTION

You said above that knowledge and intelligence can be used to understand what is true, right, and good simultaneously. Does that mean that the Absolute Truth can also be understood through theoretical knowledge and reasoning?

2.3.20 (236)
सवात्मना चोत्तरयोः
svātmanā cottarayoḥ

svātmanā—one's own self; ca—and; uttarayoḥ—rise, deliver, north;

TRANSLATION

(The knowledge must) also arise or spring of its own accord.

COMMENTARY

The knowledge we acquire theoretically or philosophically rests in our memory, which can be recalled or even sometimes forgotten. This knowledge is accessible to the soul, but it is different from the soul. The content of the knowledge may be spiritual, but it is not considered realized knowledge. Until this realization is attained, mistakes are repeated, and these mistakes are then corrected by the faculty of judgment to obtain the truth, right, and good.

Thus, without the realization, the mind, the intellect, the ego, and the moral sense are distinct. The mind produces meanings, but they may not be true, right, or good. The intellect, ego, and moral sense then correct these meanings. However, when perfect realization is attained, then there is no need for the instruments of judgment, separate from the instrument of thinking. Rather, whatever is thought is always true, right, and good. Now, we must understand that the mind automatically gives rise to thoughts; these are said to arise in the mind like waves in an ocean. With our intellect, ego, and moral sense, we suppress these waves. But when the mind is perfectly purified, then there is no need to suppress anything, nor is there any necessity to produce only the true, right, and good thoughts mediated by the instruments of judgment. Therefore, the purification of the mind means that only the Absolute Truth appears in the mind, and this truth, right, and good doesn't need to be curtailed. This merger of the instruments of judgment into the mind, and the unceasing production of the thoughts in the mind is referred to here by the term *svātmanā* here.

QUESTION

Some people argue that because the knowledge of the infinite can exist in the soul, therefore, the soul too must be infinite. On the other

hand, if the soul is itself finite, then how can he know the nature of the infinite? So, the realization of the Absolute Truth must entail the infinity of the soul's existence.

2.3.21 (237)

नाणुरतच्छरुतेर् इति चेत् न इतराधिकारात्

nāṇuratacchruter iti cet na itarādhikārāt

na aṇuḥ—not atomic; atat-śruteḥ—as the scriptures state; iti cet—if it be said; na—not so; itarā-dhikārāt—due to the other being its position.

TRANSLATION

If it is said that the soul is not atomic because the scriptures state (that he can attain the knowledge of the Absolute Truth which is also infinite), we say no; due to the other (being small rather than infinite) being its (real) position.

COMMENTARY

The impersonalist makes a mundane argument about the soul's size. Since the soul is small, and the Absolute Truth is big, therefore, the big cannot fit into the small. If, on the other hand, the big fits into the small, then the small must be as big. The impersonalist doesn't realize that knowledge is like a tree. The soul is the root of his knowledge tree, and this root can be atomic, but the tree doesn't have to be atomic. Therefore, the atomic soul can acquire the knowledge of the infinite because the tree is infinite, but the root is atomic. As a result, the argument about the infinite not 'fitting into' the atomic is unacceptable.

The real reason that the soul doesn't know the full truth is because this knowledge is acquired only in proportion to our service to the Lord. As the demand for service grows, the knowledge also grows. The impersonalist has no demand for serving the Lord. He only has a demand to become the Lord. But the Absolute Truth is never known in this way. He is known on a need-to-know basis. Why do you need to know? Well, you may want to serve the Absolute Truth, and some information is required. Our knowing is not based on *wanting* to know—e.g., I want to know everything! Curiosity isn't a sufficient reason for the Absolute Truth to be known. He is only known by the *need* to know.

Just like the chauffeur of a rich man doesn't need to know everything about the man he drives around. He just needs to know the schedule at which he must bring the car around. The chauffeur cannot ask his boss—tell me everything about yourself before I will drive you around. Unless I know everything about you, how can I drive the car for you? Just as silly as this sounds, it is equally silly to demand knowing the Absolute Truth before we start serving that truth. The conclusion is that one must not try to know the Absolute Truth. We must rather try to serve the Lord, and whatever is needed to serve the Lord will be automatically provided by the Lord based on our needs to serve Him.

However, those who aren't devoted to the Lord need the knowledge to develop the devotion. For example, a chauffeur will normally demand a salary from his boss, unless the boss was the president of a country. If the boss is the president of the country, then the chauffeur would feel privileged to drive the car, rather than asking the boss for a salary. In the same way, knowledge of the Absolute Truth invokes devotion. That knowledge however doesn't mean that the chauffeur knows the president intimately. He may however know the president intimately if he performs the service well. Thus, philosophy is needed to invoke devotion, and then devotion is needed to get intimate knowledge.

Many people confuse these two forms of knowledge. They argue: if the Lord is obtained by devotion, then why cultivate knowledge? The short answer is that real devotion doesn't spring without true knowledge. The devotees without the philosophical knowledge are like chauffeurs driving around ordinary people. The chauffeur may chat with the passengers, and this friendship is confused with devotion. But if the passenger refuses to pay, then the friendship disappears. In the same way, without philosophy, devotion is temporary. The so-called devotee loses all faith in the Lord the moment he encounters problems. But if philosophical knowledge is acquired, then the chauffeur knows that he is driving the president of the country, and even his own life is less important than the life of the president. The chauffeur will keep silent unless he is spoken to. So, there are no overt signs of devotion. But that is real devotion.

QUESTION

Are you saying that there is a difference between knowing the infinite and being infinite? That the soul can know the infinite, but that doesn't make him infinite? If so, what is the difference between knowing and being infinite?

2.3.22 (238)

स्वशब्दोन्मानाभ्यां च

svaśabdonmānābhyāṃ ca

svaśabda—His own words; unmānābhyām—from measurable; ca—and.

TRANSLATION

From being measurable by His words also.

COMMENTARY

When we look at a tree, there is a picture of the tree in our minds. To hold this picture, we don't have to be equal to or larger than the tree. Also, when we know the tree, we don't become the tree. This is because we have a representation of the tree, not the tree itself. Similarly, when we know the Lord, we have a representation of the Lord, which is in one sense the Lord and in another sense not the Lord. The tree projects itself into our minds, and the Lord—when known—projects Himself into our consciousness. Having this projection of representation of the Lord within us doesn't make us equal to or larger than the Lord, because there is a difference between the object and the symbol representing it. By the existence of symbolism, the Lord can have a name, which is a sound representation of the Lord. However, if we don't call the Lord's name, the Lord doesn't cease to exist. So, by symbolism, knowing is not being that thing; even if we know the Lord, we don't become God. Likewise, even though we are finite, we can still know the infinite by a symbol representation.

QUESTION

The impersonalist says that the problem of the finite knowing

the infinite would not arise if the consciousness was present everywhere because then its omnipresence would lead to omniscience and dissolve the contradiction between being in one place and knowing many things simultaneously.

2.3.23 (239)
अवरोधश्चन्दनवत्
avirodhaścandanavat

avirodhaḥ—no contradiction; candanavat—like sandalwood.

TRANSLATION

There is no contradiction (between being situated in one place and knowing many things simultaneously) just like sandalwood (can be in one place and its smell can spread far and wide away from the sandalwood itself).

COMMENTARY

The distinction between being and knowing is again being asserted here. In the previous sūtra, it was said that these are different because the infinite can be known by the finite and yet this knowing doesn't entail that the knower has also become infinite. In this sūtra it is said that knowing many things is not contradictory to being in one place. If you are seeing an apple, then you are still in the same place, but your consciousness has spread to the apple. This spreading is not contradictory to being in one place because the soul exists in three modes. The soul's desire is still in the same place, but his consciousness has spread. Therefore, the soul is in one place, and yet he is in many places.

Here, the sūtra gives the example of the use of perfumes. You wear a drop of perfume, and everyone around you smells the perfume. Sandalwood has been used as a perfume for ages, and a little amount of sandalwood produces a faint aroma over a very large area. So, by analogy, the notion of being in one place, and spreading to many places—by its effect—is stated in this sūtra.

This problem in well-known in modern science as wave-particle duality. The particle is one place, but its effect—the field or the wave—the particle spreads everywhere. In classical physics, each field extends infinitely into space, but quantum fields are not like that; they spread by the emission of a particle, which is supposed to 'travel' to the destination, while a reverse particle (represented by the complex conjugate of the wave) travels in the opposite direction. This problem is called 'entanglement' because both forward and backward waves are moving simultaneously (one from source to destination, and the other from destination to the source). Even though a particle travels between two objects—which makes the interaction local—the concurrent propagation of forward and backward particles makes this interaction non-local.

When this model is applied to perception, we can say that our consciousness is 'reaching out' into the apple, and the apple is 'entering into' our consciousness. And yet, even as the apple and the self are interacting, they are not becoming unified (even with the non-locality of bidirectionality). This is because what we call consciousness or awareness is only one aspect of the soul. It is what we can call the 'relation' to the world, which defines the world in relation to us, and us in relation to the world. The focus of our awareness—i.e., which object it is directed toward—is under control of our will. For instance, in the yoga practice, we can withdraw the consciousness from the worldly objects, and then neither our consciousness enters the world, nor the world enters our consciousness. Even as consciousness spreads everywhere, the will that causes this spreading is situated in one place, which we can call the soul. Specifically, the non-local aspect of consciousness is called *sat*, the local aspect is called ānanda, and result of the local and non-local is cognition and action or *chit*. In short, we develop a will, which causes the consciousness to interact with something else, and the interaction then produces cognition and conation.

So, the claim that because my consciousness can spread to many places in order to know the external world and therefore the self is non-localized can be rejected by the simple analogy that the sandalwood tree is in one place but its effect of smell—like the spreading of consciousness—is everywhere. Thus, we reject the superficial contradiction between locality and non-locality; both locality and non-locality are real, the locality causes the non-locality because if this wasn't the case, then our consciousness would permanently be spread to everything in the world, and it could not be withdrawn by the use of choice.

QUESTION

The problem of consciousness spreading applies not just to the spreading into the external world, but also the spreading within the body. We are aware of the different parts of our body—such as hands and legs—so someone can argue that since consciousness spreads in the body, so it cannot be in one place. By extension, one could say that consciousness must also be non-local.

2.3.24 (240)

अवस्थितिविशेष्यादिति चेत् न अभ्युपगमाद्धृदि हि

avasthitivaiśeṣyāditi cet na abhyupagamāddhṛdi hi

avasthiti—situated; vaiśeṣayat—in individuals; iti cet—if it be said; na—not; abhyupagamāt—from being engaged; hṛdi—in the heart; hi—certainly.

TRANSLATION

If it is said that (the soul is situated) in the individuals (i.e., all over the body due to awareness) (we say) no, from being engaged in the heart certainly (we can say that it is then spread all over the body).

COMMENTARY

Like the claim of the soul spreading all over the universe due to awareness was rejected in the previous sūtra, in this sūtra, the claim that the soul spreads all over the body due to awareness of the body is rejected in this sūtra. The soul is situated in the heart, as the root of the tree which is the body. Thus, a person can be brain dead, but not heart dead. If the heart has stopped working, then the person is considered dead. Similarly, spiritual bliss is experienced in the heart, but its effects—such as hair standing on end, the wavering of the voice, trembling of the body, etc.—are spread to the rest of the body. The bliss in the heart can be continuous, but the symptoms may sometimes not be manifest.

Thus, we distinguish happiness from pleasure. The body feels pleasure, but the heart feels happiness. If someone touches your hand, you can feel comforted or relaxed in the skin, but not happiness. The happiness arises in the heart, even for ordinary sensations. This is especially true for spiritual bliss, which is experienced in the center of the chest, not all over the body. The symptoms of this bliss can spread to all over the body—such as hairs standing on end or the body quivering, or tears coming out of eyes—but these are the symptoms of the bliss in the heart, not the bliss itself. The symptoms are cognitive and can be seen by others, but the bliss is personal and only experienced by the individual. The awareness is therefore non-local; however, the source of awareness is local.

QUESTION

If you are saying that the soul is situated in the heart, then what causes the movement of consciousness all over the body and all over the world?

2.3.25 (241)
गुणाद्वा लोकवत्
guṇādvā lokavat

guṇāt—owing to the guna; vā—movement; lokavat—as in the world.

TRANSLATION

(The) movement (of consciousness) all over the world is due to guna.

COMMENTARY

When we perceive the world, our consciousness moves out into the world, and the world moves into our consciousness, thus resulting in a bidirectional field propagation. The cause of this movement in our heart is desires, which are produced due to *guna* or material tendencies. Similarly, the objects (of the mind and the senses) have material tendencies to be attracted toward these desires. These tendencies are potentials and they generally lie dormant, but when the desire arises in the heart, the objects are attracted to the mind and the senses, and the senses and the mind are attracted to the objects. This mutual attraction is due to the innate tendencies and can be loosely called the 'force' of attraction (or repulsion—in case our desire is opposed to certain things). Then we seek these kinds of objects in the external world, trying to fulfill these desires. In simple words, the desire for an object contains the object in a subtle form because the desire refers to the object. In the same way, the objects contain the desires, or the intended purpose in subtle form, as the object exists for a purpose. When the purpose in our senses matches the purpose in the objects, the senses and the objects are mutually attracted due to this matching. This then results in the forces of attraction and repulsion driven by the guna.

In material science, we imagine that objects are naturally attracted to each other due to physical forces, which means that the attraction must spread everywhere and all the time. This view of attraction—which existed in classical physics—has failed in atomic theory because the so-called force of attraction requires the emission and absorption of a particle and these particles are not always emitted or absorbed. The point of emission and absorption is also not predictable, which means that the application of force (i.e., when the force is applied or not applied) is unpredictable. This unpredictability leads to the probabilistic nature of atomic theory. This sūtra offers a remedy to the problem—the cause of the force is not the mechanical attraction or repulsion; it is rather the potentials which exist in complementary forms in the object and in the senses; the potential in the senses and the mind is called 'desire' and the potential in the objects is called 'ability'. When the desire arises, it is naturally attracted to the ability; likewise, the ability is naturally attracted to the desire. This attraction between desire and ability is called 'entanglement' in modern science; when the objects are entangled, then the interaction occurs bidirectionally. And the cause of this entanglement is the guna that lead to desire in the heart.

Both desire and ability are called guna, but they are separated in Sāñkhya as senses and their objects. The desires become the senses, and the objects become the sensations. The conditioning due to guna means that some tongue likes spicy food, while another tongue likes sweet things. Some eyes desire green, while other eyes desire yellow. So, the guna create predispositions in the senses and the objects, and due to these predispositions, science can model them as probabilities. However, science can't explain how these predispositions get entangled, then attracted to each other, finally resulting in an interaction. The cause is time, which converts the predisposition in the mind and the senses into a desire. Unless time acts, desires don't arise, the attraction to the objects isn't created (although the predisposition exists), and experience isn't created. Thus, guna are the causes of attraction, and the movement of awareness.

QUESTION

But there are so many scenarios in which the desire is created by perception rather than perception caused by desire. Thus, for example, we might see tasty food, and then suddenly develop hunger even though we weren't hungry before seeing the food. How can we say that the cause of the movement of consciousness is guna when perceptions can also lead to desires within us?

2.3.26 (242)
व्यतरिको गन्धवत्
vyatireko gandhavat

vyatirekaḥ—the mutual-exclusion (the object i.e., the soul, which constitutes the spreading of our awareness); gandhavat—like odor.

TRANSLATION

The mutual exclusion (the soul, or the spreading of consciousness from the soul) (can be caused by the perception of sensations) just like odor.

COMMENTARY

An analogy like that of a sandalwood tree is used here—in the sense that both speak about the spreading of smell—but there is a difference. In Sāñkhya philosophy, there is a difference between the objects and the sensations; the objects are called bhūta and the sensations are called tanmātra. These tanmātra include sabda, sparsha, rūpa, rasa, and gandha or sound, touch, form, taste, and smell. The use of gandha here indicates the existence of a tanmātra or a sensation, and the implication is that just like desires can attract us to objects, similarly, the perceptions can also result in the drawing out of consciousness.

In simple terms, object perception can lead to desire, just as desire can lead to object perception. The original claim that the cause of movement is guna is not affected by this clarification because the guna exist both in the senses as well as in the observer. As we noted above, there are two forms of these guna—namely, possibility and desire. The possibility is feminine, and the desire is masculine. While the overall material energy is feminine, a further distinction between masculine and feminine is made within this material energy. Just as the feminine can agitate the masculine into desire, similarly, the objects of the senses and the mind can agitate the mind and senses into desire. There isn't hence a strict causality from possibility to desire, or desire to possibility, because either possibility or desire can result in the creation of the other.

QUESTION

So, you are stating that experience is caused by the interaction of possibility and desire, and these are divisions within the material energy, and each of them can be the cause of the other, so should we not call it 'mutual causality'?

2.3.27 (243)
तथा च दर्शयति
tathā ca darśayati

tathā—thus; ca—also; darśayati—the experience is created, or the philosophy (of perception) states.

TRANSLATION

Thus (through the interaction of the guna present in the senses and the objects) the experience is created, or the philosophy of perception states.

COMMENTARY

Through the influence of modern science, we have become accustomed to linear models of causality in which a cause creates the effect, but the effect could not create the cause. Therefore, if we say that our desires in the mind are the cause of the bodily activity, then the body could not create desires. Conversely, if the body is the cause of the activity, then the mind must be causeless. These linear models of causality emerged from the understanding of objects, which can cause a change to another object only if they have the same properties. For instance, a billiard ball can push another billiard ball because they have the same properties of mass, momentum, energy, etc. This model fails when we start speaking about two different kinds of things—e.g., mind and body. The problem of mutual causality arises because the body can change the mind, and the mind can change the body. In fact, the same experience can be caused by either the body or the mind. Thus, we cannot say that the body or the mind are *necessary* and *sufficient* conditions for their reciprocal effects. Hence, if the cause is not necessary and sufficient, then it cannot be considered a cause.

These models of causation are inappropriate for understanding experience. Instead of billiard ball causality, if we begin with perception as the model of interaction, then we can extend this model to ordinary interactions as well. For instance, we can say that inherent in each thing is not just a possibility but also a purpose. Both possibility and purpose lie in an unmanifest state, and they are manifested by the other. Thus, possibilities can manifest a purpose, but it requires a purpose to exist in unmanifest form. Similarly, the purpose can make the possibility manifest, but there must be a possibility to begin with.

This sūtra gives us the clue that we must think in terms of mutuality and complementarity of possibility and purpose. If the possibility exists, then it can create a purpose. Similarly, purpose can activate the possibility. Thus, if you are looking for a weapon, a kitchen knife will be perceived as a weapon, and the possibility of being a weapon would be realized out of the many alternatives. Likewise, if you see the possibility of food, you can develop hunger for food. So, mind and body are mutually capable of causing the other and this becomes obvious when we understand these in terms of desires and possibilities.

The desire is still superior to the possibility because the mind cannot just control the body, but it can also control itself. If the body creates a desire in the mind, the mind can reject it. But if the mind has a desire, and the body can enact it, then the actions would be enacted. Therefore, the mutual causality between the mind and the body should not make the mind 'at the same level' as the body; the mutual causation doesn't entail the similarity of types in the two.

QUESTION

Whenever we speak of mutual causation, we are unable to

separate the cause from the effect. In science, we call this inseparability non-linearity, due to which we can never speak of the self and the world as separate things. If we lose this separability, then we lose the sense of realism—i.e., that I exist independent of the world, or the world exists independent of me. Without such separability and realism, how can we say that we are choosing to see? The inseparability would entail an infinite causal chain in which the possibility created the desire, but that possibility was created by desire, and so on, ad infinitum.

2.3.28 (244)

पृथगुपदेशात्

pṛthagupadeśāt

pṛthak—separate; upadeśāt—on account of the teaching.

TRANSLATION

The (possibility and desire, or matter and mind) are said to be separate.

COMMENTARY

The philosophy of materialism recognizes an external reality but claims that the mind is also material; so, the desires are produced from matter. This matter, however, cannot exist in a state of possibility, because then there would be no desires. If matter doesn't exist in a state of possibility, then there is no free will, because we cannot choose what to experience and what to avoid. Specifically, we cannot withdraw our consciousness from the objects of perception. The philosophy of idealism, on the other hand, rejects the existence of an external reality, and claims that all that we see is merely a phantasm of the mind. It is produced by our desires, so it exists as our will. This, however, fails to explain why we are suffering in this world—if everything is a product of the mind, and is caused by our free will, then everything we experience should make us happy. After all, at every moment our desires are being fulfilled by experience!

The existence of an external reality enables our choice; thus, realism is necessary for free will. Similarly, the separation of the will from the external possibility is necessary to explain why we aren't happy—the external world is not always in accordance with our will. Hence, the separation of the will and the possibility is necessary to explain why we have will, and why it is sometimes not fulfilled. The claim that will causes possibility, which then causes will, thus producing an infinite cycle of causes doesn't come close to understanding the nature of the two. For instance, even though possibilities can cause our will, not every possibility will create a desire in us. In fact, we might look at certain things and be revulsed by them. So, even as a desire is created in us, there are certainly predispositions toward what we will like or hate. So, the creation of the desire is within the possibilities of desires, or innate tendencies of likes and dislikes. Similarly, even though our desires can manifest the possibilities, the external reality is still a definite set of possibilities from which we select. The mutual creation of will and possibility pertains to the activation of a preexisting dormant reality, rather than to the creation of something that doesn't exist. Hence, when we say that will was created due to possibility, the potential for that will preexisted in us, and was activated by the presence of possibility.

Since both will and possibility exist in such potential forms prior to being excited, therefore, they are mutually separate and individuals, even though their interaction can activate a dormant state into a reactivated one. The mutual causation doesn't collapse the distinction between will and possibility. As a result, we must reject both materialism and idealism; there is an objective external world, although it is not an object. There is similarly potential for enjoyment within us, although it might not always be manifest as desire or pleasure. The capacity for enjoyment and the ability to fulfill the desire are separate realities, and their mutual causation changes the causal model, not their separability.

This is a form of the Bhedābheda that we have seen in the masculine and feminine aspects of the Absolute Truth. The will and the possibility are separate, and yet they are identical because every will can be fulfilled, and every possibility can be desired. Due to the one-to-one mapping between the will and the possibility, we can say that they are non-different. And yet, they are still different because the will and the possibility can remain separate. (i.e., without experience). This distinction becomes unavoidable when we recognize that the will and the possibility in the material world are not one-to-one mapped: we might have desires that cannot be fulfilled, and we might have possibilities that we don't desire. And yet, we seek to fulfill the desires by using available possibilities, which entails that the two are separate and yet when the experience is produced, it is only through the combination of will and possibility, so at the point of experience we can say that the two have become non-different.

QUESTION

If the will and the possibility are separate, then how do they combine? What is the cause of their interaction, and what brings about their combination?

2.3.29 (245)

तद्गुणसारत्वात् तु तद्व्यपदेशःप्राज्ञवत्

tadguṇasāratvāt tu tadvyapadeśaḥ prājñavat

tadguṇa—its qualities; sāratvāt—due to the essence; tu—but; tadvya-padeśaḥ—that pervades; prājñavat—as awareness or consciousness.

TRANSLATION

(Each of the two) exist due to the essence of their qualities, but they intersect or enter each other as the awareness or consciousness (of the other).

COMMENTARY

The senses and the mind are said to be the manifestation of sat-tva-guna, which represents desire. The objects of the senses and the mind are manifestation of tamo-guna or the possibilities of fulfilling the desires. Their interaction is caused by a third entity called prāṇa which manifests due to rajo-guna. Each of these three guna are material representations of spiritual qualities in the soul. The desire is a representation of the ānanda potency. The objects are the manifestation of the *chit* potency. And the connection between the objects and the senses is created by the *sat* potency. Here, the term *sāratvāt* is used which indicates the 'essence', or 'in a primordial state'. This primordial state is the possibility for enjoyment or desire in the ānanda potency.

It is the possibility for fulfilling the desire in *chit* potency. And it is the possibility of connecting the desire to its objects in the *sat* potency. We have also previously called them emotion, cognition, and relation, where emotion is the desire, cognition is the object, and relation is the connection between the desire and the objects that fulfill it.

The cause of the interaction between will and possibility is that in both there is a third ability to form relations. Thus, when the will excites the possibility, it is through a relation, which we can call consciousness or awareness. In matter, this 'awareness' has a material counterpart that we can call 'structure'. When structure is established, two entities start interacting; the structure also defines their mutual roles. This means that two material objects do not always interact, regardless of how physically close they are. They interact only after a relation is formed between them, and this relation—also being a potential—is activated. Hence, either the cognition, the emotion, or the relation can be causes of experience. For instance, we can have desire, which then drives our relation to the world to pick something that will fulfill our desire. There can be a potential for fulfilling the desire, which then drives the object into our awareness and produces a desire. Finally, a relation can sometimes be established without a prior desire or the ability to fulfill the desire, and both ability and desire may then be activated. In different situations, these three entities become dominant or subordinate; the dominant entity becomes the cause of the subordinate entities. That is, either emotion, relation, or cognition can give rise to the others.

QUESTION

If we can fulfill our desires just by directing our consciousness to the desired objects, then why are so many of our desires always unfulfilled?

2.3.30 (246)

यावदात्मभावत्विाच्च न दोषःतद्दर्शनात्

yāvadātmabhāvitvācca na doṣaḥ taddarśanāt

yāvat—as soon as; ātmabhāvitvāt—due to the desire in the soul; ca—also; na doṣaḥ—absence of defect; taddarśanāt—from that being seen.

TRANSLATION

As soon as desire arises in the soul, also that is seen (i.e., the desire is fulfilled as soon as the desire arises in the soul) in the absence of defect.

COMMENTARY

The term *doṣaḥ* used here should be contrasted with *guna* previously. In one sense, *guna* are qualities, but in another sense (contrasted to doṣaḥ), they are also 'good' qualities; the term doṣaḥ then means 'bad' qualities. All illnesses and diseases for instance are attributed to the presence of doṣaḥ instead of guna. But what is doṣaḥ? It is the state when the guna are either excessive or debilitated. For example, the debilitation of the senses can lead to loss of sensation or desire for sensation, while the guna in excess can cause hypersensitivity or excessive desire. The modes of nature are expected to remain in a 'balance', but when this balance is disturbed, then doṣaḥ are created. So, doṣaḥ is nothing but guna although in an excessive or debilitated state. When one mode goes out of balance, then the other modes either become dominant or debilitated. And this change in the normal balanced state creates illnesses and diseases. This sūtra asserts that all discrepancies in desire fulfillment can be called doṣaḥ.

The causes of this imbalance are not noted here, but they could be attributed to our senses, the objects of the senses, or the relation between the objects and the senses. Each of these is described according to the three modes. But the cause of this imbalance can either be our desires which become habits over time, or these could be due to the consequences of previous actions, or it could be exaggerated effects of the time, place, and circumstance a person is in (which are again caused due to conscious or unconscious memories). Here, only the general principle of 'good' qualities becoming 'bad' is being noted.

QUESTION

Some people say that if our desires are controlled, then they die slowly. Do our desires go away if we suppress them or they remain unfulfilled?

2.3.31 (247)

पुंस्त्वादिवित् त्वस्य सतोऽभविय्यक्तयियोगात्

puṃstvādivat tvasya sato'bhivyaktiyogāt

puṃstvādivat—like the origin of masculinity; tu—certainly; asya—its; satah—eternally; abhivyaktiyogāt—from manifestation upon union or contact.

TRANSLATION

Just like the origin of masculinity (in the Supreme Lord), its (the soul's) (desires) are certainly eternal, and they are manifest from union or contact.

COMMENTARY

In this sūtra, the emergence of the desire in the soul is compared to the emergence of desires in the Lord. The term *puṃstva* indicates masculinity or virility. The Lord's desire to enjoy exists as a possibility in Him. But it can be activated by the Lord's energy when the feminine looks at the masculine, and the masculine is excited to enjoy with the feminine. The soul has the same potential for enjoyment, but his desires can be either like the Lord's (i.e., to enjoy by domination) or like the Lord's energy (i.e., to enjoy by serving the Lord).

Of course, the soul can give up both these kinds of desires and remain situated within Brahman, but the potential for enjoyment can never be destroyed. This potential is the essential innate property of the soul, and sense or mind control can restrain the soul's enjoyment but cannot destroy the potential for such enjoyment. This sūtra states indicates that desire for enjoyment can spring up any time in the soul when it contacts the material or the spiritual energy. Thus, the claim of the impersonalist that desire and enjoyment exist only in the material world is rejected by stating that the virility in the soul—and this virility can be masculine or feminine (although the term used here is masculine)—is eternally existent, and it springs into desire in contact with its objects.

QUESTION

I can understand how you are describing the separation of the Absolute Truth into masculine and feminine, and extending this to the emergence of desire in the soul, and how it enjoys with the Lord or with the material energy. But doesn't this separation between masculine and feminine complicate the philosophy of the Absolute Truth? Isn't a single reality much better in comparison instead of saying that there are two inseparable aspects of this reality?

2.3.32 (248)
नतियोपलब्ध्यनुपलब्धिप्रसङ्गोऽन्यतरनियमोवान्यथा

nityopalabdhyanupalabdhiprasaṅgo'nyataraniyamovānyathā

nityopalabdhi—perpetual perception; anupalabdhi—non-perception; prasaṅgaḥ—the incidents or outcomes or episodes; anyatara—either; niyamaḥ—limitation of the power; vā—or else; anyathā—otherwise.

TRANSLATION

(Without the philosophy of masculine and feminine), either of two outcomes would follow: perpetual perception (by the union of desire and possibility) or non-perception (by the separation of desire and possibility). In either of these two cases, there will be limitations on both (the will cannot withdraw from enjoyment, and the possibility cannot control the will's emergence).

COMMENTARY

This sūtra refutes two opposite claims simultaneously— (1) there is one Absolute Truth and it has no aspects such as feminine and masculine, and (2) there are two separated realities (masculine and feminine) such that their interaction is unnatural. The sūtra notes that if we take the first position, then there is no possibility of ending the experience, and if we take the second position then there is no possibility of starting the experience. Some impersonal philosophers take the first position and say that matter doesn't really exist. The material experience is an illusion created by the self within the self. The sūtra argues that if this were the case, then there would be no way to end the material experience because the soul is eternal and therefore the illusion would also become eternal. Other impersonal philosophers take the second position and say that the soul and the material energy are very different such that their combination is very unnatural. The sūtra argues that if the combination was unnatural, then it should not arise in the first place to even produce a material experience.

If either of these conditions is granted, then either the enjoyment cannot begin or if it has begun it cannot end. The beginning and end of the material experience entails that the soul has free will to engage or withdraw. Similarly, the material energy has the power to entice or hinder the enjoyment. By this enticement, the soul is allured to enjoy, but by the hindrances, the soul suffers and becomes detached from enjoyment. Its ability to be attracted or detached constitutes the soul's free will, and merging the soul with matter, or separating the soul from matter would not explain the phenomena (*prasaṅgaḥ*).

Topic 14

QUESTION

This description of mutual causation between the masculine and the feminine is unsatisfactory because it doesn't say why each side must act in the first place. If the feminine is the cause of the activation of the masculine, what causes the feminine to become activated? If we say the cause is masculine, then it leads to an infinite circularity of causality. How can you resolve this problem?

2.3.33 (249)
करता शासत्रारथवत्त्वात्
karta śāstrārthavattvāt

karta—the actor; śāstrārthavattvāt—from just like engaging in a discussion between them (which is like a debate on the real meaning of the scriptures).

TRANSLATION

From the actors (masculine and feminine) being engaged in a mutual discussion (which is aimed to obtain a better understanding of each other).

COMMENTARY

The ideas of linear causation are based on a criterion in logic in which a premise leads to a conclusion, or a cause leads to an effect. According to this model of causation, either the feminine or the masculine must be the original cause; but since they are both potentials (of desire and the power to fulfill that desire), one of them must come first and cause the other. This is the point at which we need to alter our notions of logic as linear causation. We must rather defer to a dialectical model of causation in which a premise exists, but it doesn't lead to a conclusion automatically unless a question is asked. The question presents itself as a problem, and the pair of question and answer constitutes a contradiction. This contradiction is resolved when the premise expands into an answer—specifically to resolve the problem posed by the emerging question.

In this case, the feminine is the premise, and the masculine is the question. The premise can exist forever, but it doesn't lead to the creation of the world unless a question is asked. But when the question is asked, then the premise becomes the answer, and the question is satisfied. However, the answer will then lead to another question, which must be answered, and so on, ad infinitum. This process of questioning and answering is described in this sūtra as śāstrārtha. This term refers to a practice in ancient times in which two debaters will sit down for a debate, and one will ask the other questions. As the questions are answered, new questions are raised based on the previous answer. And this process continues until one of two conditions is satisfied— (1) there are no more questions to be answered, and the questioner is satisfied, or (2) some question is not answered, and the questioner is dissatisfied. This process of dialectical inquiry was used to check the consistency and completeness of a theory. For instance, if a theory is incomplete, then some question would remain unanswered. And if the theory is inconsistent, then the questioner can point out the contradictions in the answers which makes a new question—which of these two answers would you like to prefer? And if a choice is made, then the original question (which was answered by the rejected answer) returns to the fore. Ultimately, under a contradiction, some question must remain unanswered. Thus, every inconsistency eventually leads to some incompleteness (as we prefer not to answer some questions, rather than provide a conflicting answer).

The literal meaning of śāstrārtha is the 'interpretation of scriptures', and this interpretation is debatable because there are many ways to interpret. How do we know which of the interpretations are correct? The short remedy to this problem is consistency and completeness: all questions must be answered, and no answer must contradict the other answers. Therefore, the method of deciding the 'interpretation of scripture' was debate, discussion, and testing the hypothesis. It was understood that the scripture can be understood in many ways; while the text is eternal, its understanding can change. A superior interpretation is one that satisfies the twin conditions of consistency and completeness.

In this sūtra, the interaction between the masculine and the feminine is compared to such a discussion. The difference is only that such debates can be finite or infinite. In the case of the material world, the soul asks the questions to material nature, and material nature gives the answers. These answers update our understanding, but we are not free to create this understanding whimsically. We are free to ask any question we want, but the answers are decided by material nature. Therefore, we cannot come up with an understanding of nature by speculation; this understanding must be based on previously asked questions. Of course, when an answer is provided, the answer is itself subject to interpretation. To clarify which interpretation is correct, we can ask further questions. But since every answer is subject to interpretation, to converge on the right answer, we must remember the previously asked questions and answers. If we forget the previous questions and answers, then the process is infinite. Therefore, enlightenment is a difficult problem because we forget.

The Lord doesn't forget the answers given by His Śakti, but He is never satisfied by the answers. He keeps seeking clarifications—i.e., posing new questions—based on the previous answers. Since the process is dialectical, the Śakti can change the Lord's questions by giving different answers to the same question. If there are infinite questions and infinite correct answers to each question, then the process of questioning can never come to an end. However, this endless process doesn't indicate an ignorance; it is rather the endless quest for understanding. The masculine understands the feminine by Her answers, and the feminine understands the masculine by His questions. These are two complementary methods of understanding—we can know the other person by what they answer, just as we can know them by the type of questions they ask.

QUESTION

If this process of questioning and answering potentially never comes to an end, then what is the point of this sequence of questions and answers? Why should someone engage in an endless sequence of questions and answers?

2.3.34 (250)

वहिरोपदेशात्

vihāropadeśāt

vihāra-upadeśāt—due to the teaching of their playing, pleasure trip.

TRANSLATION

This is described as their play or pastime.

COMMENTARY

The purpose of the manifestation of the world is the enjoyment of pleasure. It is not a goal that ends, because pleasure can be enjoyed eternally. Therefore, we should not think of the process of questioning and answering as a finite sequence that comes to an end. Indeed, questions are asked only because we want to be happy. Answers to a question are accepted if they make us happy. If the process of discussion is itself the source of pleasure, why must it end? This sūtra states that there is no purpose in this process other than pleasure itself.

QUESTION

You are saying that the purpose of the masculine and the feminine is to know each other. But don't we speak about self-knowledge as the main goal?

2.3.35 (251)

उपादानात्

upādānāt

upādānāt—due to the appropriation (of meaning to the self).

TRANSLATION

(Self-knowledge is obtained) by appropriating (the other-knowledge).

COMMENTARY

The masculine and the feminine are different due to being will and possibility. But they are non-different because every will can be fulfilled, and every possibility is desirable. Thus, if you see some possibility, you know that it can be desired. Similarly, if you see some desire, you know that it can be fulfilled. So, knowledge of the other is also non-different from self-knowledge. The impersonalist thinks that self-knowledge is the goal of existence, but as it has been noted in an earlier sūtra, if the knower and known are merged together, then there is no cessation of perception. It follows that everything must always be known, and there cannot be a sequence of questions and answers that lead to discovery, which then results in a new type of pleasure at every moment. When the process of self-knowledge only involves the self, then this knowledge is unchanging. But when it involves the self and the other, then it evolves. This evolution should not be confused with the material temporariness; it is an ever-deepening understanding of the same truth; what was previously known doesn't become false after you know something new; the previous knowledge is rather nuanced, complemented, and exemplified by the new discovery.

QUESTION

Are you indicating that self-knowledge is non-different from knowledge of the other because each side knows the other through their actions?

2.3.36 (252)

वयपदेशाच्च क्रयियायाम् न चेन्नर्दिदेशवपिरयय:

vyapadeśācca kriyāyām na cennirdeśaviparyayaḥ

vyapadeśāt—on account of mention; ca—also; kriyāyām—in respect of action; na cet—if it were not so; nirdeśa-viparyayaḥ—the reference (would have been) of a different kind.

TRANSLATION

If it were not the case that the action (of one side) describes (the other side), then the reference (or purpose of each side) would be different.

COMMENTARY

In this sūtra, the nature of non-difference is being exemplified further. The masculine and the feminine are non-different not just because all the desires are possible, and all the possibilities are desirable. It is also because the desires and the possibilities are mutually referencing each other. In short, the desire exists because it is possible, and the possibility exists because it is desirable. Each side can be called the reason or purpose for the existence of the other. The sūtra also states that if this mutual justification or purpose wasn't there, then the mutual actions by which the other is mentioned would also not exist. Each side would be self-absorbed, and the will would never be fulfilled, while the possibility would never be realized. That would entail the end of all manifestation.

QUESTION

Can this sequence of questions and answers not come to an end? Doesn't this process have a limit that culminates in the completeness of knowledge?

2.3.37 (253)
उपलब्धविदनयिमः
upalabdhivadaniyamaḥ

upalabdhivat—just like perception; aniyamaḥ—no limitation.

TRANSLATION

Just like perception, (the process of discussion) has no end.

COMMENTARY

Most people today believe that if perfect knowledge were possible, then it will also have an end. That is, we will someday know everything there is to be known, and nothing would be known after that. Unless everything is known, we cannot call our knowledge perfect.

If perfection is attained, life becomes boring after that because there is nothing more to be known. Therefore, we must choose between an ignorant life and a boring life. An ignorant life will be exciting because there is much to be known. And a boring life would be full of knowledge because there is nothing left to be known. Now perfection that leads to liberation must also lead to an endlessly boring existence. On the other hand, ignorance must be bliss—because there is so much yet to be known.

Many devotees too have a similar viewpoint. They think that whatever had to be known is already known, and it is now time to put it into practice. But since this practice doesn't reveal anything new, therefore, the person quickly loses interest in the practice too. By treating spiritual life as a practice, rather than a process of discovery, they lose both the discovery and the practice.

This sūtra indicates that perception and discussion are both infinite. Hence, we can never know the Absolute Truth completely. There will always be room for new things to be found, and for new things to be discussed. Does this entail that the spiritualist also doesn't know the truth? No. The ignorance in the material world is that the new knowledge repudiates the previous knowledge. The ignorance in the spiritual world is that the previous understanding is never falsified, but new information is endlessly added to the existing understanding. For example, we can look at a forest from a distance, and not see the trees. Then when we come closer, then we see the trees. Then we come even closer and we see the leaves. An even closer examination reveals that the leaves have veins in them. And we can then zoom out and look at another leaf, another branch, or another trunk, and then again zoom in and look closer at more details.

Does this mean that your knowledge of the forest was false? No. There is a forest, and it is not an ocean or a river or a mountain. That knowledge is correct, and if the forest was all that existed, then the knowledge is also complete. However, this knowledge is *abstract* rather than *detailed*. The soul is liberated when it obtains the abstract knowledge of the whole, because this is the whole truth. But the details are within that abstraction, and because they are infinite, they are never completely known. This doesn't they cannot be known. It just means that life is an infinite journey of constant discovery of the details. Those details do not refute the previous understanding of the whole truth, or of the previously discovered details. It just nuances and enhances that knowledge.

Thus, we can say that nobody knows everything. However, that ignorance is not the same as one possessing false beliefs. Thus, material and spiritual ignorance are different—in the former case you believe in falsities, and the in latter case you don't know all the truths, although you know the whole truth.

QUESTION

Even if the Lord is infinite, should we not suppose that this process can come to an end because the knowers are finite? After all, don't they ever become satisfied with knowing enough, and end the process of continual knowing?

2.3.38 (254)
शक्तविपिर्ययात्
śaktiviparyayāt

śaktiviparyayāt—due to being contrary to the nature of śakti.

TRANSLATION

(Being finite) is contrary to the nature of śakti.

COMMENTARY

While previous sūtras have accepted that the soul is finite and atomic, this sūtra states that even the soul's knowledge can be infinite, and this infinity is attributed to the Śakti. The finitude of the soul is that it can focus on one thing at a time, while the Lord can focus on everything at once. The infinity of the soul is that it has infinite capacity for memory, which comes from the Śakti.

At present we recall one thing from the past at any one time, but we have the capacity to recall numerous things. Similarly, in the spiritual world, the soul knows many things, but it remembers one thing at a time. On the other hand, the memories are destroyed in the material body, and many of the unpleasant memories are blocked. But in the spiritual world, the memory is eternal, and nothing previously experienced is ever forgotten. If the soul were finite, it could only remember a finite past. This doesn't happen because memory is afforded by the Śakti. If the soul is outside the Śakti, then it has no memory, and hence no past. If the soul is within Śakti, then the soul has a past, which can be recalled eternally. As the memories are destroyed in the material world, the 'size' of the universe—i.e., the information that needs to be stored in the universe—remains finite. But, since the past is remembered in the spiritual world, therefore, the spiritual world constantly expands, as the past events are never forgotten.

Effectively, the memory of the past is not in the soul, but in the Lord's Śakti. This idea has been previously described as the 'collective unconscious' in Jungian psychology, where our memory is not our individual property, but a property of the entire universe, although we get to access many parts of this memory, and our shared values and ideals include those that existed in the past that is long gone. The past is ever-present in the Śakti, but it is selectively recalled by the soul. Like we don't have to be infinite to access an infinite library of information, similarly, the soul doesn't have to be infinite to recall the past. The Śakti is the library of information, and She fulfills the soul's desires to know. Thus, when the finite takes shelter of the infinite, then the finite acquires some of the capacities of the infinite. The finite can still only read book at a time from the library, but he has access to the library of infinite information.

QUESTION

Your descriptions of the separation of the soul and the Lord, who are then engaged in constant mutual enjoyment, seem contrary to the concept of samadhi in which the distinction between the soul and the Lord is lost.

2.3.39 (255)

समाध्यभावाच्च

samādhyabhāvacca

samādhi-abhāvāt—due to the absence of samadhi; ca—also.

TRANSLATION

Due to the absence of samādhi also (the soul and the Lord enjoy).

COMMENTARY

The term *samādhi* is made up of two roots—*sama* (which means uniformity without a distinction) and *adhi* (situated at). Thus, *samādhi* refers to the soul merging into Brahman, which lacks diversity (*sama*). The soul has inner contradiction between its three modes, and one of the results of this conflict is that every answer produces a new question. However, in Brahman, the *sat, chit,* and *ānanda,* are not in conflict, because the soul has a relation to the self, fully knows the self, and because the soul is finite, there is nothing more to be known. This produces a static knowledge of the self—i.e., there is nothing new to discover about the self at every moment. Thus, in one sense, the desires of the soul come to an end, although the soul still has the potential for desire. This *sūtra* states that association with the Lord cannot be called *samādhi* because the soul is not self-absorbed; he is rather absorbed into the nature of the Lord.

Thus, a distinction is drawn between the dissolution of two separate identities (i.e., the soul and the Lord) and their union (yoga) through mutual knowledge. If you see an apple, your consciousness is merged with the understanding of the apple. And yet, you are not identical to the apple. You still know that you are different from the apple, and your knowledge is *about* the apple. In the same way, the soul is merged in the Lord because his consciousness is absorbed in the thoughts, sensations, and pleasure of the Lord. And yet, this merger of consciousness is not the dissolution of their separate identities.

QUESTION

If the soul decides to enter samadhi, and become self-absorbed rather than being absorbed in the knowledge of the Lord, does it mean that the experience of the Lord and the interactions with Him no longer exist for the soul?

Topic 15

2.3.40 (256)
यथा च तक्षोभयथा
yathā ca takṣobhayathā

yathā—just as; ca—also; takṣa—cutting through; ubhayathā—both ways.

TRANSLATION

Just as (the soul withdraws from the Lord) also (the Lord withdraws from the soul); (the disconnection between soul and Lord) cuts both ways.

COMMENTARY

In the previous sūtra it was stated that the soul and the Lord enjoying with each other mutually are not in samādhi (i.e., they are different individuals). In this sūtra, the same point is made by stating that if the soul enters samādhi then the connection to the Lord (i.e., the consciousness and experience) are severed mutually. That is, if the soul is not engaged with the Lord, then the Lord is also not engaged with the soul. They exist as separate individuals, who have the potential to know each other, but that potential remains unrealized. The relationship to the Lord is therefore about mutual devotion and affection. If the soul wants to ignore the Lord, then the Lord doesn't force Himself upon the soul.

Topic 16

QUESTION

Does this severance of the relationship between the soul and the Lord permanently close the doors to a relationship in the future? Or is this absorption in Brahman a temporary state, which can also be altered in the future?

2.3.41 (257)
परात्तु तच्छ्रुतेः
parāttu tacchruteḥ

parāt—from the Supreme Lord; tu—but; tat—that (the soul); śruteḥ—so declares the śruti.

TRANSLATION

The śruti states that the soul has but emerged from the Lord (so there can never be a permanent disconnection between the soul and the Lord).

COMMENTARY

It has previously been noted that the soul is always connected to the Supreme Lord even in Brahman (through the agency of His prāṇa). This sūtra confirms that the soul can rise above Brahman and enter the pastimes of the Lord. The entry into Brahman is not a limitation to entry into the Lord's pastimes. In effect, what we call 'eternity' is not contrary to the possibility of change.

QUESTION

You have earlier said that the soul enters the Lord's association due to devotion. But how does he enter the undifferentiated state called Brahman?

2.3.42 (258)

कृतप्रयत्नापेक्षस्तु विहितप्रतिषिद्धावैयर्थ्यादिभ्यः

kṛtaprayatnāpekṣastu vihitapratiṣiddhāvaiyarthyādibhyaḥ

kṛtaprayatna—one who endeavors; apekṣaḥ—future prospect or expectation; tu—but; vihita—injunctions according to scriptures; pratiṣiddha—forbidden or prohibited; vaiyartha—uselessness; ādibhyaḥ—due to etc.

TRANSLATION

One who works according to scriptural injunctions, rejecting what is prohibited, and avoiding what is useless, etc. without expectation of future results (is entitled to enter the undifferentiated state called Brahman).

COMMENTARY

This sūtra describes the philosophy of karma-yoga and how it leads to Brahman realization. The cornerstone of karma-yoga is performing the prescribed duties, not indulging in sinful actions, avoiding all useless actions, but doing what needs to be done without the expectation of results (positive or negative). Generally, people over-endeavor in actions where they expect a positive result, and they neglect the actions where the outcomes are feared to be undesirable. Thus, the person creates good or bad karma, which entangles him in the cycle of repeated birth and death. Karma-yoga, however, liberates the soul from the cycle of birth and death, and leads to the Brahman state. As we have discussed before, the soul is bound to the material world due to guna and karma. When actions are performed without desire, then the guna or the ropes of desire are broken. And when the actions are performed in this way, then the cycle of karma is also broken. This liberation from the material world is the end of guna and karma, in which the soul is self-absorbed. But this self-absorption is incomplete because other souls, including the Supreme Soul, remain unknown.

Topic 17

QUESTION

The practice of karma-yoga is very difficult, because how can we act without thinking about the results of our actions? Is it possible that someone who is unable to practice karma-yoga can also attain the Brahman realization?

2.3.43 (259)

अंशो नानाव्यपदेशात् अन्यथा चापि दाशकितवादित्वमधीयत एके

amśo nānāvyapadeśāt anyathā cāpi dāśakitavāditvamadhīyata eke

amśaḥ—part; nānāvyapadeśāt—on account of the many descriptions; anyathā—otherwise; ca—and; api—also; dāśakitavāditvam—being cheating servants etc.; adhīyate—in the followers (of the Lord); eke—some.

TRANSLATION

Besides the parts (devotees) described in many ways (previously), in some cheating servants who follow the Lord additionally also (Brahman attained).

COMMENTARY

A cheating servant is one whose faith and commitment to the master are based on getting something in return. In this world, we can see that people bear loyalties to each other if they are rich and powerful, and those loyalties are broken if the master loses his power or wealth. The soul can similarly serve the Lord because the Lord is rich and powerful because by association, the soul obtains something in return. Since the Lord is always rich and powerful, therefore, this loyalty may never be broken, and it might seem that the soul is devoted to the Lord like others who are devoted without self-interest. But, such a servant, who is only devoted to his self-interest, and seems devoted to the Lord because he gets something in return, is called a 'cheating' servant here.

Such devotees accept that God is great because He supplies their necessities, but they are not interested in God. Their self-interest manifests in the desire for happiness, and the avoidance of suffering, which also manifests in the quest for liberation. Most devotees of Lord Śiva, for example, worship Him for liberation or sometimes material gain, because He grants boons easily. They may call themselves devotees of Lord Śiva, but their real devotion is to themselves. Thus, for example, they might chant the mantra *śivoham* or that "I am Śiva". Since Lord Śiva is detached from the material existence, by chanting this mantra, one may get liberated from the cycle of birth and death. This sūtra mentions that some (*eke*) souls are liberated by this process, which means that even if one has selfish interests, one must still have reverence toward the Lord. They must admire and respect the Lord, even if they are using Him for self-interest.

QUESTION

Even the practitioners of cheating religion expend much effort in worshiping the deities, offering them something in exchange for something else. If one is unable to do such worship, is there another way for getting liberated?

2.3.44 (260)

मन्त्रवर्णाच्च

mantravarṇācca

mantravarṇāt—due to the letters of the mantra; ca—also.

TRANSLATION

By the accurate pronunciation of Vedic mantras as well (one can get liberated from the material existence into the state called Brahman).

COMMENTARY

The Vedic mantras are manifestations of śabda-brahman or the sound representation of Brahman. For instance, the mantra OM, which is comprised of three letters—A, U, and M—is said to the origin of the varṇamāla or the garland of letters (there are 50 letters in the Sanskrit varṇamāla). These three letters represent the three primordial aspects of the soul—*sat*, *chit*, and ānanda—and by chanting this mantra, one can realize that one is eternal and can be situated in relation to oneself, that the external world is not necessary for self-awareness and self-knowledge, and that this self-awareness itself brings happiness. The mantra OM simply means "I am". Similarly, mantras such as ahaṁ brahmāsmī or "I am Brahman" means that I am beyond the material existence. The sound vibration of these mantra can liberate the soul from the bondage to the cycle of birth and death, and if one cannot worship the Lord, this sūtra suggests that one can chant such mantra if they want to be liberated from life and death.

QUESTION

The chanting of mantras generally requires a person to give up their material lives, sit in an isolated place, and meditate on the sound of the mantra. What if someone is not able to give up their material life for the changing of mantra in isolated places? Is there a path for liberation for such souls as well?

2.3.45 (261)
अपि च स्मर्यते
api ca smaryate

api—also; ca—and; smaryate—those who follow the smriti (such as Manu Smriti which prescribes the rules of living a regulated pious human life).

TRANSLATION

Even those who follow the principles of smriti (such as Manu Smriti).

COMMENTARY

The previous sūtra recommended the chanting of mantras from the śrutī, and this sūtra recommends that if one cannot follow the mantras of the śrutī, then even leading a regulated life as prescribed in the smriti is a practical way for getting liberated. We have earlier discussed how the terms śrutī and smriti are used loosely in the Vedic system. It is said that śrutī is words spoken by God, but Bhagavad-Gita, and many Purāṇa where the Lord speaks directly are termed as smriti. Meanwhile, even in the Upanishads, there are numerous narrations of conversations between self-realized souls instructing their disciples, not necessarily the words spoken by the Lord. The exact meaning of these terms is understood only based on the context, and in this case, the term smriti refers to the texts such as Manu Smriti which prescribe the four-fold classification of human society into Brahmana, Kshatriya, Vaisya, and Sudra, and their respective duties. The sūtra states that if one follows the prescriptions of Manu Smriti correctly, he can be liberated from the cycle of birth and death. In short, if society is organized properly according to the principles of Manu Smriti, just following the rules and regulations of social organization can lead us to Brahman.

QUESTION

If good social organization can lead us Brahman, then shouldn't the worship of demigods, such as Sun, Moon, stars, etc. also lead to liberation? You have rejected this process earlier, but would you recommend it now?

2.3.46 (262)
पूरकाशादविन्नैवं परः
prakāśādivannaivaṃ parah

prakāśādivat—like light etc.; na—is not suitable; evaṃ—for this; parah—the path toward transcendence (i.e., the attainment of Brahman).

TRANSLATION

The worship of the luminaries (such as sun, moon, stars, etc.) is not suitable for this process of attaining transcendence (i.e., liberation into Brahman).

COMMENTARY

In the previous sūtra, the proper organization of society according to the principles of Manu Smriti was recommended as a path to liberation, but in this sūtra, the worship of demigods is rejected for the purpose. Thus, we can see how proper social organization has greater importance than the worship of demigods; many people think that they are on the same level, and because the worship of demigods is rejected, therefore, the principles of social organization can also be rejected. From the previous sequence, we can see that karma-yoga, the chanting of certain mantras (such as OM), and social organization are preferred over demigod worship. This assumes significance because the Mīmāṃsā system, which worshipped the demigods, was dominated by Brahmanas. Buddhism rose as a reaction to the dominance of the Brahmanas, and it flattened society, removing the erstwhile class structure. Thus, two birds were hit with the same stone, but only one should have been hit. The rejection of demigod worship is not the rejection of the system of four classes according to this sūtra. The principles of Varṇāśrama have been slightly modified with time, such as rejecting the killing of animals by the Kshatriya, the consumption of intoxicants by the Sudra, and elevating the position of women who are qualified to lead society. But underlying all these changes is an understanding that there is a transcendental society where animals are not killed, intoxicants are not consumed, and women have equal or greater role in society as the men.

Therefore, both personalism and impersonalism accept a classful society, although they reject the worship of demigods. There is considerable false propaganda today that because we are all souls, and therefore children of God, and because we merge into oneness, therefore, everyone should be treated equally. The classful societies of the past had a superior role for kings and priests, who worshipped the demigods. As the demigod worship was demolished, the classful system also disappeared. But here the demigod worship is clearly separated from a classful society—the obedience of the rules of a classful society are said to lead to Brahman, whereas the demigod worship is explicitly rejected.

QUESTION

It has become very difficult to follow the rules of good social organization in modern times. We are forced to do things that we are not supposed to do, and we are often unable to do things that we are expected to do. For those who cannot follow the rules of a good social organization, what is the way?

2.3.47 (263)

स्मरन्तिच

smaranti ca

smaranti—those who remember (at the time of death); ca—and.

TRANSLATION

Even those who can remember (the Lord at the time of death) (can get liberated from the material existence and become situated in Brahman).

COMMENTARY

There are many reasons to remember the Lord at the time of death. First, when a person is sinful, they fear death because it is now the beginning of the repayment of the sins, and they might remember the Lord out of this fear. Second, a person might be suffering in the present life and is prepared to die to alleviate this suffering, but he is also looking for a better material body in the next life; they might remember the Lord to give them a better next life. Third, a person may be enjoying this life, and doesn't want to leave this body; since death entails separation from the body, wealth, and family, therefore, he might cry due to the incumbent separation, and he might pray to the Lord to prevent the death. Fourth, one might be detached from this world—neither sinful, nor suffering, nor enjoying, and may want to be liberated from the cycle of birth and death; they can remember the Lord to give them liberation from the cycle of birth and death. Fifth, a devotee will remember the Lord out of love, because he always remembers Him in good or bad times. The result of remembering the Lord depends upon the mood or intention underlying the remembrance.

In the progression of sūtras, we can see that the seeker is trying to find the minimal requirement for liberation. He first rejects the devotion to the Lord. Then he rejects karma-yoga, then the chanting of mantras, then the regulations of the social order. Due to the rejection of karma-yoga, the person is not aspiring for detachment and liberation. Due to the rejection of the chanting of mantras, he is not interested in spiritual endeavors. Due to the rejection of the restrictions of social order, he is not even interested in a responsible life. In short, the seeker is asking—what is the appropriate method for liberation for one who is not devoted to the Lord, isn't detached from the material world, doesn't want to undertake any spiritual activity, and doesn't like social rules and regulations? The only reason for such a person to remember the Lord at death is that they haven't done anything to deserve a better life, and they are about to lose their present life. Such a person only remembers the Lord unwillingly for a moment, just like an atheist in a state of shock and fear, might occasionally say: "Oh, my God".

This sūtra then says that even such a person can get liberated into Brahman due to their remembrance of the Lord at the time of death. However, the reality is that most people don't even remember the Lord despite such concessions. Most of our recall or memory works as part of the intellect. For example, when we see a cow, then the intellect recalls the images of the cows from the memory to say that "this is a cow". But under fear, the intellect stops working. Therefore, when we see death, our intellect doesn't say: "now I'm seeing the Lord". Therefore, the intellect cannot help us remember the Lord under great fear. This remembrance is possible if we have felt a more powerful emotion than the fear of death. The fear of death is the most powerful material emotion and to feel something other than this fear, one must feel an even more powerful emotion that conquers the fear. Therefore, the Lord's remembrance is easily achieved by devotees, but there are accidental cases in which it can be achieved by others.

QUESTION

What is considered sinful life due to which a person is cast repeatedly into the cycle of birth and death and is disqualified from liberation into Brahman?

2.3.48 (264)
अनुज्ञापरिहारौ देहसम्बन्धाज्ज्योतिरादिवत्
anujñāparihārau dehasambandhājjyotirādivat

anujñāparihārau—injunctions and prohibitions; dehasambandhāt—on account of the connection with the body; jyotirādi-vat—like light etc.

TRANSLATION

(Those who do not follow) the injunctions and prohibitions (even of) the body (such as cleanliness, eating, sex, etc.) and do not believe in the existence of the demigods (who deliver good and bad karma) (are disqualified).

COMMENTARY

Those aspiring for the Lord's devotion or liberation from matter don't worship the demigods, but they don't disregard their existence or role in the material world. For instance, they understand that the universe is governed by moral laws whose results (good or bad) are delivered by the demigods. They don't worship the demigods because these results are bound to come depending on our actions, and demigod worship cannot mitigate the good or bad results of our actions. Nevertheless, they don't reject the existence of the demigods precisely because that rejection would entail the rejection of good and bad karma, and once the law of karma is rejected, then people will descend into immoral activities. All morality comes down to the actions of the body, combined with a mental state. For instance, just thinking of harming someone does not entail sin unless an action by the body is performed.

However, if the action is performed without the intention of harming, then the deed involves a reduced sin.

To save us from these sins, the scriptures provide many injunctions (of what to do) and prohibitions (of what not to do). In the last but one sūtra, the injunctions of social life were described—i.e., the things that one must do. And in this sūtra, the prohibitions of social life are referenced—i.e., the things that one must not do. These include regulations about eating, cleanliness of the body and the surroundings in which we live, sex regulations, what can and cannot be said, etc. The devotees of the Lord can do anything for the pleasure of the Lord, and they are not implicated by karma because their intentions are pure devotion to the Lord. But those who don't have such devotion have to follow rules and regulations related to the body. Liberation from material existence of course involves the purification of the mind. But if someone cannot even follow the purification of the body through regulations (and has an impure or uncontrolled mind) then he is disqualified from any type of transcendence.

QUESTION

Does this mean that only purification of the body is necessary? What about the actions of a person? Do they qualify or disqualify a person from liberation?

2.3.49 (265)

असन्ततेश्चाव्यतिकिरः

asantateścāvyatikaraḥ

asantateḥ—discontinuous; ca—and; avyatikaraḥ—not acting reciprocally.

TRANSLATION

Those who neglect their reciprocal duties or perform them inconsistently (i.e., sometimes they do and sometimes they don't) (are forbidden).

COMMENTARY

In an earlier sūtra, a cheating religion was described as a system of worship in which the person serves the Lord only to obtain something in return. Practically everyone in this world works for selfish reasons. Thus, a laborer toils because he is paid a salary. People remain honest because they fear the punishments. But some people are even lower; they cannot perform the reciprocal duties, even to avoid punishment. This class of people believe in exploiting others and using them for their interest, but do not reciprocate the good they have received, or reciprocate inadequately (i.e., sometimes they reciprocate and at other times they don't). Maddened by their power, they feel invincible. These people are said to be disqualified from the pursuit of transcendence. As we have said, devotees are the most unselfish, as they serve the Lord and other souls without expecting returns. Those aspiring liberation are next, as they work for their own benefit, but they don't use others for their needs. Lower than those aspiring for liberation are those who engage in honest give-and-take transactions—i.e., they give and take reciprocally; they don't exploit, and they are not exploited. But the lowest of all these classes is those who exploit others.

Note that this sūtra follows the previous one where the rules and regulations of the body, such as regulated eating, sleeping, sex, cleanliness, etc. were prescribed. So, the implication is that there are people who follow all such bodily regulations—they lead a healthy lifestyle, refrain from intoxicants, regulate their sex-life, etc.—and yet their goal is only to keep a body and mind healthy enough to exploit others. Prime examples of such a class of people is present-day high-ranking members of society who use their wealth and power to extract more than they are giving back. They may come across as very clean, family-oriented, healthy, well-educated, and articulate people. And yet, their exploitative and deceitful activities disqualify them from any spiritual attainments.

QUESTION

There are many altruistic people who perform many kinds of charities. They are giving back more than they are taking from others. So, we can say that they are not exploitative, because they are performing more than their fair share of reciprocal duties. Are they qualified for the pursuit of transcendence?

2.3.50 (266)
आभास एव च
ābhāsa eva ca

ābhāsaḥ—an appearance or pretense; eva—only; ca—also.

TRANSLATION

(The performance of charities creates) the appearance or pretense (of religiosity) only; (such people are) also (disqualified from transcendence).

COMMENTARY

In former times, kings used to perform a great yajñā worshiping the demigods, and after the yajñā was complete, they would give away a lot of their wealth in charity. Such charities are meant to earn good karma, and the performance of yajñā elevates the person to heavenly planets. Therefore, they are materially good for the performer, but they are not considered spiritual activities for the simple reason that even if you perform some charity, you cannot give to anyone more than what they will otherwise get due to their own karma. The person receiving the wealth in charity is destined for this wealth due to his past pious activities, just like one might inherit wealth from their parents due to a good birth without having to work for it. The person who performs charity gains good karma but the person receiving it was entitled for it anyway. In modern times, for example, many people are either unqualified, uneducated, disabled, or simply unfortunate to not get a job. The government provides them with food and minimal shelter and medical care, which constitutes charity. But we should not suppose that these people receiving the charities are receiving something *ex gratia*. They are entitled by their karma to live a certain level of life, which means that they don't get the pleasure of working, earning, and being able to decide how they want to spend the earning; they are limited to a bare essential survival, because nature has ensured this fate for them.

When religion is mixed with such pious activities—such as by giving away free food, opening schools and colleges, or running low-cost medical facilities for the poor and incapable—an illusion or appearance of religiosity is created in which the main purpose of transcendence is forgotten and temporary purposes of serving the body, saving the environment, or helping people in their day-to-day materialistic lives passes off in the name of religiosity. Many people are greatly impressed by such activities because we have become so accustomed to exploitation that we equate any generosity and piety to transcendence. Of course, charity is better than exploitation for the person who indulges in such activities. However, from the perspective of the receiver, both outcomes are decided by their karma. Thus, whether you are being exploited by others or receiving charity from them, your actions are key determinants of these outcomes. The person who is performing such charity is pious, but not a transcendentalist. His piety is called a pretense or appearance of religion here.

QUESTION

There are many people situated in the renounced order of life. They follow all the rules and regulations of the body, they believe in the existence of demigods and the law of moral consequences, they don't exploit others and they stay away from unnecessary social and political engagements knowing that transcendence lies beyond this body. Does the renunciation of the material world by such people enough qualification for attaining transcendence?

2.3.51 (267)

अदृष्टानियमात्

adṛṣṭāniyamāt

adṛṣṭa-aniyamāt—cannot see that there are no rules or restrictions.

TRANSLATION

(The renunciates) cannot see that there are no rules or restrictions (for the practice of transcendence); (renunciation alone doesn't lead to transcendence).

COMMENTARY

In India, and in other cultures, there are traditions in which people become monks at an early age, renouncing mundane pleasures, detaching themselves from society, strictly following the rules and regulations of the body, and not indulging in any kind of exploitative or reciprocal business activities. This renunciation is good because it frees up time and energy for spiritual practices. But many of these renunciates don't perform any spiritual practices, such as chanting mantra or meditating on the Lord. They only believe in performing extreme forms of austerity, standing under the sun or rain, tolerating hot and cold, eating whatever nature provides, and torturing the body in various ways. But this renunciation doesn't achieve much because the accumulated pile of good karma is postponed, and the accumulated pile of bad karma is reaped by self-torture. Ultimately, the person is not liberated because even though the bad karma may be reduced or destroyed, good karma remains, and the person will be forced to take birth to enjoy this good karma. Thus, penance without a spiritual practice is merely the torture of the body and not transcendence.

In this sūtra, it is also noted that such people don't realize that transcendence is not restricted to renunciation; even those who are engaged in karma-yoga, or chanting the mantras from śrutī, or doing their Varṇāśrama duties, or worshiping the Lord asking for liberation, are better placed in the path of transcendence rather than those who are simply torturing the body. While rules and regulations of the body are necessary, this sūtra states that they are insufficient. One cannot be freed from the bondage of life and death by austerities, although one's sinful karma can be destroyed by such austerities. Formerly, austerities were prescribed for the destruction of bad karma, but the good karma is destroyed only when one develops a spiritual understanding of the self.

The soul is ānandamaya or having a natural inclination toward pleasure. So, how can austerity—which is contrary to pleasure—be considered a natural state? It can at best be a temporary provision for destroying sinful reactions. One cannot perform austerities forever because of the ānandamaya nature of the soul. So, unless the soul becomes situated in transcendental pleasure—either of the self or of the Lord—austerities will eventually end and the soul will fall back to material enjoyment, repeating the cycle of birth and death.

QUESTION

The Brahmins perform sandhyā-vandana three times a day. They say that by this process the body and the mind are purified, and by the chanting of Gāyatri during this process, one can attain spiritual realization. Is this true?

2.3.52 (268)

अभसिन्ध्यादष्विपि चैवम्

abhisandhyādiṣvapi caivam

abhisandhyādiṣu—in those regularly following Sandhya etc.; api—even; ca—and; evam—like this.

TRANSLATION

(The Brahman cannot be attained) even in those who are thus following the regular practice of Sandhya (the chanting of Gayatri three times a day).

COMMENTARY

The term Sandhya refers to three times in a day—sunrise, sunset, and mid-noon. These times have been used for chanting the Gayatri, which worships the sun. Just like the soul emanates from the body of the Lord as light, similarly, the energy of the sun is considered a material counterpart of the Lord from whose body the light illuminates the universe. Analogically, the sun is called Sūrya Nārāyana, because the soul emerges from the body of Lord Nārāyana at the time of creation and goes back into His body at the time of annihilation. However, the sun's worship is not considered transcendental because the words *bhu*, *bhuvar*, and *svarga* in the Gayatri refer to the three planetary systems in which the sun's light is manifest. The light of the sun doesn't reach the four upper planetary systems, nor does it reach the seven lower planetary systems, or the 28 hellish planets. Therefore, the Gayatri mantra is ineffective in all these places. The purpose of the Gayatri is to understand that our bodies and minds are sustained by the sun's light, and the connection between our body and the sun is established through prāṇa. The chanting of Gayatri can help a person maintain a strong body and mind, because the sun is the signifier of physical and mental health (the senses, the mind, and the intellect).

Therefore, even though the Brahmana chanted the Gayatri three times a day, the chanting did not define the qualification to be a Brahmana. The real definition of a Brahmana is one who is learned about the nature of Brahman—*brahma jānāti iti brahmana*. Just like humans may brush their teeth but brushing the teeth doesn't define our humanity; it is prevalent, but neither necessary nor sufficient. Similarly, Sandhya has been popular among the Brahmanas, although this practice does not define the essence of being a Brahmana. With the passing of time, such rituals have remained and become the defining characteristics of Brahmana. Thus, we can find many people today who wear the sacred thread, and chant the Gayatri three times a day, and yet have no understanding of Brahman. Thus, it is sometimes said that in the kali-yuga simply wearing a thread would identify someone as Brahmana. This sūtra rejects the practice of Sandhya as the sole qualification for the attainment of transcendence.

QUESTION

Many people believe that transcendence can be achieved simply by living in holy places, and if one dies in a holy place, one is automatically elevated to the spiritual world. This seems quite an easy way to attain transcendence.

2.3.53 (269)

परदेशादिति चेत् न अन्तर्भावात्

pradeśāditi cet na antarbhāvāt

pradeśāt—due to place; iti cet—if it be said; na—not so; antarbhāvāt—from the internal state.

TRANSLATION

If it is said that (one can attain transcendence simply) due to the place (of birth, death, or living) (we say) not so; it is based on the internal state.

COMMENTARY

All places in Vedic philosophy are not the same. Space is structured like a tree, which means that locations in this space are higher and lower. The higher places affect a greater number of aspects of our lives, and the lower places affect fewer aspects of our life. The spiritual world is the highest place, and a minor discrepancy in the spiritual world immediately leads to a fall. Within the material world too, there are higher and lower places, and good deeds in the higher places produce greater benefit, just as the sinful activities in these places produce greater suffering. Hence, it is said that we must perform good deeds in holy places, as any sinful deeds in those holy places produce greater sin.

Thus, there was a tradition to discuss spiritual topics in holy places to amplify the understanding. Many sacrifices were also performed in the holy places because they produce greater benefits. However, the holy places are not the only determinant of a person's spiritual standing. If that were so, then an advanced devotee of the Lord could not exist in the material world, because the material world is considered a fallen place. The ultimate determinant is a person's internal state, and the Lord's devotion can therefore exist everywhere.

However, as time passes, and the spiritual understanding declines, people start associating the place itself with holiness, rather than understanding that the place facilitates the results, but is not the sole cause of the results. Every religion identifies some holy places, and people visit these places frequently. This sūtra rejects the conception that birth, death, or living in a holy place is enough for transcendence. Even if the actions in a holy place produce greater benefits, ultimately it is the internal transformation that counts, not the place. The same transformation could also be attained in other places, although a person may have to endeavor harder for similar results. The holy places make spiritual transformation easier, but they are not substitutes for our efforts.

SECTION 4

Topic 1

QUESTION

You have earlier (in sūtra 1.3.4 (67)) rejected the use of prāṇa for attaining the Lord and said that this is only possible through devotion. Does this hold true for attaining the Brahman stage? Many yogis believe that they can attain Brahman by the practice of prāṇa control; since the soul is transported from one body to another by the influence of prāṇa, it is said that the prāṇa can also liberate the soul into Brahman. What is the conclusion on this understanding?

2.4.1 (270)

तथा प्राणाः

tathā prāṇāḥ

tathā—in the same way; prāṇāḥ—the five vital airs in the body.

TRANSLATION

In the same way (transcendence cannot be attained just by) prāṇa.

COMMENTARY

We have earlier distinguished between three types of prāṇa. The first type of prāṇa works under the control of guna and karma, which are in turn under the control of time; due to this prāṇa, we breathe without conscious effort, the blood circulates without our knowledge, the immune response works without our intervention, etc. Likewise, diseases appear without our inviting them. The second type of prāṇa works under the control of the soul, due to which the soul can reject the automatically created desires produced out of guna (under the influence of time), and the soul obtains mastery over the body and the mind. This prāṇa is responsible for the effects of free will translating into the body and the mind because by exercising this prāṇa we can control the body and the mind. The third type of prāṇa connects the soul to the Lord, due to which Brahman has been called prāṇa earlier. The attainment of Brahman requires the rejuvenation of this connection to the Supreme Lord, and it is activated only when the soul establishes its relation to the Lord, which is also called sambandha. Once this relation is established, typically, the soul also serves the Lord, which is called abhidheya, leading to pleasure which is called prayojana. However, it is possible that after the soul has established a relation, the service and the concomitant pleasure are absent. This occurs when the relation is *śānta* or one of silent appreciation. The service to the Lord begins with the *dasya* (the relation of a master and servant). It progresses with *sakhya* (the relation of friendship), *vātsalya* (the parent-child relation), and *mādhurya* (amorous relation). In the *śānta* relation, the soul understands that God is great, and the soul is small. In this silent appreciation, the soul appreciates the Lord from a distance, just like we might admire a person in our heart, but not express that admiration through words of glorification, or actively participate in serving the person we admire.

The term prāṇa here refers to the material energy by which the soul controls his desires, and the yogis aspire for this control to obtain mastery over the mind and the body by the control of prāṇa (which is also called prāṇayāma). By controlling our breath, we can control our thoughts, and relax the body.

In the aṣṭāṅga-yoga system, prāṇayāma is the 4th step toward self-realization. Following this, the yogi practices *dhyāna* (establishing a relation to the Lord), *dhāraṇā* (full cognition of the Lord), and *samādhi* (being absorbed in the pleasure attained from the cognition of the Lord). These last three steps involve the use of the spiritual prāṇa that connects the soul to the Supreme Soul, and it is triggered only when the soul develops devotion toward the Lord, although the devotion is only developed only till the point of silent appreciation. The mere control of the material prāṇa thus doesn't lead even to Brahman.

QUESTION

But you have earlier said that the soul is bound to material nature due to guna and karma. If the guna are dissolved, then the karma will also be eventually dissolved, and the soul can get liberated from material existence. Since the soul has the capacity for controlling the desires emerging from guna, and it can reject these desires, can't the soul get liberated by controlling its desires?

2.4.2 (271)

गौण्यसंभवात्

gauṇyasambhavāt

gauṇi—covered by the guna; asaṃbhavāt—from being impossible.

TRANSLATION

(Becoming free of guna) from being impossible for one covered by guna.

COMMENTARY

Suppressing our desires doesn't mean freedom from desires. The material prāṇa operates under the control of guna and karma, while the soul's prāṇa operates under the soul's control. By this control, the soul can suppress one's desires, but that suppression doesn't mean freedom from material desires.

Material guna represent our habits, desires, and proclivities. To be free of the guna means to change the purpose of our life, which requires a new purpose. Simply the rejection of the material purpose is insufficient, and the soul being extremely small, cannot make himself the purpose of its existence. Thus, the real method for liberation is to make the Lord the purpose of our existence. If this purpose doesn't appear, then no matter how much we try to reject the material purposes—in relation to this world—we cannot completely reject these purposes. This fact is seen in many meditators who don't become devotees of the Lord, and after long periods of meditation, they come back to material purposes—e.g., opening hospitals, schools, engaging in politics, etc. One such example of returning to material purpose is described in the life of Sage Viśvāmitra who became envious of Sage Vasiṣṭha (who was a devotee of Lord Rāma), and performed severe austerities for thousands of years, but could not free himself from sex desire, the hunger for power and superiority, etc.

Many people falsely presume that liberation is being free of all desires. However, to become free, you must have the desire to be free of desires, which is also a material desire. "I don't want this" is not a spiritual desire, because the mere reference to what we don't want can exist only if that thing exists. If we keep thinking about what we don't want, we keep that thing alive in our minds. The spiritual desire begins by wanting the self and becoming self-absorbed. By self-absorption, the world is automatically forgotten. But one cannot remain self-absorbed because the soul is the potential for relation, cognition, and emotion, but in self-absorption, these are not fulfilled. How can we be satisfied with seeing the unfulfilled potential? Can a musician be happy thinking that he can play music, without ever playing music? This is the cause of the soul's fall.

Thus, desires can never be completely overcome. They can be suppressed in the material world, and they can remain in a potential state in the soul. But ultimately, the suppression and elimination of desire fail. Freedom from material desire is not the rejection of all desire; it is the desiring of the Lord. Thus, anyone who wants to be freed from guna need only desire the Lord.

QUESTION

Can the material entanglement not be ended by knowledge? The practitioners of jñāna-yoga claim that liberation is obtained through knowledge.

2.4.3 (272)

परतज्ज्ञानुपरोधाच्च

pratijñānuparodhaccha

pratijñāna—toward knowledge; uparodha—interruption; ca—also.

TRANSLATION

As one progresses toward the knowledge (of the Supreme Absolute Truth), the material nature (of a person) is also interrupted (by knowledge).

COMMENTARY

This sūtra indicates that knowledge is helpful but is not the ultimate answer to the cycle of birth and death. As one acquires transcendental knowledge, one's material activities begin to cease, but they don't fully come to an end until devotion for the Lord is established in the heart. Regular hearing of the scriptures, for instance, destroys most of the material desires, but doesn't end them completely. This end is achieved only when the Lord is perceived. Therefore, liberation too is attained only through devotion, although spiritual knowledge can certainly arrest and interrupt the progression of material entanglement. With spiritual knowledge, a person realizes the value of human life, and starts endeavoring toward transcendence. But material attachments are not easily destroyed. No amount of knowledge can change a person's heart. Only when a superior kind of happiness is experienced are material desires destroyed.

QUESTION

But finding the Lord in the heart as Paramātma—as you have recommended earlier—is also not easy. Isn't there a way that a person can enter meditation while practicing prāṇa without seeking the Paramātma in the heart?

2.4.4 (273)

तत्पराक्श्रुतेश्च

tatprākśruteśca

tat—that; prāk—first; śruteḥ—hearing; ca—also.

TRANSLATION

To do that (i.e., achieve transcendence without meditating on Paramātma), one must first hear (the names of the Lord) as well (as prāṇa control).

COMMENTARY

In the Śrīmad Bhāgavatam, a process that combines the yogic practices along with the chanting of mantras is described in the narration about Maharaja Dhruva, who was given this process by Sage Nārada. Dhruva stood on a single leg, controlled his breath, and began pratyahāra or reducing in eating; gradually he stopped eating, drinking, and even breathing; such was his mastery of the prāṇa that the breathing of the other living entities in the universe was curtailed because Maharaja Dhruva had controlled his breath. However, this wasn't the only practice he was following; he also continuously chanted the mantra *om namo bhagavate vāsudevāya*. With this meditation, the Lord automatically appeared in his heart, and he was able to meditate upon Him.

This sūtra refers to the mastery of prāṇa along with the hearing the sound of the mantras, thus meditating on the sound, by which the Lord automatically is revealed in the heart, a process previously prescribed by Sage Nārada.

QUESTION

The meditation on the Lord in the heart is performed silently. Should these mantras also be chanted silently in the mind along with breath control?

2.4.5 (274)

तत्पूर्वकत्वाद्वाचः

tatpūrvakatvādvācaḥ

vācaḥ—the speech; tatpūrvakatvāt—from being prior (to the hearing).

TRANSLATION

The speech (vocal utterance) from being prior (to the hearing).

COMMENTARY

The mind is the sense that perceives meanings of the words, just as the senses of hearing and speaking utter those words. When the meaning of the mantra is firmly established in the mind, then vocal utterances are not necessary. But for the beginner, vocal utterances are essential because only by meditating on the sound is one's mind purified to even understand the meaning. This sūtra recommends audible chanting of the mantra followed by the hearing (which was prescribed in the previous sūtra) along with breath control.

Topic 2

QUESTION

What is the role of prāṇa in chanting and hearing? How is the process of prāṇa control noted earlier related to the process of chanting and hearing?

2.4.6 (275)
सप्त गतेर्वशिेषतित्वाच्च
sapta gaterviśeṣitatvācca

sapta—seven; gateḥ—centers, places of refuge; viśeṣitatva—the agency of instantiation or individuation; ucca—is called or described as.

TRANSLATION

(The prāṇa is) the agency of instantiation or individuation; it is described or said to have seven centers or places of refuge (called the chakra).

COMMENTARY

The prāṇa is the agency that divides the whole into parts and connects the parts to the whole. If the whole is the mammal, and the part is the cow, then the following three facts hold true about the division of the mammal into the cow: (1) the cow is an *instance* of mammal, (2) the cow is a *part* of mammal, and (3) cow is a *detail* about mammals. These three properties of being an instance, a part, and a detail are ascribed by the term *viśeṣitatva*, which stands for 'more specific', 'more detailed', or 'individual'. The process of converting the abstract into contingent is said to proceed through seven levels, in which the whole—at the topmost level—is successively divided into parts through seven stages. These seven stages are noted in both Sāñkhya and Yoga philosophies.

In Sāñkhya, the stages are called objects, sensations, senses, mind, intellect, ego, and moral sense. In Yoga philosophy, these seven stages are identified with centers of prāṇa organized hierarchically and identified as chakras called Mulādhāra, Svādhiśthāna, Manipura, Anahata, Viśuddha, Ajna, and Sahasrāra. The spiritual aspirant is expected to raise themselves through these levels. One begins by the objects, or the uttering of the sound. Then one progresses into the sensation which is hearing. Over time, the senses are purified, and one develops an attachment to hearing. After this attachment, one realizes that the name of the Lord refers to the Lord; this realization occurs in the mind. Then by the intellect one realizes that the Lord is the Absolute Truth. By the ego, subsequently, the soul develops devotion to the Lord. And by the moral sense, one becomes a servant of the Lord. Once this servitude is attained, the cognition of the Lord and the pleasure of the Lord attained by that cognition are spiritual.

The ascent of the prāṇa under the control of the soul can take one to the point of establishing a relationship to the Lord. However, the soul doesn't have the power to see the Lord by this prāṇa. This seeing or revelation is due to the prāṇa controlled by the Lord, and He appears when He so desires. Thus, we can be situated in the relationship to the Lord, but we cannot force the Lord to appear. There is hence value in our effort—to bring us to the point of a relationship to the Lord. But after this, the Lord is only seen through His grace.

By practicing the control of prāṇa, the process of sensual, mental, intellectual, emotional, and moral purification can be accelerated, because there is a parallel between the ascent of prāṇa and the purification of the senses, mind, intellect, ego, and the moral sense. This doesn't mean that the Lord is controlled by our prāṇa, and that we 'attain' spiritual realization by our efforts. We have the power to establish a relationship to the Lord and to serve Him. But ultimately, the Lord will appear only when He sees devotion and love in us.

QUESTION

The prāṇa you are talking about is present all over the body, such as in hands and legs as well. Then what is so special about the chanting of mantras relative to this breath control? Can't the same breath control be practiced along with the activities of the other senses, such as those of the hands and legs?

2.4.7 (276)
हस्तादयस्तु स्थिते$'$तो नैवम्
hastādayastu sthite'to naivam

hastādayaḥ—hands etc.; tu—but; sthite—being situated; ataḥ—therefore; na—not; evam—like this;

TRANSLATION

(The prāṇa is) but situated in the hands etc. and therefore this process is not (highly recommended, or not a suitable method of advancement).

COMMENTARY

The Lord can be served by all the senses of the body, not just the tongue and ears. The serving by hands or legs is neither superior nor inferior to the service by the tongue; ultimately, the quality of the service depends on how deep the realization of the person is—i.e., whether it just permeates the gross body, or even the senses, the mind, the intellect, the ego, and so on. When a yogi performs prāṇayāma, the body remains static, and only the ear and the tongue are involved in serving the Lord. To make progress in this path, one would have to remain situated in this state for long periods of time. In contrast, one who can serve the Lord through all the senses—e.g., the hands, legs, etc.—doesn't need to make these senses still and idle. He can keep serving the Lord through the entire body, and while it seems that the person's prāṇa is not being controlled, the fact is that the person is constantly being purified through this service. Therefore, if one insists on using prāṇa control, the previous sūtra recommended that one also chant the names of the Lord while doing such meditation. But since we know that prāṇa is not just activating the senses of hearing and chanting, but every other sense and the main cause of spiritual progress is the sound rather than the prāṇa itself, therefore, engaging the entire body into the Lord's service is a preferred method rather than the control of prāṇa itself.

Topic 3

QUESTION

If prāṇa is the agency for individuation, and these individuals become atoms, then shouldn't the cause of individuation be also considered atomic?

2.4.8 (277)

अणवश्च

aṇavaśca

aṇavaḥ—atomic; ca—also.

TRANSLATION

(The prāṇa is) is also atomic.

COMMENTARY

We have discussed how experience is created by the combination of three factors— ability, opportunity, and desire—through the power of prāṇa. In the previous sūtra, prāṇa was described as the agency that divides and expands the abstract ideas into contingent ideas. This division produces the three types of possibilities—abilities, opportunities, and desires—like the trunks, branches, and leaves expanding from a root. These expanded spaces constitute the 'unmanifest' world—i.e., something that is yet not experienced. Experience is then created by a *choice* that combines an ability, an opportunity, and a desire.

The 'atomism' of prāṇa is the indivisibility of choice. The spaces of ability, opportunity, and desire exist as atoms, and the choice that combines these atoms is also atomic, although it produces an experience. The choices occur in sequence; therefore, the atoms of choice are temporal: they are created and destroyed. While they exist, the experience is also sustained. Thus, we distinguish between the atoms of space (desire, possibility, and opportunity) and time (choices). Due to these atoms, experience has a spatiotemporal division.

The atoms of time—the smallest durations of experience—define the units of time. The smallest unit is called Truti, and it is approximately 1/3 microsecond. Thus, every second of experience involves millions of choices, and hence millions of atoms of prāṇa. This makes us think that the experience is continuous, rather than discrete. When a yogi slows the prāna, then time also slows, because a fewer number of choices are made. Thus, the mind, the senses, and the intellect remain still and steady, rather than fleeting and changing. By the control of prāna, the yogis can elongate their lifespan, and the underlying science for that longer life is that what we call 'time' is produced by choices, which are atomic. If we can slow down the succession of atoms, then we can slow down time. In this state, we can observe individual atoms of experience and how they are created from possibilities by the application of choice.

Topic 4

QUESTION

You have earlier said that the prāna transports the soul from one body to another, implying that the soul is being controlled by prāna. In the above sūtra, you are saying that the successive states of experience are choices, which I take to mean are being produced by the soul. So, in one case you are saying that the prāna is forcing the soul to move, and in another case, you are suggesting that the prāna is being controlled by the soul. Which of these is the case?

2.4.9 (278)

शरेष्ठशच

śreṣṭhaśca

śreṣṭhaḥ—being superior; ca—as well.

TRANSLATION

(The prāna can) also be the controller (just like the soul can be controller).

COMMENTARY

We have discussed how the three kinds of prāna work: (1) the material prāna is controlled by guna and karma, (2) the soul's prāna is controlled by the soul, and the Lord's prāna is controlled by the Lord. Due to the first prāna, the soul is dragged by prāna. Due to the second prāṇa, the soul controls the body and mind and can form a relationship to the Lord and perform loving service to Him. And due to the third prāṇa, the Lord controls even the soul. Hence, the soul can be controlled by matter, and the soul can control matter. Similarly, the Lord can be controlled by the soul, and the soul can control the Lord. These are not contradictory claims once the nature of prāṇa is completely understood.

Topic 5

QUESTION

So your main point seems to be that because devotion to the Lord is the development of desire, and this desire is ultimately in the control of the soul, rather than the control of prāṇa (or its antecedents like karma and Causal Time), therefore, prāṇa cannot be considered the cause of the soul's liberation?

2.4.10 (279)
न वायुक्रिये पृथगुपदेशात्
na vāyukriye pṛthagupadeśāt

na vāyukriye—not the action of the air; pṛthak—separately; upadeśāt—on account of its being mentioned.

TRANSLATION

(Devotion to the Lord) is not the (result of the) action of the prāṇa; it is always taught to be separate (and transcendental to the material elements).

COMMENTARY

After delving into details about the nature of prāṇa and explaining how prāṇa control helps to control the mind and the body, this sūtra states that the prāṇa is not the cause of devotion in the soul. Prāṇa can be used to control the mind and the body, and to the extent that the mind and the body impose needs and desires upon the soul, the control of prāṇa is useful in concentrating the mind and controlling the body. Prāṇa control is therefore not completely useless as it can be employed in meditation of the Lord by suppressing bodily and mental urges. But, once these urges have been suppressed, the prāṇa cannot lead to the development of devotion toward the Lord. Without that devotion, there is no happiness, and after some time, the need for enjoyment will give way to the urges of the body and the mind, and the effect of prāṇa control will be lost. Thus, prāṇa control is a useful method for stopping the noise generated by the body and the mind so that the soul can meditate on the Lord. But in this role of control, we cannot say that prāṇa is the cause of the devotion to the Lord.

QUESTION

Does that mean that when the devotion is developed, then the control of the body and the mind (through the agency of prāṇa) becomes unnecessary?

2.4.11 (280)

चक्षुरादिवित्तु तत्सहशषिट्यादभि्यः

cakṣurādivattu tatsahaśiṣṭyādibhyaḥ

cakṣurādivat—like eyes etc.; tu—but; tat-saha-śiṣṭyādibhyaḥ—being controlled or disciplined along with that (the prāṇa that controls the senses).

TRANSLATION

(The senses) such as the eyes etc. are but disciplined along with that (the prāṇa, which is controlled by the development of the devotion to the Lord).

COMMENTARY

In the previous sūtra, it was said that the devotion to the Lord is not caused by prāṇa, although prāṇa can help control the body and the mind. This sūtra now goes a step further and states that if devotion to the Lord is developed, then the prāṇa is automatically controlled by that devotion. In short, the control of prāṇa is inadequate in producing devotion, and it is unnecessary after devotion is developed. It may be useful in mind-body control when devotion hasn't yet been developed, for the practice of developing such devotion. The term *tat-śiṣṭya* means the 'disciplining of that', which ultimately indicates the control of the prāṇa that then controls the senses and the mind. Thus, a cascading hierarchy of control—from the devotion to the Lord to the control of the prāṇa to the control of the mind, to the control of the senses—is indicated here. When devotion to the Lord develops, the mind is filled with emotions about the Lord, and the pleasure of the mind and the senses in relation to the world becomes insignificant. The pursuit of higher desires makes lower pursuits insignificant.

QUESTION

It was earlier said that the soul is connected to the Lord through prāṇa, and just as we control the parts of our body through prāṇa, similarly, the Lord can control the soul through the (spiritual) prāṇa. In short, this (spiritual) prāṇa was the instrument of control of the soul. But now you are saying that the devotion to the Lord is an innate property of the soul, and it cannot be forced by the prāṇa, so does this imply that the Lord doesn't force devotion on the soul?

2.4.12 (281)
अकरणत्वाच्च न दोषःतथाहि दर्शयति
akaraṇatvācca na doṣaḥ tathāhi darśayati

akaraṇatvāt—due to not being an instrument; ca—and; na—not; doṣaḥ—faults or discrepancies; tathā hi—because thus; darśayati—He is seen.

TRANSLATION

(Upon the development of devotion, the prāṇa) ceases to be the instrument of control (of the Lord), and this is not considered a fault or discrepancy because only through such (unforced devotion of the soul) is He (the Lord) seen.

COMMENTARY

The spiritual prāṇa is like a rope that binds the soul and the Lord. The Lord can use this rope to pull the soul towards Himself, but He doesn't do that, unless the soul pulls first. This is the nature of the

Lord and His Śakti—the Śakti must pull the Lord first, and the Lord will then pull the Śakti. In the material world, the soul is controlled by karma, which is ultimately in the control of the Lord. But once the soul is free from karma, the Lord doesn't exert control over the soul. The soul is free to be devoted to the Lord or be a passive/silent observer of the world or remain self-absorbed. In that sense, the prāṇa ceases to be a *karana* or instrument of the Lord. And yet, this freedom of the soul to pursue its own goals is not considered a fault—e.g., that the Lord is no longer in control of the soul. In fact, the contrary is now stated, namely, that the soul can control the Lord by this prāṇa if he so desires. A symptom of that control is that the Lord now appears before the devotee, compelled by the devotee's love.

In this regard, we must note that all vision (even material vision) is caused through an interaction between two objects. As we discussed before, our senses have desires, and the material objects have purposes to be used for the senses. When the senses interact with the objects, the desire in the senses is created and the purpose in the objects is activated. This activation then results in a stronger interaction, which makes the desire and purpose even stronger. Thus, through an iterative process, the senses and their objects come 'close' to each other: this proximity is not physical; it is caused by their mutual interaction. The stronger the interaction, the greater is the perceived proximity. (This is the inverse of the modern scientific idea that greater proximity results in a stronger interaction). Similarly, when the devotion in the soul arises, the strength of that desire forces an interaction by which the Lord becomes visible to the soul—i.e., proximate. Proximity is therefore an *effect* of the interaction, not a *cause*. That is, the Lord doesn't come close to us before we see Him. We rather desire the Lord very strongly, and the desire results in an interaction by which proximity grows, and ultimately, we see the Lord. If we understand the process of material vision, then we can also understand the process of spiritual vision because both processes are caused by an interaction resulting in a proximity and when there is proximity, we get clarity of vision and we think we are 'seeing' the object.

Practicing devotees sometimes ask: Why can't the Lord come closer to me, become visible to me, or show signs of His existence to me, so that I can firm my faith in the Lord's existence? We must note that such kind of accidental appearance before us is caused by karma—e.g., due to good karma we can meet things, to which we get attracted and the karma then fulfills the desire. The Lord is, however, not controlled by karma. It is the strength of desire in us that evokes a desire in the Lord, and these two desires gradually become stronger due to mutual inter-action. They then bring the soul and the Lord face to face.

QUESTION

If the Lord can be controlled by the spiritual prāṇa, does it mean that the spiritual prāṇa is also like material prāṇa, which controls material objects?

2.4.13 (282)
पञ्चवृत्तिर्मनोवद्व्यपदिश्यते
pañcavṛttirmanovadvyapadiśyate

pañcavṛttiḥ—having five natures; manovat—just like the mind (has five natures); vyapadiśyate—it pervades in all directions, or it is thus asserted.

TRANSLATION

(The material and spiritual prāṇa) have a five-fold nature, just like the mind (has a five-fold nature); by this nature, the prāṇa exists everywhere (i.e., wherever the consciousness of the soul or the Lord is directed by desire).

COMMENTARY

This sūtra gives further insights into the process by which an inter-action occurs, and how things become visible (as was noted in the pre-vious sūtra). This insight comes from the five-fold nature of the mind, which is said to proceed through five stages called thinking, feeling, willing, knowing, and acting. The thinking stage of the mind involves a cognitive understanding of an object, which we can call the picture of the object. It comes to us suddenly due to recollection, just as waves arise automatically in the ocean. When a memory suddenly arises, we either like it or dislike it. This like or dislike constitutes the feeling stage. If we dislike the idea, the picture is pushed out of our recol-lection. If, however, we like the idea, then the liking is subjected to a judgment—e.g., is the thing that we are desiring also true, right, and good? For instance, we might develop a craving for sugar, but we have been forbidden from eating sugar, then the judgment of true, right, and good will stop the desire immediately. If the judgment agrees to proceed further (or is overwhelmed by the desire), the mind proceeds into the willing stage—I have decided to get this object. To obtain the object, one must know how to obtain it; this is called the knowing stage which involves procedural knowledge of how to get the things we want. Finally, we must apply this knowledge and act upon it—which is called the acting stage—that converts procedural knowledge into actions. The result of these actions is that one comes closer to the destination. As one comes closer, another cycle of thinking, feeling, willing, knowing, and acting occurs. That is, at every step, we evaluate if we still want this object, if we will like to have it, if it is worth the effort we are putting in, if we should change the method of getting it, and if alternative methods will get us to the destination easier and faster.

The working of the prāṇa is compared in this sūtra to the cyclic process of thinking, feeling, willing, knowing, and acting. As we can see, each step of the process involves a decision or a choice. As we come closer to the results we are working toward, the thoughts of the object to be attained automatically arise in the mind, which then strengthen the desire, which then strengthen our resolve to pursue the goal, which clarify the process by which we can move further, and the clarity and resolve drive us to endeavor harder as we get closer. In short, the prāṇa is described as a reflection of the working of the mind.

In many places, the five-fold nature of the prāṇa is also called *prāṇa, samāna, apāna, vyāna* and *udāna*, which represent ingestion, digestion, excretion, assimilation, and production. This five-fold process can be applied to the mind in analogy to the body—e.g., the mind ingests ideas, breaks them down into simpler ideas that are already understood, which can be called 'digestion', excretes or rejects some ideas that don't fit our current understanding, then assimilates the accepted ideas with the rest of our conceptual worldview, and finally uses the newly acquired knowledge to produce new things.

The prāṇa is an intermediate level of reality between the mind and the body. Thus, the understanding of prāṇa can be modeled after the actions of the body—e.g., ingestion, digestion, assimilation, excretion, and production. Or, it can be modeled after the actions of the mind—e.g., thinking, feeling, willing, knowing, and acting. In this sūtra, the comparison is made to the working of the mind, rather than to the working of the body. Therefore, this sūtra should not be viewed as referring to *prāṇa*, *samana*, *apana*, *vyana* and *udana*, even though in most other contexts, a five-fold division will entail these five.

Topic 6

QUESTION

You have previously called the prāṇa as being atomic and described it as comprising choices. You are now stating that choices can further be divided into five parts—thinking, feeling, willing, knowing, and acting. Doesn't this entail that the atomism should be understood as five types of choices?

2.4.14 (283)
अणुश्च
aṇuśca

aṇuḥ—atomic; ca—as well.

TRANSLATION

(The five-fold division of the prāṇa and the mind, as noted in the previous sūtra, can be applied to) atomism as well.

COMMENTARY

Many people think that the existence of choice will not alter the understanding of matter; at best, the choices will select material possibilities. In this sūtra, this idea is challenged by suggesting that when an atom is a choice, and there are many kinds of choices, then there are many kinds of atoms. Atomism simply means indivisibility, which is characterized by a choice—a choice is a unit that can break into parts, but you don't necessarily break it apart. If your choices divide the things into smaller parts, then atomism can refer to the smallest division that can be performed by choice. But, if you don't use the choices to divide, then atomism can also represent the individual choice, which need not be picking something small. For instance, we can choose the

Absolute Truth, and that 'atom' of choice will include everything that exists. There is hence a difference between the ideas that atoms are indivisible and the idea that the atoms are small things. In this case, the indivisible is not necessarily small. The Absolute Truth is therefore an 'atom' in the sense that it cannot be reduced to smaller things. And yet, many smaller things are part of that Absolute Truth. This type of atomism is understood only using concepts such as cow and mammal. The concept mammal cannot be reduced to its members—cows, dogs, cats, horses, etc. And yet, cows, dogs, horses, cats, etc. are part of mammal.

Since thinking, feeling, willing, knowing and acting all involve choices, therefore, the atomism can also be construed in multiple ways. The atom of thought, or an idea, is different from the atom of feeling or emotion. Similarly, the acquisition of a relation to a goal is different from the idea (after all we can have an idea, and not decide to make it a goal), or the feeling (after all, we can like or dislike something but not make it the mission of some pursuit). Procedural knowledge is also an atom, although different from descriptive knowledge. And actions that put these procedures into actions are also atoms. When we begin with a physical world, then atoms are the smallest things that exist. If instead we begin with the postulate that everything can be experienced, then the different categories of experience constitute different kinds of atoms.

Topic 7

QUESTION

If we classify the atoms according to our mental states, then don't we have the problem about the interaction of the mind with an objective world? Would it not entail that we can obtain anything in the world simply by our will?

2.4.15 (284)
ज्योतिरादयधष्ठिानं तु तदामननात्
jyotirādyadhiṣṭhānaṃ tu tadāmananāt

jyotirādi-adhiṣṭhānam—presiding over luminaries etc.; tu—but;

tat-āmananāt—on account of not thinking or understanding about that.

TRANSLATION

(The association of mental states to atomism doesn't create problem because) the demigods are presiding over the material elements and the luminaries, although we don't necessarily see them or understand their role (and that their mental states are involved in giving us the results of our actions).

COMMENTARY

Our experiences are the combination of ability, opportunity, and desire. To eat tasty food, I must desire tasty food, I must have the opportunity to get tasty food, and I should have the ability to eat. The mental states in the last sūtra referred to the combination of ability and desire, and this sūtra states that mental states are fulfilled by the presiding deities of elements who deliver karma. In Sāñkhya philosophy, there are 24 primary elements, and each element has its own presiding deity. Thus, for example, Brahma is the presiding deity of the moral sense, Rudra of the ego, Surya of the intellect, and Chandra of the mind. In the same way, five planets—Jupiter, Mercury, Mars, Venus, Saturn—are the presiding deities of the five gross elements. This simply means that these personalities arrange our encounter with the world at different levels.

We don't see the demigods, but we can see the effects of the demigods, which appears in the fact that some people are rich while others are poor, some enjoy prosperity while others live through poverty, some receive good moral upbringing during childhood while others are born in immoral families, some are lucky to find good teachers while others end up in bad schools, etc.

Atomism is personalized when we treat the mind also as comprised of atoms. But this atomism only consists of our abilities and the reflections of desire which lead to goal formation. Atomism is further personalized due to demigods when they are said to be delivering the results of our desires, and objects by which our abilities to sense and act are converted into sensations and actions. If we do not personalize atomic theory, then it will remain incomplete. This personalization is not subjectivity, because there are many modes in nature. The 'how' mode of explaining is impersonal, but 'who' and 'why' are personal. If science tries to explain 'how' we eat an apple, then, it can talk about the successive states of my body and the apple, and how they come to interact. But this is an incomplete explanation. Completeness is obtained only when we say 'who' gets to eat the apple, and 'why' they get to eat the apple instead of others.

The role of the demigods in delivering karma has been previously discussed. So, why is it being discussed again? The answer is that we are now getting into details about their role and connecting it to the nature of atoms. Modern science assumes that atoms are moving automatically—e.g., due to properties like mass and charge in them—but this idea is rejected here. The atoms are moving because the demigods are causing them to move. But the demigods are also not independent; they are only delivering the consequences of our actions. Therefore, in one sense, we are in control because we reap the consequences of our actions. In another sense, the demigods are in control since they decide which consequence is reaped when and where. Thus, what will happen where is not in our control. But whether it will happen to us, and whether it will be done by us, is within our control. Thus, some people will go hungry and there is nothing we can do about it. What we can do is two things—(1) if they are destined to receive food, then we can be involved in giving it to them, and (2) we can decide by our good actions that we will not have to go hungry.

By the consideration that a person can only change his own destiny, a person is selfish. But by the consideration that others' destiny can be fulfilled by us, we can be altruistic. This altruism doesn't mean that we are changing the world. It only means that within the scope of whatever is destined to happen, we can participate in the good outcomes and avoid the bad outcomes. The devotee of the Lord, however, goes beyond these conceptions of selfishness and altruism. He offers to others the representations of the Lord. These offerings are mainly in the form of knowledge of the Lord, but they can be in the form of food offered to the Lord, a chance to see the Lord in His deity form, etc.

QUESTION

If the objects of our senses are under the control of the demigods, then the demigods too have senses. If our senses are controlled by the demigods, then who controls the senses of the demigods?

Alternately, who is the presiding deity of the elements for the demi-gods, if they are the presiding deities for us?

2.4.16 (285)
पुराणवता शब्दात्
prāṇavatā śabdāt

prāṇavatā—one possessing the prāṇa; śabdāt—from the scriptures.

TRANSLATION

The owner of the prāṇa (the Supreme Lord) is said (in the scriptures) (to be the final presiding deity or controller for everyone, including demigods).

COMMENTARY

In the previous sūtra, atomism was connected to the demigods. In earlier sūtras, material atoms were connected to the prāṇa. And now in this sūtra, the connection between atomism, demigods, and prāṇa is being made. If each of these have been understood individually in the past, then they are now being described collectively in this sūtra. This is the process of diversity leading to unity. There is also the reverse process of unity resulting in diversity. Thus, the argument goes from the root toward the leaves, and from the leaves toward the root. By employing the top-down process from root to leaves, we enunciate religion. But by using the bottom-up process from leaves to root, we describe science. Thus, there is no contradiction between religion and science, but there is a difference: religion goes top-down, and science goes bottom-up.

A demigod may provide us with the opportunity to enjoy a sense object. In doing so, he is exercising his power and control, and that use of power also constitutes the demigod's enjoyment. The demigod's power is in turn enabled by a higher demigod, who is also enjoying in granting that opportunity to the lower-level demigod who then enables the enjoyment of the humans. In this way, everything we enjoy involves the enjoyment of many other higher beings. Ultimately, the Lord who controls all the demigods is the provider of opportunities for all the demigods, which enables their enjoyment. So, He is the ultimate presiding deity for every material element and enjoyment, and just as lower-level demigods deliver the karma for the humans, the higher-level demigods deliver the karma for the lower-level demigods. Ultimately, the Supreme Lord, delivers the karma for the highest-level demigod—Brahma—to create the opportunity for him to control the lower-level demigods, who then control the lower-level living entities. If the Supreme Lord did not create an opportunity for Brahma to exercise his will, and enjoy his karma, then the lower-level demigods and humans won't be able to exercise their wills either. Thus, in each enjoyment, there many levels of enjoyers exercising their power and karma.

The Supreme Lord, however, is not constrained by karma, because His power is His Śakti, who is always serving Him, and He doesn't need karma to obtain His power. The souls in the material world suffer from the fear of losing their power, but the Lord is fearless because He never loses His power. The enjoyment of the humans, demigods, and Brahma are finite, and they end with time. But the enjoyment of the Lord is eternally facilitated by His Śakti.

QUESTION

To become the presiding deity for a lower-level living entity, the higher-level living entity must have a longer lifetime, because only then can he control which living entity enters a specific type of body and life opportunity.

2.4.17 (286)
तस्य च नित्यत्वात्
tasya ca nityatvāt

tasya—His; ca—also; nityatvāt—on account of permanence.

TRANSLATION

(Ultimately this entails) the eternity of the Supreme Lord as well (because He is the presiding deity for all the other lower temporary demigods).

COMMENTARY

One of the amazing features of transcendental literatures is that they connect the knowledge of the material world to the Lord. Such literatures are not afraid to delve into the questions of space and time, matter and causality, or karma and rebirth. However, they deliver this knowledge by connecting it to the Lord. Thus, someone may ask about the body, the material elements, the mind, the process of perception and judgment, etc. and even as answers to these questions are given, the ultimate truth is also given. In fact, the former always implies the latter. This sūtra shows how after discussing atomism, prāṇa, the demigods, and how the Lord is the controller of the world, we now come to the transcendental truth—that the Lord is eternal. This is important because in each country there is a supreme ruler, under whose authority subordinate administrators do their work. But these rulers die and are replaced by other rulers. By extension, one could argue that the Lord is a ruler in so far as the material world exists. If the world ceased to exist, then the Lord would also cease to exist.

This sūtra eliminates that argument by saying that the Lord is not just temporarily supreme, but He is eternally supreme. Transcendence begins with eternity, and supremacy follows this eternity. This is because supremacy is needed if there are many individuals, one of whom is supreme. But if these individuals are within the One, then the supremacy is not demonstrated, although eternity is. Now, the impersonalist argues: the supremacy is temporary, and because the Lord is temporarily supreme, the notion of "God" is only temporary. If these individuals enter the Lord, then nobody is superior or inferior. Therefore, we don't have to worship the Lord since we can merge within the Lord. This merger is expected to dissolve the difference between God and the soul.

However, as we have discussed earlier, this kind of whole-part relation is construed on physical analogies, such as the ocean and the drop within it, and it rests upon the idea that the Lord and the soul are quantitatively different but qualitatively similar. This identity doesn't exist when the whole and the part are meanings, because now they are also qualitatively different. Thus, the mammal and the cow are both quantitatively and qualitatively dissimilar. Reality is known at many levels of detail and abstraction. The impersonalist thinks that the Lord knows all the facts, and the soul doesn't know them. Therefore, the Lord is quantitatively different from the soul, but ultimately all knowledge is merely facts. This is false. Knowledge is both facts and theories. The theories are deeper than the facts, and there are shallower and deeper theories. The knowledge of the Lord is not merely the facts, but also all the deeper explanations of these facts. He is therefore qualitatively different from the soul.

His supremacy is His qualitative difference from the soul. His supremacy as described in the previous sūtras, and the eternity of this supremacy is described in this sūtra. This means that the theories emerge before the facts. The explanation is the cause, and the cause then produces the effects. We can see some of these effects, but the Lord sees the effects and their explanations.

Vedic cosmology provides descriptions of the hierarchy of control in the material world, in which each living entity lives for 100 years, but the definition of a 'year' varies for each type of living entity. Thus, for instance, what constitutes a year for us, constitutes a day for the demigods (of which 6 months in the year are considered day, while the next 6 months are night). At successively higher levels of control, the controllers also have a much longer lifespan. Thus, a Manu—who has control for a period of a Manavantara and constitutes 72 cycles of four-ages (satya-yuga, tretā-yuga, dvāpara-yuga, and kali-yuga)— lives only for a fraction of Brahma's day as there are 14 Manus in a single day of Brahma. Brahma's lifetime adds up to approximately 311 trillion solar years. But the Supreme Lord is eternally situated in His abode to create and destroy the universes innumerable times, to create the opportunities for others to enjoy. His desire is part of every other fulfillment, so He is indirectly enjoying as everyone enjoys. His enjoyment is the control of nature for everyone's enjoyment.

Topic 8

QUESTION

The senses and the objects of the senses are present everywhere. How do the demigods control the interaction between the senses and their objects?

2.4.18 (287)

तं इन्द्रयियाणि तद्व्यपदेशादन्यत्र श्रेष्ठात्

ta indriyāṇi tadvyapadeśādanyatra śreṣṭhāt

te—they; indriyāṇi—the senses; tadvyapadeśāt—from designated as that (i.e., the masters of the senses); anyatra śreṣṭhāt—from another superior place.

TRANSLATION

They (the demigods) from being designated (as the masters of) the senses (control the access of the objects for the senses) from another, superior place.

COMMENTARY

The causes of experience are divided into three parts in Sāṅkhya philosophy: ādibhautika, *ādiatmika*, and ādidaivika, or the objects, the senses, and the demigods. In modern science, we think that objects are directly interacting with the senses, and there is nobody in control of our perception. But such a theory cannot explain why someone is rich while another person is poor, why someone is intelligent while another person is not, etc. The demigods are responsible for ensuring that everyone gets their due according to their karma. Thus, even the food that we eat every day is provided by the demigods due to karma. This food can come from many different sources—we can grow the food, we can purchase it from someone, someone can give us the food in charity, etc. Karma simply ensures that we will get the food, but the source of that food is not predetermined. This source is decided based on both guna and karma—e.g., someone has the requisite *karma* to give food, and they want to give the food. Sometimes, karma will override guna and a person will be forced to give even if he or she doesn't want to give. Sometimes, guna will override karma and a person will give to someone who he wants to give. These arrangements of provider and consumer are made by the demigods. The mechanism of this type of causality involves establishing a relation between a provider and a consumer.

At the advent of modern science, it was believed that every object exerts a force on every other object; so, for example, our bodies are exerting a gravitational force on the sun, just as the sun is exerting a gravitational force on us. This meant that everyone had access to everything in this world, which is patently false. Later developments in science have shown that objects occasionally interact with each other only when they have become 'entangled' with each other, and during an interaction the causality flows in both directions—from source to destination and from destination to source. There are not good explanations of this causal model in classical or modern science, because we are used to thinking of the interaction in terms of the interacting objects alone.

The fact is that these interactions are created by demigods who 'entangle' objects with each other such that they can interact. This entanglement is based on a combination of our desiring and our deserving, and by this entanglement we fulfill our desires and reap our karma. This entanglement is prior to the exchange of energy by which force is exerted, so we cannot attribute 'force' as the cause of entanglement. And without understanding the cause of this entanglement all other causal explanations become incomplete. The short answer to this problem is that objects don't get entangled; the objects enter different relations or roles which are mutually entangled. We call these roles by names such as 'consumer' and 'provider'; these are not objects, but roles of give and take. The demigods move the individuals into these roles based on their karma.

Scientists believe that to change an object a force must be applied on it. They may not realize that this force is exerted after a role is changed, and the changes to these roles are not due to forces. The causality in matter is conditional on the interaction: *if* you eat a medicine, then you will be cured or *if* you eat food, then your hunger will be satisfied. But that doesn't mean you automatically access the medicine or the food. So, the modern notions of material causality are incomplete: they say that something is possible but cannot predict which possibility becomes real for whom. The power of the demigods is to enable access to opportunities that can be utilized (by our desires). By wielding this power, the demigods are said to be in a 'superior position'; this superiority refers to their ability to exert control over our life, not necessarily to everyone else's life. The demigods, for instance, don't control the life in the lower planetary systems, nor do they control the living entities who are situated in positions above them. So, their control is also limited, and universal. Their position of power is also enabled and controlled by higher living entities, which means that their positions are not permanent. Only the position of the Supreme Lord is eternal.

Finally, the demigods are only said to be controllers of the senses in this sūtra. This means that all desires cannot be fulfilled, even if we have the karma. The objects of desiring—e.g., flying machines—are not created by demigods. They are produced due to time. If we desire, and the object is possible, and the karma is manifest at the present, then the person can fly. Thus, the causality has many causes—the soul, his guna and karma, matter and the effect of time.

QUESTION

The distinction between the Lord and the demigods seems to be based on the distinction between a person and a role. The Supreme Lord is eternally situated in His role as the supreme controller, but the roles of the other demigods are temporary. Why do we distinguish between the person and a role?

2.4.19 (288)
भेदश्रुतेः
bhedaśruteḥ

bheda—the difference; śruteḥ—as stated in the śrutī.

TRANSLATION

The scriptural texts differentiate between them.

COMMENTARY

Every organized system requires a hierarchy of controls, and this hierarchy requires a distinction between a person and the role played by the person. The 'person' here is represented by their desire and the role constitutes their deserving. These two must be distinguished because every desiring person cannot acquire a position unless they are also deserving. Similarly, every deserving person doesn't get to fulfill their desires immediately—they may need to wait for the right time to arrive for fulfilling their desires. The restrictions of deserving do not apply in the spiritual world, and experience is controlled only by desire. Therefore, the only qualification to see and serve the Lord is a desire. These desires are spiritual, and they automatically spring from the soul, due to which they are often called causeless. They are also always manifest to serve the Lord. Therefore, the devotee doesn't say—I desire to see the Lord, because I would be delighted by it. That kind of desire is not considered spiritual. But if a causeless desire springs in the soul, the Lord and His Śakti fulfill it.

QUESTION

But we can see that there are many people who acquire powerful positions due to their preexisting wealth or connections. They seem to have the good karma, they are obviously desirous of these positions, but they may not be qualified. Shouldn't we say that that karma and desire are insufficient to decide the most deserving person, as they must also be skilled in doing their job?

2.4.20 (289)
वैलक्षण्याच्च
vailakṣaṇyaccha

vailakṣaṇya—uniqueness, specialization; ca—also;

TRANSLATION

(In addition to good karma and desire, the person) must be qualified also.

COMMENTARY

The law of karma ensures justice for all the souls—you get what you deserve, and that deserving is decided by previous actions. However, it is possible that a person with good karma is incapable of fulfilling the demands of the role. Hence, there are two types of qualification—the ability and the entitlement. The entitlement is fulfilled by karma, but many incapable people may also ascend powerful positions in society due to entitlement, not due to their ability.

Karma is like money, which can be spent to purchase the things that we want. But once we obtain these things due to karma, we may still not know how to use them. Nature allows such outcomes, and even unqualified people ascend powerful positions if they desire it, and if they have the karma, even if they don't have the ability. Thus, it is seen that even demigods commit mistakes. They might be envious of other demigods or even humans, and might compete with them, instead of focusing on their own roles and responsibilities. The demigods have the desires for power, and they have the karma for power, but they don't necessarily have all the abilities. Such abilities are obtained only by devotees. If a pure devotee of the Lord ascends a position of power, then he doesn't work by his own intellect. He rather works by the guidance of the Lord, and whatever he may be missing, the Lord supplies the necessities. Therefore, the devotees do not fail the duties of their position due to their inabilities.

If a person neglects their duties deliberately, the laws of nature produce a greater karma. If a person neglects their duties due to inability, the laws of nature still punish, although the punishment is lesser. Therefore, incapable people must not accept the roles they cannot fulfill—simply because they are offered such positions, and they would like to enjoy the position of power. One should rather understand their abilities against the demand for the position. If the demands exceed their abilities, then a person must renounce that position, and allow someone more qualified to accept the position. Even if there is no one more qualified, an unqualified person must not accept a position beyond his abilities—on the pretext of doing 'serving the greater good'. But if such a position has been accepted by mistake, it must be quickly renounced. That renunciation will save the unqualified person from subsequent suffering.

QUESTION

How can unqualified people ascend to positions of power, simply due to good karma? Shouldn't the laws of nature allow only those people who are both qualified (to play the role) and have the good karma (to obtain the role)?

2.4.21 (290)

संज्ञामूरतकिलृप्तिसितु तरवृतकुरवत उपदेशात्

saṃjñāmurtiklṛptistu trivratakurvata upadeśāt

saṃjñā—designation or naming; murti—form or deity;

klṛptiḥ—conforming; astu—in this way; trivrata—the vow of three times a day; kurvata—those who perform; upadeśāt—based upon the teaching.

TRANSLATION

(Qualifications can be obtained by those who) designate a deity based upon the teaching (of the scriptures) and perform the vows (of worshipping the designated deity) three times a day (again, according to the scriptures).

COMMENTARY

The worship of the demigods has been decried many times before, but in this sūtra, it is being recommended. To understand this recommendation, we must distinguish between the three aspects of experience we have discussed previously—desire, opportunity, and ability. We might have desires, but they remain unfulfilled unless we have the right karma. The opportunities to fulfill the desires are given to us by karma. But, if we have the desire, and get the opportunity, but don't have the ability, we will not be able to use the opportunity well. The demigod worship is recommended if one wants to obtain the ability to deal with the present opportunities. This doesn't entail a change in the situation or getting better opportunities, because the demigods cannot change our karma. However, the demigods can give us the power to deal with the present situation better. The result of this betterment is that our responses to the problems will be more effective and appropriate; instead of fumbling through the problems, we can provide correct and measured responses to them.

Therefore, whether we pray to the Lord or to the demigods, we should never ask for improving our situation. We should rather ask for giving us the ability to deal with the situation. This ability can mean a stronger body or mind, greater moral and emotional courage, and the strength to keep doing our duties even under adverse and difficult circumstances. The worship of demigods for getting a better life is futile. But the worship of the demigods for getting better abilities to deal with whatever life we are getting is still appropriate. The devotees of the Lord take shelter of the Lord and ask for His help in giving them strength, courage, patience, and tolerance to deal with difficult situations. They also beg the Lord for the power to spread His glories. It is said that by the mercy of the guru, a dumb man can speak, and a lame man can cross mountains. Thus, all kinds of worship—of the Lord, of the guru, or of the demigods—are only meant to obtain the abilities by which we handle the difficulties of life, even as we can use the same abilities for spreading the glorification of the Lord.

The devotees know how to engage powerful people in the Lord's service. They don't have to shy away from wealthy or powerful people, in the name of renunciation. The demigod worship is similarly accepted, after numerous previous rejections, provided it is sought not for enjoyment, but for betterment of our abilities to fulfill our duties. Thus, a person with a poor intellect can worship Sarasvati to understand the scriptures. A person with a disturbed mind can worship Chandra to perform their duties. And a warrior fighting the moral battle can worship Durga or Kali to obtain the power that can help them win these battles. Arjuna obtained weapons of various kinds before the battle of Mahabharata by worshipping the demigods. If the intention is the Lord's service or even the strength to perform one's mundane duties, then the demigod worship is accepted. Thus, everything described in the Vedic texts is ultimately for a single purpose—the service of the Lord. The soul conditioned by selfishness, however, falsely construes this knowledge to be meant for his enjoyment.

QUESTION

You earlier said that the demigods are delivering our karma by which our roles are decided. You are now also saying that the demigods can give us better abilities (of the body and the mind) making us more capable of dealing with circumstances. How are these abilities delivered to the living entities?

2.4.22 (291)

मांसादि भौमं यथाशब्दमितरयोश् च

māṃsādi bhaumaṃ yathāśabdamitarayoś ca

māṃsādi—flesh etc.; bhaumaṃ—from the earth; yatha—just as; śabdam—the sound; itarayoh—the other two (i.e., the guna and karma); ca—also.

TRANSLATION

Flesh etc. (the body of abilities) are formed from the earth, just as the sound (is formed) from the other two (i.e., guna and karma) as well.

COMMENTARY

We have earlier discussed the three modalities of existence—universal, individual, and contextual. The type of body—e.g., tiger, tree, bird, fish, etc.—are universals. The guna is the soul's desire, which differentiates the soul materially from other souls, and constitutes the individual mode. The universal and the individual combine, the soul gets a type of body (e.g., cat or dog or human) due to its guna. Now, the third mode—of contextuality—decides the environment in which this body is placed, and this contextual modality is due to karma.

This sūtra draws a comparison to speech. The meaning is the universal, and its expression as words are the individual instantiation of that meaning. However, those words are also spoken in some context—e.g., to some people.

This process is cyclic, which means that after we express some meaning, the other person also expresses other meanings. By this expression, our desires change, and we tap into different universals, and speak different words. We might also change the context, and speak to other people, or stop speaking to the person we were speaking to earlier. Thus, causality begins in our guna or desires when we obtain a type of body. Then by the interactions of this body with its environment, the body develops slowly—e.g., we eat some food, we acquire some knowledge, we develop some aspirations, and learn some values. This development then shapes the meanings, and their expressions.

The worship of demigods enhances this process as the demigods can give the person not just the things that they deserve due to their karma but also portions of their ability by which these things enhance their effects. For instance, if Sarasvati—the deity of knowledge—is worshipped, then the effort invested in learning will produce better knowledge with the assistance of Sarasvati. As we become better equipped with knowledge, strength, health, etc. we are better prepared for the good or bad situations that come naturally due to karma.

In Vedic philosophy, even the mind is sometimes included in the body, because both are considered the coverings of the soul. Thus, in this sūtra, a gross material example of bodily flesh being generated from the element earth is given, to make the point that the food we get to eat is fixed by our karma but the same food can build a stronger body by the grace of demigods. Of course, the abilities in the demigods are also provided by the grace of the Supreme Lord. So, one who worships the Lord is said to eventually develop all the great qualities of all the demigods—not just a specific demigod. This internal strength or ability in the mind and the body of a person is not a permanent quality; it can rather come and go; sometimes the mind and the body become very strong and we can do difficult things easily. Sometimes even simple things become very difficult because the mind and the body are weakened. The strength and weakness of the body and the mind can be obtained through the grace of the Lord (or the demigods) without being conditioned by karma. Thus, we can see descriptions in Vedic texts where people perform yajñā or austerities to get the benedictions from demigods that gives them strong bodies and minds.

QUESTION

You are saying that the health of the body and the mind can be improved by the grace of demigods. Since this health has many components, coming from the different elements of matter, is there a separate demigod for each such element that gives us not just the element but also the ability to consume it?

2.4.23 (292)

वैशेष्यात्तु तद्वादस्तद्वादः

vaiśeṣyāttu tadvādastadvādaḥ

vaiśeṣyāt—due to the specialization; tu—but; tad-vādas—they are called; tad-vādaḥ—by that name.

TRANSLATION

For each kind of material specialization, there is a demigod who is called by the same name (as the type of specialization that he or she represents).

COMMENTARY

There are innumerable kinds of talents, abilities, and specializations in this world. Some people are artists, others are musicians, writers, orators, philosophers, scientists, cooks, dancers, etc. Each such specialization has a personification in a demigod who specializes in that area. These demigods represent the parts of the ability, talent, and specialization in the Lord. Thus, the Lord is full of all talents, but each demigod only personifies one such type of talent.

When the ability of a demigod is present in a person, the demigod is said to have become immanent in that person. Otherwise, the demigod is always transcendent by the fact that he delivers the specific type of karma or objects. Thus, for instance, Sarasvati is delivering knowledge to everyone (according to their karma). But some of these people acquire an extraordinary ability to understand, assimilate, and transmit that knowledge. The goddess Sarasvati is said to be 'present' in them. In a previous sūtra, the term *anyatra śreṣṭhāt* was used to describe how the demigods control the world from another, superior place. In this sūtra, the power to give opportunities is contrasted to their power to deliver abilities by being present by their portion in a person's body.

The Vedic texts describe a form of incarnation called śakti-*āveśa* *avatār* in which the Lord appears as ability in the body and the mind of a soul. Veda Vyās, the author of Vedānta Sūtra, is, for instance, considered śakti-*āveśa* *avatār*. In every millennium, at the dawn of kali-yuga, a different soul appears as Veda Vyās, who converts the oral Vedic tradition into a written one. This conversion is entrusted to an empowered soul, who is called Veda Vyās. Veda Vyās, however, is not the Lord, and yet empowered with the Lord's powers.

When Śukadeva Goswami spoke the Śrīmad Bhāgavatam, his father (Veda Vyās), his grandfather (Parāśara), and his father's spiritual master (Nārada Muni) were present in audience. Even though Veda Vyās is an empowered incarnation, and the author of Śrīmad Bhāgavatam, he doesn't consider himself qualified to speak on the Śrīmad Bhāgavatam. Why? Why are the author, the author's father, and the author's guru in the audience, while the disciple and son speaks? The answer is that the devotee is superior to the empowered incarnation. If the devotee speaks, then even the Lord listens in rapt attention.

नाहं वसामि वैकुण्ठे योगनिां हृदये न च ।
मद्भक्ता यत्र गायन्ति तत्र तिष्ठामि नारद ॥

O Nārada, I do not reside in Vaikuṇṭha, nor do I dwell in the hearts of the yogis; I am firmly situated wherever my devotees are singing.

The description of the Lord by the devotees is superior to the Lord's description of Himself, or the description by an empowered incarnation of the Lord. The Lord describes Himself analytically by indicating His powers. But the devotees speak about the Lord's sweet nature, which the Lord doesn't speak of Himself. Thus, Vedānta Sūtra and the Śrīmad Bhāgavatam are both conclusions of the Vedas. The Śrīmad Bhāgavatam is called the ripened fruit of the tree of Vedic knowledge (*nigama-kalpa-taror galitaṁ phalaṁ*). The Vedānta Sūtra is also that ripened fruit, or the conclusion of all knowledge in the Vedas. However, the Śrīmad Bhāgavatam is made sweeter by the biting of the fruit by Śukadeva Goswami (*śuka-mukhād amṛta-drava-saṁyutam*), but the Vedānta Sūtra is not. The Śrīmad Bhāgavatam we read is not the Śrīmad Bhāgavatam that was written by Veda Vyās. It is rather Śukadeva Goswami's exposition of what Veda Vyās wrote. Expositions of the original text by the devotees are superior to those authored by the empowered incarnation of the Lord. If we understand the Vedānta Sūtra devotionally, then they are non-different.

The conclusion is that power is inferior to devotion. Many people call advanced devotees a *śakti-āveśa avatār*, thinking this to be a glorification of the devotee. But the Lord's devotee is superior to the empowered incarnation. Those enamored by power, magic, and mystical abilities, think of the devotees as possessing power. The devotee has no power. He is helplessly in love with the Lord. And the Lord provides whatever he needs. This is not an inferior position. It is rather superior to anyone possessing Lord's empowerment.

In summary, the demigods can be worshipped to obtain the strength to serve the Lord. But empowerment by the demigods, or even by the empowered incarnations of the Lord present as *śakti-āveśa avatār*, are inferior to devotion. Hence, if possible, one must only remain devoted to the Supreme Lord.

INDEX

Big Bang 104

Brahma 62, 64, 68, 92, 199, 207, 228, 278, 303, 606, 609, 611

Brahman 6, 7, 33, 34, 35, 36, 42, 44, 45, 52, 54, 56, 58, 59, 60, 61, 62, 64, 65, 66,
67, 68, 77, 85, 87, 90, 91, 92, 93, 94, 95, 96, 98, 99, 100, 102, 104, 106, 107,
108, 109, 110, 116, 117, 118, 121, 124, 128, 129, 130, 131, 132, 133, 134,
135, 138, 139, 140, 141, 142, 143, 144, 146, 149, 150, 151, 157, 158, 159,
168, 186, 212, 225, 230, 231, 235, 248, 249, 250, 283, 284, 344, 347, 370,
376, 377, 403, 404, 453, 457, 458, 459, 473, 477, 510, 533, 534, 539, 557,
568, 569, 570, 571, 572, 573, 574, 575, 576, 577, 578, 584, 587, 588

Brahmana 221, 299, 300, 305, 574, 584

Brahmanas 210, 221, 575, 585

Buddhi 69

Buddhism 1, 6, 16, 18, 29, 30, 31, 33, 34, 35, 77, 95, 96, 98, 266, 575

Causal Ocean 228

Chaitraratha 296, 297

Chāndogya Upaniśad 143, 302

Chandra 188, 190, 288, 292, 293, 606, 618

Chārvāka 24

Chatuśpāda 61, 62, 65, 66, 67

Cintyabhedābheda 66

classical physics 26, 197, 423, 472, 544, 548

Completeness 1

conflict 81

consistency 1

Cosmic Man 75, 206

Descartes 30

Dhruva Loka 208

Durga 63, 618

dustbowl empiricism 27

Dvaita 18, 37, 38, 39, 41, 45, 46, 54, 55, 56, 58, 60, 76, 77, 80, 369

Earth 70, 103, 119, 141, 142, 245, 247, 318, 344, 525, 527, 531

Edmund Husserl 28

empiricism 197, 198, 282

Ether 70, 103, 142, 245, 247, 318, 525, 527, 531

Euclidean geometry 119, 120

ex nihilo 31, 32, 33, 495

feminine 47, 52, 53, 54, 68, 85, 89, 129, 364, 365, 366, 367, 368, 369, 370, 375,
376, 377, 421, 550, 553, 557, 558, 559, 560, 561, 562, 563, 564

Fire 70, 103, 142, 245, 247, 318, 344, 527, 531

Garbhodakaśāyi 62, 205

Gāyatri 136, 137, 139, 140, 141, 298, 299, 583

Gödel 15

Goloka 62, 64, 65, 138, 142, 149, 159, 249, 250, 496, 509

Govardhan 326, 327

helical progression 86

Hierarchical 84

Hume   27, 191, 283
Idealism   26, 30, 77, 258
Immanuel Kant   27, 283
impersonalism   123, 422, 426, 459
indistinguishability   57
inverted tree   160, 162, 340
Jambudvīpa   208, 219
Jīvā Goswami   167
jñāna-indriya   71, 72
Kalā   69
Kāla   69
Kāli   63
Kāmadeva   188
Kārana Ocean   228
Kāraṇodakaśāyī   62, 64, 65, 135, 205
karma-indriya   71, 72
Kṛṣṇa   53, 56, 59, 62, 64, 65, 66, 99, 100, 155, 172, 209, 210, 242, 244, 259, 260,
        279, 286, 295, 302, 304, 308, 319, 322, 325, 327, 335, 343, 354, 356, 371,
        381, 464
kṣetrajña   126, 129, 131, 148, 167, 200, 201
Kshatriya   221, 296, 300, 574, 575
Kshatriyas   210, 221, 296
Kṣīrodakaśāyī   62, 205, 412
Kubera   188
Lakshmi   68, 314, 329, 371
left-wing   29
madhyamā   245, 312, 313
Mahabharata   167, 301, 302, 303, 618
mahad-yoni   129, 130
mahattattva   74, 103, 142, 204, 231, 283, 450, 530, 531, 532
Mahattattva   69
mano-maya   68, 70, 73, 75
Martin Heidegger   28
masculine   47, 52, 53, 54, 68, 85, 89, 364, 365, 366, 367, 368, 369, 370, 375, 376,
        377, 421, 550, 553, 557, 558, 559, 560, 561, 562, 563, 564
materialism   236, 434, 552, 553
Materialism   24, 30, 77, 79
māyā   6, 7, 8, 9, 33, 34, 35, 36, 45, 52, 54, 59, 60, 77, 100, 226, 239, 370, 407, 450,
        452, 469, 499, 534
Mīmāṃsā   77, 190, 191, 192, 193, 194, 195, 196, 198, 207, 216, 291, 293, 294,
        303, 350, 351, 354, 415, 575
modalities   2, 3, 4, 10, 13, 15, 16, 17, 18, 21, 23, 24, 25, 26, 27, 28, 34, 35, 37, 43,
        55, 57, 58, 59, 62, 64, 66, 71, 73, 74, 75, 76, 77, 79, 80, 84, 256, 261, 263,
        396, 619
monotheism   487
Monotheism   31, 32, 77

www.ingramcontent.com/pod-product-compliance
Lightning Source LLC
LaVergne TN
LVHW042341190726
843493LV00005B/878